The Macrodynamics of Capitalism

Second Revised and Enlarged Edition

Peter Flaschel

The Macrodynamics of Capitalism

Elements for a Synthesis of Marx, Keynes and Schumpeter

Second Revised and Enlarged Edition

Springer

Prof. Dr. Peter Flaschel
Department of Economics
and Business Administration
Bielefeld University
Universitaetsstrasse 25
33615 Bielefeld
Germany
pflaschel@wiwi.uni-bielefeld.de

ISBN: 978-3-540-87931-2 e-ISBN: 978-3-540-87932-9

Library of Congress Control Number: 2008937135

First edition published with Peter Lang Verlag, 1993

Printed on acid-free paper

springer.com

Preface

This book provides an introduction to advanced macrodynamics, viewed as a disequilibrium theory of fluctuating growth. It builds on an earlier attempt to reformulate the foundations of macroeconomics[1] from the perspective of real markets disequilibrium and the conflict over income distribution between capital and labor. It does so, not because it wants to support the view that this class conflict is inevitable, but with the perspective that an understanding of this conflict may help to formulate socio-economic principles and policies that can help to overcome class conflict at least in its cruder forms or that can even lead to rationally understandable procedures and rules that turn this conflict into a consensus-driven interaction[2] between capitalists or their representatives and the employable workforce.[3]

The book starts from established theories of temporary equilibrium positions, the forces of real growth, and the conflict over income distribution, represented by basic modeling approaches, which it considers in detail in its Part I in order to prepare the ground for their integration in Part II of the book. In this way we inspect what types of models of disequilibrium, income distribution, and real growth we have at our disposal, as models that have proved to be of real interest and sound from a rigorous modeling perspective. We stress in this regard that the book concentrates on non-market-clearing approaches, does not assume that only microfounded models make sense with regard to an understanding of the real world, and – above all – does not

[1] P. Flaschel (1993). Macrodynamics. Income Distribution, Effective Demand and Cyclical Growth. Frankfurt, M. Peter Lang. This book was the starting point for a very fruitful collaboration with Carl Chiarella from the University of Technology, Sydney, in particular, involving many visits and joint projects in Sydney as well as in Bielefeld, see in particular, Chap. 1 and the references quoted there. The matured Keynesian AD-AS model presented in Chaps. 8 and 9 are an important example of the outcome of this collaboration.

[2] With respect to the occurrence and discussion of such consensus situations see P. Flaschel, R. Franke, and W. Semmler: Kaleckian investment and employment cycles in postwar industrialized economies. In P. Flaschel and M. Landesmann (Eds.): *Mathematical Economics and the Dynamics of Capitalism*. London: Routledge, 2008.

[3] We here consider only the social structure of such societies in highly stylized form and thus abstract from the fact that any adult person can in principle be an employer, be employed or even be self-employed at one and the same time.

rely on the jump-variable technique of the rational expectations school, which turns saddle point instability into always convergent dynamics by assumption.[4]

In Chap. 5 we provide in this respect a first example how these models can help to understand current economic controversies, for example, about inflation, and how to bring about disinflation. It shows that a Marxian reinterpretation of the baseline Monetarist model of inflation, stagflation, and disinflation may be more to the point from a factual viewpoint than Friedman's initial and later attempts to explain these phenomena against the background of a Walrasian understanding of the working of the economy. Reinterpreting the monetarist baseline model in this way may indeed remove unnecessary detours in the understanding of the occurrence of stagflation phenomena and thus provide arguments that both parties who are interacting in this framework, firms (responsible for price inflation) and workers (at least partially responsible for wage inflation), can use in the arguments exchanged with each other. Coherent and rigorous models and their factual explanations, stating the variables they seek to explain and the equilibrium conditions and laws of motion used for this purpose in a systematic way, are an important tool, quite independent from the current belief that only models that are microfounded (within the representative agent framework) are acceptable as tools of analysis.[5]

In Part II, we proceed to integrated models of effective demand, income distribution dynamics, and monetary growth. We show there that the textbook neoclassical model of AD-AS growth (based on the old neoclassical synthesis) is logically inconsistent, basically since it marries Keynesian and Walrasian concepts in a contradictory way. The neoclassical synthesis of Patinkin et al., extended and reformulated as a general AS-AD model of business fluctuations and economic growth, is therefore no solid basis for a Keynesian theory of the macroeconomic working of capitalist economies, basically since there is a logical contradiction between its Keynesian theory of effective demand and the Neoclassical postulate that assumes that prices are equal to marginal wage costs (due to perfect competition). Part II therefore ends with a negative conclusion concerning an integration of the baseline models discussed in Part I.

In Part III, starting with Chap. 8 and concluding this discussion, also from the empirical point of view, in Chap. 9, we then provide a solution to these inconsistencies by assuming that gradual adjustment processes do not only characterize wage level formation, but also price level formation and also quantity adjustment processes. In this way we show that a matured and coherently formulated disequilibrium AD-AS monetary growth model can be obtained from the old neoclassical synthesis, which can serve as a baseline model of the interaction of the trade cycle with the distributive cycle in a growing monetary economy. This model type is – from a formal perspective, as we show – very similar to the now fashionable New Keynesian model of the business cycle (the new neoclassical synthesis), but differs radically from it in its implications and the explanation of the occurrence of cyclical growth.

---

[4] This technique is investigated and criticized in detail in Chap. 7 of the book.

[5] We know from Walrasian theory that nearly everything can be microfounded from first principles if a sufficient degree of heterogeneity among the interacting economic agents is assumed.

Our matured AD-AS monetary growth model has interesting dynamic implications and stability features (intuitively understandable from the feedback mechanisms that characterize the model's dynamics), can be applied successfully to the observed macrobehavior of actual economies and also gives rise to interesting simulation studies. It reveals in this respect that a proper synthesis of the Marxian distributive cycle with the Keynesian theory of the business cycle leads to a model of the interaction of "short-phased" Keynesian business fluctuations with long-phased fluctuations in inflation and income distribution that can explain factual observations, but that also needs further thorough investigation to really determine its potential as a theory of the short-, the medium-, and the long-run evolution of capitalism. The integration with Schumpeterian microprocesses of creative destruction, and the long-wave theories that are associated with this view of the working of capitalist economies, is also of high desirability here, but must be left for future research in this book.

In Chap. 10, we focus instead on another aspect of Schumpeter's research, his seminal work on "Capitalism, Socialism and Democracy"[6] and use its theory of a competitively organized (Western) socialism as starting point and foundation for a modeling attempt of the current politico–economic discussion of a new concept for the working of capitalism, the debate on so-called flexicurity systems and the combination of economic flexibility and social security they intend to establish. This approach provides an alternative model for our understanding of modern capitalist economies compared to the Chaps. 8 and 9 where we considered the actual working of orthodox types of capitalist economies.

In closing, I thank Toichiro Asada, Carl Chiarella, Ekkehardt Ernst, Reiner Franke, Christian Proaño, and Willi Semmler for suggestions and discussions that helped to improve the contents of this book. I also have to thank them, as co-authors, for allowing me to use joint work with some of them in Part III of this book. Indirectly, the book also owes much to my former colleagues Michael Ambrosi, Jörg Glombowski, Klaus Jaeger, Michael Krüger, and Elmar Wolfstetter during my time at the Free University of Berlin and to Gangolf Groh during the time he was at Bielefeld University. I also thank Christian Proaño for polishing the outlook of this book in an excellent way. The views expressed in this book are, of course, nevertheless entirely my own as are all remaining errors and mistaken views of this attempt to reformulate the foundations of macrodynamics from a Keynes–Marx–Schumpeter understanding of the interaction of effective demand with the distributive cycle and the social structure of accumulation.[7]

Bielefeld, *Peter Flaschel*
August 16, 2008

---

[6] New York: Harper & Row, 1942.

[7] See in this respect also the work of L. Taylor (2004): Reconstructing Macroeconomics. Structuralist Proposals and Critique of the Mainstream. (Cambridge, MA: Harvard University Press) for a contribution that in my view is similar in intention and spirit to the approach chosen in this book.

Contents

Notation

Steady state or trend values are indicated by a sub- or superscript "o". A dot over a variable $x = x(t)$ denotes the time derivative, a caret its growth rate; $\dot{x} = \mathrm{d}x/\mathrm{d}t$, $\hat{x} = \dot{x}/x$.

Y^{s}	Aggregate supply
$Y \equiv Y^{\mathrm{s}}$	Aggregate income
Y^{d}	Aggregate demand
L^{s}	Labor supply
L^{d}	Labor demand
L	Employment
K	Capital stock
K^{p}	Desired capital stock (reference: Y)
Y^{p}	Potential output (reference: K)
C	Aggregate planned consumption
I	Aggregate planned investment
G	Government expenditure ($g = G/K$)
T	Real taxes ($t = T/K$ or $t = T/Y$)
$\overline{I}, \overline{C}, \overline{A}, \ldots$	Autonomous demand components
S	Aggregate savings
$S_{\mathrm{p}}, S_{\mathrm{g}}$	Private and government savings
$B^{\mathrm{s}}, B^{\mathrm{d}}$	Demand and supply of bonds
$\overline{B}$	Stock of bonds
$B_{\mathrm{p}}, B_{\mathrm{g}}$	Private and government bonds
δ	Rate of depreciation
$y = Y/L$	Labor productivity (part III: z)
$\sigma = Y/K$	Output-capital ratio (part III: y, index p: planned)
$v = K/Y$	Capital coefficient (index p: planned)
$k = K/L$	Capital intensity
$l = L/K$	Labor intensity
$l^{\mathrm{s}} = L^{\mathrm{s}}/K$	Full employment labor intensity
g^{p}	Planned rate of growth

g_{w}	Warranted rate of growth
g^*	Expected rate of growth
$n = \widehat{L}^{\mathrm{s}} = \dot{L}^{\mathrm{s}}/L^{\mathrm{s}}$	Natural rate of growth
m	Growth rate of labor productivity
$g_0 = n + m$	Steady growth rate
p (or P)	Price level ($p = \ln P$ in the latter case)
$\pi = \hat{p}$	Rate of inflation
$w\,(W)$	Real wages (nominal wages)
p_{B}	Price of bonds
$V = L/L^{\mathrm{s}} = 1 - U$	Rate of employment ($\bar{\cdot}$ natural rates) (e in III)
$\Theta = Y/Y^{\mathrm{p}}$	Rate of capacity utilization ($\bar{\cdot}$ natural rates) (u in III)
u^{w}	Utilization rate of the employed labor force
c	Marginal propensity to consume
s	Marginal propensity to save
s_{w}	Savings ratio (out of wages)
s_{p}	Savings ratio (out of profits)
t	Time (if not $t = T/K, T/Y$)
g	Rate of growth (if not $g = G/K$)
c	Consumption per head (if not: propensity to consume)
r	Rate of interest or rate of profit
z	Rate of interest (if r: rate of profit)
$u = WL/pY$	Share of wages (v in part III)
$\Pi = 1 - u$	Share of profits
Π^*	Expected share of profits
$\overline{M}^{\mathrm{s}} (\overline{M}, M^{\mathrm{s}}, M)$	Money supply
M^{d}	Money demand
$m^{\mathrm{s}} = M^{\mathrm{s}}/p$	Real money supply ($m_l^s = M^s/L^s$, $m_k^s = M^s/K$)
$m^{\mathrm{d}} = M^{\mathrm{d}}/p$	Real money demand
$\rho = \dot{M}^{\mathrm{s}}/M^{\mathrm{s}} = \widehat{M}^{\mathrm{s}}$	Growth rate of money supply
$A = 1 + a$	Mark-up factor
Y_0, p_0, etc.	Steady state values (or short-run equilibrium values)
$Y^{\mathrm{d}*}, \pi^*$, etc.	Expected aggregate demand, rate of inflation, etc.
$Y_{\mathrm{t}}, g_{\mathrm{t}}$	Discrete time values of $Y, g, \ldots$
$F_{\mathrm{K}}, F_{\mathrm{KL}}, F_{\mathrm{l}}$	Partial derivatives of the function F
$\dot{p}, \ddot{p}$	Time derivatives (also Dp, D^2p)
$\widehat{p} = \dot{p}/p$	Percentage rate of change (here of prices p)
$\dot{p}_+, \widehat{p}_+$	Right hand derivatives and rates of growth
$\Delta Y = Y - Y_{-1} = Y_t - Y_{t-1}$	First differences
$Y^{\mathrm{s}'}, L'$	Derivative of the functions Y^{s}, L

Chapter 1
Goodwin Growth Cycles in a Keynes Trade Cycle Framework and Beyond

1.1 Overview

This book on macrodynamic theories and models of monetary growth, (in-)stability, and cycles attempts *in the first place* to draw the attention of the reader to the fact that there is one important, but unconventional prototype approach to these topics that has been and still is fairly neglected in systematic (textbook) presentations of the development of macrodynamic models – whether old or new: The Goodwin (1967) model of the Marxian analysis of cyclical growth of a capitalist economy.[1] There exist meanwhile numerous articles and also monographs on this growth cycle model, which extend it in various directions.[2] Yet, the typical overshooting mechanism of Goodwin's growth cycle analysis of the conflict between capital and labor about income distribution has never really received the explicit attention which it deserves in the (textbook) treatments of macrodynamics – in particular when it is compared with other well-known and equally basic prototype models of growth and cycles, such as (in chronological order) Hicks' model of the trade cycle, Solow's model of capital accumulation and its various extensions, or the Monetarist prototype models of inflation and stagflation.[3]

In our view, there exist furthermore many fairly conventional macrodynamic models in which this approach is partly, indirectly, or implicitly present, but where the relationship to the Goodwin model is neither investigated nor even noticed. It is one basic working hypothesis of this book that this growth cycle mechanism will indeed be present in any model that really attempts to introduce a wage/price spiral and its dynamics into an otherwise more or less conventional type of model of monetary growth dynamics – if such an approach is not so reduced and simplified

---

[1] See, however, Chiarella and Flaschel (2000), Flaschel (2001), Chiarella, Flaschel, and Franke (2005) and related work for advanced studies of the Goodwin growth cycle approach in a Keynesian trade cycle setup.

[2] See Flaschel and Landesmann (2008) for a recent collection of essays in the Goodwin tradition.

[3] See also Solow (1990) for a discussion of the merits and the empirical content of the original Goodwin model.

P. Flaschel, *The Macrodynamics of Capitalism: Elements for a Synthesis of Marx, Keynes and Schumpeter, Second Edition,*

that it does not treat all of the basic markets of a macroeconomic approach explicitly (as, e.g., the approach we shall consider here in Chap. 5).[4] Thus, if a macrodynamic model is sufficiently complete and elaborated in its temporary equilibrium part as well as in its representation of the laws of motion of a capitalist economy (including the detailed formulation of wage/price adjustments), there will be a Goodwinian component involved in the dynamics that it generates.[5]

To demonstrate this, the book will make use – in Part II – of one important prototype monetary growth model in the main, which at first does not seem to bear any relationship to the Goodwin growth cycle approach. Instead, somewhat simplified (and also modified) variants of this model were often used in the literature for comparing and contrasting presentations of the debate between Monetarists, Keynesians, or New Classical economists as, for example, in the book of Stein (1982).

One explanation for the fact that Goodwin-like features were not noticed in the treatment of such models is given by the observation that these models were normally so complex that a general analytical treatment was not available at that time so that these models had to be and were reduced in various respects to allow for definite stability considerations, comparative dynamics, and policy applications.[6] The prototype model chosen in Part II of this book, that is, Sargent's (1987; Chaps. 1 and 5) complete Keynesian or AS–AD model of business fluctuations, for example, was – in the case of adaptive expectations – treated by Sargent by means of a mixture of analytical and graphical tools, which seemed to suggest, but did not prove, a Friedmanian story for its possible dynamic reactions to monetary disturbances. Yet, as we shall see in Chaps. 6 and 7, the basic assumption of Sargent on the asymptotic stability of this model is not correct in general, which implies that this model is in fact not yet a complete one as far as the basic condition of economic viability is concerned, and that it must be modified to guarantee this basic economic condition.

Such modifications – which have to take into account the source of the instability of the model, the so-called Mundell-effect – will then give rise to the typical overshooting phenomenon of the Goodwin growth cycle type in this model, too. Despite its unorthodox background, the Goodwin model of cyclical growth thus must be considered as providing a fairly standard component in the discussion of economic growth and the fluctuations that occur around it. There exists definitely no good reason which allows for an exclusion of this model from the existing toolbox of macroeconomic model buildings or the diagnosis of their principal components.

These working hypotheses will be pursued in this book by presenting an introduction to the Goodwin approach to cyclical growth, which starts from the classical model of capital accumulation and Marx's critique of it. The Goodwin model is then

---

[4] Or if it is not of the market clearing type (where the effects of significant under- or overemployment are excluded from consideration).

[5] The baseline Goodwin model to the conflict over income distribution and the resulting self-sustained growth cycles are introduced and investigated in detail in Chap. 4 in part I of this book.

[6] See, however, the work of the group Asada, Chiarella, Flaschel, Franke et al. for progress in this direction.

derived as a fairly natural extension of this critique,[7] which may or may not be integrable into the model of only the first section of Marx's (1954) chapter on the "Law of Capitalist Accumulation" in "Capital," Vol I, Chap. 23. This introduction of the Goodwin model will then be followed by some extensions of it, which attempt to make it a more complete model of the Marxian reserve army cycle, in particular, in the light of the discussion of its structural instability. Our main point of view thereafter is to what extent this model can provide an alternative perspective to the Monetarist claim of the asymptotic stability of capitalist economies. This alternative perspective consists in the first instance in a different concept of the stability of capitalist economies, which are here analyzed as being viable (reproducible), but generally not in the extreme way that there is a steady state point attractor for the evolution of such economies. As it will be demonstrated, order (reproducibility) can arise and prevail through the occurrence of fluctuations in the use of the various real and financial resources of the economy. In other words, it will be shown that fluctuations in economic activity are here a necessary ingredient for the dynamic viability of such economies in the long run.

We then proceed in the direction of our working hypotheses by making use of a fairly standard model of monetary growth, which was used by Sargent (1987) to show how Monetarist conclusions can be derived from it. This is an interesting attempt that strives to derive Friedmanian propositions from a seemingly Keynesian model of business fluctuations (which Friedman never did consistently). Our alternative attempt here is to show to the reader that it is, however, much more likely that Goodwinian propositions will follow from such a model type. We do not claim, however, that this will be definitely demonstrated in the present textbook already.[8] Yet, on balance, we expect that the reasoning put forth in the Chaps. 6 and 7 for a partly Goodwinian interpretation of the Sargent model will appear at least comparable in weight and important to the constructions and results that are provided by Sargent himself in his attempt to derive Monetarist assertions from an elaborate AD–AS model of Keynesian business fluctuations. Moreover, we provide in Part III (Chaps. 8 and 9) an extension of the Sargent model, which reflects the work of Chiarella et al. by providing a prototype approach that is based on their work and that compares its achievements with the currently fashionable New Keynesian approach to AS–AD dynamics.

The Sargent (1987) model of monetary growth dynamics therefore here serves as a test model for our general hypothesis that any elaborate model of monetary growth (which allows for unemployment and its interaction with a fully specified dynamic wage/price module and which avoids the extreme assumption of uniform rational expectations) will be more likely Goodwinian than Monetarist. This model and its closely related modifications have, due to the complex interactions they can generate, indeed many interesting and often still unexplored features, which cannot

[7] Though not necessarily as a model that does justice to Marx's further ideas on the "General Law of Capitalist Accumulation."

[8] The reader is referred here again to Chiarella and Flaschel (2000) and the work that builds on this book.

be exhaustively discussed in this book, but which have meanwhile been investigated extensively in the work quoted above.

There is no room here to provide a detailed analysis of other approaches to monetary growth as they exist in the literature.[9] Our proof of the assertion on the general validity of the Goodwin growth cycle perspective as an important explanation of the cyclical viability of capitalist economies remains therefore restricted here to one model example – and its variants – in the main.[10] Yet, the Keynesian approaches to temporary equilibrium, the trade cycle, and the real growth dynamics we are surveying in Chaps. 2 and 3 are only complete when they are synthesized with the Goodwin distributive cycle into a coherent whole as we attempt it on the basis of conventional AD–AS analyses of monetary growth (considered in Part II) and their coherent reformulation in Part III of the book.

In the second place, this book also provides a systematic, though selective, discussion of Keynesian, Marxian, and Neoclassical views on the dynamics of a capitalist economy. It starts this discussion – in Part I, Chap. 2 – by contrasting basic alternative views on the short run determination of output, employment, and interest, that is, the concept of temporary equilibrium that underlies the study of economic evolution. It will be shown here that the elementary textbook presentations of Keynes vs. the Classics are still alive, since their modern counterparts have remained in spirit fairly close to them. This chapter also provides a brief introduction into Keynesian IS–LM analysis – the most general temporary equilibrium model of this introductory chapter on Keynes and the Classics. This model and its specific interpretation will be of use later on when this Keynesian approach is made a complete model of monetary growth in Part II of the book.

For the remaining chapters of Part I of the book, we start, however, from a much more simplified concept of temporary equilibrium, the simplest type of a Keynesian goods market model one can think of, to summarize and supplement (in its Chap. 3) the medium and long run multiplier–accelerator analyzes of the Keynesian theory that ruled the roost in the 1950s and the 1960s. Of central interest here is the discussion of the destabilizing or depressing forces in economic growth as they can be derived from Harrod's and Domar's analysis of investment behavior and economic dynamics.

Though there emerges here an important prototype model for local economic instability (in the boom) or of the stability of a depressed situation, we shall not make detailed use of these approaches in the following. Exceptions are the multiplier–accelerator extensions of the Goodwin growth cycle model in Chap. 4 and to some extent the appendices to Chaps. 5 and 6. The main reason for this is that our later prototype model of AD–AS growth – following Sargent's (1987, Chap. V) approach – makes use of a (neo)classical alternative to the investment accelerator of Chap. 3,

---

[9] A simple further example is given in the appendix of Chap. 5, where a Neokeynesian alternative to the Monetarist standard model of this chapter is investigated with respect to the Goodwinian features it may contain.

[10] See Rose (1990), Stein (1982) for further early examples of complete models of monetary growth that can be exploited in the direction of our approach.

which cannot be extended in a straightforward way to include problems of changing capacity utilization and accelerator dynamics.

Chapter 4 then introduces another basic prototype model, that is, the Goodwin growth cycle model already discussed earlier. We here start from the classical model of capital accumulation and its stationary state and Marx's constructive critique of its assumptions and its conclusions. This allows us to derive the Goodwin approach to cyclical growth by means of a systematic variation of the classical model. The multiplier–accelerator analysis of the preceding chapter is then integrated into the Goodwin approach in Chap. 4 in a preliminary way. It will again give rise to global instability problems, which are only partly overcome at the end of this chapter by an appropriate choice of the accelerator mechanism. In this chapter we also continue the discussion of fiscal policy rules started at the end of Chap. 3.

In Chap. 5, finally, we study a third kind of prototype model, that is, a Monetarist model of inflation and stagflation. We here review basic Monetarist propositions on stability, the role of expectations, and monetary policy and then contrast the Monetarist background of this model with a reinterpretation of it that directly derives from a Postkeynesian reformulation of its structural equations. Adding to this critique of the one-sided Monetarist interpretation of certain formal laws of the economy, we then contrast the Monetarist view on the viability of capitalist economies (which stresses the asymptotic stability of their balanced growth path and the inappropriateness of activist government policies in such an environment) with a Marxian analysis of the long run viability of capitalist economies, where the central structural characteristic of the Monetarist model – the so-called NUR-hypothesis – is deprived of its basis (and where an orthodox fiscal policy rule may contribute to economic stability, as we have already seen it in Chap. 4).

The conclusion of this part of the book – and also of its more elaborate Part II – is that the Monetarist treatment of the process of capital accumulation is either intimately (but only implicitly) related to a Marxian view of the working of a capitalist economy or fairly misleading. There thus emerges a model of the economy at the end of this first part and – in more elaborate form – also in Part II of this book, which might be called a Marx–Keynes–Friedman synthesis, but one which has nothing to do with the Walrasian approach to general equilibrium and the macroeconomic market clearing approaches that derive from it and which thus might not be accepted in general as being Friedmanian. Yet, since this synthesis offers an explanation of steady state unemployment and of the overshooting phenomenon of stagflation, it should at least bear some resemblance with the Monetarist way of explaining these two important stylized facts.[11]

In Part II we introduce a synthesis of the temporary equilibrium IS–LM model of Chap. 2 with the Solow growth model of Chap. 3 and the dynamics of the wage/price module we have considered in Chaps. 4 and 5. Chapters 6 and 7 then present and explore Sargent's attempt to derive Friedmanian hypotheses – discussed by means of a specifically tailored model in Chap. 3 – also in this context of a full-fledged

[11] See also Dornbusch and Fischer (1987) for an introduction of a basic model of inflation, unemployment, and stagflation, which attempts to provide a bridge between a Monetarist and a Keynesian analysis of these problems.

Keynesian IS–LM and Solovian growth model. These chapters – as well as the final Chaps. 8 and 9 on this topic – therefore synthesize the approaches of the preceding chapters to some extent and they show that this synthesis of fairly conventional elements of macroeconomic analysis may lead eventually not so much to hypotheses of a Friedmanian type, but of a type that stresses the cyclical nature and the overshooting mechanisms of the capitalist way of generating economic viability and economic reproducibility in the long run. This basic hypothesis of the book therefore demands for its proper – future – critique a model that is equally complete in its collection of static as well as dynamic structural equations for the explanation of growth, stability, and cycles and long run unemployment cum inflation. Independent of this discussion, Chaps. 6 and 7 also provide a detailed introduction into the analysis of a prototype textbook monetary growth model, which shows some of the typical results such a model gives rise to as well as some of the defects such a prototype construction still contains.

In this respect *a third essential aim* of this book is to show in its Chaps. 6 and 7 in Part II that there are several problematic features contained in such a standard approach to a Keynesian analysis of monetary growth and fluctuations that need to be dealt with. These (perplexing) features are given as follows:

- The striking but implausible contrast that is here claimed to exist between adaptively formed and myopically formed perfect foresight expectations of the short-run rate of inflation
- The problematic composition that is customary in such Keynesian aggregate demand and supply analyzes that make use, on the one hand, of the concept that firms are constrained by effective demand and which employ, on the other hand, a price-taking and profit-maximizing behavior of firms in the motivation of their standard marginal productivity real-wage relationship, and finally and most importantly
- The extreme type of assumption employed in such models, which makes the money wage a dynamically endogenous and thus at least somewhat sluggish variable, while the price level is treated as statically endogenous, that is, as perfectly flexible (independent of the period length of such models).

We shall see in Chaps. 6 and 7 that these features are closely related with each other and that a removal of the last problem – by making use of an adjustment principle of prices toward some target level as the proper supplement to the assumption of sluggish wages – will also take care of the first two problematic features previously mentioned (and also some severe instability problems of the model). The result will be that there is no longer a real difference visible then between the case of an adaptive formation of expectations – if adjusted sufficiently fast – and the case of myopic perfect foresight (which in its implications is then simply given as the limit case of adaptive expectations adjusting with infinite speed). The saddle-point features of conventional AD–AS models of monetary growth appear therefore to be the consequence of an implausible mixture of Walrasian and Keynesian elements, where the Walrasian component is not so much given by the assumption of the marginal wage-cost pricing rule, but by the presupposition that the price level will always adjust with infinite speed to such a target level. This extreme flexibility of the cost-determined price level is the real trouble maker in Keynesian demand restricted models of monetary growth.

Furthermore, we shall also see in Chap. 7 that the original introduction of Sargent and Wallace (1973) of the saddlepoint stability approach by means of Cagan's model of hyperinflation is incorrect, as this model can also be used to justify a quite different analysis of the dynamics of the price level, which does not give rise to the jump variable methodology of the rational expectations approach.

Part III is devoted to provide – on the basis of what we have learned in Part II – what we would like to call matured Keynesian AD–AS analysis, that is, a modeling approach that builds on the Hicks–Patinkin type of Neoclassical synthesis, but removes from it through suitable extensions the inconsistencies we have discussed in Part II. In contrast to the New Keynesian approach, where households behave in a Walrasian manner, and where monopolistic competition underlies price dynamics, and where purely forward-looking rational expectations rule out (if determinacy is given) all nonconvergent dynamics, we thus develop the Neoclassical synthesis, stage I, further into a Keynes–Marx (Goodwin) synthesis[12] in place of a complete break with anything that was considered Keynesian before the establishment of the so-called New Keynesian model building.

In Chap. 8 of the book we therefore formulate a general dynamic AD–AS model based on gradually adjusting wages and prices, perfect foresight of current inflation rates, and adaptive expectations concerning the inflation climate in which the economy operates. The model consists of a general wage and a price Phillips curve, a dynamic IS curve as well as a dynamic employment adjustment equation (Okun's law) and a Taylor interest rate rule. The model can be reduced to a 3D dynamical system by a suitable choice of the Taylor rule and implies strong stability results, in particular, for an appropriately chosen interest rate policy rule. Through instrumental variables GMM system estimation with aggregate time series data for the U.K. economy, we obtain parameter estimates that support the specification of our theoretical model and its stability implications. We contrast these results with the standard (formally similarly structured) New Keynesian model with both staggered wage and price setting, where determinacy of the implied dynamics represents a severe analytical problem and where (if determinacy can be achieved) inertia-free stability is obtained by the very choice of the solution method (which places the economy in a unique way on its stable submanifold). The considered two theories of the business cycle are therefore in direct opposition to each other, so that one of these scientific endeavors is or must become a failure sooner or later.

Chapter 8 extends our approach to a matured type of AD–AS analysis by means of a semi-structural model that is close (formally seen) in its building blocks to the New Keynesian baseline model with both staggered price and wages, but that differs radically from it in its solution methods and its economic implications. We estimate the model again – now for the US economy and the Eurozone – and show that it performs quite well in these application, leading to fairly similar results for these

[12] Based in particular on Keynes (1936, Chap. 22) and Marx (1954, Chap. 23).

two economies. We conclude that a matured type of Keynesian AD–AS analysis exists that can be easily compared with the New Keynesian approach to macrodynamics and that provides an alternative for all those who do not believe that rational expectations and the jumps to stable submanifolds they are depending upon are the relevant approach to applied macrodynamics from the descriptive point of view.

The book will be closed by a chapter where the impact of Schumpeter's approach to economic analysis becomes visible. In Schumpeter's (1942) book, "Capitalism, Socialism, and Democracy," the question is raised whether "capitalism can survive" and the various socio-economic aspects by which the functioning of after World War II capitalism may be threatened are discussed there in detail. In the subsequent part of the book the question of whether "socialism can work" is answered by and large in an affirmative way. The crucial side condition is, however, whether the concerned countries are in a state of maturity or not, leading to his conclusion that the road to socialism is prepared by the Rockefellers, Vanderbilts, etc., but not by the eastern type of socialism, that is, it is a Western type of competitive socialism where the human factor plays an important role, in particular, the integration of the bourgeois component of the working population. In the following part of the book, the issue of "socialism and democracy" is extensively discussed and another type of democracy – than the classical one – is considered on the basis of a Schumpeterian concept of the process of competition for political leadership.

We will not reconsider these considerations of Schumpeter in our final chapter of the book. Instead, we move on to the contemporaneous discussion of the so-called flexicurity capitalism, a topic that is currently extensively discussed on the informal level within the European Union. It is meanwhile far from clear whether there are economic limits to the functioning of capitalism, to say the least. Yet, there are social consequences of the way capitalism is by and large working in the World economy in the twenty-first century that may make it incompatible with human rights and democracy in the longer run.

Concerning the declaration of human rights it is stated there with respect to basic income and minimum wages:

1 Everyone has the right to work, to free choice of employment, to just and favorable conditions of work, and to protection against unemployment.
2 Everyone, without any discrimination, has the right to equal pay for equal work.
3 Everyone who works has the right to just and favorable remuneration ensuring for himself and his family an existence worthy of human dignity, and supplemented, if necessary, by other means of social protection.
4 Everyone has the right to form and to join trade unions for the protection of his interests.

United Nations (1998, article 23): Universal Declaration of Human Rights, 1948 (http://www.un.org/Overview/rights.html).

This article 23 from the United Nations' declaration of Human Rights does not only represent a normative statement, but can also be justified from the economic point of view in the context of analysis of the process of capital accumulation. We believe that capitalism has been and still is a very robust system of resource allocation and income distribution that can adjust to many social restrictions (neglecting, however, its possible financial instability on this level of analysis) if these restrictions are justified from a normative point of view. However, besides vulnerable financial markets, most capitalist countries exhibit long-lasting degradation processes of human work and whole families in significant parts of the working population, growing inequalities in income and wealth distribution, growing hostilities between social classes on both sides of the distribution scale, and significant decay in the acceptance of the outcomes of the democratic processes (in existing democracies, or plutocracies, ignoring here one-party systems of various types).

To make capitalism work in the long-run we surely need its flexibility, that is, Schumpeter's process of creative destruction through the entrepreneur or (with respect to Schumpeter Mark II) the large companies that reorganize or routinize the process of technical change on a large scale throughout the world economy. But combining this with the ruthless capitalism of the past and today may be destructive for the further function of the capitalist economies that have become democracies. In the times of conflict between the Western capitalist countries and the Eastern socialist countries (and even before that time) Welfare State elements were introduced into the working of such ruthless competition with very different degrees, for example, in the Nordic states of Europe as compared, for example, with the US economy. On the basis of the evolution of the Nordic countries, the concept of flexicurity has been introduced now into the discussion on labor market reform and societal progress.

Defining in this respect flexibility by unrestricted hiring and firing (but changes in the technologies of firms as restricted by human rights and ethics), one here adds the concept of social security (employment, but not job security, and basic income needs) in order to design a social structure of accumulation that does not allow for a systematic degradation of human beings and family structures, as we can observe it in particular in the large countries of the European Union, for example. Such a flexicurity model of capitalism – reformulating and improving the Schumpeterian description of Western competitive socialism – has been formulated in its principles on various occasions and is also confronted with workfare instead of welfare state constructions and the like in the contemporaneous discussion within the European Union.

Chapter 10 will provide in this respect a formal baseline model of flexicurity capitalism and will extend this model by credit, financial markets, and Keynesian goods market problems in its course. It will also discuss skill formation and utilization, but will also provide a broader view on the education system of such economies, in particular with respect to the equal opportunity principle, the need for life-long learning, and more. This type of model extends Schumpeter's views as expressed in his work "Capitalism, Socialism, and Democracy" and it will also allow for all forms of dynamic entrepreneurships, small-, middle-, or large-sized ones and driven by Keynesian "animal spirits" or routinized R&D units and thus preserve the process of creative destruction that was nearly absent in past Eastern Socialism.

1.2 Methodological Considerations

Mainstreams macroeconomics generally – at least with respect to heterodox approaches – insists on the following three methodological principles in order to judge whether a macrodynamic model makes sense or not:

- Microfoundations of the representative agent type (disaggregated with respect to age structure in so-called OLG models, however)
- Market-Clearing on all markets (i.e., in general the use of algebraic equations in place of dynamic error adjustment equations)
- Rational Expectations (which ensure that the economy is always on its stable submanifold in its deterministic core)

We will collect in this brief section some arguments that we believe show that such a methodological approach to the study of macrodynamic systems is much too narrow and one-sided to allow for a fruitful analysis of actual behavioral possibilities, the stock-flow interactions they imply, and the complex dynamics this may create outside the narrow range of ideal baseline considerations of rational expectations type (often characterized by ad hoc modifications needed to address relevant empirical issues). Indeed, since the *assumption* of rational expectations by the economic agents has become an undeniable *truth* for many economists, the stability of the economy (and the well behaved impulse-response functions generated after anticipated and unanticipated shocks) implied by its mathematically highly complex and economically highly questionable rational expectations solution (which is mathematically of a structurally unstable type)[13] has become a "goes without saying" matter in the mainstream economic literature. Hand in hand with this development, the study of possibly unstable or divergent paths of the economic has become superfluous for the majority of the profession. However, as, for example, the recent financial crisis, and more generally, simple common sense would suggest, not all agents are or *have the capability* to be fully rational at all times, so that the modeling and study of *nonrational* macroeconomic dynamics is just as, if not more, important as the study of dynamics generated solely under the assumption of fully rational and all-knowing agents.

By contrast, the theme that is common to *all* economic theories is the existence of short-term budget restrictions, which when all debt items are properly specified must be fulfilled at all moments in time.[14] The type of behavior that takes place within given budget equations (or *restrictions* if credit rationing takes place) is, however, open to discussion, since there is no unique way to rationalize the behavior of economic agents (who may use different optimization routines when solving problems of differing complexity). And coordination between the plans of agents

[13] See Chiarella, Flaschel, Franke, and Semmler (2008) for their detailed treatment and for example for cases where the addition of one further state variable (in the course of a model generalization) completely alters or even overthrows earlier economic outcomes instead of only making them more general.

[14] The way intertemporal budget equations are made binding ones is, however, not so obvious as it is usually assumed in the mainstream approaches to such issues.

acting on a specific market may be very different, not only depending on the specific form of the market, but also on the restrictions economic agents experience when operating on it.

In the following subsections we briefly consider each of the above items in isolation before we come to a general evaluation of the importance of these items in their interaction.

1.2.1 Microfoundations

In our view the basic objection to the Robinsonian representative agent approach is given by the simple observation that capitalism is in the minimum based on the interaction of two representative agents (Robinson as principal and Friday as agent). We claim that capitalism cannot be sensibly modeled under the assumption that a ceteris paribus reduction in wages simply reappears as profits in the income statement of the representative agent, who therefore may benefit in fact from not employing himself (Two souls alas! are dwelling in my breast; Goethe, Faust, 1097–1132).

The conflict about income distribution (and new techniques of production) is a very fundamental conflict in a capitalist economy. It may even be claimed that it is the core element in the explanation of the dynamics of capitalism, shaping Keynesian goods market dynamics (based on the wage-led profit-led distinction) as well as Schumpeterian cycles in the economic and the social structure of accumulation in significant ways. The long-run nature of this conflict is exemplified with respect to the short- and long-phase cycles it implies for the case of the US economy in Flaschel, Tavani, Teuber, and Taylor (2008) and Proaño, Flaschel, Diallo, and Teuber (2008). This situation is not solved by so-called Overlapping Generations (OLG) models, since the distinction between capitalists and workers is not a matter of age. Instead, if this distinction is made, we would get four types of economic agents from it, since social affiliations tend to be stable in time and are thus quite the opposite of the case considered in the single agent OLG framework.

There are of course more than just the two considered social classes, but our argument is not directed towards finding the most appropriate calls representation for a given economy, but to establish what should be assumed in the minimum in the investigation of the dynamics of capitalist economies. On the basis of such a minimum framework, one should then formulate a situation which is more general than the case of classical saving habits where only savings out of profits are allowed for. In a modern capitalist economy, both capitalists and workers save so that personal income distribution will be different from functional income distribution and there will be wealth accumulation also on the side of workers, the long-run effects of which have to be investigated.

There will be the evolution of unions, pension funds, and more and workers' preferences may also change in the course of wealth accumulation. Yet, these are secondary issues that should be kept apart from the baseline version of the model that attempts to investigate the dynamics of wages, profits, and wealth in a society where interests differ about the evolution of these magnitudes.

There is, however, a second argument that questions the validity of the arguments put forth by those that insist on the representative agent approach. Households in this approach are often modeled in a Walrasian manner, as not only price takers, but also as seing no (income) restrictions for the supply they are offering through their optimizing procedures. With respect to the Walrasian framework, we know, however, from the theorem proved by Sonnenschein, Mantel, and Debreu[15] that nearly everything can be microfounded, once enough heterogeneity is assumed between economic agents. What therefore is the value of a Robinson Crusoe type of microfoundation of certain demand and supply schedules? The answer is that nothing can be proved in this way to be superior to well-specified supply and demand relationship (formulated within well-specified budget restrictions).

The argument can only be a methodological one, namely to avoid situations where this type of well-specified behavior is neglected by assuming supply and demand relationships that are inconsistent with the stock–flow interactions generated by the budget restrictions of the various types of agents. This implies that these latter restrictions should always be carefully specified, but that the matter of what agents actually optimize within these constraints should at the least be a matter of dispute, if not even be a matter of empirical investigation that cannot be subjected to theoretical analysis alone. All this also holds outside the counterfactual general equilibrium analysis of Walrasian production economies. It should be used to demand rigor on the side of stock–flow specifications of the considered economy, but – in the interest of pluralism – not be used to just refuse coherent modelings of this type simply because they are not based on the presentative agent assumption or related modeling devices.

1.2.2 Market Clearing

A basic empirical fact is that the actual data generating process in macroeconomics – with respect to annual data like the inflation rate over the last 365 days – is by and large a daily one, since the annual average inflation rate is updated in the actual process at least every day (and the data collection frequency is now also often much less than a quarter). This suggests that empirically oriented discrete-time macromodels mirroring the actual data generating process should be iterated with a short period length and will then in general provide the same answer as their continuous-time analogues. Concerning expectations, the (slower) data collection process may, however, be of importance and may give rise to certain (smaller) delays in the revision of expectations, which, however, is overcome by the formulation of extrapolating expectation mechanisms and other ways by which agents smooth their expectation formation process. We do not expect here that this implies a major difference between period and continuous time analysis if appropriately modeled, a situation which may, however, radically change if proper delays as for example gestation lags

[15] The reader is referred to vol. 38 of the journal *History of Political Economy* (2006) for a variety of articles that discuss the implications of this theorem.

are introduced. Yet even this situation may only lead to continuous time systems involving certain moving delay terms and not to the period models with a uniform, totally synchronized period over all the markets in the economy, as they are customary now, for example, in the New Keynesian approach to macrodynamics.[16]

Sims (1998, p. 318) states in this regard:

> The next several sections examine the behavior of a variety of models that differ mainly in how they model real and nominal stickiness ... They are formulated in continuous time to avoid the need to use the uninterpretable "one period" delays that plague the discrete time models in this literature.

We completely agree with such a statement. We conclude from it that the use of general equilibrium approaches with market clearing on all markets in the economy in continuous time is very unlikely to represent a reasonable assumption for the real markets of the economy. Instead, there are gradual adjustment processes at work that respond, for example, to unintended inventory changes. We thus claim here that continuous time disequilibrium dynamics is much more relevant for the study of actual market economies than macrodynamic period models with their artificial synchronization of all activities (their virtual bunching at, e.g., four points during the year). This is directly obvious for macrodynamic models of dimension one, where there is convergence in continuous time and chaotic dynamics in period versions of the model when the period length becomes sufficiently large, but it also applies to statements of Erceg et al. (2000) when uniformly synchronized period lengths of 2 years are considered with respect to their economic implications.[17]

Of course, there exist processes that are synchronized with certain calendar dates, like monthly wage payments or the mentioned data collection snapshots of the economy, which are often taking at given points in time. The question, however, is whether these synchronized activities are so important that they challenge the usage of continuous time models with their compelling implication of using disequilibrium formulations at least for the real markets of the economy rather than the assumption of equilibrium at all moments in time.

We moreover conclude that period models that give different answers than their corresponding continuous time analogues should be interpreted with caution if they are intended to apply to the actual behavior of actual economies. Such model types may be very misleading if we attempt to use them for macroeconomic policy advice.

1.2.3 Rational Expectations

We here consider the rational expectations (RE) methodology only with respect to their deterministic continuous-time core (if there is one). In the deterministic case. The existence of uniquely determined rational expectations solutions (called

---

[16] See Flaschel, Groh, Proaño, and Semmler (2008, Chap. 1) for a detailed study along arguments of this type.

[17] See Erceg et al. (2000, p. 302).

determinacy) are based on eigenvalue calculations and the local search for unstable submanifold, as in Woodford's (2003) appendices, such that a one-to-one correspondence between forward-looking variables and the number of unstable roots can be established. This guarantees determinacy in the reaction of nonpredetermined variables by means of the so-called jump-variable technique, which by assumption then allows to put the economy in a unique way onto the stable submanifold of the full phase space of the dynamics (or – in the case of anticipated events – onto a bubble towards it that lands exactly on this stable manifold when anticipations are realizing). In the considered core case, rational expectations are therefore much more than just model-consistent expectations, since they select – by jumps of the forward-looking variables – from the set of all future paths with only model-consistent expectations (if possible) the single path that converges to the steady state of the economy as time goes to infinity. This type of omniscient agent is assumed to the representative household's behavior as well as to decision making within firms.

Our basic objections to such a solution to the local stabilization of an in general unstable (saddlepoint) economy through a schematic application of a mathematical algorithm are the following ones:[18]

- What are the microfoundations for this choice of behavior for the whole economy in models where the area of economic outcomes, that is, the stable manifold depends on the interaction between independent households' and firms' demand, supply, and pricing decisions? Who is coordinating the macroeconomically endogenous parameters of the partial decision problems of households and firms over the considered horizon?
- How do agents master the complex RE calculations that are needed to guarantee such a macroeconomic performance (in particular, if information is costly)?
- In a nonlinear context: Why do they have REs in loglinear approximations around the steady state and apply their global RE calculation (since they must know all unbounded trajectories) routines to the loglinear approximation instead of checking how the nonlinear stable submanifold looks like, representing a problem when the limit sets of all trajectories are all globally seen bounded ones?
- Increasing the dimension of an economic model simply by adding, for example, some stock-flow interaction may lead to totally different jumps than in the initially given situation, for example, when the capacity effects of investment are added to the model. The behavior of the economy is therefore structurally unstable, not only with respect to local approximations of the model, but also with respect to the number of state variables, even if they do not involve additional behavior from the side of the economic agents.
- Assuming, for example, a PPP-UIP model with RE may lead to policy advices that must recommend increases in money supply in order to fight inflation, that is, perfectness in the neoclassical sense implies policy conundrums.

[18] See, for example, Chiarella et al. (2008) and in this book Chap. 9 for more details on the statements of this list. See also Colander (2006) for a collection of essays that attempt to go beyond Post-Walrasian DSGE macroeconomics.

- There is no rigorous determinacy discussion for theoretical models of staggered wage and price setting and even more in applied DSGE models, where this problem is thus only implicitly dealt with (in an ad hoc numerical manner).
- Purely forward-looking models of New Keynesian type perform poorly with respect to empirical applications and need often to be modified in an ad hoc fashion to improve their empirical accuracy.
- Rational expectations approaches represent a very cumbersome method for getting impulse-responses that correspond to empirical observed patterns.
- Rational expectations approaches are very limited with respect to even slight generalizations in the considered model frame, for example, with respect to an adequate treatment of the investment decisions of firms.
- Rational expectations approaches are nearly noncommunicable to an educated public outside the narrow range of true followers of this methodology.

Taken together, we would claim here that the RE methodology may be a rigorous strategy to solve for the performance of a model economy numerically, but it is far away from producing realistic baseline cases (with staggered wages) that are solvable from the theoretical perspective. Moreover, its solution strategy is structurally unstable (at least in the case of anticipated events), from the mathematical perspective a highly complex type of behavior, and subject to bizarre reactions of the agents of the economy (in times of severe contractive shocks) or bizarre policy conclusions (in perfectly open economies). We refer the reader again to Chiarella et al. (2008), Flaschel et al. (2008), and Asada, Flaschel, and Proaño (2008) for more details on the validity of these statements.

1.2.4 A Short Summary

On the basis of what has been discussed earlier, it appears that the rational expectations approach (coupled with representative agents microfoundations and market clearing) is just the wrong axiomatic starting point for an applicable macrodynamic analysis that therefore demands for complicated epicycles (habit formation, indexing, etc.) in order to reconcile this approach with empirical observations. It is a very restrictive if not even very hypothetical way to model the working capitalist economies. It represents very inefficient or cumbersome way to reproduce (or even understand) the factual behavior of actual economies.

If we accept that continuous-time approaches are more appropriate than over-synchronized quarterly models of the real-financial market interaction on the macrolevel, if we go on from this observation to corresponding disequilibrium AD–AS models as investigated in Flaschel et al. (2008), where agents may have myopic model-consistent expectations (to simplify without significant loss of generality the analysis to a certain degree), if we vote for principal-agent problems on the macrodynamic level (to avoid the two-souls problem), and if we are prepared to accept that economies may be locally unstable around their steady state position, but can be tamed by behavioral nonlinearities when they depart by too much from their steady state position, we might be able to find interesting new insights and policy conclusions not attainable within the New Consensus of mainstream macroeconomics.

A gentle warning: All these assertions are attributable to the author of the present book and may not necessarily be shared or formulated in this way by the co-authors of the work here quoted. Moreover, the present critique is one that in fact argues for methodological pluralism and should not be understood as suggestion to abandon the approaches here characterized by representative agent microfoundations, market clearing, and rational expectations. In fact it may be an interesting scientific experience to see how far approaches to macroeconomic dynamics can be developed in the pursuit of a particular research strategy.

One scientific postulate for macroeconomic research should, however, be respected in economic modeling by all schools of thought, namely that budget restrictions and stock–flow interactions always need to be carefully formulated and investigated, also already on the level of partial model building. What agents are in fact doing within these budget restraints is, however, be a matter of scientific dispute and is therefore open for pluralistic solutions.

1.3 A Baseline Model of a Capitalist Economy

In this section we build a simple macro-model, which is microfounded, considers disequilibrium by way of real wage rigidity (in the form of a conventional real wage Phillips curve, based on myopic perfect foresight with respect to the price inflation rate), and assumes heterogeneous agents, in fact two, the representative worker and the pure capitalist, both with their own utility function[19] and with differing ownership in the total capital stock of the economy (which may change in time). We use a continuous-time framework with a stationary population of both types of agents, the first normalized to "one" in number and the second a (small) portion of "one." Workers maximize a Cobb–Douglas utility function $C_{\mathrm{w}}^{\alpha_{\mathrm{w}}} I_{\mathrm{w}}^{1-\alpha_{\mathrm{w}}}$, with C_{w} their planned consumption and I_w their planned investment in the capital stock they own (all capital items depreciate with the rate δ).[20] The temporary budget restriction of workers is given by

$$C_{\mathrm{w}} + I_{\mathrm{w}} = \omega L^{\mathrm{d}} + \rho K_{\mathrm{w}}, \quad \rho = (Y - \delta K - \omega L^{\mathrm{d}})/K = y - \delta - \omega l^{\mathrm{d}},$$

where Y, L^{d} is gross output and employment, K_{w} the capital stock owned by workers, and ρ is the rate of profit of the economy (ω the real wage). We assume fixed proportions in production, that is, y, l^{d} are given magnitudes here for reasons of simplicity.

---

[19] This two-class Pasinetti model is considered in Greiner (2001) with life cycle utility functions in place of the simple utility functions used here to get Pasinetti type capital stock dynamics (with bequest) in the simplest possible way.

[20] The distribution of wealth may be different between workers, due to fluctuating real wages and bequest, but this does not matter on the macrolevel, since they will be shown to save all with the same rate out of their current income.

Utility maximization then implies for workers the gross savings = gross investment relationship:

$$I_{\mathrm{w}} = (1-\alpha_{\mathrm{w}})[\omega l^{\mathrm{d}} + \rho k_{\mathrm{w}}]K, \quad k_{\mathrm{w}} = K_{\mathrm{w}}/K.$$

Pure capitalists also maximize a Cobb–Douglas utility function $C_{\mathrm{c}}^{\alpha_{\mathrm{c}}} I_{\mathrm{c}}^{1-\alpha_{\mathrm{c}}}$ with C_{c} their planned consumption and I_{c} their planned investment in the capital stock they own. We assume that $\alpha_{\mathrm{w}} > \alpha_{\mathrm{c}}$ holds true with respect to the utility generated by consumption and that capitalists do not work, but consume on the basis of their profit income solely. The temporary budget restriction of capitalists is therefore given by

$$C_{\mathrm{c}} + I_{\mathrm{c}} = \rho K_{\mathrm{c}}, \quad \rho = y - \delta - \omega l^{\mathrm{d}},\ K_{\mathrm{c}} = K - K_{\mathrm{w}},$$

where K_{c} is the capital stock owned by capitalists.

Utility maximization then implies for capitalists' gross savings = gross investment relationship:

$$I_{\mathrm{c}} = (1-\alpha_{\mathrm{c}})\rho k_{\mathrm{c}} K, \quad k_{\mathrm{c}} = K_{\mathrm{c}}/K.$$

The dynamic of the real wage is given by a conventional type of Phillips curve (expectations augmented and based on myopic perfect foresight), that is,

$$\hat{\omega} = \dot{\omega}/\omega = \beta_{\mathrm{w}}(e-\bar{e}), \quad e = L^{\mathrm{d}}/L = l^{\mathrm{d}}/l,$$

where e denotes the rate of employment and $\bar{e}$ the given NAIRU level of this rate (L the stationary labor supply). Since $e = l^{\mathrm{d}}/l$ and l^{d} is a given magnitude (and the working population a stationary magnitude) we have two state variables ω, e and their laws of motion in this model so far:

$$\hat{\omega} = \beta_{\mathrm{w}}(e-\bar{e}), \quad \hat{e} = \hat{K} = I_{\mathrm{w}}/K + I_{\mathrm{c}}/K - \delta.$$

The latter law of motion gives (when investment behavior is inserted)

$$\hat{e} = (1-\alpha_{\mathrm{w}})[\omega l^{\mathrm{d}} + \rho k_{\mathrm{w}}] + (1-\alpha_{\mathrm{c}})\rho k_{\mathrm{c}} - \delta.$$

We therefore have to make use of a third state variable in order to close the model, given by $k_{\mathrm{c}} = K_{\mathrm{c}}/K$, the percentage of the capital stock that is owned by capitalists. This finally gives

$$\hat{e} = (1-\alpha_{\mathrm{w}})[\omega l^{\mathrm{d}} + \rho(1-k_{\mathrm{c}})] + (1-\alpha_{\mathrm{c}})\rho k_{\mathrm{c}} - \delta$$

and for the new state variable the law of motion

$$\hat{k}_{\mathrm{c}} = \hat{K}_{\mathrm{c}} - \hat{K} = (1-\alpha_{\mathrm{c}})\rho - (1-\alpha_{\mathrm{w}})[\omega l^{\mathrm{d}} + \rho(1-k_{\mathrm{c}})] - (1-\alpha_{\mathrm{c}})\rho k_{\mathrm{c}}.$$

The dynamical system implied by our simple model therefore reads

$$\hat{\omega} = \beta_{\mathrm{w}}(e-\bar{e}), \tag{1.1}$$

$$\hat{e} = \hat{K} = (1-\alpha_{\mathrm{w}})(y-\delta) + (\alpha_{\mathrm{w}}-\alpha_{\mathrm{c}})\rho k_{\mathrm{c}} - \delta = g(\omega, k_{\mathrm{c}}),\ g_{\omega} < 0 g_{k_{\mathrm{c}}} > 0, \tag{1.2}$$

$$\hat{k}_{\mathrm{c}} = (1-\alpha_{\mathrm{c}})\rho - g(\omega, k_{\mathrm{c}}), \tag{1.3}$$

with all parametric expressions in front of the state variables ω, e, k_c being positive ($\rho = y - \delta - \omega l^d$).

The interior steady state solution of these dynamics, where $I_w = \delta K_w, I_c = \delta K_c$ holds, are given by

$$e_o = \bar{e}, \tag{1.4}$$

$$\rho_o = \delta/(1-\alpha_c), \tag{1.5}$$

$$\omega_o = (y - \delta - \rho_o)/l^d = \frac{(1-\alpha_c)(y-\delta)-\delta}{(1-\alpha_c)l^d}, \tag{1.6}$$

$$k_c^o = \frac{\delta - (1-\alpha_w)(y-\delta)}{(\alpha_w - \alpha_c)\rho_o}. \tag{1.7}$$

The steady state values of the real wage and the percentage of the capital stock of capitalist are positive if and only if there holds

$$\alpha_w \quad > \quad (y-2\delta)/(y-\delta) \quad > \quad \alpha_c,$$

with the left inequality as equality relationship implying $\omega_o = 0$ and the right one implying as equality relationship $k_c^o = 0$. Workers' propensity to consume must therefore be sufficiently large and capitalists' consumption propensity sufficiently low to guarantee in the first case the existence of capitalists at the steady state and in the second case that workers get in fact remunerated for their work.

The matrix of partial derivatives of this dynamical system at the steady state and when reformulated as differential equations is given by

$$J = \begin{pmatrix} 0 & \beta_w \omega_o & 0 \\ g_\omega e_o & 0 & g_{k_c} e_o \\ -(1-\alpha_c) l^d k_c^o - g_\omega k_c^o & 0 & -g_{k_c} k_c^o \end{pmatrix}.$$

It is easy to show that the trace and the determinant of this Jacobian matrix are both negative and that the sum a_2 of the principal minors of order 2 is positive. The Routh–Hurwitz stability conditions, see the mathematical appendix, are therefore fulfilled if also the expression -trace $J \cdot a_2 + \det J$ can be shown to be positive. For this expression we get from the above Jacobian (with the constant c being positive)

$$g_{k_c} k_c^o \beta_w \omega_o(-g_\omega e_o) - \beta_w \omega_o g_{k_c} e_o - (1-\alpha_c) l^d k_c^o = c[(\alpha_w - \alpha_c)k_c^o - (1-\alpha_c)] < 0$$

We thus have the somewhat astonishing result that the steady state of this economy is nearly stable, but that the fourth Routh–Hurwitz stability condition is in fact hurt, implying that there must be eigenvalues with positive real parts so that the dynamics becomes divergent sooner or later. This locally unstable dynamics can, however, be made convergent, for example, in the following simple manner. Assume that the propensity to consume α_c of capitalists depends positively on the rate of employment e, meaning that they invest less in situations of increasing employment, since they consider such a situation as undermining their bargaining position on the labor market. This implies as modified Jacobian the matrix

$$J = \begin{pmatrix} 0 & \beta_w \omega_o & 0 \\ g_\omega e_o & -\alpha_c^{'}(\bar{e})\rho_o k_c^o & g_{k_c} e_o \\ -(1-\alpha_c)l^d k_c^o - g_\omega k_c^o & -\alpha_c^{'}(\bar{e})\rho_o(k_c^o+1) & -g_{k_c}k_c^o \end{pmatrix}.$$

This extension of the model increases term-trace $J \cdot a_2 + \det J$ without altering its det-component. Choosing $\alpha_c^{'}(\bar{e})$ sufficiently large will therefore make this expression positive. This happens by way of a Hopf bifurcation, leading to Goodwin (1967) type, but damped oscillations around the steady state as considered in detail in Chap. 4 of this book, since the determinant of the matrix J prevents the occurrence of zero eigenvalues.

We have built in this section the in-our-view simplest type of a continuous-time model of capitalism with a microfounded principal-agent structure (and thus not two souls in one breast), with conflict and disequilibrium on the labor market and gradually adjusting real wages (derived from a conventional type of expectations-augmented Phillips curve coupled myopic perfect foresight on price inflation), with all budget equations specified and an implied coherent stock–flow interaction, which can give rise to damped oscillations around its interior steady state position where capitalists coexist with workers and thus own part of the capital stock.

Given this situation we therefore do not move to a case where pure capitalists would disappear and where some sort of peoples' capitalism would come about with workers as the representative agent. Of course, one may ask how the economy and with it the model will change if workers' part of the capital stock is run under other conditions than the one of the pure capitalists, since workers do not only get income from firms (through firm bonds), but may also be able to decide on the way these firms are run (through equities). Moreover, Keynesian demand problems may enter the scene when investment projects financed through paper credit markets are added to the model. Schumpeterian long-phase waves may also be added through microprocess of creative destruction, which may create continuing increases in labor productivity Y/L^d and bounded fluctuations in the output-capital ratio y.

Such model extensions are, however, not the topic of this section, which was solely designed to show the minimal type of structure one should allow for in the theoretical as well as the empirical investigation of the fundamental forces that drive capitalism, which in our view is the sometimes more, sometimes less intensive conflict about income distribution between two types of agent (and the conditions of capitalist production), with long-phase cycles in the evolution of social structures of accumulation, as they were classified in Schumpeter's (1939) work on business cycles and long-phased waves.

Using the here proposed modeling strategies, the book will provide in its course elements for a synthesis of Marx' reserve army mechanism with Keynes' trade cycle analysis, but will not go into the micro details of the Schumpeterian view on the cyclical evolution of capitalism ranging from his character of the restless dynamic entrepreneur (and his imitators) to the bureaucratic mega-corporation with its routinized R&D work. Instead, in the final chapter of this book, we will go on from the model of this section with workers normally considered unskilled in such a framework (and capitalists considered skilled) to a model with skilled and high skilled workers in a framework where flexibility is combined with social security (flexicurity) and where – in place of the stationary class formation processes here assumed – the principle of equal opportunities may find successful application. Also in this model type, we will have real wage rigidities and Keynesian business fluctuations, but no Marxian reserve army mechanism anymore, through the assumption of an employer first (but possibly also: last) resort. The minimum model of capitalism we have constructed in this section will thus there be confronted with a similarly basic structure of a matured type of capitalism to which some modern forms of capitalism may lead us through social consensus about reforms of the welfare state and the progress paths this may generate.

Part I
Temporary Equilibrium, Distribution-Driven Demand Cycles, and Unbalanced Growth

The rise of wages therefore is confined within limits that not only leave intact the foundations of the capitalist system, but also secure its reproduction on a progressive scale. The law of capitalistic accumulation, metamorphosed by economists into pretended law of Nature, in reality merely states that the very nature of accumulation excludes every diminution in the degree of exploitation of labor, and every rise in the price of labor, which could seriously imperil the continual reproduction, on an ever-enlarging scale, of the capitalistic relation. It cannot be otherwise in a mode of production in which the laborer exists to satisfy the needs of self-expansion of existing values, instead of. on the contrary, material wealth exist to satisfy the needs of development on the part of the laborer. As, in religion, man is governed by the products of his own brain, so in capitalistic production, he is governed by the products of his own hand.[1]

[1] Marx, K. (1954). *Capital, Volume I*. London: Lawrence and Wishart, p. 582.

Chapter 2
Keynes, the "Classics," and the "New Classics": A Simple Presentation of Basic Differences

2.1 Introduction

This chapter reformulates *the static foundations* of "Keynesian macrodynamics" and *their proper interpretation* in an economically consistent and complete way. It is one of its aims here to lay the ground for a critique of conventional representations of "Keynesian dynamics" by indicating how certain deficiencies of these dynamic models can be attributed to a wrong understanding of their static components, that is, of the *Keynesian concept of temporary equilibrium* and the adjustment processes that are compatible with it. Its central purpose thus is to provide a clear picture (model) of the basic steps and components of Keynes' revolution of macroeconomic thinking.

This will be done by taking as starting point the conventional synthetic model of "Classical Macroeconomics" and by providing a description of it as consistent and complete as possible, in particular with regard to its representation of Say's Law [the central point in Keynes' attack on the "Classics"!]. In our view, this Law has not yet been given a sufficiently exact expression in this type of model, which also implies that an exact critique à la Keynes of the defects of this Law has generally not been provided in the literature so far.

Completing the conventional "Classical Macroeconomic model" and showing how a Keynes' type of revolution can be incorporated into it by means of basically *only one change* in its components is the objective of the first part of our following considerations. Yet, such a project would not be of too great importance if it would only clarify the starting chapter of a correct presentation of the theory of employment, interest, and money, that is, if it only served as a didactic introduction into the first stage of the development toward today's macroeconomics. In the second part of this chapter we therefore in addition attempt to exemplify that important macroeconomic textbook models of temporary equilibrium can be reformulated and extended in such a way that they will be recognized as fairly simple modernization of the above basic representation of Classical Macroeconomics. These models to some extent improve the consistency of the Classical approach, yet, as we shall see,

P. Flaschel, *The Macrodynamics of Capitalism: Elements for a Synthesis of Marx, Keynes and Schumpeter, Second Edition,*

also deprive it of important applications and conclusions, which were available in the original Classical setup of this approach. Modifying the "Classics" in this way to obtain a prototype model of the "New Classical economics" is important for an evaluation of the advances of this new approach to macrostatics and -dynamics. *And furthermore*, as we shall see, the obtained example of a New Classical model allows – just as its Classical predecessor – a revolution à la Keynes and consequently only provides us with a more precise, but eventually still pre-Keynesian type of analysis.

Some Observations

To start our investigations let us first – in the light of our above remarks – exemplify some basic flaws in the application and interpretation of the macroeconomic theory of aggregate demand and supply. The conventional (textbook) analysis of the aggregate demand and supply schedules $Y^{\mathrm{d}}, Y^{\mathrm{s}}$ is normally based on a diagram as shown in Fig. 2.1.

The aggregate demand curve $Y^{\mathrm{d}}(p)$ of this diagram is generally viewed as being derived from money *and goods market equilibrium*, that is, from the conventional IS-LM model, by varying prices p parametrically. It consequently represents more than just aggregate demand $C+I$ and will therefore be called the effective demand schedule $Y^{\mathrm{d}}(p)$ in the following. The so-called aggregate supply curve $Y^{\mathrm{s}}(p)$ is generally viewed, on the other hand, to determine for a given money wage that level of planned output (where with regard to given prices p) profits are maximized by price-taking firms. The economic background of this relationship will be reformulated in the following.[1]

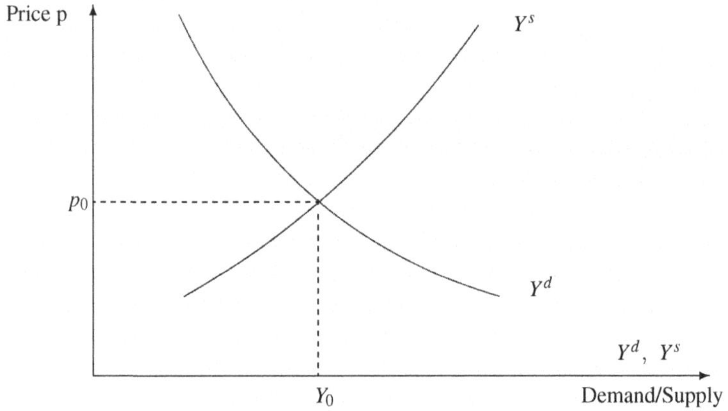

Fig. 2.1 Aggregate "demand" and "supply"

[1] By making use of the argument that $p(Y^{\mathrm{s}})$ must be interpreted to represent the supply price of producers when they expect to sell Y^{s}, which inverts the causality normally associated with the (p,Y^{s})-schedule, cf. also the following.

The discrepancy between aggregate demand and supply is then often used to show the direction into which the price level will change – by making use of the standard *microeconomic* formulation of the so-called *law of demand and supply* [cf. the Fig. 2.1 and, e.g., Barro (1990, Chap. 20)]. This, however, is not a convincing starting-point for a proper understanding (and explanation) of the interaction of Keynesian *"aggregate"* demand and supply schedules. We cannot simply confront the goods-market equilibrium point $Y^{\mathrm{d}}(p)$ with a level of planned output Y^{s} that is different from it by referring to price-taking and profit-maximizing firms. A different context consequently has to be found to interpret and explain Fig. 2.1. Disequilibrium in this diagram, as we shall see, has to be analyzed in the vertical or price direction, not in the horizontal or quantity direction. This means that, for given prices p and the corresponding situation of an IS-LM equilibrium $Y^{\mathrm{d}}(p)$, it should be viewed as showing the level of competitive (supply) prices, which may be above or below the actual one. Price (setting) adjustment on the basis of this discrepancy may (or may not) move actual prices toward competitive ones, yet this happens – by definition – without any disequilibrium in the market for goods. This is the correct interpretation of a possible disequilibrium in Fig. 2.1,[2] which thus describes correct demand anticipations of producers and a disequilibrium between potential supply and actual market prices.

The consideration of equilibrium in the market for goods is in general based on a consumption function of the type $C(Y^{\mathrm{s}},\ldots)$, where planned consumption expenditures have been assumed to depend on planned *output* Y^{s}.[3] Hence, though a

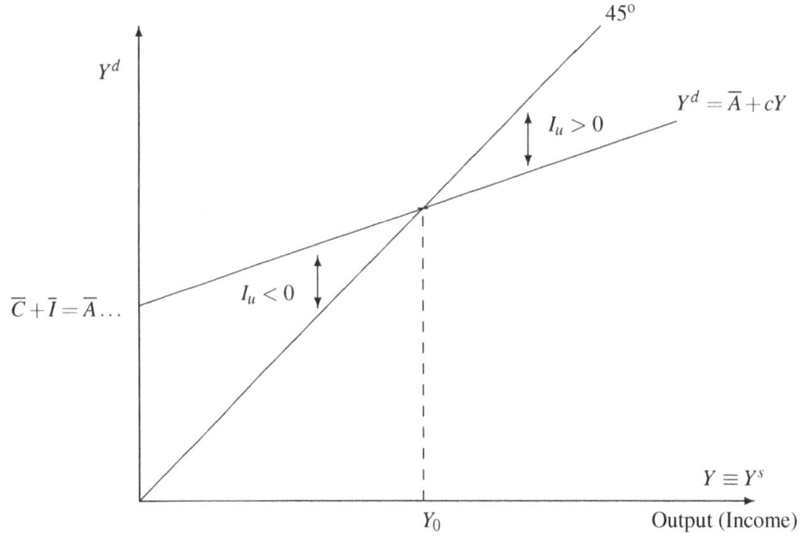

Fig. 2.2 The dynamic multiplier process

[2] See Chaps. 6 and 7 for an application of this interpretation of disequilibrium price movements.

[3] This is often concealed by employing the ambiguous symbol Y instead of Y^{s}, but is revealed when unintended inventories are used to characterize disequilibrium situations as in the Fig. 2.2.

difference in Y^d and Y^s is allowed for in the literature (and used for the purposes of the above wrong type of disequilibrium analysis), the same seems not to be true for the treatment of planned income Y and planned output Y^s.

This fact is exemplified by the depicted misinterpretation of the standard 45°-cross-diagram shown in Fig. 2.2, which is quite common in the literature [see Dornbusch and Fischer (1987, Chap. 3) for an example].[4] The diagram not only shows the equilibrium point of effective demand Y_0, but also interprets situations of disequilibrium by means of I_u (= unintended investment). It shows in addition how adjustment toward equilibrium is assumed to take place – via the information provided by the unintended investment. Yet, situations which differ from the equilibrium Y_0 and the directions of adjustment which are derived from them cannot be interpreted in an economically meaningful way in the light of the above understanding of the symbol Y. This follows, for example, in case of $I_u > 0$, from the simple fact that planned "income" Y is then greater than money income actually received: $Y^d(Y)$, that is, producers suffer from "income illusion" in that they count as income the value of goods I_u, the future of which is fairly uncertain. And indeed, Dornbusch and Fischer (as well as many other textbooks) describe the adjustment toward equilibrium Y_0 in a way which cannot explain how the income that has gone into (accumulated) unintended inventories will be realized in the end. Such an interpretation of the core model of the theory of aggregate and effective demand is therefore very misleading and does not provide us with a firm background for an understanding of the Keynesian notion of effective demand – and its applications in economic dynamics.[5]

The above two examples show that the situation surrounding the concept of effective demand $Y_0(= Y_0^d = Y^d(p_0))$ is often at least not well represented (or even understood) [see Sargent (1987, Chap. 2) for a further example into this direction]. In many applications of the above IS analysis this may cause no harm, since a correct representation of the assumptions underlying it is not needed in such cases. Yet, there exist also examples – in particular models with unintended inventories, but also dynamic IS-LM equilibrium models – where wrong or inconsistent extensions of this temporary equilibrium concept are proposed and studied.

To overcome such problems, a reconsideration of Keynes' central critique of the Classical theory, that is, his way of rejecting Say's Law, will be of great use. Hence, we shall first study the elements by which Say's Law can be given explicit and nontrivial expression in an elaborate version of the macroeconomic model of the Classics. This will be done in Sect. 2.2 by an adequate completion of Ackley's (1969) extensive, but still incomplete description of Classical Macroeconomics and Say's Law. Section 2.3 then shows how the "Classical structure" of Ackley's model can be completely overthrown – in a way which in our view is similar to Keynes' reasoning – simply by thoroughly distinguishing between saving and lending and

---

[4] An alternative interpretation of this adjustment process assumes a (Robertson) lag between income and consumption demand and proceeds by means of goods market equilibrium toward the point of effective demand Y_0. This alternative thus avoids the problem of unplanned inventory accumulation.

[5] We shall not consider inventory disequilibria in this book, which means that this problem ($Y \equiv Y^s$) will not be treated here in its full depth, cf., however, Sect. 6.3 for a simple further discussion of it.

their respective determinants. Consequences of this distinction and the modifications of Ackley's model deriving from it, however, also concern the money market, which then can no longer be of a Classical type. Such additional modifications of Ackley's Classical model will be introduced in a first step by means of Barro's (1990) approach to general macroeconomic equilibrium [the New Classical Macroeconomics], that is, they will appear, in Sect. 2.4, as a reformulation of our version of the Classical Macroeconomic model (Sect. 2.2) without the Keynesian aspects that were introduced into it in Sect. 2.3. These latter aspects are again added in Sect. 2.5 – now to the New Classical model of Barro – where we shall see that Keynes' original claim on the generality of the "General Theory" is still true – despite all progress that is nowadays maintained with regard to recent developments of macroeconomic theory.

In sum, the aim of this chapter is, on the one hand, to isolate as precisely as possible the basic logical flaw in the Classical system and to go on then to show the limitations of current seemingly consistent reformulations of this approach. We shall show, on the other hand, how Keynes' type of analysis can be obtained through minimal modifications and extensions of both the Classical and the "New" Classical Macroeconomics.

2.2 Classical Macroeconomics

The following provides a brief presentation of how Ackley's (1969)[6] incomplete Classical model must be completed to allow for an unambiguous and consistent interpretation of the interaction of its simple behavioral relationships.[7] We have chosen here Ackley's presentation of Classical Macroeconomics from the many textbook versions that exist of it, since it is in many respects the most complete treatment of this synthetic Classical model.

Since this model allows for downwardly rigid money wages $\overline{W}$ (this assumption will be discussed later on), a central element in the discussion of Ackley's model is given by the *Classical aggregate supply function* (Fig. 2.3).

Here, $Y_{\mathrm{f}}^{\mathrm{s}}, p_{\mathrm{f}}$ characterize the point of full employment of the labor force for the given wage $\overline{W}$:

$$L^{\mathrm{s}}\left(\frac{\overline{W}}{p_{\mathrm{f}}}\right) = L^{\mathrm{d}}\left(\frac{\overline{W}}{p_{\mathrm{f}}}\right), \quad \frac{\overline{W}}{p_{\mathrm{f}}} = Y^{\mathrm{s}'}(L^{\mathrm{d}}).$$

Prices $p > p_{\mathrm{f}}$ imply that the real wage is below its equilibrium level, that is, labor demand L^{d} [based on Keynes' (1936, p. 5) Classical postulate No. I] exceeds the supply of labor L^{s}, in which case it is assumed that money wages react instantaneously,

6 See, for example, also Felderer and Homburg (1984) and Hillier (1991) for recent presentations of this synthetic model and note that Sargent's (1987) and McCallum's (1989) versions of the Classical model are in fact already models that synthesize Keynes and the Classics.

7 Our following presentation assumes that the reader has already some background knowledge with regard to the synthetic Classical model of textbook economics.

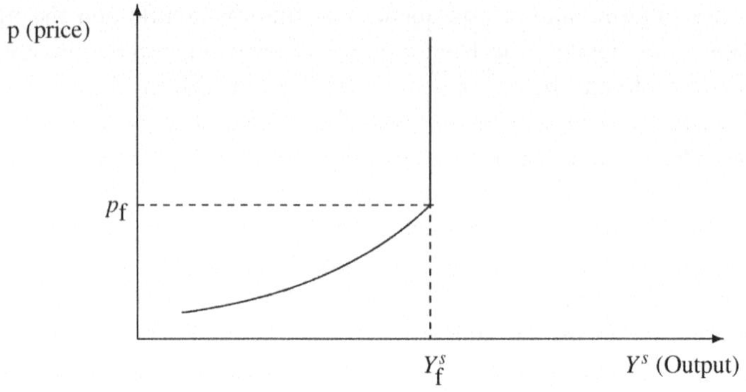

Fig. 2.3 Aggregate supply

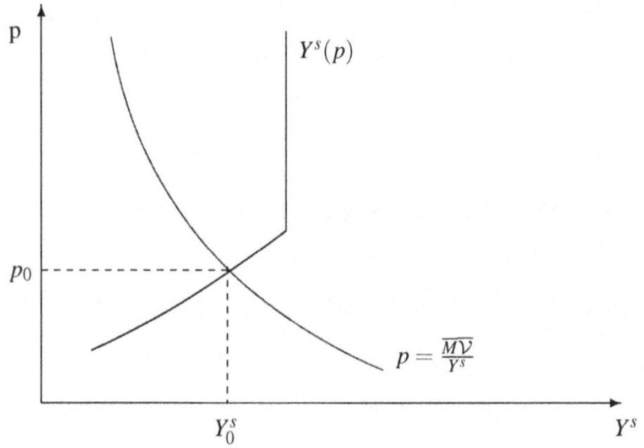

Fig. 2.4 Classical underemployment equilibrium

that is, rise to restore labor market equilibrium. This explains the vertical part of the aggregate supply schedule, while its downward sloping part gives expression to the fact that real wages are too high then to allow for full employment output.[8]

Combining the aggregate supply curve with the *strict quantity theory of money*[9]

$$\overline{M} \cdot \overline{V} = pY^s \tag{2.1}$$

then gives us two equations from which supply side equilibrium output Y^s_0 and equilibrium prices p_0 can be uniquely determined – as is obvious from the Fig. 2.4.

And the standard production function relationship[10] $Y^s(L)$ will then determine actual employment L_0 and the rate of unemployment $U_0 = \frac{L^s - L_0}{L^s}, L^s = L^s\left(\frac{\overline{W}}{p_0}\right)$,

[8] See Glahe (1977, p. 27) for further explanations of this schedule.

[9] See Crouch (1972, p. 173) for example.

[10] See Sargent (1987, Chap. 1).

which is positive for sufficiently low equilibrium prices p_0, that is, for sufficiently high wages $\overline{W}$ or low quantities of money $\overline{M}$.

Keynes (1936, p. 5) described the above situation with the following words: The Classical theory of employment – supposedly simple and obvious – has been based, I think, on two fundamental postulates, though practically without discussion, namely:

> *I. The wage rate is equal to the marginal product of labor ... II. The utility of the wage when a given volume of labor is employed is equal to the marginal disutility of that amount of employment.*

And after discussing the theoretical background and the empirical relevance of the second postulates he concludes on p. 16: "We need to throw over the second postulate of the Classical doctrine and to work out the behavior of a system in which involuntary unemployment in the strict sense is possible."[11] We shall see in Chaps. 6 and 7, however that there are also logical as well as empirical reasons, which imply that the above first postulate should be dismissed from a Keynesian theory of effective demand, as well.

Ackley's above version of Classical Macroeconomics is turned into a complete four-market macroeconomic model by *adding the capital market and its equilibrium condition* as in the Fig. 2.5 (see his p. 142 and compare also Keynes (1936, Chap. 14) for a discussion (of the defects) of this diagram).

By way of the terminology chosen, the Fig. 2.5 suggests that it is not only the capital market, but also the *goods market* that is represented by it. This is indeed the case as can be shown by *adding budget constraints* to the above model. These constraints are not discussed in Ackley (1969), an omission which there gives rise

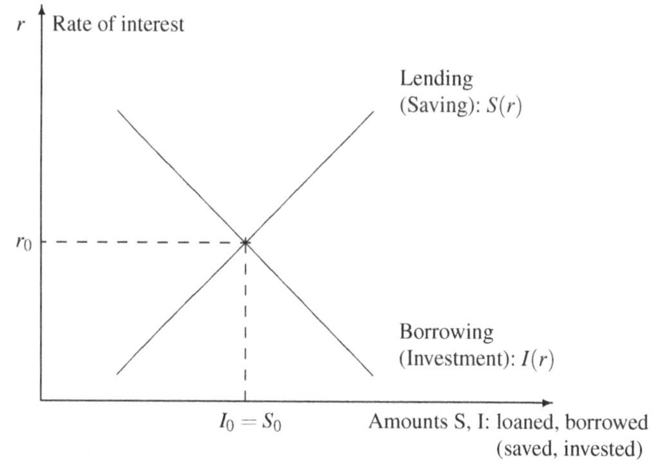

Fig. 2.5 Goods- and capital-market equilibrium

[11] He then interpreted the above situation (Y_0^S, p_0) as an underemployment equilibrium with no involuntary unemployment in the strict sense (see his discussion of various types of classical unemployment in his Chap. 2 and also our discussion of it at the end of this section).

to a considerable amount of vague verbal statements, for example, with regard to the implicitly employed type of "Say's Law" and also the only implicitly present concept of aggregate demand Y^d.[12]

In a Classical world, saving normally can either mean "investing directly" or "lending." The identity for consistently made *saving plans* consequently reads in view of this distinction:

$$pS \equiv pI_{\text{direct}} + \frac{1}{r}(B^d - \overline{B}), \tag{2.2}$$

where B^d denotes the total (stock) demand for (perpetual) bonds, $\overline{B}$ the set of perpetuities (consols) already in existence and where $\frac{1}{r}$ is the (current) price of this type of bonds.[13] Similarly, *planned investment* must be assumed to fulfill the following consistency requirement regarding the financing of investment

$$pI \equiv pI_{direct} + \frac{1}{r}(B^s - \overline{B}) \tag{2.3}$$

Here, B^s denotes the stock supply of bonds, that is, $\frac{1}{r}(B^s - \overline{B})$ represents the currently planned amount of money borrowing for investment purposes. Subtracting (2.2) from (2.3) gives

$$p(I - S) \equiv \frac{1}{r}(B^s - B^d). \tag{2.4}$$

This identity can now be used to provide justification for Ackley's I-S-diagram (Fig. 2.5), which for the sake of clearness should at first be represented by

Figure 2.6, and identity (2.4) imply that it is the job of the rate of interest *to coordinate lending and borrowing*[14] and that it, in doing so, *at the same time equates savings with investment*: $S(r_0) = I(r_0)$, *and thus brings forth equilibrium in the goods market as well*, if the following conventions are adopted to interpret the left hand side of (2.4):[15]

$$\left.\begin{array}{lcl} \text{Planned real income } Y & \equiv & \text{Planned output } Y^s \\ \text{Planned saving } S & \equiv & Y - C \equiv Y^s - C \end{array}\right\}, \tag{2.5}$$

where C denotes planned consumption. These two identities represent well known assumptions or definitions of macroeconomic theory. They immediately give rise to

$$\left.\begin{array}{lcl} p(I - S) & \equiv & p(Y^d - Y^s) \\ Y^d & \equiv & C + I \end{array}\right\}, \tag{2.6}$$

---

[12] cf. also Felderer and Homburg (1984) and Hillier (1991) in this regard.

[13] See Crouch (1972, pp. 60ff.) for details and note that interest payments are given by $\bar{B}$ in this case. For simplicity we shall assume that this is the only interest-bearing asset in the present model. Note also that the government sector is only introduced into this model in Sect. 2.8.

[14] Compare, e.g., Mill (1965, Chap. XXIII) with regard to such a view.

[15] Note here, that income Y is here composed of $Y \equiv WL^d + \Pi + \bar{B}$ (Π = profits) and that all direct investment is here made by households who earn the profits $\Pi = Y - WL^d - \bar{B}$ with regard to their past investments (see Chaps. 6 and 7 for the integration of profits into the investment decision).

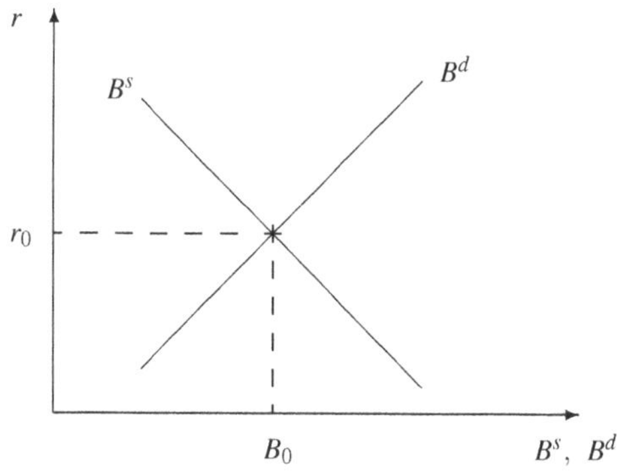

Fig. 2.6 The classical bond market

that is, the equivalence of I, S-equality and product-market equilibrium (as was claimed earlier).

We are now in the position to describe in detail the type of *Say's Law* that we have introduced by our above completion of Ackley's Classical model. Following Mill (1965, pp. 571/2) we have modeled the following two statements:

I. THE SUPPLY OF COMMODITIES IN GENERAL CANNOT EXCEED THE POWER OF PURCHASE

which in the above model is represented by the assumption $Y \equiv Y^s$. This assumption – to our knowledge – has remained unquestioned as far as macroeconomic model building is concerned[16]

II. THE SUPPLY OF COMMODITIES IN GENERAL NEVER DOES EXCEED THE INCLINATION TO CONSUME

In terms of our model this quotation from Mill's text can be represented by $Y^d = Y^s \equiv Y$ for any given Y^s, and must be viewed upon as an equilibrium condition: Aggregate demand Y^d is made equal to aggregate supply Y^s if $Y \equiv Y^s$ (assertion I) holds and if the rate of interest performs its job to equilibrate the demand and the supply for loans [$B^d = B^s$; note here that Mill – in trying to prove the above phrase – restricts his attention to the case $S \equiv I_{\text{direct}}$, while his discussion of loans and the rate of interest is confined to a later chapter of his "Principles"]. In our view, therefore, the formulation of *Say's Law* which is consistent with Ackley's (standard) version of Classical Macroeconomics should be

$$\left.\begin{array}{rcl} p(Y^d - Y) & \equiv & \frac{1}{r}(B^s - B^d) \\ Y & \equiv & Y^s \\ B^s(r_0) & \equiv & B^d(r_0) \end{array}\right\}, \tag{2.7}$$

[16] See Crouch (1972, p. 142) for an explicit representation of this hypothesis, and Keynes (1936, p. 20) for a verbal statement in this regard which, however, did not hinder him to attack Mill's identical statement of this fact (see his p. 18).

that is, *it consists of two macroeconomic identities* [the first of which relates the desire and the ability to purchase with what is happening in the market for loans, while the second claims that planned income should equal planned output under all circumstances] *and an equilibrating mechanism* [which – via the market for loans – creates as much desire to spend as there is ability to purchase]. This form of Say's Law overcomes the weaknesses of its purely verbal presentation in Ackley (1969) by giving it an exact content within the model that is employed by him.[17] We thereby now know that the interpretation of Fig. 2.5 should be restricted to capital market phenomena [unless we in addition assume $I_{\text{direct}} \equiv 0$] and that moreover "lending" and "saving" cannot in general be treated as synonymous. Finally, we now have a clear idea why *the goods market* can be eliminated from the complete set of markets of Ackley's Classical Macroeconomics and which concepts we should choose to discuss the determination of the rate of interest.

The above completion of his model *disqualifies* Ackley's (1969, pp. 138f.) attempt (also present in more recent macro-models) to interpret the quantity theory *as a theory of aggregate demand* by means of its following reformulation

$$Y^{\text{d}} \equiv \frac{\overline{M} \cdot \overline{V}}{p}, \tag{2.8}$$

since aggregate demand Y^{d} has already been determined by $Y^{\text{d}} \equiv I + C \equiv Y^{\text{s}} + I - S$.[18] The quantity theory cannot be used consistently for a description of aggregate demand in a Classical model in which the above elaborate form of Say's Law is assumed to be valid.[19] Yet, though the quantity theory and Say's Law must be carefully distinguished with regard to their meaning and range of applicability, we shall see in the next section that they stand and fall together if the distinction between saving and lending is developed further.

The description of our version of a Classical model is now complete. Figure 2.4 determines equilibrium output Y_0^{s} and the price level p_0 and thus (as already indicated) employment L_0 and the rate of unemployment U_0 (which we assume to be positive). The rate of interest, in clearing the market for bonds, then creates the necessary demand for the predetermined output Y_0^{s}. The model implies that unemployment can be lowered only if either money wages fall, whereby $Y^{\text{s}}(p)$ is shifted downward, or if the quantity of money (here still of helicopter type) is raised,

---

[17] Felderer and Homburg (1984, Chap. 4) use instead of Y the notional concept $Y + w(L^{\text{s}} - L^{\text{d}})$ and thus include the labor market in their derivation of the aggregate budget constraint. The consequences of this approach (Lange and Patinkin) is that Classical underemployment equilibria (due to rigid wages) as they are, for example, discussed in Keynes (1936) are then impossible. This is therefore not a good starting point for a discussion of the macroeconomic controversy about the causes of unemployment and therefore not a good representation of pre-Keynesian macroeconomics.

[18] $= Y^{\text{s}}(p) + \frac{B^{\text{s}} - B^{\text{d}}}{rp}$! Note here, that in the above general form of a Classical model the quantity theory has to be formulated by means of $p \equiv \frac{\overline{M} \cdot \overline{V}}{Y^{\text{s}}}$ to be consistent with the remainder of the model, a formulation which can be related to the Cambridge-interpretation of this theory.

[19] See Keynes (1936, p. 183), for a harsh critique of mixing the quantity theory with the theory of aggregate demand.

whereby the other curve in Fig. 2.4 is shifted upward.[20] Hence, unemployment is caused by an imbalance between the level of money wages and the existing quantity of money, implying that it mainly depends *on the labor market* and the behavior of economic agents in this market (in relation to productivity and prices) how unemployment will develop over time.[21]

Glahe (1977, p. 25) gives several arguments why money wages may be downwardly rigid – in relation to the prevalence of imperfect competition in the main. Yet, also in the case of atomistic competition downwardly rigid money wages can be assumed to prevail – even if all unemployed workers are willing to accept lower wages. Such a situation is given if (e.g.) account is taken of the existence of firms that behave as follows:

- Wages are *set by firms* (and not by a Walrasian auctioneer)
- It is *not profitable for a firm* to hire new laborers at lower wages than are paid to those already in the work force of this firm (assuming homogeneous labor for simplicity)
- It is *not profitable for a firm* to cut the wages of all of its employees simultaneously
- It is *not profitable for a firm* to exchange its complete labor force against the cheaper work that can be obtained from the pool of the unemployed.

The reasons underlying the statement not profitable, of course, relate to the costs involved in the undertaking of such actions. Broadly speaking these costs consist of various types of productivity losses, which we shall not, however, consider here in more detail. Leaving extreme situations aside, it appears fairly obvious that firms will not try immediate wage cuts whenever the state of the labor market seems to allow for such an action – even in the presence of an atomistic labor market and a large pool of unemployed workers ready to work for less than the prevailing money wage $\overline{W}$ [see Chick (1983, pp. 74 ff.) for further arguments of this kind and Blanchard and Fischer (1989, 9.4) for a brief formal discussion of such efficiency wage hypotheses].

Wage rigidity of this basic type combined with our Classical model (which has been supplemented by an explicit and "consistent" version of Say's Law), however, imply that *involuntary unemployment and Say's Law are not incompatible with each other* as it is claimed in Keynes (1936, pp. 15 ff.), cf. our above remarks. Classical economists could have discussed the existence of men involuntarily unemployed (had they wished to do so) without destroying at the same stroke the logic of Say's Law in the market for goods.[22]

[20] We here neglect the effects of capital accumulation and of technological change.

[21] See also Modigliani (1944) for a set of related observations on Classical (Sect. 2.2) vs. Keynesian (Sect. 2.3) model building.

[22] Note in this regard that Fig. 2.4 and $Y^s(p)$ can also be interpreted in terms of the wage fund theory where minimum nominal wages are fixed by law or opinion [as discussed by Mill (1965, p. 356)]. This way of interpreting Fig. 2.4 clearly shows that the supply of labor (and the labor market) should not be included in Mill's discussion of the impossibility of a general glut (Say's Law), in contrast to the Walrasian interpretation of Say's Law à la Lange and Patinkin! Assuming

Hence, in exploring the logical flaws of the Classical model as presented above, we should concentrate on its view of the goods market and not on Keynes' claim that it is logically impossible to have involuntary unemployment within a Classical framework.[23] Instead, our aim should (and will) be to explore in how far the working of the goods market must be viewed as more complicated than it is suggested by Say's Law, how this complication contributes to an analysis of the extent of involuntary unemployment factually observed, and why the remedy of lowering money wages to cure unemployment may represent an ineffective or even dangerous proposal (as was claimed by Keynes).

These points will be examined in the following by developing further the distinction between *saving* and *lending* in a monetary economy. We thereby shall be able to demonstrate that – despite the existence of a Classical labor market *as well* as a Classical capital market – there will be a complete reversal in the causal explanation of unemployment. Our aim here, on the one hand, is to preserve (for purpose of comparison) the Classical elements of the above presentation as far as possible, while demonstrating, on the other hand, how the outlook on the mechanism of the economic system can be changed into a Keynesian one if saving and lending are properly distinguished. It is hoped that we are able thereby to demonstrate that very slight changes in the setting of a known model can have large consequences on its implications and that valuable insights can be gained by such a procedure. This demonstration should be valuable for didactic purposes, too, and it provides a good example, of how sensitive a conventional model may react with regard to seemingly minor qualifications in its analytical framework.

2.3 A "Keynes Revolution" in the Classical Model

The model considered in Sect. 2.2 obviously tries to provide a complete macroeconomic picture of a *monetary* economy, in which one type of input is used to produce one type of output, roughly related to the sphere of circulation by means of a medium for transactions (money), which can also be lent and borrowed. Though still in rudimentary form the four kinds of markets usually distinguished in a macroeconomic model are all present in this Classical model.

However, as a brief inspection of the identities (2.2) and (2.3) shows, money has not yet been fully integrated into the equations of this model. Money is used and thus held for transaction purposes and consequently must enter the budget identities of savers (and investors) unless they never plan to change their cash holdings (which, however, cannot be sensibly assumed in general). The obvious modifications of (2.2) and (2.3) are

---

that wages are paid out of past funds or assuming $Y \equiv Y^s$ clearly gives (2.7) as the basic description of Say's Law [where the labor market is not involved!].

[23] The above model thus shows that Keynes' (1936, Ch.2) labor market test for "involuntary unemployment in the strict sense" is not a sound test. This must be so, since one cannot test the nonworking of Say's Law (which concerns the goods- and the bond-market) by reference to the labor market alone.

$$pS \equiv pI_{\text{direct}} + \frac{1}{r}(B^{\text{d}} - \overline{B}) + (M_{\text{S}}^{\text{d}} - \overline{M}_{\text{S}}), \tag{2.9}$$

$$pI \equiv pI_{\text{direct}} + \frac{1}{r}(B^{\text{s}} - \overline{B}) - (M_{\text{I}}^{\text{d}} - \overline{M}_{\text{I}}), \tag{2.10}$$

where $\overline{M}_{\text{S}}$, $\overline{M}_{\text{I}}$ denote the actual money holdings of savers and investors and $M_{\text{S}}^{\text{d}}, M_{\text{I}}^{\text{d}}$ their desired ones. On the basis of the definitions of Y and S (see Sect. 2.2) we now get instead of (2.4)

$$pI - pS \equiv pY^{\text{d}} - pY^{\text{s}} \equiv \frac{1}{r}(B^{\text{s}} - B^{\text{d}}) + (\overline{M} - M^{\text{d}}), \tag{2.11}$$

which is the so-called Walras-Identity of Flows or Keynesian aggregate budget restraint for our monetary economy $[\overline{M} \equiv \overline{M}_{\text{S}} + \overline{M}_{\text{I}}, M^{\text{d}} \equiv M_{\text{S}}^{\text{d}} + M_{\text{I}}^{\text{d}}]$.

An immediate and important consequence of this simple correction of the Classical model of Sect. 2.2 with regard to the holding of money is that the equilibrium situation in the market for bonds as depicted in Fig. 2.6 now no longer informs us unambiguously on the state of the goods market *and* on the behavior of excess demand on this latter market. It is now logically quite possible (and even plausible, if the economic content of the savings function is taken into account) to have at one and the same time the relationships $p(Y^{\text{s}} - Y^{\text{d}}) \equiv p(S(Y^{\text{s}}) - I(r))$ and $B^{\text{d}}(r), B^{\text{s}}(r)$ without any direct logical contradiction between them. It is therefore completely admissible under the logically compelling extension (2.9) and (2.10) of the Classical model to incorporate a simple Keynesian consumption – or savings function – into this model, since the goods and the capital-market now have ceased to represent just two sides of the same coin (as it is suggested by Ackley's bond market diagram, cf. Fig. 2.5). The definition of nominal savings $p(Y^{\text{s}} - C)$ is now clearly quite different from the definition of extra lending $B^{\text{d}} - \overline{B}$, because the latter is referring to the bond market and not to the demand gap on the market for goods. The confusion between saving and lending is one of the basic reasons on which the Classical view that "supply will create its own demand" (Say's Law) rests, a confusion which is also present in Keynes' (1936, p. 178) presentation of the Classical and his own theory of interest – despite his clear vision on the proper determinants of savings.

Adding a simple Keynesian savings function $S \equiv S(Y^s)$ to the model of Sect. 2.2 implies that Ackley's Fig. 2.5 is to be replaced by Figs. 2.6 and 2.7, that is, we now need two diagrams to characterize bond and product market equilibrium.[24]

The Classical bond market determines as in Sect. 2.2 the equilibrium rate of interest r_0 (Fig. 2.6), this rate determines as before the amount of *planned* investment, *which now however determines equilibrium output and income* [where planned saving is equal to planned investment]. The sequence of determinants that results from this new situation consequently is[25]

[24] Note here that we do not yet revise explicitly the now inconsistent formulation of the money market, that is, the quantity theory of money of the Classical model. This market is left implicit in the following reconsideration of bonds- and goods-market equilibrium. The money market will be made explicit again in Sect. 2.4 and its IS-LM reformulation in Sect. 2.5.

[25] Cf. also Keynes (1936, Chap. 18) with respect to this simple sequence of causations (which, e.g., still neglects the so-called Keynes effect as a possible repercussion effect, see Sect. 2.5).

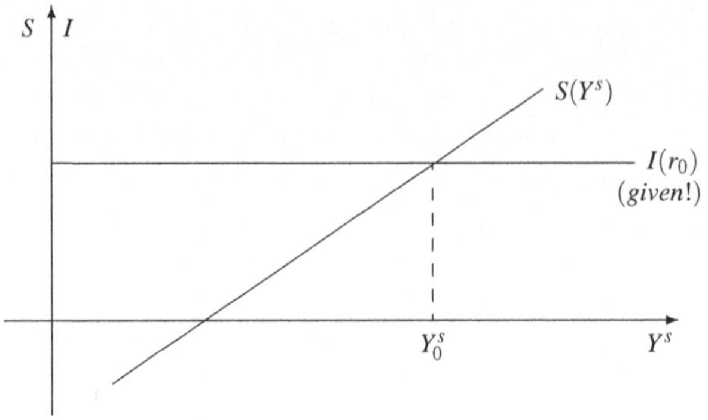

Fig. 2.7 The Keynesian IS-diagram

$$r_0 \rightarrow I_0 \rightarrow Y_0 \rightarrow L_0 \rightarrow p_0 \left[= \frac{\overline{W}}{Y^{s'}(L_o)} \right],$$

that is, the conditions that prevail on our Classical bond market now determine output Y_0 as well as employment L_0 and competitive prices p_0. Downwardly flexible money wages W will in this changed situation only give rise to downwardly flexible prices p_0 (a wage-price spiral) and will thus lead to monetary instability solely, that is, no improvement in employment conditions will result from this type of flexibility (if it were available).

The causal nexus that made rigid money wages $\overline{W}$ the important element in the explanation of unemployment in the previous section is now completely removed from the model – simply by drawing a sharp distinction between lending and saving behavior and its central determinants. Wage policy – and in the above situation also monetary policy – cannot improve the prevailing (un-)employment situation.[26] It is not the money wage that is too high to allow for full employment, but it is the rate of interest (based on bond market equilibrium) that is not sufficiently low to imply an amount of investment that will (via the multiplier process) raise income and output to its full employment level. To quote Keynes (1936, p. 185): "A decreased readiness to spend will be looked on in quite a different light if, instead of being regarded as a factor which will, *cet. par.*, increase investment it is seen as a factor which will, *cet. par.*, diminish employment."

This change in implications illustrates the basic difference between the model of this and the preceding section in a very pronounced way, in contrast to Keynes' (1936, Chap. 14) considerations, however, without any change in the Classical theory of interest (à la Mill) simply by drawing a sharp distinction between the determination of this rate and the forces that determine the equilibrium in the market for goods.

Besides our addition of a Keynesian savings function to the Classical model of Sect. 2.2, there is, however, yet another change implicitly involved in the proposed modification of Ackley's Classical Macroeconomics. From the assumption made on savings behavior there follows by means of identity (2.11)

[26] See, however, Mill (1965, p. 656) for qualifications with regard to this point.

$$M^{\mathrm{d}} = \overline{M} + p[S(Y^{\mathrm{s}}) - I(r)] + \frac{[B^{\mathrm{s}}(r) - B^{\mathrm{d}}(r)]}{r}, \tag{2.12}$$

that is, by assuming the savings relationship $S(Y^{\mathrm{s}})$ we have implicitly removed the quantity theory (see Fig. 2.4) from the model of Sect. 2.2. The assumed goods- and capital-market behavior thus imply an interest-elastic money demand function due to the fact that the aggregate budget restraint [by which we have removed the money market from an explicit treatment in this section] must hold true.

The above money demand function, of course, is a very peculiar one, though it already indicates why the rate of interest should become an argument in this demand function. Of course, this function should be replaced by Keynes' or a Keynesian money demand function in the end. Obviously, this demands further changes and modifications in the demand and supply functions of other markets (goods, bonds) to make them a consistent whole and may well give rise to so many simultaneous dependencies that the above simple causal sequence may again become completely obscured by these extra modifications. Such a procedure should, however, not be adopted too hastily – in the name of mathematical generality of the finally accepted behavioral relationships. It is not the ideal of the Walrasian view (that everything depends on everything else) that macroeconomic model building should and does strive for. On the contrary, simple, yet informative models are still in need that are simultaneously *logically consistent* [or, alternatively, as clear as possible with regard to the gaps that have still to be filled], *give a clear impression of the basic macroeconomic forces* (which are assumed to determine income, employment, etc.), and which mainly *utilize conventional means in demonstrating their possibly new view* about the dominant forces that direct the macroeconomic behavior of the economy. It is in this sense that we have tried to show how a Keynesian view of these forces can be provided by only slight, minimally necessary improvements of an otherwise strictly Classical model.

It is stated in Ackley (1969, p. 137) that there can be no doubt about the logical completeness and consistency of his "Classical theory" and that Keynes was surely wrong in attacking it as logically incomplete or inconsistent. Yet, we have shown in this and the preceding section that Ackley's model is neither complete (it neglects the budget restraints of, e.g., savers and investors) nor that it can be considered consistent (it illegitimately identifies lending and saving behavior, which is only possible if money does not enter the budget restraints, implying an economy that cannot really be considered to represent a monetary one).

The assumptions that have to be used to attach a proper interpretation to the two diagrams in the introduction to this chapter should now be obvious. The curve $Y^{\mathrm{s}}(p)$ in Fig. 2.1 is better and more suggestively written as $p(Y^{\mathrm{s}})$, which together with $Y^{\mathrm{s}} \equiv Y^{\mathrm{d}}(p)$, that is, no error on the side of producers with respect to the level of effective demand at given prices p leads us to a confrontation of actual prices p and competitive prices $p(Y^{\mathrm{s}})$ outside the equilibrium point p_0. Situations different from p_0 thus represent disequilibria in prices and not in quantities, that is, the standard interpretation of this diagram is fairly misleading.

An interesting example of this type of confusion is given by Benassy's (1984) non-Walrasian model of the business cycle where producers adaptively modify their demand expectations in an IS-LM-context of the type of Fig. 2.1 (see also Sect. 2.5). Such a simple modification of the conventional IS-LM-model (with endogenous prices) by means of an investment function $I(r, Y^{d^*})$ which now also depends on expected demand Y^{d^*} and which is supplemented by a money-wage Phillips-curve *and* the adaptive mechanism

$$\dot{Y}^{d^*} = \mu(Y_0^{s} - Y^{d^*}) \tag{2.13}$$

cannot, however, be regarded as a consistent modification and extension of this model, since the IS-LM-part of the model already assumes

$$Y^{s} \equiv Y^{d^*} \equiv Y_0 \equiv Y_0^{d} \tag{2.14}$$

as we have seen above. Hence, this treatment of expected demand is not a convincing representation of the behavior of producers (2.14) and investors (2.13) in an IS-LM-context.[27]

Similarly, the IS-LM-model does also not allow for disequilibrium in the market for goods (and money) without a fairly detailed revision of the assumptions (2.14), that is, we cannot formulate a price-level and interest-rate dynamics as in Sargent (1987, pp. 58 ff.) on the basis of these two imbalances solely – without any modification in the assumptions made on producers' expectations of aggregate demand. Imbalance in the market for goods does no longer admit for the above type of perfect anticipation (2.14) of producers' sales situation and thus necessarily leads in a Keynesian context to a much more complicated dynamics than is given by Sargent's (1987) Walrasian or notional pure price adjustment rules.[28]

Finally, we note that also the situation we have considered in Fig. 2.2 will give rise to a more complex dynamics than is considered there, since in such a disequilibrium situation the magnitudes "output," "aggregate demand," "income," "expected demand," and "expected income" should at first all be carefully distinguished making it possible thereafter to formulate which of these magnitudes can in fact be set equal to each other (to simplify the dynamics) on the basis of assumptions that look reasonable in the presence of such a disequilibrium situation. It is our opinion here that goods market disequilibrium will give rise to considerable complexities (including a more complicated inventory dynamics than has been considered in this type of literature so far). The equilibrium concept of "effective demand" Y_0 (which excludes the analysis of errors on the side of producers) is the central approach to avoid all such complexities (by assumption). Yet, if it is used as a shortcut for the problem of producers to form reasonable expectations on aggregate demand, we should not forget the assumptions on which it is based to avoid that it will be incorporated into a model that is not consistent with it.

---

[27] Unless they are reinterpreted as some sort of long-run expectation.

[28] Note here that only an adjustment rule of the type $\dot{p} = \alpha(\frac{\overline{W}}{Y^{s'}(L_0)} - p)$ represents a good starting point for the further investigation of possible imbalances in Fig. 2.1, because of the assumed IS-LM equilibrium.

2.4 New Classical Macroeconomics

We shall now provide a brief discussion of the New Classical Macroeconomics by making use of the market clearing approach of Barro (1990) in its most developed form, that is, where the four basic markets of a minimally complete macroeconomic model are all present.[29] We shall then see that this model adds only minor improvements to the full employment situation of the Classical model of Sect. 2.2 (making it also more consistent thereby), while neglecting in its analysis of the classical causes of unemployment completely as they are, for example, discussed in Keynes (1936, p. 7). In Barro's (1990) textbook approach to macroeconomics much stress is laid on an explicit discussion of aggregate consistency requirements which in conjunction with the market-clearing approach are then used to determine general equilibrium on the macroeconomic level. Barro starts with the model of a Robinson–Crusoe economy and proceeds by introducing first a credit-market, then the money market, and finally the labor market into this model. It is somewhat astonishing, however, that in the final stage of his approach the consistency requirements – which receive so much attention throughout the book – are no longer explicitly discussed. Furthermore, the fact that equilibrium in the goods- and the labor-market are interdependent in this final version of his models and have to be determined simultaneously can be represented in a way that is much easier to understand and to manipulate than Barro's own presentation of it. And finally, on the basis of these two additions of Barro's approach to macroeconomics, we shall be able to show that Barro's model corresponds very well – with regard to its method as well as its results – to the other types of macromodels here considered and can therefore be usefully compared with them.

Appending the budget restrictions of households (and the Walras-Law they imply) to Barro's final basic form of a market-clearing model will make it again a complete and consistent model. Furthermore, this will also allow us to give a concise list of the differences and improvements of Barro's model with respect to the Classical model of Sect. 2.2 (this list will be fairly short). Finally, this new presentation of Barro's model will make the comparison with a conventional IS-LM-extension (Sect. 2.5) of our Keynes model (Sect. 2.3) very easy and will also allow us to show

---

[29] Barro (1990) treats the IS-LM model only in a closing chapter of his macroeconomic textbook and therefore considers macroeconomics by and large from a new-classical perspective solely, see the summarizing Fig. 2.11 in this chapter. This figure summarizes our result that IS-LM is indeed a generalization of this pre-Keynesian type of approach. It thus suggests that temporary equilibrium analysis must overcome this very limited stage of analysis if it truly wants to be applicable to the real world. Subsequent textbooks like Mankiw (1994) have given IS-LM analysis again more weight in their framework, while Blanchard (2006) even presents IS-LM as well as AD-AS as the core of his analysis of the medium- and the long-run. For a discussion of the AD-AS framework from a variety of perspectives, see also Dutt and Skott (2006), while Carlin and Soskice (2005) reformulate the AD-AS framework – as in Blanchard (2006) – towards a treatment of models of imperfect competition as well as a treatment of Neo-Wicksellian or New Keynesian approaches to monopolistic competition. Our approach in this chapter is further developed in Flaschel, Groh, and Proaño (2007) and Asada, Chiarella, Flaschel, and Franke (in preparation).

that the latter can be obtained from Barro's model in a way such that Keynes (1936, Chap. 1) claim on the generality of the General Theory (again) becomes obvious [see Sect. 2.5].[30]

Briefly characterized, Barro's final basic model (implicitly) starts from the following (current) budget restriction of households (and firms) [31]:

$$pC + pI + \Delta B + M^{\mathrm{d}} \equiv WL^{\mathrm{s}} + pY^{\mathrm{s}} - WL^{\mathrm{d}} + (1+\bar{r})\overline{B} + \overline{M}. \qquad (2.15)$$

We have formulated this constraint directly on the aggregate level, where we in addition know that the stock of Barro's one-period fix-price bonds $\overline{B}$ held by private sector as a whole must be zero in each moment of time [we do not yet consider a government sector and have assumed – as in Barro (1990) – that all planned profits $pY^{\mathrm{s}} - WL^{\mathrm{d}}$ and all income expectations concern the household sector solely].[32]

On the basis of given current prices $p, W, \frac{p}{1+r}$ for present and future commodities Barro proposes to adopt the following behavioral relationships as the result of rational choice in an intertemporal context ($w = \frac{W}{p}$ the real wage rate):[33]

$C = C(w,r)$: Consumption, $C_w > 0, C_r < 0$
$L^{\mathrm{s}} = L^{\mathrm{s}}(w,r)$: Labor supply, $L^{\mathrm{s}}_w > 0, L^{\mathrm{s}}_r > 0$
$M^{\mathrm{d}} = pm^{\mathrm{d}}(Y^{\mathrm{s}},r)$: Money demand, $m^{\mathrm{d}}_{Y^{\mathrm{s}}} > 0, m^{\mathrm{d}}_r < 0$
$I = I(r)$: Investment, $I_r < 0$
$Y^{\mathrm{s}}(w), L^{\mathrm{d}}(w)$: Firms' output and employment decision, $Y^{\mathrm{s}}_w < 0, L^{\mathrm{d}}_w < 0$

We only note (but do not treat this problem any further here) that these equations are not consistently derived from the (intertemporal) budget restrictions underlying (2.15), yet that they do not obviously appear as being inconsistent. Our aim is to make use of the above approach of Barro to compare its strengths and weaknesses with the other prototype models of this chapter. The above restriction (2.15) implies the following type of *Walras-Identity (Micro-Version)*:

$$p(C + I - Y^{\mathrm{s}}) + W(L^{\mathrm{d}} - L^{\mathrm{s}}) + (B^{\mathrm{d}} - B^{\mathrm{s}}) + (M^{\mathrm{d}} - \overline{M}) \equiv 0,$$

[30] To not overload our reformulation of Barro's final market-clearing approach we exclude depreciation, inflation, etc. and any discussion of permanent effects from our following considerations. Note also that we do consider here only direct investment for simplicity. For the case of credit-financed investment see (2.9) and (2.10) and for an integration of equities Sargent (1987, Chap. 1).

[31] With regard to the magnitude ΔB we have departed from our earlier notation and follow Barro who uses excess demand ΔB of the household sector for simplicity instead of the more explicit notation $B^{\mathrm{d}} - B^{\mathrm{s}}$. Note also that we have implicitly made use of discrete time in the presentation of this identity, which avoids the dimensional problems of the stock/flow-distinction of continuous time models.

[32] Note here that we follow Barro's approach in this and the following section as closely as possible, which in particular means that we here exclude the speculative motive from liquidity preference, because of the type of bonds that is assumed: $p_{\mathrm{B}} = 1$ instead of $p_{\mathrm{B}} = \frac{1}{r}$ as in Sects. 2.2 and 2.3.

[33] This function is based on an optimal transaction balance approach [where, however, real balances effects have been excluded from consideration].

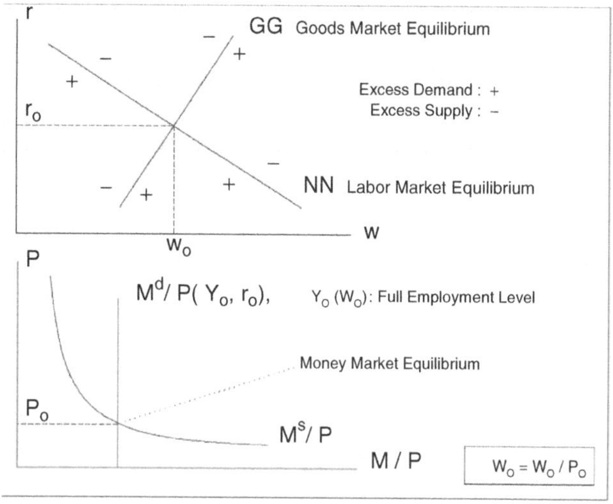

Fig. 2.8 The Barro model

which in turn implies the following formulation of *Walras' Law (Micro-Version)*:[34]

> *If three of the four markets of the economy are in equilibrium, the fourth must be in equilibrium, too.*

This law allows us to ignore the bond-market and its equilibrium condition in the presentation of Barro's market-clearing model (Fig. 2.8)[35]

$$C(w,r)+I(r) = Y^{s}(w), \tag{2.16}$$
$$L^{d}(w) = L^{s}(w,r), \tag{2.17}$$
$$pm^{d}(Y^{s},r) = \overline{M}. \tag{2.18}$$

These three remaining equations show that Barro's model dichotomizes (as does the Classical model!) with regard to the money-market and the determination of nominal values. Yet, in contrast to our Classical model the labor- and the goods-market are now interdependent as is the determination of real wages w and the interest rate r. In direct analogy to the conventional determination of IS- and LM-curves, (2.16) and (2.17) can be viewed to give rise to a positively sloped GG-curve and a negatively sloped NN-curve in w,r-space. Both curves depict the set of equilibria of (2.16) and (2.17), respectively, and they give rise to the following graphical representation of the model (2.16)–(2.18).

---

34 This law, in particular, implies that any labor market disequilibrium must be accompanied by at least one further disequilibrium in this macromodel, which makes disequilibrium analysis more demanding than in the Keynesian underemployment model considered in the next section.

35 Cf. here Barro's (1990, p. 144) brief discussion of this final basic market-clearing model ($W = wp$!).

This model can be easily manipulated – just as the conventional IS-LM-model – for various comparative-static exercises, which are, however, not of interest here, since we are dealing with different conceptualizations of the macroeconomy in this chapter solely.

Instead, our task is to assemble the differences between the above general equilibrium approach to macroeconomics and our former synthetic Classical model. These differences are given by the following:

- The inclusion of intertemporal substitution effects into household decisions:

$$C(w,r), C_w > 0, C_r < 0, \qquad L^s(w,r), L^s_w > 0, L^s_r > 0$$

- The influence of the interest rate on optimal real transaction balances $m^d(.,r)$
- The use of Walras' Law (2.15) in place of Say's Law (2.7), by employing the national income concept $Y \equiv Y^s + w(L^s - L^d)$ for households' decision making

The first two modifications enrich the Classical model, but they do not alter its outlook significantly. The effect of the third, however, is significant, since we lose thereby an important property of the Classical model, namely the possibility to analyze the consequences of a money wage, which has been set too high [which in the Classical model implied unemployment despite the presence of goods-, credit-, and money-market equilibrium, see our reformulation of Say's law]. Such an analysis is no longer possible in the above model of the New Classical Macroeconomics, since labor market disequilibrium now implies disequilibrium in at least one further market.

If there is disequilibrium in the above model, it is of such an extent that its treatment lies outside the possibilities that this model offers. *Therefore, this New Classical Macroeconomics has to restrict itself to the consideration of full equilibria only!*

Barro's (1990, p. 145) conclusion is that the introduction of the labor market does not alter his basic market-clearing approach significantly, so that it suffices to consider this approach without this market for the most part of the book. Only in his Chap. 11 on unemployment it is, of course, necessary to reintroduce this market. But an inspection of this chapter shows that the term "reintroducing" does not mean "extending the model so that it now allows for the discussion of unemployment as well."

In sum, we therefore find that this New Classical Macroeconomics improves (to some extent) the analysis of the behavioral relationships, but that it achieves this in a way, which severely limits its applicability. In our view, the Classical model is therefore still to be preferred over this New Classical version, since it does not exclude the analysis of the causes of unemployment from its final formulation.

2.5 IS-LM-Analysis as a Generalization of the New Classical Model

I have called this book the *General Theory of Employment, Interest and Money*, placing the emphasis on the prefix *general*. The object of such a title is to contrast the character of my arguments and conclusions with those of the *Classical* theory of the subject, upon which

I was brought up and which dominates the economic thought, both practical and theoretical, of the governing and academic classes of this generation, as it has for a hundred years past. I shall argue that the postulates of the Classical theory are applicable to a special case only and not to the general case, the situation which it assumes being a limiting point of the possible positions of equilibrium. Moreover, the characteristics of the special case assumed by the Classical theory happen not to be those of the economic society in which we actually live, with the result that its teaching is misleading and disastrous if we attempt to apply it to the facts of experience.

J.M. Keynes (1936, p. 3).

This quotation from the General Theory can be easily "mapped" into the above GG-NN-diagram when one notes that Keynes (1936, Chap. 2) explicitly accepts the marginal productivity relationships $L^{\mathrm{d}}(w), Y^{\mathrm{s}}(w)$ we have used in Barro's model.

Keynes' interest was to analyze massive unemployment on the basis of a demand-determined goods-market equilibrium. To obtain such an analysis from the above simple model let us again assume that the money-wage $\overline{W}$ (set by firms and workers interactively) is much too high in comparison to the money wage W_0 momentarily needed to reach a full equilibrium in Fig. 2.9. As already stressed, the model of Sect. 2.4 is incapable of implying a reasonable answer for such a situation, since it does not allow a determination of income Y_{o} in such a case as the Fig. 2.9 makes clear.

Let us furthermore assume (ad hoc) that by the experience of massive unemployment households will revise their income plans and substitute $\overline{W}L^{\mathrm{d}}$ for $\overline{W}L^{\mathrm{s}}$ (perhaps not exactly, but it may represent the better proxy than $\overline{W}L^{\mathrm{s}}$, see Barro and Grossman (1971), for example, for a similar approach). The Walras-Identity of the preceding section will thereby be modified to the following *Walras-Identity (Macro-Version):*

$$p(C+I-Y^{\mathrm{s}})+(B^{\mathrm{d}}-B^{\mathrm{s}})+(M^{\mathrm{d}}-\overline{M})\equiv 0$$

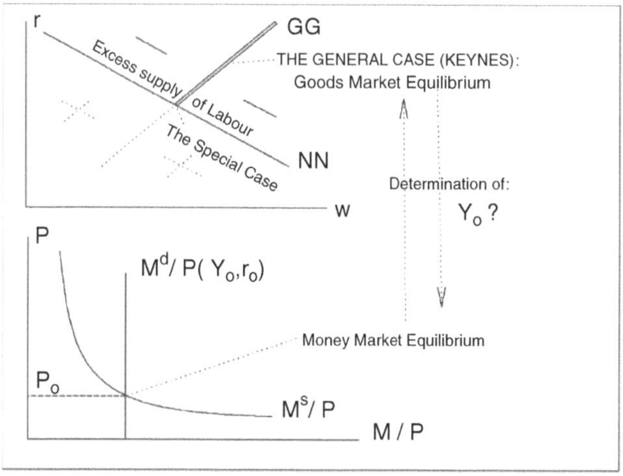

Fig. 2.9 The Barro model and the "General Theory"

and *Walras' Law (of Flows)* has obviously to be rephrased on the basis of this identity (in a well-known fashion). The change from $(pY^s - WL^d) + WL^s$ to pY^s in the budget equation of households then suggests the following change in the *expenditure behavior* of households:

$$C(w,r) \longmapsto C(Y,r), Y \equiv Y^s,$$

which, of course, is to be supplemented by $C_Y \in (0,1)$ with respect to Keynes' views on this matter.

As a consequence of this we no longer have Barro's interdependence of the goods- and the labor market, but now obtain an interdependence between the goods- and the money-market plus the determination of prices by marginal costs. This leads us in a well-known fashion to the depicted conventional IS-LM-model (with endogenous prices, see Fig. 2.10), which nevertheless exhibits a striking formal similarity with our presentation of Barro's approach in Fig. 2.8.

We have thereby shown how the conventional IS-LM-model (with endogenous prices)[36] is obtained in a fairly simple and straightforward way as a generalization of the general equilibrium model of Barro,[37] a fact that provides an interesting illustration for the above quotation from Keynes' General Theory. Fifty years after the appearance of this book, Barro's contribution thus seems to provide a more consistent [yet not too consistent][38] model of pre-Keynesian Macroeconomics which, on the

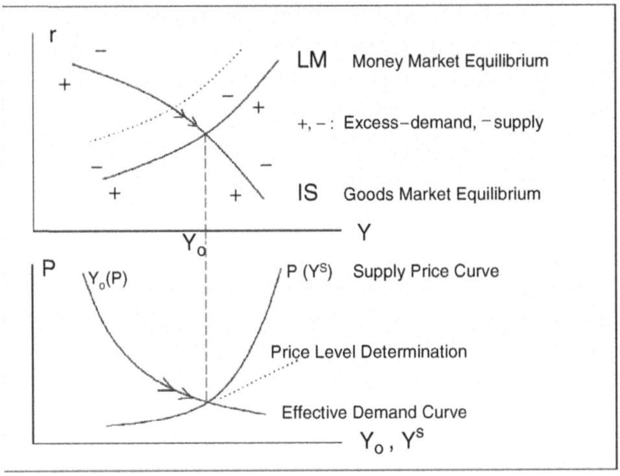

Fig. 2.10 IS-LM as a generalization of the new classical model

[36] See Turnovsky (1977, Chap. 2) and Sargent (1987, Chap. 2) for its detailed formal discussion with respect to given or endogenous prices p. See furthermore Sargent (1987, Chap. 1) for the so-called classical variant of this IS-LM model.

[37] Note here, however, that this *generalization in applicability* has been achieved by a *modification* in the assumed behavior of households.

[38] Cf. his derivation of the demand for money, his discussion of government expenditures and their effects on the private sector, etc. ...

one hand, remains a good starting point for explaining the innovations introduced by the Keynesian concept of temporary equilibrium with deficient effective demand. On the other hand, we have seen that our original Classical model is not changed very much by Barro's modifications and extensions as far as its general equilibrium situation is concerned, while its underemployment equilibrium has been lost through this particular type of its revision. Today's orthodoxy again does not feel much need or pressure to develop a serious macrotheory of unemployment.

Remark: We have seen (in Sect. 2.4) how Barro's New Classical model can be completed with regard to the inclusion of the labor market and we have shown (in this section) how it can be modified and extended in a plausible way to give rise to the conventional IS-LM-model. In his Chap. 20 Barro, too, provides an introduction into Keynesian IS-LM analysis. In this chapter he furthermore adds a Keynesian theory of inflation by means of the equation[39]

$$\pi_t = \lambda(Y_t^{\mathrm{d}} - Y_t^{\mathrm{s}}), \quad \pi_t = \frac{\Delta p_t}{p_t}.$$

As we have seen in the introduction, this equation represents an inconsistent addition of the law of demand and supply to the Keynesian IS-LM- framework![40]

We conclude from this comparison of Barro's New Classical model with a correctly interpreted IS-LM-model that the former could be a good guide to the latter, if it is presented in an appropriate way so that its special character becomes obvious and if the latter is not mixed with partial ideas from ordinary (Walrasian) demand and supply analysis. Such a statement should not convey, however, that macroeconomics in general and Keynesianism in particular has been and should be further improved by a thorough analysis of individual and aggregate budget constraints to be added to its new or standard behavioral relationships in a consistent way.

2.6 Keynes' Notes on the Trade Cycle

> Since we claim to have shown in the preceding chapters what determines the volume of employment at any time, it follows, if we are right, that our theory must be capable of explaining the phenomena of the trade cycle.
>
> J. M. Keynes (1936, p. 313).

Following this introductory remark of Keynes in his "Notes on the trade cycle" we shall here briefly recapitulate his observations on the main source and the pattern of the cyclical fluctuations, which characterize the evolution of capitalist economies. By this section, we only intend to sketch some basic medium run implications of

[39] Cf. also Sects. 9.2 and 9.3 for a characterization of this approach toward a theory of inflation, which is there called a Classical cross-dual rule of price level adjustment in contrast to the Keynesian dual one treated thereafter (in Sects. 9.4 and 9.5).

[40] See, however, Sect. 9.3 for a related (hybrid Keynes–Wicksell) approach toward a theory of price inflation.

the temporary equilibrium analysis of this chapter. It will therefore not provide a thorough presentation or even elaboration of Keynes' ideas on this process. Yet, since most textbooks of macroeconomics often introduce IS-LM analysis without discussing its medium and long-run dynamic implications à la Keynes,[41] this brief outlook on his views in this matter may help to stimulate further interest in Keynes' own approach to the analysis of the trade cycle – and the role that expectations play in his arguments.

There are three main elements that can be used from the above IS-LM analysis for an analysis of the phenomenon of the business cycle:

- The marginal propensity to consume
- The marginal efficiency of capital
- The state of liquidity preference

The marginal propensity to consume out of income has already been introduced in the preceding section. Elements that may explain shifts in this propensity (and thus shifts in the IS-curve, without, however, having been introduced into this analysis yet) are among others:

- Changes in income distribution
- Changes in perceived wealth and disposable income
- Changes in the rate of time-discounting

cf. Keynes (1936, Chaps. 8 and 9). Shifts in the marginal propensity to consume decrease or increase the Keynesian multiplier and thus have expansionary or contractionary effects on the level of activity of the economy.

The marginal efficiency of capital, cf. Keynes (1936, Chap. 11), is defined in reference to certain time series $Q_1, \ldots, Q_n, n \geq 2$ of prospective returns or yields of investment projects. Without going into the details of its definition,[42] it can be seen that such an approach makes investment heavily dependent on expectations of returns over a considerable amount of time. It follows that investment demand may be very volatile and consequently may be of central importance for an explanation of the trade cycle.

Multiplier effects (including its changes) may add to this volatility and its impacts. Nevertheless, in Keynes' view, they mainly transmit fluctuations in investment demand to those of income and employment, but do not by themselves explain the business cycle.

Changes in liquidity preference, cf. here Keynes (1936, Chap. 15), refer to the stock of accumulated savings and are – as investment demand – highly dependent on the "state of confidence." This, of course, is particularly true for the speculative motive for holding cash balances, which through sudden changes in expectations may give rise to "discontinuous" changes in the rate of interest.

[41] Cf. here Chaps. 6-8 for the formal difficulties that are involved in the discussion of IS-LM models of cyclical growth.

[42] See Keynes (1936, pp. 135/6) for his original proposal of such a definition.

We may summarize the above provisionally by the use of three additional parameters γ, η, and λ in the three behavioral relationships, which underlie the IS-LM-part of the model in Sect. 2.5:

$$C(\underset{+}{Y}, \underset{-}{r}, \underset{+}{\gamma}), \quad I(\underset{-}{r}, \underset{+}{\eta}), \quad \frac{M^d}{p}\left(\underset{+}{Y}, \underset{-}{r}, \underset{+}{\lambda}\right). \tag{2.19}$$

These parameters express that the employed behavioral relationships may be subject to changes, which are not explained by the IS-LM-model, but are added to it from the outside in an ad hoc fashion, due to the fact that an endogenous treatment in particular of the marginal efficiency of investment is at least a very demanding task.

> "By a *cyclical* movement we mean that as the system progresses in, e.g. the upward direction, the forces propelling it upwards at first gather force and have a cumulative effect on one another but gradually lose their strength until at a certain point they tend to be replaced by forces operating in the opposite direction; which in turn gather force for a time and accentuate one another, until they too, having reached their maximum development, wane and give place to their opposite. We do not, however, merely mean by a *cyclical* movement that upward and downward tendencies, once started, do not persist for ever in the same direction but are ultimately reversed. We mean also that there is some recognizable degree of regularity in the time-sequence and duration of the upward and downward movements.
>
> There is, however, another characteristic of what we call the trade cycle which our explanation must cover if it is to be adequate; namely, the phenomenon of the *crisis* - the fact that the substitution of a downward for an upward tendency often takes place suddenly and violently, whereas there is, as a rule, no such sharp turning-point when an upward is substituted for a downward tendency.
>
> J. M. Keynes (1936, pp. 313/4).

Keynes then starts his discussion of such fluctuations in investment, income, employment, etc. from the late stage of a boom period. In this stage of the boom, it may become apparent for investors – due to the past effects of capital accumulation on the abundance of physical capital and the costs of production – that their views on the marginal efficiency of capital demand a significant revision ($\eta \downarrow$). Such a revision of ideas – when it becomes generalized – may lead to a significant change in η and thus a fall in effective demand (via the multiplier process), which in turn may aggravate the pessimism that has become established ($\eta \downarrow\downarrow$). The cumulative upward trends of the boom may thereby become reversed and turned into cumulative downward trends in income and employment.

It appears as plausible that this decline (or collapse) in the marginal efficiency of capital (η) will give rise to an increase (or upward jump) in the liquidity preference parameter λ, that is, a (sudden) increase in the demand for money. IS-LM analysis implies that this will lead to a (sharp) increase in the rate of interest r and consequently to a further decrease in investment and income. Negative expectations are thereby confirmed and strengthened. It follows that the parameters η and λ may interact in such a way that there results a collapse in economic activity. (Of course, also milder forms – as the recessions of the sixties – are conceivable in the above framework).

The upper turning point for economic activity is thus explained by the interaction of free parameters of the model, which bring a boom that is gradually losing force to an end – since the gradual change in η, λ has endogenous consequences (on I, Y, and r) that confirm the opinions that are responsible for this change in behavior. Finally, one effect of the boom may also have been that the marginal propensity to consume has risen (e.g., due to an increase of the share of wages in national income). The parameter γ may therefore also contribute to the decline in economic activity by its subsequent decline.

Let us assume for our following discussion of the lower turning point in economic activity that there has been a long period of economic prosperity, so that the above described moments all work with sufficient strength and induce a depression of considerable strength. Economic activity now being low means that the rapid accumulation of "capital" in the past has created a significant amount of idle capital-goods. It is obvious that this excess capacity in production must disappear before there can be any recovery in the parameter that characterizes the marginal efficiency of capital. A considerable amount of time will elapse therefore during which now unprofitable investments of the past are eliminated in physical or in value form. Such a process of capital depreciation will not in general accelerate, since there is a floor to the level of gross investment (above zero) that helps to maintain a low level of economic activity. Once the capital stock has been reduced so far to be in line again with the prevailing level of activity, a return to a more optimistic view on investment profitability becomes possible and may come about. The forces that have operated downward in the development of the depression may now come to help to allow a spreading optimism to gather force. Rising investment and thus rising income and economic activity confirm the positive change in the parameter η, eventually leading to a further increase in it. An improving state of confidence may give rise to a decline in λ, the liquidity preference parameter, and thus to a decline in the rate of interest, giving further force to the spreading investment optimism. The resulting cumulative upward effects may, of course, in some cases be weak and thus only lead to a minor recovery, but may in other cases be strong enough to generate once again a boom of significant duration and strength.

This brief sketch of cumulative upward or downward working forces and the gradual appearance of counteracting elements that bring an end to such upward or downward tendencies must suffice here as an outline of the potential of IS-LM-analysis to explain business fluctuations. The central role of the parameter η (in comparison to the other two parameters[43]) in the explanation of such fluctuations should be obvious from the statements just made.

No such analysis is possible when the Classical model is used instead (because of its reliance on Say's Law in the main). Business fluctuations in the market clearing approach are then, for example, explained by introducing local markets and misperceptions of agents in such a setup, see Barro (1990, Chap. 19), Sargent (1987, Chap. 18) for details, or by so-called real business cycles, see Blanchard and Fischer (1989, Chap. 7).

Keynes' approach to explaining the trade cycle has not received much attention in the discussion on growth and instability that developed after the appearance of the

[43] Which play the role of amplifiers.

General Theory (see the next chapter). This may in particular be due to the strong psychological influences that appear in his explanation of the cycle as, for example, in the following statement (p. 317):

> ... it is not so easy to revive the marginal efficiency of capital, determined, as it is, by the uncontrollable and disobedient psychology of the business world.

Instead of the above speculative type of interaction of primarily psychologically determined magnitudes (the parameters η, γ, λ), dynamic economic analysis has turned to the analysis of interactions of a more mechanical type in the sequel: the multiplier/accelerator-approaches. Various results of these endogenous interactions (of S and I) will be considered in the following chapter.

2.7 Conclusions

We have started in this chapter on temporary equilibrium from a completed version of the prototype model of so-called classical macroeconomics, which is used in the literature to explain by it the advances of Keynesian economics. This model has indeed allowed us to give a clear description of Keynes' rejection of (a sophisticated version of) Say's Law. At the same time it enabled us to reconsider the advances of the New Classical economics, and to show that they are in fact of a very pre-Keynesian nature, which moreover again allow for a Keynesian revolution [just as in the basic Classical model], leading thereby toward a (correctly interpreted) conventional type of IS-LM model. We have shown the basic flaw in the Classical model (the incorrect identification of saving with lending), and have seen how this flaw is overcome in its New Classical version, at the expense of reducing the validity of the model to full equilibrium situations solely, that is, to a special and not too interesting case from which Keynes wanted to depart.

We have furthermore seen that very small changes – if they concern an important error in a prototype model – may have large consequences such as the following:

- The wage paradox (a declining nominal wage rate does no longer improve the situation on the labor market in the "Keynes model" of Sect. 2.3)!
- The savings paradox (increased saving – instead of lowering the rate of interest and thereby raising investment – leads to a decrease in output and employment in this simple revolution of the Classics)!

The procedure applied and the results obtained in this chapter may be summarized in the form of the Fig. 2.11.[44]

This diagram shows in compact form the hierarchical relationships that exist between the various macroeconomic models we have considered in this chapter by pointing to the main elements of change involved when going from the special or

[44] See the appendix with regard to a brief presentation of Wicksell's contribution to these macroeconomic approaches.

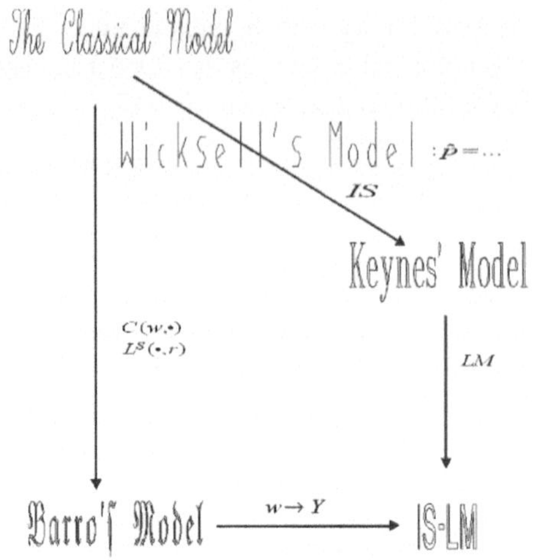

Fig. 2.11 Basic macroeconomic models

Table 2.1 Types of aggregate budget constraints

No.	Macroidentity	Goods-M.	Bond-M.	Money-M.	Labor-M.
1.	Say (crude form)	X			
2.	Say (sophisticated form)	X	X		
3.	Keynes (general form)	X	X	X	
4.	Keynes (reduced form)		X	X	
5.	Say (Lange version)	X	X		X
6.	Walras (barter form)	X			X
7.	Walras (general form)	X	X	X	X

older situation to the more elaborate or newer one. We think that this way of restructuring the relationships between basic prototype models of macroeconomic analysis will contribute to a clarification of the real advances in macroeconomic theory.

Since the chapter has laid much stress on various types of aggregate budget constraints, we shall close it with a brief survey on them as well as further interesting alternatives of such aggregate consistency relationships of macroeconomic model building.[45]

In the Table 2.1,[46] the symbol X characterizes those markets that are included in the formulation of the corresponding identity. Note here, that we did only make use of the identities 2, 3, and 7 (and their background) in this chapter. Identity 1 (i.e.,

[45] The names used to characterize the macroidentities in Table 2.1 indicates the context into which the respective identity has to be placed.

[46] The identity 3 and the following one are normally called Walras' Law of Flows and Stocks, respectively, which, however, is a fairly misleading denomination since both of these identities correspond to the Keynesian notion of an underemployment equilibrium and thus do not address questions of a Walrasian type [note here, however, that we have called identity 3 in Sect. 2.4: Walras Identity (macro-version) to stress its relationship with the corresponding general equilibrium identity of Sect. 2.3 (here No. 7)]. As can be seen form the Table 2.1 and our discussion in Sects. 2.1 and 2.2, the two aggregate restrictions 3 and 4 have nevertheless more in common with the type of Say's identity, which precedes them (No. 2) than with the constraints 5–7 in the Table 2.1.

$I \equiv S$) is often used in real models of (cyclical) growth such as Solow's or Goodwin's growth model. Note, furthermore, that identity 4 is not really an aggregate budget constraint, but a partial one, namely that of shareholders for their portfolio decision [which may be considered a useful approximation to No. 3 in appropriate types of models]. Note finally that the $(n-1)$-market version of Say's Identity (Lange and Patinkin discussion of Say's Law) does not supply us with a *Classical* version of this Law which – for example, due to the wage fund theory, that is, due to the fact that wages are paid out of past proceeds – should not contain the labor market.[47] Say's Law should be considered as a predecessor of the above "Keynes' Law" – as demonstrated in this chapter – and not as an incomplete version of the most general type of Walras' Law, that is, of the aggregate budget constraint of the New Classical Macroeconomics. Much of the confusion of the Lange and Patinkin discussion simply originates from the fact that Say's Law is discussed there from the perspective of notional Walrasian excess demand functions and the corresponding concept of macroeconomic general equilibrium instead of making use of a truly Classical or Keynesian type of analysis of this Law.[48] We conclude that a proper analysis of aggregate budget constraints still remains a vital issue in macroeconomic theory.

Having discussed here various concepts of temporary equilibrium as the fundament for the following presentations,[49] we now start our investigation of the explanations of growth and cycles in a capitalist economy. In view of the present chapter it is natural to start from Keynesian models of the goods-market (IS-equilibrium), which soon after the appearance of the General Theory were extended to the analysis of economic growth and which became the leading explanations of growth and cycles in the fifties and the sixties.

Appendix: Wicksell's Cumulative Process. An Intermediate Case Between the "Classics" and "Keynes"

Consider again the Classical model of Sect. 2.2 and let us now add a "banking sector" to its (modified) restrictions (2.9) and (2.10) for savers and investors in the following simple way

$$M^{\mathrm{s}} - \overline{M} \equiv \frac{1}{r}(B_{\mathrm{b}}^{\mathrm{d}} - \overline{B}_{\mathrm{b}})$$

[we should change our former notation $B^{\mathrm{d}}, B^{\mathrm{s}}$ to $B_{\mathrm{S}}^{\mathrm{d}}, B_{\mathrm{I}}^{\mathrm{s}}$ here to allow again the use of $B^{\mathrm{d}}, B^{\mathrm{s}}$ for aggregate magnitudes]. Through this addition, identity (2.11) now assumes the following form:

[47] This fact, as we have seen, allows the analysis of underemployment equilibria also in a Classical context, independent of the very restrictive assumptions of the wage fund theory.

[48] This may not be too obvious from Patinkin's (1965) own analysis of these concepts, since the case of a production economy is not thoroughly analyzed in his book.

[49] See here in particular Chap. 6.

$$p(Y^{\mathrm{d}} - Y^{\mathrm{s}}) + \frac{1}{r}(B^{\mathrm{d}} - B^{\mathrm{s}}) + (M^{\mathrm{d}} - M^{\mathrm{s}}) \equiv 0 \tag{2.20}$$

Note here that we have employed the corrected budget restrictions of Sect. 2.3 in the derivation of this aggregate identity, but that the model of Sect. 2.2 will otherwise remain unchanged, that is, remain classical in nature with regard to the assumed behavioral relationships. Only the budget constraints are now made consistent with the given existence of money and no modification of the savings function as in Sect. 2.3 is added. This partial revision of the Classical model nevertheless represents an important intermediate step, in that it will allow us to provide a simple and precise description of Wicksell's cumulative process of price-level changes.

To demonstrate this let us assume – as in Ackley (1969, pp. 158 ff.) – that the price level is temporarily fixed and that the money market consequently cannot [and need not] be in equilibrium in each moment of time. The strict version of the quantity theory thereby gives way to a more sophisticated version of it, where – as we shall see in a minute – the natural rate of interest (at which the product market is in equilibrium, see Fig. 2.5) may be different from the interest rate that is actually established through the operation of the bond-market (because of monetary disturbances as they may result from the above type of money supply by the banking sector).

We are now in the position *to show* – in contrast to the simple quantity-of-money approach of Sect. 2.2 – how monetary factors and their changes affect the price level – namely via deviations between the actual (market) rate and the natural rate of interest. Assume that the market rate of interest is flexible and clears – as it should do – the bond market: $B^{\mathrm{d}}(r_{00}) = B^{\mathrm{s}}(r_{00})$, cf. Fig. 2.6 in Sect. 2.2. At this rate of interest it is – in contrast to the Classical model of Sect. 2.2 – not generally true that the goods market must also be in equilibrium then, cf. Fig. 2.5. Such a disequilibrium situation may come about because of the behavior of banks that – in an attempt to attract borrowers and to stimulate investment – supply extra money to reduce the market rate r_{00} below the level r_0 at which $I = S$ holds true.[50] Consumption and investment demand is increased through this excess supply of money and the resulting low rate of interest. This excess supply is thus accompanied by an excess demand for goods [cf. the above aggregate budget restraint (2.20)].

In such a situation it is natural – for the Classical model – to assume that prices will respond to goods market disequilibrium in the following way:[51]

$$\dot{p} = \alpha[I(r_{00}) - S(r_{00})], \quad \alpha = \text{const} > 0. \tag{2.21}$$

This additional equation makes this intermediate type of model again a determined one. Furthermore, this state of a bond market equilibrium is unstable with respect to its goods market consequences, that is, the goods market cannot achieve equilibrium by the above assumed price level dynamics as long as the banking sector continues to supply the economy with extra money to keep the market rate of interest r_{00} below

[50] See, for example, Patinkin (1965, p. 529) for a brief description of such a situation.

[51] Cf. also our discussion of the so-called Keynes–Wicksell model in Sect. 9.3.

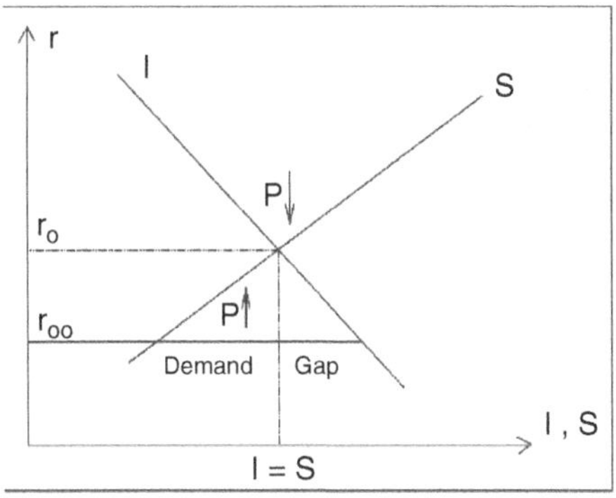

Fig. 2.12 The quantity theory, thc goods market, and inflation

the level of the natural rate r_0 (which would clear the goods market). There will consequently be cumulatively rising prices or inflation as long as monetary policy is conducted in this way [see, however, Patinkin (1965, pp. 591 ff.) for a discussion of the forces, which may restrict banks in this type of behavior].

The above simple extension of the Classical model thus provides a clear picture of the process by which too high a quantity of money influences the behavior of prices by its creation of an inflationary gap in the market for goods (Fig. 2.12). We see that an even simpler modification of the Classical model than that of Sect. 2.3 (on Keynes) can provide us with a Wicksellian view of the working of a market economy.

Chapter 3
After Keynes: Real Growth and (In-)Stability

3.1 Introduction

Theories of economic growth and business fluctuations after Keynes developed from two seminal contributions: Harrod's (1939) "Essay in Dynamic Theory" and Domar's (1946) article on "Capital Expansion, Rate of Growth, and Employment." In many textbooks of the sixties and seventies these two approaches to economic dynamics were treated as nearly identical or at least as very similar as, for example, in Jones (1975, Chap. 3). Yet, reading these two articles will soon convince the reader that such a similarity is only due to those of their assumptions which ensure that their models will imply a steady state solution, that is, a growth path where all variables are growing at a constant rate. The similarity between Harrod's and Domar's approach thus mainly relies on its similarity for this special case and it ends where nonsteady behavior is discussed by these two authors.

Harrod's (1939) dynamic theory consists (in his own words) in a marriage of the "acceleration principle" and the "multiplier theory," which means (as he states it on p. 14):

- "That the level of a community's income is the most important determinant of its supply of savings,"
- "That the rate of increase of its income is an important determinant of its demand for saving," and
- "That demand is equal to supply."

Instead of "demand for saving" we use the term "investment" today to describe the "acceleration principle" or the investment function employed here to get a complete determination of the equilibrium in the market for goods.

The above approach sounds fairly Keynesian and it is in fact Harrod's main aim to supplement the static method of thinking about Keynesian underemployment equilibrium by a new method of thinking, namely to "think dynamically" (cf. his p. 15), which is of much more importance to him than the particular model that he uses for its introduction. Keynes, as the editor of the journal where Harrod's article finally appeared, nevertheless saw many problems in Harrod's way of thinking. His

P. Flaschel, *The Macrodynamics of Capitalism: Elements for a Synthesis of Marx, Keynes and Schumpeter, Second Edition,*

exchange with Harrod on this article is documented in Moggridge (1973, p. 321 ff.) providing the reader with an interesting example of how difficult it is to argue in words, rather than by means of a (radically) simplifying set of assumptions and an explicit model based upon them.

After having discussed (among other things) his "Fundamental Equation" (for the steady-state), Harrod (1939, p. 22) continues:

> But now suppose that there is a departure from the warranted rate of growth. Suppose an excessive output, so that g exceeds g_w.[1] The consequence will be that v, the actual increase of capital goods per unit increment of output, falls below v^p, that which is desired. There will be, in fact, an undue depletion of stock or shortage of equipment, and the system will be stimulated to further expansion. g, instead of returning to g_w, will move farther from it in an upward direction, and the farther it diverges, the greater the stimulus to expansion will be. Similarly, if g falls below g_w there will be a redundancy of capital goods, and a depressing influence will be exerted; this will cause a further divergence and a still stronger depressing influence; and so on. Thus in the dynamic field we have a condition opposite to that which holds in the static field. A departure from equilibrium, instead of being self-righting, will be self-aggravating. g_w represents a moving equilibrium, but a highly unstable one.

Keynes commented[2] on the third sentence of this quotation (beginning with: The Consequence will be...): "This is the crux of the whole theory, from which the rest follows. But you have not made the faintest attempt to prove it." It has indeed been somewhat difficult to rationalize Harrod's ideas on dynamic instability by means of the concepts used in the above quotation solely. And it is even more difficult to provide a sound model for the following further conclusion from Harrod's instability analysis (p. 24):

> We may define general over-production as a condition in which a majority of producers, or producers representing in sum the major part of production, find they have produced or ordered too much, in the sense that they or the distributors of their goods find themselves in possession of an unwanted volume of stocks or equipment. By reference to the fundamental equation it appears that this state of things can only occur when the actual growth has been *below* the warranted growth – i.e., a condition of general over-production is the consequence of producers in sum producing too little. The only way in which this state of affairs could have been avoided would have been by producers in sum producing more than they did. Over-production is the consequence of production below the warranted level.

Attempts to provide mathematical models for such a view will be considered in Sect. 3.3 of this chapter. They may represent far-reaching simplifications of Harrod's views on how his instability principle works, but it is only by means of such simplifications that it becomes possible to present clearly the basic achievements of Harrod's analysis, which is not possible – by contrast – by means of broad verbal characterizations of the *quantitative* interaction of the asserted two basic adjustment mechanisms of a capitalist economy. Reformulated in this way, Harrod's (1939) observations on dynamic instability are still of great importance, since they concern a paradoxical element in the working of such an economy – a situation that

[1] The actual and the warranted rate of growth of total output (we have changed Harrod's notation into ours, see also Sect. 3.3).

[2] In a letter to Harrod, 19 September 1938, see Moggridge (1973, p. 340).

is much more worthwhile to be investigated thoroughly than those conclusions of mathematical model building, which just confirm in detail what is already considered to be obvious.

In contrast to Harrod's essay, Domar (1946) presents his analysis of (the problems of) growth in a capitalist economy in much more detail and by means of a simple mathematical model throughout. We shall present in Sect. 3.4 of this chapter an alternative modeling of his basic ideas and in particular one of his central results:

> Thus the failure of the economy to grow at the required rate creates unused capacity and unemployment.

The way of its derivation in Domar (1946) clearly shows that Domar's analysis concerns the convergence toward a dynamic underemployment equilibrium (with regard to labor *and* capital), that is, the *stability* of a situation of depression. This quite obviously has not much in common with Harrod's instability principle! In our view, these two types of analyses concern two different phases of the business cycle, since Domar's approach describes stable situations of a depressed economy, while Harrod's analysis concerns the unstable situation of a booming economy.

Furthermore, these two types of partial descriptions of the dynamics of the macroeconomy are not inconsistent with the very broad picture that Keynes gave in his "Notes on the trade cycle" [see Chap. 2 of this book].

In a famous article, Solow (1956) attempted to show that Harrod's results rested on the decisive assumption of a macrotechnology with fixed capital-output and capital-labor ratios (no substitution). He stated in this regard (see the first page of his article):

> But this fundamental opposition of warranted and natural rates turns out in the end to flow from the crucial assumption that production takes place under conditions of *fixed proportions*. There is no possibility of substituting labor for capital in production. If this assumption is abandoned, the knife-edge notion of unstable balance seems to go with it. Indeed it is hardly surprising that such a gross rigidity in one part of the system should entail lack of flexibility in another.

Yet, Solow's contribution – as a critique of Harrod's instability principle – is invalid in two related aspects:[3]

- He again assumed Say's Law, thereby avoiding the use of an independent investment function and the Keynesian problem of deficient effective demand.
- He considered the stability of the "natural" rate of growth (of the labor force) and not that of the warranted rate of growth.

Despite this defect of Solow's argument as a counter argument against Harrod's "instability problem," his model has become one of the most popular model of the literature on economic growth. This has lead in many contributions to the following important and consequential separation of the theory of the business cycle from that of economic growth. While the former medium-run theory uses the principle of

---

[3] See in this regard also footnote 15 in Sen's Introduction to Sen's (1970) reader on growth theory, where he quotes Solow with a statement on the proper contents of Solow's (1956) growth model.

effective demand as a constraint to profit-maximizing output-plans of producers, the latter theory assumes that it can ignore this principle in its explanation of the *long-run* trends of a capitalist economy, which therefore can be analyzed as if Say's Law would be valid.[4] The basics of this latter approach will be presented in Sect. 3.5.

There have not been many attempts to reject Solow's above-quoted claim by means of an explicit mathematical model, which again includes the principle of effective demand. One contribution in this direction is Nikaido's (1980) paper, which we shall discuss here in Sect. 3.6. Goods-market equilibrium is there again treated in a nontrivial way, but now in the context of a neoclassical growth model (with factor substitution).

Having thus shown that the assumption of "fixed coefficients" is not the crucial element in Harrod's instability assertion, we return again to the simpler type of a "macrotechnology," that is, to fixed proportions. On the basis of such a technology description, we then consider the Hicksian theory of cycles and growth, which Hicks (1950, pp 3 ff.) characterized as being derived from three immediate progenitors: Keynes' multiplier theory, Clark's acceleration principle, and Harrod's theory of growth. These three aspects were married by Hicks in his "Contribution to the Theory of the Trade Cycle," which in some parts differs significantly from Keynes' Notes on this subject[5], but which nevertheless (due to its formal structure and completeness) has become the leading prototype model of macroeconomic dynamics in the fifties and sixties.

This prototype model of an analysis of cycles and growth – but not of cyclical growth – will be discussed in Sect. 3.7. The final section of this chapter will then provide a fiscal policy application of this trade cycle analysis, that is, it will treat the question in how far the Hicksian cycle can be controlled in its amplitude, can be damped, or even made disappear by choosing appropriate rules for public expenditures.

In an appendix to this chapter, we shall finally briefly present and compare some close relatives to the nonlinear Hicks model of the trade cycle, which have recently been used in the literature again to demonstrate the usefulness of the modern tools of nonlinear dynamic analysis. We shall make use of these results on traditional nonlinear models in Chap. 7, where we analyze the dynamics of an instable model of monetary growth in a different way than is customary in the literature on such monetary instabilities.

3.2 Basic Assumptions and Tools

Mathematical economic models are made for many purposes, – legitimate and also illegitimate ones. In all cases, however, they contribute to the discussion of economic assertions and hypotheses in a positive way, in that it is much easier to detect

---

[4] cf. Chap. 2 for a discussion of this Law and its defects.

[5] in particular with respect of the use it makes of the acceleration principle in contrast to Keynes' analysis of business investment behavior.

their inconsistency or incompleteness than it is the case with a model that is mainly presented in verbal terms [as, e.g., Harrod's (1939) model].

In this book we do not intend to make use of mathematical models of economic interactions as "maps" (and thus parts of an"atlas") of the "real world," since it is by no means clear how we should understand the notion "real."[6] In our following considerations of economic growth and cycles, we shall instead use models – and the assumptions on which they are based – as (it is hoped: interesting) hypothetical "economic worlds," the behavior of which can then be studied on the basis of the underlying set of assumptions.

Assumptions are here primarily not justified by their realism, but by the degree in which they are considered as "standard," that is, the degree of acceptance of using them in basic models to derive – or disqualify – typical results of the various approaches toward growth and its possibly cyclical nature. An example of this methodology has already been considered in Chap. 2. Our understanding of Keynes' critique of pre-Keynesian theory is that he accepted most of the assumptions of the economic theory of his times not primarily because they were beyond any doubt, but because he could not have argued in a convincing way with his fellow-economists had he not used their way of thinking and modeling the working of a whole economy. We saw in Chap. 2 – in a (with regard to Keynes) certainly very simplified model – that we basically had to change only *one* assumption in a very natural way to obtain very different, that is, here Keynesian conclusions from an otherwise purely neoclassical model.

To boil down one's economic views on the complex interactions in a whole economy to a few relationships that are formulated as exactly as possible should not be viewed as a loss in realism, but as a gain in clarity, whereby either the merits of one's theoretical insight become clearly visible (to the "standard" economists) or whereby the defects of one's approach can be shown by finding out the crucial assumption(s) on which its essential conclusions are based – and with which they will fall once these assumptions are no longer accepted as standard or basic.

Our approach – one among others – to macroeconomic theory and its applicability thus concentrates on the methodological aspect of economic model building. The basic assumptions of a given epoch in macroeconomic theorizing provide the skeleton for the method of thinking, with the help of which one can hopefully formulate new – and perhaps controversial – insights in a way that is clearly understandable to those who are trained in using these assumptions to structure their thinking about economic interactions.

At this point it is, however, necessary to state that we shall exclude here one type of modern procedure for modeling macroeconomic interdependence in space and in time, perhaps the one that is now the most honored one, that is, the derivation of macroeconomic relationships from representative agents and their optimizing behavior. Valuable as this (in the end always partial) approach to economics

[6] All our thinking – and particularly that in economics – rests on concepts created by the human brain. There is not something like "the objective reality."

may be in certain domains of economic theorizing, and it is by and large – at present – inadequate or at least too restrictive for approaches that attempt to treat the following:

- A complete model of the macroeconomy where all basic markets are present
- The existence of mass unemployment in such models
- The problem of the coordination of savings and investment plans
- The existence of social classes and their saving habits
- The dynamics of the conflict over income distribution
- The unbalanced evolution of temporary equilibria over time

In this matter, one has to decide whether one wants to approach macroeconomic interaction by means of very limited, but concise microfounded scenarios of basically full-employment economies or whether it is perhaps more important to first provide an understandable (but not always concise) picture of the imperfections in the working of a capitalistic economy – as a prototype description to whose details the microfounded analysis may then be applied.

Using an approach to macroeconomic theory as in Sargent (1988) does not really allow for the pursuit of the above described aims in our view and is therefore excluded from this introduction into theories of often unstable or cyclical growth. These theories may therefore appear as somewhat old-fashioned from the viewpoint of the current fashions in macroeconomic theorizing. Yet, there exist also approaches towards complex nonlinear economic dynamics which take their point of departure from the models of the goods-market, which we shall discuss in the following, cf., for example, Chiarella (1990), Hommes (1991), Lorenz (1989), Puu (1991), and Zhang (1991).

Basic assumptions of the above characterized type (to be employed in the following unless alternative assumptions are stated explicitly) are the following:[7]

Assumption 1:

There is only one commodity produced in the given (closed) economy which can be used for consumption and investment purposes. There are no resale markets for this commodity.

This assumption is completely standard in macroeconomic theory. The next interesting step in this regard would be to assume a two-commodity world with one pure consumption and one pure investment-good. Such an extension will not be considered in the present book.

Assumption 2:

(Total) output Y is produced by labor L and capital K (accumulated past investment) according to the following production function with fixed coefficients σ, y:

$$Y = \min\{\sigma K, yL\} = \min\{K/v, L/a\}.$$

[7] The reader is referred to Jones (1975) for a more detailed presentation and discussion of these assumptions.

The parameters σ and y are called output-capital-ratio and (aggregate) labor-productivity, respectively[8] [capital depreciation $\delta K, \delta$ the depreciation rate, will be explicitly considered in later parts of the book only].

Instead of such a production function with fixed coefficients we shall employ in later portions of the book a so-called neoclassical production function $Y = F(K,L)$, which allows for a smooth factor substitution, with F_L, F_K denoting the marginal product of labor and capital. A compact introduction into the properties of such functions is given in Sargent (1987, I. 1), cf. also Jones (1975, Chap. 2) in this regard.

Remark: We shall denote in the following by $\dot{x}$ the time derivative of a variable x and by $\hat{x} = \dot{x}/x$ its rate of growth. Calculations that use rates of growth often can be simplified by means of the following rules for growth rate calculations: $\widehat{xy} = \hat{x}+\hat{y}, \quad \widehat{x/y} = \hat{x}-\hat{y}$. These rules apply to continuous time modeling and will be often applied in this book.[9] In discrete time they have to be replaced by $\widehat{xy} = \hat{x}+\hat{y}+\hat{x}\hat{y}$ and $\widehat{x/y} = \hat{x}-\hat{y}-\widehat{x/y}\cdot\hat{y}$, as can easily be established by starting from the right hand side of the $\widehat{xy}$-expression.

If technological change is included into the above input–output approach – with fixed coefficients – it is generally at first included in the form of Harrod-neutral technical progress

$$\hat{y} = \dot{y}/y = m = \text{const}, \qquad \hat{\sigma} = 0,$$

that is, output per head grows at a constant (positive) rate m, while the output-capital ratio remains constant over time.[10]

Assumption 3:

In growth theory, the following simplest form of a Keynesian savings function has often been used

$$S = sY, \qquad s = \text{const}.$$

Standard extensions of such a savings function in the post-Keynesian tradition are given by

$$S = s_p(rK) + s_w(wL) = s_p(Y - wL) + s_w(wL), \quad 0 \le s_w < s_p < 1,$$

that is, instead of assuming that a fixed proportion of national output and income is saved, it is assumed that such fixed proportions only apply to profit–income $Y - wL$

[8] Or in reciprocal form: capital- and labor-coefficient or capital-output and labor-output ratio v and $1/y$. In addition to that, we denote by $k = K/L$ and $l = L/K$ the capital- and labor-intensity ratio in production.

[9] See Jones (1975, 2.5) for further details.

[10] See Jones (1975, Chap. 7) for a detailed presentation of the basic concepts for analyzing the effects of technological change, in particular by means of the above type of a neoclassical production function.

and wage–income wL separately (w the real wage).[11] The neoclassical alternative to such a macro ad-hoc approach, which attempts to integrate the most basic feature of observed social structures, is given by the so-called overlapping generations model where savings is derived from the optimizing behavior of the different generations that are alive at a point in time (and not from the social structure of a capitalist economy).

Assumption 4:

Assumptions regarding investment behavior may differ considerably even in basic macroeconomic approaches (and also in this chapter). One may, for example, use a simple acceleration principle

$$I = (Y^* - Y)/\sigma = v(Y^* - Y), \quad v = 1/\sigma \text{ the capital coefficient,}$$

where net investment is determined by the capacity that is needed for the expected future change in the demand for goods (Y^* the expected demand of "the next period," Y the current level).

This principle can – under certain conditions – be generalized to the so-called capital stock adjustment principle

$$I = I(Y,K), \qquad I_Y > 0, \quad I_K < 0,$$

where it is assumed that investment depends positively on current output and negatively on the accumulated capital stock.[12]

An alternative formulation of investment behavior makes it dependent on the rate of return on this asset (in comparison to the rates of returns on financial assets).[13] Such an approach ($I/K = I(F_K - (r - \hat{p}))$) will be considered later in this book (in Chaps. 6 and 7) and may, of course, also be synthesized with the capital stock adjustment principle.

Assumption 5:

Goods market equilibrium: $I = S$.

Our final basic assumption concerns the change in the amounts of the employed two factors of production through time, which is formulated here in the simplest possible way:

[11] This Kaldorian savings function has been criticized by Pasinetti for its neglect of laborers' capital income, see Jones (1975) for details and necessary modifications, for example. We shall avoid the so-called Pasinetti paradox which resulted from this critique in this book by assuming $s_w = 0$ in our treatments of differentiated saving habits.

[12] A special case is given by $I(Y/K)$, where Y/K may be considered as a measure of "capacity utilization." The capital stock adjustment principle is discussed in detail in Matthews (1970).

[13] cf. Sargent (1987, Chap. VI) for details.

Assumption 6:

The growth of the production factors L^s, K is determined by the laws of motion: $\hat{L}^s = n = \text{const}$ and $\dot{K} = S(= I)$. The rate n is the so-called natural rate of growth.

These assumptions – and simple modifications of them – will generally suffice for the purposes of the present chapter, which is devoted to the post-Keynesian theory of growth and instability and its critiques. It is obvious that the present set of assumptions concentrates – following Harrod's assumptions quoted in Sect. 3.1 – on the market for goods and is thus of a very partial nature still. Of course, at least all the elements of the conventional temporary equilibrium IS-LM model of Chap. 2 have to be considered later to arrive at a complete picture of a closed monetary economy exhibiting cycles and growth.

We shall start in this chapter by means of very simple models of economic dynamics (one-dimensional differential or difference equations of order one with no complex nonlinearities). In these cases, we often simply use graphical tools to study the stability properties of such models [The reader who wants more mathematical details here is referred to the book of Gandolfo (1983)]. Graphical tools – phase diagram presentations – are also often employed for two-dimensional dynamical systems, which – as well as all systems of higher dimension – will be given in the form of differential equations throughout this book. In such cases graphical information will, in general, not be sufficient to determine the stability properties of the studied dynamics unambiguously. The methods we shall then use in addition are briefly enumerated as follows:

- *Local stability analysis* (by means of the linear part or the Jacobian J – the matrix of the partial derivatives at the steady state – of the dynamics under consideration, see Sect. 4.2),
- *Olech's theorem* (for two-dimensional system, cf. Sect. 4.8)
- *The Poincaré–Bendixson theorem* (for two-dimensional system, cf. Sect. 3.8)
- *The Routh–Hurwitz theorem* (for two, three, or more dimensions, cf. Sect. 3.8)
- *Liapunov's direct method* (making use of so-called Liapunov functions, cf. Sect. 4.8)

The theory of two-dimensional differential equations – and often much more – is extensively treated in addition to the already given reference in Hirsch and Smale (1974), Andronov and Chaikin (1949), Coddington and Levinson (1955), Yan-Qian et al. (1984), and Jordan and Smith (1977), and it is surveyed in Brock and Malliaris (1989) and Guckenheimer and Holmes (1983).[14] Local stability analysis is contained in most books on ordinary differential equations, as, for example, (and in a compact form) in Hirsch and Smale (1974). Liapunov's direct method is explained in detail in Hirsch and Smale (1974) and also in Brock and Malliaris (1989), where also a statement of the Routh–Hurwitz theorem can be found. Finally, Olech's theorem – as well as related theorems – are considered in Hartman (1964).

[14] The last book treats extensively the difficulties that are already involved when the dimension of a nonlinear dynamical system of dimension two is increased by one to dimension three.

We shall not make use in this book, however, of the more advanced techniques of studying nonlinear systems, such as bifurcation theory or chaos theory and related approaches. Such methods are either not necessary or not easily available for the economic models which are of interest in our selective approach to macrodynamics.[15] Some references that survey these newer methods and also inform the reader on the above more standard techniques of local or global stability analysis (by an integrated treatment of a variety of related economic models) are Beltrami (1987), Lorenz (1989), Puu (1991), and Zhang (1991). These books should also be consulted for further references on the literature on dynamical systems, which are of use in the study of economic dynamics.

3.3 Unstable Warranted Growth (Harrod)

The central theme of Harrod's (1939) first essay on dynamic theory is the following set of assertions, cf. Jones (1975, Chap. 3):

- There is only one rate of growth of output that confirms the expectations of entrepreneurs in view of their decision to expand productive capacity ($g_{\mathrm{w}} = s/v^{\mathrm{p}}$).
- This "warranted rate of growth" is unstable since divergence from it produces forces that tend to increase this divergence.
- The existence of a so-called golden age, where the "warranted rate of growth" coincides with the so-called "natural" rate of growth n, is highly improbable.

There are many further ideas in Harrod's (1939) essay, which should be investigated in this context. We shall, however, concentrate ourselves here on the above claim that Harrod's warranted rate of growth is surrounded by centrifugal forces. This is obviously not yet a global statement on economic dynamics. Further investigations are therefore needed, when account is taken of the fact that the macroeconomy cannot solely be governed in its overall behavior by an accelerating divergence from its possibility to grow steadily.

It is stressed in Harrod's (1939) essay that it is not the often destabilizing effect of lagged feedbacks, which is at the core of his explanation of the instability of balanced growth in a capitalist economy. To demonstrate his results in a dynamic model which excludes lags of any significance, we shall therefore first use a continuous-time formulation of Harrod's basic assumptions to show the dynamic instability of his warranted rate of growth.

As is obvious from the quotation in Sect. 3.1, the basic assumption of Harrod's approach to dynamics is the Keynesian theory of the multiplier (in its equilibrium formulation), that is, on the basis of Sect. 3.2:

---

[15] See, however, for example Farkas and Kotsis (1992) for extensions of the growth cycle model of Chap. 4, which make use of bifurcation theorems that were originally established for related models of "theoretical biology." Such (and other) important theorems of theoretical biology cannot be discussed or applied in the present investigation due to limitations of scope and of time.

$$I = S = sY \qquad \text{or} \qquad Y = \frac{1}{s}I. \tag{3.1}$$

For investment behavior it may, for example, then be assumed that its dynamics $\hat{I} = \dot{I}/I$ is governed by the following type of acceleration equation:

$$\hat{I}(v) = s/v^{\mathrm{p}} - a(v - v^{\mathrm{p}}), \quad a = \text{const.} \tag{3.2}$$

Such a behavioral function, of course, demands explanation, which may be as follows:

- The rate s/v^{p} is Harrod's warranted rate of growth g_{w}, which is thus determined by the following two given: the desired capital-output ratio $v^{\mathrm{p}} = K^{\mathrm{p}}/Y\ (= 1/\sigma^{\mathrm{p}})$ and the rate of savings $s = S/Y (= I/Y)$:

$$g_{\mathrm{w}} = s/v^{\mathrm{p}} = (I/Y)/(K^{\mathrm{p}}/Y) = I/K^{\mathrm{p}},$$

  that is, the rate of growth of the capital stock that guarantees goods–market equilibrium through time at this constant rate (which is thus "warranted"): $g_{\mathrm{w}} = \hat{I} = \hat{K}^{\mathrm{p}} = \hat{Y}$.
- Deviations of the actual capital-output ratio $v = K/Y (= 1/\sigma)$ from the desired one (v^{p}) produce negative effects on investment, that is, its rate of growth: if v exceeds v^{p} $(K > K^{\mathrm{p}})$, this rate is reduced (and v.v.)

This kind of investment behavior will be sufficient to make explicit the links between Keynesian multiplier theory and the acceleration principle, which Harrod proposed to combine without using lags (as in Samuelson (1939), see Sect. 3.7.) to obtain the result of their unstable interaction, an assertion that he does not discuss very thoroughly (as Keynes already remarked, see Sect. 3.1).

To discuss these links, the following mathematical derivation from the above two equations (3.1), (3.2) is of help (v^{p} = const by assumption):

$$\begin{aligned}
\widehat{v/v^{\mathrm{p}}} &= \hat{v} - \widehat{v^{\mathrm{p}}} = \hat{v} = \hat{K} - \hat{Y} = I/K - \hat{I}, \\
&= (sY)/(vY) - s/v^{\mathrm{p}} + a(v - v^{\mathrm{p}}), \\
&= (s/v) - (s/v^{\mathrm{p}}) + a(v - v^{\mathrm{p}}).
\end{aligned}$$

Note, that we have applied here the rules of growth rate calculations for continuous time (see Sect. 3.2) and have made use of the multiplier theory $I = sY$ as well as the definition of the actual capital-output ratio $v = K/Y$.

In the situation where the actual capital-output-ratio "v" coincides with the desired one (because the multiplier has created – through an appropriate amount of investment – just the necessary amount of national income Y), we immediately get $\hat{v} = \hat{v}^{\mathrm{p}}$, that is, firms will then continue to invest an amount that *warrants* $g_{\mathrm{w}} = s/v$ as the rate of growth of the economy. There thus exists a steady state for this economy, which moreover is uniquely determined ($v = v^{\mathrm{p}}$, but $g_{\mathrm{w}} \neq n$ in general).

If, however, the realized ratio $v = K/Y$ is different from the desired one ($v^p = K^p/Y$), we get for the above dynamics (locally) the following picture (if in addition $a(v^p)^2 - s > 0$ holds true at its steady state).[16]

This follows since the derivative of the function $\widehat{v/v^p}(v)$ at v^p is given by

$$-\frac{s}{(v^p)^2} + a.$$

If the above inequality is given, we consequently have that v will rise to the right of v^p and fall to its left , that is, we get Harrod's centrifugal forces near $v = v^p$.[17]

The above sketch of proof of Harrod's instability assertions has attempted to stay close to Harrod's own formulation of this situation. However, this continuous-time approach to economic dynamics exhibits two great disadvantages, which imply that it is not yet a satisfying modeling of such an instability assertion:

- Its investment function (3.2) assumes the "warranted" rate of growth g_w has to be known to firms and incorporates it directly into the formulation of their investment demand, instead of deriving it from the multiplier–accelerator interaction.
- It does not treat the expectations of firms explicitly.

The necessity of formulating the investment schedule of firms independently from any a priori knowledge of the warranted rate of growth can be easily solved as follows:[18] Let us denote by $\sigma^p = Y^p/K (= 1/v^p)$ the (given) output-capital ratio as it is desired by firms and let $\sigma = Y/K (= 1/v)$ be the actual output-capital ratio. Following Harrod, it is then natural to assume that investment – as a percentage of the capital stock – will be increased if the actual output-capital ratio is above the desired one and decreased in the opposite case. This leads to the following formulation of an accelerator equation:

$$\hat{g}_K = \widehat{I/K} = \alpha(\sigma - \sigma^p), \quad \alpha > 0.$$

Supplemented again by the multiplier equation $Y = I/s \quad (\hat{Y} = \hat{I})$ this gives rise to

$$\hat{\sigma} = \widehat{Y/K} = \widehat{I/K} = \alpha(\sigma - \sigma^p) \quad \text{or} \quad \dot{\sigma} = \alpha(\sigma - \sigma^p)\cdot\sigma.$$

The economically meaningful steady state of this dynamic equation is given by $\sigma = \sigma^p = I/(sK) = g_K/s$, which is again Harrod's determination of the warranted rate of growth of income and the capital stock $g_K = g_Y = s\sigma^p = s/v^p$. If, however, investment plans are such that $Y/K = I/(sK)$ exceeds σ^p, implying that actual

[16] Crudely speaking, this demands with regard to empirically observed magnitudes of s and v the validity of the inequality $a > 0.01$.

[17] This is obvious from Fig. 3.1 and is also easily obtained from a formal discussion of the differential equation that precedes this picture (e.g., by means of a so-called Liapunov-function $L(v) = \int_{v^p}^{v}((s/x) - (s/v^p) + a(x - v^p))x\,dx$, see Brock and Malliaris (1989, Chap. 4) for details on the use of such an instrument (here in a case of instability: $\dot{L} > 0$) and note its trivial nature in the case of only one differential equation.

[18] This variant of the Harrod model has been suggested to me by Rajiv Sethi.

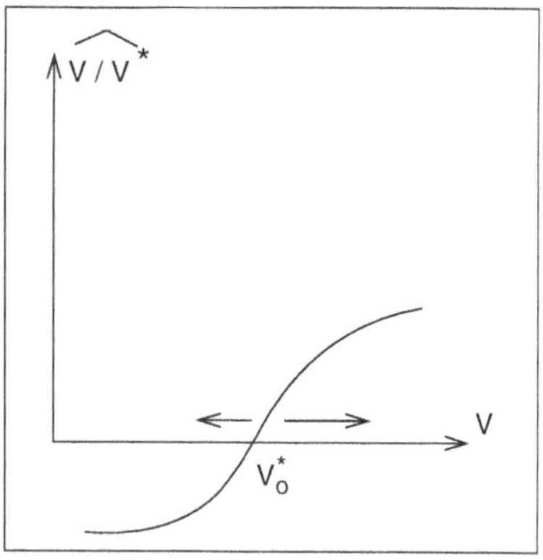

Fig. 3.1 Harrod's growth instability of the goods-market ($v^* = v^p$)

growth g_K exceeds the warranted rate $s\sigma^p$, then firms will increase investment and thus the rate of growth of the capital stock, which lets the actual rate of growth of the economy diverge farther and farther from the warranted rate of growth. Of course, the opposite reasoning applies to a level of investment which lets the economy grow less than the warranted rate of growth. These results of the model can be depicted in the same way as those of our earlier Harrod model (see Fig. 3.1). Note here, finally, that this instability result now holds for any size of the parameter α.

The lack of an explicit treatment of the formation of expectations can be overcome by making use of a very simple, but ingenious discrete-time model of Sen (1970, p. 10 ff.), which, in our view, provides the best of all basic approaches to Harrod's instability analysis.[19]

In Sen's presentation of Harrod's approach to dynamic theory, we find the following reformulation of the basic equations of the model:

$$I_t = S_t = sY_t, \tag{3.3}$$

$$I_t = v(Y_t^* - Y_{t-1}). \tag{3.4}$$

Investment is now governed by expectations on the level of output Y_t^* that can be sold at the current market period t. Firms here thus attempt to create the amount of additional productive capacity that is needed for the expected increase in sales.

To make the mathematical analysis of this approach an easy task, the following harmless deviation from the conventional definition of rates of growth is very helpful:

$$g_t = \frac{Y_t - Y_{t-1}}{Y_t}, \quad g_t^* = \frac{Y_t^* - Y_{t-1}}{Y_t^*}.$$

Growth rate calculations are thus not of the form of a percentage of the beginning-of-period amount (of sales), but are given by means of an end-of-period denominator (as point of reference). This is a pure matter of convention, which does not include any assumption on economic behavior.

[19] Cf. also Jones (1975, Chap. 3) in this regard.

On the basis of these two definitions, it is easy to check[20] that

$$g_t = 1 - (1 - g_t^*)(\frac{s}{v}/g_t^*)$$

must hold true as relation between the actual rate g_t and the expected rate of growth g_t^*. We here define the warranted rate of growth by s/v and note that an explicit reference to a desired capital-output-ratio v^p is no longer needed in this formulation of Harrod's instability hypothesis.

Instead we now add the following *adaptive expectations mechanism*

$$g_{t+1}^* = g_t^* + \alpha(g_t - g_t^*), \alpha \in [0,1] \tag{3.5}$$

to the above model to make it complete. Inserting the above equation into this equation immediately gives the following difference equation:

$$g_{t+1}^* - g_t^* = \alpha \frac{(1-g_t^*)(g_t^* - \frac{s}{v})}{g_t^*}$$

as the fundamental law for expected growth generated by the interaction of the multiplier theory (3.3), the accelerator assumption (3.4), and the assumed adaptive formation of expectations (3.5).

This fundamental equation then gives rise to[21]

$$g_t^* \gtrless \frac{s}{v} \Longleftrightarrow g_{t+1}^* \gtrless g_t^*,$$

that is, again the cumulative (local) instability of the warranted rate of growth $g_w = \frac{s}{v}$. The basic result of this section consequently is that steady growth may be plagued by centrifugal forces on the market for goods, which may accelerate (decelerate) growth toward some, yet unknown, upper (or lower) limit where a different type of economic dynamics will come into being. Harrod's above analysis may therefore be regarded as a partial contribution to the theory of the trade cycle solely, since it may help to explain accelerating or decelerating forces (upswing or downswing), but it does not yet contribute anything to an analysis of turning points of economic fluctuations.[22]

[20] By inserting the definition of g_t^* on the right hand side and by making use of the equilibrium condition $sY_t = I_t = v(Y_t^* - Y_{t-1})$, that is, $\frac{s}{v} = \frac{Y_t^* - Y_{t-1}}{Y_t}$, which reduces the second bracket on the right hand side of this equation to Y_t^*/Y_t.

[21] As long as $1 - g_t^* > 0$ and $g_t^* > 0$ can be assumed to hold true, that is, as long as the expected growth rate of the economy is positive and below 100%. Note here, that the above is only intended as a local instability around the steady state value $g_w = s/v > 0$.

[22] A rational expectations critique of Harrod's local instability result would basically assume that firms are always capable of calculating the warranted rate of growth and would thereby make the centrifugal forces of this model irrelevant. In our view, this is, however, a reformulation of the model, which avoids paradoxical instability problems by assumption, since any less perfect mechanism than that of myopic perfect foresight should be plagued at least to some extent by the centrifugal forces we have analyzed earlier.

3.4 Stable Depressions (Domar)

Domar's (1946, p. 137) article starts from the observation that the standard Keynesian system (see here, Chap. 2) does not yet provide us with any tools for deriving the equilibrium rate of growth. And he continues in the next paragraph:

> Because investment in the Keynesian system is merely an instrument for generating income, the system does not take into account the extremely essential, elementary and well–known fact that investment also increases productive capacity. This *dual* character of the investment process makes the approach to the equilibrium rate of growth from the investment (capital) point of view more promising: if investment both increases productive capacity and generates income, it provides us with *both* sides of the equation the solution of which may yield the required rate of growth.

To determine the equilibrium rate of growth from this dual character of the investment process, Domar uses the assumptions of our Sect. 3.2 – up to its formulation of an investment function. The parameter σ is characterized by him as describing (average) production capacity,[23] which together with the capital stock K that is presently in existence gives potential (normal) output $Y^{\mathrm{p}} = \sigma K$. Since σ is considered as given, we can easily calculate the capacity effect that new investment has, for example, by means of continuous-time analysis:

$$\dot{Y}^{\mathrm{p}} = \sigma \dot{K} = \sigma I. \tag{3.6}$$

Dual to this capacity effect of investment expenditures is their income generating effect, which on the basis of Sect. 3.2 is again simply given by

$$Y = \frac{1}{s} I, \tag{3.7}$$

that is, the multiplier theory of the determination of national income and production (goods–market equilibrium). These two equations taken together now determine the equilibrium rate of growth à la Domar, where the supply side effect of investment stays in line with the demand that is induced by this investment, that is, where the capacity effect of investment equals its income effect.

Differentiating (3.7) gives $\dot{Y} = \dot{I}/s$, that is, this equilibrium condition reads

$$\sigma I = \dot{Y}^{\mathrm{p}} \overset{!}{=} \dot{Y} = \dot{I}/s \qquad \text{or}$$

$$\hat{I} = \dot{I}/I = \sigma s.$$

We obtain therefore that investment must grow to perpetuate goods market equilibrium and it must grow at a definite rate $g = \sigma s$ in the present simple growth model.[24] Note that this rate is identical to Harrod's warranted rate of growth: s/v.[25]

---

[23] Cf. Domar (1946) for further details.

[24] Domar's crude estimate for this rate is $g = 3.6\% = 30\% * 12\%$.

[25] This gives the main reason why Harrod's and Domar's theory are often treated under one and the same heading (as if they were identical, which, as we shall see, are not), see Evans (1969, 14.2) for a typical example.

The above result can also be obtained by an explicit consideration of the degree of (macroeconomic) capacity utilization $\Theta = Y/Y^p$. Differentiating this definitional equation logarithmically gives on the basis of the assumptions in Sect. 3.2:

$$\begin{aligned} \hat{\Theta} &= \hat{Y} - \hat{Y}^p = \hat{I} - (\sigma I)/(I/s) \cdot (Y/Y^p) \\ &= \hat{I} - \sigma s \cdot \Theta \end{aligned} \tag{3.8}$$

The conditions for equilibrium growth then are $\Theta = 1 (t = 0), \hat{\Theta} = 0$ (for all $t \geq 0$), which immediately gives rise to

$$\hat{I} = \sigma s = \hat{Y} = \hat{Y}^p = \hat{K}.$$

Hence, though there is considerable difference in the models of this and the preceding section (we have not yet considered investment behavior explicitly here, but have only investigated its equilibrium path so far!), the steady state result of both types of approaches is the same, namely that the equilibrium or warranted rate of growth is given by $\sigma s = s/v$.

Domar (1946) then goes on to explore what happens when investment does grow at some constant percentage $\bar{g}$, which is not equal to the equilibrium rate σs. The consequences of this assumption can easily be obtained from our above differential equation (3.8), which then reads

$$\hat{\Theta} = \bar{g} - (\sigma s) \cdot \Theta.$$

Graphically this gives rise to the following dependence of the percentage rate of change of capacity utilization on the degree of capacity utilization,[26] which clearly shows the basic difference between Domar's and Harrod's approach to disequilibrium growth.[27]

The stable equilibrium capacity utilization rate Θ_0 of this new situation is given by

$$\Theta_0 = \bar{g}/(\sigma s) \gtrless 1 \quad \text{if} \quad \bar{g} \gtrless \sigma s.$$

The case $\bar{g} > \sigma s$, of course, demands that potential capacity Θ must be understood to include sufficiently large planned reserve capacity, since the consequences of reaching capacity barriers are not considered explicitly here. We assume in the remainder of this section that such capacity barriers can be safely ignored.

Domar was particularly interested in the case where $\bar{g}$ is below the equilibrium rate σs, that is, where the fraction $1 - \bar{g}/(\sigma s)$ of the full capacity will remain idle in the steady state. In this case one might object that it is not sensible to assume a constant rate of growth $\bar{g}$ of investment projects, in particular if the economy has proceeded from above to this depressed level of capacity utilization [e.g., 50% if $\bar{g} = 1.8\%$ and s, σ as in the above footnote].

---

[26] Domar (1946) makes use of certain limit considerations instead.

[27] On the basis of goods-market equilibrium $I = S$.

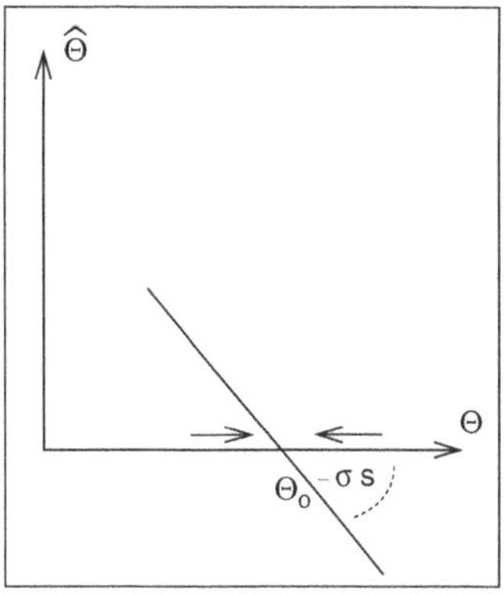

Fig. 3.2 The Domar case of a stable depression

Van Rijckeghem (1966) has investigated the case where the rate of growth $\bar{g}$ of investment will be reduced when capacity utilization falls. He assumed the following simple relationship between this rate and capacity utilization Θ:

$$\hat{I} = \bar{g} - a(1-\Theta), \quad a = \text{const} > 0.$$

This modifies the above differential equation (3.8) in the following way:

$$\begin{aligned}\hat{\Theta} &= \bar{g} - a(1-\Theta) - (\sigma s)\Theta, \\ &= (\bar{g} - a) - (\sigma s - a)\Theta.\end{aligned}$$

The above characterization of a stable (medium run) depression-equilibrium, cf. Fig. 3.2, consequently remains valid[28] as long as $\sigma s > \bar{g} > a$ holds true, that is, as long as the reaction of the growth rate of investment I to changes in the utilization of capacity Θ is sufficiently weak (as it may be in the case of a deep depression). In such a case we get for the long run degree of capacity utilization:

$$\Theta_0 = \frac{\bar{g} - a}{\sigma s - a} > 0,$$

which may be very low if the parameter a is close to $\bar{g}$. Note here, that the condition for the positivity of Θ is stronger ($a < \bar{g}$) then that which guarantees its stability ($a < \sigma s$).

We cannot pursue here any further the question what happens if $a < \bar{g}$ is not fulfilled. We have shown, however, that Domar's approach need not give rise to cumulative instability as was the case – and the central point of view – in Harrod's approach to economic growth. Nevertheless, an investment behavior that reacts with sufficient sensitivity to capacity utilization problems will undermine Domar's view

[28] A formal proof by means of a simple Liapunov function ($\dot{L} < 0$ now) is again as easy as in the preceding section.

on economic dynamics and will give rise to Harrod-like conclusions.[29] Yet, in the light of our discussion of Keynes' Notes on the Trade Cycle, we may conclude that the parameter a may be small during its depressed phase (since investment is then near to its floor), while it may be larger (too large for Domar's result) in the boom phase of the cycle, then leading to accelerating growth à la Harrod, for example. For this latter phase a marriage of Harrod's expectations-oriented with Domar's capacity-oriented approach may be worthwhile. It may then provide a more complete picture for that phase of the cycle where forces that are propelling it upwards are gathering force by having a cumulative effect on one another (see also Keynes (1936, pp. 313/4) in this regard).

Domar's approach to the stability of a growing economy, on the other hand, may be viewed as a particular contribution to effects of a sudden decrease in the rate of investment and the (for some time) stable depression that will be the consequence of such a sudden decrease.

It is, however, noteworthy here that neither the Harrod nor the Domar model considers the role Keynes' concept of the marginal efficiency of capital may play in situations of accelerating or decelerating growth.

3.5 Stable Full Employment Growth (Solow)

We have already discussed, in Sect. 3.1, why Solow's (1956) "contribution to the theory of economic growth" does not provide a valid critique of Harrod's knife-edge growth analysis. Our earlier verbal arguments will be supplemented here by an explicit formulation of his growth model which, on the one hand, will substantiate our critique of the message that Solow added to his model. On the other hand, this model is so fundamental for many other models in macrodynamics that its brief presentation is in any case justified even if its original motivation is not sound. (We see in Sect. 3.6, Solow's assertion on the validity of Harrod's contribution is not only unproved, but in fact incorrect).

The Solovian growth model starts from the following set of new assumptions that replace the corresponding assumptions of the Harrod model:

Technology is now described by means of a so-called neoclassical production function[30]

$$Y = F(K,L),$$

which exhibits constant returns to scale and marginal products of capital F_K and of labor F_L, which are positive and decreasing: $F_{KK} < 0, F_{LL} < 0$.[31]

[29] Note that $av^{\mathrm{p}} < s/v^{\mathrm{p}}$ guarantees local asymptotic stability in the first type of Harrod model considered in the preceding section.

[30] See Jones (1975, Chap. 2) for further mathematical conditions on such a production function and a detailed analysis of its properties. We assume, for simplicity, that the depreciation rate δ of the capital stock is equal to 0 here.

[31] One generally also assumes $F_{KL}(= F_{LK}) > 0$, that is, the marginal product of one factor increases if more of the other factor becomes available.

There is only the direct investment of savings, that is, Say's Law is assumed to hold true in its most simple form:

$$I \equiv S$$

Finally, a flexible real wage w is assumed, which guarantees the full-employment of the labor force at each moment t of time by means of the following marginal productivity condition:[32]

$$w = F_L(K, L^s).$$

The growing labor force ($\hat{L}^s = n$) is therefore always fully employed and the profit-maximizing output can always be sold as there is no Keynesian problem of effective demand: all output that is not consumed is (voluntarily) invested into new capital formation, that is, in a continuous time approach:

$$\dot{K} \equiv S.$$

By assumption (by the unmodified use of the neoclassical production function) also capital is always fully employed.

So far no assumption of Harrod's approach in the form it was presented in Sect. 3.3 has been made. But there is indeed *one* assumption where Solow's and Harrod's approach are identical, that is, assumption 3 of Sect. 3.2 on the savings function[33]

$$S = sY,$$

yet without any kind of multiplier theory here as there is no independent investment behavior in this neoclassical growth model.

For labor supply it has already been assumed that its rate of growth is constant through time: $\hat{L}^s = n =$ const and that the model is closed by means of the full employment assumption with regard to this primary factor supply.

It is obvious that Solow's growth model – despite many opposite statements in the literature – has not much in common with Harrod's or Domar's approach. There are neither expectations on sales or their rate of growth nor capacity utilization problems based on an independent investment behavior. The problem of coordinating independent savings and investment behavior is thus absent from the model. No multiplier interacts with the accelerator principle to generate economic dynamics. Instead, this dynamics results solely from increases in factor supplies on the basis of the assumption of their full employment, as the following will further clarify. Solow's critique of Harrod's results is thus of quite a different nature than the Keynes critique of the classical model we have modeled in Chap. 2: the latter removes only one central logical flaw from the classical model and overthrows thereby nearly all of its conclusions (despite its acceptance of many other questionable assumptions). Solow's approach, on the other hand, removes Harrod's problem by assumption and

[32] See Jones (1975, Chap. 2), and the following, for the details of this neoclassical theory of income distribution, which determines the shares of labor and capital by their marginal products *and* the assumption of their full employment.

[33] This assumption is dropped in modern presentations of the neoclassical growth model (which instead of it make, for example, use of the so-called overlapping generations approach and the savings function that is derived from it).

simply considers a quite different world where full-employment growth determines output and factor incomes without any demand problems on the market for goods. This is, of course, not a valid way by which the conclusions of a quite different model can be criticized.

Let us start with the investigation of Solow's model. For the supply of the factor capital we know from the above

$$\dot{K} = sF(K,L), \text{ where } L = L^s$$

due to the full employment assumption. Let us denote labor intensity L/K by l. Because of the assumption of constant returns to scale, we can reduce the dynamic analysis of this growth model to the movements of this ratio l:

$$\hat{l} = n - \hat{K} = n - sF(1,l) = n - sf(l), \quad (3.9)$$

where $f(\cdot) = F(1,\cdot)$ denotes the above production function in its so-called intensive form (here expressed by means of labor intensity in the place of capital intensity $k = K/L$). The economic and mathematical conditions that are generally placed on the original production function $F(K,L)$ imply the following standard form[34] (Fig. 3.3) for this function $f(l) = \sigma, \quad \sigma = Y/K$.[35] Because of $w = F_L(K,L) = F_L(1,K/L) = f'(l)$, this intensive form of the production function also allows a simple graphical presentation (Fig. 3.3) of the determination of the functional distribution of income between labor and capital [see Jones (1975, Chap. 2) for further details]:

Equation (3.9) is the so-called fundamental equation of Solow's growth model. In words it simply states that (the growth rate of) labor intensity must rise or fall according to the difference that exists between labor force growth and the growth

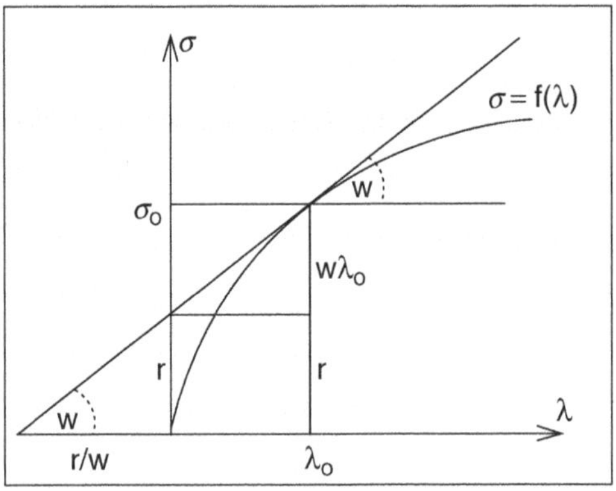

Fig. 3.3 Income distribution under perfect competition and continuous factor substitution

[34] $r = f(l) - f'(l)l = F_K$ the rate of profit (a residual), see Sargent (1987, Chap. 1) for details ($\lambda = l$ in the Fig. 3.3).

[35] Note here, that Jones uses capital intensity $k = 1/l$ for his presentations of the Solow growth model.

rate of the capital stock $sf(l)$. This fundamental equation can easily be transformed into its more common form (which uses capital intensity $k = K/L$ instead of labor intensity $l = 1/k$) by making use of the following relationships:

$$\tilde{f}(k) = F(k,1) \;=\; f(l)/l \text{ or } f(l) = \tilde{f}(k)/k,$$

which give (because of $\hat{k} \;=\; -\hat{l}$) :

$$\hat{k} = sf(l) - n = s\tilde{f}(k)/k - n, \;\text{ i.e.,}$$
$$\dot{k} = s\tilde{f}(k) - nk.$$

This last equation gives rise to the following alternative formulation of Solow's fundamental dynamic law:

- nk is the amount of capital per currently employed laborer that is needed to employ the current additions to the labor force nL^s without a change in the capital intensity k (the needed capital widening)
- $s\tilde{f}(k)$ is the amount per laborer that is actually invested
- The change in capital intensity k is then determined by the difference of these two terms (the resulting capital deepening).

Given the fundamental dynamic equation (3.9) of Solow's growth model, the analysis of the stability of the steady state of this model is a simple matter, since the dynamics is once again only of a one-dimensional type (Fig. 3.4). A graphical presentation will again suffice to convince the reader of the validity of the most important assertions of the Solow model. These assertions are as follows:

- There is a unique steady-state value l_0 if it is assumed that the following Inada conditions hold true: $f(0) = 0, f(\infty) = \infty$.
- This steady-state value is globally asymptotically stable, that is the economy approaches n, the natural rate of growth, in the course of time by an appropriate change in the labor intensity that is used in production.

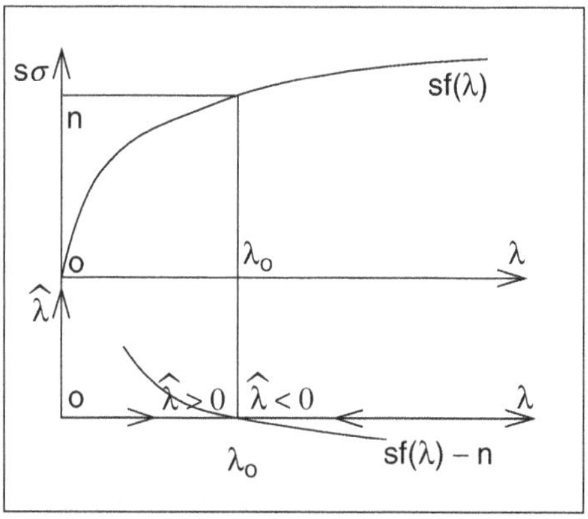

Fig. 3.4 The dynamics of the neoclassical growth model ($\lambda = l$)

- The steady-state value of l_0 – as well as of consumption per head c = (1-s)$\tilde{f}(k)$[36] – depend on the rate of savings s, but the final rate of growth of the economy is independent of it.
- In the steady-state we have

$$n = sf(l_0) = s\sigma_0 = s/v_0,$$

that is, the equality of Harrod's warranted rate of growth s/v with the natural rate of growth n. There is thus no longer a conflict between these two rates.

Solow's model does therefore exhibit none of the problems listed for Harrod's approach towards economic dynamics in Sect. 3.3.[37] The stability of the natural rate of growth path is achieved through variations in capital productivity σ (or the capital-output ratio $v = 1/\sigma$) by means of an appropriate change in labor or capital intensity in the course of capital accumulation. From the perspective of supply, based on Say's Law ($I \equiv S$) and the full employment of the supplied factors, there is thus no problem involved in the process of capital accumulation, since the factor that is more scarce in relation to the other (with regard to the steady state ratio l_0) will always grow faster, so that a nonsteady value of the labor intensity l will always be modified in the direction of its steady state value l_0.[38]

Yet, this analysis not only assumes that real wages w are manipulated at each moment in time such that full employment results. In addition to this counterfactual statement, it also depends on the classical view that supply will (always) create its demand, that is here, every income that is not consumed will be invested.

3.6 Harrodian Instability in the Neoclassical Growth Model (Nikaido)

Nikaido's (1980) article provides various growth models à la Solow, which in addition include an investment behavior that is independent of savings behavior in order to show the irrelevance of smooth factor substitution $Y = F(K,L)$ for the (in)stability properties of such a growth model. In this section we shall briefly consider the model of his Sect. 3.3 to demonstrate that the inclusion of an independent investment function[39] in addition to the simple Keynesian saving hypothesis $S = sY$

---

[36] The magnitude c will be maximized when the savings rate s is chosen such that $n = f'(k)$ holds true ($S = sY = rK = Y - wL$), which gives the so-called golden rule of accumulation (in which case investment is exactly equal to profits – as if $s_w = 0, s_p = 1$ would hold true).

[37] As we already know, due to the quite different setup of the Solow model in comparison to Harrod's.

[38] An alternative approach (by Kaldor) makes the savings rate s endogenous (dependent on income distribution) in order to avoid Harrod's two problems.

[39] Note here, however, that not all types of an independent investment and savings behavior will create problems for Solow's growth model, as can be shown by means of the microeconomics that underlies the investment behavior in the Barro model of Sect. 2.4 [where $F_K = r$ is always true].

of the preceding section will, on the one hand, indeed again question the stability assertion of the Solow model and will, on the other hand, show that the inclusion of the Keynesian multiplier will imply the existence of two types of market regimes in such a model, since either effective demand or maximum supply can then be the force that determines goods–market behavior for each moment of time. The inclusion of such alternative restrictions for goods market behavior, however, is not without problems, since it may imply that important parts of the plans of economic agents cannot be realized. There is thus the problem of rationing, and furthermore, of the proper feedbacks of such a situation of rationing on the conditions of demand and supply. Such problems will not be treated in great depth in the following,[40] where we, following Nikaido (1980), only attempt to show in a first step how an independent investment behavior may be integrated again into the model of Sect. 3.5 and what the consequences of such an integration will be.

Solow's growth model will be modified in two major ways to allow the multiplier theory to be reintroduced into its structure:

- First, actual output is now determined by the minimum of Keynesian effective demand $Y^K = I/s$ and the maximum supply of goods $F(K,L^s)$ that is possible with the presently given capital stock K and the labor supply L^s: $Y = \min\{I/s, F(K,L^s)\}$.
- Second, firms will now react in their investment plans with regard to the discrepancy between $Y^K = I/s$ and $F(K,L^s)$, in that they take effective demand Y^K – whether realized or not[41] – as a signal that induces them to accelerate (or decelerate) the planned growth rate of their capital stock K: $\widehat{I/K} = \alpha(Y^K - F(K,L^s))/K, \alpha = \text{const.} > 0$.

As in Solow's model, capital is assumed to be always fully utilized. In addition to this, we also assume full employment $L = L^s$ of the labor force (and a corresponding real wage that clears the labor market). Nevertheless, firms adjust to a deficient effective demand $Y = I/s$ by choosing their output (and thus actual labor time) in accordance with it: $Y^K = F(K,L), L < L^s$, that is, they do not react immediately by firing laborers in such a situation. This assumption of labor hoarding (for $I/s < F(K,L^s)$) justifies the use of $F(K,L^s)$ as a benchmark in the above investment function and it can be justified itself by restricting the following stability analysis to a neighborhood of its full employment steady state.

The above type of investment function is – appropriately reformulated – closely related to the second type of such a function we employed in the section on Harrod. To see this we simply have to interpret the ratio $F(K,L^s)/K = Y^p/K$ as the output-capital ratio that is desired by firms: $\sigma^p = Y^p/K$, while $\sigma = \frac{I/s}{K}$ is now used to denote the output capital ratio that corresponds to effective demand (which is not the actual

---

[40] See Sect. 5.5 in this regard.

[41] Note here that we now for the first time employ a model were $I \neq S$ can hold true. Note also that the equilibrium concept $I/s = I + cI + c^2I + \ldots$ (effective demand) is used here as a proxy for expected demand, which may be a problematic procedure in the case where $Y < Y^K$ holds true. We follow Nikaido's assumption here, since it makes the comparison with our second version of a continuous time Harrod model particularly simple.

one $\sigma_a = Y/K$ if labor supply restricts the output of the economy). This first measure is – in the light of the preceding remark on L and L^s – so to speak a neoclassical full employment version of Harrod's intended capacity, while the second provides a (still crude) measure for demand pressure on the market for goods. We then get again from these two definitions

$$\hat{\sigma} = \hat{I} - \hat{K} = \widehat{I/K} = \alpha(\sigma - \sigma^p) = \alpha(\sigma - f(l^s)),$$

which – up to the new interpretation of σ^p and σ and the fact that σ^p is now an endogenous variable of the model – is the same form of relationship as was employed in Sect. 3.3.

In addition to this consequence of the assumed investment behavior, it is furthermore assumed in Nikaido (1980, p. 114) that $\dot{K} = sY$ holds throughout, that is, consumption plans are always realized while investment plans may remain in the state of orders.[42] The effect of an accumulation of such orders is not considered, which in sum shows that there remain certain feedback mechanisms to be included into such a Keynesian variant of a neoclassical growth model in its further discussion. It is, however, not to be expected that the inclusion of such feedbacks will again ensure the asymptotic stability of this model in the sense of Sect. 3.5.[43]

As in this earlier section, we can now derive the intensive analog of the supply equation for new capital goods, which here reads

$$\hat{l}^s = n - \hat{K} = \begin{cases} n - I/K = n - s\sigma \;\; if\; Y = I/s, & \text{(the Keynes-regime I = S)} \\ n - sf(l^s) \qquad\quad if\; Y = F(K, L^s), & \text{(the Solow-regime } S < I\text{)} \end{cases}$$

since $\hat{K} = \dot{K}/K = sY/K$ must hold true in each moment of time.

This dynamic law together with the above reformulation of Nikaido's investment function in sum gives a system of two differential equations in the two variables l^s and σ. Note, that this system of differential equations is defined by different equations in situations of excess supply ($Y < F(K, L^s)$) and excess demand ($Y < I/s$) on the market for goods, that is, that it in fact represents a system of differential inequalities.

To investigate the stability of this differential inequality system, it suffices here to consider its phase diagram to see that its steady state again is plagued by centrifugal forces in general. We stress again the local character of this analysis – now due to the above choice of a Harrodian investment function in this otherwise neoclassical model of capital accumulation.

The unique steady state equilibrium of this system fulfills $I/s = F(K, L^s)$ at each moment of time and $sf(l_0) = n$, that is, it is identical to the full employment steady

[42] This amounts to the assumption that I/s is relevant as an expression for expected demand, but is irrelevant with respect to the growth rate of the capital stock in the case of a full employment of the (hired) labor force.

[43] See Dutt (1990, 2.3.1) and Ito (1980) for a regime switching approach to the Solow model via the market for labor instead of the market for goods, which in this case gives rise to an asymptotically stable adjustment process, cf. here Sect. 4.3.

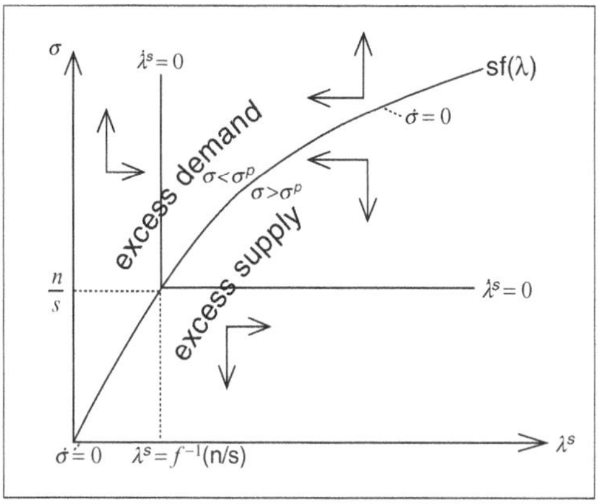

Fig. 3.5 Harrodian instability in the neoclassical growth model ($\lambda = l$)

growth path of the Solow model. However, already a brief glimpse at Fig. 3.5 shows that this steady state path can no longer be an asymptotically stable one.

Indeed, calculating the Jacobian of this system for the Keynesian effective demand regime, we get

$$J = \begin{pmatrix} \alpha\sigma_o & -\alpha\sigma_o f'(-l_o^s) \\ -s l_o^s & 0 \end{pmatrix},$$

which gives that the local dynamics at the steady state of the unrestricted Keynes-regime is of a saddlepoint type – as it is depicted above (there restricted to the Keynes-domain: $\sigma < \sigma^p$). In the Solow-regime we instead have that the second dynamical law is independent of the first one and identical with Solow's fundamental growth equation, which again provides an asymptotically stable adjustment of the (full employment) labor intensity l^s to its steady state value l_o^s. The first dynamic law is in this case – up to its dependence on the full employment output-capital ratio l^s (which makes it a nonautonomous differential equation) – directly comparable to the Harrod knife-edge case and it leads to the self-referencing explosive movements of the demand determined output capital ratio σ as depicted above in the upper left hand part of the figure. Also Solow's full employment steady state solution is thus surrounded by centrifugal and not by centripetal forces if the accelerator principle is included into the formulations of its adjustment mechanisms (despite the fulfillment of $n = s\sigma$ in this type of model).

The above dynamics shows that the investment function is indeed the crucial element in the formulation of stability problems à la Harrod. Properties of technology and smooth factor substitution are not of relevance in this matter. They thus can be safely excluded from any first formulation of a new economic theory – be it Keynesian or Neoclassical or something else, since facts of technology should (and do) not modify the basic story of an(y) economic theory.[44] Because of this result we shall now return to the simple technology with fixed coefficients (of Sect. 3.2) for

[44] See Sect. 9.1 for further arguments into this direction.

the remainder of this chapter in order to proceed from the local (in-)stability analysis of the Harrod and Domar multiplier/accelerator type to the global analysis of this economic dynamics as it has been formulated by Hicks (1950) in his "Contribution to Theory of the Trade Cycle." Such a global point of view becomes unavoidable if it is taken for granted that the growth path of an economy is surrounded by centrifugal forces (Harrod) – and not by centripetal ones (Solow), due to an interaction of investment and savings behavior of the multiplier–accelerator type.

A model which in its treatment of the market for goods can be usefully contrasted with the above model will be introduced in Chap. 6. This model will replace the Harrodian investment function by a neoclassical one and will thus ignore the instability problems discussed in this chapter. In the place of such an instability, we will there study instability problems as they arise from the wage/price sector of the economy.

3.7 The Keynesian Trade Cycle Model (Hicks)

Hick's program in writing his "Contributions to the Theory of the Trade Cycle" was to achieve a synthesis of Keynes (the multiplier theory), Harrod (dynamic instability of steady growth), and Clark (the acceleration principle) and also to add mechanisms to this model, which keep its unstable growth pattern within economically meaningful bounds. In a final chapter of his book he also considered monetary phenomena by adding a LM-equation[45] to his consideration of IS-dynamics. Such a complication will be left aside in the following, which is concentrated on the core model of his approach, and thus also neglects the many details he discusses in his book concerning the partial treatment of the components of his nonlinear multiplier–accelerator approach.[46]

The multiplier–accelerator interaction of Hicks' (1950) model is usually modeled by means of a simple modified version of Samuelson's (1939) treatment of such an interaction.[47] This version is given by the following three equations (in discrete time):

$$C_t = cY_{t-1}, \tag{3.10}$$

$$I_t = v(Y_{t-1} - Y_{t-2}), \tag{3.11}$$

$$Y_t = C_t + I_t + A. \tag{3.12}$$

[45] See, for example, Evans (1969, p. 406) for some details on this.

[46] Cf. again Evans (1969, p. 400f.).

[47] There exist a variety of more refined economic approaches to this multiplier–accelerator interaction, which primarily make use of extensions of the accelerator principle, most notably by Kalecki, Kaldor, and Goodwin [see Evans (1969, 14.1) and the appendix to this chapter for details.] Such models have received revived interest in the recent past, because of the complex nonlinear dynamics they can give rise to, cf., for example, Chiarella (1990), Lorenz and Gabisch (1989), Puu (1991), and in particular Hommes (1991), who gives a detailed treatment of the Hicks trade cycle model and its extensions.

In comparison to Sen's model (3.3), (3.4) of Harrod's approach, we have now a consumption (or savings) function which is lagged by one period (a so-called Robertson Lag). Furthermore, investors are here purely backward looking by using the last observed change in sales instead of the currently expected one for their investment decision. Equation (3.12) finally again describes goods–market equilibrium, now, however, with an additional term A, which is assumed to be positive and stands for "autonomous demand." This term will be of use later on when adding growth to this model of the business cycle.

The above model gives rise to the following difference equation of order two

$$Y_t - (c+v)Y_{t-1} + vY_{t-2} - A = 0.$$

A particular solution to this equation is

$$Y_0 = \frac{1}{1-c}A = \frac{1}{s}A. \tag{3.13}$$

By means of this solution the above dynamic equation can be reduced to a homogeneous difference equation making use of the variable $Z_t = Y_t - \frac{1}{s}A$, which describes the deviations of output and sales from the above stationary solution:

$$Z_t - (c+v)Z_{t-1} + vZ_{t-2} = 0. \tag{3.14}$$

The procedure for solving such a homogeneous linear difference equation is to assume that its solution must be of the form $Z_t = \lambda^t Z_0$ and to determine λ by inserting this form into the above equation [the details of this approach are, e.g., given in the appendix to Chap. 13 in Evans (1969)]. In the present case this gives rise to

$$\lambda^2 - (c+v)\lambda + v = 0 \qquad \text{or}$$

$$\lambda_{1,2} = \frac{c+v \pm \sqrt{(c+v)^2 - 4v}}{2}$$

as the two solutions for the parameter λ of this approach.

Let us consider the case of real roots $\lambda_{1,2}$ first. In this case, $Z_t = \lambda^t Z_0$ will behave explosively or converge to 0 $\quad (Y_1 \longrightarrow \frac{1}{s}A)$ if $|\lambda| < 1$ or $|\lambda| > 1$, respectively. Assume, second that $\lambda_{1,2}$ are (conjugate) complex roots of the above equation and let us denote by $|\lambda|$ the absolute value of these two solutions. It is well-known [see again Evans (1969)] that the real solutions to (3.14) will then be of the form

$$Z_t = |\lambda|^t[\delta\cos(\Theta t - \varepsilon)], \tag{3.15}$$

where Θ is determined by

$$\lambda_{1,2} = a \pm ib = |\lambda|(\cos\Theta \pm \mathrm{i}\sin\Theta)$$

and where δ and ε are given by initial conditions (values that describe the displacement from the equilibrium $Z = 0$ if such a displacement occurs). The solutions to (3.14) are thus of a cyclical type in the case of complex roots with increasing (decreasing) amplitude if $|\lambda| > 1(|\lambda| < 1)$ holds true.

The case $|\lambda| = 1$ describes the boundary case between explosive and implosive behavior of the solutions both for real (monotone) and complex (cyclical) roots of the above equation. It is easy to check that $|\lambda|^2 = v$ must hold true in the complex case, so that this boundary is given by $v = 1$ (c arbitrary) as long as complex roots come about.

This will be the case if $c < 2\sqrt{v} - v$ holds, since $(c+v)^2 - 4v = 0$ implies $c = 2\sqrt{v} - v$ (due to the positivity of the parameter c).

In the real case, the root

$$\lambda_1 = \frac{c+v+\sqrt{(c+v)^2-4v}}{2}$$

dominates the other (smaller) root and thus needs to be considered solely ($Z_t = a_1\lambda_1^t + a_2\lambda_2^t \to a_1\lambda_1^t!$).

For $v < 1$ we get in this case (due to $c < 1$):

$$\lambda_1 < \frac{1+v+\sqrt{(1+v)^2-4v}}{2} = \frac{1+v+1-v}{2} = 1,$$

that is, the implosive type of behavior. And for $v > 1$ we get in a similar way (by making use of $c > 2\sqrt{v} - v$)

$$\lambda_1 > \frac{c+v+\sqrt{4v-4v}}{2} > \sqrt{v} > 1,$$

that is, the explosive type of behavior.

The Fig. 3.6 summarizes these results in a graphically intuitive way:

This figure in particular shows that explosive cycles will occur in the domain where $c < 2\sqrt{v} - v$ and $v > 1$ hold true simultaneously, that is, for accelerator coefficients that are larger than one and marginal propensities to consume which are sufficiently low. This is exactly the constellation of parameters that Hicks assumed to underlie his trade cycle model (in its most basic form). Through this choice,

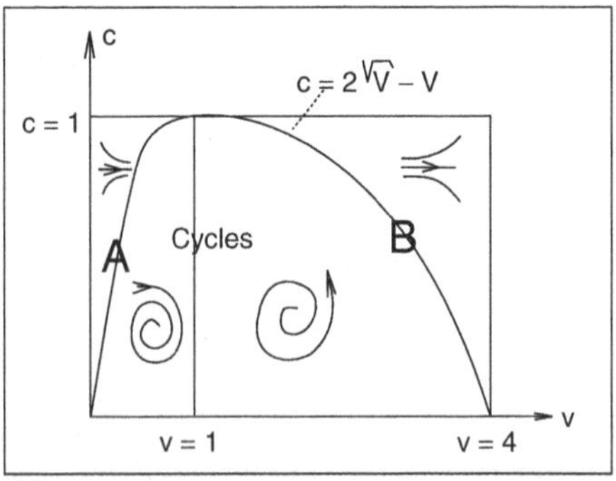

Fig. 3.6 The four stability regions of the Samuelson–Hicks model

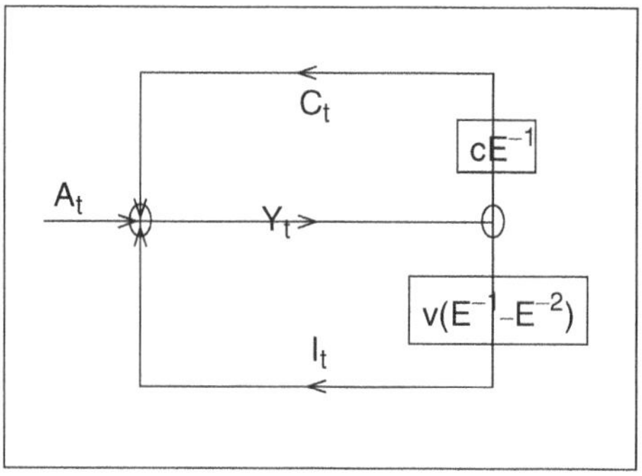

Fig. 3.7 The income–expenditure circuit of Hicks trade cycle model

the important alternative of an asymptotically stable private sector (Regime A, see the Fig. 3.6) of the economy is excluded from consideration.[48] Furthermore, this also excludes Harrod-like growth paths from consideration (which only becomes possible under regime B when the marginal propensity to consume is assumed to be sufficiently high).

Hicks' choice of parameters thus has the effect that the above approach so far can only provide a theory of the cycle (3.15) around a stationary level of national income (3.13) (Fig. 3.7). To allow also for steady growth in such an approach a trend component has to be added therefore,

$$A_t = (1+g)^t A \tag{3.16}$$

that is, it is now assumed that autonomous expenditures grow with a constant rate g over time. Furthermore, since the cycle around this trend has been assumed to be of an explosive nature, upper and lower bounds on economic activity have to be introduced to keep model of cycles and growth economically viable. It is a customary assumption – but not a plausible one – that these ceilings (full capacity) and floors (maximum depreciation) to output movements grow with the same rate as autonomous expenditures (3.16).

Because of the linearity of the system (3.10)–(3.12), (3.16) we know that the above solution Z_t describes the deviation from any particular solution of this system (with δ and ε as initial displacement parameters that depend on the particular solution that is chosen). An especially important particular solution of the above inhomogeneous system of difference equations is given by its steady-state solution, the rate of growth of which is determined by the exogenously given rate of growth of autonomous expenditures. This solution must therefore be of the form $Y_0(1+g)^t$, where Y_0 remains to be determined through the amount of autonomous expenditures A given at time $t=0$. Inserting $Y_0\,(1+g)^t$ into the difference equation of this growth dynamics:

$$Y_t-(c+v)Y_{t-1}+vY_{t-2}=A\,(1+g)^t$$

[48] Which is the basis of the stochastic approach to the explanation of the trade cycle phenomenon, see Lorenz and Gabisch (1989) for details and references.

gives

$$Y_0 = \frac{(1+g)^2}{(1+g)^2-(c+v)(1+g)+v}A = \frac{(1+g)^2}{(1+g)(s+g)-vg}A = \alpha(g)A, \quad (3.17)$$

where $\alpha(g)$ is the so-called Hicksian supermultiplier[49] and where $s = 1-c$ is the savings rate [note, that $\alpha(0) = \frac{1}{1-c} = \frac{1}{s}$ gives the ordinary Keynesian multiplier – in the situation of no growth].

It is easy to check that the derivative of $\alpha(g)$ is given by

$$\alpha'(g) = \frac{v(1-g)/(1+g)-c}{(s+g-vg/(1+g))^2},$$

which (as well as $\alpha(g)$) is well defined if

$$\frac{s+g}{v} > \frac{g}{1+g}$$

holds and which is positive if

$$\frac{1-g}{1+g} > \frac{c}{v}$$

is true in addition. In this case, we have for $g > 0$

$$\alpha(g) > \frac{1}{1-c} > 0,$$

that is, steadily increasing autonomous expenditures have a larger multiplier effect on the current level of national income Y_0 than stationary ones (as far as steady state solutions are concerned).

The general solution to (3.10)–(3.12), (3.16) now finally is

$$(1+g)^t \frac{(1+g)^2}{(1+g)(s+g)-vg} A + |\lambda_1|^t[\delta\cos(\Theta t-\varepsilon)],$$

where Θ is determined by $\lambda_1/|\lambda_1| = \cos\Theta + i\sin\Theta \quad (\cos\Theta = (c+v)/(2\sqrt{v}))$ and where δ and ε are the two initial conditions needed to supply a unique solution for the above difference equation of order 2.

To sum up, this is the solution to the following circular flow of income of the unlimited Hicksian multiplier–accelerator model with exogenous growth.[50]

A possible result of this goods–market interaction is provided in Fig. 3.8. This figure shows the case of a cyclically explosive multiplier–accelerator interaction, which comes about for accelerator coefficients $v > 1$ and marginal propensities to

---

[49] This multiplier shows the steady state effect of an increase in autonomous expenditures A at time $t = 0$.

[50] E the shift operator: $EY_t = Y_{t+1}$, i.e., $E^{-1}Y_t = Y_{t-1}$ etc.). Circles are used in such block diagrams to denote points of summation, while the rectangles show the operators acting on the flows passing through them [See Allen (1967, 5.8) for the details of such block-diagrammatic representations].

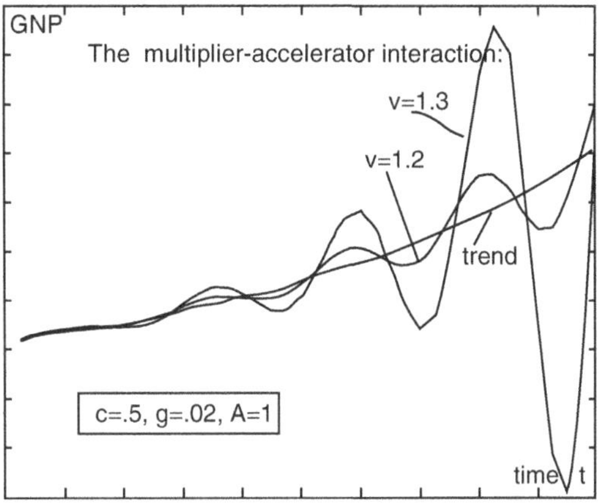

Fig. 3.8 The dynamics of the unrestricted multiplier–accelerator model

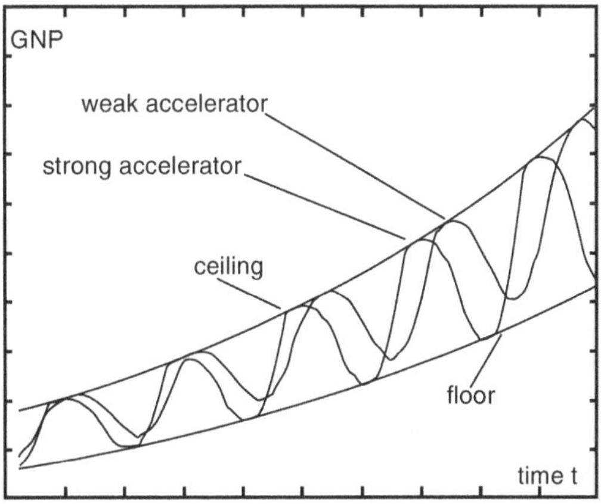

Fig. 3.9 The restricted multiplier–accelerator model

consume c that are sufficiently low. It represents the type of choice of parameters that underlies the Hicksian trade cycle explanation.

This figure immediately shows the necessity of adding extra forces to this model to keep its dynamics within reasonable bounds. The simplest way of doing this is to add the Hicksian ceilings and floors already mentioned earlier. This will give rise to the following modified types of behavior (where the ceiling, the floor, or both delimiters can be operative) (Fig. 3.9).

These simulations in particular show a result that is typical for the Hicksian trade cycle model, namely that ceilings (and floors) are only very briefly operative during each cycle. In the case of the floor (a depressed economy), this may be modified by assuming that the accelerator becomes inoperative for a while (due to the existence of excess capacities). But for the ceiling, this idea does not appear to be a plausible one. The cycle that is generated by the Hicks model therefore bears no close resemblance to the form of the business cycle that was (and to some extend still is) believed to be typical (at least) for the fifties and the sixties of this century,[51] see Fig. 3.10.

[51] See Evans (1969, pp. 418/9) for details on this stylized cycle.

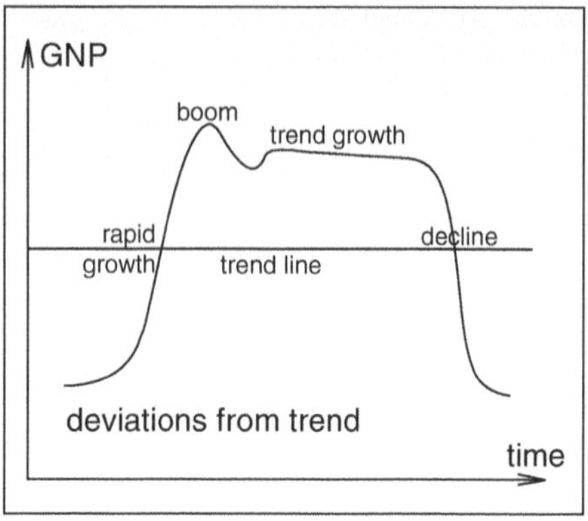

Fig. 3.10 The stylized business cycle of the fifties and sixties

One basic critique of this model therefore was that it is not capable of generating this typical asymmetry in the pattern of the cycle.

Yet, it is easily possible to name many further weak points of this goods–market model of the trade cycle, as, for example, the following

- Its lack of a treatment of other markets than the market for goods
- Its ignorance of wage/price-effects and the question of income distribution
- Its additive treatment of the explanation of cycles and growth
- Its neglect of Keynes' concept of the marginal efficiency of capital
- Its schematic, additive treatment of upper and lower bounds.

Despite all these weaknesses, Hicks' trade cycle model nevertheless represents the first complete approach to the problem of modeling viable cycles and growth. Though its solution to this problem must be viewed as being fairly mechanical and purely driven by the interactions of the quantities of goods demanded and supplied (thus excluding prices from it), it was and still is conceptually important, in particular with regard to the modeling of accelerating forces and viability mechanisms (which keep these forces within reasonable bounds).

3.8 Three Types of Economic Regulation (Phillips)

It has been an issue in the late sixties whether the business cycle is or can be made obsolete.[52] That it is not obsolete has meanwhile been proved by the facts. It is nevertheless interesting to study – here in a multiplier/accelerator-context – possible economic policies that at least in principle might be capable of removing cyclical patterns from economic activity. To show this possibility, we shall use in this section a model of Phillips and various stabilization policy devices introduced by him to macroeconomics from control theory.[53]

[52] See in particular Bronfenbrenner (1969).

[53] For details with regard to the following the reader is referred to Allen (1967, Chap. 18).

We return in this section to continuous time analysis and shall use here (for notational simplicity) the operator D for the time derivative of a variable. We shall investigate the following disequilibrium multiplier–accelerator model, where Y^{d} denotes aggregate demand, Y aggregate supply and where autonomous expenditures A are a given magnitude.[54] The model's equations are

$$Y^{\mathrm{d}} = C + I + A, \tag{3.18}$$

$$C = cY, \tag{3.19}$$

$$I = (T_{\mathrm{o}}D + 1)^{-1} vDY, \tag{3.20}$$

$$A = \bar{A} = \bar{C} + \bar{I}, \tag{3.21}$$

$$Y = (TD + 1)^{-1} Y^{\mathrm{d}}. \tag{3.22}$$

Equations (3.20) and (3.22) need explanation (while all others are simple and already well known from earlier models). Transformed back to our standard notation, the accelerator equation (3.20) reads[55]

$$\dot{I} = \frac{1}{T_{\mathrm{o}}}(I^{\mathrm{p}} - I) = \frac{1}{T_{\mathrm{o}}}(v\dot{Y} - I),$$

which says that the endogenous component of current investment plans (I) will be revised (with an adjustment lag of length T_{o}) according to the discrepancy that exists between them and the extra capacity ($I^{\mathrm{p}} = v\dot{Y}$) that is needed for the current change in output (a new formulation of the accelerator). In the same way (3.22) is shown to be equivalent to

$$\dot{Y} = \frac{1}{T}(Y^{\mathrm{d}} - Y),$$

which is a dynamic multiplier formulation of the effects of goods–market disequilibrium (and which justifies why we have termed this approach a disequilibrium model).[56]

The usefulness of the operator D becomes apparent in the derivation of the dynamic law that governs this economy. Inserting (3.19)–(3.22) into (3.18) gives ($T_{\mathrm{o}} = 1$):

$$(TD + 1)Y = cY + \frac{1}{D+1} vDY + A.$$

By multiplying this equation with $D + 1$ we then obtain

$$(D+1)(TD+1)Y = (D+1)cY + vDY + (D+1)A, \text{ i.e.}$$
$$(TD^2 + (1+T)D + 1)Y = (D+1)cY + vDY + A.$$

[54] Which includes both investment and consumption demand, which are therefore separated here from the endogenous components of these two types of demand.

[55] Since (3.20) is equivalent to $T_{\mathrm{o}}(D+1)I = vDY$. We shall assume $T_{\mathrm{o}} = 1$ in the following (by means of an appropriate choice of the time unit).

[56] In this section – as well as in the following appendix – we thus depart from our basic assumption of goods–market equilibrium by making use of a simple textbook-version of the dynamic multiplier.

Transformed back to ordinary notation this gives rise to

$$T\ddot{Y} + (T + 1 - c - v)\dot{Y} + (1 - c)Y = A$$

or

$$\ddot{Y} + \left(1 + \frac{s - v}{T}\right)\dot{Y} + \frac{s}{T}Y = \frac{1}{T}A. \tag{3.23}$$

For the stationary state Y_0 we then immediately get $Y_o = A/s$, that is, the usual static multiplier formula.

To investigate the (in)stability of the model, we have to examine the characteristic equation of the homogeneous part (A = 0) of the second order equation (3.23), which describes the deviations $Z = Y - A/s$ from the stationary state A/s:

$$\lambda^2 + \left(1 + \frac{s - v}{T}\right)\lambda + \frac{s}{T} = 0,$$

which gives

$$\lambda_{1,2} = -\frac{1}{2}\left(1 + \frac{s - v}{T}\right) \pm \sqrt{\frac{(1 + \frac{s-v}{T})^2}{4} - \frac{s}{T}}.$$

The roots of this equation will be complex (and thus imply cycles) if and only if[57]

$$\left(\sqrt{T} - \sqrt{s}\right)^2 < v < \left(\sqrt{T} + \sqrt{s}\right)^2$$

holds true[58] (and these cycles will in addition be explosive for $T + s < v$).

Following Phillips (1954), there exist three simple fiscal policy rules of which it may be hoped that one or a combination of them will allow to remove the above explosive cyclical pattern from the model under consideration. These policy rules are (G government expenditures, α's parameters):

$$\begin{aligned} \text{Proportional control:} \quad & G = \alpha_p(-Z), \\ \text{Derivative control:} \quad & G = \alpha_d(-\dot{Z}), \\ \text{Integral control:} \quad & G = \alpha_i\left(-\int_0^t Z(s)ds\right) \qquad (\dot{G} = -\alpha_i Z). \end{aligned}$$

It is here assumed that these controls are directed toward deviations Z from the original steady growth path $Z = Y - A/s$, that is, they operate on the solution Z of the homogeneous differential equation corresponding to (3.23). It is furthermore assumed by Phillips that the above types of government expenditures represent intended figures which thus will realize in general with an implementation lag τ only, so that actual expenditures G_a follow a law of the following type

[57] The condition $T > 0$ is thus a necessary condition for the occurrence of cyclical behavior.

[58] Since $(1 + \frac{s-v}{T})^2/4 < \frac{s}{T}$ is equivalent to $|T + s - v| < 2\sqrt{s}\sqrt{T}$, which is equivalent to $\pm(T + s - v) < 2\sqrt{s}\sqrt{T}$ which implies the above double inequality that encloses the parameter v.

$$G_{\mathrm{a}} = \frac{1}{\tau D+1} G \quad \text{or} \quad \dot{G}_{\mathrm{a}} = \frac{1}{\tau}(G - G_{\mathrm{a}}),$$

where intended government expenditures G are given by a combination of the above three policy rules:[59]

$$G = -\left[\alpha_{\mathrm{p}} Z + \alpha_{\mathrm{d}} \dot{Z} + \alpha_i \int_0^t Z(s)\,\mathrm{d}s\right], \ \alpha_{\mathrm{p}}, \alpha_{\mathrm{d}}, \alpha_i \geq 0.$$

Government thus observes (at t=0, and thereafter) deviations from the original stationary state level of income, their time rate of change (increasing or decreasing), and the over the past accumulated deviations from this level and lets each of these observations influence its intended expenditures with strength $\alpha_x, x = p, d, i$ (where α_x can, of course, also be zero). The question now is which of the above types of control are the most effective ones in removing (explosive) cyclical patterns from the model (and also permanent reductions in its stationary level) and which combination of these rules might still do better.[60]

Starting from a stationary situation, a permanent dip in autonomous expenditures by $-\Delta A$ results at first in the following situation of no control – if the above mentioned conditions for a (mildly explosive) cyclical behavior hold true ($\Delta Y_o = -\Delta A/s$):

There is thus caused (in the absence of any policy) a permanent decrease in national income plus an explosive temporary disequilibrium movement around this new permanent level.

To answer the question on policy effectiveness posed above, we have to investigate the following inhomogeneous dynamical system

$$(TD+1)Z = cZ + \frac{1}{D+1} vDZ - \Delta A + \frac{1}{\tau D+1} G,$$

where the expression for G is as above.

Again, the D-operator is very useful in reformulating this differential equation (of order 4) as follows:

[59] Note that derivative control may act as a brake here, which may slow down anticyclical government expenditures of the proportional type even much before a full correction in the level of income is achieved – if income is rising from below toward its original level. This implies a somewhat problematic symmetry for this type of control that treats alike situations well below and well above the original stationary level (which only differ in the sign of the existing disequilibrium, but not in their time rate of change). In its present form a derivative control thus strictly behaves like an inverse accelerator which also explains (part of) the success this method has in stabilizing this economy.

[60] Turnovsky (1977) investigates Phillips' stabilization policy rules in the context of dynamic multiplier models and obtains results that can be usefully compared with the ones that are obtained here.

$$(TD+1)(D+1)(\tau D+1)Z = (D+1)(\tau D+1)cZ + (\tau D+1)vDZ \\ -(D+1)(\tau D+1)\Delta A + (D+1)G,$$

which gives rise to

$$T\tau D^3 Z + (T\tau + T + \tau - \tau c - \tau v)D^2 Z + (T+1+\tau - c - \tau c - v)DZ + (1-c)Z \\ = -\Delta A - \alpha_p DZ - \alpha_d D^2 Z - \alpha_i Z - \alpha_p Z - \alpha_d DZ - \alpha_i \int_0^t Z(s)\,ds \quad \text{or}$$

$$T\tau D^3 Z + (T + \tau(T+s-v) + \alpha_d)D^2 Z + (T+s-v+\alpha_d+s\tau+\alpha_p)DZ \\ + (s+\alpha_i+\alpha_p)Z = -\Delta A - \alpha_i \int_0^t Z(s)\,ds, \quad s = 1-c.$$

In a pure study of the stability of such a dynamics it is admissible to remove the integral (if $\alpha_i > 0$ holds) from this dynamic equation by applying the operator D to it. This gives rise to $T\tau D^4 Z + (T+\tau(T+s-v)+\alpha_d)D^3 Z + (T+s-v+\alpha_d+s\tau+\alpha_p)D^2 Z + (s+\alpha_p+\alpha_i)DZ + \alpha_i Z = 0$. We shall use this equation now to show that a suitably large choice[61] of the parameter α_d, the magnitude of the derivative control parameter, will always produce an asymptotically stable solution Z, that is, will remove any business cycle from the model in the end [the other policy rules are assumed to be inactive for the time being].

Let us denote the characteristic polynomial of the above last differential equation by

$$a_0\rho^4 + a_1\rho^3 + a_2\rho^2 + a_3\rho + a_4 = 0,$$

where the a_i are given by the coefficients of the above equation. According to, for example, Brock and Malliaris (1989, pp. 75/6), *a necessary and sufficient criterion for asymptotic stability* of such a dynamical system is given by the following conditions (the so-called Routh–Hurwitz conditions for local asymptotic stability):

$$a_1 > 0, \quad \begin{vmatrix} a_1 & a_0 \\ a_3 & a_2 \end{vmatrix} > 0, \quad \begin{vmatrix} a_1 & a_0 & 0 \\ a_3 & a_2 & a_1 \\ 0 & a_4 & a_3 \end{vmatrix} > 0 \quad \text{and} \quad \begin{vmatrix} a_1 & a_0 & 0 & 0 \\ a_3 & a_2 & a_1 & a_0 \\ 0 & a_4 & a_3 & a_2 \\ 0 & 0 & 0 & a_4 \end{vmatrix} > 0.$$

If we at first assume $\alpha_i = 0$, we can ignore the last determinant $(a_4 = 0)$. The first three Routh–Hurwitz conditions are then equivalent to

$$a_0, a_1, a_2, a_3 > 0 \quad \text{and} \quad (a_1 a_2 - a_0 a_3)a_3 - a_4 a_1^2 = (a_1 a_2 - a_0 a_3)a_3 > 0.$$

The positivity of the coefficients of this characteristic polynomial can be easily established by choosing α_d sufficiently large ($\alpha_d > v - (T+s)$, e.g., is sufficient in the unstable case $v - (T+s) > 0$, if $\tau \le 1$ holds true[62]). And the condition $a_1 a_2 > a_0 a_3$ can be achieved in the same way, since $a_1 a_2$ depends positively on α_d, while the

[61] In view of the size of the other parameters of the model.

[62] $\alpha_d > \tau(v - (T+s))$ otherwise.

term a_0a_3 does not depend on it.[63] We thus have proved that the isolated application of a derivative control rule – if applied with sufficient strength – must lead at least to damped oscillations around or a monotonic adjustment[64] to the new stationary state and will thus (in the longer run) remove any significant cyclical behavior from the given multiplier–accelerator model.

The above stability result obviously holds true in this general form only for derivative control and not for the other two types of control mechanisms. Nevertheless, though derivative control allows to control the cycle of the preceding figure at least to that extent that its amplitude can be reduced to an unimportant magnitude by it, it does not at all correct for the initial decline $-\Delta A/s$ in national income, since α_{d} is not part of the static multiplier formula.

With regard to proportional control ($\alpha_i = \alpha_{\mathrm{d}} = 0$)) one can show by means of simplifications of the above model, see Allen (1969, Chap. 18), that its effects will be mixed, since it, on the one hand, allows an improvement in the long-run level of national product, but will, on the other hand, introduce cycles, for example, in cases where no cycle existed before the use of this type of regulation. The correction in level implied by this policy can be easily calculated from the above ($\alpha_i = 0$ still) by solving it for the new stationary value of this dynamics:

$$(1-c+\alpha_{\mathrm{p}})Z_0 = -\Delta A, \quad \text{i.e.,} \quad Z_0 = -\frac{\Delta A}{s+\alpha_{\mathrm{p}}}.$$

This is indeed a smaller value for the permanent decline of the national product, but not yet a return to the original level ($Z_0 = 0$).

A complete correction in the long-run level of national product is only possible when integral policy is being active, which can be seen as follows: The above differential–integral equation can be rewritten in the following way:

$$\begin{aligned} T\tau D^3Z &+ (T+\tau(T+s-v)+\alpha_{\mathrm{d}})D^2Z + (T+s-v+\alpha_{\mathrm{d}}+s\tau+\alpha_{\mathrm{p}})DZ \\ &+ (s+\alpha_i+\alpha_{\mathrm{p}})Z = -\Delta A + G_i, \qquad DG_i = -\alpha_i Z. \end{aligned}$$

The unique stationary solution of this system is $Z_{\mathrm{o}} = 0$ and $(G_i)_{\mathrm{o}} = \Delta A$. This can either be established by an endogenous (steady state) reaction in the level of G_i or through the dynamics of the model ($Z \to 0, G_i \to \Delta A$).[65] This means that there will be full correction of the dip in income in the end (cf. Fig. 3.11) – if the system is asymptotically stable.

---

[63] The above condition on α_{d} is already sufficient to also imply $a_1a_2 - a_0a_3 > 0$ (if $\alpha_{\mathrm{p}} = 0$ holds true).

[64] Conditions for the monotonicity of the solution curves are not easy to find here, since the Routh–Hurwitz conditions do not contain anything about it and since the transformation formulas that exist for calculating the roots of the polynomials of degree 3 and 4 are already complex to provide a definite answer in the present context.

[65] Note that $\int_0^t Z(s)\,\mathrm{d}s$ can only react with a delay to any exogenous disturbance $\Delta A \neq 0$, that is, we cannot obtain the steady state solution from the original formulation of the above dynamics without any reformulation of it.

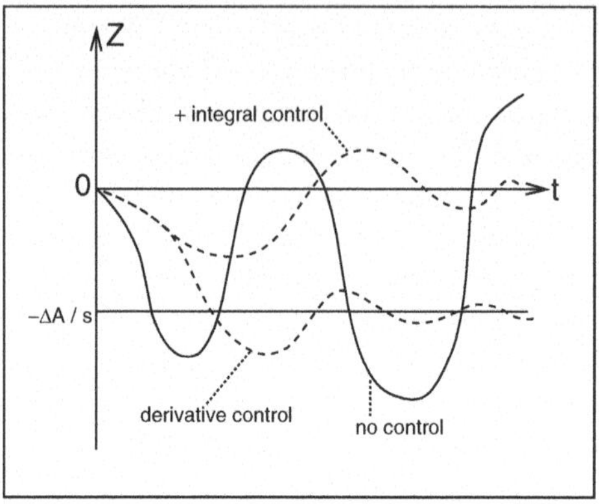

Fig. 3.11 Multiplier–accelerator models and economic regulation

We have seen that a derivative policy can iron out fluctuations, but cannot achieve anything with regard to persistent level changes. Integral policy, on the other hand, achieves complete correction in the level. Both derivative and integral policies seem therefore at least to be needed to allow for the possibility of a full control over the cycle as well as the level of activity. Yet, we have so far only proved that derivative control irons out persistent fluctuations in the case of no integral control. If integral control is used in addition to a derivative control, the last two of the above determinants in the Routh–Hurwitz stability criterion have to be considered in addition, which gives rise to the following additional inequalities to be proved to hold true:

$$(a_1a_2 - a_3a_0)a_3 - a_4a_1^2 > 0 \quad \text{and} \quad a_4 > 0.$$

It is obvious that $a_4(= \alpha_i)$ must be positive when integral control is exercised. By the above, we furthermore know that the coefficients a_i depend (positively) in the following way on the control parameters α:

$$a_0, a_1(\alpha_d), a_2(\alpha_d + \alpha_p), a_3(\alpha_p + \alpha_i), a_4 = \alpha_i.$$

There exist various ways by which one can achieve that the value of $(a_1a_2 - a_3a_0)a_3$ (already known to be positive) can be made larger than $a_4a_1^2 > 0$. The simplest, and generally applicable, case is that of a sufficiently strong derivative control and a sufficiently weak (but positive) influence of the integral policy. This is but a slight variant of the case we have already analyzed $(\alpha_i = 0)$. Yet, there is here in general some conflict between fighting the cycle (by α_d) and reestablishing the level (by α_i), since the latter policy – if exercised with sufficient strength – can endanger the asymptotic stability that is achieved by the former policy (α_d).[66]

Of course, any real application of this analysis would have to take the actual magnitudes of the coefficients $a_0, \ldots, a_4$ (approximately) into account and would have to tailor the use of α_d, α_i, and α_p in the light of their magnitudes. Choosing, for example, $\alpha_d > v - (T + s)$ (as above), and α_p such that $a_1a_2 > a_1^2$ holds true, and finally the policy lag parameter τ sufficiently small – such that $a_1^2(s + \alpha_p) - a_3^2a_0$

[66] See Phillips (1954) and Allen (1969, 18.3–7) for further details.

is fulfilled – will establish again the asymptotic stability of the dynamics now for any level of the – level correcting – integral control.[67] This is in the end a more important result than the statement "α_d sufficiently large," since a derivative term which is really large also has the effect of making the overall adjustment toward equilibrium very slow.[68]

Since the above is, however, only a simple example for the possibilities of economic regulation by means of fiscal policy *rules*, we will conclude our discussion of this type of model now.[69] We have learned in particular that a derivative fiscal policy rule may be an important stabilizer in an economy, which is subject to internally generated fluctuations.

3.9 Conclusions

We have considered in this chapter various models that – interpreted as partial contributions to an analysis of cycles and growth – provide important elements for the construction of a complete theory of cyclical growth and economic policy. Such contributions were given by the following:

- Harrod's theory, which we interpreted as an explanation of rapid growth and its instability
- Domar's model of the stability of a state of depression
- Solow's analysis of the simple interaction of the supply side factors
- Phillips' design of fiscal policy rules

The Hicksian model, on the other hand, because of its attempt to provide a seemingly complete picture of the cycle, does not appear to be as suggestive as these other approaches, since it

- is based on a fairly mechanical interaction of quantities demanded on the market for goods solely,
- treats growth, ceilings, and floors in a purely exogenous fashion, that is, does not contribute anything to their explanation.

It thus aims at completeness at a stage in dynamic theorizing where the gathering and analysis of further partial ideas on economic dynamic forces is still needed. Such ideas are nevertheless contained in this approach and can be appended to the list given above

- The role of lags in the shaping of economic dynamics
- The role of nonlinearities in the creation of viable economic growth mechanisms

---

[67] Since we have $a_3 - a_4 = s \cdot \alpha_p$.

[68] The eigenvalues of the purely derivative policy case will then approach the values 0, 0, −1.

[69] For examples, numerical magnitudes, explicit solutions, and further assertions on such policies, the reader is again referred to Allen (1969, Chap. 18).

Hicks' full model furthermore stands in striking contrast to Keynes' Notes on the Trade cycle we have considered at the end of the preceding chapter. The latter approach is sketchy and broad. It discusses the cycle by means of many undetermined (exogenous) parameters by speculating about their possible change and interacting influence and it stresses business psychology as being very important. The former, by contrast, is narrow and exhibits only a few, more or less technically determined parameters, which completely determine the motion of the system. Psychology and expectations are completely absent from this approach.

The analysis of cycles in the fifties and sixties followed the Hicksian approach by and large. The explanation of fluctuations thereby remained limited to goods–market phenomena in the main (sometimes appended by monetary aspects and rate of interest considerations). Labor market effects (and the wage-price sector of the economy) consequently received little attention during this period – until by the occurrence of stagflation (stagnation and inflation) the real process itself – and the Monetarist critique – demanded for such an analysis.[70] Yet, as we shall see in the following chapter, cyclical phenomena that relate to unemployment are not difficult to be established – through the role that income distribution plays in the laws of motion of a capitalist economy. Approaching economic dynamics from this perspective has the significant advantage that cycles and growth, that is, cyclical growth, can be explained at one and the same time. This is done by means of certain natural nonlinearities and the endogenous turning-points they create, without any help from assumptions about specific lags à la Hicks. But, once again, also this "new" approach will provide only a further partial explanation for the course of economic evolution, though one that has been very neglected in the general presentations of macrodynamics.

Appendix: Nonlinear Approaches to Multiplier–Accelerator Analysis

In this section, we shall briefly review two approaches, one by Kaldor (1940) and the other by Goodwin (1951), that make use of a nonlinear accelerator (or stock adjustment) principle in their study of multiplier–"accelerator" interactions. The formal structure and the general reasoning of these models will be of use later on (in Chap. 7) in the context of price adjustment process and inflationary expectations. We therefore will not consider here in detail the economic motivations that were put forward by these two authors to justify their particular choice of nonlinearity, but instead will stress the economic and formal similarities between the two models. In addition, further extension and modifications of these two models, which make them more different from each other, will not be considered here. The reader interested in details and extensions of these two approaches to the nonlinear theory

[70] See, for example, Rose (1967), Bergstrom (1962) for exceptions in this regard.

of the trade cycle may consult Allen (1967, Chap. 19), Chiarella (1990, Chap. 2/3), Evans (1969, Chap. 14), Lorenz and Gabisch (1989, Chap. 4/5), and Lorenz (1989, Chap. 2) for further details.

Opposite to their date of origin, we shall start here from the Goodwin trade cycle model, which in our version – up to the nonlinearity now involved – is identical to the linear Phillips model of Sect. 3.8, where we have considered a multiplier–accelerator model of the following type:

$$Y^{\mathrm{d}} = C + I + A, \tag{3.24}$$

$$C = cY, \tag{3.25}$$

$$I = (D+1)^{-1}\varphi(vDY), \quad \varphi' \equiv 1, \tag{3.26}$$

$$A = \bar{A} = \bar{C} + \bar{I}, \tag{3.27}$$

$$Y = (TD+1)^{-1}Y^{\mathrm{d}}. \tag{3.28}$$

We have shown in Sect. 3.8 that this model is capable of generating explosive cycles just as the period version of the Hicks model of the trade cycle considered in Sect. 3.7. For this latter model, we have also presented the simple (inequality) approach by which Hicks kept its explosive multiplier/accelerator dynamics within economically meaningful bounds. Goodwin (1951) has modified this inequality approach towards nonlinearity by proposing that the introduction of two smooth nonlinearities into the above accelerator principle (3.26) is also sufficient to obtain the Hicksian result (of a stable limit cycle), now from the above continuous-time model without any further use of difference or differential inequalities. In addition, this form of a trade cycle model can easily be tailored in such a way that it will give rise to the asymmetric stylized business cycle format presented in Fig. 3.10 of Sect. 3.7.

To make use of such a proposal we assume now in addition for (3.26) of the above model that there is an absolute floor to net investment, which is determined by the maximum scrapping rate of the capital stock ($I > -I_{\min}, I_{\min} > 0$) and that there is also an absolute ceiling for the rate of output of capital goods ($I < I_{\max}, I_{\max} > 0$) – due to a full employment barrier on the labor market, for example.[71] We assume furthermore that actual investment behavior is described as earlier, yet now by means of a smooth strictly increasing function φ (of the capacity vDY needed to satisfy a given change in final demand DY), which is now equal to the identity mapping only in a neighborhood of the stationary state and is elsewhere characterized by the conditions $\varphi' < 1$ and[72]

$$\lim_{x \to -\infty} \varphi(x) = -I_{\min}, \quad \lim_{x \to +\infty} \varphi(x) = I_{\max}.$$

The form of this function implies that net national product is limited from below and from above – because of the multiplier – by the following two values:

---

[71] The details in the economic motivation of these two constraints on net investment and disinvestment may be different in the various representations of these two models and do not matter here very much.

[72] See Allen (1967, p. 379 ff.) for details and graphical representations.

$$Y_{\min} = (A + I_{\min})/s, \quad Y_{\max} = (A + I_{\max})/s.$$

The idea of Goodwin's (1951) nonlinear accelerator analysis of the persistence of business cycles is to use this new functional relationship $\varphi(vDY)$ in place of the former term vDY in the above investment function and to show by means of the resulting differential equations that such a model must exhibit a stable limit cycle (if it has been explosive in the linear case we considered in Sect. 3.8).[73]

To show this we shall now make use of a system of two differential equations in place of the differential equation of order two employed in Sect. 3.8. These two differential equations are obtained from the above model by solving it for the two dynamic variables $DI = \dot{I}$ and $DY = \dot{Y}$, which gives rise to

$$\dot{I} = \varphi(v(A + I - sY)/T) - I, \tag{3.29}$$

$$\dot{Y} = (A + I - sY)/T, \quad s = 1 - c. \tag{3.30}$$

The stationary state of this dynamical system is given by $\dot{Y}_o = \dot{I}_o = 0$, which implies $I_o = 0$ and $Y_o = A/s$. And for the Jacobian of this system at the stationary state we get

$$J = \begin{pmatrix} v/T - 1 & -vs/T \\ 1/T & -s/T \end{pmatrix}.$$

This implies for the determinant of J the expression $\det J = s/T > 0$ and for the trace of this matrix $(v - T - s)/T$ which, of course, gives rise to the same (in)stability result as in Sect. 3.8 (see there also for the conditions of a cyclical behavior). We assume again that the parameter values of the model are such that it is locally unstable ($v > T + s$).

To investigate (graphically) whether the system can nevertheless be globally stable and will exhibit a stable limit cycle around its stationary state, we have to determine the isoclines $\dot{I} = 0, \quad \dot{Y} = 0$ of this dynamics. They are given by (in this order)

$$Y = \frac{I + A}{s} - \frac{T}{vs}\varphi^{-1}(I), \quad Y = \frac{I + A}{s}.$$

By means of these isoclines we can derive the following phase portrait for the above dynamical system.

The graphs in Fig. 3.12 of the isoclines indicate that the $\dot{Y}$-isocline will always be steeper than the $\dot{I}$-isocline as far as positive slopes are concerned. We see in addition that the positive slope of $\dot{I}$-isocline at the stationary state $(v - T)/(vs)$ must be larger than $1/v$ in order to imply instability and that it will be always less than $1/s$ for all choice of the parameter value v. We see furthermore that the slope of the $\dot{I}$-isocline will approach $-\infty$ when net investment I is approaching the boundary values $I_{\min}$ and $I_{\max}$, which it in fact can never do.

[73] Which (in contrast to the Hicks model) must stay away from the above two outward bounds, that is, which has turning points before these absolute bounds are reached.

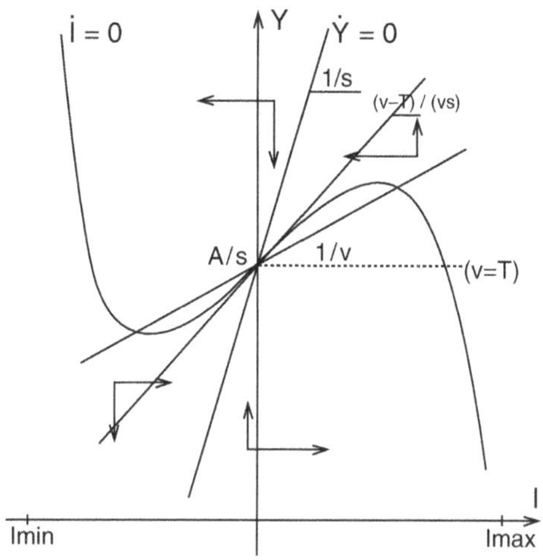

Fig. 3.12 Goodwin's nonlinear accelerator model

This phase portrait will now imply that there must exist a stable limit cycle if the slope of the isocline $Y = \frac{I+A}{s} - \frac{T}{vs}\varphi^{-1}(I)$ further away from the stationary state is such that the following type of box can be found with respect to the graph of this function.

This picture shows that there exists a compact subdomain of the whole phase space where the dynamics points into the interior of this domain everywhere on its boundary. This situation then allows the application of the *Poincaré–Bendixson theorem* (see Hirsch and Smale (1974, p. 248)), which says that

> any nonempty compact limit set[74] of (such) a C^1 planar dynamical system, which does not contain a stationary point, must be a closed orbit,

that is, must be the image of a nontrivial periodic solution. It is intuitively clear that the above compact box cannot be left by any trajectory (which starts in it). These trajectories furthermore cannot approach the stationary point due to the type of instability of this point (not a saddle). The limit sets of all these trajectories must therefore fulfill the conditions of the above theorem and are thus all of the closed orbit type.

Such a closed orbit will be a semistable limit cycle if it attracts trajectories that are different from it (i.e., we then have at least one-sided stability of this cycle). The limit cycle will be stable (two-sided stability) if there is an open region around this cycle such that all points in this region give rise to trajectories that are attracted by it. We state without proof that a system such as the one we depicted earlier will not only have a closed orbit, but will in fact exhibit just one limit cycle, which will be a globally stable attractor for all other trajectories of this dynamical system in the above depicted domain.[75]

[74] See Hirsch and Smale (1974, p. 198).

[75] A proof of this fact is not straightforward and is generally missing in the literature on such cycle models – also in the case of the Kaldor model that will now be considered along similar lines, cf. Yan-Qian et al. (1984) for the details of such a stability analysis.

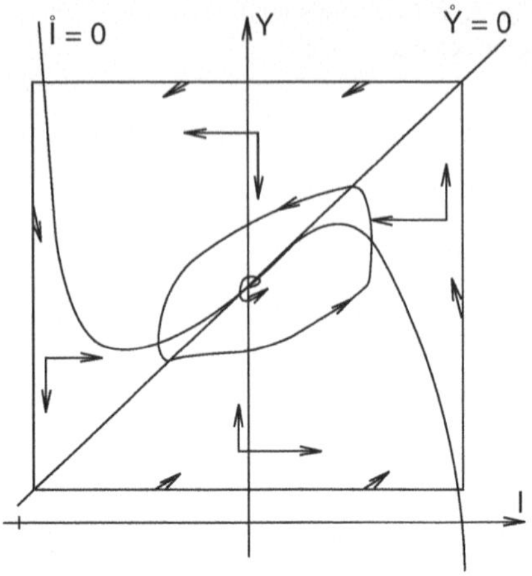

Fig. 3.13 Goodwin's non-linear accelerator and the Poincaré–Bendixson theorem

For economic purposes, it is, however, not necessary to have a unique and stable limit cycle under all circumstances. Figure 3.13 shows that all points close to the boundary of the box as well as all points close to the stationary state of the dynamics cannot lie on a limit cycle, but will be attracted by one (not necessarily the same) in the interior of the box. We thus have the result that persistent economic fluctuations must emerge – after some finite time interval – from such a nonlinear multiplier–accelerator approach for all historically given combinations of the capital stock K and national income Y that are situated in this invariant domain. The precise nature of these fluctuations may depend on the historically given starting position of the trajectories if the function φ is of a more general shape than the one that underlies Fig. 3.13. Note, finally, that the analysis of economic regulation of Sect. 3.8 can be applied here and be used to remove the persistent cycle from this Goodwin model.

Let us now contrast this model with the Kaldor (1940) model of the trade cycle which, in our formulation, employs instead of the above two differential equations the following two laws of motion:

$$\dot{K} = I(Y,K), \quad I_Y > 0, I_K < 0, \tag{3.31}$$

$$\dot{Y} = \gamma(I(Y,K) - sY + \bar{C}) = \gamma(\bar{C} + cY + I(Y,K) - Y), \tag{3.32}$$

with the unique and strictly positive equilibrium $I(Y_o, K_o) = 0, Y_o = \bar{C}/s$.

The new thing in this model is the alternative type of investment behavior it assumes, which is given now by a so-called capital stock adjustment principle.[76] The second equation of this dynamic model is again the dynamic multiplier process, which is reformulated here by means of a given adjustment speed parameter γ in place of the adjustment lag coefficient $T = 1/\gamma$.

Following Kaldor (1940) we assume with regard to this multiplier process that it is unstable at the stationary state of the economy ($\dot{K}_o = 0, \dot{Y}_o = 0$), that is, the marginal propensity to spend $c + I_Y$ is assumed to be greater than 1 ($s < I_Y$) in

[76] See Matthews (1970) for a detailed comparison of this principle with the accelerator principle we have used before.

this (medium run) equilibrium situation $K_o, Y_o = \bar{C}/s$. This instability condition is intended to play the same role as the instability condition of the Goodwin model $v > 1/\gamma + s$, yet – as Chang and Smyth (1971) have shown – a stronger condition is in fact necessary here to achieve this aim, namely $\gamma(I_Y - s) + I_K > 0$. In this case, the Jacobian at the steady state of the above dynamical system will have a positive trace (and a determinant that is always positive). The stationary equilibrium is thus either an unstable node or an (unstable) source in this case.[77]

The basic idea of Kaldor's approach to an explanation of the trade cycle is (again) that the investment function is n (increasing) nonlinear function of national income Y and that it is fairly insensitive to changes in Y for small as well for large values of income Y. The simplest case for Kaldor's cycle model is given by the following situation of goods market equilibria as well as disequilibria.

This diagram shows that there can be three (or more[78]) IS-equilibria in such a model, two stable ones ($I_Y < s$) for high as well as low values of national income, and an instable one in between ($I_Y > s$). The economy will then – if the dynamic multiplier process works with sufficient strength – always be near either to a boom or a depressed situation (the instable situation in between characterizing the average situation). Yet, it was assumed above that the growth (or the decline) in the capital stock exercises a negative influence on the level of net investment. In the above boom situation, we thus get that the I-curve shifts downwards, whereas in the depressed situation, where net investment is negative, we have a shrinking capital stock and thus an upward shifting I-curve. These shifts of the I-curve will continue until a point is reached where the upper IS-equilibrium (the case of a downward shifting I-curve) and the lower IS-equilibrium (the case of its upward shift) disappears (AC and BC, respectively).[79] In such a case the economy switches to the alternative stable equilibrium, and thus falls into a depression in the initial case of a boom equilibrium and into a boom in the opposite situation. The model thus generates – under suitable further mathematical conditions – a succession of booms, which all change into depressions after a while and vice versa. This is the intuitive idea behind Kaldor's model of the trade cycle.

This model therefore also suggests that there should exist stable limit cycles in the evolution of the K, Y-dynamics to which all relevant trajectories are attracted. To show this (again solely) by graphical means, we assume once more that the slope (now) of the $\dot{Y} = 0$-isocline is such that a box of the following type can be drawn in an economically meaningful subdomain of the whole phase space. This box is normally chosen in the literature such that it contains parts of the boundary of the nonnegative orthant so that only $K > 0, Y > 0$ can be assured by it (see Chang and Smyth (1971), e.g.). This, however, is not a sensible procedure, since the forces that restrict the dynamics to a compact domain cannot be formulated by making use of the "catastrophe" values $K = 0, Y = 0$, where savings and investment behavior

---

[77] See Fig. 4.2 in Chap. 4.

[78] If there is more than one point of inflection of the I-curve in the above diagram (which may give rise to more than only one limit cycle).

[79] See Evans (1969) and Lorenz and Gabisch (1989) for a detailed graphical presentation of these assertions.

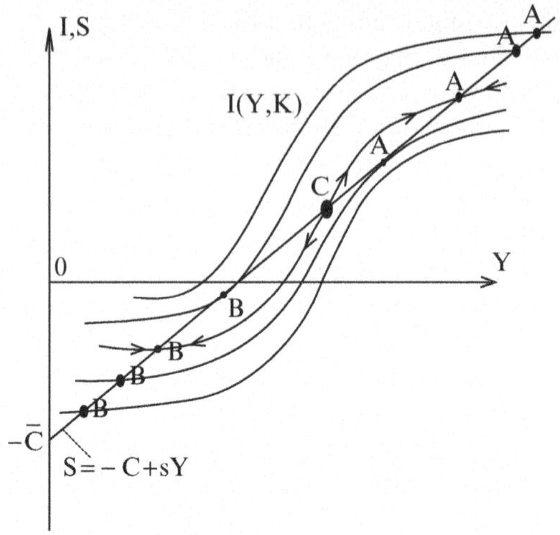

Fig. 3.14 Kaldor's trade cycle model (A's, B's the stable, and C's the unstable IS-equilibria)

will be of no reliable nature. An economically meaningful procedure must restrict the dynamics to a compact domain that uses economically sensible limits for the possible fluctuations in net national income in particular.

To motivate the above graphs a little bit further, let us assume in addition that the investment function reads as follows:

$$I = \varphi(Y) - bK, \quad \varphi' > 0, b > 0,$$

where the graph of φ is of a shape as it is depicted in the Fig. 3.14. The $\dot{K} = 0, \dot{Y} = 0$ isoclines are in this case given by

$$K = \frac{\varphi(Y)}{b} \text{ and } K = \frac{\varphi(Y) - sY + \bar{C}}{b}.$$

The slope of the first isocline is positive throughout, while the slope of the second is positive by assumption in (a neighborhood of) the stationary state (Fig. 3.15). Since the slope of the function φ is small far off the stationary state value Y_0, the slope of the second isocline must, however, become negative then in a way as it is shown earlier. This situation allows for the same type of reasoning as in the case of Goodwin's nonlinear accelerator with regard to the existence of limit cycles.

Comparing the details of the dynamics that is generated by these two models, there seem to exist significant differences, but this is not really true. In fact, making use of the following simple form of the capital stock adjustment principle, $I = vY - K$ makes the model of Goodwin and Kaldor identical to each other (if $\varphi' \equiv 1$ holds true in the Goodwin case), since we then get from this adjustment principle

$$\dot{I} = v\dot{Y} - \dot{K} = v\dot{Y} - I.$$

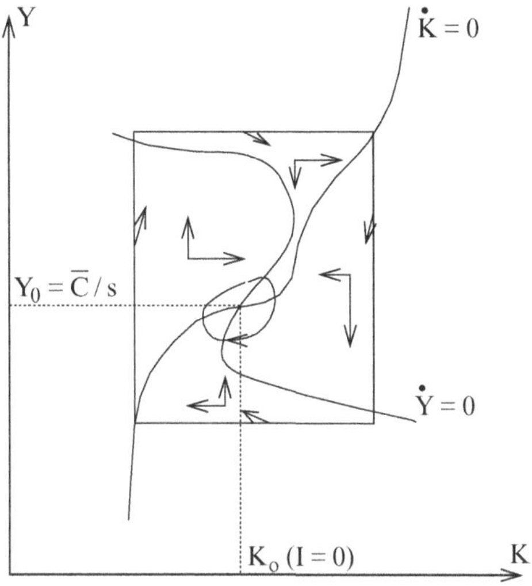

Fig. 3.15 The construction of a limit cycle for the Kaldor model

In this linear case, the models are thus only using different phase diagrams to characterize the resulting dynamics. There follows that the difference in the nonlinear case is primarily given by the specific nonlinearity that has been assumed by the two authors, which is given by a nonlinear accelerator (followed by a lagged adjustment of actual investment to this accelerator mechanism) in the Goodwin case and by a nonlinear connection between investment and the absolute level of output in the Kaldor case. Hicks' (1950, p. 9) critique of the Kaldor trade cycle model as an insufficient alternative to his own model is therefore partly misleading, since the adjustment principles that are employed in each case differ only in the particular shape assumed for these two adjustment principles to generate their cycles.[80]

There is, however, also one implied difference that is worthwhile of being noted. Varian (1979) has discussed Kaldor's trade cycle model from the perspective of catastrophe theory, which studies the singularities of potential functions like, for example, the following one (for the Kaldor model):

$$V_K(Y) = -\int_{Y_0}^{Y} \gamma(I(y,K) - sy + \bar{C})\,\mathrm{d}y, V_K' = -\gamma(I(Y,K) - sY + \bar{C}, V_K'' = -\gamma(I_Y - s).$$

The variable Y is called the state variable and the variable K the control variable in this context. The above one-parameter family of potential functions for the dynamic multiplier process reflects the stable cases of this adjustment process by minima ($I_Y - s < 0$) and the unstable ones by maxima ($I_Y - s > 0$) of the function V_K. The catastrophe manifold or the set of all singular points $V_K' = 0$ of this parameterized family of functions V_K is in this case given by the set of all IS-equilibria of the Kaldor model and it is described again by the curve $\dot{Y} = 0$ as in Fig. 3.16.

[80] The conditions for instability of the stationary state are $v > T + s$ in the first case and $\varphi'(Y_o) > Tb + s$ in the second.

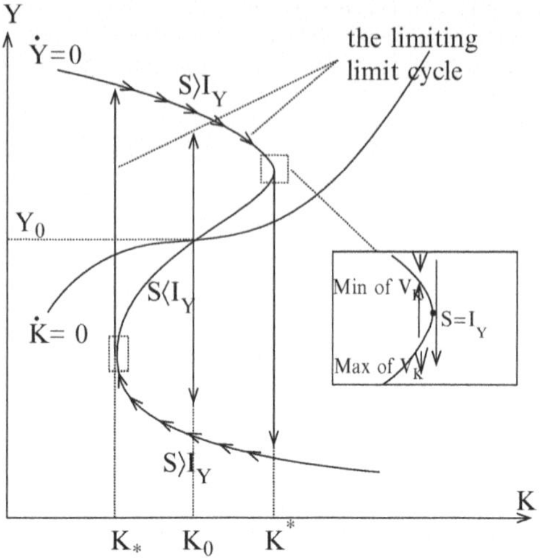

Fig. 3.16 The limit cycle of the Kaldor model from the "viewpoint of catastrophe theory"

The bifurcation set (in the space of control variables K) with regard to this catastrophe manifold is given by the two points K_* and K^* in Fig. 3.16, that is, by the two points where the multiplier turns from stability to instability with respect to a change in the level of income Y.

Catastrophe theory now investigates the type of singularity that occurs at such bifurcation points, which is here given by the simplest form that exists, the so-called fold catastrophe, at each of the two bifurcation points K_*, K^*.[81] It thus studies the above graph of $\dot{Y} = 0$ from a local perspective to determine the various shapes of the catastrophe manifold at points that correspond to points in the bifurcation set. Because of its local character, such an analysis, however, does not contribute much to the study of the dynamics that is associated with Fig. 3.16. It mainly says that the stability of positions on the upper leaf of this fold will get lost at the fold and that some sort of sudden change or jump must then occur. But since this analysis is restricted to a small box in the above phase space, it cannot say anything more on what is occurring. The same thing, of course, applies to the lower leaf of the above goods–market equilibrium curve. The local analysis of the above catastrophe manifold is thus not very illuminating – due to the straightforward character of the fold catastrophe.[82]

Our interest in Fig. 3.16 lies in the global situation it represents and the intuitive story that may be related with it (as well as the formal means that may be applied to it). To this end we now assume that the adjustment speed in the above

[81] See Poston and Stewart (1978, Chap. 9) for further details on the concepts of catastrophe theory in general and on the fold catastrophe in particular.

[82] This situation changes when the next type of catastrophe is considered, the so-called cusp, since this type will allow a meaningful type of local dynamic analysis, see Varian (1979) for an economic application of it.

dynamic multiplier process is (close to) infinity. Adjustment in the vertical direction of Fig. 3.16 is therefore (nearly) instantaneous (as indicated by the above arrows). The motion of the system is consequently always close to the above two stable leaves of the graph of $\dot{Y}_0 = 0$ – up to the two points represented by the bifurcation set where a large jump in the variable Y must occur from the upper part of the equilibrium manifold to the lower one or vice versa. Such a situation of very rapid change occurs at regular instances, since the capital stock is increasing in the upper stable part of this manifold and it is shrinking in the lower part according to the investment levels that are realized in these two cases.

Kaldor's trade cycle result can thus also be explained by means of such a special case of adjustment speeds. Equilibrium income is then either high and slowly declining due to the increase it implies for the stock of capital – until there is an immediate (or very rapid) transition to a very low new equilibrium level for it – or it is low and slowly increasing due to the decline in the capital stock that then occurs – until it reaches a level where a rapid upturn sets in to bring it back to the high levels that prevailed before the downturn.

This is the verbal description of a so-called relaxation oscillation analysis, which due to its global approach may provide a better means for studying the dynamics of the Kaldor model than is given by the above local approach of catastrophe theory. Relaxation oscillations may come about when a time lag (or a speed of adjustment) in a dynamic model approaches 0 (∞). One of the differential equations then collapses into an algebraic equation, which decreases the dimension of the dynamics by one. It is tempting then to rationalize the limit case of infinite adjustment speeds by means of some kind of jumping hypothesis – as we have done it in the above Kaldor model. Yet, careful mathematical analysis is necessary here to really demonstrate the equivalence of the dynamics for high as well as infinite adjustment speeds.[83] Examples of how to analyze such limiting discontinuous oscillations where one of the differential equations has become an equilibrium condition are given in Chiarella (1990, Chap. 2/3).

We have seen above that stagnant booms or slowly recovering depressions – with rapid changes in between – characterize the Kaldor trade cycle dynamics. A similar situation as the above twofold fold of the Kaldor model is not directly visible for the phase diagram of the Goodwin multiplier–accelerator cycle model, since the curve of goods market equilibria is a straight line in this case, the nonlinearity now being present in the other isocline of this model. The question arises whether the Goodwin model will also allow for a relaxation oscillation interpretation or whether it will differ in this respect from the Kaldor model. Chiarella (1990, 3.3) provides the formal details that such an interpretation is indeed possible if the phase space of the dynamics is reformulated in an appropriate way. A different method for calculating the function that characterizes the relaxation oscillation must therefore be applied in this case to determine from it again the limiting limit cycle as in the Kaldor model.

---

[83] Cf. Chap. 7 for an example of an erroneous imposition of jump conditions in such a limit case.

In closing this section on the contents and similarities of Kaldor's and Goodwin's approach to persistent economic fluctuations, we shall provide here an alternative presentation to the $Y, \dot{Y}$-phase space analysis of Chiarella (1990) of the relaxation oscillations that occur in the Goodwin model. This presentation is again only in graphical terms so that the reader must be referred to Chiarella's book for the mathematical details of it.

To find a function that can be utilized to depict the relaxation oscillation, let us first reformulate the dynamic equations of the Goodwin model in the following way:[84]

$$\dot{I} = \varphi(vX) - I, \quad X = \dot{Y}, \tag{3.33}$$

$$\dot{X} = \frac{1}{T}(\dot{I} - sX) = \frac{1}{T}(\varphi(vX) - I - sX). \tag{3.34}$$

These equations are obtained from the original ones by differentiating the second with respect to time and by introducing for their representation the new variable $X = \dot{Y}$. The dynamics is now given in term of the variables $\dot{Y}, I$, which gives rise to Fig. 3.17 of it.[85]

This diagram reveals the formal similarity of the Goodwin model with that of Kaldor as it was represented earlier. The difference mainly is that the fast adjusting variable is now the time rate of change of national income (or net investment), and not the level of these magnitudes as in the Kaldor model. This is due to the distinguishing fact that we have a nonlinear accelerator in this case and not a nonlinear relationship between levels as in the Kaldor model. Instead of the stable or instable dynamic multiplier relationship of this latter model, we here employ the second of the above equations (for $X = \dot{Y}$) to describe the fast adjustment of $\dot{Y}$ to

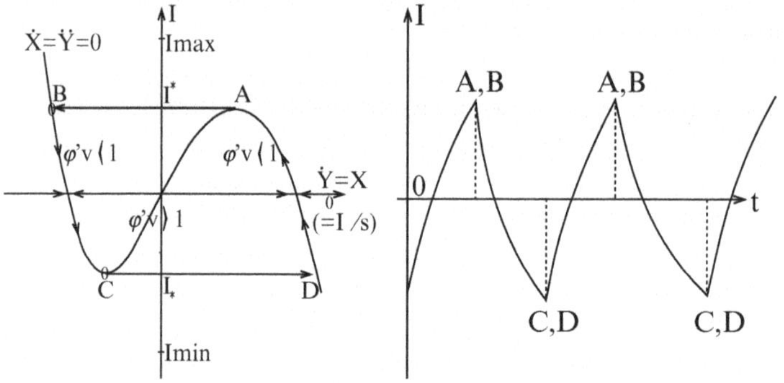

Fig. 3.17 Relaxation oscillations in the Goodwin model and the path of investment activity

[84] See Allen (1969, p. 381) for an alternative presentation by means of a single differential equation in the variable Y.

[85] See again Allen (1969, pp. 381/382) for an alternative verbal and graphical presentation of the resulting dynamical situation (in terms of the variables $Y, \dot{Y}$; a presentation in the variables $I, \dot{I}$ would have been equally possible here).

the left or right stable branch ($\varphi' v - s < 0$) of the equilibrium manifold $\dot{X} = 0$ if the adjustment lag T tends to infinity. Since the variable I is a continuous variable in this case, the variable Y must here be continuous, too, also in the limit case $T = 0$ (where $Y = (A + I)/s$ and $\dot{Y} = \dot{I}/s$ must hold true). It is thus only the time rate of change of these variables that can jump in the case where the stable solution to the left or to the right will disappear due to the continuing rise of net investment I that occurs to the right and the decrease of it to the left. The path of investment and income will thus be of the above depicted type in the case of no output lag.

Chapter 4
Distributive Stability by the Reserve Army Mechanism: Marx's Contribution

4.1 Marx's Point of Departure: The Classical Theory of Capital Accumulation

Central propositions of Ricardo's Principles of Political Economy[1] and the Classical theory of income distribution and accumulation are the assertions that (real) profits and (real) wages must fall in the long-run to their minimum values, while the rent of landlords will increase in the course of this process. The Classical authors then concluded that the economy will in general be approaching the stationary state, since commercial crisis – which interrupt this process – are only temporary phenomena and since technological change will be too weak (in the agrarian sector) to reverse this tendency towards stationarity.[2]

To provide a clear-cut picture of the above assertions of the Classical authors, we follow Samuelson's (1978) version of the Classical model, since Marx's critique of the Classical theory of capital accumulation can be reformulated with regard to this model in a particularly simple and illuminating way. Samuelson's model makes use of the following technological and economic assumptions:

1. As in Chap. 3 capital K and labor L are applied in fixed proportions: $K/L = y/\sigma$, a magnitude which – due to the absence of technological change – will be set equal to one by an appropriate choice of units in the following. In difference to the preceding chapter, we here consider the agrarian sector of the economy (as being representative for the whole economy). Capital and labor inputs are thus subject to the Classical law of diminishing returns, which is here formulated as follows:
$$Y = f(\min\{K,L\}), \quad f' > 0, f'' < 0, \tag{4.1}$$
where Y stands for (real) output.
2. For the competitive equilibrium which is assumed to prevail at each moment of time, it is assumed that both factors K, L^s are always fully employed ($L = L^s$)

[1] Third Edition: 1821 (Chap. IV); cf. Sraffa (1970) for details.

[2] Contrast this with Domar's analysis that a capitalist economy must grow to avoid economic crisis.

P. Flaschel, *The Macrodynamics of Capitalism: Elements for a Synthesis of Marx, Keynes and Schumpeter, Second Edition,*

and that the real rates of wages w and of profits r are uniform. Because of (4.1) we must have $f'(K) = f'(L) \geq w + r$ on the marginal (or worst) land that is used for production, since the price for renting it cannot become negative. Competition with the best unused land (which due to our technological assumptions has "nearly" the same productivity) then in addition implies $f'(K) = f'(L) = w + r$, that is, no (absolute)rent (following Ricardo) on the worst land that is in use.[3] Total rent is then – because of diminishing returns to extensive agrarian production – given by

$$R = f(K) - f'(K)K \tag{4.2}$$

and positive.[4]

3. Economic evolution is driven in the Classical model by the following two dynamic relationships:

$$\widehat{K} = \dot{K}/K = \alpha(r - \overline{r}), \quad \alpha(0) = 0, \quad \alpha' > 0, \tag{4.3}$$

where $\overline{r}$ is the exogenously given minimum rate of profit where capital accumulation comes to an end, and

$$\widehat{L} = \dot{L}/L = \beta(w - \overline{w}), \quad \beta(0) = 0, \quad \beta' > 0, \tag{4.4}$$

where $\overline{w}$ is the so-called subsistence wage at which population growth (or decline) becomes stationary. Equation (4.3) is a special formulation of the Classical investment (and savings) function, which is based on the simple version of Say's Law (only direct investment). Equation (4.4) is the so-called population law of Classical economics.

We have assumed – following Samuelson – that the labor market is in permanent equilibrium (or that it exhibits a constant rate of employment as time evolves), that is,

$$\alpha(r - \overline{r}) = \alpha(f'(K) - w - \overline{r}) = \beta(w - \overline{w}), \tag{4.5}$$

which defines a functional relationship $w(K)$ with $w'(K) < 0$ by the implicit function theorem. This function characterizes real wage/capital stock combinations w, K, which guarantee the persistence of full employment in the course of time. According to Samuelson (1978, p. 1421) the background of this function is given by the following characterization of "ruthless competition":

$$L^s > K : w = 0, \quad K > L^s : r = 0,$$

where $w + r = f'(\min\{K, L^s\}), L^s \gtreqless K$. Surplus supply is thus acting in an extreme way on the remunerations of the productive factors (and their laws of growth).

---

[3] Here based on the assumption of a uniform rate of profits r and of wages w due to Classical competition.

[4] Since we have $L^s = L = K$ in competitive equilibrium, we can neglect the symbol L in the following.

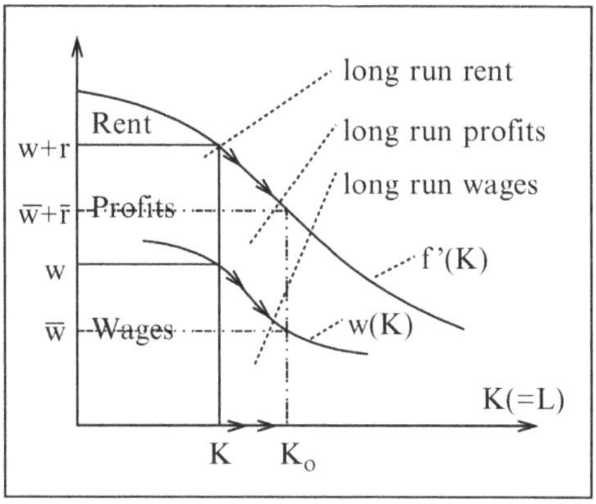

Fig. 4.1 The Classical theory of accumulation

The above function $w(K)$ now implies that the dynamics of this economy is subject to a single law of motion, which is given by

$$\widehat{K} = \alpha(f'(K) - w(K) - \overline{r}) = \beta(w(K) - \overline{w}).$$

Since the function on the right hand side of this equation is strictly decreasing $(w'(K) < 0!)$, we thus know that the stationary state $[f'(K_0) = \overline{w} + \overline{r}!]$ must be globally asymptotically stable.

Graphically, the above approach to capital accumulation can be summarized as in Fig. 4.1.[5]

This figure shows that the temporary equilibrium at K (with its determination of the distribution of income: $wL + rK + R = Y$) will indeed evolve toward the stationary level K_0 (where we have $\overline{w}L_0 + \overline{r}K_0 + R_0 = Y_0$). In the course of this process, real wages fall from w to $w_0 = \overline{w}$ – due to the $w(K)$-relationship – and the rate of profit $r = f'(K) - w(K)$ decreases too, since the right hand side of (4.5) is falling with the increase in K. Because of the above equilibrium condition for the market for labor, we know that the wage rate and the rate of profit will "reach" their minimum levels simultaneously. Finally R, on the other hand, must increase, since $R'(K)$ is equal to $f'(K) - f'(K) - f''(K)K = -f''(K)K > 0$.

The above model therefore provides a good illustration of central Classical hypothesis on the consequences of the process of capital accumulation.

Taken literally, it is to be expected that the subsistence wage of the assumed population law must be fairly low. In a developing capitalist economy, we may therefore expect that there will exist many voices that recommend that actual real wages should not fall to this level, but should be limited from below by a historically determined minimum wage $\widetilde{w}$ (resulting from legislation, at the time of Ricardo: the

[5] Note with regard to this figure that the above implies

$$R = f(K) - f'(K)K = \int_0^K f'(x)\,dx - f'(K)K,$$

which justifies the following graphical representation of total rent R.

so-called "poor laws"). Yet, the establishment of such a floor to the real wage (above $\overline{w}$) only has destructive consequences: population growth will continue in such a case, but capital accumulation will nevertheless come to a halt – due to the law of diminishing returns. Unemployment and misery must therefore be the consequence of such a policy. In the words of Ricardo, see Sraffa (1970, p. 105) the following conclusion results:

> These then are the laws by which wages are regulated, and by which the happiness of far the greatest part of every community is governed. Like all other contracts, wages should be left to the fair and free competition of the market, and should never be controlled by the interference of the legislature.
>
> The clear and direct tendency of the poor laws is in direct opposition to these obvious principles: it is not, as the legislature benevolently intended, to amend the condition of the poor, but to deteriorate the conditions of both poor and rich; ...

It is thus the "natural" wage rate $\overline{w}$ that should govern the evolution of wages over time!

4.2 Marx's Critique of the Classical Theory of Accumulation

Marx's (1954, p. 597) comment on the results of the preceding section was this: "A beautiful mode of motion .... " The battle between capital and labor is instead analyzed by him in the following way:

> ... a rise in the price of labor resulting from accumulation of capital implies the following alternative: Either ... Or, on the other hand, accumulation slackens in consequence of the rise in the price of labor, because the stimulus of gain is blunted. The rate of accumulation lessens; but with its lessening, the primary cause of that lessening vanishes, i.e., the disproportion between capital and exploitable labor-power. The mechanism of the process of capitalist production removes the very obstacles that it temporarily creates. The price of labor falls again to a level corresponding with the needs of the self-expansion of capital, whether the level be below, the same as, or above the one which was normal before the rise of wages took place. We see thus: In the first case, it is not the diminished rate either of the absolute, or of the proportional, increase in labor-power, or laboring population, which causes capital to be in excess, but conversely, the excess of capital that makes exploitable labor-power insufficient. In the second case, it is not the increased rate either of the absolute, or of the proportional, increase in labor-power, or laboring population, that makes capital insufficient, but, conversely, the relative diminution of capital that causes the exploitable labor-power, or rather its price, to be an excess. It is these absolute movements of the accumulation of capital which are reflected as relative movements of the mass of exploitable labor-power, and therefore seem produced by the latter's own independent movement.
>
> Marx (1954, pp. 580/1).

Instead of the monotonic laws derived in the preceding section, Marx here develops the picture of an "industrial cycle" as the consequence of the growth of capital "on the lot of the laboring class." Growth will – according to the above quotation[6] –

[6] We interpret the passage following: "Either ..." as characterizing a particular phase of such a cycle.

consequently be accompanied by fluctuations in economic activity, which originate from changing labor market conditions and their effect on the distribution of income between capital and labor. Furthermore, this cyclical process is not viewed by Marx as something that describes forces that are active near a steady state. Instead, this cycle is the basic mechanism that guarantees the viability of the capitalistic system in the long run, in Marx's (1954, p. 582) words:

> The rise of wages therefore is confined within limits that not only leave intact the foundations of the capitalistic system, but also secure its reproduction on a progressive scale.

Since the population law is at the heart of Marx's critique of Classical accumulation theory we want to model this critique at first by removing only this law from the model of the preceding section – replacing it by the Marxian hypothesis of the effect of the reserve army on the evolution of wages. Our procedure here is therefore similar to the one we have used for a critique of the "Classical model" of Sect. 2.3.

Instead of (4.4) we therefore make use of the following type of a real-wage Phillips-curve

$$\widehat{w} = h(V) = h(L/L^s), \quad h' > 0, \tag{4.6}$$

where we assume in addition that there is some level V_0 of the rate of employment V between 0 and 1 where $h(V_0) = 0$ holds true. This percentage V_0 describes in the present model (by means of $1 - V_0 = U_0$) the (least) percentage amount of reserve army (of unemployed) that is necessary to keep wages away from rising.[7]

Since the model now distinguishes between employment $L(=K!)$ and labor supply L^s, the $w(K)$ curve of the preceding section – which synchronized capital and labor growth – has no longer any meaning here. The model that results now exhibits two dynamical laws instead of only one:

$$\widehat{K} = \alpha(f'(K) - w - \overline{r}), \tag{4.7}$$

$$\widehat{w} = h(K/L^s). \tag{4.8}$$

The stationary state of this model is given by $K_0 = V_0 L^s$ and $w_0 = f'(K_0) - \overline{r}$. We assume that this state lies below (to the left) the stationary state of the Classical model, that is, the labor supply L^s – which is presently considered as given – is not (yet) at a level that would bring the economy within the reach of the Malthusian biological subsistence limit as far as the production conditions that presently prevail are concerned: $w_0 = f'(K_0) - \overline{r} > \overline{w}$.

The Jacobian of the right hand side of above dynamical system is given by

$$J = \begin{pmatrix} \alpha' f'' & -\alpha' \\ h'/L^s & 0 \end{pmatrix},$$

[7] Compare here Marx's (1954, pp. 600 ff.) description of the segments of the labor market.

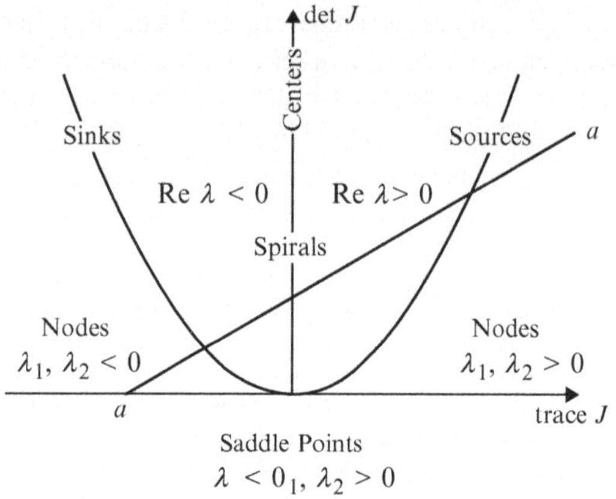

Fig. 4.2 Determinant/trace-stability characterizations

that is, it fulfills tr(ace) $J < 0$, $\det J > 0$, and $J_{21}, J_{12} \neq 0$ throughout the positive orthant $\mathbf{R}^2_+$ of $\mathbf{R}^2$ – which according to the Fig. 4.2 implies that the equilibrium point $z_o = (K_o, w_o)'$ is a local sink.[8]

By an appropriate version of Olech's theorem,[9] we can therefore conclude that the above dynamics is globally asymptotically stable in $\mathbf{R}^2_+$ with regard to its unique stationary state (K_0, w_0). And by means of local stability analysis we can furthermore investigate the conditions under which the response of this system to disturbances will be of a cyclical nature. Because of the fact that the characteristic polynomial of the matrix J is given by $\lambda^2 - \operatorname{tr} J \cdot \lambda + \det J$ in the two-dimensional case, the fundamental eigenvalue characterizations of the local dynamics of systems of dimension 2 can easily be translated into a $\operatorname{tr} J / \det J$-diagram as follows:[10]

We already know that the equilibrium of the system must be a sink. To have that it will be a spiral in addition we must according to Fig. 4.2 furthermore establish that $4\det J = 4\alpha' h'(w_0 K_0 / L^s) > (\alpha' f'' K_0)^2 = (\operatorname{tr} J)^2$ holds true at the stationary state[11]. This expression immediately reveals that, for example, a sufficiently steep Phillips-curve or sufficiently slowly decreasing marginal products will give rise to cyclical movements in the adjustment toward equilibrium. In the place of Fig. 4.1 we thus

---

[8] Local stability analysis or stability in the first approximation is based on the following approximation of the original dynamics $\dot{z} == f(z)$:

$$\dot{z} \approx f(z_o) + f'(z_o) \cdot (z - z_o), f(z_o) = 0, J = f'(z_o),$$

see Amann (1983, III) and in particular Arrowsmith and Place (1982) for details.

[9] Note here that the variable transformation $x = \ln K$ and $y = \ln w$ transforms system (4.7) and (4.8) into $\dot{x} = \alpha(f'(e^x) - e^y - \bar{r})$, $\dot{y} = h(e^x / L^s)$, which has the same type of Jacobian as the above growth rate system and which allows for an application of the Olech theorem in its original form, see the appendix to this chapter for details.

[10] See, for example, Amann (1983) for details.

[11] Note here that the above Jacobian has now been recalculated to include the terms that follow from the growth rate formulation on the left hand side of the above dynamics.

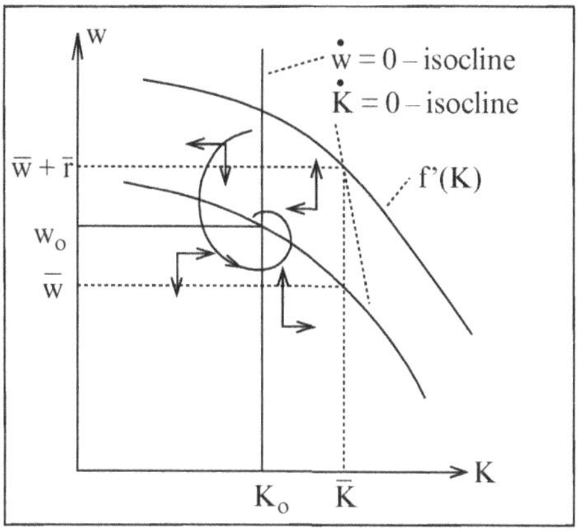

Fig. 4.3 A new type of w/K-interaction in the Classical model

get the picture shown in Fig. 4.3. As in Sect. 2.3 a single new behavioral relationship is therefore capable of producing quite a different outlook for the economic mechanism that is at work.

The above result represents, nevertheless, only a first step into the direction of Marx's view on the dynamics of a capitalistic economy, since the above approach still requires exogenous shocks for the creation of economic fluctuations. Furthermore, a defender of the Classical approach may object that the above is only a medium run picture of the economy, and that the population law will exercise its influence in the very long run. While Marx may therefore been right in asserting that the "industrial cycle" is not determined by variations in the absolute number of the working population, but by the varying proportions in which the working-class is divided into active and reserve army (p. 596); this statement may nevertheless only be true for a limited amount of time, while Classical forces will again come into being once population pressure and capital accumulation has moved the system sufficiently close to the Classical stationary state.

A simple attempt to formalize this view is given by the following modification of the above model, which reintroduces the population law into it (yet, now in combination with Marx's reserve army mechanism) and which in addition assumes that accumulation has pushed the system to a point where the marginal product of land has become so low that it is close to the minimum requirement $\overline{w}+\overline{r}$ for the factors that are applied to this land. In such a case wage increases are fairly limited and we may expect the Phillips-curve to be flat.

Adding again (4.4)[12] – but not (4.5)! – to the dynamics (4.7) and (4.8) makes this system a three-dimensional one with $\overline{w}, \overline{K}, L^s = \overline{K}/V_0 > \overline{L} = \overline{K}$ as the new stationary state. The Jacobian of this extended dynamics is

$$J = \begin{pmatrix} \alpha' f'' \cdot K & -\alpha' \cdot K & 0 \\ h' \cdot w/L^s & 0 & -h' \cdot wK/(L^s)^2 \\ 0 & \beta' \cdot L^s & 0 \end{pmatrix}.$$

[12] We here assume for simplicity that there are poor laws that guarantee the subsistence level to the unemployed (paid out of rent).

The characteristic polynomial is in this case given by

$$\lambda^3 - \text{tr}\, J \cdot \lambda^2 + a_2\lambda - \det J,$$

where a_2 is determined by

$$\alpha' h' \cdot (wK/L^s) + \beta' h' \cdot wK/L^s), \quad \text{and where}$$

$$\text{tr}\, J = \alpha' f'' \cdot K; \quad \det J = h'\alpha'\beta' f'' \cdot wK^2/L^s.$$

Applying again the necessary and sufficient conditions for local asymptotic stability of Sect. 3.8 we immediately see that all coefficients a_1, a_2, a_3 of the above polynomial are indeed positive ($a_0 = 1$). And for the final condition $a_1a_2 - a_3 > 0$ we get from the above

$$-\alpha' f'' \cdot (\alpha' h' + \beta' h') \cdot wK^2/L^s + h'\alpha'\beta' f'' \cdot wK^2/L^s = -\alpha' f'' \cdot \alpha' h' \cdot wK^2/L^s > 0.$$

We simply assert here that the Classical stationary state – just proved to be asymptotically stable – will be approached monotonically if wage-reactions to unemployment are slow (of course, β' can be safely assumed to be small as well).

Marx's claim that the process of capitalistic accumulation is essentially independent from the labor supply and its rate of change thus still rests on shaky grounds, since the Classical laws of accumulation will here still succeed in the end and remove thereby any scope for the working of the reserve army mechanism.

There is, however, one further basic assumption in Marx's (1954, Chap. XX, Sect. 1) approach, which overcomes this critique. This is the assumption of a given 'organic composition of capital'[13] which in modern terms is represented by the assumption of a constant capital coefficient v (or of a constant capital productivity σ) already made in Sect. 3.2. This (standard) assumption will replace the – for industrial societies – implausible agrarian law of diminishing returns (4.1). It will be used in the following section to obtain Goodwin's (1967) version of the Marxian growth cycle.

4.3 Goodwin's Distributive Growth Cycle Model

Replacing the pessimistic view on technology of the Classics by Marx's assumption of constant capital productivity (but still neglecting technological change) gives rise to the following dynamic model:

$$K/Y = v = 1/\sigma \quad (K = L), \tag{4.9}$$

$$\widehat{w} = h(K/L^s), \quad h' > 0, h(V_0) = 0, \tag{4.10}$$

[13] We shall not consider here Marx's attempt to derive his own version of a falling rate of profit by means of technical change, which increases labor productivity at the cost of an increasing capital-output ratio.

$$r = (\sigma K - wL)/K = \sigma - w, \tag{4.11}$$
$$\widehat{K} = \alpha(r - \overline{r}), \quad \alpha' > 0, \alpha(0) = 0, \tag{4.12}$$
$$\widehat{L^s} = \beta(w - \overline{w}), \quad \beta' > 0, \beta(0) = 0. \tag{4.13}$$

There is no longer any rent R; in fact the model now considers the manufacturing sector as being representative and does not pay any attention to agrarian production.

This model can be reduced to an autonomous system of differential equations of dimension two in the following way ($V = L/L^s = K/L^s$):

$$\widehat{w} = h(V),$$
$$\widehat{V} = \widehat{K} - \widehat{L^s} = \alpha(\sigma - w - \overline{r}) - \beta(w - \overline{w}).$$

The steady state of this system is determined by $V = V_0$ and

$$\widehat{K} = \alpha(\sigma - w - \overline{r}) = \beta(w - \overline{w}) = \widehat{L^s}.$$

For a capitalist economy it is natural to assume that $\sigma = Y/K$ is larger than $\overline{w} + \overline{r}$, that is, the minimum rate of profit allows for a wage $w_\sigma = \sigma - \overline{r}$ that is larger than the subsistence level $\overline{w}$. We then have the situation shown in Fig. 4.4.

This assumes that the positions of these two curves are such that they will intersect indeed. Turning to the dynamics of the above system, it is easy to establish the phase diagram 4.5 for it (which already suggests the existence of cyclical movements!).

This diagram furthermore suggests the final conclusion that can be established for this model (not by graphics, but by means of the following calculations), namely that all orbits of the given dynamical system will be closed curves, that is, its cycles are neither damped nor explosive and every solution to it is of this simple cyclical type.

To prove this assertion we shall construct a Liapunov function for this system and then apply Theorem 1 in Hirsch and Smale (1974, p. 193) on the stability

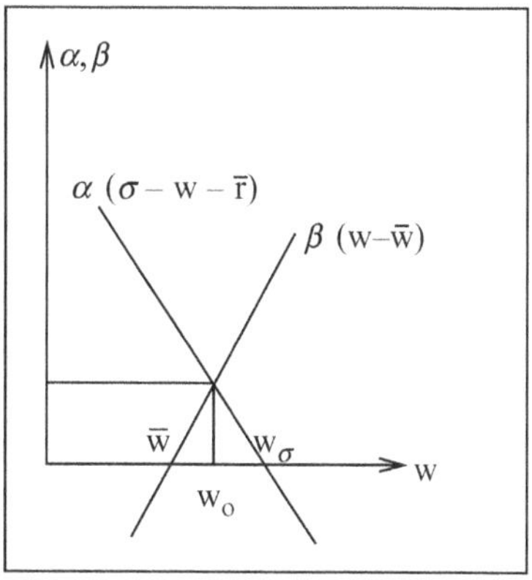

Fig. 4.4 Reformulating the Classical model

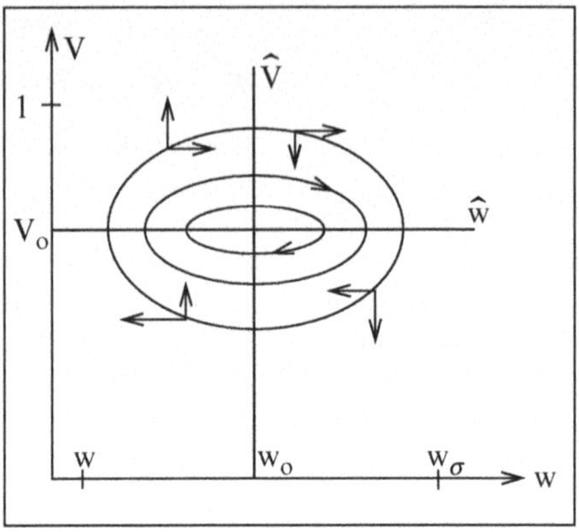

Fig. 4.5 The Goodwin growth cycle model

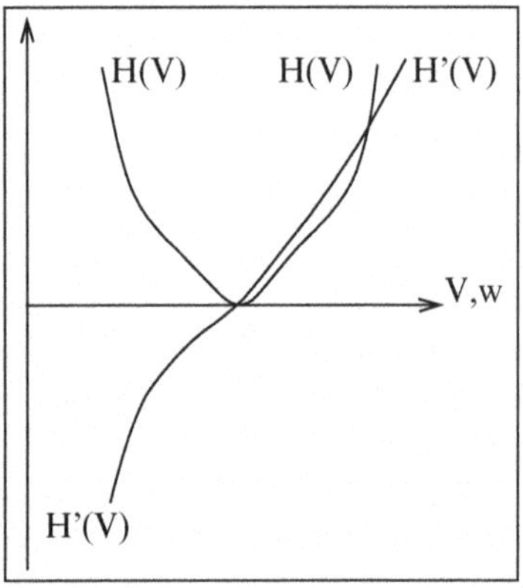

Fig. 4.6 Building a Liapunov function for the above dynamics

implications of such a construction.[14] Let us denote by H and I the primitives (integrals) of the functions $h(V)/V$ and $-(\alpha(\sigma - w - \overline{r}) - \beta(w - \overline{w}))/w$ for positive V and w which in addition fulfill $H(V_0) = I(w_0) = 0$. We denote by L the "sum" of these two functions, that is, $L : \mathbb{R}^2_+ \mapsto \mathbb{R}, L(w,V) = I(w) + H(V)$. Obviously $L(w_0,V_0) = 0$. Furthermore $L(w,V) > 0$ if $(w,V) \neq (w_0,V_0)$, since the functions H and I must both be as in Fig. 4.6.

With regard to the above dynamical system and this function L, we finally have[15]

$$\dot{L} = L_V \dot{V} + L_w \dot{w} = h(V)\widehat{V} - (\alpha(\sigma - w - \overline{r}) - \beta(w - \overline{w})) \cdot \widehat{w}$$

$$= h(V)(\alpha(\sigma - w - \overline{r}) - \beta(w - \overline{w})) - (\alpha(\sigma - w - \overline{r}) - \beta(w - \overline{w}))h(V) \equiv 0.$$

This function is therefore constant along the trajectories of the considered dynamics. This implies that the equilibrium (w_0, V_0) is Liapunov-stable, cf. again Hirsch

[14] Cf. the appendix to this chapter, which offers a general stability proof for the above cross-dual type of dynamics.

[15] $\dot{L}$ is the derivative along the trajectories of this system, and L_V, L_w is the partial derivatives of the Liapunov function L.

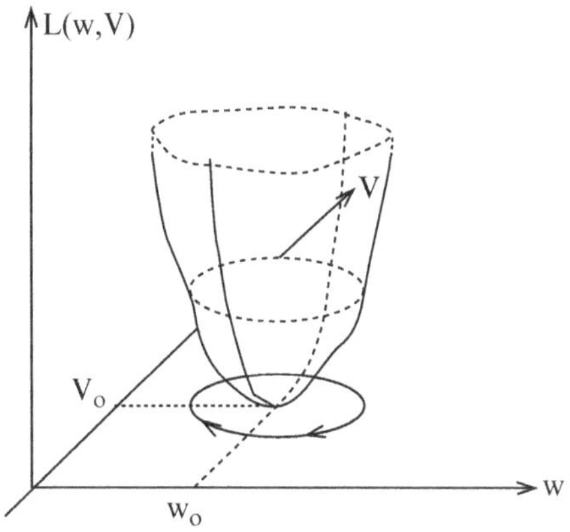

Fig. 4.7 The Liapunov function and the implied center dynamics

and Smale (1974, p. 193) and Sect. 4.9 of this chapter. Furthermore, in the simple situation we are facing, it is not difficult to see that the function L must be of a form as it is depicted in the following Fig. 4.7,[16] which implies that the orbits of the considered dynamics – which are the projections of the level curves of the function L into the phase plane – must all be closed curves as shown for one case.

This wage-rate/employment-rate dynamics is therefore always strictly periodic – with phase length and amplitude of the cycles being determined by initial conditions.

An important consequence of this new approach to Marx's reserve army mechanism is that the population law (4.13) is now deprived of its Classical consequences. A constant capital-output ratio is sufficient to establish this result (without any help from assumptions about technological change). The labor force will grow – in the steady state – with the rate $n = \beta(w_0 - \overline{w})$, but so will the capital stock: $n = \alpha(r - \overline{r})$, due to the fact that w_0 and r_0 are both larger than their minimum values $\overline{w}, \overline{r}$ (see Figs. 4.4 and 4.5). Two basic modifications of the Classical approach are consequently in the end sufficient to overthrow its Classical content and make it a Marxian model of cyclical growth.[17]

It is now very simple to modify the above model once again so that *Goodwin's (1967)* meanwhile well-known *growth cycle model* will be established. It is first of all not sensible to make use of the Malthusian population law in the analysis of steady states of developed *capitalist* economies. Population growth is instead often considered as being exogenously given and constant (the natural rate of growth that we have introduced in Chap. 3), that is, the above endogenously determined n is turned into an exogenous magnitude right from the start. Furthermore, instead of

[16] That the equilibrium point z_o is a local minimum of the function L is easily shown by means of: $L'(z_o) = 0$ and $L''(z_o)$ positive definite.

[17] Marx's characterization of such a growth cycle mechanism, however, differs in at least one very important respect from the analysis of this section, since Marx (1954, p. 581) asserts that the rate of accumulation (investment) has to be considered as the independent variable in this industrial cycle, which surely is not the case for the growth cycle we consider in this section (see Sects. 4.6 and 4.7 for a first integration of independent investment behavior into this model).

the Ricardian investment function (4.12) it is now assumed in this model that all profits are accumulated, while all wages are consumed. Instead of (4.12) this gives

$$\widehat{K} = \dot{K}/K = rK/K = r = (\sigma K - wK)/K = \sigma - w = \sigma(1 - w/\sigma) = \sigma(1-u),$$

where u is the share of wages in national income ($\widehat{u} = \widehat{w}$ in the present context!). The above dynamical system thereby becomes

$$\widehat{u} = h(V), \quad \widehat{V} = \sigma(1-u) - n \quad (= g(u)), \tag{4.14}$$

which establishes the same type of dynamic behavior as the former model.[18] This is Goodwin's variant of the Marxian growth cycle[19] [which in general also assumes that labor productivity Y/L grows at the constant rate m to be deducted from both of the above two equations then to integrate this Harrod-neutral type of technical change into this model. Again, this does not modify the models behavior].

It is no exaggeration to state that the Goodwin growth cycle model represents just as important a prototype model as the Solow growth model (Sect. 3.5). Robert Solow himself has recently expressed his admiration for this compact model, see Solow (1990), where he discusses its background, its strength, and its weaknesses as well as its empirical importance. Yet, despite its importance, Goodwin's model has been largely neglected in mainstream economics and the textbook literature.[20]

4.3.1 A Simple Synthesis of the Goodwin–Solow Type

Goodwin's model has often been criticized as representing a structurally unstable modeling of cyclical growth. Indeed, many small perturbations of the structure of the model will destroy the closed orbit structure of its trajectories and lead, for example, to explosive or implosive fluctuations instead. Yet, such a change in qualitative mathematical properties does not necessarily imply that the economics of the model has been changed in a significant way. To provide an example for this claim, an important extension of the above model will now be introduced, by which we in addition attempt to demonstrate to the reader that Solow's and Goodwin's model are in fact only two sides of the same coin. As in Sect. 3.6, we introduce a neoclassical production function $Y = F(K,L)$ here into Goodwin's growth cycle model

[18] The Liapunov function is in this case given by $\int_{V_o}^{V} h(x)/x\,\mathrm{d}x - \int_{u_o}^{u} g(y)/y\,\mathrm{d}y$, see the appendix to this chapter.

[19] See Goodwin (1967, pp. 57/8) for a brief verbal description of this growth cycle result.

[20] The neoclassical variant of this growth cycle mechanism uses basically the same adjustment equations – if it discusses labor market disequilibrium – but it applies them to a neighborhood of the point of full employment instead of the Marxian long run rate of unemployment and thus has to use regime switching methods to discuss the stability of the full employment equilibrium, see Dutt (1990, 2.3.1) for an example in the case of fixed proportions in production and Ito (1980) for the case of continuous substitution–which we now add to the Goodwin growth cycle model in the following extension of it.

to test how its behavior will be changed by the possibility to substitute capital for labor in the face of a rising price of labor. This possibility modifies the model in the following way:

$$Y = F(K,L), \quad F_K, F_L > 0, F_{KK}, F_{LL} < 0, \tag{4.15}$$

$$w = F_L(K,L), \tag{4.16}$$

$$\widehat{w} = h(L/L^s), \quad h' > 0, h(V_0) = 0, V_0 \in (0,1), \tag{4.17}$$

$$r = (F(K,L) - wL)/K, \tag{4.18}$$

$$\widehat{K} = r, \quad \widehat{L^s} = n \tag{4.19}$$

Of the above equations, (4.15) and (4.16) – though in principle known from the Solow model – must still be explained. Since capital K and wages w are here given in each moment of time, this equation states that employment L – and thus also labor intensity $L/K = l$ – is chosen in a way that makes its marginal product equal to the real wage. Because of the properties of the neoclassical production function (see Sect. 3.6[21]) we thus obtain the following inverse relationship

$$w = F_L(1,l) = f'(l) \quad \text{or} \quad l = l(w), \quad l' < 0$$

for the reaction of labor intensity with respect to changes in real wages. Making use of this relationship allows the following reduction of the model to a system of differential equations in the two variables w and $l^s = L^s/K$:

$$\widehat{w} = h(l(w)/l^s),$$

$$\widehat{l^s} = \widehat{L^s} - \widehat{K} = n - (f(l(w)) - wl(w)).$$

The steady state of this system is given by $n = f(l(w_0)) - w_0 l(w_0) = r(w_0)$ and $l_0^s = l(w_0)/V_0$, cf. Fig. 3.3 in Sect. 3.6. For the Jacobian of this dynamical system $\dot{w}, \dot{l^s}$, we get at the steady state

$$J = \begin{pmatrix} wh'l'/l^s & -wh'/l^s \\ (l^s)^2 & 0 \end{pmatrix}.$$

This matrix structure again fulfills the conditions of Olech's theorem in its growth rate form (see Sect. 4.9), which implies that the above dynamics is globally asymptotically stable.

To see whether convergence toward the steady state is accompanied by cyclical movements or not, we apply again Fig. 4.2 of Sect. 4.2 and thus have to consider the following terms:

$$4\det J = 4h'wl^s, (\operatorname{tr} J)^2 = (h'l')^2 (w/l^s)^2.$$

Note again that this calculation is only valid at the steady state $l = l^s$ and that it was here applied to the original system $\dot{w} = \ldots, \dot{l^s} = \ldots$ and not to its growth rate formulation. To get cyclical movements we need

[21] Cf. also Jones (1975, Chap. 2).

$$4\det J > (\operatorname{tr} J)^2 \quad \text{or } 4lw > h'\varepsilon(w)^2, \quad \text{where } \varepsilon(w) = l'(w)w/l.$$

We consequently get that the slope of the Phillips-curve h' and the elasticity $-\varepsilon(w)$ of the $l(w)$-curve are of decisive importance for the generation of cyclical movements, which are the more likely the flatter the curve h[22] or the smaller the elasticity of substitution $-\varepsilon(w)$ in production.

A more Goodwin-like reformulation of this dynamics is given by its following representation:[23]

$$\begin{aligned}\hat{w} &= h(V), \quad V = L/L^s,\\ \hat{V} &= \frac{l'(w)}{l(w)}\dot{w} - (n - (f(l(w)) - wl(w)))\\ &= \varepsilon(w)\hat{w} + g(w) = \varepsilon(w)h(V) + g(w), \quad g(w) = r(w) - n,\end{aligned}$$

where $g'(w) = -l < 0$ must hold true for the function $g(w)$ and where $\varepsilon(w)$ is defined as above. By means of the Liapunov-function

$$L = \int_{V_o}^{V} \frac{h(x)}{x}\,\mathrm{d}x - \int_{w_o}^{w} \frac{g(y)}{y}\,\mathrm{d}y,$$

we then immediately get

$$\dot{L} = h(V)\hat{V} - g(w)\hat{w} = \varepsilon(w)h(V)^2 \leq 0,$$

which again allows to prove the (global) asymptotic stability of the steady state solution – now by means of Liapunov's direct method[24] in place of Olech's theorem.

We conclude for this synthesis of Solow's and Goodwin's approach to economic growth that Solow adds stability to the Goodwin cycle, while Goodwin makes Solovian adjustment paths cycle – if (for example) the reaction of real wages to unemployment is sufficiently slow. These two important prototype models are therefore in no way in opposition to each other, but clearly show that there is a bridge between Marxian and Neoclassical ideas as far as the labor market is concerned and that it will depend on empirical judgments (on reaction speeds, elasticities, etc.) to decide which of these approaches will give the more convincing picture of economic dynamics in the end.[25]

---

22 In contrast to the result we have obtained for the cycle model of Sect. 4.2!

23 This dynamics gives rise to a phase diagram like the one of Fig. 4.5, but now with a negatively sloped $\dot{V} = 0$ isocline in place of the vertical one of this figure.

24 By means of Theorem 3 in the mathematical appendix or also by means of the more general Theorem 2 in Hirsch and Smale (1974, p. 196) applied to the set $P = L^{-1}([0,c]), c > 0$ ($\varepsilon = 0$ the original Goodwin case).

25 Adding Harrod neutral technical change to this Goodwin–Solow synthesis will give rise to a model that exhibits in its steady growth solution all the Kaldorian stylized facts (see Jones (1975, Chap. 1) for their enumeration) – including a steady state rate of unemployment not contained in Kaldor's list of the stylized facts of economic growth.

4.3.2 A Simple Goodwin–Harrod Synthesis

In his article on Goodwin's growth cycle model Solow (1990, pp. 37/38) states in view of its reliance on Say's Law in the most simple form ($I \equiv S$):

> This utter passivity of the demand side in the Goodwin model leaves me uncomfortable. One might be willing to precede tentatively on that basis so far as trend growth is concerned. That is what I did in the 1950s after all; but I was even then quite explicit that the problem of matching demand with productive capacity was left hanging. That aspect of the integration of growth and cycle theory is still unsettled and almost unexplored. In a model that has a characteristic maintain cycle around trend it seems even more risky to treat demand as adapting passively to fluctuation in production. But the gap is not easy to fill, at least not simply.

A direct way of integrating Harrod's multiplier–accelerator analysis into the Goodwin growth cycle model (4.14) is given by the following approach:

Define as in Sect. 3.3 the actual output-capital ratio σ by Y/K and the normal (or desired) one by $\sigma^p = Y^p/K$ ($< \bar{\sigma}^p$, the upper boundary on capacity utilization). The magnitude $\Theta = Y/Y^p \gtreqless 1$ is the degree of capacity utilization of the existing capital stock ($1-\Theta$ the percentage of capital goods that is involuntarily left idle). Labor productivity $y = Y/L$ of the employed units of labor grows with the constant rate m ($V = L/L^s$ the degree of employment).

Defining the magnitude x by $(LK)/(YL^s)$ gives $\sigma x = V$ and $\hat{x} = \widehat{K} - (n+m)$. The Phillips-curve of the Goodwin model can then be written as

$$\hat{w} = h(V) = h(x\sigma) \text{ or } \hat{u} = h(V) - m = h(x\sigma) - m.$$

Continuing along Harrodian lines (see Sect. 3.3) we have on the market for goods

$$I/K = S/K = s_p(1-u)\sigma, \quad \widehat{I/K} = \alpha(\sigma - \sigma^p),$$

where S/K is the (profit-oriented) classical savings function of the Goodwin model and $\widehat{I/K}$ the capacity-oriented investment function of firms. This type of IS-LM equilibrium[26] gives rise to $\widehat{I/K} = \widehat{1-u} + \hat{\sigma} = \frac{u}{1-u} \cdot \hat{u} + \hat{\sigma}$, which gives our second differential equation for the intended Goodwin–Harrod synthesis:

$$\hat{\sigma} = \alpha(\sigma - \sigma^p) - \frac{u}{1-u}(h(V) - m).$$

For the remaining dynamic variable V we finally get

$$\begin{aligned} \widehat{V} &= \hat{\sigma} + \widehat{K} - (n+m) \\ &= \alpha(\sigma - \sigma^p) - \frac{u}{1-u}(h(V) - m) + s_p(1-u)\sigma - (n+m). \end{aligned}$$

26 Where the Keynesian equilibrating output-capital ratio is determined in a Kaldorian fashion as a function of $g_K = I/K$ and $u: \sigma(g_K, u)$.

This is a three-dimensional nonlinear dynamical system based on a Harrodian type of goods-market equilibrium in place of Say's Law of the original Goodwin approach.

A dynamical representation of this model which is easier to manage is obtained by using the variable x in place of the rate of employment V, which gives rise to

$$\begin{aligned}\hat{u} &= h(x\sigma) - m,\\ \hat{x} &= s_p\sigma(1-u) - (n+m),\\ \hat{\sigma} &= \alpha(\sigma - \sigma^p) + \frac{u}{1+u}[h(x\sigma) - m].\end{aligned}$$

A further alternative representation that focuses on the profit share Π instead of the wage share u is

$$\begin{aligned}\hat{\Pi} &= -\frac{1-\Pi}{\Pi}(h(V) - m), \quad \Pi = 1-u,\\ \hat{g} &= \alpha(g/(s_p\Pi) - \sigma^p), \quad g = \widehat{K} = s_p\sigma\Pi,\\ \hat{V} &= \alpha(g/(s_p\Pi) - \sigma^p) + \frac{1-\Pi}{\Pi}(h(V) - m) + g - (n+m).\end{aligned}$$

Of these alternative representations of a Goodwin–Harrod synthesis, we choose the first one for an analysis of its dynamic properties.

Calculating the Jacobian of this system at the steady state gives

$$J = \begin{pmatrix} 0 & h'u_0 & h'u_0 \\ -s_p\sigma_0 x_0 & 0 & s_p(1-u_0)x_0 \\ 0 & \frac{u_0}{1-u_0}h'\sigma_0 & \alpha + \frac{u_0}{1-u_0}h'\sigma_0 \end{pmatrix} = \begin{pmatrix} 0 & + & + \\ - & 0 & + \\ 0 & + & + \end{pmatrix}.$$

This Jacobian clearly shows the dynamic contributions of the Goodwin as well as of Harrod's model. In sum it gives rise to

$$a_1 = \text{trace } J > 0, \;\; a_3 = \det J = s_p u_0 \sigma_0^2 x_0 \alpha h' > 0$$

and $a_2 = ?$, $a_1a_2 - a_3$, 0 with respect to the other Routh–Hurwitz conditions (see Sect. 3.8).

The above dynamics is therefore locally unstable. The characteristic polynomial of its Jacobian J is of the form

$$p(\lambda) = \lambda^3 + a_1\lambda^2 + a_2\lambda + a_3 = 0.$$

This form implies (by calculating the extrema of this function[27]) that there must always be one positive eigenvalue and two conjugate complex ones with a negative

[27] A local maximum always exists at $\lambda = 0$ with $p(\lambda) = -b$.

real part.[28] The behavior of this synthesis is thus a mixture of the Harrodian knife-edge property and the cyclical features of the Goodwin model with asymptotic stability instead of the former neutral one as far as the cycle is concerned. Yet, by including Harrod's accelerator mechanism, we have turned the Goodwin model into a nonviable one,[29] which demands completion.[30]

To investigate such a situation in more detail, we shall make use in the remainder of this chapter of an approach that was used in the literature to investigate the effectiveness of fiscal policy in the context of the Goodwinian growth cycle and its modifications.

We have just seen that it may not be easy to fill the gap observed by Solow (1990) in a satisfactory way. Following Wolfstetter (1982), we shall attempt this anew in Sect. 4.6 by means of an alternative investment function of the accelerator type [similar to the one first used in Sect. 3.3 of Chap. 3 to discuss the Harrod model]. Before that, we shall supply (in Sect. 4.4) a somewhat completed picture of the Marxian growth cycle, which we believe to be more in line with our above quotations from "Capital" than is the case for the growth cycle model we have investigated in this section. We shall then – again following Wolfstetter (1982) – consider the consequences of Keynesian and Classical fiscal policy rules in such a Marxian revision of the model (Sect. 4.5). Of course, a Keynesian policy rule cannot yet be considered as very reasonable in such a context where Say's Law is assumed to hold true. This provides another reason why – following the above proposal of Solow – Keynesian effective demand problems have to be integrated into this growth cycle model (in Sect. 4.6). The consequences of such an integration of fiscal policy rules are then discussed in the remainder of this chapter. We shall see that the conclusions obtained rest on shaky grounds still, but have to wait until Chap. 8 of this book before more definite conclusions for a Keynesian approach to goods- (and money-) market equilibrium can be reached on the basis of a Goodwinian treatment of the market for labor and the wage-price sector.

---

[28] This can easily be shown by means of the sign structure of the coefficients of $p(\lambda)$.

[29] We note in passing that also the Kaldor model of Sect. 3.10 gets into problems when reformulated from a Harrodian growth perspective:

$$\hat{g}_K = \alpha(\sigma - \sigma^p),\ \sigma^p \text{ given (see Sect. 3.3)},$$
$$\hat{\sigma} = \beta(g_K - s\sigma),\ \sigma = Y/K,\ g_K = I/K,\ s\sigma = S/K$$

The second equation of this dynamic system is a reformulation of Kaldor's dynamic multiplier in the context of a growing economy. The steady state of the model is given by $\sigma_0 = \sigma^p, g_K^0 = s\sigma^p$ and it is of a saddle-point type as the following calculation of the Jacobian of the above dynamics reveals

$$J = \begin{pmatrix} 0 & \alpha g_K^0 \\ \beta\sigma_0 & -\beta s\sigma_0 \end{pmatrix} = \begin{pmatrix} 0 & + \\ + & - \end{pmatrix},$$

[30] For example, in a way that may give to the Shil'nikov scenario, see Lorenz (1989, p. 167) for details. Note, furthermore, that the limit case $\alpha = \infty$ formally establishes the Goodwin model, but that this limit case has no similarities with the cases where $\alpha \to \infty$ is assumed.

4.4 A Simple Completion of the Goodwin Growth Cycle Model

In the remainder of this chapter,[31] we shall reexamine Wolfstetter's (1982) *symmetry assertion* that a Classical as well as a Keynesian fiscal policy rule is capable of stabilizing a Marxian growth cycle whose instability derives from problems of effective demand – provided that both policies are exercised with sufficient strength. This assertion is a very surprising one, since Goodwin's growth cycle model attempts to model the formation and subsequent removal of a profit squeeze situation by means of the reserve army mechanism. A Keynesian fiscal policy (which does not pay attention to this mechanism) should be expected to hinder, yet not remove this mechanism, thereby making the Marxian "Bereinigungskrise," longer and probably more severe – in striking contrast to Wolfstetter's stability analysis and the above symmetry assertion.

To allow a thorough reexamination of Wolfstetter's provocative claim, we shall introduce several new aspects into his extension of Goodwin's growth cycle model by a government sector:

1. A representation of this model must be found, which exhibits *local instability* and which takes account of the fact that the employment rate cannot exceed and the share of wages cannot reach the value "1," which here will guarantee *global stability*. This is a situation which is more in line with Marx's characterization of the profit squeeze mechanism than the common variants of Goodwin's growth cycle, which are still unsatisfactory in this regard.
2. The inclusion of problems of effective demand into this growth cycle may indeed destabilize this cycle further (see our above integration of Harrodian aspects into this model), yet it should not lead to the extreme kind of destabilization such that fiscal policy is absolutely necessary to prevent its immediate collapse.
3. The above "symmetry assertion" must be tested for those magnitudes of the fiscal policy parameters that at least roughly correspond to factual magnitudes (which are definitely limited).
4. A purely qualitative analysis – as it is undertaken in Wolfstetter's article – will in general be incapable of analyzing or solving tasks 2 and 3 in a satisfactory way. It has therefore to be supplemented by simulation studies.

The above four points represent the problems we see in Wolfstetter's introduction of fiscal policy into the Goodwin model. In the following, we therefore investigate these four points step by step. Our central finding will be that there is in fact no symmetry between the above two types of fiscal policies in the context of the Marxian growth cycle. However, the models used to prove this in the following have still their problematic features, as can be seen, for example, from some of the simulations that follow. The questions raised by Wolfstetter therefore need and deserve further elaboration.

[31] This section as well as the following three make use of the author's paper "Fiscal policy in an accelerator-augmented classical growth cycle" published in Flaschel (1988). Further extensions of the Goodwin model towards the integration of the effects of public policy into such a context are provided in Glombowski and Krüger (1984).

A well-known extension of the Goodwin model of cyclical growth toward a treatment of nominal magnitudes is given by the following two dynamic equations [see Wolfstetter (1977, 3.4.1) for their detailed introduction]:

$$\hat{u} = h(V) - m - (1-\eta)\lambda[(1+a)u - 1], \tag{4.20}$$
$$\hat{V} = s_p\sigma - (n+m) - s_p\sigma u = h(u). \tag{4.21}$$

These equations model the dynamic interaction of money-wage fixing, price-setting, profits, and accumulation now again in a technological world with fixed proportions. In these equations we denote by

u	the share of wages (steady state u_0)
V	the employment rate (steady state V_0)
m	the growth rate of labor productivity ($y = Y/L$), a constant
n	the growth rate $\hat{L}^s$ of (labor) population L^s, a constant
g_o	$n+m$
σ	the output-capital ratio Y/K, a constant
s_p	the savings rate (with respect to profit income; $s_w = 0$)
$\hat{W}$	the growth rate of money wages W
$\hat{p}$	the rate of inflation $\dot{p}/p$
a	mark-up factor on wage-unit-costs, a constant ($A = 1+a$).

The above dynamics is based on the following new structural equations and assumptions for the Goodwin growth cycle model:

$$\hat{W} = h(V) + \eta\hat{p} \qquad \text{[a money-wage Phillips-curve]},$$
$$\hat{p} = \lambda[(1+a)u - 1] \qquad \text{[a mark-up theory of inflation]}.$$

Here, η and λ denote positive parameters. The function $h(V)$ is of the same form as in the preceding section. Yet, instead of a real wage Phillips curve, we have now assumed a nominal form of it, which explicitly shows how inflation enters real wage determination. Note that we are back at the situation of a real wage curve as employed in the preceding section in the often assumed case [$\eta = 1$!]. In general, however, this new labor market curve demands the addition of a theory of inflation. This is done here in the particularly simple way of assuming that the time rate of change of prices p is given by the discrepancy between marked up unit wage costs and actual prices p (λ the speed of adjustment):[32]

$$\dot{p} = \lambda[AWL/Y - p].$$

We note finally that we added Harrod neutral technical progress in comparison to our earlier Goodwin approaches. This assumption is standard for these types of models.

[32] There is here no self-reference of the rate of inflation onto itself (or its expected value), since there is no exogenous driving force for the formation of the rate of inflation in this model. By a specific choice of the parameter A, it is assumed in Wolfstetter (1982) in addition to the above that the steady state rate of inflation $\hat{p}_0$ is zero, which provides a further reason for this lack of self-reference.

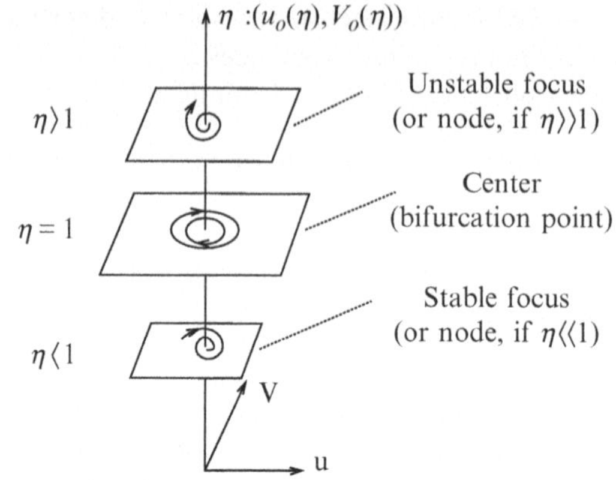

Fig. 4.8 A "quasi-linear" Hopf bifurcation diagram

In sum, (4.20) and (4.21) state that the percentage change of the share of wages u depends positively on the rate of employment V and (for $\eta < 1$) negatively on the level of u (because of the assumed mark-up theory of inflation) *and* that the percentage change of the rate of employment V is governed by savings out of profits per unit of capital $s_p\sigma(1-u)$ diminished by the growth rates m, n of the labor force and labor productivity.

It is easily shown – again by means of Olech's theorem (Sect. 4.9)[33] – that the above model's behavior can be characterized as depicted in Fig. 4.8 [see, for example, Flaschel (1984) for details].[34]

The depicted behavior is valid locally as well as globally and it is incomplete in the same way the unrestricted (linear) multiplier–accelerator model of Sect. 3.7 was not yet complete, since it does not remain restricted to economically meaningful values of u, V in the case $\eta > 1$ (of explosive cycles) and it is not yet a complete endogenous theory of the "business cycle" in the case of $\eta < 1$ (implosive cycles).

It is our opinion that a locally unstable steady state (here caused by $\eta > 1$) should be a key characteristic of a model of the Marxian theory of accumulation, yet that in addition to this feature reproductiveness, (i.e., outward stability or economic viability) should also be true, at least as long as the Marxian type of capital

[33] An alternative proof strategy is given by employing the following Liapunov function (in the case where Wolfstetter assumption $Au_0 = 1$ holds true):

$$L = \int_{V_0}^{V} (f(x) - m)/x \,\mathrm{d}x - \int_{u_o}^{u} h(y)/y \,\mathrm{d}y,$$

which gives

$$\dot{L} = (1-\eta)\lambda[Au - 1]h(u) \gtreqless 0 \quad \text{for} \quad \eta \gtreqless 1, u \neq u_o,$$

see Theorem 3 in Sect. 4.9 for details.

[34] Despite the presence of nonlinear terms this type of Hopf-bifurcation is qualitatively of a linear type.

using labor saving technological change[35] is not yet included into such a model [as is the case for the above dynamics (4.20) and (4.21)!]. To introduce such viability mechanisms that attempt to model the idea of the reproducibility of capitalism along the lines described in Marx (1954, p. 582e):

> The rise of wages therefore is confined within limits that not only *leave intact* the foundations of the capitalistic system, but also secure its reproduction on a progressive scale,

we here start with the following simple extension of the above model (4.20) and (4.21):

$$\hat{u} = h(V) - (1-\eta(u)) \cdot \lambda(u)[(1+a)u - 1] - m, \tag{4.22}$$
$$\hat{V} = s_p i(V) \cdot (1-u)\sigma - (m+n), \tag{4.23}$$

where

1. $\lambda(u) \geq 0, \quad \lambda'(u) \geq 0, \quad \lambda(u) \to \infty$ for $u \to 1$, and $\lambda(u) = 0$ if $u \leq \frac{1}{1+a}$,
2. $\eta(u)$ fulfills $\eta(u_0) > 1$, $\eta'(u) \leq 0$ (and $\eta(u) < 1$ for $u > u_0$ and near to 1),
3. $i(V) = \begin{cases} 1 \text{ for } & 0 \leq V \leq 1-\varepsilon, \quad \varepsilon > 0 \quad \text{small} \\ 0 \text{ for } & V \qquad\qquad \geq 1 \end{cases}$

(all functions are supposed to be sufficiently smooth).

The mark-up pricing rule behind the term $\hat{p}(u)$ in (4.22), that is,

$$\dot{p} = \lambda(u)\left[\frac{(1+a)W}{y} - p\right],$$

is modified by assumption 1 to that extent that it is now assumed that the adjustment speed λ of price changes (which are driven by the discrepancy between marked up wage-costs per unit of output and actual prices) increases (to infinity) as the share of wages approaches 1. Furthermore, the occurrence of deflation has been excluded from the present form of the model, which helps to avoid the existence of problematic types of steady states. Assumption 2 states that wage earners demand more than just the rate of inflation $\hat{p}$ in their money-wage claim if the wage share is at its steady value u_0 ($m > 0$!). This and the negative relationship between the aspiration factor η and the share of wages u can be motivated as follows:

Since the output-capital ratio σ is constant, we have

$$g = \hat{Y} = \hat{K} = s_p i(V)(1-u)\frac{Y}{K} = s_p i(V)(1-u)\sigma.$$

Therefore $g \gtreqless g_o = m+n$ if $u \gtreqless u_0$. It is thus implicitly assumed in assumption 2 that η relates positively to the actual rate of growth g, with $\eta = 1$ already occurring at

[35] This concerns Marx's analysis of the falling rate of profit which, however, is highly controversial and need not concern us here.

a point below normal growth g_o. Assumption 3, finally, says that it is of no use to further accumulate capital if there is no labor force available for the new capital goods.

Model (4.22) and (4.23) represents an elementary completion of (4.20) and (4.21) by projecting the reaction patterns of the distributional conflict and the accumulation process into the price/wage-sector and a simple capital formation equation. Inflation is the means by which the rate of profit is defended against money wage claims, which are too high and a simple fall in the rate of growth of capital is here assumed as reaction to the full employment barrier.[36]

Proposition 1. *Assume $s_p = 1$ for simplicity and also that $h(V_0) = (1 - \eta(u_0)) \cdot \lambda(u_0)(Au_0 - 1) + m$,*[37] *$u_0 = 1 - g_o/\sigma$ has a meaningful solution $(u_0, V_0) \in (0,1)^2$ within the range where $i(V)$ is still constant ($\equiv 1$). Assume further, $\eta'(u_0) = 0$ (or small). The model (4.22) and (4.23) then has at least one (stable) limit cycle around its unique and unstable steady state solution u_0 and V_0.*

This proposition represents a fairly obvious application of the Poincaré–Bendixson Theorem. Calculating the Jacobian of (4.22) and (4.23) at the steady state gives[38]

$$J_1 = \begin{pmatrix} -(1-\eta(u_0))\hat{p}'(u_0) \cdot u_0 & f'(V_0)u_0 \\ -\sigma V_0 & 0 \end{pmatrix},$$

that is, we have $\det J > 0$ and trace $J > 0$. The steady state (u_0, V_0) is thus an unstable node or focus.[39] And with regard to an analysis of global stability and the existence of limit cycles we will put up with the following phase portrait (and skip the details of the proof) (Fig. 4.9).[40]

Remarks. 1. Note that the $\dot{u} = 0$-isocline should not touch the horizontal axis [cf. Assumption 2 in this regard].

2. In contrast to Wolfstetter (1977, 1982), we do not assume here $A = 1/u_0$, that is, a noninflationary steady-state: $\hat{p}(u_0) = 0$.
3. $\hat{p} < 0$, that is, deflation, is, however, excluded to avoid that $\hat{u}$ may depend negatively on u for small u and V near full employment (this would imply a falling share of wages despite a situation of near full employment). Furthermore, additional interior and stable points of rest are avoided thereby.

---

[36] This assumption can be justified through a simple reinterpretation of the standard one-good model by assuming that it includes luxury goods as well. In a sufficiently small neighborhood of full employment capitalists, then simply prefer to use their inputs as (non transferable) luxury goods instead of investing them (irreversibly) into capital formation.

[37] $A = 1 + a \geq 1/u_0$.

[38] We here assume $\eta'(u_0) = 0$ for simplicity and thus neglect the term $\eta'(u_0)\hat{p}(u_0)u_0$ in J_{11}.

[39] These assumptions (which imply local instability) do not yet look very convincing. Further destabilizers can, however, easily be introduced, for example, by means of production lags, wage-drift lags, etc., yet they are difficult to treat from a purely qualitative point of view.

[40] The following picture corresponds approximately to the numerical values of the simulation example of this section.

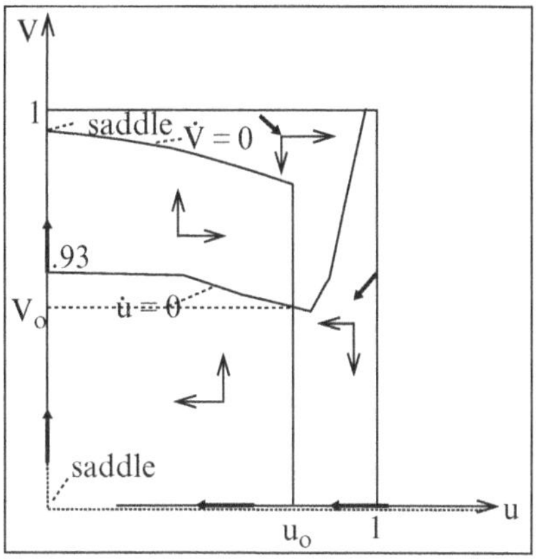

Fig. 4.9 A simple, but complete version of the Marxian growth cycle

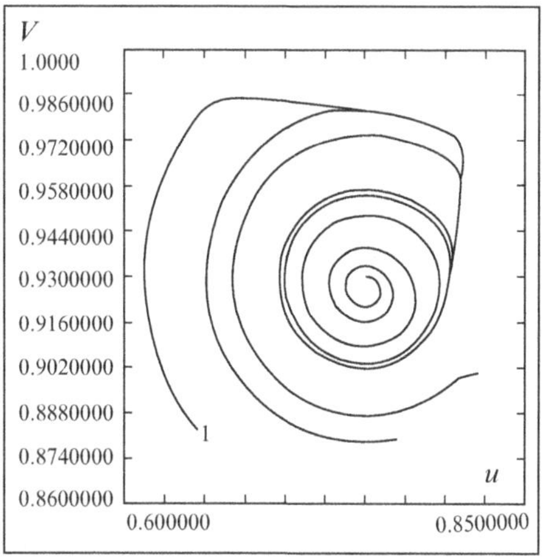

Fig. 4.10 A limit cycle in a Marxian analysis of cyclical accumulation

The above model shows explicitly (some of) the forces that keep the dynamics of a Marxian growth cycle within economically meaningful bounds. Paired with the instability of the steady state this implies that each trajectory will be attracted by some closed curve in the relevant (u,V)-domain. The model therefore provides a simple example for Marx's view on capitalistic accumulation as it is expressed in the above quotation from "Capital." Note that this explanation of positive profits is quite different in nature from the type of "explanation" that is offered by the so-called Fundamental Marxian Theorem on the equivalence of positive profits and positive surplus values [which in fact gives no explanation at all, but only establishes a relationship between two different basic magnitudes of Marx's "Capital"].

We conclude this simple analysis of a more appropriate representation of the "Marxian growth cycle" as it is given by the model (4.20) and (4.21) with a simulation study of the model (4.22) and (4.23) (Fig. 4.10):
Parameter values and functions:

$m = 0.03, n = 0.02, \sigma = 0.2,\; a = 0.5(u_o = 0.66), h(V) = \rho V - \gamma, \rho = 1,\; \gamma = 0.9,$ $i(V) = -50V + 50$ on $[0.98, 1]$ and $\equiv 0$ or 1 outside this interval, $e(u) = 1 - \eta(u)$ the continuous piecewise linear function with $e(0) = -0.5$, $e(0.72) = -0.05$, $e(0.78) = -0.05$, $e(1) = 0.5$, $\lambda(u)$ the continuous function with $\lambda' \equiv 0$ on $[0, u_o]$, $\lambda' \equiv 4$ on $(0.66, 0.75]$, $\lambda' \equiv 400$ on $(0.75, 1]$.

4.5 Government Stabilization Policies

To discuss the effects of fiscal policies, Wolfstetter (1982) introduces a public sector into the model (4.20) and (4.21) in the following way:

$$G/Y = t + \mu(V_0 - V), \tag{4.24}$$

$$T = t(Y + zB), \tag{4.25}$$

$$G + zB \equiv T + p_B\dot{B}. \tag{4.26}$$

The new symbols in these equations and the identity denote:

t	tax rate (a fixed parameter)
T	taxes
G	government expenditures
B	stock of government bonds
z	rate of interest
p_B	bond price
μ	reaction parameter

Equation (4.24) describes an expenditure policy rule that implies a constant proportion t of government spending in national income for the steady state. And outside the steady state it implies $\dot{G/Y} = -\mu\dot{V}$.[41] A Keynesian policy would attempt to counteract the cycle and would therefore be characterized by $\mu > 0$, whereas a (Neo)Classical policy would reduce expenditure in the slump and is thus characterized by $\mu < 0$ [see Wolfstetter (1982) for further details, also with regard to the following].

Taxes T are a constant proportion of the tax base $Y + zB$, with z the rate of interest. The parameter p_B is the price of new bonds $\dot{B}$. Since a portfolio decision is not included in Wolfstetter's extension of Goodwin's model, it is necessary to assume that bonds and capital goods are characterized by the same rate of return $r = (1-u)Y/K$. The simplest way of doing this, which at the same time avoids any misunderstanding of the terms p_B, z in the above equations, is to assume fix-price bonds ($p_B = 1$) with a rate of return always equal to r. This is an admissible assumption, since all bonds are issued by the government, which thus simply has to guarantee that the prevailing rate of profit will always be assumed as point of reference for current interest payments $zB = rB$.

Introducing (4.24)–(4.26) into our model (4.22) and (4.23) modifies it in the following way: (4.22) remains unchanged since wage- and price-formation rules are

[41] In the language of Sect. 3.8 this is a proportional fiscal policy rule, which assumes that the government knows the steady state value of the rate of employment.

by assumption not modified by government policy and since u is still defined by $WL/pY = (W/p)/(Y/L) = w/y$ [w the real wage, y output per head].

The growth of the capital stock is now, however, governed by [42]

$$i(V)[(1-t)(Y-wL+rB)-\dot{B}], \tag{4.27}$$

that is, by profits (including interest) after tax minus that investment that is going into government bonds instead of real capital formation. Note that – because of Say's law – there is no goods-market problem in this model, that is, the aggregation of all components of goods demanded will necessarily be identical here with the supply of goods here:[43]

$$\begin{aligned} C &\equiv (1-t)uY, \\ I &\equiv (1-t)(1-u)Y+(1-t)rB-\dot{B}, \\ G &\equiv T-(1-t)rB+\dot{B} \equiv tY-(1-t)rB+\dot{B}, \quad \text{i.e.,} \\ C+I+G &\equiv (1-t)uY+t(1-u)Y+tY \equiv Y. \end{aligned}$$

Equation (4.27) implies by means of (4.24)–(4.26):

$$\begin{aligned} \dot{K} &= i(V)[(1-t)(Y+rB-wL)-(G+rB-t(Y+rB))], \\ &= i(V)[Y-(1-t)wL-tY-\mu(V_0-V)Y], \\ &= i(V)[(1-t)(Y-wL)+\mu(V-V_0)Y]. \end{aligned}$$

On the basis of this modification, (4.23) now reads

$$\hat{V} = i(V)\sigma[(1-t)(1-u)+\mu(V-V_0)]-(m+n), \tag{4.28}$$

which together with

$$\hat{u} = h(V)-m-(1-\eta(u))\lambda(u)[(1+a)u-1] \tag{4.29}$$

constitutes the new system of differential equations to be investigated.

Note first that this new model is qualitatively identical to (4.22) and (4.23) if $\mu = 0$ holds [$u_0 = 1-g_o/\sigma$ is then to be replaced by $u_0 = 1-g_o/(\sigma(1-t))$]. And for an arbitrary parameter μ we get for the $\dot{V} = 0$-isocline

$$u = (1-t-g_o/(\sigma \cdot i(V))+\mu(V-V_0))/(1-t),$$

which gives nearly the same sort of isocline as in Sect. 4.4 if $|\mu|$ is sufficiently small [the vertical part is now downward sloping if $\mu > 0$ and will pass through the same steady state as before, that is, the one belonging to $\mu = 0$]. The $\dot{u} = 0$-isocline is, of

[42] The hypothesis underlying the reaction function $i(V)$ is that capitalists stop physical investment when the full employment ceiling is reached, but they, of course, have no problem in further investing in government bonds in such a case.

[43] Equivalently, we have $I \equiv S_p - \dot{B} \equiv S_p + S_g \equiv S$, $S_p = (1-t)(Y+rB)-C$, $S_g = t(Y+rB) - rB - G$.

course, strictly the same as before, that is, the outward bounds which it and $\dot{V} = 0$ determine are of the same type as in Fig. 4.2.[44]

For the Jacobian of (4.22) and (4.28) we get (under the assumptions of Sect. 4.4):

$$J_2 = \begin{pmatrix} -(1-\eta(u_0))p'(u_0)u_0 & f'(V_0)u_0 \\ -\sigma(1-t)V_0 & \sigma\mu V_0 \end{pmatrix}$$

and therefore a further destabilizing force with regard to the steady state for the Keynesian policy rule ($\mu > 0$). The Classical rule ($\mu < 0$), on the other hand, adds a stabilizing term to the characteristics of steady equilibrium.[45]

In the case of the original Goodwin model ($\eta \equiv 1$) these two policy alternatives consequently give rise to two sharply distinguished cases (of the type depicted in Fig. 4.8, with the bifurcation parameter $\mu = 0$ now instead of $\eta = 1$), since we then have

$$J = \begin{pmatrix} 0 & + \\ - & \sigma\mu V_0 \end{pmatrix}.$$

This sharp distinction also extends to larger regions of the (u,V)-space $(0,1)\times(0,1)$. An alternative to the proof in Wolfstetter (1982) is provided by the following approach:

Proposition 2. *The continuous function* $L : (0,1)\times(0,1-\varepsilon) \to \mathbf{R}$ *defined by*

$$L(u,V) = \int_{V_0}^{V} (h(\tilde{V}) - m)/\tilde{V}\, \mathrm{d}\tilde{V} - \int_{u_0}^{u} [\sigma(1-t)(1-\tilde{u}) - (m+n)]/\tilde{u}\, \mathrm{d}\tilde{u}$$

fulfills the following conditions:

(1) $L(u_0,V_0) = 0$ *and* $L(u,V) > 0$ *for* $(u,V) \neq (u_0,V_0)$
(2) $\dot{L} < 0 \quad (\dot{L} > 0, \dot{L} = 0)$ *for* $\mu < 0 \quad (\mu > 0, \mu = 0)$
in $(0,1)\times(0,1-\varepsilon) - \{(u_0,V_0)\}$

The well-known closed orbit structure of the Goodwin case $\mu = 0$ *(see Sect. 4.3) around the equilibrium* u_0, V_0 *in addition determines compact domains, which are positively (negatively) invariant with regard to the dynamics* $\mu < 0\ (\mu > 0)$. *By*

---

[44] There is, however, one important difference to the characteristics of the steady state for $\mu = 0$, that is, before the introduction of an active anticyclical government policy, in that the steady state, that is here, the steady state path of the government debt is not uniquely determined by the model. In fact, given an initial debt B_o, this debt can be financed without time limit and without influencing the dynamics of the system by means of the rule $rB_o = trB_o + \dot{B}_o$, that is, $\hat{B}_o = (1-t)r$. This rule does not modify the investment function of this economy in the steady state – independent of the level B_o that prevails at time t=0. It is thus to be expected that there is hysteresis present in the model as far as the relative level of long run debt is concerned.

[45] Note here that large values of μ may give rise to two and more intersections between $\dot{u} = 0$ and $\dot{V} = 0$ and also to a further equilibrium on the V-axis (if $\mu > 0$ becomes so large that the intersection of the $\dot{V} = 0$-isocline with the u-axis is removed).

Theorem 2 in Hirsch and Smale (1974, p. 196) this implies the situation of global (in)stability of the type it is analyzed and depicted in Wolfstetter (1982, p. 381).

Proof. Differentiating L along the trajectories of the dynamics (4.28) and (4.29) gives, Obvious, since $h(\tilde{V})/\tilde{V}$ and $-[\sigma(1-t)(1-\tilde{u})-(m+n)]/\tilde{u}$ are both strictly increasing functions. Furthermore,

$$\begin{aligned}
\dot{L} &= [(h(V)-m)/V]\cdot\dot{V} - [(\sigma(1-t)(1-u)-(m+n))/u]\dot{u} \\
&= (h(V)-m)\cdot\hat{V} - (\sigma(1-t)(1-u)-(m+n))\cdot\hat{u} \\
&= (h(V)-m)[\sigma((1-t)(1-u)+\mu(V-V_0))-g_o] \\
&- [\sigma(1-t)(1-u)-g_o](h(V)-m) \\
&= (h(V)-m)\mu(V-V_0) = \mu[(h(V)-m)(V-V_0)] \\
&\gtreqless 0 \text{ for } \mu \gtreqless 0 \text{ and } V \neq V_0.
\end{aligned}$$

Remark. The stability of (u_0, V_0) in the case $\mu > 0$ is always supplemented by the fact that region $(0,1)^2$ is invariant if (4.22) [and not $\eta \equiv 1$] holds true. Furthermore, Proposition 1 of Sect. 4.4 need not hold true here (if the interior equilibrium becomes non-unique). There may, for example, exist large values of $\mu > 0$, which allow for a stable equilibrium $(u_{00}, V_{00}) > (u_0, V_0)$, which is highly inflationary [note that $1-\eta(u_0)$ will become positive for $u > u_0$ sufficiently large].

The central result of this section: that Keynesian fiscal policy will be destabilizing while a Classical policy will do the opposite (and may even eliminate the limit cycle of Sect. 4.4, see the following simulations) is not too surprising. This is already noted in Wolfstetter (1982). A Keynesian policy (ceteris paribus) raises

$$\dot{B} = \mu(V_0 - V)Y + (1-t)rB$$

[in comparison to the steady state characterization $\hat{B} = \dot{B}/B = (1-t)r$], if $V_0 > V$ and lowers it in the opposite case. It consequently supplies extra funds for physical capital accumulation in the boom and absorbs such funds in the depression. This clearly makes the process of overaccumulation (and underaccumulation) of capital on which this model's cycle rests more pronounced. By contrast, a Classical rule would absorb funds in the boom and supply extra funds during the depression and thereby establishes a force that counteracts this cycle-maker. The following simulations (Fig. 4.11a–d) illustrate the various situations we have just described (note that in addition to the parameters of Sect. 4.4 we have assumed here for the new parameter t the value 0.2):

In the above remark we noted that large $|\mu|$ may give rise to new and also problematic situations, which should, on the one hand, be considered in more detail than we have done here. On the other hand, economically relevant magnitudes of $|\mu|$ can be estimated (very crudely) as follows:

$$t = 30\%, \quad \max|V-V_0| \leq 0.1, \max|\mu(V-V_0)Y| \leq 0.1\cdot tY, \text{ i.e.}$$
$$\max|\mu(V-V_0)| = \max|\mu|\ |V-V_0| \leq 0.1t, \quad \text{i.e., } 0.1|\mu| \leq 0.1t, \text{ i.e. } |\mu| \leq 0.3.$$

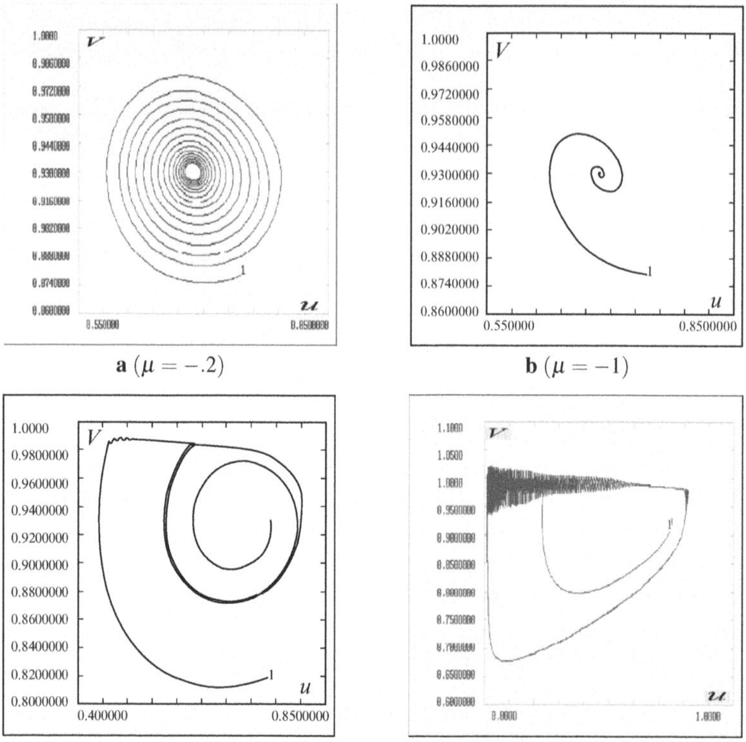

a ($\mu = -.2$) **b** ($\mu = -1$)

c ($\mu = .2$) **d** ($\mu = 1.9$)

Fig. 4.11 Classical policy (**a**,**b**) and Keynesian policy (**c**,**d**)

The problematic situations depicted in Fig. 4.11d can therefore safely be excluded from consideration. However, these extreme situations do nevertheless indicate that the enforcement of the turning points of the above cycle within the domain $(0,1)^2$ (see the behavior of the dynamics near the two points A, A' in Fig. 4.11c) must still be considered as rather preliminary in its formulation.

4.6 Independent Investment Behavior and Stabilization Problems

To allow for a proper test of the Keynesian policy rule, Wolfstetter (1982, p. 387) introduces the following investment function into the Goodwin growth cycle model:[46]

[46] See Phillips (1961) for the tradition of using such investment functions and compare its alternative formulations in Sects. 3.3 and 3.8. Note, too, that the formulation $\hat{I} = g_0 + a(v_p - v), v = 1/\sigma$ is – among the investment functions we have considered in Chap. 3 – the one that is closest to the present approach, which is of the form $\dot{g} = \varepsilon(g_o + (\frac{\sigma}{\sigma^p} - 1) - g)$, ε the speed of adjustment toward the momentarily desired level.

$$\widehat{K} = I/K = \frac{\varepsilon}{D+\varepsilon}\left[g_0 - \left(1 - \frac{x}{x_0}\right)\right] \tag{4.30}$$

where ε is an adjustment parameter and where x and x_0 denote the actual and the desired degree of capacity utilization. Since x_0 is exogenously given, we can simplify to $x_0 = 1$ [$x = Y/Y^p$, where Y^p is given by σK].

The introduction of a new equation $I = S = (1-u)\sigma K$ (goods market equilibrium) and a new variable x which allows for the realization of this equilibrium implies instead of model (4.22) and (4.23) the following set of dynamic equations (see Wolfstetter (1982) for further details):

$$\widehat{u} = h(V) - m - (1-\eta(u))\widehat{p}(u), \tag{4.31}$$
$$\widehat{V} = \sigma x(1-u) - (m+n) + \widehat{x}, \tag{4.32}$$
$$\dot{x} = [\varepsilon(g_0 - 1 + x - \kappa) + \sigma x\,\dot{u}]/(\kappa/x), \tag{4.33}$$

where $\kappa = \sigma x(1-u)$ and where $\widehat{p}(u) = \lambda(u)\cdot[Au-1]$, $A = 1+a$ gives the rate of inflation.

The first equation is the same as before if – as it is assumed – actual output Y experiences the same (constant) rate of growth of labor productivity $Y/L = m$ as normal output Y^p.[47] It again describes the conflict over the distribution of actual income based on a money-wage Phillips-curve and a mark-up pricing rule. The second equation has been modified slightly in comparison to (4.23), since we now have $\dot{K} = x(1-u)Y^p$ and

$$\widehat{V} = \widehat{L/L^s} = \widehat{(Y/Y^p)}\cdot\widehat{(L/Y)}\cdot\widehat{(Y^p/K)}\cdot\widehat{(K/L^s)} = \widehat{K} - m - n + \widehat{x}$$

by definition. The third equation, finally, is new and is derived in the following way: Goods-market equilibrium $I = S$ implies $I/K = S/K$ or $\frac{\varepsilon}{D+\varepsilon}(g_o - 1 + x) = \sigma x(1-u))$. This in turn gives $\varepsilon(g_o - 1 + x - \sigma x\cdot(1-u) = \sigma\,\dot{x}\,(1-u) - \sigma x\,\dot{u}$ and thus

$$\dot{x} = \frac{\varepsilon(g_o - 1 + x - \sigma x(1-u)) + \sigma x\,\dot{u}}{\sigma(1-u)}.$$

Introducing the relative magnitude $\Theta = V/x$ allows to rewrite (4.31)–(4.33) as follows

$$\widehat{u} = h(\Theta x) - m - (1-\eta(u))\cdot\lambda(u)[Au-1], \tag{4.34}$$
$$\widehat{\Theta} = \sigma x(1-u) - (m+n) = \sigma x(1-u) - g_0, \tag{4.35}$$
$$\dot{x} = \frac{\varepsilon(g - 1 + x - \sigma x(1-u)) + \sigma x\cdot\dot{u}}{\sigma(1-u)}. \tag{4.36}$$

Following Wolfstetter, we assume the existence of a meaningful steady state solution (which for $A = 1/u_0$ is the same as that of model (4.20) and (4.21)). The Jacobian

[47] Note here that we allow for $Y > Y^p$ in this approach to an IS-extension of the Goodwin model.

at these equilibrium values is given by ($\eta'(u_0) = 0$ as in Sect. 4.4):

$$J_3 = \begin{pmatrix} -\widehat{p}(u_0)(1-\eta(u_0))u_0 & h'(\cdot)u_0 & h'(\cdot)\Theta_0 u_0 \\ -\sigma\Theta_0 & 0 & \sigma(1-u_0)\Theta_0 \\ \frac{(\varepsilon-\widehat{p}'(u_0))(1-\eta(u_0))u_0}{1-u_0} & \frac{h'(\cdot)u_0}{1-u_0} & \frac{\varepsilon(1-\sigma(1-u_0))+\sigma h'(\cdot)u_0\Theta_0}{\sigma(1-u_0)} \end{pmatrix}.$$

Comparing the Jacobian J_3 with J_1 of Sect. 4.4, we see that destabilizing factors have entered the system even if we follow Wolfstetter and assume that the original system $\begin{pmatrix} J_{11} & J_{12} \\ J_{21} & J_{22} \end{pmatrix}$ is asymptotically stable ($\eta < 1$).

In the first instance this is due to the positive dependence of $\dot{x}$ on $x(J_{33} > 0!)$, a Harrodian knife-edge situation à la Phillips (1961). We have ($\eta < 1$)

$$\text{trace}\, J = -\widehat{p}(u_0)(1-\eta)u_0 + \frac{\varepsilon(1-g_o+\sigma h'(\cdot)u_0\Theta_0}{\sigma(1-u_0)} > 0$$

if, for example, the parameter ε is chosen sufficiently large, which implies instability. And for $\det J$ we get

$$\begin{vmatrix} -\varepsilon & 0 & -\varepsilon(1-g_o)/\sigma \\ -\sigma\Theta_0 & 0 & g_o \\ J_{31} & \frac{h'(\cdot)u_0}{1-u_0} & \frac{\varepsilon(1-g_o)}{g_o}\cdot\Theta_0 \end{vmatrix}$$

$$= \varepsilon(1-g_o)\Theta_0 \cdot h'(\cdot)u_0/(1-u_0) + \varepsilon g_o \frac{h'(\cdot)u_0}{(1-u_0)} \cdot \Theta_0 = \varepsilon\Theta_0 h'(\cdot)u_0/(1-u_0) > 0,$$

which implies that the above model will be unstable – quite independent from any stabilizing influence from money illusion ($\eta < 1$). The question arises how this instability of the "private sector" of the economy can be removed. In analyzing this question, Wolfstetter (1982) arrives at a surprising symmetry conclusion: suppose that fiscal policy is introduced in the above model (4.31)–(4.33) in the manner of Sect. 4.5. Then – in striking contrast to Sect. 4.5 – he gets in this new situation that *both* policies will stabilize the economy provided that are exercised with sufficient strength ($|\mu| \gg 0$). An alternative proof of this result will be given below.

From a Marxian perspective, however, this result looks rather unconvincing: *if* the conflict between capital and labor is the central conflict in the evolution of capitalistic societies and *if* Marx's basic form of the general law of accumulation is at least correct in its analysis of the cyclical nature of capital accumulation, *then* it is to be expected that a policy which hinders the "Bereinigungskrise" by making the slump less deep (and which speeds up accumulation in the boom – the Keynesian policy rule $\mu > 0$!) should make accumulation less and not more stable!

Starting point of Wolfstetter's (1982,3.) analysis is the model (4.20) and (4.21) of Sect. 4.4, with $s_p \equiv 1, \eta = \text{const} \in (0,1), \lambda = \text{const}, h(V) = \rho V - \gamma, \text{and} \widehat{p}(u) = \lambda[u/u_0 - 1]$. We shall follow him in this regard not to overload the presentation of the model when government activities are included. Transferred into the form of an explicit system of differential equations his model (3.2), (3.15) and (3.18) reads[48]

$$\widehat{u} = \rho\Theta x - (1-\eta)\lambda A^0 u + (1-\eta)\lambda - (\gamma + m) = a_2 V + a_1 u + a_0, \Theta x = V, \tag{4.37}$$

$$\widehat{\Theta} = \sigma\kappa - (m+n) = \sigma x[(1-t)(1-u) + \mu(x\Theta - V_0)] - g_o, \tag{4.38}$$

$$\begin{aligned}\widehat{x} &= \frac{\varepsilon(g_o - 1 + x - \sigma\kappa)/\sigma + x((1-t)\,\dot{u} - \mu x^2\,\dot{\Theta})}{\kappa + \mu\cdot\Theta\cdot x^2} \\ &= \frac{\varepsilon(g_o - 1 + x - \sigma\kappa)/\sigma + x(1-t)(a_0 + a_1 u + a_2 V)u - \mu x^2\Theta(\sigma\kappa - g_o)}{\kappa + \mu\cdot\Theta\cdot x^2}.\end{aligned} \tag{4.39}$$

The last equation of this system follows from

$$\dot{\kappa} = \begin{cases} \dot{x}\,\kappa/x - x(1-t)\,\dot{u} + x\mu\Theta\,\dot{x} + x^2\cdot\mu\,\dot{\Theta} \\ \varepsilon(g_o - 1 + x - \sigma\kappa)/\sigma \end{cases},$$

which gives

$$\dot{x}\,(\kappa/x - x\mu\Theta) = \varepsilon(g_o - 1 + x - \sigma\kappa)/\sigma + x(1-t)\,\dot{u} - x^2\mu\,\dot{\Theta} \quad \text{or}$$

$$\widehat{x}(\kappa + \mu x^2\Theta) = \varepsilon(g_o - 1 + x - \sigma\kappa)/\sigma + x(1-t)u[a_0 + a_1 u + a_2 V] - \mu x^2\Theta[\sigma\kappa - g_o].$$

The equilibrium values for this system are (for $A = A^0 = 1/u_0$)

$$u_0 = 1 - g_o/(\sigma(1-t)), \quad \Theta_0 = V_0 = \frac{m+\gamma}{\rho}, \text{ and } x_0 = 1.$$

To investigate the behavior of system (4.37)–(4.39) near the steady-state and for large parameters μ, the following simplification (approximation) of (4.39) is very helpful: dividing both the numerator and the denominator of this equation by μ gives for μ sufficiently large the approximate equation

$$\widehat{x} = \frac{-\varepsilon x(x\Theta - V_0) - x^2\Theta(\sigma\kappa - g_o)}{\Theta x^2 + x(x\Theta - V_0)} =: \frac{Z}{N}. \tag{4.40}$$

This equation is of help as a first approximation to the Jacobian of the full system. It gives in connection with (4.37) and (4.38)

$$\widetilde{J} = \begin{pmatrix} -u_0(1-\eta)\lambda A^0 & u_0\rho & u_0\rho\Theta_0 \\ -\Theta_0(1-t)\sigma & \Theta_0\sigma x_0\mu & \Theta_0(g_o + \sigma\cdot\mu\Theta_0) \\ (1-t)\sigma & -\widetilde{J}_{22}/\Theta_0 - \varepsilon/\Theta_0^2 & -\widetilde{J}_{23}/\Theta_0 - \varepsilon/\Theta_0 \end{pmatrix}.$$

Note here that the numerator N of (4.40) is zero at the equilibrium so that the partial derivatives of (4.40) are equal to Z_i/N, with $N = \Theta_0 x_0^2$, $i = u, \Theta, x$. The characteristic polynomial of $\widetilde{J}$ is thus given by $x^3 - (\text{trace } J)x^2 + a_2 x - \det J$, where a_2 is given by

48 $A^o = 1/u_o$, the mark up that allows for an inflation-free steady state.

$$a_2 = \begin{vmatrix} \widetilde{J}_{11} & \widetilde{J}_{12} \\ \widetilde{J}_{21} & \widetilde{J}_{22} \end{vmatrix} + \begin{vmatrix} \widetilde{J}_{11} & \widetilde{J}_{13} \\ \widetilde{J}_{31} & \widetilde{J}_{33} \end{vmatrix} + \begin{vmatrix} \widetilde{J}_{22} & \widetilde{J}_{23} \\ \widetilde{J}_{32} & \widetilde{J}_{33} \end{vmatrix}.$$

We then get for the coefficients of this polynomial

$$\text{trace}\, J = -u_0(1-\eta)\lambda A^0 - g - \varepsilon/\Theta_0 < 0 \qquad (\text{ if } \eta < 1),$$

$$\det \widetilde{J} = \begin{vmatrix} -u_0(1-\eta)\lambda A^0 & u_0\rho & u_0\rho\Theta_0 \\ -\Theta_0(1-t)\sigma & \Theta_0\sigma\mu & \Theta_0(g_o+\sigma\mu\Theta_0) \\ 0 & \varepsilon/\Theta_0^2 & \varepsilon/\Theta_0 \end{vmatrix} \begin{vmatrix} -u_0(1-\eta)\lambda A^0 & u_0\rho & 0 \\ -\Theta_0(1-t)\sigma & \Theta_0\sigma\mu & \Theta_0 g_o \\ 0 & \varepsilon/\Theta_0^2 & 0 \end{vmatrix}$$

$$= -u_0(1-\eta)\lambda A^0(\varepsilon/\Theta_0^2)(\Theta_0 g_o) = -(1-\eta)\lambda A^0 \cdot \varepsilon u_0 g_o/\Theta_0 < 0,$$

$$a_2 = -u_0(1-\eta)\lambda A^0\Theta_0\sigma\mu + u_0\rho\Theta_0(1-t)\sigma + u_0(1-\eta)\lambda A^0(J_{23}/\Theta_0 + \varepsilon/\Theta_0)$$
$$+u_0\rho\Theta_0 J_{21}/\Theta_0 + \varepsilon g_o/\Theta_0.$$

For $\eta < 1$ we consequently get the Routh–Hurwitz conditions, cf. Sect. 3.8,

$$\text{trace}\, J < 0, \quad \det J < 0 \quad [a_2 > 0].$$

And with regard to the final Routh–Hurwitz condition there holds

$$-(\text{trace}\, J)a_2 + \det J > 0$$

since a_2 depends positively on μ and det J does not. For large values of μ this therefore confirms that a Classical policy *as well* as the Keynesian policy rule make the above model asymptotically stable, which again establishes the assertion made in Wolfstetter (1982).

Remarks. (1) The assumption $\eta < 1$ is essential for the obtained result. For the original Goodwin model ($\eta = 1$) computer simulations show that the Classical rule introduces asymptotic stability into the model while the Keynesian rule does not (for any $\mu > 0$).

(2) If the parameter η is > 1 (so that the private sector (4.20) and (4.21) is already unstable in the context of Goodwin's model, see Fig. 4.8), one can show for η sufficiently near to 1: trace $J < 0$, det $J > 0$ (and $a_2 > 0$). Both policies consequently fail in this case, however, large they are exercised.

Returning to Wolfstetter's analysis ($\eta < 1$), we want to argue now that his results are problematic in at least two respects:

(a) As shown in Sect. 4.5, the parameter μ should for economic reasons be less than 0.3. This may prevent an applicability of Wolfstetter's result.

(b) Left to itself ($\mu = 0$) the private sector may not, of course, be asymptotically stable. However, its type of instability should not be of a completely erratic nature (at least in the short-run).

Both aspects were out of reach for the type of qualitative analysis given in Wolfstetter (1982). However, the following Figs. 4.12 and 4.13 – based on computer simulations of the above model for $m = 0.03$, $n = 0.02$, $\gamma = 0.9$, $t = 0.2$, $\varepsilon = 0.2$, $\sigma = 1/3$, $\rho = 1$, $\eta = 0.8$, $\lambda = 1$ – clearly show that the above policy rules are far from

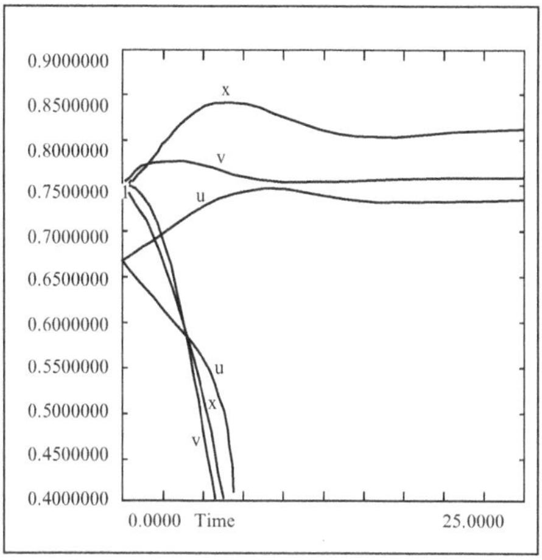

Fig. 4.12 A comparison of Classical and Keynesian fiscal policies for small values of $\mu(\pm 0.2)$

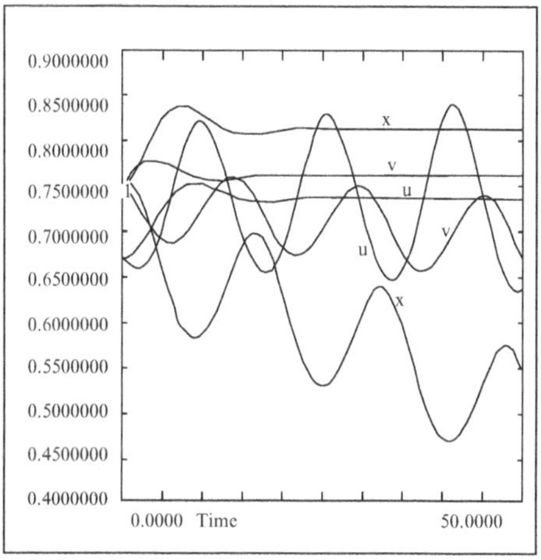

Fig. 4.13 A comparison of both policies for large values of $\mu(\pm 3)$

being equivalent over economically relevant ranges of policy parameters μ. The first figure also indicates that the private sector (when left to itself $\mu = 0$) will collapse within the time-span of 1 year. We consequently have to conclude that the above symmetry assertion is doubtful and that the Goodwin model with an independent investment behavior needs some reformulation to approach this question on a firmer basis.

4.7 The Nonequivalence of Classical and Keynesian Stabilization Policies

Inspection of (4.31)–(4.33) makes it obvious that there is no simple way of stabilizing this model with independent investment behavior in the way we have solved this task for the model (4.20) and (4.21) in Sect. 4.4. Following a proposal of Wolfstetter we therefore start to improve the model of Sect. 4.6 (with regard to its analyzed weaknesses) by making use of a simplifying limit case of this model ($\varepsilon = \infty$). This reduces the model's dynamics again to only two dynamical laws, whereby additional stabilizers of the private sector's reaction pattern can be designed much easier than for the general case (4.31)–(4.33). We shall provide here only a brief survey of the modifications to be made and of the results obtained from them.

As already stated, our first modification of model (4.31)–(4.33) concerns the investment function (4.30). On the basis of the assumption "$\varepsilon = \infty$," that is, of no adjustment lag in investment behavior, it will now read

$$I/K = g_o + c(x/x_0 - 1), \tag{4.41}$$

where $x_0(=1)$ represents normal capacity use. The new parameter c takes account of the fact that changes in capacity utilization are not necessarily transferred 1:1 into percentage investment plans.

Using (4.41), the new savings–investment equilibrium reads (cf. (4.36)–(4.38); $s_p = 1$ again)

$$\frac{I}{K} = g_o + c(x-1) = \sigma x[(1-t)(1-u) + \mu(V - V_0)] = \frac{S}{K}, \tag{4.42}$$

that is, we now get a *static* relationship between x and u, V:

$$x = \frac{c - g_o}{c - \sigma[(1-t)(1-u) + \mu(V - V_0)]}. \tag{4.43}$$

This static equation makes it possible to attempt a global dynamic analysis of the type introduced in Sect. 4.4 for the case of Say's law. As in that situation, something concerning the full-employment ceiling must be said, however. Note here that we did not use the function $i(V)$ of Sect. 4.4 to modify S/K near full-employment as in that section. This is no longer adequate in a model that differentiates between the act of saving and that of investment. It is, however, also not adequate to apply $i(V)$ in the spirit of Sect. 4.4 to simply limit investment behavior I/K thereby. Goods-market equilibrium concerns *value magnitudes* (of I and S), whereas $i(V)$ has been introduced to describe the development of the capital stock K as an index for employment near the full employment ceiling. Such an index is of the nature of a physical magnitude, that is, its growth is not necessarily properly described by I/K even in our one-good model with disembodied technical progress. When approaching full-employment the same amount of investment I may (even in such a model) be assumed to result in less and less growth of K as an index of employment, speeding up instead the growth rate of labor productivity $y = Y/L$. In addition to (4.42), we consequently should assume

$$\widehat{K} = \dot{K}/K = i(V)[g_o + c(x-1)] \neq I/K, g_o = m+n \tag{4.44}$$

in combination with $m = m(V)$, $m'(V) \geq 0$ to describe the technological side of the process of capital accumulation (the function i is of the same type as in Sect. 4.4). Summing up, the revised model consists of the following four equations:

$$\widehat{u} = h(V) - m(V) - (1-\eta(u))\lambda(u)[Au-1], \tag{4.45}$$
$$\widehat{V} = i(V)[g_o(V) + c(x-1)] - g_o(V) + \widehat{x}, \tag{4.46}$$
$$g_o(V) = m(V) + n, \tag{4.47}$$
$$x = \frac{c - g_o(V)}{c - \sigma[(1-t)(1-u) + \mu(V-V_0)]}. \tag{4.48}$$

Inspecting (4.46) in the light of Fig. 4.9 shows that the invariant domain $(0,1)^2$ of this figure need no longer have this property here, due to the occurrence of $\widehat{x}$ in (4.46) [which makes the $i(\cdot)$-reaction insufficient for this purpose]. Problems for the condition $\dot{V} < 0$ at $V = 1$ arise to the right of the $\dot{u}$= 0-isocline, cf. again Fig. 4.9. We expect that this will not endanger the stability (viability) of the dynamics (4.45) and (4.46) within the range of economically meaningful values of u, V.

We again make the assumptions of Sect. 4.4 and assume in addition $A = 1 + a = 1/u_0$, $(f-m)'(V) > 0$, $c > g_o(V)$ sufficiently[49] large, and $m(V) \equiv m =$ const near V_0. The steady-state hence is the same as before

$$V_0 = f^{-1}(m) = \frac{m+\gamma}{\rho}$$

[if $h(V) = \rho V - \gamma$], $u_0 = 1 - g/[\sigma(1-t)]$.

Logarithmic differentiation of (4.48) gives

$$\widehat{x} = \frac{g_0'(V)}{c - g_0(V)}\dot{V} + \frac{(\sigma[\mu\dot{V} - (1-t)\dot{u}])^2}{(c - \sigma[(1-t)(1-u) + \mu(V-V_0))^2]}. \tag{4.49}$$

Inserting (4.48) and (4.49) into (4.46) then leads to

$$\widehat{V} = \left[1 - \frac{g_0'(V)V}{c - g_0(V)} + \frac{\sigma \cdot \mu \cdot V}{c - \sigma[(1-t)(1-u) + \mu(V-V_0)]}\right]^{-1}$$
$$\cdot \left\{ i(V)\left(g_0(V) + c\frac{c - g_0(V)}{c - \sigma[(1-t)(1-u) + \mu(V-V_0)]} - 1\right)\right.$$
$$\left. - g_0(V) - \frac{\sigma(1-t)u}{c - \sigma[(1-t)(1-u) + \mu(V-V_0)]}\widehat{u}\right\}.$$

[49] To make this more precise demands an investigation of the positivity of $c - \sigma[(1-t)(1-u) + \mu(V-V_0)]$ for all economically meaningful values of u, V. Note here that this positivity implies an unstable reaction of capacity use x and a stable reaction of prices p to demand/supply imbalances $I \neq S$ (see (4.43)). Equation (4.43) therefore has to be interpreted with some care. I thank Peter Skott for making me aware of this point.

The assumption on $m(V)$ near V_0 and the fact that $i(V_0) = 1$ then imply for the basic case $\mu = 0$

$$\begin{aligned}\widehat{V} &= c\left(\frac{c - g_0(V)}{c - \sigma(1-t)(1-u)} - 1\right) - \frac{\sigma(1-t)}{c - \sigma(1-t)(1-u)} \cdot \dot{u} \\ &= q(u,V) - k(u)\cdot \dot{u} \ \text{ with } q_u < 0, q_V \le 0 \text{ and } k'(u) < 0.\end{aligned}$$

The above calculations now allow for the investigation of the stability of the steady state u_0, V_0

$$\begin{aligned}J_{11} &= -(1-\eta(u_0))\widehat{p}'(u_0)u_0 > 0,\\ J_{12} &= (f-m)'(V_0)u_0 > 0,\\ J_{21} &= [q_u(u_0,V_0) - k(u_0)\cdot J_{11}]V_0,\\ J_{22} &= [q_V(u_0,V_0) - k(u_0)\cdot J_{12}]V_0.\end{aligned}$$

This gives for the steady state u_0 and V_0:

$$\text{trace}\, J = -(1-\eta(u_0))\widehat{p}'(u_0)u_0 + [-k(u_0)J_{12}]V_0 \gtreqless 0$$

and

$$\begin{aligned}\det J &= J_{11}J_{12} - J_{12}J_{21}\\ &= -J_{11}k(\cdot)J_{12}u_0V_0 - (q_uJ_{12} - k(\cdot)J_{12}J_{11})u_0V_0\\ &= -J_{12}q_uu_0V_0 > 0.\end{aligned}$$

Whether the equilibrium u_0, V_0 is stable or not consequently solely depends on the strength of the destabilizing term $-(1-\eta(u_0))\widehat{p}'(u_0)u_0$ in the trace of J. In striking contrast to the results obtained in Sect. 4.6 this modified model is thus locally unstable if and only if the conflict over income distribution is sufficiently intense [$\eta(u_0) > 1$ and $\lambda(u_0)$ sufficiently large, for example]. When this situation prevails, we again get the limit cycle result of Sect. 4.4 and have consequently removed from the private sector's behavior the implausible type of instability we investigated in Sect. 4.6.

As seen earlier, an immediate application of the Poincaré–Bendixson theorem to prove this last assertion is not possible. Yet, the following computer simulations show that[50]

[50] The parameter values and functions employed are those of Sect. 4.4 with the following additional values for the new parameters: $t = 0.2, c = 1$. The labor productivity coefficient $m(V)$ rises from 0.03 to 0.05 near the full employment ceiling $V = 1$. Note with respect to Fig. 4.14, for example, that there exists also a completely instable limit cycle (1) in this picture (not shown), which separates the basin of attraction of the steady state and that of the limit cycle that shows up in this figure.

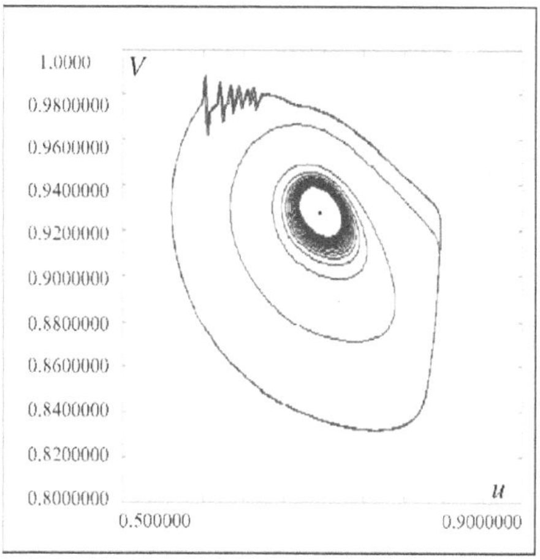

Fig. 4.14 The case of no fiscal policy

(a) The private sector exhibits again the Marxian type of reproducibility (see Sect. 4.4) despite the presence of an independent investment function of a Postkeynesian variety.
(b) The results of Sect. 4.5 on the nonequivalence of Classical and Keynesian fiscal policy carry over to this new situation where problems of effective demand and of capacity utilization are present.

This indicates that the analysis of Sect. 4.6 is not conclusive and that its symmetry assertion may rest on shakier grounds than the opposite claim.

The situation in the Fig. 4.15 is an unusual one, since there may here exist – besides the outer stable limit cycle that is generated by global forces – in the case of an asymptotically stable steady state solution a completely unstable limit cycle in the interior of it (see Fig. 4.15a, c in particular). This limit cycle encloses the basin of attraction of the steady state, which is here fairly small in the situation of no fiscal policy (Fig. 4.14). The central effect of Classical policy in the depicted situation is to enlarge this basin of attraction, thereby making the steady state of the economy "more stable." Keynesian fiscal policy on the other hand reduces the size of this basin of attraction and thus has again an adverse effect on the stability of this economy – in the sense of so-called corridor stability!

4.8 Conclusions

We have introduced in this chapter the Marxian analysis of the stability of capitalism – which in its most basic form claims its continuing reproduction on a progressive scale – by way of Marx's critique of the Classical model of capital accumulation. We have shown in this way that there exists a straightforward revision of assumptions, which leads us from the model of the Classical stationary state to the Goodwin model of a Marxian growth cycle. We have furthermore seen

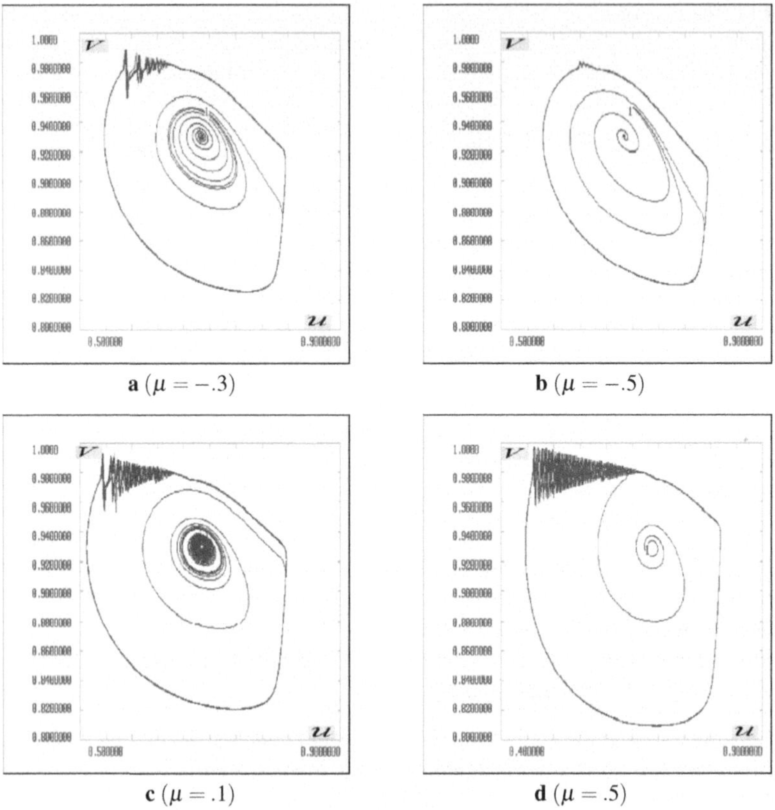

Fig. 4.15 Classical policy (**a**,**b**) and Keynesian policy (**c**,**d**)

that this approach allows an easy synthesis of Goodwin's Neomarxian and Solow's Neoclassical growth model by introducing the Marxian reserve army mechanism into the latter model. This is a point of contact between Neomarxian and Neoclassical theory, which deserves further attention and discussion far beyond this simple synthesis.

We have then made the Goodwin model more complete as a representation of the Marxian growth cycle, in that we have added to it forces which, on the one hand, destabilize its steady state, but which, on the other hand, make this dynamics globally stable (viable or reproducible). In the resulting limit cycle context, we have discussed the stabilizing power of a fiscal policy of the Phillips' proportional control type. It was shown that an orthodox policy – which slowed down accumulation in the boom phase of this growth cycle and which encouraged investment in the depression – was the better policy with respect to the stability of the model than a more Keynesian one. The explanation of this fact is, however, not difficult in the context of the Goodwin model, which relies on Say's Law in its discussion of the over- or underaccumulation of capital vis à vis the labor supply. It is therefore to be expected that results will change when a Keynesian goods demand problem is introduced into such a dynamic model.

We have seen in Sect. 4.6 that this is indeed the case making use of an investment function of the accelerator type, which deprived the private sector of the economy of any characteristic of viability – the basic story behind the Marxian growth cycle model. Disregarding these shaky grounds of the model, it was shown there that there might now be an equivalence between the Keynesian and the Classical policy rule of this model – if both are exercised with sufficient strength.

Subsequently, we have modified this IS-extension of this growth cycle model somewhat and considered anew its stability properties as well as the stabilizing powers of fiscal policy, which attempts to be countercyclical. The nonequivalence of Classical and Keynesian fiscal policies was reestablished for this revised IS-growth model. This suggest in our view that Keynesian fiscal policy can be judged as being problematic in the long run context of the conflict over income distribution on which according to Marx the viability of a capitalist economy may rest. In contrast to a more orthodox policy rule, Keynesian fiscal policy here contributes to the destabilizing factors of the model, which may explain from a different perspective why Keynesian policy has become ineffective in the seventies and the eighties of this century – the period of crisis in Keynesianism and of political success of Monetarism. This chapter thus also raises doubts on the effectiveness of Keynesian fiscal policy in the longer run.

Appendix: Stability Analysis

A. A Growth Version of Olech's Theorem

The original version of the theorem of Olech – which we shall have to modify for our purposes in the following – reads as follows [compare Ito (1978, p. 312 and the mathematical appendix of this book)]:

Theorem 1 *Given an autonomous differential equation system*

$$\dot{x} = f(x,y), \quad \dot{y} = g(x,y), \quad (x,y) \in \mathbf{R}^2 \tag{4.50}$$

with continuously differentiable functions $f, g : \mathbf{R}^2 \to \mathbf{R}$, *which possesses exactly one stationary point* $(x_0, y_0) \in \mathbf{R}^2$, *that is, a point where* $\dot{x}$ *and* $\dot{y}$ *are both zero. This equilibrium point* (x_0, y_0) *is globally asymptotically stable if the Jacobian J of (4.50) fulfills the following three conditions:*

$$\begin{aligned}
traceJ &= f_x + g_y < 0 \qquad : \forall (x,y) \in \mathbf{R}^2, \\
detJ &= f_x g_y - f_y g_x > 0 \qquad : \forall (x,y) \in \mathbf{R}^2, \\
Either\ f_x g_y &\neq 0 \quad : \forall (x,y) \in \mathbf{R}^2 \quad or \quad f_y g_x \neq 0 \quad : \forall (x,y) \in \mathbf{R}^2.
\end{aligned}$$

In place of Ito's (1978) generalization of this theorem, the following modification of it is often sufficient in the case of a dynamical system that is based on growth rate formulations.

Theorem 2 *Assume as given an autonomous differential equation system on* $\mathbf{R}^2_+$ *of the kind (4.50), the left hand side of which is, however, now based on growth rates* $\widehat{x}, \widehat{y}$ *instead of time derivatives* $\dot{x}, \dot{y}$ *and which again exhibits a unique equilibrium solution* $(x_0, y_0) \in \mathbf{R}^2$. *Assume additionally with respect to the above trace condition that* f_x, g_y *are now both strictly negative throughout. The conditions for global asymptotic stability of the equilibrium point* (x_0, y_0) *are – up to this change – the same as in preceding theorem.*[51]

Proof. Instead of $\dot{x} = f(x,y)$, for example, the following dynamic equation is now given $\widehat{x} = f(x,y)$. The transformation $z = \ln x$ then yields $\dot{z} = f(e^z, y) = \widetilde{f}(z,y)$, which (taken together with the other dynamic equation and its variable transformation) implies the above three conditions of Theorem 1 under the assumed circumstances. The interval $(0, +\infty)$, which includes by assumption x_0, will be mapped onto the entire real line $\mathbf{R}$ through this transformation of the variable x, so that the fully transformed system is again defined on the entire $\mathbf{R}^2$.

Corollary 1. *If in the above two theorems the conditions on the trace are reversed, then the equilibrium* (x_0, y_0) *is totally unstable in the large, that is, the reversed solution curves of this system all converge to the equilibrium* (x_0, y_0).

Proof. The system $(-f, -g)$ then satisfies the conditions of the preceding theorems. Its solution curves $(\widetilde{x}(t), \widetilde{y}(t))$ fulfill $(\widetilde{x}(t)), \widetilde{y}(t) = (x(-t), y(-t))$ with respect to arbitrary initial conditions $(x(0), y(0))$ and corresponding curves (x,y) of the system (f,g).

B. Liapunov's Direct Method of Stability Analysis

Liapunov's stability theorems (see also the mathematical appendix to this book) that make use of so-called Liapunov functions are discussed in Hirsch and Smale (1974) and other books on ordinary differential equations, cf. also Sect. 3.2 in this regard. We shall here briefly present a general formulation of such a theorem from Beltrami (1987, p. 42). This theorem is then illustrated by means of a typical example, a so-called cross-dual type of dynamics, which we have studied in this chapter in the specific form of the Marxian theory of capital accumulation.

Theorem 3 (Barbashin–Krasovskij[52]**).** *Let* z_o *be an isolated equilibrium of an ordinary system of differential equations, which is defined on an open set* U *of* $\mathbf{R}^2$.

[51] This theorem can be similarly formulated in cases where only part of the dynamics is based on rates of growth formulations, that is, for mixtures of the above two theorems. Only for those variables which are based on a growth rate formulation is the restriction of the domain of definition to the interval $(0, +\infty)$ then necessary and also possible.

[52] See Barbashin, E. A., & Krasovskij, N. N. (1952). On the stability of motion in the large (in Russian), Dokladü Akad. Nauk SSSR 86, 453–456. This reference has been provided to me by M. Farkas.

Let L be a Liapunov function on U, that is, a smooth nonnegative function L on U that is zero only at z_o and that fulfills $\dot{L} \leq 0$ in U. Suppose V is the subset of U in which $\dot{L} = 0$ holds. If V contains no invariant subset other than z_o itself, then z_o is asymptotically stable.

This theorem in particular implies asymptotic stability if V consists of the point z_o solely, which is the standard case for the application of this theorem in the economic literature (cf., however, the model examples of this and the next chapter for more general applications, where we also referred to the more general theorem on global stability in Hirsch and Smale (1974, p. 196) for analyzing such cases).

A cross-dual dynamics (of dimension two) is a system of two ordinary differential equations on an open set U of $\mathbb{R}^2_+$ that is of the following type:

$$\hat{x} = f(y), f' > 0, f(y_o) = 0 \quad \text{at some} y_o > 0,$$
$$\hat{y} = g(x), g' < 0, g(x_o) = 0 \quad \text{at some} x_o.$$

Such a system can easily be shown to be Liapunov-stable. For this purpose let F and G be the primitives of $f(y)/y$ and $-g(x)/x$ (which in addition fulfill $F(y_o) = 0, G(x_o) = 0$), respectively, that is, for example, $F'(y) = f(y)/y$. The function $L(x,y) = F(y) + G(x)$ then fulfills

$$L \geq 0, \dot{L} = -g(x)f(y) + f(y)g(x) \equiv 0$$

(as can be easily checked[53]) and thus provides a Liapunov function that proves the stability, but not the asymptotic stability of the equilibrium point of such a system. We note that the set V here consists of the whole range of definition U of the above dynamics.

Asymptotic stability can be obtained from such a system if the above dynamics is modified in the following way by means of two further functions p, q:

$$\hat{x} = f(y) + p(x), \quad p' \leq 0, p(x_o) = 0,$$
$$\hat{y} = g(x) + q(y), \quad q' \leq 0, q(y_o) = 0,$$

if the restricted subset V, which now derives from these extra terms, is as in the above theorem, which is the case if the function p or q is strictly decreasing. The proof of these assertions is again easy, since we now get for the time derivative of the function L (as defined above)

$$\dot{L} = -g(x)p(x) + f(y)q(y) \leq 0.$$

[53] It is 0 only at the equilibrium point of the system.

Chapter 5
Inflation, Stagflation, and Disinflation: Friedman – or Marx?

5.1 Introduction

It has often been claimed that the postwar occurrence of stagflation (stagnation + inflation[1]) represented an entirely new phenomenon, which in addition could not be explained satisfactorily by the macrodynamic approaches of that time. In a certain sense this is surely correct. Yet, it is nevertheless quite astonishing that a simple reflection of Marx's reserve army mechanism, which is not too alien to neoclassical thinking, as we have seen in Sect. 4.3, is sufficient to offer a possible explanation for such an occurrence.

Indeed, making use of the simple completion of the Goodwinian growth cycle model we have presented in Sect. 4.4, it is immediately clear that a mechanism, which in particular exhibits recurrent "overshooting" of the wage share whenever employment reaches its peak level, must lead to inflationary pressure – at least – during the early phase where employment is beginning to decline again. In the model of Sect. 4.4, this is immediately obvious because of the simple mark-up theory of inflation that has been used there. This approach – if it offers a valid explanation for cyclical movements in the distribution of income – also implies that stagflation must have existed since the time this overshooting mechanism came into operation. The lack of any observation of a (serious) stagflation before the seventies of this century need not represent a contradiction in this respect.[2]

Solow (1990, p. 38) wonders whether Goodwin's growth cycle model should be interpreted as a model of the business cycle at all: "Goodwin cycles are something else. What could that something be?" We have argued in Sects. 4.2–4.4 that the question of the economic viability of a capitalist economy is at the heart of the analysis from which this growth cycle model has emerged (Marx's Capital, Vol. I) (Fig. 5.1). Significant departures from the steady state thus have to occur to make

[1] We define the term "stagflation" here by the joint occurrence of a rising rate of unemployment as well as a rising rate of inflation, which is only one of various possibilities that exists in the context of a growing economy, see Sect. 5.2 for details.

[2] See the numerical simulations in Chap. 9.5 in this regard.

P. Flaschel, *The Macrodynamics of Capitalism: Elements for a Synthesis of Marx, Keynes and Schumpeter, Second Edition,*

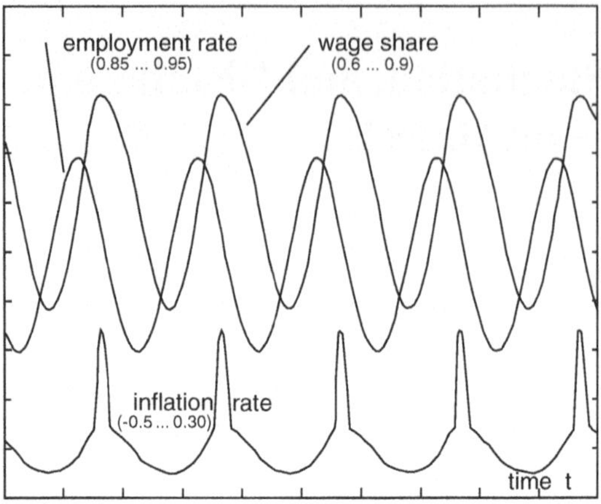

Fig. 5.1 The interaction of the rate of employment, the wage share, and the rate of inflation in the Marxian growth cycle model of Sect. 4.4

this idea applicable – for example, in the simple way of Sect. 4.4. Therefore, significant changes in economic behavior are involved in each of the four turning points of the cycle (where one variable reaches its peak while the other continues to increase or decrease). Such a regulation mechanism for the economic viability of capitalist economies surely must have changed a lot during the evolution of capitalist societies. It is therefore quite possible that the interplay of wage dynamics, price dynamics, and capital accumulation before World War II has been such that stagflation phenomena were weak in magnitude, short-lived and thus of no importance to the public and the economist. In any case, there are nearly no empirical analyses which start from or built on the Goodwin growth cycle model in this question. Empirical underpinning must therefore be put aside in the following. Instead, the above numerical simulation – of the model of Sect. 4.4 – must suffice here as an illustration of the working of this mechanism with respect to the generation of unemployment and inflation.

We observe with regard to the figure that the reaction of the rate of inflation is sometimes fairly extreme (at the end of the stagflationary period). This is due to the extreme type of reaction functions we have assumed in Sect. 4.4 for our numerical simulations.[3] Inflation that exceeds wage inflation is here the means by which it is prevented that the wage share can approach "one" in situations where employment is near to its peak level.

Modern macroeconomic theory has, however, not used this line of reasoning in its approach toward an explanation of stagflation. It instead started from the following famous passage of Friedman's (1968, p. 8) presidential address:

---

[3] Note here that the models of Chap. 4 are real models that neglect any influence from the side of money. Note furthermore that we have excluded deflation from the model of Sect. 4.4 by the choice of the mark-up mechanism.

> We have added only one wrinkle to Wicksell – the Irving Fisher distinction between the nominal and the real rate of interest. Let the monetary authority keep the nominal market rate for a time below the natural rate by inflation. That in turn will raise the nominal natural rate itself, once anticipations of inflation have become wide-spread, thus requiring still more rapid inflation to hold down the market rate. Similarly because of the Fisher-effect, it will require not merely deflation but more and more rapid deflation to hold the market rate above the initial 'natural' rate.
>
> This analysis has its close counterpart in the employment market. At any moment of time there is some level of unemployment which has the property that it is consistent with equilibrium in the structure of *real* wage rates. At that level of unemployment real wages are tending on the average to rise at a 'normal' secular rate, i.e., at a rate, that can be indefinitely maintained so long as capital formation, technological improvements, etc., remain on their long-run trends. A lower level of unemployment is an indication that there is an excess demand for labor that will produce upward pressure on real wage rates. A higher level of unemployment is an indication that there is an excess supply of labor that will produce downward pressure on real wage rates. The 'natural rate of unemployment', in other words, is the level that would be ground out by the Walrasian system of general equilibrium equations, provided there is imbedded in them the actual structural characteristics of the labor and commodity markets, including market imperfections, stochastic variability in demands and supplies, the cost of gathering information about job vacancies and labor availabilities, the cost of mobility, and so on.[4]

The *natural rate of unemployment* (NUR) and its role as a center of gravity in the movement of Phillips curves that are based upon it subsequently became one centerpiece in the analysis of inflation and unemployment, see, for example, Frisch (1983) for the details in this development. "Unnaturally" low rates of unemployment (caused by excessive monetary or fiscal policy), the inflationary pressure they can create, and the acceleration of this pressure by inflationary expectations were and are the ingredients in the modeling of the causes of stagflation from this point of view.

In his review of inflation theory, Frisch (1983) in particular presents a very simple, yet complete monetarist growth model that allows a straightforward analysis of the interactions among the growth rate of money supply, the growth rate of real income, the rate of inflation, and the rate of unemployment.[5] This model starts from a price-inflation Phillips-Curve, which is then combined with Okun's law of the employment consequences of growth and the strict quantity theory of money as the ceiling to growth and inflation to derive the dynamics of these relationships under various assumptions on inflationary expectations.

In the following investigation, we intend to show by means of simple modifications of this "monetarist" model that the building blocks of it which are responsible for its monetarist implications, i.e., the given "natural" rate of unemployment (and

---

[4] See Friedman (1968, p. 9) for an enumeration of economic forces which may induce a change in this "natural rate of unemployment" and note that he intended to use this term "to try to separate the real forces from the monetary forces."

[5] In a revised presentation of this model [see Frisch and Hof (1981, pp. 158 ff.)] it is no longer maintained that this textbook version of inflation and unemployment is "exclusively 'monetarist,' because the quantity equation is linked with the real sector through the Phillips curve and Okun's Law" [see also Dornbusch and Fischer (1987) and Turnovsky (1977) for a detailed introduction into such a baseline model of the wage-price sector and its dynamics].

the stable NUR-hypothesis that is built upon it) as well as the exogenously given trend growth of the potential output, must be rejected as overly simplified and misleading for a proper analysis of stagflation. To show this, we present in Sect. 5.2 a generalized continuous-time version of Frisch's model and a brief survey of its main implications. Section 5.3 then questions the usual interpretation of its natural or inflation-neutral rate of unemployment (NAR or NAIRU[6]) by showing that a quite different and endogenous interpretation of it may be much more plausible in explaining the high natural rates of unemployment that were observed in the recent past. Section 5.4 finally will show that the above critique of the assumed stable relationship between "unnatural" unemployment and unanticipated inflation is indeed justified, and it will also question the relevance of assuming a given growth rate of potential output. Both Sects. 5.3 and 5.4 will derive their alternative views concerning natural unemployment and its relation to inflation by integrating two different aspects of the conflict over income distribution into Frisch's model, aspects which are complementary to each other, but will not be integrated into a consistent whole in this chapter.[7]

It is thus beyond the scope of this chapter to provide a convincing and complete alternative to Frisch's prototype monetarist model. Our more modest aim here is to question radically the theoretical usefulness of starting from given rates of natural unemployment and potential output growth by assuming certain stable relations with regard to these rates. The problems which concern that part of unemployment that is not correlated to unexpected inflation and which concern capital shortage or abundance (and thus cyclical accumulation) are too important to be treated as exogenous, even in a simple model of stagflation. Yet, endogenizing these significant aspects of real economic development will imply that the stable relationship of the NUR–hypothesis type (or its conventional NAIRU reformulation) cannot sensibly be assumed.

5.2 A "Monetarist Baseline Model"

We introduce in the following[8] a non-linear version of the monetarist "textbook" model of Frisch (1983) in order to present the so-called NUR-proposition and other standard monetarist assertions based on the concept of a natural unemployment rate (NUR or NAIRU).[9] The significance of this rate – and of the proposition named after it – will be examined critically in two further sections, where especially the employed Phillips curve will be shown to be of a rather dubious nature.

---

[6] The nonaccelerating-inflation rate of unemployment which is part of the interpretation of the natural rate of unemployment $\bar{U}$ we shall make use of in the following.

[7] See Chaps. 6–8 in this regard.

[8] Sections 5.2–5.4 of this chapter are a revised version of the author's paper Flaschel (1984).

[9] cf. with regard to this model also Sargent's (1987, p. 117) footnote 1 and his subsequent attempt to provide a much more elaborate model of the Friedmanian hypotheses now considered. We will return to the Sargent model in Chaps. 6 and 7.

The following four equations represent the generalized version of Frisch's (1983) "monetarist model" we shall work with:

$$\overline{p} = \pi + g, \tag{5.1}$$

$$\pi = \eta\pi^* + f(U - \overline{U}), \tag{5.2}$$

$$\dot{U} = h(g - \overline{g}), \tag{5.3}$$

$$\dot{\pi}^* = k(\pi - \pi^*). \tag{5.4}$$

The functions f, h, and k of this model fulfill $f(0) = h(0) = k(0) = 0$ and $f' < 0$, $h' < 0$, and $k' > 0$ (η a given parameter). We here use π, π^* for actual and expected inflation. The symbols $U, \overline{U}$ denote the actual and the natural rate of unemployment (where $\overline{U}$ stands for "exogenous"). The rates $\bar{p}$, $\bar{g}$, and g finally are the rate of growth of the money supply and of real GNP ($\bar{g}$ the trend rate of growth). The endogenous variables that are determined by the model are π, π^*, g, and U.

Equation (5.1) is the well-known simple quantity theory relationship between the growth rate of the money supply $\overline{p}$, on the one hand, and the rate of inflation π as well as the growth rate of real income g, on the other hand: $\hat{M} = \hat{p} + \hat{Y}$ (the velocity of the circulation of money being constant). This equation will not be questioned here, but will be used as the simplest approach to the formulation of a monetary ceiling that is acting on the development of nominal GNP and, thus, on the sum of the rate of real growth and inflation. Equation (5.2) represents a slightly generalized version of an inflation-rate Phillips curve on the basis of a given natural unemployment rate: $\overline{U}$. The parameter η in front of π^*, the expected rate of inflation, need not be equal to "1," as it is often assumed by monetarist.[10] This equation asserts (for $\eta = 1$) a strict positive correlation between anticipation errors in the inflation rate and deviations of actual from natural unemployment[11] (which becomes less strict when η departs from unity). "Okun's Law" (5.3) describes the time rate of change $\dot{U}$ of the unemployment rate U in its dependence on the difference $g - \overline{g}$ between actual and natural growth $\overline{g} = m + n$ [the sum of labor productivity growth m and population growth n; a more detailed application of these two component rates m and n is postponed to Sect. 5.4]. The Phillips curve and Okun's Law regulate the breakup of exogenous monetary impulses into growth and inflation. They represent the field for possible modifications in the following sections, while (5.4), the standard assumption of an adaptive change in inflationary expectations,[12] will only temporarily give way to other, from an analytical point still simpler assumptions concerning the formation of such expectations.

Equations (5.1)–(5.4) can easily be reduced to the following autonomous, nonlinear system of differential equations in the variables U, π^*:

$$\dot{U} = h(\overline{p} - \eta\pi^* - f(U - \overline{U}) - \overline{g}), \tag{5.5}$$

$$\dot{\pi}^* = k(f(U - \overline{U}) - (1 - \eta)\pi^*). \tag{5.6}$$

---

[10] See, for example, the mixed empirical results surveyed in Santomero and Seater (1978, VI.A).

[11] See Dornbusch and Fischer (1987, Chap. 13) for a derivation of this curve which is not based on a price-taking behavior from the side of firms as it is assumed in the Lucas supply curve approach.

[12] See Frisch (1983, Chap. 2) for details.

Evaluated algebraically, this system implies the uniquely determined steady-state solution ($\dot{U} = \dot{\pi}^* = 0$):

$$\pi_0 = \pi_0^* = \overline{\rho} - \overline{g}, \tag{5.7}$$
$$U_0 = \overline{U} + f^{-1}((1-\eta)\pi_0^*), \tag{5.8}$$

where it is assumed that $(1-\eta)\pi_0^*$ lies within the domain of definition of the function f^{-1}. [For the sake of simplicity we will, however, generally not explicitly state such additional assumptions, as, for example, those which would assure the condition $0 \leqq U < 1$]. In the steady-state, the economy grows with the given trend $\overline{g}$ and with constant inflation (or deflation) $\pi_0 = \overline{\rho} - \overline{g}$.[13] This rate π_0 can be called the "inflation ceiling"; that is, higher inflation rates π are necessarily related with subnormal growth rates g, due to the assumed strict quantity theory of money [see Rowthorn (1980, p. 170) for further comments on this notion]. It follows that the difference between the natural unemployment rate $\overline{U}$ and the steady-state rate U_0 carries the same sign as the inflation ceiling π_0 if $\eta < 1$ holds true, which constitutes a long run trade-off between steady state unemployment and steady state inflation [it is zero – and the trade-off nonexistent – if $\eta = 1$ holds].

Dynamic evolution apart from the steady-state can easily be derived again by means of Olech's Theorem[14] [see Sect. 4.2], and it is illustrated by the phase diagram shown in Fig. 5.2.

According to Olech's Theorem, the system is globally asymptotically stable, when for the Jacobian J (or the linear part) of the right-hand side of (5.5) and (5.6), that is,

$$J = \begin{pmatrix} J_{11} & J_{12} \\ J_{21} & J_{22} \end{pmatrix} = \begin{pmatrix} -h'f' & -\eta h' \\ k'f' & -(1-\eta)k' \end{pmatrix} \tag{5.9}$$

---

[13] Assumed to be positive in the following graphical representations.

[14] An alternative stability proof (for the case $\eta = 1$) is the following: It is easy to show (for $\eta = 1$) that the function

$$L(U,\pi^*) = -\int_{\overline{U}}^{U} k(f(x-\overline{U}))\,\mathrm{d}x + \int_{\overline{\rho}-\overline{g}}^{\pi^*} h(\overline{\rho}-\overline{g}-y)\,\mathrm{d}y$$

provides a Liapunov function for this dynamics, since we have $L > 0$ for $(U,\pi^*) \neq (\bar{U}, \rho - \bar{g})$ and:

$$\begin{aligned} \dot{L} &= L_1 \cdot \dot{U} + L_2 \cdot \dot{\pi}^*, \\ &= -k(f(U-\overline{U}))h(\overline{\rho}-\pi^*-\overline{g}-f(U-\overline{U})) + h(\overline{\rho}-\overline{g}-\pi^*)\cdot k(f(U-\overline{U})), \\ &= -k(f(U-\overline{U}))\cdot h'(\cdot)(-f(U-\overline{U})) = +k(f(U-\overline{U}))\cdot f(U-\overline{U})\cdot h'(\cdot) < 0 \\ &\quad \text{for} \quad U \neq \overline{U}, \end{aligned}$$

by means of the mean value proposition (noting the fact that $\dot{L} = 0$ contains no invariant subset other than the unique equilibrium itself, cf. Sect. 4.9 on this additional stability condition). The private sector is thus shown to be (globally, Hirsch and Smale (1974, p. 196) asymptotically stable by means of a suitably chosen potential function L.

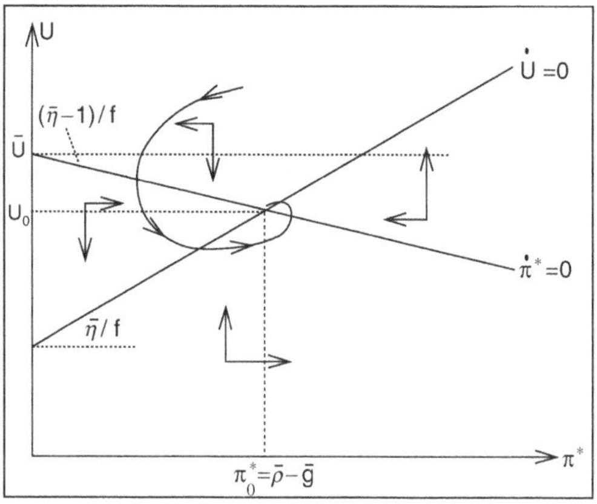

Fig. 5.2 The monetarist model in the linear case and a long-run trade-off between π_o and $U_o = \bar{U} - \frac{1-\eta}{f}\pi_o$

the inequalities trace $J = J_{11} + J_{22} < 0$, $\det J = J_{11}J_{22} - J_{12}J_{21} > 0$, and $J_{11}J_{22} \neq 0$ or $J_{12}J_{21} \neq 0$ are valid everywhere in $\mathbb{R}^2$.[15] These conditions are indeed fulfilled if $\eta \leq 1$ holds true – due to the assumptions made for system (5.1)–(5.4). In this case, the trajectories of system (5.5) and (5.6) all approach the steady-state values (5.7) and (5.8) as $t \longrightarrow \infty$.

Making use of the isoclines $\dot{U} = 0$, $\dot{\pi}^* = 0$, that is, of the curves:

$$U = \overline{U} + f^{-1}(\pi_0 - \eta\pi^*) \quad (\text{or} \quad U = \bar{U} + \frac{1}{f}(\eta\pi^* - \overline{\rho} - \overline{g}) \quad \text{in the linear case), and}$$

$$U = \overline{U} + f^{-1}((1-\eta)\pi^*) \quad (\text{or} \quad U = \bar{U} + \frac{\eta - 1}{f}\pi^* \quad \text{in the linear case),}$$

this situation can be depicted in a phase diagram for the globally stable case $\eta \leq 1$, in the way shown in Fig. 5.2.

The isoclines $\dot{U} = 0$, $\dot{\pi}^* = 0$ separate the four possible types of movement in the phase space (π^*, U).[16] The figure seems to suggest a cyclical behavior of the variables π^*, U. An analysis of the eigenvalues of (5.9), however, demonstrates that, similar to the difference equations considered in Frisch (1983), locally cyclical behavior (complex eigenvalues) will arise only under a further condition, namely for example that $h'f' < 4k'$ (for $\eta = 1$) holds true, that is, for an adaptive expectations mechanism that operates with sufficient strength. Such a cyclical dynamics implies that π^* and $-U$ cannot always run in phase, a situation which must hold true for the variables $\pi = \eta\pi^* + f(U - \overline{U}), -U$ as well.

---

[15] For an economically meaningful model we must, however, prove that the rate of unemployment stays in the interval (0,1) for any adjustment path that starts in this interval. This can, for example, be easily shown if one in addition to the above assumes that $f(-\bar{U}) = +\infty$ and $f(1-\bar{U}) = -\infty$ hold true.

[16] The $\dot{\pi}^* = 0$-isocline will be given by $U \equiv \bar{U}$, if $\eta = 1$ holds true.

The area in Fig. 5.2 below the curves $\dot{U} = 0$, $\dot{\pi}^* = 0$ shows the potential domain for a "perverse" phase synchronization (stagflation), which in fact occurs in the left hand part of this region. The larger this domain becomes, the "steeper" the curve f becomes, that is, the more sensitively the rate of inflation responds to variations of the actual rate of employment. Figure 5.2 finally shows that there exists a long-run trade-off between inflation and unemployment in the case $\eta < 1$, since the long-run equilibrium value of U_0 will be lower than $\bar{U}$ if $\pi_o > 0$ holds; it will be lower when the parameter $\bar{p}$ chosen is higher). Monetarists do not, however, believe that this situation is a proper description of the long-run of a capitalist economy. They instead generally assume $\eta = 1$, and we shall follow them in this regard from now on.

In addition to the above phase diagram, a representation of the implied dynamics in (π, U) – space is also of interest – to properly locate the area of actual stagflation. To provide such a representation let us assume for simplicity that the above model is described by linear functions, that is, we replace the functions f, h, and k by suitably chosen parameters $-f$, $-h$, and k. It is then easy to derive the following system of differential equations from the above model:[17]

$$\dot{\pi} = -fh(\bar{g} - \bar{p} + \pi) + kf(\bar{U} - U),$$
$$\dot{U} = h(\bar{g} - \bar{p} + \pi).$$

These differential equations, of course, must imply the same stability properties for the above model and they give rise to the phase diagram in the actual magnitudes π, U shown in Fig. 5.3.[18]

It is easy to see that the stagflation area will be enlarged by a decrease of the parameter h or an increase of the parameter k. We also, once again, can see that stagflation is caused by "unnaturally" low unemployment, which gives rise to an increasing rate of inflation and thus to rising inflationary expectations. As expectations about inflation try to catch up with actual inflation, the rate of unemployment must

---

[17] Making use of $\dot{\pi} = \dot{\pi}^* - f\dot{U}$.

[18] Note that the positions of the isoclines of this diagram both depend on the rate of growth of the money supply, and not only the curve $\dot{U} = 0$ as it were true in Fig. 5.2. Recall that we have defined stagflation at the beginning of this chapter by a rising rate of unemployment ($\dot{U} > 0$) plus a rising rate of inflation ($\dot{\pi} > 0$), see Fig. 5.3 (this definition may also be extended to phases where one of the two rates remains constant). In the case of the above model this implies as a further feature of stagflation that the rate of growth must be less than normal, and in the setup of the next section it implies that the capacity utilization rate of firms will be declining as well. In Sect. 5.4, however, a rising rate of unemployment will come about in situations where the capital stock (which is there always fully employed) will grow with a rate that is lower than the steady state rate $n + m$. Our use of the term stagflation thus does not necessarily coincide with situation where

- both inflation and the rate of unemployment are above their steady state values, or
- U is rising and π is above its steady state value, or where
- the rate of growth g is falling and the rate of inflation π is rising.

These situations will define different subdomains in the above phase space (Fig. 5.3) in general. In our use of the word stagflation characterizes the initial phases of recessions and depressions – where in the above model the rate of employment is still above the steady state rate of employment, see Fig. 5.3.

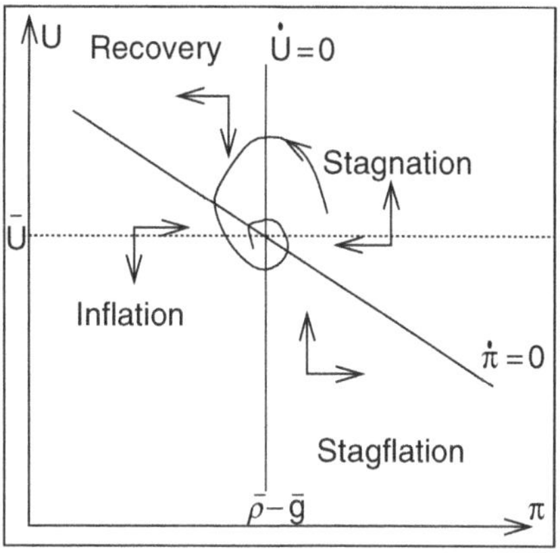

Fig. 5.3 Areas of pure inflation, stagflation, and stagnation in the monetarist model

begin to rise again (from the low level it had reached). This slows down the further increase in the rate of inflation until this rate starts falling again. It must become equal to the still rising expected rate of inflation exactly when the "normal" level of unemployment $\bar{U}$ is again reached. Before this point is passed, however, the actual rate of inflation must indeed have started falling, since it is only in this way that an adaptive expectations mechanism can fully catch up with the actual rate of inflation. From this point onwards we enter the region where only stagnation prevails, which in turn will come to an end when the natural rate of inflation $\pi = \bar{\rho} - \bar{g} = \pi_0$ is passed.

To start the discussion on the NUR-hypothesis (5.2), the monetarist type of Phillips curve, let us reconsider this equation in more detail. The NUR-hypothesis[19] contradicts the conventional Phillips-curve trade-off in so far as it implies [for $\eta = 1$, i.e., in the monetarist case] "that a fixed relation exists, not between economic aggregates and the rate of inflation, but between these aggregates and the difference between the actual rate of inflation and expectations about the rate of inflation" (Grossman, 1980, pp. 6/7). The overly simplified Phillips-curve menu of Samuelson–Solow type is thereby modified to a quite different kind of stable relationship.

This new hypothesis is generally considered to derive from the assumption of a natural rate of unemployment $\overline{U}$ à la Friedman: "ground out by the Walrasian system of general equilibrium equations" (see our above quotation) if interpreted in terms of real world imperfections. Deviations of unemployment U from natural unemployment $\overline{U}$ are then viewed to correlate negatively with deviations of actual inflation π from expected inflation π^* and this is explained by (various types of) microeconomic misperceptions of the behavior of aggregate magnitudes, which may prevail among the agents of this Walrasian economy.[20] This microeconomic general-equilibrium motivation of the NUR-hypothesis (5.2), $\eta = 1$, might be called the *Speculative Walrasian Natural Unemployment Rate* (SW-NUR)

[19] Here in fact also the NAIRU.

[20] See Cukierman (1984), for example.

from a macroeconomic point of view as it is developed in the present chapter.[21] Disregarding this speculative Arrow and Debreu background of the structural equation (5.2),[22] however, means that this equation then simply states that natural unemployment prevails if and only if inflation is fully anticipated and that deviations from this unemployment rate correlate in a stable and predictable way with unanticipated inflation. We shall denote this *black-box* type description of the natural rate hypothesis by BB-NUR in the following. Finally, the natural rate of unemployment may also be defined as that rate which is compatible with the steady-state development of a given macroeconomic system. Following the literature,[23] this very broad definition of natural unemployment will be called the *nonaccelerating inflation rate of unemployment* (NAIRU) in the following.[24] All three interpretations, the SW-NUR, the BB-NUR, and the NAIRU, are used interchangeably in Frisch (1983).[25] However, no complete formal derivation of the SW-NUR-approach à la Friedman has been presented to date in the context of a monetary growth model. Consequently, this definition will only be of minor importance in our examination of the NUR, the NUR-hypothesis, and the NUR-proposition, to which this chapter is devoted.

On the basis of the NUR-hypothesis (5.2), restricted to the case $\eta = 1$, the following set of core monetarist assertions very easily follow from the above model (5.1)–(5.4):

A. *Short-term proposition*: If a given steady-state is disturbed by an increased rate of monetary expansion $\bar{\rho}$, the actual unemployment rate will fall below the natural rate, if expectations concerning inflation (were to) remain at the initially correct level (e.g., $\pi_0 = 0$). Monetary policy can under such circumstances indeed lower the rate of unemployment below the natural rate.
B. *Neutrality proposition*: Every such disturbance of the steady-state moves, after the adaptive expectation adjustment process (5.4) sets in, toward a new steady-state (with inflation $\bar{\rho} - \bar{g}$) and will consequently result, in the end, in a positive or higher rate of inflation solely (if the original increase in the rate of money supply is maintained).
C. *Acceleration proposition*: Every attempt of the monetary authority to counter this long-run neutrality to perpetuate the employment effect of the short run requires a continuously increasing rate of monetary expansion $\bar{\rho}$, which implies accelerating inflation.
D. *Stagflation Proposition*: If such a behavior of the monetary authority is stopped or even reversed toward a restrictive monetary policy, there will be at least one subsequent period of stagflation, before the steady state can be reached once

[21] Since it is not integrated into such a model.

[22] Since it lacks any thorough proof in a consistently formulated model of the Arrow–Debreu variety.

[23] See Blanchard and Fischer (1989, p. 544) for example.

[24] Note here that the NAIRU can be defined in any model that allows for steady growth. It therefore does not depend on a particular view on the economy as it is implicitly underlying a structural equation such as the BB-NUR.

[25] Compare in particular his page 49 and note that a partial justification for his formulations is provided by the NUR-proposition to be presented below.

again. It follows that the above course of monetary policy is contradictory and damaging to the economy.

E. *Long-run-expectations proposition*: If the expectations regarding inflation, in contrast to (5.4), are oriented toward the actual inflation ceiling π_0 (= π^*), then all adjustments to the steady-state $\overline{U}$, $\overline{g}$ are monotonic and independent of the parameter $\overline{p}$, that is, of its variations.

F. *NUR-proposition*: If inflation is always fully anticipated, the economy (5.1)–(5.3) cannot depart from the steady-state.

G. *Regressive expectations proposition*: If expectations are governed by $\dot{\pi}^* = k(\bar{p} - \bar{g} - \pi) = k(\pi_o - \pi), k > 0$, the dynamics of the system will be determined by the single differential equation $\dot{\pi} = (k + fh)(\bar{p} - \bar{g} - \pi)$ and will be of a monotonically stable type.[26]

H. *Rational Expectations Limit Proposition*: If agents attempt to learn the above parameter $k + fh$ (which determines the evolution of the actual change in the rate of inflation in this model), they will drive the value of k and $k + fh$ toward infinity, which will lead to an infinitely rapid adjustment of the rate of inflation towards its steady state value in the end (i.e., the case of the NUR-proposition).

These statements immediately follow from what has been shown for the system (5.1)–(5.4), if one observes that it suffices to discuss the differential equation (5.5) when considering (A) and (E) [in the latter case the movement of the unemployment rate U is simply governed by $\dot{U} = h(f(U - \overline{U}))$], that (5.5) is no longer in effect when (C) is under consideration, and that (B) and (D) has already been treated in the stability analysis following (5.7) and (5.8). Propositions (G) and (H) finally only show how proposition (F) can be obtained by taking regressive expectations to their perfect foresight limit (as in Dornbusch's (1976) model of overshooting exchange rate dynamics, yet without any overshooting result in the present situation).[27]

Proposition (F) – which is trivial in the context of the model (5.1)–(5.4) – states that the BB-NUR- and the NAIRU-definitions of the natural unemployment rate are here in fact equivalent. This, however, is mainly due to the overly simplified hypothesis (5.2), the monetarist type of a stable Phillips curve relationship. Furthermore, the determination of natural unemployment $\overline{U}$ is left completely unexplained in the context of the above model. Should this be "standard" for the monetarist view on the dynamics of a capitalistic economy (which we believe to be the case), it can be criticized for at least two reasons. First, since the natural rate $\overline{U}$ is exogenously given, we are still free to associate any interpretation with it, which is consistent with the structural equations (5.1)–(5.4), see the next section for a detailed proposal in this direction. We need not accept the SW-NUR of Friedman and others, unless it

[26] Note that we have assumed here a linear form of the Phillips curve and of Okun's law once again. Note also that such an approach demands a reinterpretation of the symbol π^* (as the expected change in the momentarily given rate of inflation π), which also demands a respecification of the Phillips curve of the model as follows: $\dot{\pi} = \dot{\pi}^* - f\dot{U}$ [see Dornbusch (1976) for a formally similar treatment there of the expected rate of depreciation].

[27] These propositions are immediately obtained from the respecification of the model we considered in the preceding footnote.

is integrated for example into the above model in an acceptable way.[28] This, however, is a task which is neither easy nor has it seriously been approached, which is the reason why we designated the Friedman interpretation of the natural rate $\overline{U}$ as speculative.[29] Second, the assumed fixity of the equation which represents the NUR-hypothesis (5.2) bears a close resemblance to the overly simplified stability assumption for the Samuelson–Solow modification of the original Phillips curve, which has justifiably been attacked by monetarists for its crude menu-view of the problem of unemployment and inflation. We shall see in Sect. 5.4 that a simple Classical model with an endogenous determination of the growth of potential output is sufficient to demonstrate that a stable relationship of the type (5.2) cannot sensibly be assumed.

Summing up the discussion of this section, propositions (A)–(G) can be illustrated as given in Fig. 5.4:[30]

This diagram shows again the futility, in the context of the present model, of wanting to operate for longer periods below the $\dot{\pi}^* = 0$-line, that is, below natural unemployment $\overline{U}$. Note here that the $\dot{U} = 0$-isocline must continuously shift to the right during process (C), so that in giving up the goal of reaching unnaturally low rates of unemployment, the dynamic process is again left to itself at the unfavorable end of the stagflation area. Furthermore, situations (C)–(F) very well illustrate the crucial role that the Phillips curve (5.2) plays in this model: together with Okun's Law (5.3) it regulates the economy in such a way that temporary deviations from a given trend will always be corrected in the end; they indeed will be eliminated the quicker, the more foresight we introduce into the process by which inflationary

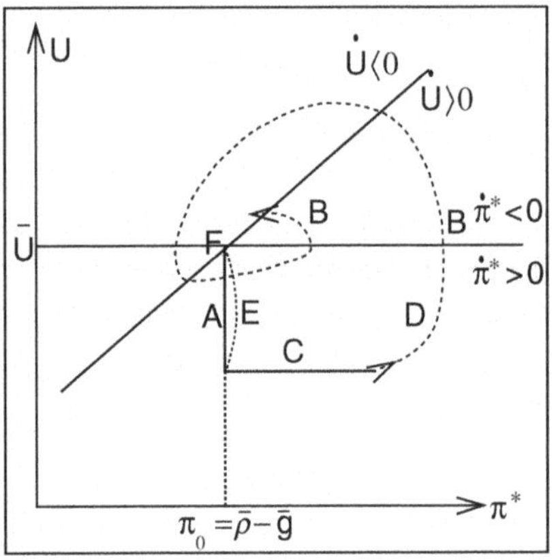

Fig. 5.4 Short term effects, A; neutrality, B; acceleration, C; stagflation, D; long term expectations, E; and perfect foresight, F

---

[28] An attempt to do this from a Post-Keynesian perspective is provided in the now following section.

[29] See, however, Pissarides (1990) for a recent approach towards a steady-state theory of unemployment by means of the so-called Beveridge curve.

[30] We here assume for simplicity that the rate of growth of the money supply is the same initially as in the end (and larger than the trend rate of growth of output). Intermediate regimes of money supply growth rates are thus only implicitly present in the Fig. 5.4.

expectations are formed. Note finally the striking contrast that exists between this model of an asymptotically stable private sector of the economy and the Hicksian trade cycle view of the stability of the private sector (see Sect. 3.7).

A final observation: One might argue that the monetarist model we have considered in this section is a too simple one in order to allow for a fair treatment of basic monetarist propositions. More elaborate models may be more convincing in this regard, such as Sargent's (1973) and Sargent and Wallace's (1975) IS-LM study of the role of rational as opposed to adaptive expectations. Yet, inspecting these models immediately shows that they heavily depend on a supply side description (à la Lucas) of the following type:[31]

$$\ln Y_t = \ln K_t + \gamma(\ln p_t - \ln p_t^*).$$

Such an approach, on the one hand, does not differ from the NUR-hypothesis of this section in a significant way. On the other hand, and much worse, this assumption on the supply side of the model amounts to assuming that the IS-LM part, which is appended to it, is operating in a near to full employment environment. Basic textbook representations – such as Dornbusch and Fischer's (1987, Chap. VII) – then already clearly show that there is not much left for a Keynesian IS-LM approach and its typical policy implications in such an environment. Sargent's (1973) conclusion is that such a model's

> structural equations ... do not differ from those of the standard IS-LM-Phillips-curve models used to rationalize Keynesian prescriptions for activist, countercyclical monetary, and fiscal policies. In fact, the statics of the model with fixed or exogenous expectations about the price level are of the usual Keynesian variety.

This statement is misleading (due to the assumed narrow definition of aggregate supply) and it is also in general wrong, as we shall show by means of a detailed analysis of Sargent's (1987) elaborate deterministic IS-LM growth model in Chaps. 6 and 7.

5.3 Conflict About Income Distribution and the "Natural" Unemployment Rate

We have shown in the last section how standard monetarist assertions can be derived from a simple macroeconomic model. These assertions will not be significantly altered if more flexible market mechanisms are allowed for to deal with aggregate demand shocks – as long as the essence of the NUR-hypothesis (5.2) is preserved, that is, as long as deviations from a predetermined natural (or equilibrium) rate of unemployment can only occur *in combination with* unanticipated inflation (or price changes). The NUR and the hypothesis built upon it consequently represent the critical steps in the monetarist arguments against an active monetary policy – or other types of demand management to combat high unemployment rates – at least with regard to their natural core.

---

[31] We neglect Sargent's stochastic term in the following equation.

In the light of existing Walrasian general equilibrium models, the idea of a natural unemployment rate à la Friedman's SW-NUR is here regarded as speculative not only because of the proposed problematic extensions of Arrow–Debreu theory it demands, but also because

> this theory has nothing simple to offer in answer to the question why is the share of wages, or of profits, what it is? ... [because, P.F.] social class is not an explanatory variable of neoclassical theory. The latter is not formulated in terms of workers and capitalists but in terms of inputs and outputs. This lack of contact between the economic theory and sociological reality may well be the most damaging criticism of the neoclassical construction.
>
> (Hahn, 1972; p. 2).

The commonly employed identification of the noninflationary natural rate of unemployment NAIRU with a Walrasian equilibrium rate of unemployment SW-NUR consequently must be regarded as premature, unless some prototype and complete model is presented in which a thorough endogenous description of this rate is given. Otherwise, the SW-NUR-view of the NUR-hypothesis (5.2) should rather be dismissed as being unfounded. There then remains only the BB-NUR-attitude to justify the model (5.1)–(5.4) of Sect. 2. This, however, is a black box description of the NUR, which not only allows a variety of monetarist interpretations of it, but also makes an interpretation admissible that is explicitly based on the existence of social classes. The spectrum of beliefs about the nature of inflation described in Laidler (1981, pp. 7f.) in fact can be enriched by a version which sharply differs from any monetarist one without changing the formal structure of (5.1)–(5.4) on which Frisch's monetarist model is based. We shall demonstrate in this section that this model indeed allows such an extremely different interpretation of its basic premise, the natural rate of unemployment $\overline{U}$.

The following new interpretation of (5.1)–(5.4) has also the advantage that the determination of the rate $\overline{U}$ is now explained by the model itself. This eliminates a grave weakness from the monetarist model of the causes of unemployment, though it, of course, is but a first step in the critical evaluation of the NUR-hypothesis and of the monetarist theory of the "business cycle" built upon it. Further steps in this direction will be taken in Sect. 4, where the NUR-hypothesis itself is criticized as representing a structural equation, which is of too crude a type.

The variation of the "monetarist model" (5.1)–(5.4) to be treated here closely follows some concepts developed in Rowthorn (1980).[32] Equation (5.1), the "budget equation" for inflation and growth, as well as (5.4), the adaptive process by which expectations about inflation are formed, will remain unquestioned in this model variant. Yet, to derive (5.2) and (5.3), which essentially determine the division of a monetary impulse $\overline{p}$ into inflation π and growth g, the following new assumptions about pricing and output behavior will be made. Instead of Frisch's Okun-Law (5.3), we shall employ now the version of Okun's (1970) original specifications of this law [see his page 136]:

[32] An alternative, detailed, and closely related analysis of conflicting income claims is given in Meade (1982), see in particular his appendix A. Furthermore, such a "conflicting claims" approach to steady state unemployment has also been investigated recently by authors as Layard and Bean (1989) among others.

$$\frac{V}{\overline{V}} = \left(\frac{Y}{Y^{\mathrm{p}}}\right)^{d} = \Theta^{d}, \qquad d > 0. \tag{5.10}$$

Here, V represents the rate of employment and $\overline{V}$ its trend value (a given parameter). Deviations of V from its trend are according to this "law" positively correlated with the degree of capacity utilization $\Theta = Y/Y^{\mathrm{p}}$ of the capital stock K. Logarithmic differentiation of (5.10) yields the equation by which we shall replace Frisch's equation (5.3):

$$\widehat{V} = d(\widehat{Y} - \widehat{Y}^{\mathrm{p}}) = d(g - \overline{g}^{\mathrm{p}}) \tag{5.11}$$

[note that Okun assumes $\overline{V} \equiv 0.96$, that is, $\widehat{\overline{V}} \equiv 0$ in particular]. As is evident from its above formulation, this equation again assumes a constant trend growth of potential output Y^{p} (a trend growth rate $\overline{g}^{\mathrm{p}}$).

Equation (5.11) only differs from (5.3), in that $\dot{V} = -\dot{U}$ has been replaced by $\widehat{V}$. Our fundamental deviation from Frisch's model (5.1)–(5.4) concerns its Phillips curve (5.2), which is here derived from the following assumption about how the inflation rate π is formed ($\eta = 1$ again):

$$\pi = c(\Pi^{*} - \Pi) + \pi^{*}, \qquad c > 0. \tag{5.12}$$

In this equation, the symbols π^{*} and π signify expected and actual inflation rates as before, while Π, Π^{*} denote the actual and the target profit share of capitalists [cp. Rowthorn (1980, pp. 150ff.) for further details on this approach]. Equation (5.12) indicates that the expected inflation rate undergoes a correction that is proportional to the aspiration gap $\Pi^{*} - \Pi$ in its transmission into actual inflation π.

To make this type of Phillips curve (5.12) analytically applicable, the determinants of the aspiration gap remain to be stipulated. Rival income claims of capitalists and workers, expressing themselves in the target share Π^{*} and in the momentary wage share $u = 1 - \Pi$, can be seen as being dependent on the demand for the commodities supplied by the respective party. That is, they can be viewed as dependent on the degree of utilization Θ of the capital stock and on the degree of "utilization" V of the labor force, respectively:

$$\Pi^{*}(\Theta), \Pi^{*\prime} > 0, \quad u(V), u' > 0. \tag{5.13}$$

Income claims are therefore here simply regulated by the respective utilization of capital and labor. But according to (5.10), the employment rate V can be substituted for Θ in $\Pi^{*}(\Theta)$ without causing a change in the assumed mode of reaction $\Pi^{*\prime} > 0$. The final form of the Phillips curve of this section consequently is

$$\pi = c(\Pi^{*}(V) - (1 - u(V))) + \pi^{*} = c(\Pi^{*}(V) + u(V) - 1) + \pi^{*}, \tag{5.14}$$

a form which, if one wishes to do so, can be interpreted as a specific foundation of the Phillips curve (5.2) we used in Sect. 2.[33]

[33] Cf. Dornbusch and Fischer (1987) for an alternative, but related foundation.

The analogy to (5.2) can be made even more obvious if one defines as natural (in applying the BB-NUR to determine natural unemployment) that rate V_0 which implies a wage share $u(V_0)$ and a target share $\Pi^*(V_0)$ which are compatible with each other as no additional inflation effects will arise apart from the inflationary expectations π^* in this case. This rate V_0 is defined by $u(V_0) + \Pi^*(V_0) = 1$ and it is uniquely determined [see (5.13)]. It will exist if $u(0) + \Pi^*(0) < 1 < u(1) + \Pi^*(1)$ holds true. By means of this rate, (5.14) can be rewritten in the following way:

$$\pi = c(\Pi^*(V) + u(V) - (\Pi^*(V_0) + u(V_0))) + \pi^*, \qquad (5.15)$$

which is the kind of Phillips curve we used in the preceding section [if V and V_0 are replaced by $1 - U$ and $1 - U_0$].

The important point with regard to this curve is that its natural rate V_0 [in general $\neq \overline{V}$, the rate which underlies the Okun curve (5.10)!] is no longer exogenously given and of the SW-NUR-type. Social classes and their particular interests – and no longer households and firms subordinated to them – are now at the center of the analysis. Conflict over income distribution is regulated by the respective power of the two classes, here measured in terms of the utilization rates Θ and V, and gives explicit content to the black box unemployment rate of the BB-NUR approach. Monetarists may – and surely will – not be content with the way we have filled the gap given by their black-box rate $\overline{U}$. Yet, they cannot disqualify the above additions to Frisch's monetarist model simply by pointing to the complex Walrasian character of their natural rate $\overline{U}$. Complexity is not an excuse that allows one to treat a rate of unemployment of more than 5% as exogenous in a complete model of macroeconomic interdependence. If a noninflationary natural rate of unemployment of basically Walrasian type worth mentioning really exists in a monetary economy,[34] then ways have to be found by which their essential determinants can be treated explicitly in a macroeconomic model of unemployment and inflation.

It should be obvious from our discussion that up to our endogenous determination of the rate $\overline{U}(= 1 - V_0)$, Frisch's standard model (5.1)–(5.4) has undergone practically no revision. Equations (5.14) and (5.11) now simply replace (5.2) and (5.3). Thus, (5.5) and (5.6) can be replaced by

$$\widehat{V} = d(\overline{p} - \pi^* - c(\Pi^*(V) + u(V) - 1) - \overline{g}^p), \qquad (5.16)$$
$$\dot{\pi}^* = k(c(\Pi^*(V) + u(V) - 1)). \qquad (5.17)$$

In view of this formal correspondence, the entire analysis presented in Sect. 5.2 is also valid for this model and need not be repeated here.

The natural unemployment rate has often been estimated in the literature as, for example, already in Batchelor (1981), principally on the basis of the NUR-hypothesis (5.2). The core result of his calculations is roughly summarized and updated – for the case of the German economy – in Fig. 5.5.[35]

---

[34] See Malinvaud (1984) in this regard.

[35] See Chiarella and Flaschel (1998) for an endogenous modeling and simulation of the evolution of the NUR in time.

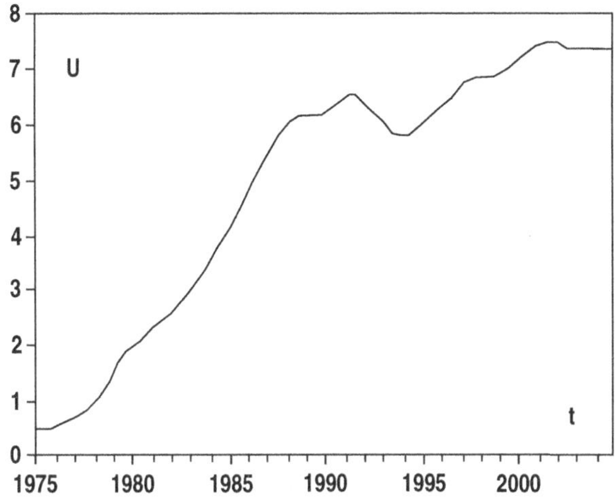

Fig. 5.5 The rise of the natural rate of unemployment in Germany

Should we conclude on the basis of this empirical evidence (which in its qualitative features is confirmed by other empirical studies) that the Walrasian world we are suggested to live in (by employing Friedman's SW-NUR as interpretation of Equation (5.2)) has become progressively imperfect to ground out this steep rise in natural unemployment? We do not think that such a conclusion – nor its basis – makes much sense. Our alternative interpretation of the observed behavior of the natural rate $\overline{U} = 1 - V_0$ (on the basis of the above reformulation of Frisch's model) is that situations of depressed growth $\overline{g}^{\mathrm{p}}$ of potential output (the occurrence of which still requires explanation) may go hand-in-hand with upward shifts in the aggressiveness of capitalist' or laborers' income claims, due to the fact that there is now less (additional) income to distribute. Such upward shifts imply that the natural rate $U_0 = 1 - V_0$ will rise, and will cause further inflationary pressure at the current rate of employment $U = 1 - V$. This pressure can be reduced – if the fight against inflation becomes of primary importance for the political decision maker – either by a wage-price freeze or by allowing for idle labor and capital, thus reversing in the end the upward shift in income claims behavior. Natural unemployment consequently should then fall again after a certain period of high unemployment and low capacity utilization – at least if there have been no severe social consequences like, for example, the development of a hard core of unemployables. We conjecture that it is this view and not Friedman's speculative Walrasian view that implicitly underlies the anti-inflationary programs put into effect in the past. This is documented to some extent by the indifference of politicians towards the rapid rise of unemployment, an attitude which can hardly be justified on the grounds of wanting to break inflationary expectations π^* alone. The disciplinary function of the $U - \overline{U} = V_0 - V$ term in the Phillips curve (5.14) is in our opinion fairly well-known, though this is seldom officially expressed.

A thorough analysis of the views expressed above, however, cannot be supplied in the context of this chapter, which mainly addresses a critique of a particular monetarist hypothesis by formulating simple alternative views, which are at least equally plausible as this monetarist construction, but which nevertheless still need elaboration. A further step in this direction is the observation that the monetarist NUR-hypothesis (5.2) is still utilized (at least formally) in the above modification of Frisch's "monetarist model" and that potential output grows at a predetermined rate $\overline{g}^p$ in this variant, too. The weaknesses still present in this section's approach to unemployment and inflation also find expression in the fact that the development depicted above concerning the natural rate $\overline{U}$ (Fig. 5.5) must be exclusively attributed to rising aggressiveness of income claims. Such a monocausal explanation of the rise in that part of unemployment which cannot be attributed to erroneous expectations about inflation $\pi^* - \pi$ is not very convincing. We need further arguments to help explain this component of unemployment.

Some such arguments will be offered in the following section using a model that discusses the consequences of the conflict over income distribution with regard to natural growth $\overline{g}^{\mathrm{p}}$, now, however, by neglecting the problem of capacity utilization Θ considered in this section. The result of this discussion will be that the NUR-hypothesis should be completely dismissed because it is not a sensible and stable relationship. This is to say that it should not be used to measure the core of the unemployed (however defined).

The models of this and the following sections stress different aspects of the conflict over income distribution, which should be integrable (but are not integrated in this chapter) by treating simultaneously the problems of the underutilization of existing capital and its varying growth over time (see Sects. 4.6 and 4.7 for an example).

5.4 A Classical Modification of the "Baseline Model"

We have seen in the last section how the interpretation of the natural unemployment rate of the BB-NUR-Approach can be radically changed and why it will depart from Okun's (1970. p. 137) exogenous benchmark rate of $\bar{V} = 4\ \%$ unemployment. The results obtained raise questions for Okun's procedure to identify this benchmark with a reasonable target for anti-inflationary politics. This latter target rate heavily depends on the developments in the conflict over income distribution, which should not be included in an output–employment relationship of mainly technological nature.

Okun (1970, pp. 132 ff.) qualifies his treatment of the technological relationship $V = 0.96(\frac{Y}{Y^{\mathrm{p}}})^{\mathrm{d}}$, however, by means of a variety of additional observations, which are normally ignored when this "law" is used for economic model building. For example, in Okun (1970, p. 137) it is observed that the growth rate g^{p} of potential output Y^{p} was not uniform throughout his sample period 1947–1960 and that "the failure to use one year's potential fully can influence future potential GNP: to the extent that low utilization rates and accompanying low profits ... hold down investment ..., the growth of potential GNP will be retarded." [see p. 134].

However, profits and thus investment may also vary even if actual output always coincides with its potential level – due to changes in income distribution! Such a possibility is ignored in the models of Sects. 5.2 and 5.3, where the growth rate of potential output $\overline{g}$ has been treated as exogenous, not subject to a retardation process at all. It is not possible in this section to present a thorough extension of the model of Sect. 5.3, which incorporates the type of retardation mentioned in Okun (1970). Instead, we shall ignore problems of the underutilization of capital below and will concentrate our interest on a further mechanism – the profit-squeeze mechanism – by which fluctuations of potential output may be generated ($Y \equiv Y^{\mathrm{p}}, \Theta \equiv 1$ in the following). This choice has the advantage that it can be treated in an analytically well-established way. Furthermore, this influence on potential output growth is of a sufficiently sweeping character to question radically the NUR-hypothesis of Sect. 5.2 (and its implications), which is the main intention of this chapter. And finally, the classical investment cycle derived from it solely abstracts from the problems of deficient demand and idle capital and, therefore, does not exclude a later integration of these effects into its dynamics, for example, along the lines we have sketched in the preceding section.

The two models we have considered so far do not allow the possibility that potential output growth g^{p} varies with actual output Y and its rate of growth g. The dynamics considered above thus should be applied only to an analysis of the short-run. In the medium run it is no longer possible to assume the rate g^{p} as given.[36] To endogenize this rate we shall – as has already been stated – start from a simple Classical view of capital accumulation, namely Goodwin's (1967) Classical growth cycle model. This model will now be appropriately modified to make it comparable to Frisch's monetarist model, that is, to allow equally well for the discussion of the impact of exogenous monetary impulses on real growth and inflation. The following description of our modification of Goodwin's original model can be brief and will concentrate on its implications in the main (see Chap. 4 for the details of such an approach).

Assume as given a conventional aggregate production relationship of the fixed coefficient form which is subject to Harrod neutral technical change. Assume furthermore a classical savings function $S = s_{\mathrm{p}} \Pi Y$ with $0 < s_{\mathrm{p}} \leq 1$, where ΠY denotes profit income. Assume finally that ex-ante investment is identical with ex-ante saving, so that the Keynesian difficulties of deficient demand (and of idle capital $\Theta < 1$, see Sect. 5.3) can be ignored. On the basis of these standard assumptions of growth theory, we get from the tautological relation

$$V = \frac{Y^{\mathrm{p}}}{\frac{Y^{\mathrm{p}}}{L} \cdot L^{\mathrm{s}}}$$

[36] As this rate refers to potential output and not to the average or steady state growth rate of output.

the following set of relationships between the rate of change of the employment rate $\widehat{V}$, the growth rate of potential output $g = g^{\mathrm{p}}$, of labor productivity growth m, of labor force growth n, and the share of wages $u = WL/(pY)$:

$$\begin{aligned}\widehat{V} &= g - m - n,\\ &= \widehat{K} - (m+n),\\ &= s_{\mathrm{p}}(1-u)\frac{Y^{\mathrm{p}}}{K} - (m+n),\\ &= s_{\mathrm{p}}\frac{1-u}{v} - (m+n).\end{aligned} \tag{5.18}$$

These equations immediately follow from our above assumptions of a constant capital-output ratio $v = K/Y = 1/\sigma$ and a Solovian investment behavior $\dot{K} = I \equiv S$ based on earned profits $(1-u)Y$ and a constant savings propensity s_{p} [m, n the given rates of growth of labor productivity y and of the labor force L^{s}]. Equation (5.18) replaces Okun's Law (5.11) by endogenizing capital accumulation K in place of capacity utilization Θ. And instead of the NUR-hypotheses (5.2) and (5.15) we here return to Phillips' original money-wage specification of this curve, augmented by a term that reflects inflationary expectation (W the money wage):[37]

$$\widehat{W} = \eta\pi^* + \widetilde{f}(V), \quad \widetilde{f}' > 0, \widetilde{f}(\bar{V}) = 0, \bar{V} = 1 - \bar{U} \in (0,1). \tag{5.19}$$

As in Sects. 5.2 and 5.3, these two equations are again supplemented by the strict quantity theory of money

$$\overline{\rho} = \pi + g = \pi + s_{\mathrm{p}}\frac{1-u}{v} \tag{5.20}$$

and by an adaptive mechanism for inflation rate expectations

$$\dot{\pi}^* = k(\pi - \pi^*), \qquad k' > 0, k(0) = 0. \tag{5.21}$$

Utilizing the definitional relation $\widehat{u} = \widehat{W} - \pi - m$, these four equations form a complete model in the four state variables V, u, π, andπ^* [when the Phillips curve (5.19) is reformulated as $\widehat{u} = \eta\pi^* + \widetilde{f}(V) - \pi - m$ by means of the above definitional relationship].

The modifications of Frisch's monetarist model (5.1)–(5.4) thus concern, as in Sect. 5.3, again only the form of division of a monetary impulse $\overline{\rho}$ into inflation[38] and growth, now by means of the following dynamic equations (5.18) and (5.19):

$$\widehat{V} = s_{\mathrm{p}}\frac{1-u}{v} - (m+n), \qquad \widehat{u} = \eta\pi^* + \widetilde{f}(V) - \pi - m$$

---

[37] In the context of an economy that exhibits a steady growth rate $n+m$, it would perhaps be more natural to assume that the wage bargain takes the constant growth rate of labor productivity explicitly into account. This is not done here, but would not change much in the arguments that follow.

[38] Here, wage-inflation instead of price-inflation as far as influences of the real part of the model are concerned.

instead of (5.2) and (5.3). Since we have restricted our attention in this section to the case where capital is fully utilized, it is no longer possible to include implicitly or explicitly a mark-up pricing procedure in the present model. This is only possible when the degree of capacity utilization is again allowed to vary (to reconcile the twofold determination of the inflation rate through the strict quantity theory of money and then added theory of mark-pricing), an additional complication that will not be treated in this chapter, since it will not alter the negative conclusions obtained below.

With regard to the curve (5.19) it is assumed that there exists $V_o \in (0,1)$, which fulfills $\widetilde{f}(V_o) = m + (1-\eta)\pi_o$. Note that this is not equivalent to the assumption of a natural unemployment rate $\overline{U}$ as it is imagined to underlie hypothesis (5.2).[39] Instead, this rate V_o rather resembles the rate V_0 derived in Sect. 5.3, despite the different types of dynamics considered in this and the preceding section.[40]

The unique steady-state values of system (5.18)–(5.21) can easily be calculated and they fulfill the equations

$$u_0 = 1 - \frac{v(m+n)}{s_p},$$

$$\pi_0 = \overline{\rho} - \frac{s_p(1-u_0)}{v} = v - (m+n) = \overline{\rho} - g_0 = \pi_0^*,$$

$$V_0 = \widetilde{f}^{-1}((1-\eta)\pi_0 + m).$$

With regard to the propositions (A)–(G) of Sect. 5.2, we may now briefly state that propositions (A) and (D) will again be true. The dynamics of system (5.18)–(5.21) can then be reduced to only two differential equations, which fulfill the assumptions of Olech's Theorem (Sect. 4.9), since expectations π^* are treated as exogenous (short-term proposition) or are given by $\pi^* = \overline{\rho} - m - n$ (long-term proposition). The proof of global stability of the whole dynamical system (5.18)–(5.21), which by means of $\pi = \overline{\rho} - \frac{s_p(1-u)}{v}$ can be reduced to three nonlinear equations in the three variables u, V, and π^*, is however no longer straightforward.

What can be shown is that this system is locally asymptotically stable[41] (by employing the Routh–Hurwitz criterion, see Sect. 3.8). This assertion leaves, however, everything concerning *practical* stability open and thereby greatly reduces the power of the neutrality proposition (B). Finally, the acceleration proposition (C) now largely falls from consideration, since a stabilization of the employment rate V, for example, above its steady state value V_0 annuls at once the whole dynamic structure of the system, which means that this proposition requires a more extensive model specification for its sensible discussion.

Though a more careful treatment of these four propositions may reveal further differences in comparison to the results obtained in Sect. 5.2, these differences are not of primary concern in this section. Our interest here lies in the NUR-hypothesis

---

[39] The SW-NUR.

[40] $1 - V_o$ the Goodwinian type of NAIRU.

[41] Independent of the size of k' in this simple framework.

and in the NUR-proposition (F) derived from it. If we abstract – as it is demanded by this proposition – from unanticipated inflation ($\pi^* \equiv \pi$), the above system (5.18)–(5.20) of differential equations is again reduced to only two equations, namely

$$\widehat{u} = \widetilde{f}(V) - m - (1-\eta)\frac{\overline{\rho} - s_{\mathrm{p}}(1-u)}{v}, \tag{5.22}$$

$$\widehat{V} = \frac{s_{\mathrm{p}}(1-u)}{v} - (m+n), \tag{5.23}$$

which imply the same steady-state values as before. For the dynamics of this system with fully anticipated inflation we now, however, get

The dynamic system (5.22) and (5.23) is globally asymptotically stable (totally unstable) if $\eta < 1$ ($\eta > 1$). And for $\eta = 1$, system (5.22) and (5.23) exhibits only closed orbits around its steady-state values u_0 and V_0, that is, the monetarist case $\eta = 1$ is not asymptotically stable in particular.[42]

The first part of this proposition is an immediate consequence of Olech's Theorem,[43] appropriately reformulated for the two situations under consideration [see the mathematical appendix in Chap. 4]. And its second part is at least plausible, since it must be the limit case between the two situations $\eta < 1$, $\eta > 1$ [see again the preceding chapter (Sect. 4.3)]. Represented in a phase diagram we thus obtain for the monetarist case $\eta = 1$ the above type of dynamics.[44]

On the basis of this diagram and the preceding proposition, the following important economic conclusions can now be drawn for the case $\eta = 1$:

(a) There is no fixed relation à la Grossman (see Sect. 5.2) between central economic aggregates of the real side of the model and the difference between actual and expected inflation in the context of this model of endogenous capital growth, since all these aggregates will fluctuate in the above model while the latter difference is here zero throughout.[45]
(b) Such a fixed relation can only be ensured if mark-up pricing of the type $p = A\frac{WL}{Y}$ (implying $\pi = \widehat{W} - m$) is introduced into the above model. However, such an extension of system (5.18)–(5.20) – in addition to the capacity utilization problems it will cause – has the unpleasant feature that it implies $\widehat{\left(\frac{W}{p}\right)} = m$ and $\overline{u} = 0$, facts which can sensibly be assumed solely for the short-run, yet not for the intermediate-run as it is considered here.
(c) Assuming $\widehat{u} = 0$ $\left[\widehat{\left(\frac{W}{p}\right)} = m\right]$ and $m = \widehat{\left(\frac{Y}{L}\right)}$ (also in the case of idle capital) allows to transform system (5.18)–(5.21) into the following system of differential equations

[42] In this case, the real part of the model is completely independent of the money supply process.

[43] A Liapunov function is also easily available here by means of an appropriate reformulation of the type of Liapunov functions we have used in Chap. 4.

[44] Because of $\pi = \bar{\rho} - s_{\mathrm{p}}\frac{1-u}{v}$.

[45] There is also no fixed relation in this type of model as it is postulated by Okun's law, since capital is always fully used in the above approach.

$$\begin{aligned}\widehat{V} &= g-(m+n), \quad g=\widehat{Y},\\ \pi &= \pi^* + f(V) - m,\\ \overline{p} &= \pi + g,\\ \dot{\pi}^* &= k(\pi - \pi^*),\end{aligned}$$

because of $V = \frac{L}{L^s} = \frac{Y}{\frac{Y}{L} \cdot L^s}$. This result indicates to some extent how the baseline model (5.1)–(5.4) of Sect. 5.2 can be obtained from the above — by ignoring the effects of a changing income distribution; $\widehat{K} = \frac{s_p(1-\bar{u})}{v} = g^p$ is then exogenously determined (and equal to $m+n$, if $\bar{u} = u_0$ holds).

(d) In the context of the above model, the BB-NUR and the NAIRU (see Sect. 5.2) are no longer equivalent, that is, the neutrality proposition (F) of Sect. 5.2 now fails: the BB-NUR here implies that each actual unemployment rate has to be characterized as natural, while only the rate V_0 can be natural with regard to the NAIRU point of view. Similarly, there now holds $g = g^p$ with regard to every actual growth situation, yet $g^p = m+n$ will in general be false! The two stable curves (5.2) and (5.3) of Sect. 5.2 thus are of a very dubious nature when reconsidered from the perspective of this simple Classical model of capital accumulation. The commonly believed equivalence between Walrasian, a perfect-foresight, and a steady-state characterization of the natural unemployment rate is completely absent from this Classical variation of Frisch's baseline model. This latter model therefore cannot be considered to provide the basis for very robust propositions of economic theory.

(e) Any measurement of the natural unemployment rate, which is based on the NUR-hypothesis (5.2) as, for example, in Batchelor (1981), compare Fig. 5.5 in Sect. 5.3, can be completely misleading if the Classical dynamics we considered above is of some relevance. Considering, for example, Fig. 5.6, its actual unemployment rates U would then all be measured as natural by this procedure – if measurement errors are neglected – which in part might provide an explanation of the steep rise of "natural rates" that has been observed by Batchelor. If the steady-state $U_0 = 1 - V_0$, the only unemployment rate which allows

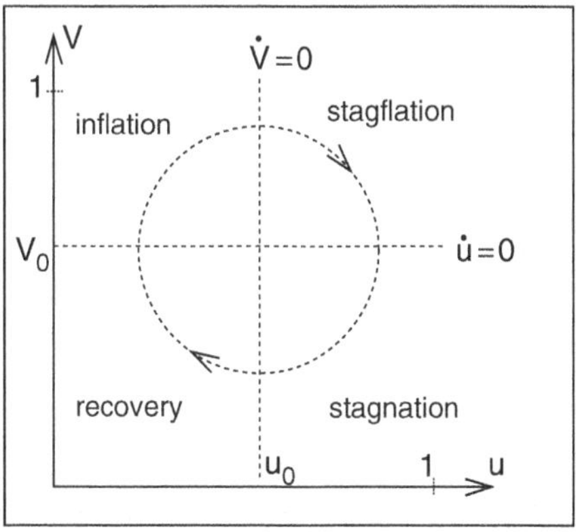

Fig. 5.6 A Goodwin–Friedman model of cyclical growth

for constant rates of inflation, is to be estimated; unanticipated inflation therefore is by no means a sufficient starting-point to determine its complementary part $U - U_0$.

(f) In the context of the above model, also the Keynesian approach of structuring unemployment into frictional, structural, and demand-deficient components must be looked at with suspicion [see Armstrong and Taylor (1981) for such an approach]. Such attempts, based on Hansen's U(nemployment)-V(acancies)-methodology, classify all unemployment U exceeding the number of vacancies as demand deficient. This last, unquestionably important component of unemployment has, however, been excluded by assumption from the above model, which leads us to the false conclusion that in this Goodwin-type model open positions and job hunters always balance each other out. Capital shortage, too little capital to employ the entire work force, seems to play no role in the above Keynesian classification of unemployment.

(g) The above model finally implies that the private sector can only be asymptotically stable if the growth rate of money supply $\overline{\rho}$ exercises some influence on natural employment V_0, which, of course, is a trade-off not very favorable to the monetarist view on the working of a capitalistic economy.

The above conclusions [drawn from a simple variant of Frisch's (1983) as well as Goodwin's (1967) model] should not be regarded as being well-established propositions derived from a framework that is also already acceptable to a monetarist inclined reader. They should be viewed rather as a starting point for a discussion, which, on the one hand, must integrate problems of effective demand, price setting behavior, financial assets, etc., but which, on the other hand, should not return to the crude view of a given natural unemployment rate and a given trend growth of potential output [to which short-term deviations will adjust in the end]. It is our conjecture that the above depicted cyclical development of the wage share u and of the employment rate V (which here follow each other with a quarter phase displacement) at least partially will remain intact in such extensions of the model. Capital shortage (and abundance) – relative to the long run trend $m+n$ – is an important macroeconomic problem and not only a logical possibility which explains the disappearance of available jobs without a deficiency in total demand. The economic system may not function so regularly as the ideal case depicted in Fig. 5.6 suggests. Yet, endogenizing that part of unemployment which cannot be attributed to misconceptions of the economic agents with regard to price behavior and also endogenizing potential output growth, for example, along the lines here suggested, will preserve the basic conclusion of this section, namely that the NUR-hypothesis and the NUR-proposition cannot be maintained in an economic model which truly investigates these two types of complications.

After correctly criticizing the crude descriptions of the unemployment-inflation trade-off developed in the sixties, monetarists have established alternative stable relationships, which in the end suffer from the same type of critique, because they take components and structures of the economic system as exogenous and stable, which are too fundamental to be treated in this way. This topic will be further pursued in Chaps. 6 and 7 by adding an IS-LM sector to the above cycle model (in place of the strict quantity theory of money and with savings determined by $s = s_w = s_p$ instead of $0 = s_w < s_p \leq 1$) and by allowing for factor substitution and the choice of technique as in the Solow model of economic growth. One striking difference to the above will then be that adaptively formed expectations can give rise to instability of the steady state solution of this extended model.

Appendix: A Neo-Keynesian Analysis of Economic Depressions

We have considered in the main part of this chapter downturns in economic activity which were due to excessive growth and the inflationary consequences of it (see Fig. 5.3). We have then attempted to show that such an occurrence may be simply due to a general dynamic law, which dominantly governs the evolutionary dynamics of a capitalist economy, that is, the reserve army mechanism, considered at length in the preceding chapter (see here Fig. 5.5). In this view, periods of stagflation are not caused by a misplaced monetary policy, for example, but are inherent to the system, which is systematically based on overshooting in its reproduction of economic growth and development. In the literature on macroeconomic dynamics, there exists, however, another approach to the analysis of cycles (and growth) which has received much more attention than the Neomarxian analysis we have presented in Chap. 4, that is, the Neo-Keynesian fixprice analysis of temporary equilibrium and of the forces that change this equilibrium position over time. A brief sketch of the procedures involved in such an approach is thus to see in how far it offers an alternative to the explanation of cycles and trends we have considered so far.

For this purpose we shall reconsider here a prototype model of Neo-Keynesian dynamics as it has been provided by Malinvaud's (1980) presentation of the interaction of profitability and unemployment. To our knowledge, Malinvaud's (1980) approach is one of the rare contributions that gives the Keynesian regime, among the regimes that are generally considered by non-Walrasian economists, the priority it can be shown to exhibit in theory as well as in practical experience, see Chiarella, Flaschel, Groh, and Semmler (2000) and Flaschel, Groh, Proaño, and Semmler, (2008) for details on such an argumentation.

We shall provide here a continuous time reformulation of Malinvaud's medium-run analysis of capital accumulation and income distribution which is based on three different types of short-term equilibrium, their dynamic links, and the sequence of equilibria these links imply. We shall argue then that Malinvaud's central result – the dominance of the position of a stable stationary Keynesian underemployment equilibrium (a Keynesian depression) over more Classical types of unemployment (which appear to be only of a transient nature) – may become questionable when the labor market is considered in a slightly more realistic way. Such a feature of the labor market has been at the core of the present chapter, namely the existence of a long-run steady state rate of unemployment and its explanation, be it Walrasian (a la Friedman) or not. Full employment, in the literal sense, is not a meaningful category in macroeconomics as a description of an equilibrium position, but is only applicable as a ceiling to macroeconomic evolution – in the way it has been considered in Sect. 3.7. Taking this fact into account will lead us again towards a model structure that is similar to the ones we have considered in Sects. 4.3 and 5.4.

Starting point of Malinvaud's Neo-Keynesian approach to economic dynamics is the simple observation that prices are generally rigid in the short-run since only this fact guarantees that they can have informational content for economic agents in a complex economic world. Notice here that this stylized fact is not uncommon to the models we have considered in Chaps. 4 and 5. What is new is that it is now employed to show that such rigid prices will give rise to different economic regimes (qualitatively different temporary equilibrium positions), depending on the (absolute) magnitude these prices can temporarily have in a monetary economy. These regimes are based on different types of disequilibria which, by the principle that the short side on a market will determine its outcome, then give rise to quantity adjustments which in turn give rise to temporary equilibria in quantities. Discrepancies in demand and supply thus lead to an adjustment toward the minimum of both, which – paying attention to the spill-over effects that this adjustment implies in a multimarket economy – can then be used to determine short-run equilibrium positions in quantities in correspondence to the prices that presently prevail. Prices consequently fail to coordinate markets in the short-run in the ideal fashion of Walrasian general equilibrium theory. Some economic agents will be rationed with regard to their "rational" optimal demand and supply schedules. Because of this rationing there will be new demand and supply functions which take such quantity constraints into account and which then form the basis of a theory of "effective" demand and supply. This new approach is discussed in Malinvaud (1980) in a macro model as a basis for an analysis of the medium-run consequences of its various temporary equilibrium positions. Such an extension of the Neo-Keynesian "fix-price" approach is necessary, since it in fact only claims that "quantities" adjust faster than "prices." It does, of course, not claim that prices do not adjust at all but solely uses as on organizing idea that output and employment adjust so quickly that their determination can be described by equilibrium conditions (or equation), while prices – like growth – have to be described by dynamic laws (differential or difference equations).

Malinvaud's (1980) analysis of temporary equilibrium positions is based on the following two macroeconomic demand functions:[46]

$$C = c_{\mathrm{w}} w + c_{\mathrm{m}} m^{\mathrm{s}} + c_{\mathrm{V}} V, \quad c_{\mathrm{w}}, c_{\mathrm{m}}, c_{\mathrm{V}} > 0, \tag{5.24}$$

$$I = i_{\mathrm{w}}(\bar{y} - a - w) + i_{\Theta}(\tilde{Y} - Y^{\mathrm{p}}), \quad i_{\mathrm{w}}, i_{\Theta} > 0, \tag{5.25}$$

where $\tilde{Y}$ is given by

$$\begin{aligned} \tilde{Y} &= \min\{Y^{\mathrm{d}}, \bar{Y}\}, \\ Y^{\mathrm{d}} &= C + I + \bar{G}, \\ \bar{Y} &= \bar{y}\bar{L}. \end{aligned}$$

46 To simplify the analysis, we directly employ linear relationships here, as in Malinvaud (1980, Chap. 4).

Furthermore,

$$Y = \min\{\tilde{Y}, Y^{\mathrm{p}}\} \quad \text{and} \quad Y^{\mathrm{p}} = \sigma K.$$

Consumption C has been assumed here to depend linearly on the real wage $w = W/p$ and on real balances $m^{\mathrm{s}} = M^{\mathrm{s}}/p$ and also on the rate of employment $V = L/\bar{L} = 1 - U$. This letter term reflects autonomous expenditures, which are modified in a simple way if employment falls short of full employment $V = 1$.

Net investment I also depends on the real wage through the term $\bar{y} - a - w$, which is output per head $y = Y/L$ minus wages per head minus minimum profits per labor unit a, which gives a simple measure of excess profits (per unit of labor). It furthermore depends on the minimum of the excess of aggregate demand $Y^{\mathrm{d}} = C + I + \bar{G}$ and full employment output $\bar{Y} = \bar{y}\bar{L}$ over full capacity use $Y^{\mathrm{p}} = vK$ (which, of course, may also be a negative quantity). Note here that use is made again of the simple production function with fixed coefficients $\bar{y} = Y/L$, $v = Y/K$ we have introduced in Sect. 3.2.

Aggregate demand Y^{d} includes exogenous government expenditures $\bar{G}$ and it is defined by

$$Y^{\mathrm{d}} = c_{\mathrm{w}}w + c_{\mathrm{m}}m^{\mathrm{s}} + c_{\mathrm{V}} + i_{\mathrm{w}}(\bar{y} - a - w) + i_{\Theta}(\bar{Y} - Y^{\mathrm{p}}) + \bar{G}$$

in the case of full employment. If employment is restricted by the available capital stock K and full capacity output Y^{p} (but not yet by the "effective" demand for goods), we instead have

$$Y^{\mathrm{d}} = c_{\mathrm{w}}w + c_{\mathrm{m}}m^{\mathrm{s}} + c_{\mathrm{V}}(Y^{\mathrm{p}}/\bar{Y}) + i_{\mathrm{w}}(\bar{y} - a - w) + i_{\Theta}(\bar{Y} - Y^{\mathrm{p}}) + \bar{G}.$$

Note here that $\bar{Y} - Y^{\mathrm{p}}$ is negative in the first case and positive in the second case. If, however, aggregate demand Y^{d} falls below full employment output $\bar{Y}$ (but not yet below Y^{p}), we have to use Y^{d} instead of $\bar{Y}$ in the i_{Θ}-expression. This shows that this concept of aggregate demand is already a special one, in that there is no difference between aggregate demand Y^{d} and that demand that is expected by investor's as the basis of their investment decision. Because of this, we shall call this Y^{d} (the point of) "effective" demand in the following:

$$Y^{\mathrm{d}} = c_{\mathrm{w}}w + c_{\mathrm{m}}m^{\mathrm{s}} + c_{\mathrm{V}}(Y^{\mathrm{p}}/\bar{Y}) + i_{\mathrm{w}}(\bar{y} - a - w) + i_{\Theta}Y^{\mathrm{p}} + \bar{G}/(1 - i_{\Theta}).$$

A similar formula is established in the above full employment case when aggregate (i.e., effective demand) is below full capacity output Y^{p}.

This demand concept becomes more complicated when it is finally assumed that employment and capacity use are constrained by it: $Y = Y^{\mathrm{d}}$. We then get

$$\begin{aligned} Y^{\mathrm{d}} &= c_{\mathrm{w}}w + c_{\mathrm{m}}m^{\mathrm{s}} + c_{\mathrm{V}}(Y^{\mathrm{d}}/\bar{Y}) + i_{\mathrm{w}}(\bar{y} - a - w) + i_{\Theta}(Y^{\mathrm{d}} - Y^{\mathrm{p}}) + \bar{G}, \quad \text{e.g.,} \\ Y^{\mathrm{d}} &= [c_{\mathrm{w}}w + c_{\mathrm{m}}m^{\mathrm{s}} + i_{\mathrm{w}}(\bar{y} - a - w) - i_{\Theta}Y^{\mathrm{p}} + \bar{G}]/[1 - c_{\mathrm{V}}/\bar{Y} - i_{\Theta}]. \end{aligned}$$

This already provides an example of how different regimes (full employment, full capacity use, deficient goods demand) may change the outlook of a simple macroeconomic model.

The above model marries a specific theory of consumption [see Malinvaud (1977) in this regard] with an investment theory which exhibit Goodwinian as well as Domar-like features. Its centerpiece is, of course, the market for goods, while both factors of production act in the most simple fashion as ceilings in this market. Note finally that labor supply $\bar{L}$ has been assumed to be constant in this model (of the medium run).

We have already noted that output and sales of firms $Y = \min\{\bar{Y}, Y^{\mathrm{p}}, Y^{\mathrm{d}}\}$ are constrained in three different ways: by labor supply $\bar{L}$ ($\bar{Y} = \bar{y}\bar{L}$), by potential output of firms $Y^{\mathrm{p}}(=vK)$, or by effective demand $Y^{\mathrm{d}}(=C(Y^{\mathrm{d}})+I(Y^{\mathrm{d}})+\bar{G}!)$.[47] The amount of excess demand on the market for goods which can be produced by the labor supply that is still available has been denoted by $\tilde{Y} - Y^{\mathrm{p}}$, which if positive says that the demand constraint for labor is not yet binding. This excess is one important driving force in net investment behavior.

This completes the description of the elements needed for temporary equilibrium analysis. We have now to solve the task to drive what kind of quantity equilibrium will in fact prevail in a given situation of a real wage $w = W/p$ of prices p and of a productive capacity $Y^{\mathrm{p}} = vK$ as well as a given full employment ceiling of amount $\bar{Y} = \bar{y}\bar{L}$. To solve this task in a prototype way, we shall neglect any influence from real balances. This will allow us to treat the model in terms of the variables w and Y^{p}, solely. We define the degree of capacity utilization (of the capital stock) by $\Theta = Y/Y^{\mathrm{p}}$ and by $V = L/\bar{L}$ the rate of employment. With regard to these ratios the following three possibilities then exist for the state of the product- and the labor-market:

$$\begin{array}{lrl} \text{K-Equilibrium:} & Y^{\mathrm{d}} = Y & [V \leq 1, \Theta \leq 1] \\ \text{C-Equilibrium:} & Y^{\mathrm{p}} = Y & [V \leq 1, \Theta = 1] \\ \text{I-Equilibrium:} & \bar{Y} = Y & [V = 1, \Theta \leq 1] \end{array}$$

These equilibria (which are called **K**eynesian, **C**lassical, and **I**nflationary equilibria, respectively) can be further subdivided as follows:

$$\begin{array}{ccccccccl} Y^{\mathrm{d}} & = & Y & \leq & \bar{Y} & \leq & Y^{\mathrm{p}} & : & \text{Weak K-Equilibrium} \\ Y^{\mathrm{d}} & = & Y & \leq & Y^{\mathrm{p}} & \leq & \bar{Y} & : & \text{Strong K-Equilibrium} \\ Y^{\mathrm{p}} & = & Y & \leq & \bar{Y} & \leq & Y^{\mathrm{d}} & : & \text{Weak C-Equilibrium} \\ Y^{\mathrm{p}} & = & Y & \leq & Y^{\mathrm{d}} & \leq & \bar{Y} & : & \text{Strong C-Equilibrium} \\ \bar{Y} & = & Y & \leq & Y^{\mathrm{d}} & \leq & Y^{\mathrm{p}} & : & \text{Weak I-Equilibrium} \\ \bar{Y} & = & Y & \leq & Y^{\mathrm{p}} & \leq & Y^{\mathrm{d}} & : & \text{Strong I-Equilibrium} \end{array}$$

A strong K-Equilibrium has in its background a further (at present still latent) force, which would imply unemployment even if the present demand deficiency could be removed by an appropriate demand management policy. A similar

[47] Inventories (and their changes) are not considered (or allowed for) in this basic prototype model.

argument applies to the case of a strong C-Equilibrium. Strong I-Equilibria, finally, exhibit a further (again still latent) force, which may contribute to already existing inflationary pressures.

To determine which of the above situations will be valid in a given real-wage rate accumulation regime w, Y^{p}, a calculation of the borderlines between the different regimes is very helpful. The primary ones among these borderlines are given by assuming equality signs on the right hand side of the above last classification and its inequality signs, which leads us to three different types of borderline equilibrium: **KC**-Equilibria, **KI**-Equilibria and **CI**-Equilibria (which are, of course, identical to CK-Equilibria, etc.).

KC-Equilibria are determined by the condition

$$Y^{\mathrm{p}} = c_{\mathrm{w}}w + c_{\mathrm{V}}(Y^{\mathrm{p}}/\bar{Y}) + i_{\mathrm{w}}(\bar{y} - a - w) + 0 + \bar{G} \leq \bar{Y},$$

KI-Equilibria by

$$\bar{Y} = c_{\mathrm{w}}w + c_{\mathrm{V}} + i_{\mathrm{w}}(\bar{y} - a - w) + i_{\Theta}(\bar{Y} - Y^{\mathrm{p}}) + \bar{G} \leq Y^{\mathrm{p}},$$

and CI-Equilibria by

$$\bar{Y} = Y^{\mathrm{p}} \leq c_{\mathrm{w}}w + c_{\mathrm{V}} + i_{\mathrm{w}}(\bar{y} - a - w) + 0 + \bar{G} = Y^{\mathrm{d}}.$$

This gives

$$\begin{aligned} \mathrm{KC} &: w = \frac{(1 - c_{\mathrm{V}}/\bar{Y})Y^{\mathrm{p}} + (a - \bar{y})i_{\mathrm{w}} - \bar{G}}{c_{\mathrm{w}} - i_{\mathrm{w}}}, \\ \mathrm{KI} &: w = \frac{i_{\Theta}Y^{\mathrm{p}} - c_{\mathrm{V}} + (1 - i_{\Theta})\bar{Y} + (a - \bar{y})i_{\mathrm{w}} - \bar{G}}{c_{\mathrm{w}} - i_{\mathrm{w}}}, \\ \mathrm{CI} &: \bar{Y} = Y^{\mathrm{p}}. \end{aligned}$$

It is plausible (in a Keynesian approach) that $1 - C_{\mathrm{V}}/\bar{Y} \geq 0$ can be assumed. Malinvaud (1980) in addition assumes that the real wage has a stronger influence on consumption demand then on investment demand: $c_{\mathrm{w}} > i_{\mathrm{w}}$. The cost-effect is thereby assumed to be less pronounced then the (mass-) purchasing effect of the real wage! And he furthermore assumes that government expenditures are determined such that $c_{\mathrm{w}}(\bar{y} - a) + c_{\mathrm{V}} + \bar{G} = \bar{Y}$ holds true. This last condition guarantees that $\bar{Y} = Y^{\mathrm{p}} = Y^{\mathrm{d}}$ must hold for the real wage $w = \bar{y} - a$ (where net investment is zero). Note here that Y^{d} is increasing with w along the line $Y^{\mathrm{p}} = \bar{Y}$ in Y^{p}, w-space so that $Y^{\mathrm{d}} \gtreqless \bar{Y}$ must be true for $w \gtreqless \bar{y} - a$ due to this last assumption.

In strengthening the first of the above assumptions, let us finally assume that $1 - C_{\mathrm{V}}/\bar{Y} - i_{\Theta} > 0$ will hold, that is, $1 - C_{\mathrm{V}}/\bar{Y} > i_{\Theta}$. This implies for the two positively sloped lines KC and KI that the KC-line will be steeper than the KI-line. The above thus gives rise to the subdivision of the Y^{p}, w-space into K, C, and I-equilibria and their boundaries KI, KC, and CI shown in Fig. 5.7.

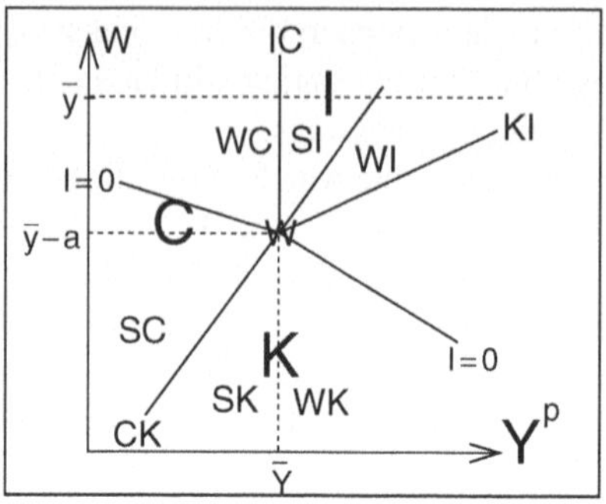

Fig. 5.7 The three regimes in Malinvaud's analysis of a Keynesian depression

It is obvious that we must have C- or K-Equilibria to the left of $\bar{Y} = Y^{\mathrm{p}}$ and K- or I-Equilibria to its right.

Furthermore, we must have K-Equilibria below CK and KI, due to the assumption $c_{\mathrm{w}} > i_{\mathrm{w}}$ (i.e., rising effective demand for rising w and a given Y^{p}). Because of $c_{\mathrm{w}}(\bar{y} - a) + c_{\mathrm{V}} + \bar{G} = \bar{Y}$ the KC-line and the KI-line must intersect the CI-line $\bar{Y} = Y^{\mathrm{p}}$ at $w = \bar{y} - a$, which gives the only point where both the goods-market and the market for labor are cleared (the Walrasian equilibrium **W**).

It is easy to separate weak and strong Keynesian equilibria (WK and SK) from each other. They are situated to the right and to the left of the $\bar{Y} = Y^{\mathrm{p}}$-line, respectively. The dividing line between weak and strong Classical equilibria (WC, SC) is to be determined from $Y^{\mathrm{p}} \leq Y^{\mathrm{d}} = \bar{Y}$, which gives rise to

$$\bar{Y} = c_{\mathrm{w}} w + c_{\mathrm{V}}(Y^{\mathrm{p}}/\bar{Y}) + i_{\mathrm{w}}(\bar{y} - a - w) + i_{\Theta}(\bar{Y} - Y^{\mathrm{p}}) + \bar{G}$$

or

$$w = \frac{(i_{\Theta} - c_{\mathrm{V}}/\bar{Y})Y^{\mathrm{p}} + (1 - i_{\Theta})\bar{Y} + (a - \bar{y})i_{\mathrm{w}} - \bar{G}}{c_{\mathrm{w}} - i_{\mathrm{w}}}.$$

For graphical simplicity we here assume that $i_{\Theta} = c_{\mathrm{V}}/\bar{Y}$ holds, which gives rise to the horizontal line in the Fig. 5.7. Weak and strong I-Equilibria, finally, are separate by the condition $\bar{Y} \leq Y^{\mathrm{d}} = Y^{\mathrm{p}}$, which implies

$$Y^{\mathrm{p}} = c_{\mathrm{w}} w + c_{\mathrm{V}} + i_{\mathrm{w}}(\bar{y} - a - w) + i_{\Theta}(\bar{Y} - Y^{\mathrm{p}}) + \bar{G}$$

or

$$w = \frac{(1 + i_{\Theta})Y^{\mathrm{p}} - c_{\mathrm{V}} + (a - \bar{y})i_{\mathrm{w}} - i_{\Theta}\bar{Y} - \bar{G}}{c_{\mathrm{w}} - i_{\mathrm{w}}}.$$

This line is obviously steeper than the KI-line and gives therefore rise to a meaningful subdivision of the I-domain. Note that also these lines, which subdivide the C-, K-, and I-domain, must run through the Walrasian point $W = (Y^{\mathrm{p}}, \bar{y} - a)$.

We briefly note here that none of the above assumptions is so restrictive that its modification will destroy the basic message of the above model that we will derive in the following. This holds true in particular for the assumptions $c_{\mathrm{w}} - i_{\mathrm{w}} > 0$ and $c_{\mathrm{m}} = 0$. It is shown in Groh (1991) that the opposite assumption $i_{\mathrm{w}} - c_{\mathrm{w}} > 0$, where the cost-effect of real wage increases dominates its purchasing power effect (a more orthodox line of reasoning), does not alter the following dynamical analysis of a Keynesian depression significantly. Falling wages will even in this situation not push up aggregate demand by so much that this Keynesian depression will be overcome. Assuming $c_{\mathrm{m}} > 0$, on the other hand, will make the model a much more complicated one, again without altering its conclusions in a significant way (Malinvaud, 1980; Soyka, 1991). If real balances $m^s = M^s/p$ count, we have to integrate the dynamics of the price level into this model explicitly. But again, falling prices will generally not raise effective demand in the Keynesian region to such an extent that the asserted Keynesian depression can be dissolved by it. These two lines of reasoning therefore do not represent a safe route, which allows to avoid that the system may become trapped in a stationary situation of zero net investment and deficient aggregate demand, where both labor and capital are unemployed.

To prove that such a trap will be the plausible outcome of the above model, we have to turn away from the above temporary equilibrium analysis and have to consider the forces that govern its medium rum behavior. To solve this task, a final line in the above figure will be of importance, the $I = 0$- or $Y^{\mathrm{p}} = 0$-line, where capital accumulation comes to a rest. This line is given by

$$i_{\mathrm{w}}(\bar{y} - a - w) + i_{\Theta}(\min\{Y^{\mathrm{d}}, \bar{Y}\} - Y^{\mathrm{p}}) = 0.$$

This line cannot pass through the I-domain, since it gives rise to a falling curve (which passes through **W**) in this case. And since it will also be falling in the C- and K-domain it will be situated in the WC-domain and the WK-domain, where it is given by

$$w = \frac{i_{\Theta}(\bar{Y} - Y^{\mathrm{p}}) + i_{\mathrm{w}}(\bar{y} - a)}{i_{\mathrm{w}}} \quad \text{or}$$
$$w = \frac{i_{\Theta}(Y^{\mathrm{d}} - Y^{\mathrm{p}}) + i_{\mathrm{w}}(\bar{y} - a)}{i_{\mathrm{w}}},$$

respectively [where $Y^{\mathrm{d}} = c_{\mathrm{w}}w + c_{\mathrm{V}}(Y^{\mathrm{d}}/\bar{Y}) + \bar{G}$ or $Y^{\mathrm{d}} = (c_{\mathrm{w}}w + \bar{G})/(1 - c_{\mathrm{v}}/\bar{Y})$]. The second line hence in the end reads

$$w = -\frac{i_{\Theta}}{i_{\mathrm{w}} - c_{\mathrm{w}}i_{\Theta}/(1 - c_{\mathrm{V}}/\bar{Y})}Y^{\mathrm{p}} + \mathrm{const},$$

which gives a line that is falling and steeper than $\dot{Y}^{\mathrm{p}} = 0$ in the C-domain if $i_{\mathrm{w}} - c_{\mathrm{w}}i_{\Theta}/(1 - c_{\mathrm{V}}/\bar{Y} > 0$ holds true (and which, of course, must again pass through the Walrasian point **W**).

The medium run dynamics of the above model is now given by the following differential equations (which replace Malinvaud's (1980) difference equations approach):

$$\dot{Y}^{\mathrm{p}} = \varphi(i_{\mathrm{w}}(\bar{y} - a - w) + i_{\Theta}(\min\{\bar{Y}, Y^{\mathrm{d}}(\cdot)\} - Y^{\mathrm{p}})), \quad \varphi > 0, \tag{5.26}$$
$$\dot{w} = \phi(\min\{Y^{\mathrm{d}}(\cdot), Y^{\mathrm{p}}\} - \bar{Y}), \quad \phi > 0. \tag{5.27}$$

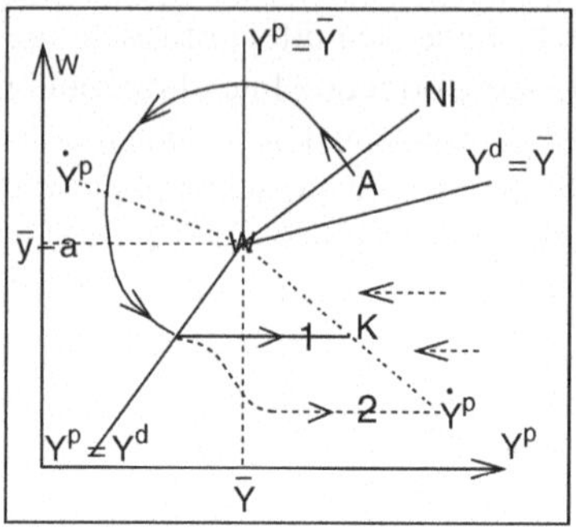

Fig. 5.8 The dynamics of the Malinvaud model

We note that the minimum in the first equation will be given by $\bar{Y}$ in the I-domain and by $Y^{\mathrm{d}}(.)$ in the K-domain, while it changes from $\bar{Y}$ to $Y^{\mathrm{d}}(\cdot)$ in the C-domain (when the dynamics passes the $w \equiv \bar{y} - a$ - line). The minimum in the second equation is given by $Y^{\mathrm{d}}(\cdot)$ in the K-domain and by Y^{p} in the C-domain. It switches from $Y^{\mathrm{d}}(.)$ to Y^{p} in the I-domain when the line NI is passed (see the Fig. 5.8). This dynamics now gives rise to Fig. 5.8 (with a strictly downward moving real wage in the K-domain):

In this diagram we have assumed that the starting-point of the trajectory to be analyzed lies in the I-domain (point A). Because of disinvestment that occurs in this whole domain, the dynamics must necessarily enter into the C-domain (since the rise in real wages which accompanies this disinvestment process remains bounded). In the C-domain, real wages start falling, since labor shortage has changed into capital shortage, as the $Y^{\mathrm{p}} = \bar{Y}$-line is passed. Nevertheless, disinvestment continues, since the real wage is too high in relation to the capacity effect of effective demand, which is still too weak in the early phase of classical unemployment. Sooner or later the $\dot{Y}^{\mathrm{p}} = 0$-isocline will, however, be reached where wages have become so low that the profitability effect in the investment function (together with $i_{\Theta}(\bar{Y} - Y^{\mathrm{p}}) > 0$) will give rise to a positive amount of net investment from then onwards.[48] Real wages continue to fall and profitability will raise net investment further, despite a falling contribution from $i_{\Theta}(\bar{Y} - Y^{\mathrm{p}})$, which changes to $i_{\Theta}(Y^{\mathrm{d}} - Y^{\mathrm{p}})$ when the $w = \bar{y} - a$-line is passed. The capacity effect will then become smaller and smaller because of two reasons ($Y^{\mathrm{d}} \downarrow Y^{\mathrm{p}} \uparrow$) instead of only one ($Y^{\mathrm{p}} \uparrow$) and it will become zero finally – and subsequently negative – when the trajectory passes the line that separates the C- from the K-domain.

In the K-domain wages will continue to fall, while investment continues to increase the capital stock, since the profitability effect dominates the now negative capacity effect $i_{\Theta}(Y^{\mathrm{d}} - Y^{\mathrm{p}})$. This situation must continue to prevail, due to the negative slope of the $\dot{Y} = 0$ curve and the positive slope of the KI-line. Real wages therefore fall without bounds, while excess capacity continues to increase due to the increase in profitability, which follows from the decrease in real wages. It is plausible that there must exist a floor to the fall in real wages (see the alternative 2

[48] Note that this profitability effect is still negative here.

in the Fig. 5.8). If this floor is reached, profitability becomes stationary, while the capital stock is further increasing, until the point is reached where excess capacity $i_\Theta(Y^d - Y^p)$ has become so large that its negative effect just compensates for the positive excess in profitability such that in sum net investment becomes zero. At this point, the economy becomes trapped in a Keynesian depression, where real wages and capacity are both stationary and where both labor and capital are in excess supply. Note here that Malinvaud (1980) assumes that real wages are constant in the whole K-domain, which instead of curve 2 gives rise to curve 1 as adjustment path in this region. This, however, is not very different from the situation we have just described.

We have already stated that neither of the alternative assumptions $c_w < i_w$ or $c_m > 0$ to the ones made above will imply sufficiently strong demand responses such that a Keynesian depression á la Malinvaud can thereby be overcome. These modifications in the behavior of effective demand are too weak (in relationship to the negative capacity effect that prevails in the Keynesian regime) to provide a remedy for the above problematic situation. In contrast to the analysis of Chaps. 4 and 5, changes in income distribution (in favor of profitability) are thus not sufficient here to lay the basis for a new upswing of the economy. Yet, we do not believe that this result is really general and characteristic for the long-run tendencies of a capitalistic economy in such a stationary environment.

A simple way of showing this is to assume that real wages w will start to rise again in the Keynesian domain before the level of *absolute* full employment $V = L/\bar{L} = 1$, that is, before the region of repressed inflation is reached again. A simple formulation of the wage-price sector which will give rise to such a behavior of real wages is, for example, given by the following two dynamical laws:

$$\hat{W} = \max\{0, \phi_1(\min\{Y^d, Y^p\}/\bar{Y} - 1)\}, \tag{5.28}$$

$$\hat{p} = \phi_2(Y^d/Y^p - 1). \tag{5.29}$$

These laws state that nominal wages rise if firms would like to expand employment – here still with respect to absolute full employment – but that this wage level W will be completely rigid in situation of less than absolute full employment.[49] Nominal prices, on the other hand, are assumed to be flexible upwards as well as downwards by means of a straightforward formulation of the law of demand on the market for goods. For the implied dynamics of the real wage we thus get

$$\hat{w} = \max\{0, \phi_1(\min\{Y^d, Y^p\}/\bar{Y} - 1)\} - \phi_2(Y^d/Y^p - 1).$$

This modification gives rise to the phase diagram shown in Fig. 5.9.

This diagram shows that the dynamics will be again of a Goodwin-like type (see Sect. 4.3) under this slight modification of the original Malinvaud model. Cyclical behavior (whether locally asymptotically stable or not) is therefore now again characteristic for this Neo-Keynesian fixprice-approach to medium run dynamics

[49] It is well-established that such a situation will already be true for a benchmark V_0, which is smaller than $V_0 = 1$, see Benassy (1984), such an approach in the context of the IS-LM model.

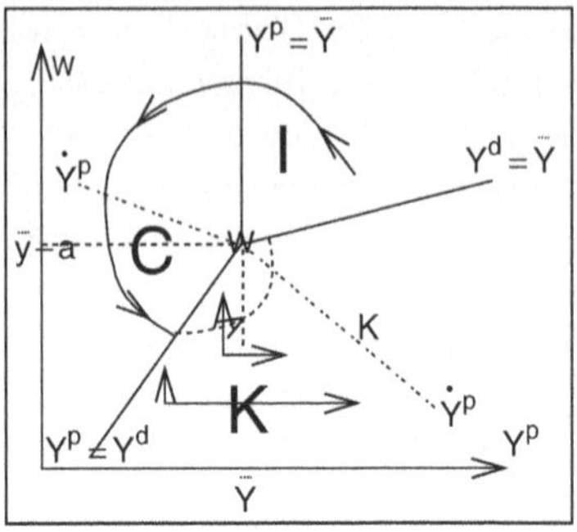

Fig. 5.9 The modified model with endogenous recovery

instead of the above claim of an ever lasting Keynesian depression – under only minor qualifications of the assumed wages/price-dynamics.

These – now separately formulated – wage/price formation rules may also be further qualified in the following ways:

- Prices may also be rigid downward so that deflation is completely excluded from the model. In this case it has to be assumed that nominal wages W rise before absolute full employment is reached in order to obtain results similar to the ones in Fig. 5.9.[50]
- We may then assume

$$\hat{W} = \phi_1(\min\{Y^d, Y^p\}/\bar{Y} - 1) + \hat{p}$$

  in the I-domain, which implies that $\hat{w}$ must be positive throughout this domain – independent of the behavior of the rate of inflation $\hat{p}$.
- In the classical domain we may nevertheless have $\hat{W} = 0,\ \hat{p} > 0$.
- There exists a region in the K-domain (not close to the Walrasian equilibrium) where wages W and prices p are both rigid, that is, where $w = const$ is implied. Keynesian depressions may then come about in the intersection of this range with the $I = 0$-line.
- Far away from the Walrasian equilibrium we have on the $I = 0$-line (due to the low values of the real wage w which then prevail) that capacity Y^p must be higher than actual sales Y^d. We should therefore expect that price deflation will come about in such a situation in the end (where $\bar{Y} \ll Y^p$! holds), so that the above depicted situation will then once again be established.

[50] It is shown in Groh (1991) that the dynamics will be of a classical type and the Keynesian depression therefore be overcome if nominal wages rise before the level $V = 1$ is reached (i.e., if the "1" in (5.28) is replaced by a value V_o, which is smaller than 1 – as it was true in the main part of this chapter for monetarist as well as Post-Keynesian approaches to medium run dynamics) and if the dynamics starts close to the Walrasian equilibrium point (as it is assumed by Malinvaud (1980)). Note here that the Walrasian point will then no longer be an equilibrium of this economy, but that a new equilibrium is born under such circumstances, which lies to the left of it in the classical domain.

We conclude from all this that it is basically the neglected existence of steady-state unemployment $U_0 = 1 - V_0$, that is, the existence of a natural rate of unemployment (or better NAIRU, be it Friedmanian or Marxian), below which nominal wages will start rising, which questions the result that is obtained in Malinvaud (1980): the Keynesian stationary underemployment equilibrium. Such an alternative approach will create a stationary state to the left of and above the Walrasian "equilibrium," which in fact cannot be sensibly claimed to represent a stationary point in a capitalistic economy. The idea of wage-inflation below the level of absolute full employment thus not only questions the results of Keynesian theory, but also that of Neo-Keynesian theory.

Part II
Conventional AD-AS Analysis: A Reconsideration

I HAVE called this book the General Theory of Employment, Interest and Money, placing the emphasis on the prefix general. The object of such a title is to contrast the character of my arguments and conclusions with those of the classical theory of the subject, upon which I was brought up and which dominates the economic thought, both practical and theoretical, of the governing and academic classes of this generation, as it has for a 100 years past. I shall argue that the postulates of the classical theory are applicable to a special case only and not to the general case, the situation which it assumes being a limiting point of the possible positions of equilibrium. Moreover, the characteristics of the special case assumed by the classical theory happen not to be those of the economic society which we actually live, with the result that its teaching is misleading and disastrous if we attempt to apply it to the facts of experience.[1]

---

[1] Keynes, J. M. (1936). *The General Theory of Employment, Interest, and Money* (p. 3). New York: Macmillan.

Chapter 6
Keynesian Monetary Growth Under Adaptive Expectations

6.1 Introduction

In this chapter[1] we shall reconsider Sargent's (1987) dynamic analysis of a Keynesian model with adaptive expectations. This analysis intends[2] to formalize the hypotheses advanced by Milton Friedman in his 1968 AEA presidential address, here for the case of adaptive expectations in an IS-LM growth context with an explicit wage-price sector, that is, for an integrated macromodel, which attempts to be a complete and consistent one.[3] In comparison to the many reduced-form models that have been used in the literature for this task (see our Chap. 5 for an example), this can be characterized as an ambitious analytical target, since it will lead to a nonlinear dynamical model which – though well-known in all of its components – is difficult to analyze and which has thus not yet received a thorough and detailed treatment in the literature. Our findings will be that this type of model will not give rise to Friedmanian conclusions in general, but can at least equally well be used to demonstrate alternative views on the working of a capitalist economy.

One important result of our analysis of this integrated approach toward Keynesian monetary growth dynamics will be that one of its conventional building blocks – the strict form of the marginal productivity theory of real wages – should be dismissed from such a model. We shall see that this equilibrium theory of the price level (where prices react so to speak with infinite speed) can come into conflict with the economic viability of such a model of monetary growth under certain circumstances. Indeed, in criticizing the classical theory of employment, Keynes (1936, pp. 5 ff.) should not only have proposed to dismiss the Classical postulate

[1] The material of this chapter represents a revised and substantially enlarged version of my paper Flaschel (1985).

[2] See Sargent (1987, p. 117).

[3] See also Turnovsky (1977) for another approach toward such integrated macromodels. In contrast to such an alternative representation we shall neglect here the dynamics of the government budget constraint, the Pigou effect, and problems of an appropriate definition of disposable income, see Sargent (1987) and Turnovsky (1977) for details on these topics.

no. 2 from a proper approach toward temporary equilibrium (and the trade cycle), but also the above Classical postulate no. 1. This will be demonstrated in Sect. 6.5 of this chapter and will be further considered in the next chapter, implying that the Sargent model must be modified as far as its treatment of the wage-price sector is concerned to make it an economically complete and consistent Keynesian macromodel of monetary growth.

Sargent's attempt to exploit a complete model of Keynesian dynamics for the demonstration of monetarist propositions therefore fails in general. This conclusion also holds for the "rational expectations" variant of this model to be considered in the next chapter. We can conclude that the basis for Friedmanian propositions in a full-fledged Keynesian dynamic macromodel is small, so that these propositions can generally be rejected as false in such an integrated approach to macrodynamics.

This chapter starts by critically reexamining the dynamic background of the Keynesian temporary equilibrium approach to economic evolution as it is proposed in Sargent (1987, Chap. II). We shall show in Sect. 6.2 that his short-run stability analysis does not pay any attention to Keynes' concept of "effective demand" in its role as a center of gravitation for the actual output of firms. Instead, a modern version of Say's Law is utilized to clear the product- and the money-market by means of their two "prices" in a Walrasian fashion.

Section 6.3 then contrasts this type of dynamic reasoning with an integrated dynamical structure, which is basically economically consistent and which in particular gives rise to the Keynesian point of effective demand via the multiplier process, when infinite adjustment speeds are assumed for an appropriate subset of the full dynamical system, that is, one which is asymptotically stable. Utilizing the concept of "effective demand" therefore serves the purpose of simplifying a consistent, but complex whole of dynamical relationships in the spirit of Keynes rejection of Say's Law. Keynesian underemployment equilibria do not disintegrate "dynamics" into adjustment processes (using hypothetical time) and evolutionary processes (which occur in "real time"), but only reduce an integrated real-time dynamics to the dynamics of temporary equilibria, whenever this latter simplification appears to be justified.

In Sect. 6.4 we then consider the stability of the full employment equilibrium of such a model from the perspective of this short run Keynesian dynamics. We there show that Keynes' (1936) claim "that a flexible wage policy is the right and proper adjunct ...is the opposite of the truth" can be demonstrated in a way that – though simplified – follows some of the arguments that he puts forth to justify this claim. We shall see that it is indeed a fairly straightforward implication of the conventional approach to macroeconomic aggregate demand and supply analysis that flexible wages will destabilize this model under certain circumstances, once the full dynamic structure of this approach is taken into account. This fact seems to have been overlooked in the literature due to its restriction on a mixture of disequilibrium and equilibrium equations in the study of the stability of full employment positions. The instability result of this section justifies the use of a standard money wage Phillips curve to describe the medium run consequences of the state of the labor market.

The medium run dynamics of Sargent's model – which makes use of such a Phillips curve – is then reconsidered in Sect. 6.5. It is shown that Sargent's long run stability considerations– which imply the long-run neutrality of open market operations – have the character of assumptions and thus lack conclusiveness. We shall in fact be able to show (by means of computer simulations and a particularly modified type of analysis) that total instability (extremely explosive behavior) will prevail in Sargent's model of Keynesian dynamics under suitable assumptions on the reaction speeds of prices and expectations. This shows that Sargent's neutrality claim is not justified for a typical IS-LM growth model.

This instability of the wage-price-sector of the model is further analyzed in the appendix to this chapter. Here, we question the meaningfulness of the conventional IS-LM approach, in particular with regard to its strict reliance on only the *short-run* rate of interest (besides output, of course) as the transmission element between money- and product-market equilibria. We shall here provide another simple medium run model for Keynes' (1936, p. 14) claim *that the workers, though unconsciously, are instinctively more reasonable economists than the classical school* in their reluctance to accept a reduction in the general level of money wages.

6.2 Walrasian Price Adjustment in Keynesian Macrodynamics?

As basis for a dynamic analysis of the Keynesian model, the following essentially standard extended IS-LM-equilibrium submodel[4] is employed in Sargent (1987):

$$Y = F(K,L), \tag{6.1}$$

$$W/p = F_{\mathrm{L}}(K,L), \tag{6.2}$$

$$C = c(Y - T - \delta K), \quad 0 < c < 1, \tag{6.3}$$

$$I = i(F_K - \delta - (r - \pi^*))K + nK, \quad i > 0, \tag{6.4}$$

$$Y^{\mathrm{s}} \equiv Y = C + I + G + \delta K \equiv Y^{\mathrm{d}}, \tag{6.5}$$

$$M^{\mathrm{s}} = pm^{\mathrm{d}}(Y,r), \quad m^{\mathrm{d}}_Y > 0, m^{\mathrm{d}}_r < 0. \tag{6.6}$$

Under appropriate assumptions, these six equations suffice to determine the six (statically) endogenous variables:

- Y Output (s supply, d demand; $y = Y/K$)[5]
- L Employment ($l = L/K$)
- p Price level
- C Consumption
- I Investment
- r Nominal rate of interest

---

[4] See here Chaps. 2, 3 and Sargent (1987, Chaps. 1, 2, and 5) for details on the building blocks of this model.

[5] In contrast to the notation employed in the second part of this book we shall use in this part – following Sargent (1987, ch.V) – the symbol y for denoting the output-capital ratio Y/K.

given the (statically) exogenous variables

K	Capital stock
W	Money wage ($w = W/p$ the real wage)
T	Taxes ($t = T/K$ assumed as exogenously given)
δ	Rate of depreciation
π^*	Expected rate of inflation ($\hat{p}$ the actual one)
G	Government expenditure ($g = G/K$ assumed as exogenously given)
L^s	Labor supply ($l^s = L^s/K$; $\widehat{L^s} = n$ exogenously given)
M^s	Money supply ($\widehat{M^s} = \rho$ exogenously given[6])
m^d, m^s	Real money demand and supply ($m_1^s = M^s/L^s, M^s/K = m_1^s l^s$)

Up to the use of the partial derivative F_K of the neoclassical production function[7] F in the investment function I, (6.1)–(6.6) describe a fairly standard aggregate demand and supply equilibrium model. Because of the use of this production function, capital is assumed to be fully employed.[8] Investment demand thus need not pay any attention to the degree of capacity utilization (in contrast to the cases we considered in Sects. 3.4 and 4.6), but is here solely dependent on the difference between the net rate of profit $F_K - \delta$ and the real rate of interest $r - \pi^*$.[9] Note finally that consumption demand is here simply assumed to be proportional to disposable income $Y - \delta K - T$. The above IS-LM model will be extended toward a Solovian growth model with Goodwinian wage adjustment features in the following and will thus provide an integration of some of the models we have studied earlier in Chaps. 2–4).

It is noted in Sargent (1987, p. 29) that

> *is important to verify that the equilibrium positions we have described are stable, i.e. that there is a tendency to return to them if the system is displaced from them. Otherwise the comparative static exercises... are of little practical interest.*

To examine the stability of the above equilibrium positions the following adjustment process is then considered by him (pp. 58 f.):[10]

$$\dot{p} = \sigma(Y^d - Y^s), \ \sigma' > 0, \tag{6.7}$$

$$\dot{r} = \beta(pm^d - M^s), \ \beta' > 0. \tag{6.8}$$

---

[6] We assume for simplicity as in Sargent (1987) that ρ will be equal to n unless the contrary is explicitly stated.

[7] See Sect. 3.5 and Sargent (1987, Chap. 1) for (mathematical) details on the marginal productivity relationships it gives rise to.

[8] This may be rationalized by the empirical argument that capital adjusts much faster to its full employment in the presence of underutilized resources than labor, so that this type of adjustment may be considered in a second step in contrast to the treatment of the unemployed labor force.

[9] Its additional dependence on the rate of growth of labor supply is needed here to allow for the existence of a steady state solution. This problematic assumption will be reconsidered in Chap. 9. See Sargent (1973a, p. 429) for an attempt of justifying this steady state form of an investment equation.

[10] Cf. here also our critique of Barro's related price adjustment formula we have briefly considered in Sect. 2.5.

It is a simple task to prove that this type of adjustment is asymptotically stable, since it is easily established that

$$(Y^{\mathrm{d}} - Y^{\mathrm{s}})(\underset{-}{p}, \underset{-}{r}), \quad m^{\mathrm{d}}(Y^{\mathrm{s}}(\underset{+}{p}), \underset{-}{r})$$

holds true under standard assumptions of IS-LM analysis (which imply that the IS-curve is downward sloping and the LM-curve is upward sloping).[11] The linear part (the Jacobian) of system (6.7) and (6.8) thus is of the following type:

$$J = \begin{pmatrix} - & - \\ + & - \end{pmatrix},$$

which implies the asserted type of stability.

The above adjustment process, however, is of a very peculiar form. Demand Y^{d} may be lower than supply Y^{s} in its course, yet income Y in the consumption function C is always determined by the conditions of supply Y^{s}. The economy behaves during its adjustment to equilibrium as if it remained continuously on the aggregate supply curve $Y^{\mathrm{s}} = Y^{\mathrm{s}}(p)$. This fact can be characterized as a partial form of Say's Law (the *ability* to purchase is never less than the supply of commodities; see Chap. 2 for a detailed treatment of this point). It is therefore not particularly convincing to see that Keynesian comparative static experiments can be justified by help of a process which is at least partly classical in its formulation.[12] Price reactions (p,r) alone seem to suffice here to guarantee the stability and meaningfulness of Keynesian underemployment equilibrium analysis, despite the fact that no such mechanism is discussed in Keynes' General Theory and the related literature. The Keynesian dynamic multiplier in particular seems to be irrelevant for the adjustment toward the Keynesian "multiplier equilibrium." In our view the above dynamic analysis therefore represents an implausible use of a Walrasian adjustment rule in a Keynesian setup – as it was commonly used in the so-called Keynes–*Wicksell* models of monetary growth of the late sixties and early seventies.[13]

To study the dynamics of his model (6.1)–(6.6) in real time, this approach is extended in Sargent (1987, pp. 117 ff.) using the following three dynamic laws, that

---

[11] See Sargent (1987, pp. 58/9) and note that we have an extended IS-LM model here, which treats the price level as endogenous.

[12] An even more classical type of adjustment process is given by its following reformulation, which can be proved to be asymptotically stable in the same simple way (cf. also Chap. 2):

$$\dot{r} = \sigma(Y^{\mathrm{d}} - Y^{\mathrm{s}}), \ \sigma' > 0,$$
$$\dot{p} = \beta(pm^{\mathrm{d}} - M^{\mathrm{s}}), \ \beta' > 0.$$

This further possibility to specify goods- and money-market adjustment processes shows that we have to choose the proper type of adjustment by judging what may be the most adequate extension and dynamic reinterpretation of the employed concept of underemployment equilibrium.

[13] Such a, hybrid, Keynes–Wicksell model of monetary growth will be analyzed in Sect. 9.3 in detail, where it will be established that price flexibility may be bad for the overall stability of its steady state. It thus appears as doubtful whether the price level should be included among the fast variables in such a context – as it is proposed in the above quotation from Sargent (1987).

is, a money-wage Phillips curve, an adaptive adjustment of inflationary expectations and a standard (Keynes–Wicksell) growth equation for the capital stock:[14]

$$\hat{W} = \phi(L/L^s - 1) + \pi^*, \quad \phi > 0, \tag{6.9}$$
$$\dot{\pi}^* = \eta(\hat{p} - \pi^*), \quad \eta > 0, \tag{6.10}$$
$$\hat{K} = i(F_K - \delta - (r - \pi^*)) + n, \tag{6.11}$$

which enrich the model by introducing into it further endogenously determined variables: $\dot{W}, \dot{\pi}^*, \dot{K}$.[15] The *statically* exogenous variables W, π^*, K are thereby made *dynamically* endogenous, that is, their time rate of change depends on certain values of the statically endogenous variables. Finally, there are two further (exogenous) dynamical relationships to be added to the above three laws of motion. They are given by (1) the natural rate of growth of the labor force $\hat{L}^s = n$ $(n > 0)$ and (2) the growth rate of the money supply $\hat{M}^s = \rho$ $(n = \rho$ in the following for simplicity).

The real dynamics (6.9)–(6.11) is contrasted by Sargent (1987, p. 32) with the dynamics (6.7)–(6.8) in the following way:

> *The differential equations set out above [(6.7) and (6.8), P.F.] should not be construed as describing the actual evolution of the system in calendar time. For as we have already pointed out, the* (statically, P.F.) *endogenous variables are assumed to jump instantaneously to satisfy the equilibrium conditions continuously through time. Consequently, we shall interpret the adjustment processes described above [(6.7) and (6.8), P.F.] as processes in which σ and β both approach infinity.*

Time is here considered as dichotomized, as it were, into a vertical and a horizontal component [(6.7), (6.8), and (6.9)–(6.11), respectively], if this method of justifying the equilibrium positions (6.1)–(6.6) is to make any sense. The hypothetical adjustment (6.7),(6.8), however, must then be regarded as a purely formal justification for the employed equilibrium method, since it is but an artificial appendix to it with no meaning for the actual evolution of this Keynesian economy.

As long as σ and β are smaller than infinity, that is, as long as an adjustment of type (6.7) and (6.8) remains visible, this adjustment is in contradiction to a Keynesian (and to Keynes' own[16]) theory of the price level. In this theory (supply) prices are determined by marginal wage costs either instantaneously or with a certain time delay (while the goods-market is cleared by income adjustments). Supply price adjustment is thus determined in Keynes' theory by output and unit wage-costs in a positive way, and not by the law of demand and supply of the market for goods, whereby an increasing output would exercise a negative influence on the dynamics of the price level p.

This correct dynamic background for a Keynesian analysis of aggregate demand and supply will be considered in integrated form, that is, together with the

[14] We need $F_{KL} > 0$ if we want (ceteris paribus) an increase in $\hat{K}$ to be associated with an increase in output and employment.

[15] We shall call such a model an IS-LM model of monetary growth independently of whether the price level is treated as a statically endogenous variable or not.

[16] See Keynes (1936, Chap. 21), and here in particular the second paragraph on p. 300.

above "real" dynamics, in the next section of this chapter providing a stability underpinning for comparative static exercises that need not divorce time into hypothetical and real components.

In our opinion, an integrated view on the dynamics of the whole structure of the considered economy (which may still look somewhat crude at first) should *precede* the formulation of equilibrium conditions. Equilibrium theory then enters the stage as a device that helps to avoid complicated or even unsolvable dynamics under the provisional assumption (or partial demonstration) that at least the part of the dynamical structure which it replaces is *asymptotically* stable. Equilibrium analysis thus is a short-cut of (parts of) a *consistently* formulated dynamic system, which sets certain of its adjustment speeds equal to infinity. An *important consequence* of this methodology is, that equilibrium conditions have to be interpreted in the light of the dynamics, which they are assumed to replace – and not, for example, by means of Sargent's separate choice of a hypothetical Walrasian type of adjustment process.

6.3 Effective Demand as a Device for Simplifying Properly Specified Keynesian Dynamics

The following reformulation of the dynamic structure of the model of Sect. 6.2 employs the same demand and supply functions as were used in this section. The dynamics behind this model is now, however, viewed to be of the following type ($M^{\mathrm{s}}, L^{\mathrm{s}}$ as in the preceding section):

$$\dot{Y} = \alpha(Y^{\mathrm{d}} - Y),\ \alpha > 0, Y^{\mathrm{d}} = Y^{\mathrm{d}}(Y, r), \tag{6.12}$$

$$\dot{r} = \beta(pm^{\mathrm{d}} - M^{\mathrm{s}}),\ \beta > 0, m^{\mathrm{d}} = m^{\mathrm{d}}(Y, r), \tag{6.13}$$

$$\dot{Y}^{\mathrm{s}} = \sigma(Y^{\mathrm{d}} - Y^{\mathrm{s}}),\ \sigma > 0, \tag{6.14}$$

$$\dot{p} = \lambda(W/F_{\mathrm{L}} - p),\ \lambda > 0, \tag{6.15}$$

$$\hat{W} = \phi(L/L^{\mathrm{s}} - 1) + \pi^*,\ \phi > 0, \tag{6.16}$$

$$\dot{\pi}^* = \eta(\hat{p} - \pi^*),\ \eta > 0, \tag{6.17}$$

$$\hat{K} = i(y - wl - \delta - (r - \pi^*)) + n. \tag{6.18}$$

Note that we now employ adjustment parameters instead of adjustment functions $\sigma(\cdot)$, etc., for simplicity. The prevalence of an equilibrium condition instead of one of the above dynamical laws can then be simply expressed, for example, by $\alpha = \infty$, that is,

$$0 = \frac{1}{\alpha}\dot{Y} = Y^{\mathrm{d}} - Y \text{ or } Y^{\mathrm{d}} = Y.$$

Note further that – following the observations made in Sect. 6.2 – the symbol Y is no longer assumed to be identical to supply Y^{s} (as is the case in Sargent's understanding of the Keynesian model). Instead, Y now denotes "planned real income" – to be distinguished from "planned output" in an economy where households do not immediately direct production plans. Equation (6.12) thus states that income plans are changed according to current demand (sale), which also directs the change in planned supply Y^s, see (6.14).[17]

Equation (6.12) is the well-known dynamic multiplier, while (6.13) relies on the liquidity preference theory of interest rate dynamics. Equation (6.14) describes an output adjustment mechanism $[Y^d = c(\cdot) + I(\cdot) + G + \delta K]$. Note here that Y^s and thus employment $L(Y^s)$, given by $Y^s = F(K,L)$, are now predetermined in each moment of time. The final new equation (6.15) generalizes (6.2). It now allows for finite adjustment speeds of the price-level p to the conventional rule of marginal cost pricing, cf. here Chap. 2 (Fig. 2.1 and the comments made on it).[18] Note that the use of this adjustment equation demands a change in the calculation of the actual rate of profit then to be used in the investment demand function, cf. (6.18). Note furthermore that the use of this formula of a delayed adjustment of prices toward marginal wage costs – in place of the instantaneous adjustment rule (6.2) – avoids the necessity of calculating the rate of inflation from the equilibrium price level in a complicated way.[19] Equation (6.15) instead simply states that the rate of inflation depends in each moment of time on the cost-push factors output (employment) and unit wage-costs while all other influences are only considered by way of dynamic repercussions as time evolves. This makes instantaneous feedbacks much simpler to understand, while the dynamics is, of course, increased thereby by one dimension and in its complexity.

If one dislikes the above extension of (6.2) toward the dynamic law (6.15), one may instead also assume one of the following dynamical laws for describing the evolution of the price level p[20]

$$\dot{p} = \lambda\,(A \cdot WL/Y^s - p), \quad A > 1,$$
$$\dot{p} = \lambda\,(A \cdot W/F_L - p), \quad A > 1,$$

in order to avoid certain problematic features of the above adjustment rule for prices p.[21] Note that the second of the above equations represents a simple generalization of (6.15) toward imperfect competition, which applies the mark-up A to marginal, instead of average labor costs. Note also that both (6.15) and (6.2) should be read as representing a theory of the price level in Keynesian economics and not as providing a theory of labor demand as textbooks often assume.[22] In place of (6.7)[23]

[17] We neglect here the role of expected demand as possibly distinct from aggregate demand Y^d as well as the role of unplanned inventory changes to make the dynamic structure of this Keynesian model not too complicated at this starting point of the investigation.

[18] McCallum (1978, p. 427) makes use of such a delayed price adjustment in a discrete time log-linear model of the medium run to investigate by it the validity of the "Lucas–Sargent proposition" for sluggish price adjustments.

[19] By means of the implicit function theorem that gives rise to $p = H(W, \pi^*, K, M^s, G, T)$, and by means of logarithmic differentiation of this formula.

[20] See Hall (1988) for a recent empirical investigation (and rejection) of the marginal cost principle and for alternative proposals of its replacement by other pricing rules.

[21] See Turnovsky (1977, pp. 29, 92) for further alternatives.

[22] See Keynes (1936, Chap. 21.II) in this regard.

[23] Which is of a classical cross-dual type.

these adjustment rules postulate a price adjustment in the tradition of Keynesian adjustment rules where prices primarily react with respect to price-cost differentials (and quantities with respect to quantity discrepancies as in (6.14), for example). These equations must be extended to include an expression for inflations if there is significant inflation (e.g., in the case where $\hat{M}^s > n$ holds true). Various ways of doing this will be considered in Sect. 6.5 and the following chapters of this book, where also cross-dual types of price adjustment procedures will be considered.

For our purposes, it is not necessary to apply one of the above alternative price setting rules in the following (which in fact would not change much in our argumentation). We shall instead make use of (6.15) to investigate the properties of its limit case (6.2): $\lambda = \infty$. If we interpret the production function and the marginal productivity rule built upon it as representing "normal" capacity utilization, the rule (6.15) simply says that producers for whom it is profitable to expand output beyond the aggregate demand constraint will use this fact of an excess of prices over marginal wage costs to lower their prices, while sales which exceed this normal capacity (but not the absolute capacity to produce) will lead to price increases to catch up with the marginal wage costs that are caused by this excessive use of capacity. The higher the parameter λ, the quicker will be the response of producers to such an imbalance between marginal wage costs and actual prices.[24] In the limit, $\lambda = \infty$ and $\sigma = \infty$ this, however, means that producers accept Y^d as quantity signal for their production plans as well as the basis for calculating their marginal wage costs, which then exactly determine the prices at which they will sell this output. They thus face a twofold constraint that leaves them nothing to decide. This strange situation – which is often present in macroeconomic modeling[25] – gives also the reason for the strange behavior of the Sargent model, in the case where inflationary expectations are sufficiently close to the actual rate of inflation ($\eta \to \infty$, see our investigations in Sect. 6.5 and Chap. 7).

We thus find that the fact that (6.15) allows for prices being greater or smaller than marginal wage costs can be justified methodologically, since it will provide a better understanding of the peculiarities of its limit case, that is, (6.2). Of course, regime switching methods together with a more convincing formulation of target prices (plus the side condition $p \geq W/F_L$) must be used in the end for a

[24] In contrast to Barro's problematic disequilibrium approach to aggregate demand and supply analysis which we have briefly considered in Sect. 2.5, we here interpret an aggregate demand and supply disequilibrium as a goods market equilibrium at which there is an imbalance between actual prices and the ones that firms intend to charge on the basis of their present marginal wage costs. As already stated, price setting behavior may attempt to establish target prices, which are higher than these – from the viewpoint of firms – minimal target prices. The exact target determination is, however, of less importance than the assumption that there is a somewhat sluggish (staggered) adjustment of prices towards their momentary equilibrium levels in interaction with the changing levels of effective demand that result from such adjustment processes. Aggregate demand and supply equilibrium thus is the situation where not only the goods- and the money-market are cleared, but where producers are also content with the level of prices that prevails in this situation.

[25] But is not viewed in this way generally, due to a price-taking interpretation that concentrates on the point where aggregate demand equals aggregate supply.

proper economic formulation of the above Keynesian model (see Turnovsky (1977, Chap. 6) and here Chap. 8 for examples).

It is possible to transform (6.12) and (6.13) into equilibrium conditions $\alpha = \beta = \infty$ without having goods market equilibrium at one and the same time, since $\alpha, \beta = \infty$ only implies that aggregate expenditure equals aggregate income $Y = Y^{\mathrm{d}} = Y_0$. The value Y_0 is what we would propose as the *definition of effective demand* $(Y = Y^{\mathrm{d}})$ for the above model. This notion thus is – by the proposed alternative dynamic background to Sargent's model – not equivalent to the prevalence of product market equilibrium. Producers may still have incorrect anticipations of this point of effective demand Y_0 and may consequently still follow an adjustment rule of type (6.14). It is supply here that has to adjust to the conditions of (effective) demand, and not vice versa, as it is suggested when use is made of $Y^{\mathrm{d}}(Y,\ldots), Y \equiv Y^{\mathrm{s}}$, that is, when the standard interpretation of the concept of real income in macroeconomic theory is employed [see Chap. 2 for more details on this modern counterpart to Say's Law]. Note here also that the above adjustment to product market equilibrium takes place in *real* time, which in particular means that a sufficient amount of inventories has been assumed to exist to avoid a treatment of supply bottlenecks. For simplicity and for reasons of comparability with Sect. 6.2, we have, however, refrained from adding an inventory adjustment process to the above dynamical equations.

Equations (6.12)–(6.15) provide a coherent economic background for the equilibrium submodel of Sect. 6.2 $(\alpha = \beta = \lambda = \sigma = \infty)$. They exhibit an unambiguous pricing behavior. They describe the dynamic multiplier in a standard IS-LM framework, which together with the output adjustment mechanism (6.14) – if stable – then provide a proper justification to the assumption of product- and money-market equilibrium, in contrast to the dubious Walrasian process (6.7) and (6.8) that is employed in Sargent (1987, pp. 58 f.) for this purpose. They will be used in the remainder of this chapter to show that there are strong economic reasons that suggest that the parameters λ, ϕ (in contrast to α, β, σ) have to be chosen sufficiently small for a viable economic environment.

With respect to the latter parameters it is easy to show the asymptotic stability of the adjustment processes (6.12)–(6.14) they are related to – independent from their particular size. For the three then dynamically endogenous variables Y, r, and Y^{s}, (6.1), (6.3), (6.5), and (6.6) imply with respect to the Jacobian of this system the following type of sign structure:[26]

$$J = \begin{pmatrix} \alpha(Y_Y^{\mathrm{d}} - 1) & \alpha Y_r^{\mathrm{d}} & 0 \\ \beta p m_Y^{\mathrm{d}} & \beta p m_r^{\mathrm{d}} & 0 \\ \sigma Y_Y^{\mathrm{d}} & \sigma Y_r^{\mathrm{d}} & -\sigma \end{pmatrix} = \begin{pmatrix} - & - & 0 \\ + & - & 0 \\ + & - & - \end{pmatrix}$$

[if it is again assumed that $Y_Y^{\mathrm{d}} < 1$ holds true].[27] It is an easy task to show that the above sign structure will satisfy the Routh–Hurwitz criterion of local asymptotic stability [see Sect. 3.8]. The substructure (6.12)–(6.14) of the whole dynamical system thus fulfills an obviously necessary condition for its replacement by the

[26] Which is well-known for the subsystem that belongs to the first two dynamic variables and which should have been used in place of (6.7) and (6.8) by Sargent.

[27] See Sargent (1987, p. 54).

particular case $\alpha = \beta = \sigma = \infty$, that is, by equilibrium conditions. This means that part of the complicated dynamics of system (6.12)–(6.18) is (provisionally) short-circuited by means of equilibrium equations, which postulate an instantaneous reaction of this substructure of the system with regard to exogenous shocks, but which are nevertheless based on a definite dynamic interpretation of their reaction. This interpretation is (1) that (6.12) and (6.13) together determine the point of effective demand Y_0, where expenditure equals (and thus confirms) expected income, and (2) that entrepreneurs correctly anticipate this point of effective demand.

It is obvious that the introduction of the point of effective demand and the assumption of its perfect anticipation by entrepreneurs considerably simplify the above dynamic structure (6.12)–(6.18). It is equally obvious, however, that the background of this simplification must be carefully kept in mind (1) to avoid misplaced conceptualizations of the employed equilibrium substructure [à la Sargent's (6.7) and (6.8)], and (2) to judge whether the line between statically and dynamically endogenous variables has been drawn in an economically convincing way. This in particular means that the parts of the model where perfect expectations have been assumed should not be in direct contradiction to the more explicit formulation of the dynamics of the system, where errors and adjustments occur.

6.4 On the Short-Run Instability of Full Employment Positions

We have seen in the preceding section that it may be justified to replace the three dynamic laws (6.12)–(6.14) by algebraic ones, that is, by equilibrium conditions. The question arises whether this methodological advice can also be extended to the dynamic law (6.15), that is, whether it is justified to include also the labor market into the equilibrium part of the model as it is done in the classical variant of the neoclassical synthesis.

From a Walrasian perspective the answer to this question is "yes." To show this, we assume as a simplifying device again the conventional identity $Y \equiv Y^{\mathrm{s}}$ in place of the adjustment equation (6.14). Following the methodology of Sect. 6.2 there then remain the following adjustment equations to be considered:[28]

$$\dot{p} = \sigma(Y^{\mathrm{d}} - Y^{\mathrm{s}}), \quad Y^{\mathrm{d}} = C(\cdot) + I(\cdot) + nK + \delta K + G, \tag{6.19}$$

$$\dot{r} = \beta(pm^{\mathrm{d}} - M^{\mathrm{s}}), \quad m^{\mathrm{d}} = m^{\mathrm{d}}(Y^{\mathrm{s}}, r), \tag{6.20}$$

$$\dot{W} = \phi(L^{\mathrm{d}} - L^{\mathrm{s}}), \quad L^{\mathrm{d}} = L^{\mathrm{d}}(Y^{\mathrm{s}}, K). \tag{6.21}$$

[28] We use the law (6.21) in place of the original Phillips curve to simplify the presentation. This does not alter the following stability results, since the variables T, G, K, L^{s}, andπ^* are all considered as being exogenously given in the present investigation of the Sargent model. Note also that we have followed Sargent's Chap. I presentation of momentary equilibria here by making use of the more general expressions C' and I' in place of the constants c, and i. Note finally that we have refrained from growth rate and percentage formulations in the above approach to short-run dynamics for reasons of simplicity.

To study the stability of this model of a Walrasian price tâtonnement, we furthermore assume that the classical version of the neoclassical synthesis is given as its appropriate background, that is, the complete "classical" model as it is defined in Sargent (1987, Chap. I).[29] This means that we assume that prices are equal to marginal wage costs ($\lambda = \infty$, which here gives a theory of employment) and that labor supply is statically endogenous and described by the function $L^s(W/p)$, $(L^s)' > 0$.[30]

Sargent (1987, I.7) approaches the stability problem of the classical full employment model in the following simplified way:

$$\dot{p} = \sigma(Y^d(\bar{Y}^s, r) - \bar{Y}^s), \quad \sigma > 0, \tag{6.22}$$
$$\dot{r} = \beta(m^d(\bar{Y}^s, r) - M^s/p), \quad \beta > 0, \tag{6.23}$$

since he implicitly assumes that employment and output stay at their full employment levels $\bar{L}^s, \bar{Y}^s$ during this adjustment process ($\phi = \infty$).[31] This is achieved by assuming that nominal wages move according to $W = w_0 p$, where w_0 is the given real wage that clears the labor market. The Jacobian of this special dynamics is given by

$$J = \begin{pmatrix} 0 & \sigma Y_r^d \\ \beta M^s/p^2 & \beta m_r^d \end{pmatrix} = \begin{pmatrix} 0 & - \\ + & - \end{pmatrix},$$

which immediately gives the asymptotic stability of this dynamics at its full employment equilibrium.[32]

It is obvious that one cannot prove the stability of the full employment equilibrium by assuming that the economy stays at the full employment level while prices and the rate of interest adjust so as to clear the goods- and the money-market. Sargent's (1987, I.7) proof of the value of comparative static exercises in the full employment context thus does not prove anything on this matter.

To study the stability of this equilibrium point from the Walrasian perspective of a pure price tâtonnement process, we have to make use of the above full (p, r, W)-dynamics instead. To this end, we assume for the marginal propensity to spend out of income the conventional condition:

$$Y_Y^d = C' + I' F_{KL} L_Y(Y, K) < 1, \quad Y \equiv Y^s(p, W), Y_p, Y_W > 0,$$

[29] An even more classical dynamics can once again be obtained by interchanging the two laws, which govern price and interest dynamics which again does not endanger the stability of this dynamics.

[30] Sargent (1987, p. 18) assumes a more general consumption function $C(Y_D, r - \bar{\pi}^*)$ for this model, which – when added here – does not modify the following stability results.

[31] One might equally well assume that the price level or the rate of interest is always at its equilibrium value ($\sigma = \infty, \beta = \infty$) and would thereby also obtain dynamical subsystems of the above three-dimensional dynamics which are asymptotically stable. There is, however, no justification for the consideration of such subsystems in a proof of the stability of full employment equilibrium.

[32] Note here, however, that Sargent's (1987, p. 30) calculation of the Jacobian of this dynamics is more complicated than the trivial calculation in the above model due to the more complex definition of disposable income Y_D he assumes for this calculation.

where the function $L_Y(Y,K)$ is given by $1/F_L$, the derivative of the employment function $L = L(Y,K)$ (see Sargent (1987, pp. 58 ff.) for related calculations).

For the Jacobian or the linear part of system (6.19), (6.20) and (6.21), we thereby obtain

$$J = \begin{pmatrix} \sigma(Y_Y^d - 1)Y_p^s & -\sigma I' & \sigma(Y_Y^d - 1)Y_W^s \\ \beta\left(\frac{M^s}{p^2} + m_Y^d Y_p^s\right) & \beta m_r^d & \beta m_Y^d Y_W^s \\ \phi(L_p^d - L_p^s) & 0 & \phi(L_W^d - L_W^s) \end{pmatrix} = \begin{pmatrix} - & - & + \\ + & - & - \\ + & 0 & - \end{pmatrix}.$$

The partial derivatives Y_p^s, Y_W^s (and similar for L^d, L^s) are related to each other by

$$Y_W^s = Y_\omega^s \cdot \left(\frac{1}{p}\right) = -\frac{p}{W} Y_W^s \left(-\frac{W}{p^2}\right) = -\frac{p}{W} \cdot Y_p^s,$$

since Y^s (and L^d, L^s) only depend on the real wage $w = \frac{W}{p}$ (and the given capital stock K). This implies that the expression $J_{11}J_{33} - J_{31}J_{13}$ (one of the principal minors of the above Jacobian J) must be zero, while the other two principal minors are positive. And for the determinant of J we get by the same argument

$$\begin{aligned} \det J &= -J_{12}(J_{21}J_{33} - J_{23}J_{31}), \\ &= \sigma I' \beta \frac{M^s}{p^2} \phi \left(L_W^d - L_W^s\right) < 0. \end{aligned}$$

Since trace J is obviously negative, we thus have that all coefficients of the characteristic polynomial of $J : \lambda^3 + a_1\lambda^2 + a_2\lambda + a_3$ must be positive. According to the Routh–Hurwitz theorem (Sect. 3.8), there remains to be shown that $a_1 a_2 > a_3$ (or $-\text{trace}\, J \cdot a_2 > -\det J$) holds true in addition to obtain the local asymptotic stability of the system (6.19), (6.20), and (6.21) at the full employment equilibrium point.

The proof of this last stability condition is also easy, since we have

$$-J_{12}J_{21}J_{33} < 0 \quad \text{and} \quad J_{12}J_{23}J_{31} > 0,$$

and since the first and positive component of $-\det J$ is also contained as a positive component in the expression $-$ trace $J \cdot a_2$. We thus have the result that pure price adjustments are capable of moving the economy back to its full employment equilibrium[33] if this equilibrium position is (slightly) disturbed by an exogenous shock. This is in line with the general view that price flexibility guarantees continual market clearing. Nevertheless, the above approach of justifying comparative static exercises of full-employment equilibria is inadequate, since it treats the "classical case" of the Neoclassical synthesis by means of a Walrasian pure price tâtonnement (as used in Walrasian general equilibrium theory) despite the existence of quantity constraints for households and firms in disequilibrium. Yet, just as the Keynesian as well as

[33] For all choices of the adjustment parameters σ, β, and ϕ!

the "classical" equilibrium position are obtained from the same general model by operating it under a different set of additional assumption,we should also obtain the disequilibrium dynamics of this model from a common super-structure of this dynamics, as the one we have considered in the preceding section.

The neoclassical/Keynesian synthesis rests on the agreement that the economy is not governed by price movements alone, but also by quantity constraints (actual current income and aggregate demand, and not only given initial endowments) and their dynamics. These quantity constraints must – at least in principle – be included in the dynamics that is used to justify comparative statics (as it is demanded by Sargent).

To provide such an analysis we have to employ the dynamic multiplier process

$$\dot{Y} = \alpha(Y^{\mathrm{d}}(Y,r) - Y), \quad Y \equiv Y^{\mathrm{s}} \tag{6.24}$$

in place of the problematic, since contradictory price adjustment rule (6.19). To avoid the more complex dynamics that uses (6.15) in addition (which will be considered later on), we assume again that its special case $p = W/F_{\mathrm{L}}(\lambda = \infty)$ holds true. This equality was also employed in the above considered Walrasian adjustment toward full employment, where it determined output Y^{s} as a function of wages W and currently given prices p. The price-taking behavior that is contained in this type of approach is now dismissed from the model, which instead assumes that the (statically endogenous) price level is determined by the marginal wage costs, which correspond to the quantity Y that is currently produced. Once again, we neglect inventory changes as an additional influence on the above simple multiplier dynamics.

For the Jacobian of this simple Keynesian revision of a Walrasian type of adjustmentprocess (with a Y, r, W-dynamics in place of the former p, r, W-dynamics) we get

$$J = \begin{pmatrix} \alpha(Y^{\mathrm{d}}_Y - 1) & -\alpha I' & 0 \\ \beta(\frac{M^{\mathrm{s}}}{p^2} p_Y + m^{\mathrm{d}}_Y) & \beta m^{\mathrm{d}}_r & \beta \frac{M^{\mathrm{s}}}{p^2} p_W \\ \phi(L^{\mathrm{d}}_Y - L^{\mathrm{s}}_p p_Y) & 0 & -\phi(L^{\mathrm{s}}_p p_W + L^{\mathrm{s}}_W) \end{pmatrix} = \begin{pmatrix} - & - & 0 \\ + & - & + \\ + & 0 & ? \end{pmatrix}.$$

This calculation has been based on the well-known relationships

$$L^{\mathrm{d}} = L^{\mathrm{d}}(Y,K), L^{\mathrm{d}}_Y > 0 \text{ and } p = p(Y,W), p_Y, p_W > 0$$

for employment and marginal cost prices of the standard aggregate supply analysis ($p = W/F_{\mathrm{L}}(Y,K)$).

We note that the substructure

$$J = DZ = \begin{pmatrix} \alpha & 0 \\ 0 & \beta \end{pmatrix} \begin{pmatrix} Y^{\mathrm{d}}_Y - 1 & -I' \\ m^{\mathrm{d}}_Y & m^{\mathrm{d}}_r \end{pmatrix} = \begin{pmatrix} \alpha(Y^{\mathrm{d}}_Y - 1) & -\alpha I' \\ \beta m^{\mathrm{d}}_Y & \beta m^{\mathrm{d}}_r \end{pmatrix}$$

is generally used to prove the stability of the simple IS-LM model (trace $J < 0, \det J > 0$), where the price level p is still exogenous. The above therefore represents a natural generalization of this standard IS-LM-dynamically approach.

In view of the aims that are pursued by Sargent's (1987, I.7) stability analysis, this represents, however, an important generalization of the IS-LM dynamics, since it will show (despite its still fairly limited perspective) that it is not legitimate to include the money wage W among the equilibrating variables without detailed justification.

The first thing that is to be noted for the above Jacobian is that its entry J_{33} – so far denoted by ? – must be zero in fact – due to the fact $L^{\mathrm{s}}_{\mathrm{p}} = -L^{\mathrm{s}}_{w}\frac{W}{p^2}$, $L^{\mathrm{s}}_{W} = L^{\mathrm{s}}_{w}\frac{1}{p}$, $p_W = \frac{1}{F_L} = \frac{p}{W}$ must hold true.

This property of the above Jacobian immediately implies that the first three Routh–Hurwitz conditions $\det J < 0$ and trace $J < 0$ as well as $a_2 > 0$ must be true for it.

And for the final condition $b = a_1 a_2 - a_3 > 0$ we get in this case

$$\begin{aligned} b &= -(J_{11} + J_{22})\alpha\beta \det Z + J_{12}J_{23}J_{31} \\ &= -\alpha\beta((J_{11} + J_{22})\det Z + \phi(L^{\mathrm{d}}_{Y} - L^{\mathrm{s}}_{\mathrm{p}} p_Y)\frac{M^{\mathrm{s}}}{p^2} p_W I'). \end{aligned}$$

This gives that the full-employment equilibrium will be asymptotically stable for all values of the adjustment parameter ϕ, which are smaller than the following positive expression (which depends on α, β):

$$\frac{-(J_{11} + J_{22})\det Z}{(L^{\mathrm{d}}_{Y} - L^{\mathrm{s}}_{p} p_Y)\frac{M^{\mathrm{s}}}{p^2} p_W I'}$$

and it will be unstable for all ϕ, which are larger than it.[34]

We conclude that it may be dangerous to include the money wage among the equilibrating variables, since this implicitly demands that very flexible, but not infinitely flexible wages should also always lead the economy to the full employment equilibrium which – as we have shown – is not the case for certain ranges of market adjustment speeds. Proposing flexible wages (as many economists do, at least by the choice of the models they analyze) is thus not a save strategy for an improvement of the working of the economy. The above instead provides simple example for Keynes' (1936, p. 14) remark:

> *Thus it is fortunate that the workers, though unconsciously, are instinctively more reasonable economists than the classical school, inasmuch as they resist reductions of money wages, ...*

[34] This stability condition shows that it is justified to expect stability if IS or/and LM equilibrium holds at each moment in time ($\alpha, \beta = \infty, \phi < \infty$), while it indicates problems for the case where the labor market is assumed to be in equilibrium as well. The meaningful Keynesian alternative to this procedure is to assume the condition $\phi = 0$ for the short run – by which the stability of temporary underemployment positions this implies is guaranteed – and to consider the consequences of changing wages only in the longer run.

Keynes (1936, Chap. 19, p. 262) explanation of the background of this statement is the following:

> *Thus the reduction in money-wages will have no lasting tendency to increase employment except by virtue of its repercussions either on the propensity to consume for the community as a whole, or on the schedule of marginal efficiencies of capital, or on the rate of interest. There is no method of analyzing the effect of a reduction in money-wages, except by following up its possible effects on these three factors.*

In the model here under consideration, the repercussions of falling money-wages concern – via falling prices – solely the rate of interest and its influence on the level of net investment. This rate will fall with falling prices and thus make investment in real capital more attractive.[35] This counteracts the fall in wages by raising output and employment, yet – as we have shown – in a way that can lead to instability if wages react to fast with respect to situations of under- or overemployment.[36] We conjecture that this may lead to overshooting processes with an ever increasing amplitude in such a flexwage economy. This conjecture is confirmed by numerical simulations of the model as is exemplified by Fig. 6.1.
This simulation shows that a contraction in the money supply leads at first to an increase in the rate of interest and a decrease in prices, output, and nominal wages. The phase diagram on the right hand side of Fig. 6.1 then shows that wages and output continue to decrease, but that output begins to recover after some time due to the expansionary effects that are caused by the decrease in wages and prices. Wages, by assumption, can begin to increase only after output has returned to its normal (full employment) level. The increasing wages and prices will then in turn

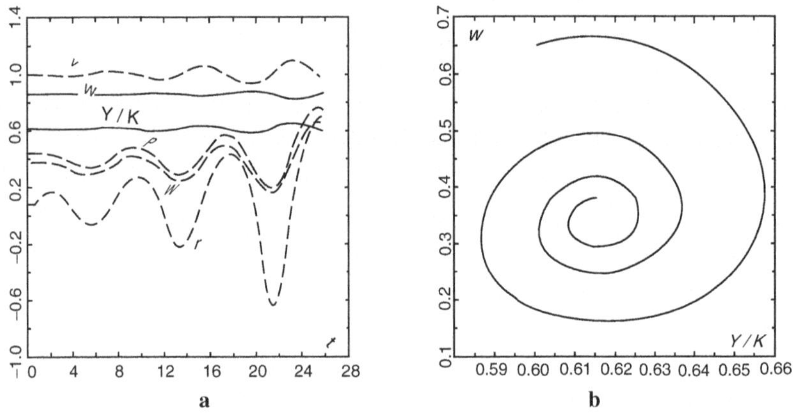

Fig. 6.1 Explosive cycles by wages that react in a too flexible way

[35] See also Keynes (1936, p. 265) in this regard.

[36] The introduction of the Pigou effect does not change this situation in an essential way, since we will then get $J_{13} < 0$ (instead of 0), which again implies the above sort of condition for the positivity of the term b (as well as the same signs for the determinant and trace of the Jacobian J).

and after the elapse of some time interval enforce that output has to start to decline again back to its normal level. Yet, when this point is reached, wages and prices start falling again, the contractionary forces continue to work (for a while) and the above cycle will be repeated again, but with an increase in its amplitude for the above choice of parameter values.[37] Note that this model contains and thus explains periods of stagflation without making use of inflationary expectations ($\pi^* = 0$ in the above simulation).

> *The chief result of this policy (of flexible wages, PF) would be to cause a great instability of prices, so violent perhaps as to make business calculations futile in an economic society functioning after the manner of that in which we live. To suppose that a flexible wage policy is a right and proper adjunct of a system which on the whole is one of laissez-faire, is the opposite of the truth.*
>
> (Keynes, 1936, p. 269).

We stress that the above provides only a very preliminary illustration for these passages from the General Theory due to the fairly restrictive form of a Keynesian IS-LM model of temporary equilibrium that is here employed. This model represents an intermediate position between the following two polar cases:

- No adjustment at all in the goods- and the money-market ($\alpha, \beta = 0$)
- A full adjustment in the goods- and money-market ($\alpha, \beta = \infty$)

In the first case we have the core of Keynes' argument that a flexible wage policy will be destabilizing, since nothing will stop the decline of wages and prices in a situation of underemployment then. The second case by contrast incorporates the full impact effect of falling wages and prices on the rate of interest (the so-called Keynes effect) and by it on effective demand. This case can be easily reduced to a single dynamic law of the following kind (by eliminating the equilibrium values of Y, r, p from its initial formulation):

$$\dot{W} = \phi(L^{\mathrm{d}}(W) - L^{\mathrm{s}}(W)), L^{\mathrm{d}}_W < 0, L^{\mathrm{s}}_W > 0.$$

This gives a wage adjustment that is globally asymptotically stable. What we have shown in this regard by our consideration of the full dynamic story is that the first case represents the approximate truth when wages react "more" flexible than income and the rate of interest with respect to situations of disequilibrium (see the above condition for the parameter ϕ), while the second case comes about when the multiplier process and interest adjustments operate with sufficient speed. On balance, the above analysis thus still supports the view that a gradual adjustment of nominal wages might be helpful in a situation of disequilibrium. It nevertheless already questions the meaningfulness of the Classical flexprice full employment equilibrium – also in the presence of the Pigou effect – as a proper description of temporary equilibrium, and this also, since less favorable cases than the above well-behaved interactions of demand and supply,[38] are easily conceivable (see Keynes

[37] Which in the present case are given by $\sigma = 0.2$, $\beta = 0.002$, $\phi = 0.002$, ($M^{\mathrm{s}} = 500$, $L^{\mathrm{s}} = 1{,}000$, $K = 2{,}000$).

[38] cf. also Keynes (1936, p. 263, case (5)) in this regard.

(1936, pp. 262 ff.) for a nonexhaustive list of such cases). Discussing conditions for the existence of full employment positions (as the Keynes- or the Pigou-effect) is not (one should say, of course, not) sufficient for proving the asymptotic stability of it.

A more refined analysis of the problems of a flexible wage policy must take into account the mentioned more complicated repercussions from wages to the level of economic activity, such as, for example, the Mundell effect, which provides an example for an adverse effect of wage deflation on aggregate demand through the latter's positive dependence on the expected rate of price inflation, see Tobin (1980) for a detailed discussion of it for example. In comparison to a recent discussion of Flemming (1987) of the effects of wage flexibility, the above is, however, much closer to Keynes' point of view, since it relies on an approach that to some extent reflects the feedback structure of the model used by Keynes. Fleming's approach, by contrast, assumes a money-wage adjustment equation, which gives rise to a stable and isolated feedback mechanism of real-wages onto themselves and thus excludes any repercussion of the IS-LM part of the model on wage dynamics (by means of the rate of unemployment). This is a rather artificial approach to Keynes' denial of the success of a flexible wage policy.

Our above instability result also suggests that the Phillips-curve relationship (6.16) of Sect. 6.3 should not be replaced by an equilibrium relationship, but that money wages should be grouped among those variables that are dynamically endogenous and whose behavior must therefore be studied in its interactions with the other dynamically endogenous variables $K, \ldots$ in their joint evolution in time.

By contrast, we have treated the price level p as a statically endogenous variable in the above stability analysis. The remainder of this chapter and the next chapter will, however, show that this will give rise to instability conclusions (of a different type) as well – now on the basis that money-wages are assumed to respond sluggishly. We thereby will arrive at the final conclusion that the classical version of the neoclassical synthesis is not a sensible model of the economy only from the viewpoint of temporary equilibrium, but also from the viewpoint of long run steady state analysis. Sluggish nominal wages and prices are thus necessary preconditions for a meaningful Keynesian IS-LM growth model, that is, one which is at least viable in its economic evolution. The conditions $\alpha = \beta = \gamma = \infty$ that establish the Keynesian concept of a temporary underemployment equilibrium are thus the most that should be assumed as equilibrium conditions and thus as simplification in the analysis of the complete dynamic structure (6.12)–(6.18) we have briefly investigated in Sect. 6.3.

Digression

The instability result of this section and the justification it provides for the use of a Phillips curve relationship instead of the assumption of perfectly flexible wages in the discussion of the interaction of aggregate demand and supply can be usefully compared with the approach that is chosen in the textbook of Dornbusch and Fischer

(1987) in their explanation of this interaction. Instead of a Neoclassical description of the functioning of the labor market (as we have used it above), these authors start from the following three simple relationships in their derivation of a dynamic schedule of aggregate supply:

$$\bar{y} = Y/L = \text{const},$$
$$p = (1+a)WL/Y = (1+a)W/\bar{y}, \hat{W} = \phi(Y-\bar{Y}) = \phi\bar{y}\bar{L^s}\frac{L-\bar{L}}{\bar{L^s}}.$$

These expressions stand for the following assumptions of their model of a medium run dynamics: constant (instead of diminishing) productivity of labor, a markup pricing rule (with – in comparison to the one we have presented in Sect. 6.3 – an infinitely fast adjustment of prices to their target level), and a money-wage Phillips curve, which is based on the natural rate assumption $\bar{L} < L^s$ (see Dornbusch and Fischer (1987, Chap. 13) for the introduction and justification of these assumptions).[39] This model is supplemented by a static aggregate demand curve by Dornbusch and Fischer, which is by and large based on the same building blocks as the aggregate demand schedule of the present chapter. We therefore shall not modify our assumptions in this regard.

The Keynesian type of an adjustment procedure (6.24), (6.20), and (6.21), whose stability properties we have investigated above, gives in the Dornbusch and Fischer case rise to the following Jacobian at its full employment point of rest:

$$J = \begin{pmatrix} \alpha(Y_Y^d - 1) & -\alpha I' & 0 \\ \beta m_Y^d & \beta m_r^d & \beta\frac{M^s}{p^2}(1+a)/\bar{y} \\ \phi W/\bar{y} & 0 & 0 \end{pmatrix} = \begin{pmatrix} - & - & 0 \\ + & - & + \\ + & 0 & 0 \end{pmatrix}$$

due to $p_Y = 0, p_W = (1+a)/\bar{y}$ in the present case. This Jacobian is closely related to the one we have considered above for the case of a Neoclassical formulation of the labor market and it gives rise to the same (in) stability conclusions as in this earlier case.

We once again conclude that it is not sensible to include the money wage among the equilibrating variables, but that this is possible – though not necessary – for the two other dynamic variables Y, and r, which can thus be assumed to clear the goods- and the money-market at each moment in time. This is exactly the limit case that is considered in Chap. 13 of Dornbusch and Fischer's (1987) textbook. In their Chap. 14 they then go on by augmenting the Phillips curve in the usual additive way by a term that reflects expectations about inflation. Such a supply side equation is then combined with a dynamic aggregate demand schedule of the type

[39] Because of the assumption of a constant labor (and capital) productivity, the investment function can be simplified to the simple textbook format $I(r), I' < 0$ in this discussion of the short-run stability of the full employment position.

$\dot{Y} = \varphi(\hat{M}^s - \hat{p})$. This model is closely related to the discussion in the next section[40] and will be briefly considered in an appendix to it.[41]

6.5 On the Instability of Long-Run Full Employment Equilibrium

We have defined in Sect. 6.3 the value of *effective demand* as that particular point of the aggregate demand function $C + I + \delta K + G$, where income expectations lead to a level of this demand that exactly confirms these expectations ($Y^d = Y, \alpha, \beta = \infty$). Assuming furthermore that output- and price-adjustment speeds are infinite ($\sigma, \lambda = \infty$), then again gives rise to the formal structure (6.1)–(6.6), (6.9)–(6.11) of Sargent's Keynesian dynamics (see Sect. 6.2), which will now be investigated with regard to its long-run properties. We have seen how this dynamical structure can be purified from all classical elements à la Say ($Y \equiv Y^s$) and Neoclassical elements of Walrasian type [see (6.7) and (6.8)]. Output is adjusting to aggregate or effective demand and not vice versa, if the Keynesian equilibrium conditions are interpreted dynamically along Keynesian lines in a consistent way.

It is claimed in Sargent (1987), p. 124), however, that even

> though this model is clearly Keynesian in its momentary or point-in-time behavior, its steady state or long-run properties are "classical" in the sense that real variables are unaffected by the money supply.

There is no formal proof for this assertion in Sargent's book, but only verbal and graphical argumentation (for the case where $\pi^* \equiv 0$ holds true, see his p. 122) which seem to suggest this assertion on the asymptotic behavior of the system. We shall, however, see in the following that the above claim on the asymptotic long-run properties of this model is in general wrong.

Yet, for the case $\pi^* \equiv 0$ ($\eta = 0$ and $\pi^* = 0$ at the beginning), that is, static steady state expectations, the assertion of asymptotic stability is indeed correct. This can be shown as follows:

In this case, (6.10) is suspended (replaced by $\pi^*(t) \equiv 0$) during the dynamic process that follows a once-and-for-all jump in the money supply. Equation (6.10) thereby becomes redundant in the discussion of Sargent's dynamical system, which makes possible a simple analytical treatment of Sargent's limit case $\lambda = \infty$, that is, $p = W/F_L$ [instead of our later alternative (6.15)]. There then remains the investigation of the following dynamical system:

$$\hat{W} = \phi(l/l^s - 1), \quad l = L/K, l^s = L^s/K, \tag{6.25}$$

$$\hat{l}^s = -i(f(l) - f'(l)l - \delta - r) = n - (1-c)f(l) - c(t+\delta) + g + \delta. \tag{6.26}$$

[40] And to the discussion in Sect. 6.2 of Chap. 5.

[41] Note here, however, that the above dynamic aggregate demand schedule should be derived from the goods-market equilibrium equation (i.e., from an equation of the type $Y = Y(M^s/p, ...)$), since output is considered a statically endogenous variable in the Dornbusch and Fischer model.

Goods- and money-market equilibrium can now be described by

$$f(l) = c(f(l) - t - \delta) + i(f(l) - f'(l)l - \delta - r) + n + \delta + g,$$
$$m_l^s l^s = (W/f'(l))m^d(f(l), r), \quad m_l^s = M^s/L^s = const.$$

Note here, that we have assumed – supplementing the simple forms of the other behavioral assumptions and following Sargent's approach – that real money demand is strictly proportional to real income Y, so that also this function allows a reduction to per capital terms. The existence of a uniquely determined steady state is then easily guaranteed. It is characterized by (for $\hat{M}^s = \rho = n$, see Sect. 6.2 and Sargent (1987, Chap. 5)):

$$\hat{K} = \hat{Y} = \hat{L} = n = \rho \text{ and } \hat{W} = \hat{p} = \pi^* = 0,$$

which gives rise to

$$f(l_o) = (n + \delta + g - c(t + \delta))/(1 - c), \quad l_o^s = l_o,$$

$$r_o = f(l_o) - f'(l_o)l_o, \quad p_o = m_l^s l_o^s / m^d(f(l_o), r_o), \quad W_o = p_o f'(l_o).$$

The comparative static properties of the temporary equilibria of this system are determined by (see Sargent (1987, pp. 120–122) for a detailed and alternative derivation)

$$\begin{pmatrix} (1-c)f' + if''l & i \\ Wm_y^d - Wf''m^d/(f')^2 & Wm_r^d/f' \end{pmatrix} \begin{pmatrix} dl \\ dr \end{pmatrix} = \begin{pmatrix} 0 & 0 \\ -m^d/f' & m_l^s \end{pmatrix} \begin{pmatrix} dW \\ dl^s \end{pmatrix}$$

or by (det the determinant of the matrix on the right hand side)

$$\begin{pmatrix} dl \\ dr \end{pmatrix} = (1/\det) \begin{pmatrix} Wm_r^d/f' & -i \\ -Wm_y^d + Wf''m^d/(f')^2 & (1-c)f' + if''l \end{pmatrix} \cdot \begin{pmatrix} 0 & 0 \\ -m^d/f' & m_l^s \end{pmatrix} \begin{pmatrix} dW \\ dl^s \end{pmatrix}.$$

The usual assumption $Y_Y^d < 1$ or $(1-c)f' + if''l > 0$ (see Sargent (1987, p. 120) for further details) gives then rise to the following comparative static results:

$$l(\underset{-}{W}, \underset{+}{l^s})), \quad r(\underset{+}{W}, \underset{-}{l^s}). \tag{6.27}$$

The Jacobian J of the above dynamical system at the steady state is thus given by

$$= \begin{pmatrix} W\phi l_W/l^s & W\phi(l_{l^s} - 1)/l^s \\ -l^s(1-c)f'l_W & -l^s(1-c)f'l_{l^s} \end{pmatrix}.$$

We therefore get the following sign structure for it:

$$J = \begin{pmatrix} - & ? \\ + & - \end{pmatrix}.$$

This already shows that trace J < 0 holds true. Furthermore

$$\det J = -W\phi(1-c)f'l_W > 0,$$

that is, this system is indeed (globally, see the appendix to Chap. 4) asymptotically stable ($l/l^s = 1$ at the steady state).[42]

The features of this stable medium-run adjustment process are discussed in Sargent (1987, Chap. V.1) by means of the graphical IS-LM apparatus in great detail. That this special case must indeed provide a stable adjustment procedure is also readily understood from the perspective of the preceding section. We therefore saw in the case of temporary full employment equilibrium (for given K, M^s and then plausible assumption $\pi^* = \bar{\pi}^*$) that the proposed adjustment to the state of full employment must be stable if the IS- or the LM-disequilibrium is removed from the dynamics by replacing it through the corresponding equilibrium assumption. In the present case we have – besides $\pi^* \equiv 0$ – both IS and LM equilibrium ($\alpha, \beta = \infty$), but now a changing stock of capital K. Nevertheless, these two equilibrium assumptions exercise their influence with sufficient strength to enforce in a similar way now the stability of the full employment steady state (in the presence of capital stock growth). These two different situations of a mixed equilibrium–disequilibrium dynamics are thus fairly close to each other in their dynamic structure and its implications (they become – nearly – identical when $i(\cdot) = 0$ (and $n = 0$) is assumed in addition). Making full employment paths stable in this way also explains why there will generally prevail a monotonic adjustment under such circumstances.[43]

The above result does not prove very much in the direction of Sargent's long run neutrality assertion. In fact, it only considers situation A, the process behind the short-term theorem of the monetarist standard model considered in Sect. 5.2. We again find that this special process ($\pi^* \equiv 0$) is an asymptotically stable one – now with regard to the originally given equilibrium. Because of the new policy assumption of an isolated jump in the money supply (with no permanent change in its rate of growth as in 5.2), monetary policy will have only temporary effects here even in the short-run, with – according to Sargent – possibly a *cyclical* adjustment back to full employment in the "long-run."[44]

---

[42] I have to thank R. Franke for making me aware of the fact that this is indeed true without any additional assumption.

[43] Because of the strongly simplified form of the adjustment mechanism of Sect. 6.4: $\dot{W} = \phi(L(W) - L^s(W))$ when aggregate demand and supply equilibrium prevails (K given).

[44] To prove the possibility of cycles for the above stable adjustment process (which are claimed to exist in Sargent (1987, (19123)), one has to investigate the conditions under which the above Jacobian gives rise to complex roots (this will be the case, if $(J_{11} - J_{22})^2 + 4W\phi(1-c)f'l_W(l_{l^s} - 1) < 0$ holds true).

Apart from this reformulation of the first assertion of the "standard monetarist model" of Chap. 5, the above result has, however, no further economic value. The parameter η will not be zero in the medium run and the consequences of this fact have therefore to be investigated.[45] In this regard, it has been shown by Franke (1992) by means of Hopf bifurcation analysis that the model will in fact lose its stability if the parameter η becomes sufficiently large, that is, if the adaptive expectations mechanism works with sufficient strength. Sargent's assertion on the long-run effects of sudden changes in the money supply consequently is in general false. To show this here too, we shall make use of computer simulations in the following and shall also supply an alternative analytical proof of this result which, on the one hand, is much simpler than Franke's approach, but which, on the other hand, is not an exact proof for his instability result (since we shall only consider an approximation to the original Sargent model). Yet, our approach will provide an intuitive idea *of the basic reasons*, which enforce that Sargent's model must become totally unstable for sufficiently high adjustment speeds of the employed inflationary expectations mechanism.

Simulating the model (6.12)–(6.18) in Sargent's form ($\alpha = \beta = \sigma = \lambda = \infty$, and adding the usual assumptions about $\hat{L}^s, \hat{M}^s$ – both equal to n – to it) gives, for example, for a parameter value $\eta = 1.6$ the following result.

In this simulation, a monetary shock hits the economy at time $t = 1$, which before this time has been following its steady state path. Figure 6.2a,b shows the explosive character of the dynamics for the most important variables of the model. In the present form the model is therefore not an economically viable one and consequently does not allow a proper discussion of the validity of Sargent's

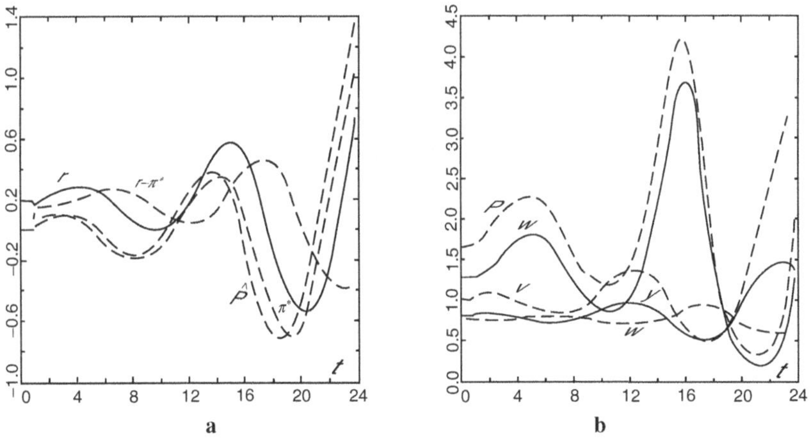

Fig. 6.2 Explosive cycles in Sargent's model of a Keynesian dynamics

---

[45] Note here that this is different for the application of the assumption $\pi^* \equiv 0$ in Sargent's (1973a) study of the Gibson paradox, since this an assumption that helps to contrast Sargent's results with the Fisher explanation of this paradox.

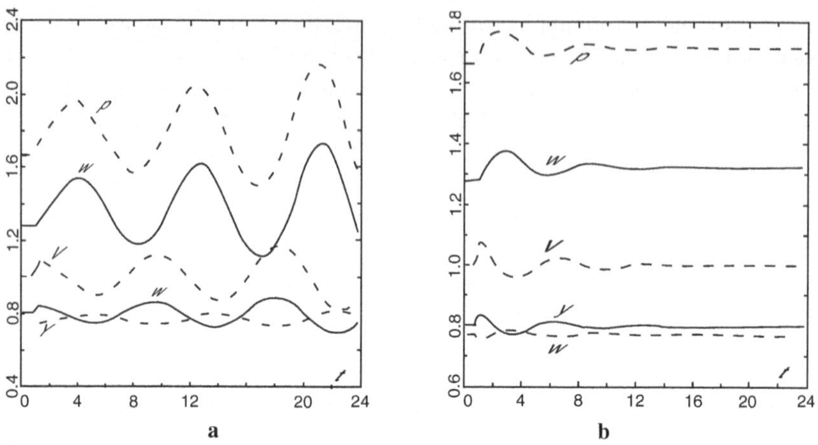

Fig. 6.3 A monetary policy rule to combat the explosive cycle of the Sargent model

neutrality proposition. It shows instead that the private sector of a fairly conventional IS-LM growth model need not at all be asymptotically stable (the reasons for this instability will be analyzed below), which disproves another important monetarist proposition.

It is interesting to ask at this stage whether there exist policy rules which are – in principle – capable of removing the (explosive) cycle from the above dynamics (Fig. 6.3a, b). In the light of the analysis of Sects. 3.8 and 4.5 the following possibilities for a derivative or a proportional control immediately suggest themselves ($g = G/K, V = L/L^s$):

$$g = \bar{g} - q\dot{V}, \quad g = \bar{g} - q(V-1), \quad q > 0.$$

Yet, as we shall see below, it is the price sector of the economy that is responsible for the above instability result. A monetary policy thus seems to be more adequate[46] than such fiscal policies and will thus be investigated briefly.[47] We therefore now assume with regard to the growth rate of the money supply the following adjustment rule:

$$\hat{M}^s = \rho - q(\pi^* - (\rho - n)), \quad q > 0.$$

This rule states that the growth rate of the money supply will be below (above) its planned steady state value ρ[48] if the expected rate of inflation π^* is higher (lower) than its steady state value (which is equal to $\rho - n = 0$ here). This rule allows the removal of both the instability and the cycle from the above dynamics, if the parameter q is chosen with care, that is, in some reasonable interval ($q = 0.5$ on the left hand side in the following simulations and $q = 2$ on the right):

[46] The initial monetary shock should here be conceived as being caused by somebody else than the monetary authority.

[47] I owe this suggestion to W. Semmler.

[48] $\rho = n$ again for simplicity.

We shall now attempt to investigate *the basic reason that is responsible for the above instability scenario* (and its possible removal). To show this analytically we shall make use of (6.15) for parameter values $\lambda < \infty$ in place of its complicated limit case $\lambda = \infty$.[49] Using the case of finite adjustment speeds in (6.15) is thus justified by its greater analytical as well as interpretational simplicity. It will make the interactions of the wage-price sector with the rest of the economy much more transparent. Furthermore, it is not very plausible for a continuous-time model to assume $0 < \phi \ll \cdots \ll \lambda = \infty$, that is, a significant qualitative difference between wage- and price-adjustments.[50]

Using the simplifying device that production is fully adjusted to the point of effective demand at each moment of time, (6.3)–(6.6) and (6.1) can be used to discuss the behavior of the remaining dynamically endogenous variables p (or $p_m = p/m_l^s$), W (or $W_m = W/m_l^s$), $\pi^*, l^s = L^s/K$.[51] This gives rise to the following set of differential equations, now be analyzed for their stability properties.[52]

$$\hat{p} = \lambda(W/(pF_L) - 1) = \lambda(W/(pf'(l)) - 1), \tag{6.28}$$

$$\hat{W} = \phi(L/L^s - 1) + \pi^* = \phi(l/l^s - 1) + \pi^*, \tag{6.29}$$

$$\dot{\pi}^* = \eta(\hat{p} - \pi^*) = \eta(\lambda(W/(pf'(l)) - 1) - \pi^*), \tag{6.30}$$

$$\begin{aligned} \hat{l^s} &= -i(f(l) - (W/p)l - \delta - (r - \pi^*)), \\ &= n - (1-c)f(l) - c(t+\delta) + g + \delta. \end{aligned} \tag{6.31}$$

Remark. Inspecting this dynamic reformulation of the Sargent model, one might object that the expected rate of inflation enters it in a fairly asymmetric way, since it influences money wage formation in a direct, additive fashion, but does not exercise a similar influence on the formation of the actual rate of price inflation.[53] Our answer to this objection is the following:

(1) There exist indeed a variety of ways by which a sluggish adjustment of prices (and the rates of inflation) toward the equilibrium where prices equal marginal wage costs (and price inflation equals wage inflation) can be postulated. We

---

[49] Since it is not easy to obtain an explicit formula for the rate of inflation (as a function of the dynamically endogenous variables W, K, π) in the case $\lambda = \infty$, see R. Franke (1992) for details in this matter.

[50] In particular if empirical applications of such a model are intended, see Duguay and Rabeau (1988) for a typical example where both adjustment speeds are chosen to be finite.

[51] The use of the auxiliary variables p_m, W_m is only necessary in the case of a variable m_l^s – as, for example, in the presence of the above money supply rule. Note, however, that the usefulness of $\hat{p}, \hat{W}$, etc. as state variables depends on the assumption $\hat{M}^s = \hat{L}^s$ (they must be replaced by other variables – which are constant in the steady state – in more general cases.

[52] Small letters (the exceptions are m^d, m^s, m_l^s) will denote that variables are now expressed in intensive form $(\ldots/K)$, cf. Sect. 6.2 for details. Note also, that $t = T/K$ and $g = G/K$ are assumed as exogenously given in Sargent (1987) as well as in the present approach. Note finally that $f(l) - wl$ is the correct measure for the actual rate of profit in the presence of (6.15) – and not $f(l) - f'(l)l$ as in the original Sargent model.

[53] See Duguay and Rabeau (1988) for a symmetric additive treatment of the expected rate of inflation in the very same situation.

have chosen above the relative departure of marginal wage costs from the actual price level, but have already pointed to alternatives to this rule, including a Wicksellian rule that takes goods-market disequilibrium as the driving force behind changes in the rate of inflation.[54]

(2) Similarly, the "inflation climate" that surrounds (6.28) can be modeled in various ways. One may add the steady state rate $\hat{M}^s - \hat{L}^s = \rho - n$ to this equation as an expression for this climate (as we have done it), or one may add the expected rate of price (or wage) inflation π^* (or $\hat{W}^*$) to it, cf. Fischer (1972) for an example. Rose (1990, p. (1955/6) makes use of an equation of the form $\hat{p}^* = \bar{\pi}^* + \lambda_1(\cdot) + \eta_1(\hat{W} - \bar{\pi}^*)$, and of a similar equation for the evolution of expected wage inflation: $\hat{W}^* = \bar{\pi}^* + \lambda_2(\cdot) + \eta_2(\hat{p} - \bar{\pi}^*)$. And finally, one might also approximate a fast working of the adaptive expectations mechanism by means of the following approach:[55] $\mathrm{d}\hat{p}/\mathrm{d}t = \lambda(\cdot)$ as an integrated expression for the rule of price formation and for expectations about the rate of inflation which – from a practical point of view – are correct or perfect.[56]

(3) In the above dynamics, we have made use of the first approach by assuming $\rho = n$ in addition. This implies that this type of analysis is confined to a neighborhood of its steady state. Making use of the additive term π^* instead of $\rho - n$ does not modify our following considerations very much as we shall see in the following. This case has the disadvantage, however, that a mechanical introduction of the myopic perfect foresight assumption $\hat{p} = \pi^*$ will reduce it immediately to an equilibrium approach[57] as far as the price level is concerned, independent of any assumption on the adjustment speed λ. In our view, this perfect foresight limit is better represented by the above rule $\mathrm{d}\hat{p}/\mathrm{d}t = \lambda(\cdot)$, which does not enforce such an independence from the parameter λ.[58] This topic will be further considered in the next chapter on myopic perfect foresight. The consequence of adding $\hat{W}$ instead of π^* to the formation rule of the price rate of inflation (e.g., as in the book of Rose (1990)) will not be investigated in any of our reformulations of Sargent's Keynesian dynamics that follow.

(4) Making use of

$$\hat{p} = \lambda(W/(pf'(l)) - 1) + \rho - n, \quad \rho = n$$

in the following is accompanied by the following interpretation of this dynamic equation. Firms are here accustomed to revising prices with the trend value of the rate of inflation $\rho - n$. If wage costs per value unit of the marginal product deviate from "1" there will be an additional effect on the rate of inflation, which

[54] This modification of the above dynamics will be considered in Sects. 9.2 and 9.3.

[55] See Asada and Franke (1990) for the empirical and theoretical importance of this dynamic equation (for $d^2 \ln p/dt^2$).

[56] $\pi^* = \hat{p}_{-h}, h \to 0$.

[57] i.e., here Keynes' postulate no.1.

[58] "Superneutrality" rests in such an approach on an adjustment speed λ that is (close to being) infinite.

makes it deviate from its trend value, but which does not yet really modify the inflation climate in which this change is operating.[59]

By employing again the homogeneity assumptions of Sect. 6.2, the IS-LM-part of Sargent's model can be reduced – in the above case (6.28) of a price level that is statically exogenous – to the following two equations for the remaining statically endogenous variables l and r [see Sargent (1987, p. (19119/20) and (6.3)–(6.6), (6.1) in Sect. 6.2]:

$$f(l) = c(f(l) - t - \delta) + i(f(l) - (W/p)l - \delta - (r - \pi^*)) + \delta + n + g,$$
$$m_l^{\mathrm{s}} l^{\mathrm{s}} = pm^{\mathrm{d}}(f(l), r), \quad m_l^{\mathrm{s}} = M^{\mathrm{s}}/L^{\mathrm{s}} = \text{const.}$$

Applying again the usual assumption on the marginal propensity to spend $Y_Y^{\mathrm{d}} < 1$, that is, here $(1-c-i)f' + iW/p > 0$, the comparative-static evaluation of the above two equations gives rise to ($f' = W/p$ at the steady state)

$$\begin{pmatrix} (1-c)f' & i \\ pm_y^{\mathrm{d}} f' & pm_r^{\mathrm{d}} \end{pmatrix} \begin{pmatrix} \mathrm{d}l \\ \mathrm{d}r \end{pmatrix} = \begin{pmatrix} iWl/p^2 & -il/p & i & 0 \\ -m^{\mathrm{d}} & 0 & 0 & 1 \end{pmatrix} \begin{pmatrix} \mathrm{d}p \\ \mathrm{d}W \\ \mathrm{d}\pi^* \\ \mathrm{d}l^{\mathrm{s}}. \end{pmatrix}$$

This implies the following sign pattern for the dependence of the statically endogenous variables on the dynamically endogenous ones (the sign-structure of the partial derivatives of the implicitly defined functions l and r):[60]

$$l = l(\underset{?}{p}, \underset{-}{W}, \underset{+}{\pi^*}, \underset{+}{l^s}), \quad r = r(\underset{+}{p}, \underset{-}{W}, \underset{+}{\pi^*}, \underset{-}{l^s}). \tag{6.32}$$

By means of the function l the system (23)–(26) can be characterized as follows:[61]

$$\hat{p} = \lambda(W/(pf'(l)) - 1) = H^1(\underset{?}{p}, \underset{?}{W}, \underset{+}{\pi^*}, \underset{+}{l^s}), \tag{6.33}$$

$$\hat{W} = \phi(l/l^{\mathrm{s}} - 1) + \pi^* = H^2(\underset{?}{p}, \underset{-}{W}, \underset{+}{\pi^*}, \underset{?}{l^{\mathrm{s}}}), \tag{6.34}$$

$$\dot{\pi^*} = \eta(\hat{p} - \pi^*) = H^3(\underset{?}{p}, \underset{?}{W}, \underset{+}{\pi^*},_{?} \underset{+}{l^{\mathrm{s}}}), \tag{6.35}$$

$$\hat{l}^{\mathrm{s}} = n - (1-c)f(l) - c(t+\delta) + g + \delta = H^4(\underset{?}{p}, \underset{+}{W}, \underset{-}{\pi^*}, \underset{-}{l^{\mathrm{s}}},). \tag{6.36}$$

---

[59] See also Boggess (1983) for such an approach.

[60] Note that there is a difference here in comparison to the case $\pi^* \equiv 0$ we have considered above, which can be easily explained by the fact that the price level has become a statically exogenous variable now.

[61] Note here, that H_{p}^1 will be negative when the parameter i is sufficiently small and positive for i sufficiently large. Note furthermore that the above comparative static results become unambiguous when the real wage is used as a state variable instead of the nominal one: $l = l(\underset{-}{p}, \underset{-}{w}, \underset{+}{\pi^*}, \underset{+}{l^s})$, since the partial derivative l_{p} represents solely the Keynes-effect in this case.

Note that we have used the standard properties $f' > 0, f'' < 0$ of the neoclassical production function f in the determination of the signs of the partial derivatives of the functions $H^1,\ldots,H^4$ and that the characterization "+" of $H^3_{\pi^*}$ will be true only *for sufficiently large values of the adjustment parameter* λ. This, however, is a meaningful restriction, since we want to reconsider Sargent's case $\lambda = \infty$ in this section. Note furthermore that both employment l and inflation $\hat{p}$ depend positively on the expected rate of inflation – due to the assumed investment behavior and because of rising marginal costs in production. The positive dependence of inflation on expected inflation, which is of the type:

$$\dot{\pi^*}_{\pi^*} = \lambda \frac{W}{p} \frac{-f''(l)}{f'(l)^2} l_{\pi^*} > 0 \quad (\rightarrow \infty \quad \text{for} \quad \lambda \rightarrow \infty),$$

will be the crucial element in the following stability investigation.

Note finally that the above proposed alternative formulation of these dynamic equations in terms of the variables p_m and W_m allows for an immediate inclusion of the above monetary stabilization rule, that is, $\hat{m}^s_l = -q\hat{p}$ $(\rho = n)$, into this dynamics. This rule adds the term $q\hat{p}$ to (6.28) and (6.29). But these are the only changes that have to be made in such a case. The Jacobian will therefore not differ very much from the one shown above (the case $q = 0$). It follows – for the case where $l_p < 0$ holds true – that the parameter q is capable of removing the positive sign from the trace of the above Jacobian, which we have established for the case of a large parameter λ. Yet, no further definite conclusions can be drawn for this extended dynamical system, unless further assumptions on the other terms in the above Jacobian are made.

It is now easy to provide the fundamental reason for our observation that the steady state of the above dynamical system will be unstable in general. According to the above, the actual rate of inflation depends positively on the expected rate of inflation, a dependence that can be increased beyond any bound by increasing the adjustment speed of the price level λ toward infinity. It follows that a suitably large choice of the parameter λ will imply that the time rate of change of inflationary expectations will depend positively on the level of these inflationary expectations, that is, the expected rate of inflation will be subject to centrifugal forces then – as the rate of growth of the Harrod model in Sect. 3.3. Increases in the rate π^* lead – via the multiplier process – in this model always to increases in employment, which in turn speeds up the rate of inflation – under the above circumstances in a way that will exceed the initial increase in inflationary expectations, thereby leading to a positive feedback of these expectations onto itself. In contrast to Harrod's knife-edge situation (Sect. 3.3), we here, however, have by choice of the model that this positive dependence does not work in isolation, but is embedded in a four-dimensional dynamics, which may and – if economically complete, also should – turn this partial instability into overall stability, for example, by sufficiently large and negative other elements in the trace of the Jacobian of the above model. Exactly this, however, is prevented when the parameter η of the adaptive mechanism also becomes sufficiently large (on the basis of a given λ that has been chosen in the above way).

In this way the trace of the above Jacobian can always be made positive, which according to the Routh–Hurwitz theorem (see Sect. 3.8) implies the instability of the above model.[62] It follows in the same way that the trace of the Jacobian can in fact be chosen as large as desired, which means that the speed of divergence from the steady state can be driven beyond any positive bound. This system therefore looses its viability in an extreme way as the parameter η approaches infinity – if the adjustment speed of prices λ is sufficiently large![63]

Remarks. In continuation of the above made remarks we observe the following:

(1) Adding π^* to (6.28) – as in Duguay and Rabeau (1988) – to treat inflationary expectations in a more symmetric fashion in the given wage–price dynamics leads to

$$\hat{p} = \lambda(W(pf'(l)) - 1) + \pi^*, \quad \hat{p}_{\pi^*} > 1.$$

This implies for (6.30) at the steady state:

$$\dot{\pi}^*{}_{\pi^*} = \eta(\hat{p}_{\pi^*} - 1) = \eta \cdot c, \quad c > 0.$$

In such a case, $\eta \to \infty$ is already sufficient to destroy the viability of the dynamics (6.28)–(6.31) independent of the size of the parameter λ.[64]

(2) In our interpretation of the dynamics (6.28)–(6.31), its collapse for high parameter values of λ and η can be explained in a very natural way. Increasing λ to a sufficient extent simply means that (some!) conditions for the generation of "hyper"-inflation come into being. If this is accompanied by sufficient increases in the expectations parameter η these two partial conditions for the onset of hyperinflation already suffice to endanger the normal working of the model.[65] Its resulting nonviability then shows that it needs further revision to allow a proper treatment of such hyperinflationary occurrences. This line of reasoning shows that the limit case $\lambda = \infty$ may not represent a meaningful approach to economic dynamics, since we can only suppress its problematic features by the assumption that η has to be sufficiently small (see Franke (1992) for details) – in place of the proper assumption that it is λ that must and can be assumed sufficiently small (see Duguay and Rabeau (1988), who employ $\lambda = 0.5$ in their empirical application of such an approach).

(3) Assuming $\hat{p} = \lambda(\cdot) + \pi^*$ as in (1) makes things even worse, since a sufficiently large parameter η is now already capable of stabilizing the model – due to the immediate positive self-reference that then exists for the expected rate of

---

[62] Of course, a complex structure such as (6.28)–(6.31) can exhibit a variety of other cases where the necessary and sufficient conditions of the Routh–Hurwitz criterion for asymptotic stability are hurt.

[63] Note here that the same argument does not immediately apply to the case $\lambda \to \infty$ (on the basis of a given finite η), since this parameter influences the trace of the Jacobian in two places in an ambiguous way.

[64] Choosing $\eta = \infty$ then enforces $W = pF_L$ as if λ were infinite.

[65] A proper analysis of hyperinflation demands further and endogenous increases in λ and η.

inflation π^*. This power of adaptive expectations to destroy the viability of the model without any change of the factual processes $\lambda(\cdot)$, $\phi(\cdot)$ in our view shows that this model needs reformulation to provide a proper approach to adaptive expectations that work with sufficient strength.[66] As already discussed this can be done by adopting $\mathrm{d}\hat{p}/\mathrm{d}t = \lambda(W/(pf'(l)) - 1)$ in place of the meaningless expression $\hat{p} = \lambda(W/(pf'(l)) - 1) + \hat{p}$. Such an approach will give rise to a meaningful economic dynamics despite the existence of expectations that are (near to being) perfect. In this way, it may be achieved that correct inflationary expectations are compatible with the Keynesian structure of the model.

(4) We remark finally that an approach of the type $\hat{p} = \lambda(\cdot) + \hat{W}^*$ will have its problems, too, since it will imply in conjunction with the Phillips curve $\hat{W} = \phi(\cdot) + \pi^*$ that there will come into being two contradictory laws of real wage determination if inflationary expectations become (nearly) correct.

In contrast to the limit case we have just analyzed, the above dynamical system can always be made an asymptotically stable one by choosing the adjustment speed of prices λ sufficiently low.

In the limit case $\lambda = 0, p \equiv p_o$, the Jacobian of the dynamics $\dot{\pi}^*, \hat{W}, \hat{l}^s$ is characterized by[67]

$$\tilde{J} = \begin{pmatrix} - & 0 & 0 \\ + & - & ? \\ - & + & - \end{pmatrix},$$

where the substructure $\begin{pmatrix} - & ? \\ + & - \end{pmatrix}$ is determined as in the case $\pi^* \equiv 0$ we have considered above, that is, its determinant is positive. We thus get $-a_3 = \det \tilde{J} < 0$, $-a_1 = \operatorname{trace} \tilde{J} < 0 \quad (\text{each } \tilde{J}_{ii} < 0)$ and

$$a_2 == \begin{vmatrix} - & 0 \\ + & - \end{vmatrix} + \begin{vmatrix} - & 0 \\ - & - \end{vmatrix} + \begin{vmatrix} - & ? \\ + & - \end{vmatrix} > 0.$$

Furthermore, $\det \tilde{J}$ is a summation component of $(\operatorname{trace} \tilde{J})a_2$, and given by $\tilde{J}_{11} \begin{vmatrix} - & ? \\ + & - \end{vmatrix}$, which implies that $a_1 a_2 - a_3$ must also be positive. The submatrix $\tilde{J}$ thus fulfills the Routh–Hurwitz conditions (see Sect. 3.8), that is, its three eigenvalues have all negative real parts. By continuity, such a situation must be true for the case $\lambda \approx 0$ as well, that is, the full matrix J must have such three eigenvalues, too. To show on this basis that the fourth eigenvalue of the Jacobian J of the complete dynamics (6.33)–(6.36) must be negative, too, it suffices to show that $\det J > 0 \quad (\lambda \text{ small})$ holds true in addition (since $\det J = \lambda_1 \cdot \lambda_2 \cdot \lambda_3 \cdot \lambda_4$). This can be proved by showing that the sign of the determinant of J is the negative of

[66] It is not very sensible to assume, on the one hand, that prices (and wages) respond sluggishly to factual changes in the environment of firms (and in the labor market) and to consider, on the other hand, situations where these same magnitudes respond very fast with respect to changes in the inflationary climate.

[67] Because of the comparative static relationships: $l = l(\underset{+}{\pi^*}, \underset{-}{W}, \underset{+}{l^s})$.

$Wl_W + l_p$, which in turn can be shown to be negative. We thereby in sum get that the full dynamics (6.33)–(6.36) must be locally asymptotically stable for all parameters λ that are chosen sufficiently small.

Formally seen, this asymptotically stable case is but a slight modification of the earlier stable case $\pi^* \approx 0$: inflationary expectations are here allowed to adjust, but they adjust to a situation where $\hat{p} \approx 0$ holds. The difference in content is that this situation is due to a very sluggish price adjustments, and not to a very sluggish inflationary expectations.

A sufficiently strong working of the rule of marginal cost pricing, on the other hand, creates a partial knife edge situation for the adjustment of inflationary expectations, which combined with a sufficiently fast adjustment of these expectations turns this partial instability into a total one and creates the explosive type of behavior we have exemplified in a still mildly explosive way in Fig. 6.2a,b above. This is an interesting wage-price sector analog to the steady growth instability observed in Sect. 3.3. And it clearly shows that the Keynesian model of Sargent is still problematic or at least incomplete in an essential way, since it does not discuss the forces that may counteract these centrifugal dynamics in the large.

Such forces can be introduced again – in a first step – in the way used to make the unstable Goodwin model of Sect. 4.4 a stable one. In this way the following improved situation (see Fig. 6.4a,b) can, for example, be established for this unstable model (if the adjustment speed in the adaptive expectations mechanism is not too high).[68] Yet, attempts to stabilize this model, that is, to restrict its dynamics to an economically meaningful region of its phase space through the choice of appropriate ceilings and floors (but not through the assumption of sluggish prices) must ultimately fail in this case, since the source of the instability of this monetary growth model cannot be controlled at all if inflationary adjustments speeds become very large. This casts considerable doubts on the validity of Sargent's equilibrium price reformulation of the model.[69]

[68] We have assumed here – on the right hand side of Fig. 6.4 – an investment constraint i(V) as in Sect. 4.4 and also a flexible parameter ϕ, which decreases with an increasing share of wages in the case of overemployment and a wage share that is above its steady state level.

[69] We only note here, that there exist numerous Keynesian models that combine Keynes' (1936, 195) classical or marginal productivity postulate no. 1 with the Hicksian IS-LM apparatus without noticing any problem (as did Keynes when he used this postulate in the "General Theory" in his chapter on the theory of prices). The use of this postulate (but also the use of the alternative price adjustment rules of Sect. 6.3) if combined with large or infinite adjustment speeds of expectations, however, implicitly introduce one further constraint into the Keynesian model of temporary equilibrium, which is already constrained by aggregate demand. If rapid price adjustment is accompanied by $\eta \longrightarrow \infty$ – which tends to remove the influence of changing prices and inflation from the Phillips theory of expected real wage determination – we finally get that real wages are no longer determined by aggregate demand and the employment it creates, but in turn determine this employment solely through their interaction with the price-sector of the economy – quite independent from the changes that occur in the level of aggregate demand. Technically speaking this means that the real wage becomes a (nearly) statically endogenous variable as λ is approaching infinity, while it is made a (nearly) statically exogenous variable of the model by means of $\eta \longrightarrow \infty$ (Firms produce what is demanded, and revise their prices very quickly in the face of their nominal marginal (or average) costs, but cannot – under the above circumstances – influence their real wage costs significantly in this way).

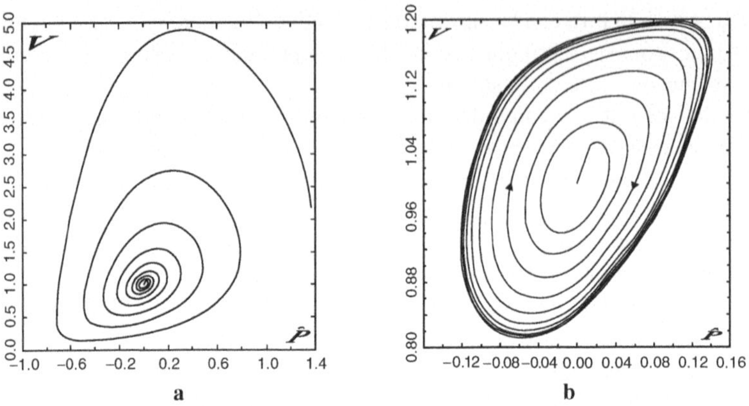

Fig. 6.4 Viability constraints (*right*) for the explosive Sargent model (*left*)

Figure 6.4a,b finally shows (to the right for a viable economic model as far as its present parameter values are concerned) that once-and-for-all disturbances of the steady state by open market operations as they are considered in Sargent (1987, Chap. V) will not lead back to these steady-state paths. It thereby once again becomes understandable why Sargent (1987, 19124) is forced to note:

> *Assuming that the system is dynamically stable, ... the final effect of the once-and-for-all jump in M, once the system has returned to its steady-state, is to leave all real variables unaltered and to increase the price level and money wage proportionately with the money supply.*

This type of reasoning and the various counterexamples given above show that *Sargent's claim that his Keynesian system has "classical" long-run properties must be rejected as invalid.*

Assuming behavioral functions which enforce *steady-states* to react neutrally to changes in money supply need not establish "Friedmanian" results for the dynamics of such Keynesian models – which indeed are already too rich in structure to allow for a general proof of standard monetarist assertions (e.g., of the type we have considered in Chap. 5). These assertions generally only come about in models that are tailored for this purpose.

Digression

Dornbusch and Fischer (1987, Chaps. 14 and 17) extend the discussion of the interaction of aggregate demand with dynamic aggregate supply to provide a simple textbook story of the IS-LM growth dynamics we have just considered. The approach they choose neglects growth[70] and makes use of an investment function that

[70] Which can be included into such an approach by way of Okun's law as we have done it in Chap. 5 of this book.

depends solely on the nominal rate of interest, that is, inflationary expectations and their adjustment only play a role in the Phillips curve of the model. The destabilizing mechanism that we have investigated in the present section is therefore still absent from their model, which should make it a viable (stable) one. Such a special case again provides a model that supports the conclusions that Sargent attempted – but did not succeed – to derive from the full IS-LM growth model.

Reformulated in continuous time and in a slightly modified way the model they use is given by the following equations:

$$\hat{p} = \phi(Y - \bar{Y})/\bar{Y} + \pi^*,$$
$$\hat{Y} = \varphi(\rho - \hat{p}),$$
$$\dot{\pi}^* = \eta(\hat{p} - \pi^*).$$

The first equation describes the formation of the rate of inflation on the basis of a money-wage Phillips curve and a static markup theory of the price level ($\hat{W} = \hat{p}$). The dynamic equation for aggregate demand has already been considered in the preceding sections (with $\dot{Y}$ in place of $\hat{Y}$). The inclusion of a mechanism describing the formation of inflationary expectations is necessary, since such expectations have now been included in the description of the Phillips curve. The parameter ρ finally is the exogenously given rate of growth of the money supply.

The steady state determination of this model is obvious ($Y = \bar{Y}, \hat{p} = \pi^* = \rho$). For the Jacobian at the steady state, we get (by inserting the first of the above equations into the following two to obtain an autonomous system of differential equations in the variables Y, π^*):[71]

$$J = \begin{pmatrix} 0 & \eta\phi \\ -\varphi & -\varphi\phi \end{pmatrix} = \begin{pmatrix} 0 & + \\ - & - \end{pmatrix}.$$

This gives rise to the following formula for the eigenvalues of the Jacobian of this dynamics:

$$\lambda_{1,2} = a \pm bi = -\varphi\phi/2\left(1 \pm \sqrt{1 - \frac{4\eta}{\varphi\phi}}\right).$$

We see that this model will be – as already expected – asymptotically stable under all circumstances, with a monotonic type of adjustment in the case of a parameter η that is sufficiently small and a cyclical dynamics for the opposite case.[72]

In the case of no uncertainty, the rational expectations alternative to adaptive expectations reduces to the assumption of perfect foresight ($\pi^* = \hat{p}$). In the present context this immediately implies (by mechanical algebraic manipulations of the

[71] An alternative way that is closer to the presentation of Dornbusch and Fischer is given by substituting the last dynamic equation into the time derivative of the first one which reduces the model to a dynamic system in the variables Y and $\hat{p}$.

[72] See Dornbusch and Fischer (1987, Chap. 17) for a graphical representation of this model, which is based – due to their special treatment of adaptive expectations – on the simpler equations $\dot{Y} = \varphi(\rho - q), \dot{q} = \phi(Y - \bar{Y}), q = \hat{p}$ (in the continuous time limit). We then, however, have that all orbits must be closed in this model – in contrast to what is shown (correctly) in Dornbusch and Fischer (1987) in the graphical representations they employ for the discrete time case.

above equations) $Y = \bar{Y}$, $\dot{Y} = 0$, and $\hat{p} = \rho$, that is, the economy will then always be in its steady state. But the Dornbusch and Fischer model suggests – in difference to the price-taking surprise stories of Lucas et al. – that unemployment is necessary to reduce prices and wages to a lower growth rate in the case of a reduction of the growth rate of the money stock. In the case of perfect foresight there is, however, no such unemployment, but nevertheless an immediate and perfect adjustment of the economy to this lower rate of monetary expansion. How come?

Perfect foresight of the above kind is but the limit case of adaptive expectations, which are updated very rapidly – at least under the side condition that inflation remains moderate (is non-"hyper"). In such a situation it should not matter very much for the dynamic evolution of the economy whether expectations are only very close to the actual rate of inflation or whether they are actually perfect. This implies that taking the limit $\eta \to \infty (\pi^* \to \hat{p})$ in the above model of adaptive expectations should lead us to an interpretation of what happens in the case when there are no forecasting errors.

This, however, is only possible under an appropriate additional assumption. We already know that the above dynamics must be convergent under all circumstances. Yet, assuming as one extreme that the parameter η becomes very large relative to the other two will imply that the dynamics must become of a strongly cyclical nature (with a phase length of the cycle that is approaching zero for $\eta \to \infty$).[73] Assuming as another extreme that the adjustment speed ϕ of wages W and thus of prices p to labor market disequilibrium becomes very large (while the other adjustment speeds remain relatively small) will imply that there will be no cyclical type of adjustment then, but that the adjustment to the steady state must become monotonic (with one eigenvalue approaching zero from below as $\phi \to \infty$).

How then do we interpret the case where perfect foresight is assumed to prevail and where the adjustment is believed to be qualitatively of the type that is given by the above algebraic solution of the model? The answer here is that this can solely be done by assuming that not only the parameter η, but also the parameter ϕ must be chosen sufficiently high to guarantee a monotonic and fast type of adjustment, that is, a very rapid and direct movement toward the new steady state. This implies that the conventional rational expectations approach to economic dynamics here appears as being dependent on the assumption of very flexible prices, to avoid interpretations of this limit situation that – due to a limited degree of wage-price adjustment – will introduce elements of an extremely cyclical nature into it.

Figure 6.5a, b illustrates these differences in the type of adjustment to the new steady state as the parameter η goes to infinity. It shows on the left hand side the case where prices react with "normal" speed ($\phi = 1$) accompanied by expectations that are nearly perfect($\eta = 100$), while on its right hand side we have a fast adjustment of prices ($\phi = 100$).[74] The economy adjusts in this case in a very fast and nearly monotonic way to the new steady state values, with only slight expectational errors (which can be further decreased by increasing the parameter η further).

[73] The eigenvalues will then be complex and the solutions of the above differential equations be built on terms of the following form: $c_0 e^{at} \cos(bt - c_1), b \to \infty$, see Brock and Malliaris (1989, Chap. 2).

[74] $\varphi = 1$ in both cases.

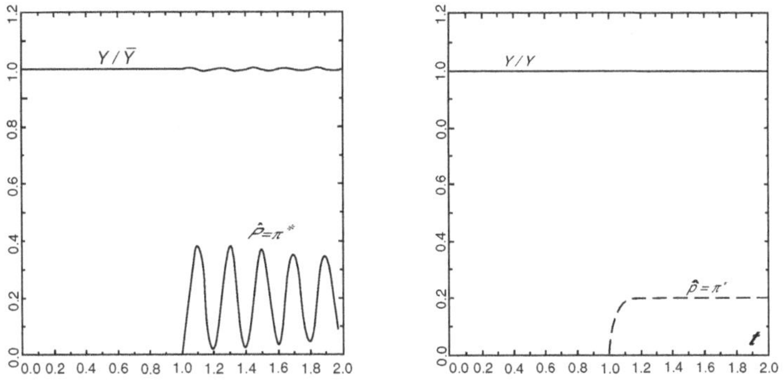

Fig. 6.5 Differences in adjustment paths with nearly perfect foresight ($\rho = 0 \to \rho = 0.2$ at $t = 1$)

We consequently see that the adjustment speed of prices ϕ may be of decisive importance for obtaining an interpretation of the limit case $\hat{p} = \pi^*$ in the direction of the rational expectations school. Assuming instead $\phi \ll \infty$ creates a situation that is better described by

$$\dot{q} = \lambda(Y - \bar{Y}), \quad \dot{Y} = \varphi(m - q), \quad q = \hat{p},$$

which – following our above remarks – is the limit of

$$\begin{aligned} \hat{p}_t &= \lambda h(Y_t - \bar{Y}) + \pi_t^*, \quad \pi_t^* = \hat{p}_{t-h}, \\ Y_t &= Y_{t-h} + \varphi h(\rho - \pi_t^*), \quad \pi_t^* = \hat{p}_{t-h} \end{aligned}$$

for a period length h that shrinks to "0." This dynamics is of the cross-dual type we considered in Sect. 4.9 and will thus imply a center-dynamics (only closed orbits) under all circumstances.

This interpretation of myopic perfect foresight stands in stark contrast to the above (algebraic) interpretation of it. It has the advantage that it does not dissolve the formulation of perfect foresight from an explicit treatment of sluggish price adjustment, but allows their joint investigation. Under the rule $\dot{q} = \lambda(Y - \bar{Y})$, the model is an unambiguous limit case of adaptive expectations, which are updated very rapidly.[75]

6.6 Conclusions

It is illuminating to compare the model of this chapter with the stochastic approaches towards aggregate demand and supply dynamics used by Sargent (and co-authors) in the discussion of adaptive vs. rational expectations as, for example, in Sargent (1973b) and Sargent and Wallace (1975).

[75] Note that assuming $\phi \to \infty$ does not make much sense in this type of model.

Sargent (1973b) makes use of a LM-curve and an IS-curve that can easily be identified as log-linear analogs of the curves of the IS-LM sector of the present chapter (but which are now formulated in discrete time by using random variables in addition). These two curves give rise to a standard aggregate demand curve in the (p, Y)-space. A further equation introduces the rule by which expectations are formed, and as in this, and the next, chapter it is adaptive vs. rational expectations that are considered here. In addition to these three equations, only one further equation is used in Sargent's (1973b) model, that is, a Lucas supply schedule or an – up to price surprises – vertical aggregate supply schedule. This single equation replaces the wage-price-output interaction on the supply side of the model of this chapter, while the capital stock is considered as given in this version of an IS-LM dynamics.[76]

Assuming a Lucas supply curve instead of an upward sloping aggregate supply schedule that is based on temporarily rigid wages as it was used in this chapter is, however, but a simplification of the full specification of the classical full-employment model (where nominal wages are perfectly flexible) as it is formulated and studied in Sargent (1987, Chap. I). This means that this approach differs significantly from the standard IS-LM-Phillips-curve model used to rationalize Keynesian prescriptions – in contrast to what is claimed in the concluding remarks of Sargent's (1973b) article. It is therefore not surprising to see that is indeed possible to derive a number of propositions of the monetarist variety in such a strictly classical variant of the IS-LM approach.

Yet, as we have seen this is no longer a task that is easy to fulfill once a standard IS-LM-Phillips-curve model is used for the derivation of such propositions. In fact, the use of an adaptive expectations mechanism then shows that the model is not yet a complete one, since it still lacks economic viability or stability in the large in the case of a flexible adjustment of the price level and expectations about it – unless one is prepared to classify such price flexibility under the heading hyperinflation.

Such an interpretation quite naturally allows for the result that the model must become an extremely unstable one in the case where the parameter λ approaches infinity.[77] The consequence of such an interpretation, however, is that the original Sargent model – as well as many other approaches to macrodynamics – represent an unacceptable model, since it is implicitly based on a condition that belongs to an analysis of the extreme case of hyperinflation without taking notice of this fact. Accepting such a point of view thus means that any treatment of the price level as a statically endogenous variable in a dynamic macroeconomic context must be replaced by a sufficiently sluggish adjustment of prices of the kind we have introduced here in Sect. 6.3 to have a model that describes the working of the economy under normal conditions. Analyzing subsequently rising adjustment speeds of prices – which should be accompanied by a faster adjustment of expectations – then implies a regime switching of the model from the conditions of moderate to explosively

[76] It is made an endogenous variable in Sargent and Wallace (1975).

[77] Independent of the particular price formation rule that is employed.

accelerating inflation à la Cagan – in particular if wages flexibility also increases and thus strengthens the positive feedback of the expected rate of inflation

$$\pi^* \nearrow \quad \Rightarrow \quad l \nearrow \quad \Rightarrow \quad \hat{p} \nearrow \quad \Rightarrow \quad \dot{\pi}^* \nearrow$$

onto itself as we have considered it in the last section.

Appendix: Wage Dynamics in a Depressed Economy

Instead of a further examination of Sargent's Keynesian model in its "long run" behavior under adaptive expectations, we shall here briefly turn to a simple and preliminary analysis of the medium-run properties of its wage-price-sector. We intend to show that plausible (and to some extend even compelling) modifications of Sargent's Keynesian dynamics will give rise to implications that can be usefully compared with some of Keynes' (in) stability conjectures.

From a post-Keynesian perspective there are at least three problems – two minor and one major – with regard to the behavioral equations of the Sargent model. To take the minor problems first, we observe that the real wage should influence the system's behavior in at least two further instances. Consumption not only depends on the level of disposable income, but also on income distribution or the real wage w. This gives rise to the following extension of (6.3):

$$C = C(Y - T - \delta K, w), \quad C_2 > 0. \tag{6.37}$$

Furthermore, the symmetry so far assumed in the Phillips curve with regard to the effects of over- and underemployment is not very plausible. Since World War II, there has been no fall in the general level of wages and it is indeed hard to imagine how such a fall may come about in the future. Instead of (6.9) or (6.16) we shall therefore assume in the following:

$$\hat{W} = \max\{0, \phi(L/L^s - 1) + \pi^*\}. \tag{6.38}$$

The major problem concerns the identity that is normally assumed between short-term and long-term rates of interest in the conventional (as well as in Sargent's) IS-LM model. This is not so in the General Theory, where we, for example, can find:

> *The monetary authority often tends in practice to concentrate upon short-term debt and to leave the price of long-term debt to be influenced by belated and imperfect reactions from the price of short-term debt.*
>
> (Keynes, 1936, p. 206).[78]

The simple IS-LM model thus not only contains one, but at least two further financial assets that are left implicit in its discussion. We conclude that "the" rate

[78] See Tobin (1980, p. 76) for a similar observation.

of interest r should be disintegrated into at least two different interest rates, the short-term money rate of interest r, which clears the money market [see (6.13)], and an expected long-term real rate of interest $\bar{z}$, which determines investment behavior. The influence of open-market operations and of the short term real rate $r-\pi^*$ on this latter rate and thus on investment may indeed be very weak or uncertain in its actual course.

A better starting point than a conventional IS-LM analysis (which assumes $r-\pi^* = \bar{z}$) in our view therefore is to start from the opposite assumption, that is, from the absence of any (clear-cut endogenous) link between the rate $r-\pi^*$ and the rate $\bar{z}$. Such a procedure has the twofold advantage that it points to an important open question of Keynesian macroeconomic models (to establish the links between the rates $r-\pi^*$ and $\bar{z}$), and it also makes comprehensible why it may be admissible to restate the "General Theory" on the basis of a given rate of interest [see Keynes (1936, p. 245)]. On the other hand, it must be stressed that the provisional device of treating "interest" in the investment function as given will lead us back to a much simpler type of multiplier theory than that of the IS-LM model. The following analysis thus remains to that extent preliminary, in that it does not aim at a complete description of all interactions that are important on the macrolevel.

We shall assume now for (gross) investment $I^{\mathrm{b}} = I + \delta K$ the following functional form

$$I^{\mathrm{b}} = I^{\mathrm{b}}(Y/K, \bar{z}), \quad I_1^{\mathrm{b}} > 0, \quad I_2^{\mathrm{b}} < 0, \tag{6.39}$$

which is formally identical with Sargent's function (6.4), but not with the investment function used in the preceding section. We shall not employ here the conventional two-factor neoclassical production function $F(K,L)$, but shall make use of the standard short-term function $F(L)$ solely. Our approach will thus leave open for further consideration the effects of investment on the given "environment of technique" K in which labor is operating. The following variations of Sargent's dynamical conclusions therefore essentially concern the wage-price-subsector of the considered economy.

In correspondence to assuming a fixed K it is, of course, sensible to assume for labor force growth $n = 0$. The dynamics of the model can thus be studied in the absolute terms of Sect. 6.2. Equations (6.37) and (6.39) then imply as equation for product-market equilibrium[79]

$$Y = C(Y - T - \delta K, w) + I^{\mathrm{b}}(Y/K, \bar{z}) + G.$$

Using again the standard assumption on expenditure propensities $Y_Y^{\mathrm{d}} < 1$, this equation implies the comparative-static results

$$Y(\underset{+}{w}, \underset{-}{T}, \underset{-}{\bar{z}}, \underset{+}{G}), \quad L(\underset{+}{w}, \underset{-}{T}, \underset{-}{\bar{z}}, \underset{+}{G}) \tag{6.40}$$

[79] Money-market equilibrium is of no importance in this analysis of the wage-price sector of the economy, since the interest rate that governs investment behavior is exogenously given in the present model.

for the partial derivatives of these (implicitly defined) functions. Neglecting for the moment the max-addition to the formulation of the Phillips curve (6.38), that is, returning to its original formulation (6.16), we get that the dynamics of this revised model is given by

$$\hat{p} = \lambda(w/F' - 1) = H^1(\underset{+}{w}, \underset{-}{\bar{z}}, \underset{0}{\pi^*}),$$

$$\hat{W} = \phi(L/L^s - 1) + \pi^* = H^2(\underset{+}{w}, \underset{-}{\bar{z}}, \underset{+}{\pi^*}),$$

$$\dot{\pi}^* = \eta(\hat{p} - \pi^*) = H^3(\underset{+}{w}, \underset{-}{\bar{z}}, \underset{-}{\pi^*}).$$

This system can be reduced to two differential equations by subtracting the first from the second equation ($w = W/p$):

$$\hat{w} = \phi(L(w)/L^s - 1) - \lambda(w/F'(L(w)) - 1) + \pi^* \quad (6.41)$$

$$\dot{\pi}^* = \eta(\lambda(w/F'(L(w)) - 1) - \pi^*) \quad (6.42)$$

The Jacobian of this system at the full employment equilibrium point

$$L(w_o) = L^s, \pi^*_o = \hat{p}_o = \lambda(w_o/F'(L(w_o)) - 1) = \hat{W} \quad (\hat{w} = 0)$$

is given by (see (6.40))

$$J = \begin{pmatrix} \phi L'/L^s - \lambda/F'(1 - wF''L'/F')w & w \\ \eta\lambda/F'(1 - wF''L'/F')\pi^* & -\eta\pi^* \end{pmatrix}.$$

The determinant of this Jacobian reads

$$\det J = -\phi L' w \eta \pi^*/L^s$$

and is thus always negative. The full employment equilibrium is therefore unstable (a saddlepoint, see Sect. 4.2). To further investigate the dynamics of this price-subsector model, the diagrams shown in Fig. 6.6 are of use.

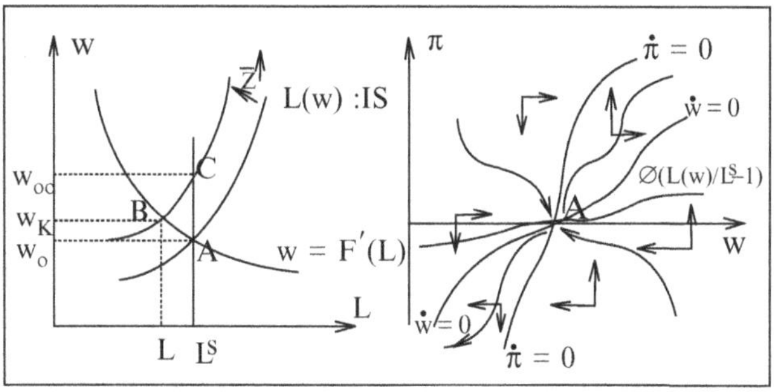

Fig. 6.6 Equilibrium curves and full employment dynamics in a modified model of the wage-price sector

The curve $w = F'(L)$ is the marginal productivity relationship of the short-term Keynesian model, while the curve $L(w)$ is the equilibrium curve implied by the above product-market equilibrium [see (6.40)]. As is customarily done, we choose as point of reference a point A where the economy works under ideal conditions. In the present model this point A is described by the situation of full employment and constant prices ($w_o = F'(L^s)$.

Assume now that the (expected) long-term real rate of interest $\bar{z}$ rises to a new level. Investment will thereby be depressed, implying that a higher level of real wages w is now necessary to ensure product-market equilibrium. The $L(w)$-curve thus shifts upwards and to the left. The wage rate w_{oo} which – via product-market equilibrium – guarantees labor-market equilibrium (point C) will now be higher than the rate w_K, which fulfills Keynes' classical postulate no.1 ($w = F'(L)$) and which allows for product-market equilibrium (see point B in Fig. 6.5).

This latter "equilibrium" point $B = (L, w_K)$ will now indeed become an equilibrium and will thus describe the situation of a stable Keynesian underemployment equilibrium, *provided that workers do react to rising underemployment as it is postulated by the Phillips-curve* (6.38). Starting, for example, from a situation of type A that exhibits neither inflation nor deflation, it is thus assumed that workers will resist any reductions in their money wage under the circumstances of a falling demand for labor (and goods).

Modifying the Phillips-curve (6.16) in the way proposed by (6.38) leaves in the above situation as adjustment rules (W = const):

$$\hat{p} = \lambda\left(W/F'(L(W/p)) - 1\right),$$
$$\dot{\pi}^* = \eta\left(\lambda(W/F'(L(W/p)) - 1) - \pi^*\right).$$

This system is stable, since its Jacobian obviously fulfills det > 0, trace < 0 [see Sect. 4.2]. By way of a temporary process of price deflation that results from the negative employment effect $L^s \to L$ (see Fig. 6.5), the point (L, w_K) is thus approached as a stable Keynesian underemployment equilibrium. Prices here adjust in a downward direction such that a new employment level L is established (higher than the one that would come about through the decrease in investment alone) by raising the initial wage rate (of the point A) to the level w_K.[80]

The resulting stable situation of a depressed economy will become much more problematic, however, if it is not assumed (as in (6.38)) that workers "are instinctively more reasonable economists than the classical school" by rejecting any claim for a general reduction of money wages W. If the earlier Phillips curve (6.16) – underlying the above local instability result – remains in force as the true description of the dynamics of the general level of money wages, there will indeed be no other equilibrium than the full employment one and the economy must collapse in this case in consequence of the assumed contradictory change in investment. This is obvious from the phase diagram of the dynamics (6.41) and (6.42) shown in Fig. 6.7.

[80] It is easy to show that point B is in fact a stable node (and not a focus).

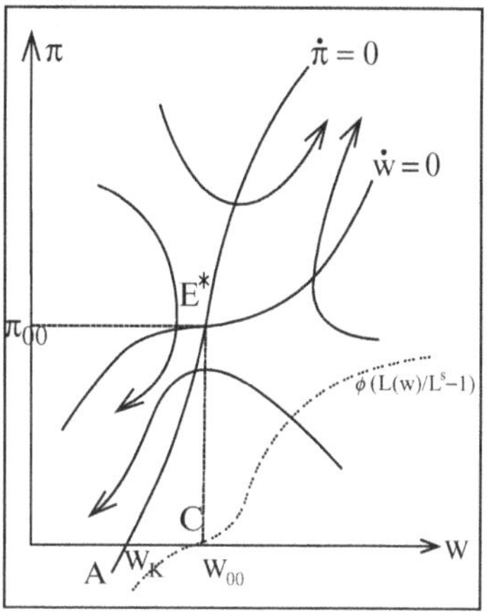

Fig. 6.7 A model with a deflationary spiral

Figure 6.7 depicts the situation B, C of Fig. 6.5, that is, the case of a too high long-term real rate of interest $\bar{z}$, by means of the phase diagram of (6.41) and (6.42). The isoclines $\hat{w} = 0$ and $\dot{\pi}^* = 0$, that is,

$$\pi^* = \lambda(w/F'(L(w)) - 1) - \phi(L(w)/L^s - 1), \quad \pi^* = \lambda(w/F'(L(w)) - 1)$$

show the particular situations where one of the two dynamical forces has come to a temporary rest. Their intersection A consequently describes the original full-employment equilibrium point of system (6.41) and (6.42). The consideration of points above and below the isoclines then finally implies the type of dynamics that is depicted in Fig. 6.6.

Before the assumed disturbance of the full employment equilibrium, the two isoclines intersected at w_0 on the horizontal axis. The decline in investment then shifts both curves to the right, but due to their above form, the curve $\hat{w} = 0$ shifts less than the curve $\dot{\pi}^* = 0$. This implies that their intersection must now lie in the positive orthant of the Fig. 6.7, that is, full employment is now coupled with price and wage inflation. Yet again, this equilibrium represents a knife-edge situation which, when disturbed in the above way, gives rise to an unending deflationary spiral with wages falling in general more rapid than prices.[81]

We have shown above that – if workers resist a reduction in their money-wage – the system will move from the point w_o to w_K in a stable fashion (solely by price deflation which increases the real wage from w_0 to w_K). Their behavior thus simply prevents that price deflation can give rise to a deflationary spiral as in Fig. 6.7. This clearly demonstrates the disadvantages of a flexible money-wage policy over money-wage resistance in situations such as the one sketched above.

Is there a way in which the full-employment point E^* of Fig. 6.6 can be made asymptotically stable again? Such a situation can indeed be established if the term

[81] Note here that the point $(w_K, 0)$ is no equilibrium point, since it is characterized by $\hat{w} = \phi(L/L^s - 1) < 0$ (and $\hat{p} = \pi^*$) in the case of flexible money-wages.

π^* in (6.41) is replaced by $\eta\pi^*$ (see Sect. 4.4 for such a proposal) with a parameter η that fulfills $0 < \eta < 1$ and is chosen sufficiently small. An easy calculation shows that the determinant of the Jacobian of system (6.41) and (6.42) will be made positive thereby, so that (under the assumption of a sufficiently large price adjustment parameter λ that establishes trace $J < 0$ in addition) asymptotic stability of the full-employment point is again ensured. Yet, this stability result demands a departure from the monetarist treatment of inflationary expectations in the Phillips curve ($\eta = 1$).

Chapter 7
A Classical Revolution in Keynesian Macrodynamics?

7.1 Introduction

In his Chap. V on the dynamic analysis of a Keynesian model, Sargent (1987) also analyzes the effects of a point-in-time change in the money supply (via open-market operations) for the case of myopic perfect foresight. However, the results he derives in this case, that is, ultra-short-run neutrality if this change in monetary policy is not foreseen and a neutralizing reaction that precedes action when this change is foreseen, look very strange when considered from the viewpoint of the Keynesian dynamics (with adaptive expectations) of the preceding chapter, in particular, since the money wage rate W is considered as reacting "sluggishly" in such models. Hence, the employed solution methods seem to be fundamentally different when the dynamic laws are changed to allow for myopic perfect foresight, where – to simplify matters – short-run expectation errors are considered as negligible by just taking the limit of an infinitely fast adjustment of inflationary expectations.

This change in solution methods and also in results is insufficiently explained and motivated in Sargent (1987) with regard to the full-fledged IS-LM growth model that is used by him.[1] Furthermore, his way of reasoning conceals important ambiguities and problematic features of the analyzed dynamic situation, which – once laid bare – will lead us to a significant reformulation of this dynamic model in order to make it a (more) consistent one. In contrast to Sargent's effort "to formalize for students the relationships among the various hypotheses advanced in Milton Friedman's AEA presidential address in 1968" (see his p. 117), we shall arrive at the conclusion that this task cannot be solved in a non-Walrasian formulation of this Keynesian dynamics (that is, in particular, based on a pattern of reaction speeds that allow for the stability of the long-run). Friedmanian hypotheses need their own type of model, and cannot be transplanted into a consistently formulated and viable Keynesian growth dynamics simply by assuming myopic perfect foresight in such a context.

[1] Note, however, that these "new" methods are in fact meanwhile fairly standard in the macroeconomic literature. Our point is that these solution methods become problematic, or even false, when a complete *Keynesian* IS-LM model of monetary growth is used in conjunction with them.

P. Flaschel, *The Macrodynamics of Capitalism: Elements for a Synthesis of Marx, Keynes and Schumpeter, Second Edition,*

In the following,[2] we shall first provide a brief alternative introduction to Sargent's dynamic model in the case of perfect foresight (in Sect. 7.2). Section 7.3 then studies and clarifies the structure of Sargent's analysis of the perfect foresight case. We will see that additional and, in this context, not well-motivated assumptions are necessary to fix a unique time path in the model that can produce the above stated results of the effects of open market operations. We shall also see that Sargent's seemingly complete Keynesian model [see (7.1)–(7.10)] is in fact still sufficiently indeterminate in this initial formulation, thereby allowing for its new results – in comparison to the case of adaptive expectations – by an appropriate manipulation of its implicit degrees of freedom. In Sect. 7.4, we shall then begin to question the consistency and the relevance of Sargent's way of closing his "Keynesian" model for myopic perfect foresight (which in fact allows him to transform the originally Keynesian dynamics into a Solovian underemployment growth model with a price level that is solely governed by expectations). Section 7.5, finally, will provide the, in our view, the basic critique of this solution procedure for a model of Keynesian dynamics. We shall see that Sargent's final version of the model cannot yet be considered as a economically consistent one, since it represents neither a "viable" model nor is composed of structural equations that are consistent with each other. Sluggish prices – besides sluggish wages – once again appear as the indispensable assumption that can ensure the stability of the steady state of such a model and thus its viability.

In the appendix to this chapter we in addition show that the solution method that is used by Sargent in this case of perfect foresight is highly implausible also when (re)considered in the setup where it has originally been introduced and motivated, that is, in the Cagan model of hyper inflation (Sargent and Wallace (1973)). We shall see there that this method is based on a much too restricted point of view and that it will change significantly in its outlook when this narrow framework is only slightly extended by means of appropriate nonlinearities.

We shall also see in this – and the following – chapter that Sargent's model of Keynesian dynamics – though simple in each of its structural components when considered in isolation – is in fact already fairly complex and sophisticated in its interactions and its properties in comparison to many other models of economic dynamics – if the observed inconsistencies are appropriately removed. It contains features of Goodwin's growth cycle model, a Wicksellian investment demand function (and price dynamics, see Chap. 8), an IS-LM-version of effective demand [where Kaldor's multiplier instability is not automatically excluded], and it also allows for capital-labor substitution governed by profit maximization. Because of its richness in structure – in contrast, for example, to the monetarist standard model we have studied in Chap. 5 – this model consequently represents an important and with regard to its complex dynamic properties still quite relevant, since still largely unexplored, starting-point for the analytical treatment of the various doctrines on the (in-)stability of the private sector of an economy and the (de)stabilizing effects of monetary (and fiscal) policies.

---

[2] This chapter provides a revised and substantially extended version of Flaschel and Picard (1986).

Of course, more modern and refined building blocks may and should be used later on in the place of the simple textbook components on which the IS-LM growth model of this and the preceding chapter has been based. However, it is our belief that most of the (in)stability considerations of the Chaps. 6 and 7 will also apply to such more refined models, since they basically state that a wage-price sector that responds to disturbances in a too flexible way provides a bridge to the occurrence of situations of hyperinflation, which – in reality as well as in theory – endanger the stability of a steady growth path of an economy in a dramatic way.

The present prototype approach to the stability of models of monetary growth in sum therefore provides the simple, but nevertheless very important result. It is not only the Classical variant of the neoclassical synthesis (the flex wage version of the Keynesian model) that is fundamentally flawed (see Sect. 6.4), but also the Keynesian variant of it (the fix wage version) as far as it is still based on perfectly flexible prices, since this introduces aspects of the inflationary process into the general formulation of such a model that should remain reserved for the stage where hyperinflation becomes a conceivable possibility. This highly problematic feature of many conventional approaches to monetary growth is revealed only when their stability (long-run viability) becomes an issue and when it is considered in a context that is sufficiently complete, that is, one that integrates the basic features of the wage-price sector with those of the markets for goods and finance.

7.2 Keynesian Monetary Growth Under Myopic Perfect Foresight

The Keynesian model on which Sargent's analysis of perfect foresight is based is described by the following set of equations

$$Y = F(K,L), \tag{7.1}$$
$$W/p = F_L(K,L), \tag{7.2}$$
$$C = c(Y - T - \delta K), \quad 1 > c > 0, \tag{7.3}$$
$$I = i((F_K(K,L) - \delta) - (r - \pi^*))K + nK, \quad i > 0, \tag{7.4}$$
$$Y = C + I + \delta K + G, \tag{7.5}$$
$$M^s = pY\,\mathrm{e}^{\beta r}, \quad \beta < 0, \tag{7.6}$$
$$\hat{M}^s = \rho \quad (\text{ here } = n), \tag{7.7}$$
$$\hat{W} = \phi(L/L^s - 1) + \pi^*, \quad \phi > 0, \tag{7.8}$$
$$\pi^* = \hat{p}_+, \tag{7.9}$$
$$\hat{K} = i(\cdot) + n \quad (\text{and} \quad \hat{L}^s = n). \tag{7.10}$$

This model ignores the bond market (and equities) by virtue of Walras' Law of Stocks. Its behavioral assumptions – up to one – are already well-known[3] from the preceding section and will not be repeated here. The new assumption is that of myopic perfect foresight, which is here formulated by means of the right hand time derivative $\dot{p}_+$[4] of the price level p at the present moment of time and which replaces our earlier assumption of adaptive inflationary expectations. It is interesting to note that this assumption $\pi^* = \hat{p}_+ = \dot{p}_+/p$ can be obtained (at least formally) from the adaptive expectations case $\dot{\pi}^*/\eta = \hat{p}_+ - \pi^*$, see (6.10) in the preceding chapter, by setting $\eta = \infty$. From a mathematical point of view, the case of perfect foresight can thus be considered a limit case of the adaptive mechanism, which should therefore reflect to some extent the properties of this more "old-fashioned" type of approach to expectations formation if these expectations are formed in a sufficiently fast way (which should – under appropriate assumptions – make the difference between actual and expected inflation very small).

Before proceeding to an analysis of this model there is one remark to be made with respect to its (implicit) subdivision of its endogenous variables into static and dynamic ones. Dynamically endogenous variables are those whose time derivative (but not the variable itself) is considered as endogenous at time t, that is, instantaneously determined in each point in time. Consequently, it is (or seems to be) assumed in the above model – if one follows the approach of the preceding chapter, see also the above formulation of the Phillips curve – that the change in money wage is determined endogenously at each moment t (by the rate of employment $V = L/L^s$), while the money wage itself is considered as given for each such t. This is, however, not the case in Sargent's treatment of the model with myopic perfect foresight.[5]

In our view, it is furthermore important to have a *disjoint* classification into statically endogenous variables (Y, C, I, L, r, and p) and dynamically endogenous variables (W and K) in a continuous time model such as the one above, that is, we should not treat both the current and the future money wage, that is, W_t and W_{t+1} or $\frac{W_{t+1}-W_t}{W_t}$ in discrete time (or $W(t)$ and $\dot{W}(t)$ in continuous time) as being both endogenously determined at each moment t. Variables that allow for equilibrium in

[3] The model exhibits a neoclassical production function (7.1), the "marginal productivity theory of employment" (7.2), a standard consumption function (7.3), a particular form of investment behavior (7.4), a special, but customary form of liquidity preference function (7.6), and a money-wage Phillips-curve (7.7). It is closed by various exogenous and endogenous growth equations, that is, assumptions on factor and money supply.

[4] It should be noted that the use of right-hand derivatives in this context is not supposed to indicate that the class of admissible functions is extended to those having differing left- and right-hand side derivative everywhere. In fact, the points where jumps are permitted to occur are determined exogenously – and even restricted to the "present" point-in-time in general (i.e., to the treatment of initial conditions whether predetermined or not). At all other points in time at least the usual assumption of absolute continuity is made with regard to the construction of the solution curves of the above dynamics.

[5] The choice of the symbol "t" for time is in conflict with our use of t for taxes per capital T/K. Since it is, however, always obvious when t is used for "taxes" or for denoting time we do not introduce a different symbol for one of these two expressions here.

each moment of time are conceived – see Chap. 6 – to adjust with infinite speed to the new equilibrium in case of a disturbance of its former position. They thus fulfill dynamical laws that are intentionally left implicit by the very approach chosen. These dynamic laws consequently cannot be used for describing the evolution of the system, that is, these variables cannot appear in the form of time rates of change in the equations that describe this evolution, since such rates do not mirror the true behavior of these variables (which is composed of discontinuous and continuous types of reaction). It is therefore in particular not sensible to formulate a differential equations for such variables *in addition* to their static determination by equilibrium conditions and thus to group such a statically endogenous variable among the dynamically endogenous ones at one and the same time. Yet, Sargent's methodology in the case of perfect foresight is precisely of this (problematic) type – at least as far as the treatment of the wage level W and the price level p is concerned.[6]

We shall study Sargent's methodology – which in its structure is well known and widely accepted, but which nevertheless is not a consistent procedure in the present context – in the next two sections. We shall see there that his results are indeed based on an (arbitrary) regrouping of the endogenous variables of the following form: Y, C, I, L, r and W statically endogenous and $K, w = W/p, p$ now dynamically endogenous. This regrouping is combined with a further subdivision of the latter variables into predetermined ones (fixed by initial conditions) and not predetermined ones (determined by terminal conditions) to overcome a knife edge situation that is present in the dynamics of the variables K, w, p of this modified model of Keynesian dynamics.

To allow for the existence of steady-states (which are needed as starting-points and reference paths in his analysis), Sargent (1987, p. 113) assumes, as already indicated earlier, that the functions F, C, and $m(r,\cdot)$ are homogeneous of degree 1. Dividing by K and expressing the resulting ratios by means of small instead of capital letters, one then obtains the following equivalent model [see Sargent (1987, p. 114) and the preceding chapter as well as Sect. 3.5 for notation and details]:[7]

$$y = f(l), f'(l) > 0, \tag{7.11}$$

$$W/p = f'(l), f''(l) < 0, \tag{7.12}$$

$$c = c(y - t - \delta), \tag{7.13}$$

$$\hat{K} = i(f(l) - f'(l)l - \delta - (r - \pi^*)) + n, \tag{7.14}$$

$$y = c + \hat{K} + n + \delta + g, \tag{7.15}$$

$$m_l^s l^s = y e^{\beta r}, \quad m_l^s = M^s/L^s, \quad l^s = L^s/K, \tag{7.16}$$

$$\hat{M}^s = \rho \quad (= n = \hat{L}^s \text{ here}), \tag{7.17}$$

[6] Note here that this critique refers to continuous time models solely. It does not yet say something for the case of discrete time models.

[7] Note that the ratios t, g are treated as exogenous in Sargent's text. This means that he employs the special assumption that the growth rates of T, G equal $\hat{K}$.

$$\hat{W} = \phi(l/l^s - 1) + \pi^*, \quad l^s = L^s/K, \tag{7.18}$$
$$\pi^* = \hat{p} \tag{7.19}$$
$$\hat{l}^s = n - \hat{K} = -i(\cdot). \tag{7.20}$$

Given initial conditions (and in fact also one terminal condition!) and given the time paths for the exogenous variables M^s, $g = G/K$, and $t = T/K$, the above model will generate (under suitable assumptions) time paths of its endogenous variables, since the statically endogenous variables y, i, c, l, r and W[8] can all be expressed as functions of the dynamic variables K, w, and p by means of the implicit function theorem. Assuming in addition, $\hat{M}^s = n(= \hat{L}^s))$ and choosing special initial conditions for the dynamic variables allows in particular for full-employment steady-state behavior with

$$\hat{W} = \pi^* = \hat{p} = 0, \quad \hat{K} = \hat{L} = \hat{Y} = n.$$

With regard to such reference paths, Sargent (1987, p. 117) then describes in verbal terms possible effects if such a steady state is disturbed at some moment t by a *once-and for all jump in money supply* M^s (engineered via an open-market operation that leaves $\hat{M}^s$ unaltered). On the assumption of myopic perfect foresight, that is, (7.9), Sargent (1987, p. 120 f.) here obtains – in contrast to the situation of an in general cyclical adjustment toward[9] long-run neutrality caused by such shocks in the case of adaptive expectations – the following two results in comparison to the steady state reference situation initially assumed to prevail:

Super-neutrality: An unexpected jump in the money supply M^s (that leaves $\hat{M}^s_+$ unchanged) implies an instantaneous jump in prices p and wages W *and* leaves all other variables unaltered.

Super-anticipation: A jump in M^s of this type that is expected at time t to occur at time $t+\theta, \theta > 0$ is reflected (from t onwards, with correct anticipation of the rate of inflation) in all earlier values of the price level p (and W, r) already and will give rise to strict neutrality from $t+\theta$ onwards.

It is easy to show that the first proposition must hold true when applied to the monetarist standard model of Sect. 5.2 (based on the monetarist assumption of a parameter η of value 1 in its Phillips curve): because of the strictly monotonic relationship there assumed to exist between the expectation error with respect to inflation and deviations from the natural unemployment rate, it follows in the case of no such anticipation errors that unemployment must be equal to natural unemployment then and thus – due to Okun's law – that growth must be on its trend value, that is, we are on the steady state. Monetary shocks (there exercised through changes in the rate of growth of the money supply) cannot influence the real sector of the economy in this case, but will give rise to a different rate of inflation solely.

Though a stochastic version of this standard model may disguise this simplistic reaction pattern somewhat and make it appear in a more favorable and interesting

[8] See the above remark and our following discussion of Sargent's reverted treatment of nominal and real wages W and w.

[9] Or away from!

light, the basic impression nevertheless should be that such a model is much too close to the conclusions it is intended to give rise to. By contrast, Sargent's attempt to derive Friedmanian hypotheses from a complete model of Keynesian dynamic represents an approach that is very demanding, in particular, since it – in the spirit of the methodology applied in Chap. 2 – attempts to show propositions that raise severe problems for Keynesian economics on its, that is, the opponents' ground, by making use of assumptions that are typical for Keynesian model building. These assumptions will – as we shall see in the following – no longer give rise to an overall stable private sector of the considered economy, a fact that then will allow – under suitable additional specifications – that the price level – and other nominal magnitudes – can react in the way that is asserted in the above two proposition.[10]

There are, however, two still puzzling facts[11] surrounding these assertions in the context of a completely specified model of Keynesian dynamics for which Sargent offers no clear-cut explanation. These are the following:

1. The standard methodology of solving a system of differential equations throughout by means of given initial conditions (as described in Chap. 6 for the case of adaptive expectations) is no longer used in this perfect foresight case.[12] Instead, the differential equation that is derived for the evolution of price level of this model is now solved by imposing (ad hoc) an, in general, fairly complicated stability requirement on it. This is done by assumption solely, and it leaves the reader totally uninformed about the general validity of such a procedure with respect to more complex (nonlinear) behavioral assumptions and more complicated disturbances of the given time paths of the exogenous variables.
2. The variable W that was *assumed* to be exogenously given at each point in time t is now able to perform jumps – to allow for the claimed super-neutrality, for example.

These two theorems look strange when viewed from the standpoint of a conventional Keynesian (IS-LM) monetary growth dynamics (with an integrated wage-price sector), which is based on given wages in each moment of time and which treats the price level in some approaches as an equilibrium variable and in other approaches as a predetermined magnitude, but never as a variable that is governed by future events solely.

A thorough explanation of this "bifurcation" in the model's implications – in comparison to the case of adaptive expectations – will be worked out in the following section. Its reconsideration in a next section will then show that Sargent's

[10] Note that there is no room for the second proposition in the monetarist model of Sect. 5.2 due to the fact that the private sector is asymptotically stable in this model.

[11] Despite the long tradition and the wide acceptance that this approach meanwhile has, it is hoped here that the reader will at least feel a little bit puzzled by this particular application of this method in the context of a full-fledged IS-LM model of monetary growth and of capital accumulation. We do not deny here that such forward-looking behavior – and its formalization – can make sense in appropriately chosen models of the medium-run.

[12] This would exclude by the very method of analysis the possibility of a reaction before a jump in an exogenous variable actually occurs – as long as this change does not feedback into the model by means of an explicitly formulated forecasting mechanism.

mathematical manipulations to obtain the above results cannot be considered as the proper solution to the incorporation of myopic perfect foresight into this model of Keynesian dynamics.

7.3 AD-AS and Macroeconomic Performance Under Myopic Perfect Foresight

The basic observation to be made in the case of perfect foresight is that (7.18) can then be reduced to

$$\hat{w} = \phi(l/l^s - 1), \quad w = W/p, \tag{7.21}$$

which gives the first differential equation of this new model. And for $\hat{l}^s = n - \hat{K}$ we can again compute by means of (7.11), (7.13), (7.15), and (7.20) as the second differential equation for this system:

$$\hat{l}^s = n - [f(l) - c(f(l) - t - \delta) - g - \delta]. \tag{7.22}$$

Inverting (7.12) $l = (f')^{-1}(w)$ then shows that (7.21) and (7.22) form an autonomous system of ordinary differential equations in the variables w and l^s (since – following Sargent – t and g are assumed to be given). This system can be solved in the usual way for each given pair of initial conditions (cf. Sect. 4.3 in this book). Its stationary solution is given by

$$(1-c)f(l_o) = n - ct + (1-c)\delta + g, \quad l_o = l^s_o = (f')^{-1}(w_o).$$

This steady state solution is uniquely determined and positive. Applying Olech's Theorem [see again Chap. 4], the stationary solution can easily be shown to be globally asymptotically stable, since the Jacobian J of systems (7.21) and (7.22) are characterized by

$$J = \begin{pmatrix} - & - \\ + & 0 \end{pmatrix}$$

in the positive orthant of $\mathbf{R}^2$. For each given vector $(w_0, l^s_0) \in \mathbf{R}^2_+$ of initial conditions (at time $t = t_0$), we have therefore a uniquely determined positive solution path $(w(t), l^s(t))$, $t_0 \leq t < \infty$, which converges to (w_o, l_o) as $t \to \infty$.[13]

In this way we can solve for all real variables of Sargent's dynamic model. Note, however, that w has become a dynamically endogenous variable now, which by its very treatment is *assumed* to evolve in a continuous fashion (which includes the present time t_o). This treatment of the variable w (together with the unambiguously continuous behavior of K or l^s) implies that the variables l, y, c, and i (and L and Y,

[13] Note that the rate of profit must remain positive throughout, implying that the share of wages will always be less than 1. Note also that the full employment labor intensity l^s is here based on the NAR-hypothesis, so that the variable l may also be larger than l^s on the adjustment path to the steady state.

etc.) must now all be continuous functions of time [compare (7.12), (7.11), (7.13) and (7.15)], that is, they are no longer capable of performing jumps in response to a sudden change in the money supply M^s. This is a trivial consequence of the *assumed* change in the treatment of the variable w.

Instead of our above procedure, Sargent (1987, pp. 120/1) specializes to the particular case of a Cobb–Douglas production function $f(l) = l^{1-\alpha}$ and a log-linear Phillips-curve $\phi(l/l^s - 1) = \gamma(ln(l/l^s))$, which allows him to give an explicit solution for the variable l (or L) on the basis of a given time path $K(t)$. This, however, is an inadmissible procedure, since L and K (or l and l^s) are mutually interdependent in their evolution! And from the integral formulation (7.17), which he obtains (on p. 121) by this method, he finally concludes that L and therefore the above set of variables cannot respond at time t to the imposition of shocks at t, without noticing that this is already a trivial consequence of treating w and l^s (or K) as continuous solutions of the differential equations (7.21) and (7.22). These variables *cannot jump because of the very method chosen* and not because of a dubious integration procedure, which tries to demonstrate that they must remain fixed in the light of a sudden jump in money supply!

The dynamical evolution we have considered so far is *completely independent* of the assumed investment behavior (7.14), money market equilibrium (7.16), and any possible solution path for prices $p(t)$. Therefore, the task of (7.14) and (7.16) of the model (7.11)–(7.20) in the case of perfect foresight now simply is to determine the rate of inflation $\hat{p}$ and the rate of interest r in such a way that goods- and money-market equilibrium is ensured for all t.

To obtain this, Sargent proceeds in the following way. He assumes – as already shown earlier – for the money demand function $m(y,r)$ the special form $e^{\beta r}y, \beta < 0$. The equation for money market equilibrium can then be solved explicitly for the rate of interest r:

$$r = (\ln M^s - \ln p - \ln K - \ln y)/\beta. \tag{7.23}$$

The variable r is subject to jumps, which ensure equilibrium in the money market whenever a jump in money supply M^s occurs. Inserting (7.23) in (7.14) and noting that $i(\cdot) + n$ is predetermined through (7.15)

$$i(\cdot) + n = f(l) - c(f(l) - t - \delta) - g - \delta$$

implies an implicit differential equation for the variable p. This equation can be made an explicit one by inverting the (here linear) function $i(\cdot)$:

$$f(l) - f'(l)l - \delta - (r - \hat{p}) = i^{-1}[(1-c)(f(l) - \delta) + ct - g - n], \qquad \text{i.e.}$$

$$\hat{p} = i^{-1}[(1-c)(f(l) - \delta) + ct - g - n] - (f(l) - f'(l)l - \delta) \tag{7.24}$$
$$+(\ln M^s - \ln K - \ln p - \ln f(l))/\beta. \tag{7.25}$$

This is the third and final dynamical law of Sargent's perfect foresight model (recall that it and (7.23) are but an equivalent expression for goods- and money-market equilibrium). Employing the solution of (7.21) and (7.22) in the condensed form $h(t)$, this differential equation can be briefly expressed as follows:

$$\hat{p} = h(w(t), l^s(t)) + (\ln M^s(t))/\beta - (\ln p)/\beta = h(t) + (\ln M^s(t))/\beta - (\ln p)/\beta. \tag{7.26}$$

This third differential equation again makes plain that the evolution of the price level has no influence on the real variables of the system, but is simply an appendix to the motion of these latter variables. The assumption of perfect foresight ($\eta = \infty$) has completely deprived the model (7.11)–(7.20) of its Keynesian features and given it an outlook of a very (neo-)classical type.

However, our main concern in the remainder of this section is not this change in the models structure at $\eta = \infty$, but the treatment of the differential equation (7.26) that Sargent uses to prove his assertions on neutrality and anticipating reaction to future action; cf. the preceding section. In Sargent and Wallace (1973) it is argued by means of a special example that one should abandon in the case of perfect foresight the requirement that the price level $p(t)$ should be a continuous function of time – if a differential equation is given for its determination – *and* that one should adopt instead a forward-looking solution procedure in such situations, that is, in our case

$$\ln p(t) = -\int_t^\infty e^{s/\beta}[h(s) + (\ln M^s(s))/\beta]\,ds\, e^{-t/\beta}, \quad t \in [t_0, \infty). \tag{7.27}$$

This explicit solution of (7.26) is the only one that is asymptotically stable, since it suppresses the explosive term ($\beta < 0!$): $ce^{-t/\beta}$ of the general solution of the differential equation (7.26) [c = 0, see Sargent (1987, p.127) for further details and note that the term $h(s)$ contains the $-\ln K$ as an item which guarantees that the above solution for p can be expressed in relative magnitudes throughout].

The rationale behind this approach is the following: if the public knows the whole future development of the function h as it is implied by the evolution of the variables w and l^s (i.e., of the real part of the model as considered earlier) *and* if it knows the future development of the money supply M^s (and of G and T), then it can make use of the explicit formula (7.27) to predict what price level should and thereby also will prevail at time t, such that at the same time myopic perfect foresight and a stable reaction to monetary shocks is always guaranteed. Using the special solution (7.27) guarantees that the price level p will converge to "1," in contrast to all other solution paths q of (7.26), which will behave in a purely explosive or purely implosive manner (approach zero in the latter case) in their deviation $x(= q/p)$ from this reference solution, due to

$$\hat{x} = -\ln x/\beta.$$

This dynamic equation describes a type of instability we have already considered when discussing Harrod's model of knife-edge growth (see Sect. 3.3). Yet, in contrast to Harrod's reflection of such an occurrence, the assumed economic agents have become meanwhile much more capable in reflecting the world (model) they live in, since they see through this instability and avoid it by simply choosing the above particular type of the solution of the linear inhomogeneous differential equation (7.26).

Centrifugal forces here exist anywhere off the steady state as in this earlier model of unstable growth, but these forces can no longer create any harm – due to the perfect behavior of agents in managing such totally unstable situations. It follows that Sen's model of Harrod's approach has been misleading to that extent as it also relied on the "stupid" assumption of adaptive expectations. Assuming instead myopic perfect foresight for this model, too,[14] will in this case immediately imply that the economy cannot leave the steady state.

Agents in Sargent's IS-LM growth model do not only have such myopic perfect foresight ($\pi_t^* = \hat{p}_t$ in place of $g_t^* = g_t$), but they in addition have to be able to choose from a continuum of possibilities of such perfect foresight paths the one that is asymptotically stable in the light of the shock that hit the economy. In the present situation there is fortunately only one such viable perfect foresight price path, which then provides the relevant theory of the price level. It has already been demonstrated by Friedman (1979) for a much simpler macroeconomic model that such a procedure can hardly be justified by a detailed microeconomic reasoning. Furthermore, as can be seen by applying Minford and Peel's (1983, Chap. 2) methodological considerations to Sargent's macrodynamic model, also purely verbal arguments – which appeal to forces not included in the model to justify the imposition of the terminal condition employed in the solution (7.27) – will look very strange in the context of this Solovian underemployment model of monetary growth.

The abandonment of the requirement that the price level $p(t)$ be continuous at all t is motivated in Sargent and Wallace (1973) only by the instability phenomena that otherwise will develop, and the elimination of the term $c\,\mathrm{e}^{-t/\beta}$ is justified by the assumption that individuals will not expect an ever-accelerating inflation of deflation if M^s *is constant in time*.[15] Problems regarding the justification of the uniqueness of a formula of type (7.27) are considered in Black (1974), Calvo (1977,) and Gray (1984) and will not be reconsidered here.

The fact that the assumption of continuity with respect to initial conditions – when solving (7.26) – leads to an economically implausible behavior of the model's variables[16] may be due to the particular approach chosen for the presentation of "Keynesian" dynamics under perfect foresight. This problem will be reconsidered in the last section of this chapter. In any case, formula (7.27) is the basis of the *super-neutrality proposition* and the *super-anticipation* proposition, which can now be summed up in the following way:

1. Suppose that at time t it becomes known that money supply $M^s(s), s \geq t$ has been misconceived and is given by $M^s(s) * \Phi$ from then on instead. Comparing (7.27) before and after this change in opinion (both for the same point in time t) implies that their difference is exactly $+\Phi$ [see Sargent (1987, p. 124) for details]. This means that p (or $\ln p$) jumps in the same way as M^s (or $\ln M^s$) does, which furthermore implies that the money wage W must jump in the same fashion, too, since $w = \frac{W}{p}$ is already fixed at time t by assumption.

[14] That is, $g_t^* = g_t$, see Sect. 3.3.

[15] an assumption which in the present model must be applied to the ratio M^s/L^s.

[16] Of "saddle-point"-type: the real sector is asymptotically stable, while the thereby implied determination of nominal values is unstable.

2. Suppose, on the other hand, that it becomes known at time t that such a change in money supply will occur at time $t+\theta, \theta > 0$. The new function for (ln)$M(s)$ must then be introduced into the price formula (7.27) at time t already, which implies a jump at t in comparison to the price–formation rule which prevailed up to t. The price-level then indeed must react before this monetary policy comes into effect. [see again Sargent (1987, p. 124) for the details of this calculation, which in addition show that the situation of point 1 must, of course, again apply from time $t+\theta$ onwards].

It is immediately obvious that (1) is but a special case of (2). We stress again that both cases demand a thorough justification that (7.27) is *the* economically meaningful solution to (7.26) *in a meaningful economic model* and that the whole procedure heavily depends on the special assumptions necessary to derive the differential equation (7.26) and the integral that solves it. [17]

Closing this section, Sargent's perfect foresight case may now be characterized as follows. Equation (7.22) would describe a Solow-type growth model if the real wage rate were always flexible enough to guarantee full employment $l = l^s$. However, because of the assumed Phillips-curve, this is not the case. Employment l is therefore in general different from full employment and evolves according to $\hat{w} = \phi(l/l^s - 1)$ and $w = f'(l)$, see (7.12) and (7.18), giving rise to a Solovian underemployment growth model. A third differential equation (7.26) concerning the price level p finally follows from adjusting the money-market and investment plans to this predetermined Solovian growth path. If this equation is solved in the conventional way by a continuous function $p(t)$, we would – instead of (7.27) – obtain the solution

$$\ln p(t) = (\ln p(t_0) + \int_0^t e^{s/\beta}[h(s) + (\ln M^s(s))/\beta]\,ds)\,e^{-t/\beta}. \tag{7.28}$$

This type of solution, is unstable with regard to once-and-for-all disturbances of the steady-state by open market operations, a very unpleasant fact for an otherwise stable Solow-type model. It is therefore replaced by solution (7.27), whereby this strange behavior is made to disappear and the above propositions are obtained. This is indeed a classical revolution in a Keynesian model of the same radical type that we have considered in Chap. 2 with regard to the opposite direction. Again, only one new assumption seems to be necessary for overthrowing completely (this time the Keynesian) conventional approach to goods-market and money-market equilibrium. Investment is now again adjusted to savings, and not the other way round as in Keynes' revolution of the Classical model of his times. This is far more than only the neoclassical synthesis à la Sargent (1987, Chaps. 1 and 2), but in fact the (neo-)classical counterrevolution to the Keynesian revolution – if this approach to monetary growth is correct.

Yet, a first skeptical impression is provided by the following observation: This model suddenly treats the money wage W in a classical manner again as a statically endogenous variable – at least in the case where jumps in the price level occur. It

[17] The above Lucas–Sargent propositions will, for example, no longer be true if the log-linear dependence of the rate of interest on p and M^s is dispensed with [see Snower (1984) for details].

thus implicitly employs two wage-reaction functions, one for the continuous case (the above type of Phillips curve) and one for the discontinuous case (the classical assumption of perfectly flexible wages). The classical features of this Keynesian dynamics therefore seem to rest at least on a partial return to pre-Keynesian assumption as far as the flexibility of the nominal wage level is concerned. This problem will be further clarified in the last section of this chapter.

Finally, when we started to consider the model (7.1)–(7.10) [(7.11)–(7.20)] for the case $\eta = \infty$, it seemed to us that a certain mathematical bifurcation must be involved when the change η is large, but finite to $\eta = \infty$ is made. Our conclusion, however, now is that it is in fact the economics of the model that undergoes a severe bifurcation at this point, while the mathematics is merely adequately manipulated to justify this bifurcation in economic thinking by formal means. The plausibility and the consistency of these completions and manipulations of the original model (7.1)–(7.10) , $\eta = \infty$, will be considered in the next section.

7.4 On the Relevance of the AD-AS Rational Expectations Model

Instability of the price level $p(t)$ in an otherwise stable surrounding has been shown to be the reason why solution (7.27) of its dynamic law (7.26) is preferred to its solution (7.28). This is clearly stated in Sargent and Wallace (1973) with regard to the simple Cagan model of price level dynamics and it holds true in the same way for Sargent's (1987) dynamic analysis of a Keynesian model. However, in our view this new device of dealing with certain problems of monetary growth models creates more difficulties that it helps to solve.

To demonstrate this, consider again formula (7.27) now rewritten in the following way:

$$\ln p(t) = -\int_t^{\infty} e^{s/\beta}[h(s) + (\ln M^s(s))/\beta + \varepsilon(s)]\, ds\, e^{-t/\beta}. \qquad (7.29)$$

Assume that $M^s(s)$ and $h(s)$ represent the correct behavior of the exogenous policy variable M^s and of the function h (as it results from the dynamics of the variables w, l^s or the real sector of the economy) over the whole future. Assume furthermore that the "error-term" $\varepsilon(s)$ that we now have included in this formula has the same simple functional properties as they are postulated in Sargent (1987) for the given money supply function M^s.[18] An explicit treatment of this error term will be of use now in judging the content of the forecasting formula (7.29).

It may, for example, be argued that it is not sensible (and practicable) for individuals to operate with such a formula for the price-level, which extends over an infinite horizon and which has as its background a growing system (possibly of a cyclical nature, but with natural growth n as its asymptotic growth rate). A special choice of the "error-term" $\varepsilon(s)$, however, helps to avoid this sort of criticism. All

[18] Assumptions that guarantee Sargent's mathematical methodology [as they are examined in Calvo (1977)] are not central for the discussion that follows.

that is needed for Sargent's kind of perfect foresight to prevail, for example, over the time interval $[t_0, T]$[19] is that $\varepsilon(s)$ is zero during this interval of time. It is thus sufficient that individuals perceive the money supply correctly over the interval $[t_0, T)$ to allow for myopic perfect foresight $\pi^* = \hat{p}_+$ during this time interval. Thereafter, everything may be wrong (e.g., because individuals have trivialized the "tail" of this formula), but this will only make the model inapplicable from time T onwards. In this way the model may be used as a model of the medium run.

Indeed, differentiation of (7.29) with regard to t immediately shows that the differential equation (7.26) will be satisfied at all points in this interval of time:

$$\hat{p} = \int_t^\infty \mathrm{e}^{s/\beta}[h(s) + (\ln M^s(s))/\beta + \varepsilon(s)]\,\mathrm{d}s\,\mathrm{e}^{-t/\beta}/\beta + h(t) + (\ln M^s(t))/\beta + \varepsilon(t)$$
$$= (-\ln p(t))/\beta + h(t) + (\ln M^s(t))/\beta + \varepsilon(t).$$

Furthermore, an economically meaningful rate of interest that guarantees money-market equilibrium can always be associated with (7.29) as long as the price-level (7.29) fulfills the inequality $M^s/(pK) < y$. Yet, it is not our interest here to justify this model with regard to its validity for such medium run analysis. Instead, we shall now show that the inclusion of such an error term will reveal serious problems of this way of solving the model (7.11)–(7.19), problems which in the end show that the model itself is not yet well-formulated as an economic model.

Inserting the error term $\varepsilon(s)$ into Sargent's price equation (7.27) represents but a simple generalization of his discussion of unanticipated monetary shocks, since the function ε will be revised in some way or another at least whenever a point in time t is reached where $\varepsilon(t) \neq 0$ holds true, meaning that this error has then finally become obvious (notice here that the additional assumption $\varepsilon_+ = 0$ is then necessary to imply the Lucas–Sargent proposition for such a case). But the observation of an error at time t may induce individuals to revise their whole expectations M^{s*} of the money supply M^s after time t giving rise to a completely new error function $\varepsilon = M^{s*} - M^s$ from t onwards.[20] Such a (from the theoretical point of view: arbitrary) revision of expectations regarding the whole future will imply that the price level will jump by an (again from a theoretical point of view) unknown amount. Within the domain of the above inequality, this says that the determination of the price level $p(t)$ in Sargent's model is completely arbitrary and subject to uncontrollable beliefs about the future, for example, with regard to periods $[T, \infty), T > t$ as considered earlier. This implies that there are many paths for the price level, which are consistent with a given steady-state of the real sector.[21]

The actual jump that occurs at a point in time t where expectations about policy actions at that point have to be revised is completely indeterminate, unless very special assumptions (as in Sargent's Chap. V) are made with regard to the revision that will be induced for the function ε for values $s \geq t$. This is the content of Sargent's theory of the price level for a Keynesian model with myopic perfect foresight. This

[19] t_0 the present point in time.

[20] Subject again to the side condition $\varepsilon_+ = 0$!

[21] This is a similar type of critique of perfect foresight models as raised in Black (1974).

level is now mainly the result of economic speculation about the future, subject only to the side condition that such speculations must be locally correct with regard to the point in time that actually prevails and must suffice (how?) the economic limits that exist for such jumps in the general level of prices.

There are further serious problems that question the meaningfulness of this approach to perfect foresight:

1. Consider for reference as in Sargent (1987, p. 123) the steady state path with $\hat{M}^s = n$ and $\hat{W} = \hat{p} = \pi^* = 0$. Assume that unexpected jumps in the money supply of the following type

$$f(s) = \ln M^s(s) \to \tilde{f}(t) = \begin{cases} \ln M^s(s), & s < t \\ \ln M^s(s) + \Phi, & s \geq t \end{cases}$$

occur at time $t = t_0 + 1, t_0 + 2, \ldots$ without any upper limit. The Lucas–Sargent proposition then implies $p(t), W(t) \to \infty$, yet this is not reflected in expected and actual rates of inflation! $[\pi^* = 0$ and $\hat{p} = 0$ for all $t \geq t_0]$. The effect on inflation of a money supply of type A (shown in Fig. 7.1) therefore cannot in general be approximated by a money supply function of type B (cf. again the Fig. 7.1), if the step function B approaches the smooth path A in any meaningful way.
Should we really believe that these two types of money supplies will generate completely different inflationary evolutions, no matter how close the approximation of the smooth supply rule by the step function is chosen?[22]
2. To ensure the solvability of the model, open market operations cannot be performed at each moment $t \geq t_0$. But what are the economic reasons that exclude jumps in money-supply except for a discrete set of points in a continuous time model that in principle should be open to such operations at each moment t?

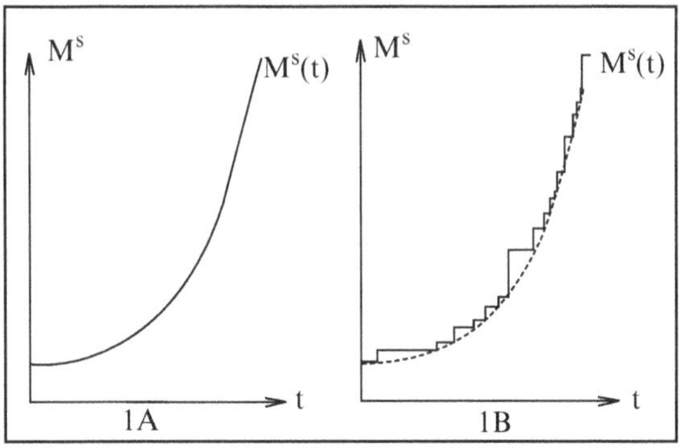

Fig. 7.1 The nonequivalence of equivalent smooth and stepwise money supply strategies

[22] Mathematically speaking, it is of course not startling to see that "C_0-convergence on the M^s-level" does not imply "C_1-convergence on the p-level." However, the economics of this model demands something of this kind, for example, by means of a redefinition of the rate of inflation in terms of a moving average or by means of a reformulated theory of price level changes.

3. With regard to the above steady-state situation ($\pi^* \equiv 0$), the Phillips-curve (7.18) of this model degenerates to $\hat{W} = \phi(l/l^s - 1) < \infty$. For the money wage W and this Phillips-curve it is stated in Sargent (1987, p. 47): "All that we require is that the value of dW/dt implied by any such relationship be finite so that W cannot jump at a point in time as a result of its interactions with other endogenous or exogenous variables." Despite all this, the money wage W is in fact allowed to jump in Sargent's perfect foresight case. The quoted logic thus cannot hold true universally.[23] The explanation for this is that there is another implicit change involved in the employed model when $0 < \eta < \infty$ (adaptive expectations) is replaced by $\eta = \infty$ (perfect foresight), since the latter case in fact makes use of a real wage Phillips-curve $\hat{w} = \phi(l/l^s - 1)$ solely, and assumes a classical money-wage equation given by $W = w \cdot p$, where w (but not p) is a continuous function of time for all $t \geq t_0$.

We conclude that Sargent's model (7.1)–(7.10) [or (7.11)–(7.20)] is neither consistent by itself nor consistently applied by Sargent (in the case $\eta = \infty$), since, on the one hand, its determination of the price level is not without ambiguities and methodological flaws, and since, on the other hand, its Keynesian Phillips-curve has implicitly been replaced by a real-wage Phillips-curve with $W = w \cdot p$ as the new equation for the determination of money wages. This variation of the original model and the new approach (7.27) to price level determination provide the scenario for short-run neutrality assertions and the like that originally appeared so odd from the methodological viewpoint of ordinary dynamical analysis. This is a classical revolt, but not a revolution in "Keynesian Economics." The task to explain to students Friedmanian conclusions by means of a full-fledged model of Keynesian dynamics remains consequently still to be solved and demands a further analysis of such much neglected, both simple and yet very demanding models of monetary growth.

7.5 A "Classical" Villain in the Keynesian Spectacle?

So far we have pointed to a variety of weaknesses of Sargent's "Keynesian dynamics under perfect foresight," but have not yet tried to understand the source of all the surprises (or troubles) this model creates for the reader accustomed to the conventional results of (deterministic) Keynesian monetary growth models. We shall now attempt to provide such an analysis. The surprisingly simple result of our following investigation will be that there is a unique element in the model, which is responsible for all of its strange behavior in the case of adaptively as well as perfectly formed expectations. The consequences of this finding are still somewhat perplexing, since it in the end suggest that models of the kind we have considered in this and the preceding chapter may lack economic viability simply because they are already too close to hyperinflationary processes that must be made inactive by the assumption that wages *and* prices are sufficiently sluggish. Continuing the analysis of Chap. 6

[23] See also the Sect. 6.5 for related observations in a much simpler model of economic dynamics.

we thus arrive at the conclusion that the true opposition in models of the neoclassical synthesis is not that between its Classical and its Keynesian variant (as in Sargent's (1987) Chaps. 1 and 2), but one between a normal Keynesian functioning of the model under both sluggish wages and prices and its economic dissolution by means of wages and prices that have become too flexible to allow for a conventional type of analysis, which must therefore be treated from the equilibrium viewpoint of saddlepoint stability and its discontinuities to avoid the explosiveness of the dynamics that is generated thereby.

To approach these topics, let us briefly return to the model with adaptive expectations ($\eta < \infty$) of Chap. 6. We have already seen there that the unstable behavior of this model for large parameters η can be explained very well, when this model is compared with a version where prices are adjusting to marginal wage costs with high, but nevertheless still finite speed. It is indeed economically not very convincing to assume for such a model that the level of money wages and that of prices *must* always be divided by the sharp distinction that the latter has to react with infinite speed, while the former cannot.[24] It thus appears as plausible to consider the alternative that their reaction speed may be very different, but that they are both finite and to assume that this alternative will inform us on essential properties of such a model equally well.

If this route towards an understanding of the adaptive as well as the perfect expectations case is accepted,[25] then marginal wage cost pricing of the type (7.2), or (7.12), should be replaced by an adjustment process towards this rule also in the case of myopic perfect foresight, which, here too, gives rise to the following pricing rule:[26]

$$\dot{p} = \lambda(W/F_L - p), \quad \text{i.e.,} \quad \hat{p} = \lambda(w/f'(l) - 1), \quad \lambda > 0. \tag{7.30}$$

The adjustment speed λ used in (7.30) may be very high compared to that which enters the Phillips-curve (7.8) and (7.18), but it should not be infinite from the very start. The idea is that the price level can nevertheless be made a fast variable, thereby which quickly removes any noteworthy discrepancy between actual prices and marginal wage costs in the case of a disturbance of this "equilibrium" relationship.

This transforms the model (7.1)–(7.10) [or (7.11)–(7.20)] back into a standard IS-LM-model as far as its equilibrium part is concerned, where the price level p (and money wages W) are now unambiguously contained among the dynamically endogenous (continuously reacting) variables, the levels of which are fixed in each moment of time.[27]

---

[24] Leaving aside the Classical variant of the neoclassical synthesis where both variables react with infinite speed, which is close to Sargent's perfect foresight solution of the Keynesian variant as we have just seen.

[25] A revision of prices of bang-bang type may be assumed on the microlevel, but is implausible on the level of aggregates. This is also stated in McCallum (1978) who then attempts to prove the Lucas–Sargent-proposition under sluggish price adjustment.

[26] Recall from Chap. 6 that this rule only applies to a neighborhood of the steady state (and that $\hat{M}^s = \hat{L}^s$ has been assumed there in addition).

[27] Leading to a model that is similar in spirit to that employed in Hadjimichalakis (1981).

The problem that p and $\hat{p}_+$ may be endogenous at one and the same point in time is consequently avoided now. And more importantly, the ambiguities we have pointed out in Sect. 7.4 with regard to Sargent's procedure are no longer present in this revised form of his model, despite the acceptance of perfect foresight as the "most neutral" device for treating expectations.

On the basis of (7.30) we get as revised dynamics in the case of perfect foresight (compare also (6.28)–(6.31) in Chap. 6):[28]

$$\hat{w} = \phi(l/l^s - 1), \tag{7.31}$$

$$\begin{aligned}\hat{l}^s &= n - \hat{K} = -i(f(l) - wl - \delta - (r - \hat{p})) \\ &= n - (1-c)f(l) - c(t+\delta) + g + \delta,\end{aligned} \tag{7.32}$$

$$\hat{p} = \lambda(w/f'(l) - 1). \tag{7.33}$$

For the IS-LM part of the model we get the following two equations for the determination of the statically endogenous variables l and r:

$$0 = f(l) - c(f(l) - t - \delta) - i(f(l) - wl - \delta - (r - \lambda[w/f'(l) - 1])) - \delta - n - g,$$
$$0 = m_l^s l^s - pm^d(f(l), r), \text{ where again } m_l^s = M^s/L^s.$$

The comparative-static evaluation of these two equations gives (due to $w = f'(l)$ at the steady state):

$$\begin{pmatrix} (1-c)w + i\lambda f''/w & i \\ pm_y^d w & pm_r^d \end{pmatrix} \begin{pmatrix} dl \\ dr \end{pmatrix} = \begin{pmatrix} -il + i\lambda/w & 0 & 0 \\ 0 & m_l^s & -m^d \end{pmatrix} \begin{pmatrix} dw \\ dl^s \\ dp \end{pmatrix},$$

which gives rise to the following sign pattern for the dependence of the statically endogenous variables on the dynamically endogenous ones[29] (case 1: λ sufficiently

[28] We have proposed in Chap. 6 to make use of $d\hat{p}/dt = \lambda(w/f'(l) - 1)$ to describe myopic perfect foresight far off the steady state (in place of the meaningless equation $\hat{p} = \lambda(\cdot) + \hat{p}$, which does not allow for such states). If this approach is used, we will have to treat a four-dimensional dynamics in place of the following three-dimensional one, making use, for example, of the variables w, l^s, $v = WK/M^s$, and $q = \hat{p}$. The resulting dynamics reads $[l_q > 0, l_v = 0, l_{l^s} = 0, l_w = ?]$:

$$\hat{w} = \phi(l/l^s - 1),$$
$$\hat{l}^s = n - (1-c)f(l) - c(t+\delta) + g + \delta = -i(f(l) - wl - \delta - r + q),$$
$$\dot{q} = \lambda(w/f'(l) - 1),$$
$$\hat{v} = \phi(l/l^s - 1) + q + i(f(l) - wl - \delta - r + q) + n - \rho.$$

We will not discuss this alternative model of myopic perfect foresight in the sequel [as well as any other alternative that can be derived from the remarks made in Chap. 6, which not in each case give rise to meaningful expressions when taken to their perfect foresight limit].

[29] The determinant of the left hand side matrix is equal to $((1-c)w + i\lambda(f''/w)pm_r^d - pm_y^d wi$, which is negative for small values of λ (case 1) and which becomes positive if λ is chosen sufficiently large (case 2), because of $f'' < 0$. This implies that the above matrix formula will be ill-defined at certain values of λ in between these two extremes.

small, case 2: λ sufficiently large):[30]

$$\text{For case 1:} \quad l = l(\underset{-}{w}, \underset{+}{l^s}, \underset{-}{p}), \qquad r = r(\underset{-}{w}, \underset{-}{l^s}, \underset{+}{p}),$$

$$\text{For case 2:} \quad l = l(\underset{-}{w}, \underset{-}{l^s}, \underset{+}{p}), \qquad r = r(\underset{-}{w}, \underset{-}{l^s}, \underset{+}{p}).$$

This implies for the Jacobian J of the above dynamics at its stationary point $w_o = f'(l_o), p_o, l_o = l^s_o$:

Case 1 (λ small):

$$J = \begin{pmatrix} \phi w l_w / l^s & \phi w(l_{l^s} - 1)/l^s & \phi w l_p / l^s \\ -(1-c) l^s w l_w & -(1-c) l^s w l_{l^s} & -(1-c) l^s w l_p \\ \lambda p(1 - f'' l_w)/w & -\lambda p f'' l_{l^s}/w & -\lambda p f'' l_p / w \end{pmatrix} = \begin{pmatrix} - & ? & - \\ + & - & + \\ ? & + & - \end{pmatrix} \begin{matrix} \cdots \hat{w} \\ \cdots \hat{l}^s \\ \cdots \hat{p} \end{matrix},$$

Case 2 (λ large):

$$J = \begin{pmatrix} \phi w l_w / l^s & \phi w(l_{l^s} - 1)/l^s & \phi w l_p / l^s \\ -(1-c) l^s w l_w & -(1-c) l^s w l_{l^s} & -(1-c) l^s w l_p \\ \lambda p(1 - f'' l_w)/w & -\lambda p f'' l_{l^s}/w & -\lambda p f'' l_p / w \end{pmatrix} = \begin{pmatrix} - & - & + \\ + & + & - \\ ? & - & + \end{pmatrix} \begin{matrix} \cdots \hat{w} \\ \cdots \hat{l}^s \\ \cdots \hat{p} \end{matrix}.$$

Asymptotic stability of system (7.31)–(7.33) at the stationary point is given if and only if the following conditions (the Routh–Hurwitz conditions, see Sect. 3.8) hold true for the coefficients a_1, a_2, and a_3 of the characteristic polynomial $x^3 + a_1 x^2 + a_2 x + a_3$ of the above matrix J: $a_1 = -\text{ trace } J > 0, \quad a_3 = -\det J > 0, \quad a_1 a_2 - a_3 > 0 (\Longrightarrow a_2 > 0)$.

It is immediately obvious for the second case of the above that this case must be locally unstable for all parameters values λ, which are chosen sufficiently large, since the expression $p_o f'' l_p / w_o$ in the entry J_{33} is a given positive number at the steady state of this model. This entry of the matrix J can therefore be increased beyond any limit by means of the parameter λ (the other entries in the trace of this Jacobian are not changed by this manipulation of the model). The trace of the matrix J can thereby not only be made positive, but also be made as large as desired. This means that at least one of the eigenvalues of the matrix J must have a real part that approaches infinity for $\lambda \to \infty$. The dynamics of this model is therefore in an extreme way an unstable one when the reaction speed of prices is increased in the attempt to establish the conventional (and Sargent's) limit case where prices are equal to marginal wage costs.

The collapse of the dynamics that we obtained in the case of adaptive expectations by choosing λ large enough and by letting η go to ∞ (see the last section of Chap. 6) is here (for $\eta = \infty$) obtained in an obviously closely related way, which

[30] A high adjustment speed of prices p thus gives rise to a perverse type of Keynes-effect, which in the case of $\lambda = \infty$ is manipulated by Sargent in such a way that there is no Keynes-effect at all in this limit case.

shows that the assumption of flexible prices is the common source of local instability in both models, which deprives them of their economic meaningfulness if this flexibility becomes too large.[31] It is also easily seen – for example, by means of the alternative pricing rules considered in Sect. 6.3 – that it is indeed not so much the specific formulation of such a rule (which here uses marginal wage costs as the target level to which prices are assumed to adjust) that causes these problems, but that it is the mere fact of flexibility that causes the breakdown of viability of this model of Keynesian dynamics if it becomes too large. The Sargent limit case – where the structure of the model undergoes a severe dichotomy as we have seen – must therefore be looked at with great suspicion.

It is this super-explosive knife-edge type of behavior that then carries over to the case $\lambda = \infty$, by dissolving the Keynesian structure of the model under perfect foresight in a way that the source of instability (which lies in the price sector!) can now exercise its effect on the behavior of prices solely. This can be underpinned further by considering in more detail the above limit process for the dynamic part of the model as well as its equilibrium subsector. The above comparative-static analysis first of all will give rise to $l(w) = (f')^{-1}(w)$ (and (7.23)) in a continuous fashion as the parameter λ approaches infinity.[32] A comparison of the Jacobians of above case 2 and its limit case we considered in Sect. 6.3:

Case 2:

$$J = \begin{pmatrix} - & - & + \\ - & + & - \\ ? & - & + \end{pmatrix} \begin{matrix} \cdots \hat{w} \\ \cdots \hat{l}^s \\ \cdots \hat{p} \end{matrix}.$$

Sargent's case:

$$J = \begin{pmatrix} - & + & 0 \\ + & - & 0 \\ ? & - & + \end{pmatrix} \begin{matrix} \cdots \hat{w} \\ \cdots \hat{l}^s \\ \cdots \hat{p} \end{matrix},$$

then shows that the first structure will indeed approach the second one by dissolving itself qualitatively into an independent real sector and a price sector that is dependent on it. Yet, though the links between these two sectors become weaker and weaker as λ approaches ∞, the instability of the latter sector increases by so much that it makes the resulting still interdependent dynamic process uncontrollable.

The final result is that the model of Sects. 7.2–7.4 is the limit of a seemingly conventionally structured Keynesian model, yet one of an extremely implausible unstable type which consequently must inherit all the bad properties of its neighboring cases. Because of this such a model must be rejected as being ill-founded.

Case 1 – by contrast – can be shown to represent a (fairly) well-behaved under standard Keynesian suppositions:

---

[31] We shall see below that both models are also closely related – and economically meaningful – for prices that are adjusted in a sufficiently sluggish way and a fast working of the adaptive expectations mechanism.

[32] This can be seen by solving the above system of linear equations with regard to dl, dr and by taking the limit $\lambda \to \infty$.

Assumption. Suppose for the steady state of the above model:

$$(1-c)f'(l)+i\lambda f''(l)/f'(l)>0 \text{ and } wl>\lambda,$$

that is, the marginal propensity to spend out of income is smaller than one and the negative effect of rising wages on investment (the direct cost effect) outweighs the positive one that is based on the accompanying increase in the expected rate of inflation (the Mundell effect).

These two assumptions restrict the parameter λ in such a way that allows the equilibrium part of the model to react as it is expected from a standard IS-LM framework $(l_w<0, l_p<0)$.

Proposition. *(a) Under the above assumption, the Jacobian J (at the steady state of the given dynamics) will be a (weak) Hicksian matrix, that is, all of its k-principal minors will have the sign $(-1)^k$, $k=1,2,3$.*[33] *(b) The matrix will become a stable matrix (which fulfills all of the Routh–Hurwitz conditions) if λ is chosen sufficiently small.*[34]

Proof. (a) The matrix J (calculated above) can be reformulated as follows (we note that the sign structure of its principal minors is the same as that of the matrix $\tilde{J}$, which it thus suffices to consider in the following):

$$J=\begin{pmatrix} \phi w/l^s & 0 & 0 \\ 0 & (1-c)l^s w & 0 \\ 0 & 0 & \lambda p/w \end{pmatrix}\begin{pmatrix} l_w & l_{e^s}-1 & l_p \\ -l_w & -l_{l^s} & -l_p \\ 1-f''l_w & -f''l_{l^s} & -f''l_p \end{pmatrix}=D\tilde{J}.$$

We already know that the principal minors of dimension one must all be negative (since $l_w, l_p<0$ in the assumed situation, $l_{l^s}>0, f''<0$). For dimension two we get

$$\begin{vmatrix} l_w & l_{l^s}-1 \\ -l_w & -l_{l^s} \end{vmatrix}=-l_w>0 \quad (J_1=-\phi w^2(1-c)\cdot l_w)$$

$$\begin{vmatrix} l_w & l_p \\ 1-f''l_w & -f''l_p \end{vmatrix}=-l_p>0 \quad (J_2=-\phi\lambda p/l^s\cdot l_p)$$

$$\begin{vmatrix} -l_{l^s} & -l_p \\ -f''l_{l^s} & -f''l_p \end{vmatrix}=0 \quad (J_3=0),$$

which shows the one exception from the Hicksian property of matrix J. Dimension three, finally, gives rise to

$$\begin{vmatrix} 0 & -1 & 0 \\ -l_w & -l_{l^s} & -l_p \\ 1 & 0 & 0 \end{vmatrix}=\begin{vmatrix} -1 & 0 \\ -l_{l^s} & -l_p \end{vmatrix}=l_p<0 \quad (|J|=\phi\lambda wp(1-c)l_p),$$

[33] See Quirk and Saposnik (1968, pp. 156/7) and Kemp and Kimura (1978, pp. 88/9) and note that one of the principal minors will be zero in fact (which we have characterized by the term "weak" in the above proposition).

[34] A Hicksian matrix only fulfills $a_1,\ldots,a_n>0$ with respect to the characteristic polynomial $\lambda^n+a_1\lambda^{n-1}+\ldots+a_n$ of the matrix J. It has the property that all of its real eigenvalues must be negative, that is, the system is stable as far as its monotonic types of adjustment are concerned.

which proves the first part of the proposition.

(b) To prove the second part of the proposition we have to show that the final Routh–Hurwitz condition (see Sect. 3.8)

$$a_1 a_2 - a_3 > 0, \qquad a_1 = -\sum_{i=1}^{3} J_{ii},\ a_2 = \sum_{i=1}^{3} J_i,\ a_3 = -|J|$$

holds true in addition.

This inequality is equivalent to

$$(-\phi w l_w / l^s + (1-c) l^s w l_{l^s} + \lambda p f'' l_p / w) \cdot (-\phi w^2 (1-c) l_w - \phi \lambda p l_p / l^s) - \phi \lambda w p (1-c) l_p$$

or

$$(-\phi w l_w / l_s + \lambda p f'' l_p / w)(-\phi w^2 (1-c) l_w - \phi \lambda p l_p / l^s) > -\phi \lambda w p (1-c) l_p (1 - l_{l^s}).$$

It will be fulfilled, for example, if $l_{l^s} \geq 1$ holds true or if λ is chosen sufficiently small (in the opposite case).

The system is thus a *locally asymptotically stable* one if the adjustment speed of prices is such that it allows for a "normal" operation of real wage and price increases (the Keynes effect) as far as the IS-LM approach is concerned and if the final Routh–Hurwitz condition $a_1 a_2 - a_3$ can be assumed to hold true.

It may, however, also happen that a still meaningful adjustment speed λ of prices toward their target level W/F_L makes this last stability condition invalid, so that *extra forces* have to be introduced to keep the dynamics within economically meaningful bounds. The result is that we may have a locally unstable, but nevertheless globally meaningful Keynesian dynamics *even in the case of perfect foresight,* which exhibits no unusual features.[35]

Yet, we know for certain that there is a limit to price flexibility in this context if the model is to remain a economically useful one. Our conclusion here was that the model will enter the region where hyperinflationary processes set in if this limit is passed. In such a case it is no longer sensible to attempt to restrict the dynamic behavior somehow by means of outward stabilizers. Instead, the approach to a hyperinflationary scenario represents a quite different economic regime, which demands much more revision of the model than only the assumption of very flexible prices (and wages) coupled with a fast or infinitely fast revision of expectations. The proper reformulation of this IS-LM growth dynamics for the case where its implicit knife-edge property becomes activated by an increase in price flexibility – and maybe also virulent – must here, however, be left to future investigations.

We close these considerations by means of some simulations of the above dynamics as well as its adaptive expectations forerunner. These simulations, on the one hand, show for the parameter values of the model we simulated in the last chapter

[35] See Flaschel (1991, 1992) for a further analysis of such cases and for details of making such an unstable core model viable – and thus complete – by means of appropriate delimiters for quantity and price reactions.

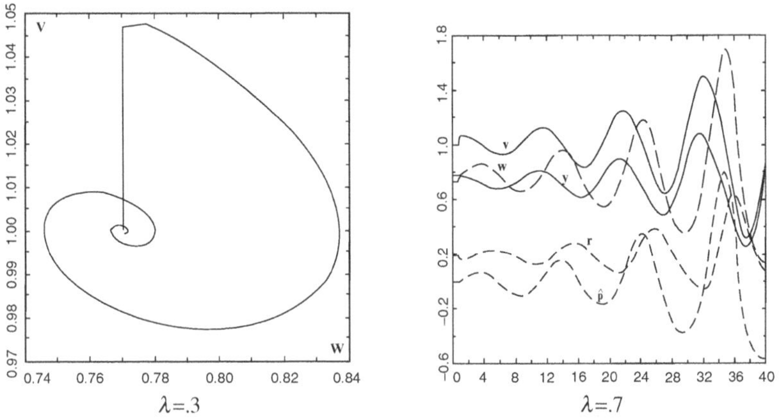

Fig. 7.2 Stability and instability in the case of perfect foresight

that an increase of the parameter λ from 0.3 to 0.7 is already sufficient in this case to turn the model from a stable to an unstable one – which still looks meaningful if its explosive tendencies are counteracted far off the steady state equilibrium. On the other hand, we see for both the stable and the unstable case that the behavior of the model is still practically the same for an infinitely fast and a fast, but finite adjustment of inflationary expectations.[36]

These numerical investigation exemplify that the striking contrast between the case of adaptive as opposed to perfect foresight is solely due to an operation of this IS-LM growth model in a region where it no longer represents a model that is economically meaningful (Figs. 7.2 and 7.3).[37]

We have started this section with the question whether there are (still) incompatible classical elements in the model of Keynesian dynamics of this and the preceding chapter and have shown that the case of a fast adjustment of the price level toward marginal wage costs – in the way it is used in Sargent (1987, Chap. V) – represents such an element that cannot be regarded as a properly formulated economic building-block of this Keynesian model. The rejection of this component of the model, however, has two aspects in it, which – even on the danger of repetition – must be carefully kept separate from each other.

[36] Note that this model – as the one of Dornbusch and Fischer we have considered in Sect. 6.6 – is again of a fairly cyclical nature for high values of η in combination with low values of the parameter λ. In contrast to the simple Dornbusch and Fischer model it does, however, lose its stability when the parameter λ is increased. This fact points to the stability illusion that is created by dynamic economic models, which – besides expectations – concentrate on only one dynamic economic law in addition.

[37] See Ball (1991, p. 446) for a similar observation that is based on another type of reasoning and note also his arguments in favor of the adaptive expectations hypothesis he puts forward in this section.

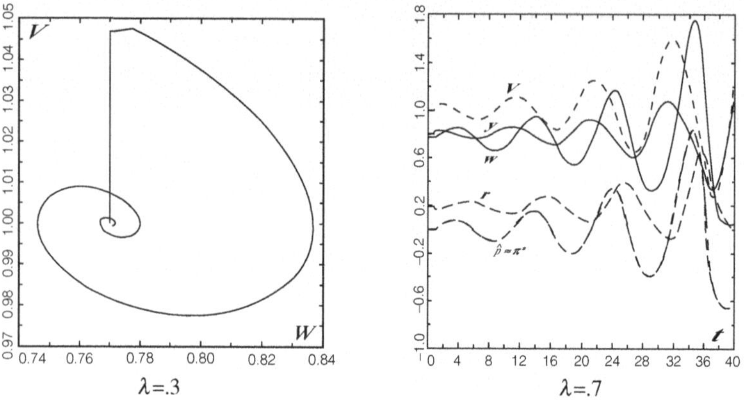

Fig. 7.3 Adaptive expectations that are close to perfect foresight ($\eta = 10$)

We have seen, *on the one hand*, that the marginal productivity postulate,[38] the conventional type of a money wage Phillips-curve and the simplifying device of assuming myopic perfect foresight come into conflict with each other in this model of Keynesian dynamics. The model with a finite adjustment speed of prices is capable of showing why this is the case. In this model, prices and wages are given in each moment of time. According to the marginal productivity rule they therefore determine employment at each point in time t. Yet, it is the essence of the Keynesian model that employment is determined by the effective demand for goods. There are thus two principles in this approach which act on employment and which will come into conflict with each other when no other variable can be found, which weakens the influence of one of these two principles with respect to the statics and dynamics of this model.

In Sargent's approach ($\lambda = \infty$) this variable is given by the rate of inflation that enters goods-market equilibrium through its influence on investment behavior. This variable can – and in Sargent's approach does – adjust investment toward savings. The goods-market is therefore again cleared in a classical fashion ($I \to S$) by means of an appropriate choice of the rate of inflation (and not by means of movements in the level of income, not even in a partial way). The restriction that effective demand was supposed to exercise on income and employment is consequently completely absent from this formulation of Keynesian dynamics.

There exist also other possibilities for resolving the above conflict between two differing theories of the determination of employment, income, interest, and real wage formation. Yet, independent of the construction of alternatives to Sargent's manipulation of a Keynesian structure, we can state at the end of this chapter that (despite Keynes' acceptance of it), it seems reasonable to dismiss the pricing rule $p = W/f'(l)$ from a Keynesian context. The reason for this claim is that this rule assumes nonrationed price-taking firms (which choose employment so as to maximize

[38] Which was explicitly accepted by Keynes (1936) as a building block of his new theory of employment.

profits). This is particularly obvious in the disequilibrium case where prices only adjust with a finite speed in the direction of marginal wage costs, where these same firms are also confronted with an effective demand constraint, and are thus also quantity-takers. We conclude that the Keynesian theory – be it static or dynamic – must be reformulated by means of a model of quantity-constrained *and price setting* firms independent of the degree of competition that may be assumed to exist. This is not only an obvious logical necessity from an economic point of view, but also much more in line with the facts. One can only wonder why Keynesian models that are based on the strict marginal productivity rule (Keynes' postulate I) are still widely used in economic theory.

Yet, necessary as such a reformulation of the Keynesian approach may be, the marginal productivity postulate by itself is not the "villain in the piece," which creates the odd-looking propositions we have started from at the beginning of this chapter. Using mark up prices based on average wage costs in place of marginal ones will create the same narrow relationship between real wages and employment in the situation where prices adjust with infinite speed to their target level and will thus create the same dichotomy of the model as the marginal productivity rule.

We have seen, *on the other hand*, that a significant difference to Sargent-type propositions can be created once the model is operated on the assumption that prices do not respond too fast to exogenous shocks. Under this assumption, the conflict between the two theories of employment observed above will disappear from the model and with it the Classical revolt in Keynesian dynamics we have analyzed in this chapter. This is so, since employment is then determined by the IS-LM part of the model in the usual way (providing the theory of short-run), while prices are adjusting in the medium run to certain target levels that will depend on the positions of the economy in between and that will in their particular formulation not exercise a strong influence on the qualitative features of its dynamic behavior (see the next chapter). The decisive (neo)classical element in the above – as well as many other – models of Keynesian dynamics therefore is the degree of price flexibility it allows for which very effectively undermines its long run stability properties if it is chosen too large. This conclusion supplements the finding of Chap. 6 that too flexible nominal wages may undermine the short-run stability properties of full employment equilibrium. The speed of price and wage adjustment is therefore the crucial element that divides macroeconomic theories of the dynamic evolution of capitalist economies – and not so much the mix of a basically neoclassical (Walrasian) assumption of price-taking agents with an otherwise Keynesian model of economic dynamics.

Sargent's (1987) attempt to obtain Friedmanian propositions from a Keynesian variant of the neoclassical synthesis fails, since he has to assume besides an infinitely fast adjustment of prices also an infinitely fast adjustment of money wages for this purpose in the end. His treatment of the case of myopic perfect foresight thus represents but a complicated detour back to the classical variant of full price flexibility ($\lambda = \phi = \infty$) of the neoclassical synthesis with all the stability problems we have investigated in this and the preceding chapter. But instability of equilibrium is not an issue that matters very much in the neoclassical approach to macroeconomics.

Appendix: On the Stability of Models of Money and Growth

This chapter would not be complete if we would not examine the basic contribution of Sargent and Wallace (1973), which provided the basis for all later analysis of the saddlepoint instability phenomenon of perfect foresight models. Our analysis, which will rationalize jumps in certain variables in a natural way, but which will refute Sargent and Wallace's specific solution to this problem, owes its ideas to Chiarella (1990, Chap. 7)[39], though it will present them in a different way here, which, on the one hand, stays close to the dynamic variables that were used by Sargent and Wallace themselves and which, on the other hand, describes the economics of the model in more detail than it is done in Chiarella (1990, Chap. 7). In this appendix, we follow Sargent and Wallace (1973) and make use of an uppercase letter to denote the price level and of a lowercase one for its logarithm ($p = \log P$), and we will use π in place of π^* to denote inflationary expectations.

From a mathematical as well as an economic point of view a natural generalization[40] of the simple Cagan model that is employed by Sargent and Wallace (1973) in their analysis of the dynamic (in)stability of models of monetary growth is given by the following model[41] of money market disequilibrium[42] and adaptively formed expectations:

$$\dot{p} = \lambda(m^s - p - \alpha(\pi)), \tag{7.34}$$

$$\dot{\pi} = \eta(\dot{p} - \pi) = \eta(\lambda m^s - \lambda p - \lambda\alpha(\pi) - \pi). \tag{7.35}$$

[39] Cf. here also Chiarella (1986).

[40] In particular, in the light of Sect. 7.5., cf. also Goldman (1972), Kiguel (1989).

[41] See Goldman (1972) for details on the assumption of a finite adjustment speed of prices P and note that the possibility of instability makes this model's outcome significantly different from the Dornbusch and Fischer model we have considered in the appendices of Sects. 6.4 and 6.5. Kiguel (1989) generalizes this model by adding a government budget constraint to its linear version and explores thereby another interesting aspect of this approach to an explanation of hyperinflationary processes.

[42] Goldman (1972, (3)) employs instead of (7.34) the linear equation

$$\frac{\mathrm{d}\log(M^s/P)}{\mathrm{d}t} = \lambda\left(\log\frac{M^d}{P} - \log\frac{M^s}{P}\right),$$

that is, $\dot{p} = \dot{m}^s + \lambda(m^s - p - \alpha\pi - \gamma)$, which can be interpreted as a special case of our following price adjustment equation. He then contrast the results that are obtained from this equation and the adaptive expectations mechanism (7.35) with what he calls the simplified Cagan model, where it is assumed that the money market is cleared at each moment in time and states (on p. 250) that "the rationalization for this procedure rests upon the assumption that the rapid adjustment of prices to disequilibrium may be approximated by the assumption of continual equilibrium." He, however, finds that these two models differ considerably (in particular, with respect to the paradox that an expansionary monetary policy may terminate a self-generating inflation), which shows in a different way that an approach that ignores adjustment mechanisms may be problematic.

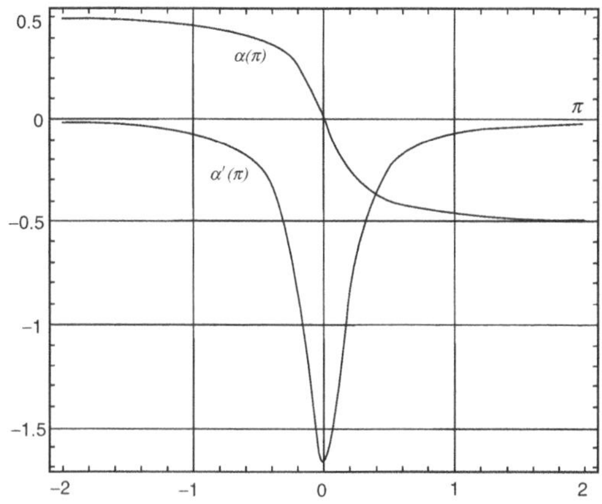

Fig. 7.4 A nonlinear formulation of the money demand function

In this model, the symbols m^s, p now denote the log of the money supply M^s (a constant[43]) and of the price level P. The time derivative $\dot{p}$ thus gives the rate of inflation $\hat{P}$, which in its difference to π, the expected rate of inflation, already explains the second equation of the model (the well-known adaptive expectations mechanism). In the first equation, the sum $p+\alpha(\pi)$ stands for the logarithm of money demand ($M^d = Pe^{\alpha(\pi)}$), which generalizes an assumption of Sargent and Wallace (1973).[44] Following Chiarella we assume for the (derivative of the) function $\alpha(\pi)$ the following general shape (Fig. 7.4), which can be rationalized by means of portfolio considerations, see Chiarella (1990, Chap. 7):

This function states that money demand will be very inelastic for very low (negative) as well as for very high (positive) values of the expected rate of inflation and will be close to $\alpha'(0)\cdot\pi, \alpha'(0) < 0$ in a certain neighborhood of the steady state $\pi = 0$ (Sargent and Wallace assume $\alpha(\pi) = \alpha'(0)\pi$ for all values of π). As in the

[43] In the case of a positive rate of growth of the money supply one has to make use of the following system (with the variables $\dot{p}, \pi, \rho = \dot{m}^s$ = const.) instead of p, π:

$$\ddot{p} = \lambda(\rho - \dot{p} - \alpha'(\pi)\dot{\pi}), \quad \dot{\pi} = \eta(\dot{p} - \pi),$$

which gives rise to the same conclusions as the case $\rho = 0$.

[44] This demand equation can – up to a constant term – also be obtained from the money demand equation (7.6) of the Sargent model of Sect. 7.5 if output Y and the real rate of interest μ are considered as given – as it may be appropriate in a model of hyperinflation:

$$M^d = P\bar{Y}e^{\beta(\mu+\hat{P})}.$$

The destabilizing mechanism that is at work in the present model is therefore of a very general type as it can be brought about by the Mundell effect in the market for goods (see Chaps. 6 and 7 and Tobin (1975)) or by a similar effect in the market for money as in the neoclassical monetary growth model of Tobin (1965), Hadjimichalakis (1981), and others. See also Calvo (1977) for further observations on the role of money demand in this context.

main part of this chapter, the parameters λ, η characterize the speeds of adjustment of prices P and expectations π.

The steady state of the above model is given by $\dot{p} = \dot{\pi} = 0$, which implies $\pi_0 = 0$ and $m^s = p_0$. And the Jacobian of the system (7.34) and (7.35) is given by (for arbitrary points of the (π, p)-phase space)

$$J = \begin{pmatrix} -\lambda & -\lambda\alpha'(\pi) \\ -\eta\lambda & -\eta(1+\lambda\alpha'(\pi)) \end{pmatrix},$$

which in turn gives

$$\begin{aligned} \text{trace } J &= -\lambda(\eta\alpha'+1) - \eta = -\eta(\lambda\alpha'+1) - \lambda, \\ \det J &= \lambda\eta > 0. \end{aligned}$$

The above dynamics will therefore be locally asymptotically stable if

$$-\alpha'(\pi_0) = -\alpha'(0) \; < \; 1/\eta \quad (\text{or} < 1/\lambda)$$

holds true and it will be instable for η and λ sufficiently large (which is similar to the observations we made in Chap. 6).[45]

Sargent and Wallace's (1973) paper now has the following restricted view with respect to the above: it, on the one hand, only considers the double limit case $\lambda, \eta \; = \; \infty$ and it, on the other hand, does so solely from a local perspective, assuming thereby that $\alpha'(0)$ characterizes the shape of the money demand function not only at or near the steady state, but also for all other values of inflationary expectations π ($\alpha(0) \; = \; 0$ in addition).

On the basis of these assumptions the above dynamic system gives rise to the following single linear differential equation:

$$\dot{p} = \frac{1}{\alpha'(0)}[m^s - p] = \gamma_1 p - \gamma_2, \; \gamma_i > 0,$$

since we then have money-market equilibrium $m^s = p + \alpha'(0)\pi$ and perfect foresight $\dot{p} = \pi$ throughout. This differential equation is the basis of Sargent and Wallace's analysis of jumps in the price level variable P, which these authors offer as the solution to the obvious instability problem of such a fundamental model of monetary growth.

It is equally obvious that this linear approach to dynamic (in)stability is very restrictive and that we should investigate its validity anew from the broader perspective of model (7.34) and (7.35), in particular, since the local aspect it implicitly contains may conflict with the global aspect of Sargent and Wallace's proposal for an economically meaningful stable solution path for the above monetary dynamics.

To discuss the instability problem of Sargent and Wallace from this broader perspective, we assume now that the parameter λ has been chosen such that

[45] See Goldman (1972, p. 253) for further details of this local approach to stability.

$\lambda > 1/\alpha'(0)$ holds true and that η is large enough to imply trace $J > 0$ on the basis of this choice of the parameter λ.

Following Sargent and Wallace's analysis, the price level will be considered at first as the fast variable (or in the limit: a jump variable) that reacts very quick (instantaneously) with respect to money market disequilibrium ($\lambda \to \infty$) :[46]

$$\dot{p} = \lambda(m^s - p - \alpha(\pi)) \quad [\text{or } p = m^s - \alpha(\pi) \text{ in the limit}].$$

For a given expectation π, this process is obviously globally asymptotically stable (approaching the equilibrium exponentially with degree λ). The isocline or equilibrium manifold $\dot{p} = 0 \quad [p = m^s - \alpha(\pi)]$ is thus attracting the price level with this strong stability property. The variable p will thus be very close to this isocline in general.

For the second isocline $\dot{\pi} = 0 \quad [p = m^s - \alpha(\pi) - \pi/\lambda]$, we get this type of stability only for points π, where $-\alpha'(\pi) - 1/\lambda < 0$ holds true [see (7.35)]. Because of the assumed shape of $\alpha'(\pi)$, this will be the case for all π that are sufficiently large in their absolute value [for $1/\lambda$ sufficiently small, cf. Fig. 7.6]. In between, the slope of the $\dot{\pi} = 0$ line must, however, become positive and thus gives rise to π-instability in a neighborhood of $\pi = 0$. We therefore get a situation as it is drawn in Fig. 7.5.

This dynamics is of the same type as that of the Kaldor business cycle model, which has been extensively studied in the literature [see Sect. 3.10 and Lorenz and Gabisch (1989) for references and various presentations of this cycle model].

One can make use of the Poincaré–Bendixson theorem to show the existence of a limit cycle for the dynamics (7.34) and (7.35), which furthermore can be shown to be stable. For the purposes of this section, it is, however, sufficient to argue intuitively by means of Fig. 7.5 and its two partial equilibrium curves, since we only want to demonstrate the existence of a valid alternative to the Sargent and Wallace procedure

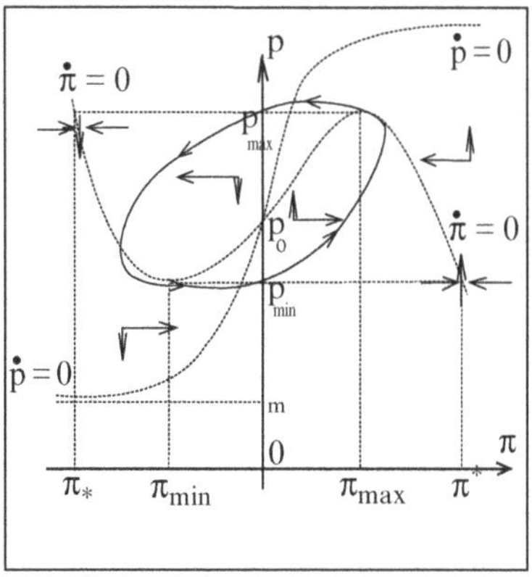

Fig. 7.5 Unstable monetary growth leads to limit cycles in the rate of inflation and the expectations about it

[46] Later on we shall, however, see that it is preferable to assume and interpret the variable π as the one that is more fast, which will thus – in the limit – jump to guarantee perfect foresight at each moment in time (up to the jump itself).

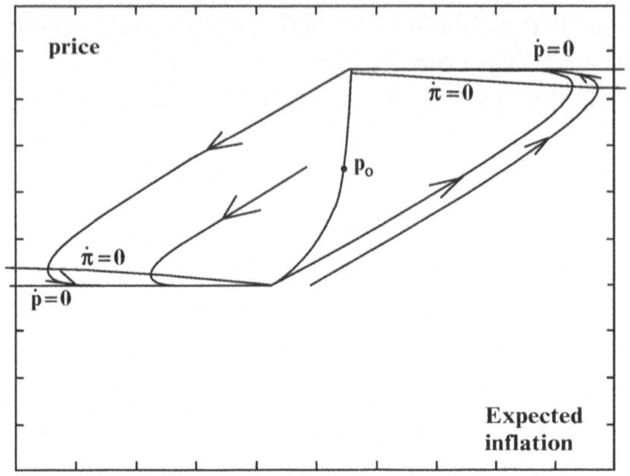

Fig. 7.6 The case of a relatively fast price adjustment

of making the model a viable one. The results on the Kaldor model are therefore assumed to be known in the following.

If the parameter λ is large (also relative to the parameter η), the $\dot{\pi} = 0$-isocline is close to the $\dot{p} = 0$-isocline in the relevant part of the π-domain. Prices will adjust quickly to the latter isocline (by strong upward and downward movements near the area where the $\dot{p} = 0$-curve is steep, see Fig. 7.6 for a still moderate example).[47]

This picture exemplifies situations where a rapid adjustment of prices is observed, while movements in expectations π are relatively slow, when the dynamics is close to the $\dot{p} = 0$-isocline.

The adjustment directions of the expected rate of inflation are shown by horizontal arrows in Fig. 7.5. If the adjustment speed η of these expectations increases (relative to λ), adjustment towards the perfect foresight path $\dot{\pi} = 0$ will be more rapid in turn and the dynamics will then stay close to the curve $\dot{\pi} = 0$. On the left hand side of this figure we have $\pi \sim \dot{p} < 0$ and therefore a shrinking level of prices. Yet, in this deflationary area, prices cannot fall below the value $p_{\min}$, which means that deflation must find an end there. There then exists, for given values of p, a stable equilibrium point for the expectations mechanism in the inflationary area on the right hand side of Fig. 7.5. If η is large, there will consequently be a nearly immediate increase in inflationary expectations towards this new attracting point. Thereafter, we have inflation at a rate that is slowly falling, that is, the price level will increase and $\dot{p}$ and π will fall during this phase of the dynamic process. Again, this comes to an end at $p = p_{\max}$, and the rapid transitory process described earlier is now working in the opposite direction. We therefore get a stable (uniquely determined) limit cycle from this dynamics, which sometimes shows slow movements in prices and their (expected) rate of change and which at other times gives rise to sudden and sharp changes in the expected rate of inflation π, whereby the preceding direction of price changes becomes reversed ($\eta = 20 \gg \lambda = 2$, in the following Fig. 7.7).

[47] We have chosen here $\eta = 2$ and $\lambda = 20$, which are still parameter values of a medium range of this dynamics. For $\lambda = 500$, for example, the upward and downward adjustment in Fig. 7.6 becomes much steeper indeed.

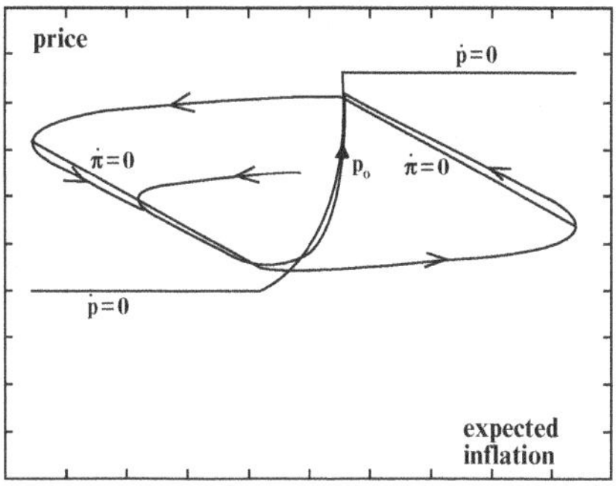

Fig. 7.7 The case of a relatively fast adjustment of inflationary expectations

Note with regard to this figure that the dynamics now stays close to the perfect foresight isocline $\dot{\pi} = 0$ and no longer to $\dot{p} = 0$ as in the Fig. 7.7. Note furthermore that this situation suggests that π should be considered as the jump variable in the end (for a fast, but finite adjustment of prices P and the limit case of myopic perfect foresight $\eta = \infty$) – and not the price level P as it is suggested in Sargent and Wallace (1973). Note finally that the two figures in Fig. 7.7 show recurrent endogenous "jumps" – independent from any (further) shock in the money supply process – once the dynamics has left the steady state.

Sargent and Wallace (1973, p. 1045) motivate their choice of the stable arm of their otherwise purely explosive dynamics $(\dot{p} = (m^s - p)/\alpha)$ by

> We assume that the public expects that, if m^s were to be constant over time, a process of ever-accelerating inflation or deflation would eventually come to an end, if only in the very remote future.

There is, however, nothing in the above more general situation that could make this sentence applicable to it, since deflationary and inflationary periods are here limited, are in addition of a decelerating and not of an accelerating nature, and interchange each other at regular time intervals. We conclude that the dynamics we have analyzed above is the correct description of the economics behind the Sargent and Wallace "limit limit" case $\eta = \infty, \lambda = \infty$. Depending on the adjustment speeds, jumps in prices or in their rate of change and expectations about it can indeed be observed in it, but they are endogenous features of a viable, but not asymptotical dynamics that works in the conventional way and they do not lead us back to the steady state (but toward a stable limit cycle).

Sargent and Wallace (1973) consider, on the one hand, only the limit case $\eta = \infty$ of such a situation. In this case, systems (7.34) and (7.35) can be reduced to one dynamical law:[48]

$$\dot{p} = \lambda(m^s - p - \alpha(\pi)) \quad \text{or} \quad \ddot{p} = \lambda(-\dot{p} - \alpha'(\pi) \cdot \dot{\pi}),$$

that is

$$\dot{\pi} = \lambda(-\pi - \alpha'(\pi)\dot{\pi}) \quad \text{or} \quad \dot{\pi} = \frac{-1}{1/\lambda + \alpha'(\pi)}\pi. \tag{7.36}$$

[48] Cf. also Kiguel (1989) for a treatment of this perfect foresight case.

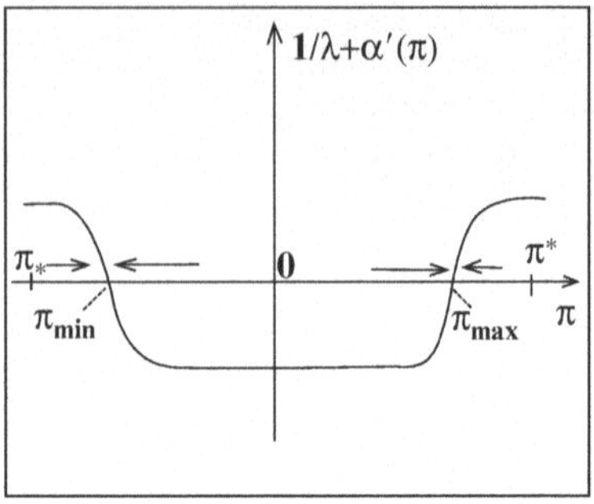

Fig. 7.8 The limit cycle for the perfect foresight case

The graph of the denominator on the right-hand side of this last equation is given by Fig. 7.8

If λ is chosen sufficiently large. The dynamic implications of (7.36), for π, are therefore as shown by the arrows in Fig. 7.8. This figure consequently implies the same type of behavior as it was analyzed above for $\eta < \infty$, since the limit procedure $\eta \to \infty$ obviously suggests that there are (now instantaneous) jumps (implicitly present) in this dynamic situation, which change π_{max} into π_* and π_{min} into π^* whenever such a borderpoint is reached. The above dynamics is thus still of limit cycle type (a limit limit cycle as it is called in Chiarella (1990)).

In Sargent and Wallace (1973) we have, on the other hand, not only perfect foresight ($\eta = \infty$), but also instantaneous adjustment of prices towards market equilibrium ($\lambda \to \infty$). With regard to Fig. 7.8 this simply means $\pi_{min} \to -\infty$ and $\pi_{max} \to +\infty$. Viewed from such limit procedures, the end result therefore simply is a "limit limit limit cycle" ($+\infty \to -\infty \to +\infty$, etc.), where the decelerating parts of inflation or deflation have now been removed from the model. In the case of such an extreme type of limit cycle dynamics, it is, however, very questionable whether λ should indeed be allowed to approach infinity.[49]

Somewhat sluggish price adjustment (here with respect to money market disequilibria – due to the simple model chosen) make visible what is hidden in the Sargent and Wallace approach to monetary (in)stability, namely that expectations may be perfect nearly everywhere and still not give rise to the jumps in the price variable p as they are proposed in the Sargent and Wallace paper from the local and linear perspective there employed. Instead perfect foresight paths are as shown in the Fig. 7.9 and they are left from time to time – for a short interval of time – due to the internal limits that here exist for decelerating inflation (to the right) and deflation (to the left). Furthermore, perfect foresight models can here again be approximated by an adaptive expectations mechanism that works with sufficient strength and thus do not lead to very different economic results in comparison to the case of adaptive expectations.

[49] If Sargent and Wallace would allow for a finite parameter λ in the consideration of their dynamics (in the nonlinear case), they would observe that a dynamics that leaves the steady state of the above Fig. 7.8 will reach the point π_{min} or π_{max} after a finite interval of time and they would then be forced to analyze, in the above way, the dynamic behavior of the nonlinear model after this point in time has been reached.

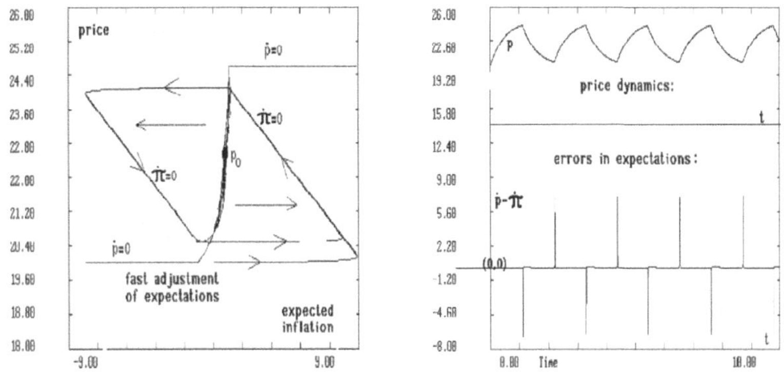

Fig. 7.9 Adaptive expectations that are close to perfect foresight

Making small errors with respect to the rate of inflation stays here close to the thus only simplifying assumption of making no errors at all with regard to immediate future development of the economy.[50]

Note with regard to these figures that the rate of inflation, crudely estimated, here cycles between -10 and $+10$, while the difference between this rate and the expected rate of inflation stays below 0.06 normally (this is only different in situations where rapid change occurs, but this is also true in Sargent and Wallace's extreme limit case, where we have $dp \neq p_+$ in such a situation). Adaptive expectations consequently remain a useful assumption in economics, even if only useful in an analysis of the mathematical manipulations made in the limit case of myopic perfect foresight.

We therefore have that models of monetary growth may be unstable with respect to their steady state, but that this instability does not prevent their conventional solution by means of a predetermined variable p – if these models are formulated by also including the nonlinear economic forces that must come about far off the steady state. This basic idea can be summarized in the following way by making use of Kaldor's original model[51] and – as far as the mathematics is concerned – naive presentation of relaxation oscillations[52] we have discussed earlier.

This picture shows three perfect foresight equilibria, two stable, and an unstable one as far as, for example, adaptively formed expectations are concerned.[53] In the stable equilibrium to the right in Fig. 7.10, we have an excess supply of money

[50] See LaSalle (1949) for the mathematical details of the statement that the dynamics of systems as the above must be qualitatively the same for small values of $1/\eta$ and for $1/\eta = 0$ – contradicting the view that the implications of myopic perfect foresight must be very different from the case of (fast) adaptive expectations.

[51] Cf. the appendix of Chap. 3 for a brief presentation of the Kaldor trade cycle model.

[52] See Chiarella (1990, 2.6) for references on such an approach as well as a brief mathematical presentation of such oscillations. See also Arrowsmith and Place (1982) and Grasman (1987) for further details on relaxation oscillations.

[53] It need, however, not necessarily be this mechanism with respect to which this asymptotic stability is proved or even only assumed.

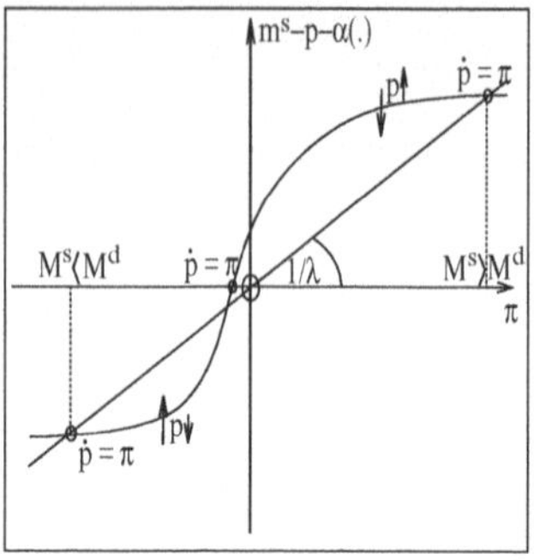

Fig. 7.10 A Kaldorian reformulation of the Cagan model under perfect foresight

and thus inflation, which attempts and indeed succeeds to reduce this excess supply. This is done by shifting the nonlinear excess supply curve $m^s - p - \alpha(\pi)$ downward, which moves the inflationary point of perfect foresight to the left towards less inflation. This process continues until a point is reached where the upper perfect foresight position coincides with the unstable perfect foresight point – and then disappears completely as the downward shift of the excess function continues. There is then only one perfect foresight equilibrium left, which, for example, under fast (nearly perfect) adaptive expectations is then rapidly approached. Thereafter, perfect foresight prevails again, but now at a point where there is excess demand for money that starts a deflationary process. This process reduces again the disequilibrium on the money market by shifting the curve $m^s - p - \alpha(\pi)$ now into the upward direction. The price dynamics thus would again make the money market disequilibrium disappear in the end if it could continue without limit. Yet, once again, there is (now a negative) rate of inflation where the perfect foresight point that is responsible for the deflation disappears and gives way to a single perfect foresight equilibrium again on the right and with a positive rate of inflation.

Money market disequilibrium dynamics – here of an extremely simple type – lets perfect foresight points consequently move in time in such a way that disequilibria are reduced, that inflation or deflation is declining, and that there is no need and no scope for letting the price level jump. This price level here functions as the relatively slow variable, which is predetermined in each moment of time and which adjusts in the direction of the above excess supply, while the fast variable is given by the expected rate of inflation which (nearly) instantaneously adjusts whenever there is need for a change in the existing perfect foresight regime. There is thus assumed a very fast mechanism – not necessarily an adaptive one – which quickly reestablishes correct anticipations whenever they have got lost and which creates a price level dynamics of the kind

$$\dot{p} = \lambda[m^s - p - \alpha(\dot{p})],$$

which is stable at the rate of inflation or deflation the expectational mechanism has led it to.

Furthermore, we once again see that the Sargent and Wallace assumption of $\lambda \to \infty$ will move the above two stable expectational equilibrium points to $\pm\infty$ and will thus make the above analysis invisible in the end. In removing two important equilibria from their model in this way, Sargent and Wallace (1973) end up with a proposal for their price level dynamics, which is – though motivated by global considerations – based on local analysis only, depends heavily on the assumption of linearity, and is inadequate from any global view on the properties of the money demand function.

Reducing dynamical models in their dimension by one by assuming infinite adjustment speeds on one market may thus lead to erroneous conclusions with respect to the proper dynamical structure that is to be assumed to underlie the reduced order system. It is not sensible to consider limit cases such as Sargent and Wallace's (1973) perfect foresight model of money market equilibrium:

$$\dot{p} = \frac{1}{\alpha}(m^s - p), \quad \alpha < 0$$

in isolation in the way they do, since it may be (and in fact here, will be) the case that very fast, but not infinitely fast reaction patterns will considerably modify the conclusions about the working of the model. Limit cases must be backed up by the consideration of limit processes that suggest the way in which infinitely fast adjustments have to be viewed and explained.

Sargent and Wallace's "perfect" agents – by contrast – do not observe any money market adjustment processes, they do not see the slight and economically irrelevant errors in their expectations, and they view the world as being linear – on the basis of the slopes of the behavioral relationships at the steady state. They then use the following explicit formula (which is also available due to the restrictive assumptions just made)

$$p(t) = \int_t^\infty e^{(s-t)/\alpha} m^s(s)\,ds$$

to predict the reactions of $p(t)$ on the basis of their assumptions about the behavior of the money supply – in a way that will not be confirmed by the model if only extremely secondary adjustment delays are introduced into it in the above way.

In view of this approach to inflationary expectations, adaptive expectations may even be claimed to be superior in comparison, since they

- avoid agents that confuse the properties of local and global situations in their formation of expectations,
- represent a sufficient (nearly perfect) response in situations that are only moderately inflationary when they react with sufficient strength (are updated sufficiently often),
- represent a response that transforms inflationary cycles into expectation cycles with a smaller amplitude, and
- are simple to manage.

Part III
Matured Keynesian AD-AS Analysis and Beyond

CAN socialism work? Of course it can. No doubt is possible about that once we assume, first, that the requisite stage of industrial development has been reached and, second, that transitional problems can be successfully resolved. One may, of course, feel very uneasy about these assumptions themselves or about the questions whether the socialist form of society can be expected to be democratic and, democratic or not, how well it is likely to function. All that will be discussed later on. But if we accept these assumptions and discard these doubts, the answer to the remaining question is clearly Yes.[1]

[1] Schumpeter, J. (1942). *Capitalism, Socialism and Democracy* (p. 167). New York: Harper & Row.

Chapter 8
Keynesian AD-AS, Quo Vadis?

8.1 Introduction

In this chapter,[1] we begin to make a big step forward in the evolution of Keynesian AD-AS analysis and present on the basis of Chiarella and Flaschel (2000), Chiarella, Flaschel, and Franke (2005), and related later work a disequilibrium AD-AS framework, which incorporates progress we have made with respect to the AS-side of the models considered in Part II of the book, the wage-price spiral of the model as we would like to call it now. This wage-price spiral, which is operating within a certain inflationary climate here, is combined in the following with a reduced form of a dynamic IS-equation,[2] Okun's law in place of a neoclassical production function, and finally a Taylor interest rate policy rule in the place of the LM-curve we have employed so far. We will consider the stability properties of this model type for arbitrary as well as estimated parameter values and will simulate the resulting dynamics numerically. The outcome of this investigation will be that the distributive growth cycle approach of Goodwin (1967), we have considered in detail in Part I of the book, is an integral part of such matured AD-AS modeling, which therefore in fact provides a synthesis of the Keynesian demand cycle with a Goodwinian distributive cycle that we have considered in Chaps. 4 and 5.

Moreover, we also compare this matured Keynesian AD-AS dynamics with the now fashionable New Keynesian approach to macrodynamics (here with both staggered wages and prices) and will see that the two model types have formally seen much in common, but differ radically with respect to their implications and the theory of the business cycle they imply. In place of the radical break with the old neoclassical synthesis that is characteristic for the New Keynesian approach (the new neoclassical synthesis), where the IS curve is basically of a Walrasian type, we provide with our disequilibrium AD-AS model an approach that can be considered as a continuation of the old neoclassical synthesis, yet one that avoids the internal

[1] This chapter is based on Asada, Chiarella, Flaschel, and Proaño (2007): Keynesian AD-AS, Quo Vadis? UTS Sydney: Working paper.

[2] See the quoted work of Chiarella et al. for fully specified IS disequilibrium adjustment processes.

inconsistencies that plagued this synthesis (see Chaps. 6 and 7) and that is based on gradual adjustment processes throughout, in place of the assumption of instantaneous market clearing and a perfectly flexible price level on the market for goods as it was assumed in the old neoclassical synthesis we have investigated in detail in the preceding chapters.

The New Keynesian and our approach to Keynesian AD-AS analysis are, as we shall show, completely incompatible with each other. The detailed investigation of this claim – that we shall pursue in the following – motivates the title of this chapter: Keynesian AD-AS, Quo Vadis?[3]

In this chapter we use – as in other recently published work – as notation w for nominal wages, ω for real wages, u for the rate of capacity utilization, e for the rate of employment, v for the wage share, z for labor productivity, y for the output-capital ratio, and finally i for the rate of interest.

8.2 Keynesian AD-AS: New or Matured?

During the last decade the New Keynesian approach to macroeconometric modeling has become standard for the study of monetary issues in the mainstream literature, despite its many shortcomings especially on the empirical level. Its advocates, however, stress its solid microfoundations as well as the "rational," forward-looking behavior of all agents. Interestingly, the log-linear representation of the baseline New Keynesian model with both staggered wages and prices as formulated by Erceg, Henderson, and Levin (2000) features remarkable similarities with the modeling of wage and price dynamics that the Chiarella et al. have developed in the past ten years, see, for example, Chiarella and Flaschel (1996, 2000) and Chiarella, Flaschel, and Franke (2005).

These two theoretical approaches to macroeconomic modeling are, though, only similar at first sight: indeed, even though the resulting dynamic equations that describe the evolution of the macroeconomy look quite similar (indeed in a striking way) in their variable and sign structure, the modeling philosophies of each approach (with the New Keynesian focusing on general equilibrium and ours stressing the properties of disequilibria in an economy) are in direct opposition to each other, due primarily to the respective modeling of (inflationary) expectations.

The contrast is due to the nonapplicability of the rational expectations solution methodology in the matured dynamic AD-AS approach we are pursuing (where stability is achieved through assumptions on economic behavior) and the strict dependence of the New Keynesian dynamics on their rational expectations solution algorithms (which are convergent by definition and work in a world where only the steady state position is stable in the deterministic core if determinacy is given in the here investigated New Keynesian model type). The difference between the two modeling approaches, that cannot be reconciled or compromised, is therefore the way expectations are formed.

[3] Venio Romam iterum crucifigi.

In our dynamic AD-AS approach we have short-run model consistent expectation coupled with medium-run inflation inertia in the real markets of the economy, made viable by the adjustment behavior in the markets for goods and for labor, whereas the purely forward looking New Keynesian baseline approach with both staggered wages and prices is restricted to the assumption of at least three unstable roots (where instability is then overcome by the choice of an appropriate mathematical solution algorithm that guarantees convergence to the steady state of the dynamics in a stochastic environment). It seems to us that one of these scientific endeavors must sooner or later exhibit serious empirical shortcomings in the explanation of the working of capitalist market economies.

We thus formulate in the tradition of conventional Keynesian macrodynamics a matured dynamic AD-AS model based of gradually adjusting wages and prices, perfect foresight of currently established inflation rates (assuming model consistent expectations) and adaptive expectations concerning the inflation climate in which the economy operates. The model consists of a wage and a price Phillips curve, a dynamic IS curve as well as a dynamic employment adjustment equation (Okun's law), and a Taylor interest rate rule, in close correspondence to the structure of New Keynesian macrodynamics with both staggered wages and prices. The model can be reduced to a 3D dynamical system by a suitable choice of the Taylor rule and displays strong stability results, in particular for an appropriately chosen interest rate policy rule.

Through instrumental variables GMM system estimation with aggregate time series data for the UK economy, we obtain parameter estimates that support (and further specify and qualify) the qualitative structure of our theoretical model and its strong stability implications. These stability implications follow from the fact that the UK economy is here measured as being both profit-led and labor-market-led, see Sects. 8.3–8.5. If, however, the model becomes unstable (by assuming the possibly counterfactual case of a wage-led economy), it instead gives rise to persistent business fluctuations when an empirically observed floor to money wage disinflation is added to the wage Phillips curve of the model. We contrast these results with the standard (formally similarly structured) New Keynesian model with staggered wage and price setting where the problem of determinacy of the implied reduced form dynamics, however, represents a severe issue and where (if determinacy can be achieved) inertia-free asymptotic stability is obtained by the very choice of the solution method.

In this chapter we contrast these two competing theories of the business cycle, focusing on the role of the modeling of expectations for the stability (and determinacy) of the system. Our study is structured as follows. In Sect. 8.3 we discuss the deterministic skeleton of the New Keynesian AD-AS model and its dynamic implications. In Sect. 8.4 we then present our alternative AD-AS model with sluggish price-quantity adjustment processes and show how it can be reduced to a 4D dynamical system of intensive form variables. In Sect. 8.5 we analyze the dynamics of the model that reduce to a study of a 3D dynamical system, since one of the intensive form dynamical variables (the expectations of the inflationary climate) does not feed back into the rest of the system, due to the interest rate policy employed in this section. In Sect. 8.6 we outline our estimation procedure and the results of the estimates for the UK economy. In Sect. 8.7 we carry out some numerical experiments with the estimated model such as its reaction to monetary policy shocks. Section 8.8 finally presents some conclusions and provides suggestions for future extensions of the model in its real and its financial sector.

8.3 The Deterministic "Skeleton" of New Keynesian AD-AS Modeling

In the literature on New Keynesian baseline models one often encounters the treatment of the case of a Price Phillips Curve (PPC), a dynamic IS curve, and a Taylor rule (TR) as the point of departure for New Keynesian and DSGE (dynamic stochastic general equilibrium) model building. A modern model of the Keynesian variety, but also older ones, should however in our view accept the proposition that both wage levels and price levels are only gradually adjusting at each moment in time, since they are macrovariables and do not perform noticeable jumps on a daily time scale, the relevant time unit for the macro data generating process and for models of the real-financial market interaction. This assertion rests on the idea that individual wage and price movements may be occurring in a staggered fashion, but that these staggered movements are not clustered in time as it is often assumed in the empirically oriented New Keynesian approaches. The data collection process by contrast may be a staggered as well as a clustered one, but this does not imply that models that have to be estimated on a quarterly data basis should then also be iterated and analyzed with as crude a period length as the rhythm of the data collection process. The foregoing statements in our view suggest that macromodels should be formulated, analyzed, and simulated as continuous processes (or quasi-continuous ones, for example with step size 1/365 with respect to their annualized data framework). This is indeed the perspective that we will pursue in this section, which allows us to use continuous time methods to analyze models that are normally formulated as period models as in the New Keynesian approaches to macrodynamics, which we will briefly reconsider from this perspective below.[4]

In our own model, treated in subsequent sections, we generally use continuous time as the modeling strategy, since this allows for stability proofs even in high order dynamical systems, which nevertheless can be simulated adequately with a very short step size. In these models, also with gradually adjusting wages and prices, we can of course consider limit cases where wages, prices, or expectations adjust with infinite speed, but these are more a matter of theoretical curiosity than of fundamental importance. Consequently, the natural starting point of the Keynesian version of the New Neoclassical synthesis and our matured approach to 'Old' Keynesian model building should be staggered wage and price setting as the baseline situation rather than one of its two limit cases (with which it may nevertheless be compared).

[4] See Flaschel, Groh, Proaño, and Semmler (2008) for detailed presentations of such arguments.

The need to have a theoretical baseline model of New Keynesian staggered wages and staggered prices type that is investigated thoroughly from the theoretical perspective concerning feedback channels and related stability issues (as we do it for our Keynesian reformulation and extension of the Old Neoclassical synthesis) has not been carried out in the literature so far, despite the fact that such model types are now heavily used in empirical applications, see Smets and Wouters (2003) for a prominent example.

In this chapter we compare the achievements of this proper New Keynesian baseline model with the AS-AD disequilibrium model that we have formulated and extended in many ways in the past, starting from the framework of Chiarella and Flaschel (2000). With respect to theoretical implications of this model class, we will find a variety of common structural elements with the New Keynesian framework, but also great differences (in particular in the treatment of expectations), where the latter is in fact responsible for the striking result that the implications of the two model types – despite strong similarities in their formal structure – have nothing at all in common with each other. In the old Neoclassical synthesis, the elements of a Keynes' (1936) model of the short-run and its implications for the theory of the trade cycle were still preserved to a certain degree, but (as we will find in this section) the New Neoclassical synthesis no longer mirrors anything from this original approach, in contrast to what we consider in this chapter as a matured synthesis of Old Neoclassical type.

The New Keynesian baseline model with both staggered wage and price setting, so to speak the Keynesian version of the New Neoclassical Synthesis, reads in its log-linearly approximated form as follows, see Erceg, Henderson, and Levin (2000) and Woodford (2003, pp. 225 ff.):

$$\begin{aligned}
\mathrm{d}\ln w_t &\overset{\text{WPC}}{=} \beta E_t(\mathrm{d}\ln w_{t+1}) + \beta_{wy}\ln Y_t - \beta_{w\omega}\ln\omega_t,\\
\mathrm{d}\ln p_t &\overset{\text{PPC}}{=} \beta E_t(\mathrm{d}\ln p_{t+1}) + \beta_{py}\ln Y_t + \beta_{p\omega}\ln\omega_t,\\
\ln Y_t &\overset{\text{IS}}{=} \ln Y_{t+1} - \alpha_{yi}(i_t - \mathrm{d}\ln p_{t+1} - i_0),\\
i_t &\overset{\text{TR}}{=} i_0 + \beta_{ip}\mathrm{d}\ln p_t + \beta_{iy}\ln Y_t.
\end{aligned}$$

It is given by a standard New Keynesian wage Phillips Curve (WPC), a New Keynesian price Phillips Curve (PPC), a dynamic IS-curve, and a conventional type of Taylor interest rate policy rule. The model is balanced in its Keynesian formulation of the New Neoclassical synthesis, since it assumes both gradual wage and price dynamics as opposed to the Classical form of the New Neoclassical Synthesis, the RBC models with both perfectly flexible wages and prices. In the above presentation of the model we assume that all adjustment coefficients α_{xy}, β_{xy} are positive and have used there d to denote the backward difference operator. The parameter $\beta < 1$ is assumed to be close to "1" and set in fact equal to "1" in the following mathematical analysis of the model. Disregarding the treatment of expectations for the moment, the structure of this model is very similar to the one we introduce in Sect. 8.4, since it mirrors in a one-to-one fashion the sign structure of our own model, though here based on a single measure of an activity gap (which in particular avoids the need to discuss Okun's law as the link between labor and goods markets gaps). Moreover, there is no impact of changing income distribution on aggregate demand, so that income distribution does not matter on the demand side of the model (due to its neglect of investment behavior and differentiated saving habits).

We consider only the deterministic core of the above dynamics, which allows us to ignore the E_t operator. Moreover we shall make use of the abbreviations

$$\pi_t^w = \mathrm{d}\ln w_t, \quad \pi_t^p = \mathrm{d}\ln p_t, \quad y_t = \ln Y_t, \quad \theta_t = \ln \omega_t.$$

All steady state values are set equal to zero (also $i_0 = 0$) due to the fact that the above model represents only a loglinear approximation around the steady state position of the underlying nonlinear model.

The above model represents – in a simple way – an implicitly formulated system of difference equations. Making use of the TR and the PPC, it can be transformed into an explicit system of difference equations giving rise to

$$\begin{aligned}
\pi_{t+1}^w &= \pi_t^w - \beta_{wy} y_t + \beta_{w\omega}\theta_t, \\
\pi_{t+1}^p &= \pi_t^p - \beta_{py} y_t - \beta_{p\omega}\theta_t, \\
y_{t+1} &= y_t + \alpha_{yi}(\beta_{ip}\pi_t^p + \beta_{iy} y_t - \pi_t^p + \beta_{py} y_t + \beta_{p\omega}\theta_t), \\
\mathrm{d}\theta_{t+1} &= \pi_{t+1}^w - \pi_{t+1}^p.
\end{aligned}$$

We argued in Asada, Flaschel, and Proaño (2008) that a discrete time model should (and, in the baseline 2D New Keynesian case considered there, also does) reflect the properties of its continuous time analogue and can thus be analyzed from this perspective. We therefore finally derive the continuous-time analogue of the above period model. This form of the model shows that all partial feedbacks now have just the opposite sign as compared to the original structural form (and also our later model of matured Keynesian AS-AD dynamics). In the continuous time limit we obtain[5]

$$\dot{\pi}^w = -\beta_{wy} y + \beta_{w\omega}\theta, \tag{8.1}$$

$$\dot{\pi}^p = -\beta_{py} y - \beta_{p\omega}\theta, \tag{8.2}$$

$$\dot{y} = \alpha_{yi}(\beta_{ip}\pi^p + \beta_{iy} y - \pi^p + \beta_{py} y + \beta_{p\omega}\theta), \tag{8.3}$$

$$\dot{\theta} = \pi^w - \pi^p. \tag{8.4}$$

Since the New Keynesian dynamics investigated here might be considered to have only forward-looking state variables when reduced to this form, the eigenvalues of the 4D continuous-time model should then all exhibit positive real parts. These eigenvalues are obtained from the Jacobian of the dynamics, given by

[5] See Asada, Flaschel, and Proaño (2008) for its derivation.

$$J = \begin{pmatrix} 0 & 0 & -\beta_{wy} & \beta_{w\omega} \\ 0 & 0 & -\beta_{py} & -\beta_{p\omega} \\ 0 & \alpha_{yi}(\beta_{ip}-1) & \alpha_{yi}\beta_{iy} & 0 \\ 1 & -1 & 0 & 0 \end{pmatrix}.$$

This matrix J implies the desired total instability of the steady state if and only if the matrix $Q = -J$ has roots with negative real parts, that is, if Q implies asymptotic stability of its steady state. We investigate therefore now the matrix

$$Q = \begin{pmatrix} 0 & 0 & \beta_{wy} & -\beta_{w\omega} \\ 0 & 0 & \beta_{py} & \beta_{p\omega} \\ 0 & \alpha_{yi}(1-\beta_{ip}) & -\alpha_{yi}\beta_{iy} & 0 \\ -1 & 1 & 0 & 0 \end{pmatrix}.$$

For the characteristic polynomial of the matrix Q we must consequently establish, see Asada, Flaschel, and Proaño (2008), that there hold the conditions

$$\lambda^4 + a_1\lambda^3 + a_2\lambda^2 + a_3\lambda + a_4 = 0,$$
$$a_1, a_3, a_4 > 0, a_1a_2a_3 - a_1^2a_4 - a_3^2 > 0.$$

These conditions then also imply that $a_2 > 0$, $a_1a_2 - a_3 > 0$ holds true. Obviously, $a_1 = -\text{trace}\ Q$ is positive. But for a_2 and a_4 we get (see Asada, Flaschel, and Proaño (2008) for details)

$$a_4 = \alpha_{yi}(1-\beta_{ip})(\beta_{wy}\beta_{p\omega} + \beta_{py}\beta_{w\omega}) > 0 \quad \text{iff} \quad \beta_{ip} < 1,$$
$$a_2 = -\alpha_{yi}(1-\beta_{ip})\beta_{py} - \beta_{w\omega} - \beta_{p\omega} > 0 \quad \text{iff} \quad \beta_{ip} > 1 + \frac{\beta_{w\omega} + \beta_{p\omega}}{\alpha_{yi}\beta_{py}}.$$

These two conditions cannot be fulfilled simultaneously, implying that the considered dynamics represented by the matrix Q are never asymptotically stable. This conclusion is confirmed finally by the fact that $a_3 < 0$ will hold throughout. The J-dynamics thus have at least one stable root, which means that the model would under the above hypothesis always be indeterminate in its bounded reactions to unanticipated or anticipated shocks.[6]

The 4D staggered-wage staggered-price New Keynesian model when considered with four forward-looking state variables is according to the above indeterminate, and thus allows for multiple solutions if shocked. This situation must consequently be eliminated from consideration, since it does not allow for a uniquely determined rational expectations solution. Moreover, this solution would – in

[6] Galí (2008, Chap. 6) claims – and illustrates this claim numerically – that the consider model type implies in particular determinacy if the Taylor principle $\beta_{ip} > 1$ holds. Using continuous time methods, we indeed prove this claim to be correct in Flaschel, Franke and Proaño (2008). This indicates that the above stability proof is in fact only a first step towards a suggested reformulation of the model by means of a backward oriented real wage dynamics as it is used in Galí (2008, Chap. 6).

the deterministic case, due to the preliminary assumption that all state variables might be forward-looking ones – be completely trivial, namely always be equal to $(0,0,0,0)$. The deterministic skeleton of New Keynesian business cycle and inflation theory would then be devoid of any economic content, in particular when compared with Keynes' (1936, Chap. 22) "Notes on the Trade Cycle" and its constituent part, the marginal propensity to consume, the marginal efficiency of investment, and the state liquidity preference.

Moreover, important feedback channels, as they have been discussed in Chiarella and Flaschel (2000) and later work, cannot carry out their roles here in the shaping of the cycle and its inflationary consequences, but would then only be manipulated appropriately in the search for a Taylor rule such that they imply four unstable roots for the Jacobian matrix of the dynamics. The implications of this New Keynesian approach to macrodynamics are consequently completely dependent on the stochastic processes that are added to this model type and thus governed literally by the Frisch–Slutzky paradigm, in that its rational expectations solutions are nothing but, in a sense, specifically iterated types of special stochastic processes, where the iteration is based on the inverse matrix of the Jacobian of the system considered above (which in the case of determinacy would be a stable matrix).[7]

Compared to the disequilibrium AD-AS model that we will formulate in Sect. 8.4, we find nevertheless many common elements in the structure of the two approaches, in particular, as far as a formal comparison of the WPC and the PPC are concerned. In addition, our model – introduced in the next section – also has a dynamic IS-curve and a specific type of Taylor rule. However we employ four gaps in place of only two and thus have to use Okun's law to link the labor market gaps to the ones on the goods market. In addition, by its origin, our model type will always use hybrid expectations formation right from the start, see Chiarella and Flaschel (1996, 2000) for its initial introduction, based on short-run model consistent expectations and the concept of an inflationary climate, which is updated adaptively. The essential difference between the two model types will, however, be their treatment of expectations, since we use neoclassical dating and model consistent cross-over expectations in the formulated wage-price spiral, in place of the forward-looking self-reference that characterizes the New Keynesian approach described earlier, and as already stated in addition hybrid ones that give inertia to our formulation of the wage-price dynamics.

We will be able to show stability of the steady state under quite meaningful assumptions on the parameters of our model. The above baseline New Keynesian approach by contrast is at present unable to provide the conditions and proofs that allow one to single out a well-determined solution path by assumption in its 4D baseline scenario. We can expand our baseline scenario relatively easily in many directions. By contrast, the New Keynesian baseline model faces many difficulties when one tries to generalize it (e.g., to the case where there is steady state inflation).

[7] If Galí's (2008, Chap. 6) numerical examples are used as guidelines for determinacy analysis, we would have to show the existence of exactly one stable root, see Flaschel, Franke, and Proaño (2008) for the details of such a proof and the trivial deterministic adjustment process this implies.

Hence, the New Keynesian model with staggered wages and prices has not yet found a starting point that has been analyzed theoretically and that can be convincing from the theoretical and the empirical perspective. It is moreover not easily extended (rigorously) beyond the range of a Walrasian approach as far as its theory of aggregate demand is concerned. Even if determinate, the rational expectations solution of nontrivial medium-scale New Keynesian DSGE models such as the one discussed in Smets and Wouters (2003) is, due to their highly complex nonlinear structure, not calculated from its original form, but solely from its log-linear approximation (see, e.g., Sims (2002)), without any discussion of whether this solution has anything in common with the RE solution in the true, nonlinear model.[8] We conclude from all of this,[9] that the New Keynesian approach to macrodynamics creates more theoretical problems than it helps to solve.

Our basic argument here is that the chosen starting point of the New Keynesian approach – purely forward looking rational expectations – is axiomatically seen to be a wrong one so that complicated additional constructions (epicycles) become necessary to reconcile this approach with the facts. In the words of Fuhrer:[10]

Are we adding "epicycles" to a dead model?

By epicycles Fuhrer means habits, indexing, adding lags, and high-order adjustment costs, which are the examples he mentions on the slides from which the above quotation has been taken.

Microfoundations, as stressed by the Rational Expectations school, are per se an important desideratum to be reflected also by behaviorally oriented macrodynamics, but agents are heterogeneous, form heterogeneous expectations along other lines than suggested by the rational expectations school, and have short-term as well as long-term views about the economy. The straightjacket postulated by the supporters of the representative agent approach is just too narrow to allow a treatment of what is known as interesting behavior of economic agents and it is also not detailed enough to discuss the various feedback channels of the macroeconomics literature.

Market Clearing, the next ingredient of such approaches, may, however, be a questionable device to study the macroeconomy in particular on its real side. The data generating process is too fast to allow for period models with a *uniform* period length of a quarter or more. So period models of this type, that deviate from their continuous time analogues, should be replaced by the latter modeling approach. In continuous time, however, it is much too heroic to assume market clearing at all

---

[8] This criticism also applies to the common econometric estimation approach of DSGE models, which also investigates solely their log-linear approximation, see again Smets and Wouters (2003).

[9] See also Asada, Flaschel, and Proaño (2008) on these matters.

[10] See comments by J. Fuhrer on "Empirical and policy performance of a forward-looking monetary model" by A. Onatstu and N. Williams; presented at the FRB San Francisco conference on "Interest rates and monetary policy", March 19–20, 2004. http://www.frbsf.org/economics/conferences/0403/jeff_fuhrer.pdf

moments in time, but real markets are then only adjusting towards moving equilibria in such an framework (as, e.g., in the modeling approach that we outline later).

Yet, neither microfoundations per se nor market clearing assumptions represent the true dividing line between the approaches we are advocating and the ones considered in this section. It is the ad hoc, that is, not behaviorally microfounded assumption of *Rational Expectations* that by the chosen analytical method makes the world in general log-linear (by construction) and the generated dynamics convergent (by assumption) to its unique steady state, which is the root of the discontent that this chapter tries to make explicit.

Smets and Wouters (2003) have extended the above baseline New Keynesian model towards a more balanced structure where there is not only consumption but also investment and capital stock growth occurring. The log-linear version of their model consists of nine structural equations, for consumption (with habit formation) and investment (with capital adjustment costs and a term representing some form of Tobin's q) and goods market equilibrium. Moreover, they then employ a price level Phillips curve (with indexation) and a reduced-form real wage PC (also with indexation). They have finally a labor demand schedule and a Taylor interest rate policy rule. In principle this is a compelling extension of the New Keynesian baseline case we have considered earlier and it also indicates the direction into which our model outlined in Sect. 8.3 should be expanded.

There are, however, several drawbacks of such an extension of the baseline case towards an empirically oriented DSGE model. To give the model sufficient inertia with respect to a meaningful empirical application, there are several ad hoc modifications of the purely forward-looking New Keynesian baseline story. Moreover, a discussion of what variables are predetermined and which ones are not (and the problem of indeterminacy) is completely bypassed. Instead various techniques for determining a unique solution are available in the form of algorithms, which solve this problem automatically and not by a theoretical inspection on the part of the model builder, see, for example, Blanchard and Kahn (1980) and Sims (2002), as well as the documentation of the Dynare system on the Dynare site. In such a black box environment, it is therefore no longer possible to design monetary policy with a view to relevant feedback channels, as we will do it in the following sections. Finally, the distinction between unanticipated and anticipated shocks can no longer be handled in the appealingly transparent form it had in the theoretical saddlepoint investigations of Blanchard (1981) and subsequent authors. Solving certain optimization problems and reducing the solution to log-linear approximations – when the model becomes too complex, though perhaps more realistic – which then are handled only by mathematical algorithms is nowadays a routine exercise which, though from an academic point of view a surely complex task, is not convincing when it comes to truly understanding how the economy is in fact working during the business cycle and even long-phase cycles (in employment, inflation and income distribution) that it is generating.

We conclude that the New Keynesian approach cannot be a viable and empirically convincing strategy for the future investigation of the fluctuating growth that we observe in actual economies. It makes the investigation of the deterministic core of the considered dynamics (if determinate) by and large a trivial exercise and reduces the nonlinear growth dynamics of market economies to log-linear approximations (within which expectations are formed that are moreover convergent by construction) and suggests that such systems when driven by appropriately chosen stochastic processes are all that one needs to have a good model of the macroeconomic real-financial market interaction, its history, and future.

There is therefore a need for alternative baseline scenarios that can be communicated across scientific approaches, can be investigated in detail with respect to their theoretical properties in their original nonlinear format, and which – when applied to actual economies – remain controllable from the theoretical point of view as far as the basic feedback chains they contain are concerned.

8.4 Keynesian AD-AS Dynamics with Sluggish Price-Quantity Adjustment Processes

In this section, we attempt to provide a viable alternative to the New Keynesian scenario we have investigated in the preceding section. Quoting again from Fuhrer:[11]

In a way, this takes us back to the very old models
— With decent long-run, theory-grounded properties
— But dynamics from a-theoretic sources

We approach this task by way of an extension of the AD-AS models of the Old Neoclassical Synthesis (NS-I) that in this chapter primarily improves the AS side, the nominal side, of this early integrated Keynesian approach (but which allows the impact of wage-price dynamics on the AD side of the model). We will call this model type DAD-DAS in the following where the additional "D" stands for "Disequilibrium." We attempt to show that this matured NS-I approach can compete with the New Neoclassical Synthesis (NS-II) with respect to an understanding of the basic feedback mechanisms that characterize the working of the macroeconomy, their stability properties, and their empirical validity. With respect to the latter we will only consider the UK economy as an example, and refer the reader to other work on the US economy and the Eurozone. Regarding microfoundations we have to face the difficulties that Fuhrer states with respect to dynamics, but will point here to some works in the literature where at least the nominal dynamics are derived from the behavior of economic agents. Nevertheless, the approach we are pursuing should be viewed as work in progress that can best be improved through a critique of its building blocks which are fairly similar to the ones of the preceding section, the NS-II, from the purely formal point of view.

In this section we thus reconsider a Keynesian D(isequilibrium)AS-D(isequilibrium)AD model as it was first introduced in Chen, Chiarella, Flaschel, and Semmler (2006), and also estimated there as well as in the later paper by Proaño,

[11] http://www.frbsf.org/economics/conferences/0403/jeff_fuhrer.pdf

Flaschel, Ernst, and Semmler (2006). We reformulate this model in such a way that it can be reduced to a 3D core dynamical system, which can be easily investigated analytically and which allows for strong stability conclusions, in particular, with respect to the role of monetary policy.

The core of the earlier theoretical framework, which allowed for nonclearing labor and goods markets and therefore for under- or over-utilized labor and capital stock, is the model of the wage-price dynamics, which are specified through two separate Phillips Curves, each one led by its own measure of demand pressure (or capacity bottleneck), instead of a single one as is usually done in many New Keynesian models, for instance in Galí and Gertler (1999) and Galí, Gertler, and López-Salido (2001).[12] The approach of estimating separate wage and price Phillips curves is not altogether new, however: Barro (1994), for example, observes that Keynesian macroeconomics is (or should be) based on imperfectly flexible wages as well as prices and thus on the consideration of wage as well as price Phillips Curves: Fair (2000) criticizes the low accuracy of reduced form price equations, and in the same study estimates two separate wage and price equations for the United States, nevertheless, using a single demand pressure term, the NAIRU gap.

On the contrary, by modeling wage and price dynamics separately from each other, each one determined by their own measures of demand pressures in the market for labor and for goods, we are able to circumvent the identification problem pointed out by Sims (1987) for the estimation of separate wage and price equations with the same explanatory variables. By these means, we can analyze the dynamics of the real wages in the economy and identify oppositely acting effects as they might result from different labor and goods markets developments. Indeed, we believe a Keynesian model of aggregate demand fluctuations should (independently of whether justification can be found for this in Keynes' General Theory) allow for under- (or over-)utilized labor *as well as* capital and gradual wage as well as price adjustments to be general enough from the descriptive point of view.

The structural form of the wage-price dynamics of our framework is given by[13]

$$\hat{w} = \beta_{we}(e-\bar{e}) + \beta_{wu}(u^w - \bar{u}^w) - \beta_{wv}(\ln v - \ln v_o) + \kappa_w \hat{p} + (1-\kappa_w)\pi^c, \quad (8.5)$$
$$\hat{p} = \beta_{pu}(u-\bar{u}) + \beta_{pv}(\ln v - \ln v_o) + \kappa_p \hat{w} + (1-\kappa_p)\pi^c. \quad (8.6)$$

We denote by $e-\bar{e}$ the employment gap on the external labor market and by $u^w - \bar{u}^w$ the excess utilization of the workforce employed by firms. In a similar way, we have that $u-\bar{u}$ the excess utilization of the capital stock. Demand pressure on the labor

[12] This model of the wage-price spiral and its coupling with an adaptively updated inflationary climate expression (representing the relative inertia that characterizes this wage-price spiral) has a long tradition in our formulations of AS disequilibrium adjustment processes, see in particular Chiarella and Flaschel (2000) and Chiarella, Flaschel, and Franke (2005) in this regard.

[13] We have stressed elsewhere, see Asada, Flaschel, and Proaño (2008) the close formal correspondence of this model of the wage-price spiral with the New Keynesian model of staggered wage and price setting. Yet we have to stress here in this regard that we employ three demand pressure gaps in this spiral in place of the single one (the output gap) that is used by New Keynesian authors. Despite this formal similarity the conclusions drawn from our macrodynamic model are in direct opposition to the ones of the New Keynesian macrodynamics.

market is therefore measured with respect to outsiders and insiders, while there is only one measure as far as the utilization of the capital stock is concerned. The demand pressure terms in both the wage and price Phillips Curves are augmented by two additional terms: first, by the log of the wage share v or real unit labor costs, the error correction term discussed in Blanchard and Katz (1999, p. 71). The second additional term is a weighted average of corresponding expected cost-pressure terms, assumed to be model-consistent with respect to forward-looking, cross-over wage and price inflation rates $\hat{w}$ and $\hat{p}$, respectively, and a backward looking measure of the prevailing inflationary climate of the economy, symbolized by π^c.[14] Indeed, while the agents in our model have myopic perfect foresight with respect to future inflation rates, there is no reason to assume that they also act myopically with respect to the past, "forgetting" whole sequences of fully observable and highly informational values of past inflation. These two Phillips curves have been estimated and investigated in detail in Chen and Flaschel (2006).

The microfoundations of our wage Phillips curve are thus of the same type as in Blanchard and Katz (1999) (see also Flaschel and Krolzig (2006)), which can be reformulated as expressed in (8.5) and (8.6) with the employment gaps $e-\bar{e}$, $u^w - \bar{u}^w$ in place of the usually employed single measure, the output gap. We use two measures of demand pressure on the labor market here, the external employment rate gap and the utilization gap within firms. Using a physical analogy they can be regarded as forming some sort of capillary system where these two pressure terms are to be related by some sort of Okun's law.

Concerning the price Phillips curve, a similar microprocedure can be applied, based on desired markups of firms. Along these lines one in particular gets an economic motivation for the inclusion of (indeed the logarithm of) the real wage (or wage share) with negative sign in the wage PC and with positive sign in the price PC, without any need for log-linear approximations. We use a capacity utilization gap in the price PC as measure of demand pressure on the market for goods (and could add a second measure here too in the form of an inventory gap). Our wage-price module is thus consistent with standard models of unemployment based on efficiency wages, matching and competitive wage determination, as well as markup pricing and can be considered as an interesting alternative to the – theoretically rarely discussed and empirically questionable – purely forward-looking New Keynesian form of staggered wage and price dynamics that we have discussed in Sect. 8.3.

Note that we have assumed model-consistent expectations with respect to short-run wage and price inflation, incorporated into our Phillips curves in a cross-over manner, with perfectly foreseen price inflation in the wage – Phillips Curve and wage inflation in the price – Phillips curve.

The across-markets or *reduced-form PC's* of the WPC and the PPC (1),(2) are given by (with $\kappa = 1/(1-\kappa_w\kappa_p)$)[15]

---

[14] This last term is obtained by an adaptive updating inflation climate expression with exponential or any other weighting schemes that incorporate medium run developments and therefore inertia with respect to the past wage and price developments.

[15] See Flaschel and Krolzig (2006), Chen and Flaschel (2006), Proaño, Flaschel, Ernst, and Semmler (2006) for details.

$$\begin{aligned}\hat{w} &= \kappa[\beta_{we}(e-\bar{e})+\beta_{wu}(u^w-\bar{u}^w)-\beta_{wv}\ln(v/v_o)\\&\quad+\kappa_w(\beta_{pu}(u-\bar{u})+\beta_{pv}\ln(v/v_o))]+\pi^c,\\\hat{p} &= \kappa[\beta_{pu}(u-\bar{u})+\beta_{pv}\ln(v/v_o)\\&\quad+\kappa_p(\beta_{we}(e-\bar{e})+\beta_{wu}(u^w-\bar{u}^w)-\beta_{wv}\ln(v/v_o))]+\pi^c,\end{aligned}$$

with inflation pass-through terms behind the κ_w, κ_p-parameters. These reduced form PC's represent a considerable generalization of the conventional view of a single-market price PC with only one measure of demand pressure, namely the one in the labor market.

Note that for this version of the wage-price spiral, the inflationary climate variable does not matter for the evolution of the real wage $\omega = w/p$, – or the wage share $v = \omega/z$ if labor productivity is taken into account. The law of motion for v is given by

$$\begin{aligned}\hat{v} &= \kappa[(1-\kappa_p)(\beta_{we}(e-\bar{e})+\beta_{wu}(u^w-\bar{u}^w)-\beta_{wv}\ln(v/v_o))\\&\quad-(1-\kappa_w)(\beta_{pu}(u-\bar{u})+\beta_{pv}\ln(v/v_o))].\end{aligned} \tag{8.7}$$

Equation (8.7) shows the ambiguity of the stabilizing role of the real wage channel, already discussed by Rose (1967), which arises – despite of the incorporation of specific measures of demand and cost pressure on both the labor and the goods markets – if the dynamics of the employment rate and the workforce utilization are linked to the fluctuations of the firms' capacity utilization rate via Okun's law. Indeed, as sketched in Fig. 8.1, a real wage increase can act, taken by itself, in a stabilizing or destabilizing manner, depending among others on whether the dynamics of the capacity utilization rate depend positively or negatively on the real wage (i.e., on whether consumption reacts more strongly to real wage changes than investment or viceversa) *and* whether price flexibility is greater than nominal wage flexibility with respect to their own demand pressure measures. All parameters shown in the first part of (8.7) thus contribute to stability if aggregate demand is profit-led, that is, decreases when the real wage is increasing, while the ones after the minus sign contribute to instability in this case (the opposite applies when aggregate demand is wage-led).

These four different scenarios can be jointly summarized as in Table 8.1. As it can be observed, there exist two cases where the Rose (1967) real wage channel operates in a stabilizing manner: in the first case, aggregate goods demand (proxied in our analysis by the capacity utilization rate) depends negatively on the real wage, which can be denoted in a closed economy as the profit-led case – and the dynamics of the real wage are led primarily by the nominal wage dynamics and therefore by the developments in the labor market. In the second case, aggregate demand depends positively on the real wage, and the price level dynamics, and therefore the goods markets, primarily determines the behavior of the real wages.[16]

[16] Note here that also the cost–pressure parameters play a role and may influence the critical stability condition that characterizes the real wage channel, see Flaschel and Krolzig (2006) for details.

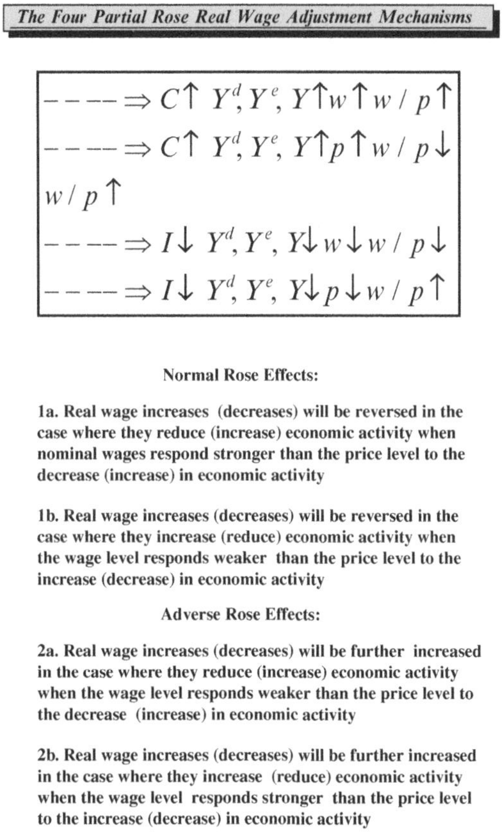

Fig. 8.1 Normal (convergent) and adverse (divergent) rose effects: the real wage channel of Keynesian macrodynamics

Table 8.1 Four baseline real wage adjustment scenarios

	Wage-led goods demand	Profit-led goods demand
Labor market-led real wage adjustment	Adverse (divergent)	Normal (convergent)
Goods market-led real wage adjustment	Normal (convergent)	Adverse (divergent)

Concerning the inflationary expectations over the medium run, π^c, that is, the inflationary climate in which current wage and price inflation are operating, they may be formed adaptively following the actual rate of inflation (by use of some linear or exponential weighting scheme), may be based on a rolling sample (with hump-shaped weighting schemes), or on other possibilities for updating expectations. For simplicity of exposition we shall make use here of the conventional adaptive expectations mechanism in the theoretical part of this chapter, namely

$$\dot{\pi}^c = \beta_{\pi^c}(\hat{p} - \pi^c). \tag{8.8}$$

The above model of an advanced wage-price spiral is considered in this chapter against the background of a fixed proportions technology, characterized by[17]

$$y^{\mathrm{p}} = Y^{\mathrm{p}}/K = \text{const}, z = Y/L^{\mathrm{d}} = \text{const}, u = Y/Y^{\mathrm{p}}, u^{w} = L^{\mathrm{d}}/L^{w}, e = L^{w}/L.$$

Potential output Y^{p} is here compared with actual output Y, which is in this model demand determined. The ratio u is therefore the rate of capacity utilization of firms. Firms employ a workforce of L^{w} workers who are employed according to actual output and thus have to supply $L^{\mathrm{d}} = Y/z$ hours of work. Their rate of utilization is therefore given by u^{w}. The rate of employment on the external labor market is finally defined by e and has already been contrasted in its implications for wage inflation with the rate u^{w} in the WPC we have introduced above.

With respect to the goods markets dynamics, we model them by means of a law of motion of the type of a dynamic IS-equation (see also Rudebusch and Svensson (1999) in this regard) here represented by the growth rate of the capacity utilization rate of firms:[18]

$$\hat{u} = -\beta_{uu}(u - \bar{u}) - \beta_{ui}((i - \hat{p}) - (i - \hat{p})_{\mathrm{o}}) \pm \beta_{uv}(v - v_{\mathrm{o}}). \tag{8.9}$$

The reduced form (8.9) has three important characteristics; (1) it reflects the dependence of output changes on aggregate income and thus on the rate of capacity utilization by assuming a negative, that is, stable dynamic multiplier relationship in this respect, (2) it shows the joint dependence of consumption and investment on the real wage/wage share (which in the aggregate may in principle allow for positive or negative signs before the parameter β_{uv}, depending on whether consumption or investment is more responsive to real wage changes/wage share changes), and (3) it shows finally the negative influence of the real rate of interest on the evolution of economic activity.

Concerning the labor market dynamics and its link to the goods market dynamics, we assume a more detailed form of the simple empirical relationship as introduced by Okun (1970) as link between the rate of capacity utilization and the employment rate in the following way:

$$\hat{e} = \beta_{eu}(u^{w} - \bar{u}^{w}), \quad u^{w} = \frac{L^{\mathrm{d}}}{L^{w}} = \frac{Y^{\mathrm{p}}}{K}\frac{L^{\mathrm{d}}}{Y}\frac{K}{L}\frac{Y}{Y^{\mathrm{p}}}\frac{L}{L^{w}} = \frac{y^{\mathrm{p}}}{zl_{\mathrm{o}}}\frac{u}{e}. \tag{8.10}$$

This law of motion states that the growth rate of the employment rate is reacting positively to the deviation of the utilization rate u^{w}, the ratio of L^{d} (employment in hours) to the workforce L^{w} of firms from its normal level $\bar{u}^{w}$. The utilization

[17] For a simple inclusion of smooth factor substitution – which makes y^{p} dependent on the real wage – see Chiarella and Flaschel (2000, Chap. 5) and see Chiarella, Flaschel, and Franke (2005) for the discussion of the role of alternative production technologies.

[18] Note here that the empirically observed controversy about income distribution does not play a role in the New Keynesian formulation of the goods market dynamics, due to its reliance on a single representative household (who receives all wage as well as profit income and who thus can be indifferent with respect to changing income distribution if total income remains the same).

rate u^w depends – as shown in (8.10) – on the rate of capacity utilization u and the employment rate e by definition, if a fixed proportions technology is assumed: $y^p = Y^p/K = const$, $z = Y/L^d = const$, and L^d the employment of the workforce of firms (in hours), and on the ratio of labor supply to the capital stock L/K, which is considered as given by l_o here (thereby ignoring the growth aspects behind the model).[19] The essential parameter here is of course the parameter β_{eu}, which characterizes the speed of the hiring and firing process of the considered economy.

The above three laws of motion therefore reformulate in a dynamic form the static IS-curve (and the rate of employment this curve implies) that was used in Asada, Chen, Chiarella, and Flaschel (2006).

Finally, we no longer employ here a law of motion for real balances (an LM Curve) as it was still the case in Asada, Chen, Chiarella, and Flaschel (2006). Instead we endogenize the nominal interest rate by using a new type of Taylor rule compared to the one that is customary in the literature, see, for example, Svensson (1998). The target rate of the monetary authorities is here determined according to

$$i = (i - \hat{p})_o + \hat{p} + \alpha_{iw}(\hat{w} - \pi^c) + \alpha_{iu}(u - \bar{u}) + \alpha_{iv}(v - v_o). \tag{8.11}$$

The target rate of the central bank i is thus here made dependent on the steady state real rate of interest $(i - \hat{p})_o$ augmented by actual inflation back to a nominal rate, and is as usual dependent on the inflation gap and the capacity utilization gap (as a measure of the output gap) and augmented by a further gap impact, the current wage share gap.[20] For the time being we assume that there is no interest rate smoothing with respect to the interest target of the central bank, which therefore immediately set its target rate at each moment in time. With respect to the inflation gap we use a wage inflation measure, since wages appear to be more flexible than prices with respect to demand pressure (in the US and the Eurozone, see Proaño, Flaschel, Ernst, and Semmler (2006) and Sect. 8.6 of this paper), and use for the time being the inflation climate as point of reference for this gap (which simplifies the dynamics to be investigated considerably). Measuring the inflation gap in terms of wages gives the labor market more weight in the reaction of the interest rate to inflation, see the reduced form PCs we have derived above. The model's behavior will, however, not be changed qualitatively if the price inflation rate is used in place of the wage inflation rate (if this rate is the one on which the Central Bank is focused).

We note that the steady state of the dynamics, due to its specific formulation, can be supplied exogenously:[21] $u_o = \bar{u}, e_o = \bar{e}, u^w_o = \bar{u}^w, v_o, \pi^c_o = \hat{p}_o = \hat{w}_o = 0, i_o = (i - \hat{p})_o$. This shows that the model has been constructed around a specific steady state position, the stability of which will be the focus of analysis in the next section.

Taken together the model of this section consists of the following four laws of motion for capacity utilization u, the goods market dynamics, for the employment

[19] This assumption is justified if it is assumed that actual labor supply always grows in line with capital stock growth.

[20] All of the employed gaps are measured relative to the steady state of the model to allow for an interest rate policy that is also consistent with the steady state.

[21] We assume for reasons of consistency: $\bar{u}^w = y^p\bar{u}/(zl_o\bar{e})$.

rate e, Okun's law, for the wage share v, describing the real wage channel, and for the inflationary climate expression π^c (to be supplemented by the derived reduced form WPC and PPC expressions as far as the wage-price spiral is concerned and with reduced form expressions by assumption concerning the goods and the labor market dynamics).[22] We note that the inflation climate here does not feed back into the rest of the dynamics due to the specific formulation of the Taylor rule of the model (where $\hat{w} - \pi^c$ is used as the expression for the inflation). The intensive form dynamics thus read

$$\hat{u} = -\beta_{uu}(u-\bar{u}) - \beta_{ui}((i-\hat{p}) - (i-\hat{p})_{\mathrm{o}}) \pm \beta_{uv}(v-v_{\mathrm{o}}), \tag{8.12}$$

$$\dot{e} = \beta_{eu}\frac{y^{\mathrm{p}}}{zl_{\mathrm{o}}}\left(u - \bar{u}\frac{e}{e_{\mathrm{o}}}\right), \quad y^{\mathrm{p}}, z, l_{\mathrm{o}} \quad \text{given} \tag{8.13}$$

$$\hat{v} = \hat{w} - \hat{p} = \kappa\left[(1-\kappa_{\mathrm{p}})\left(\beta_{we}(e-\bar{e}) + \beta_{wu}\left(\frac{y^{\mathrm{p}}}{zl_{\mathrm{o}}}\frac{u}{e} - \bar{u}^w\right) - \beta_{wv}\ln(v/v_{\mathrm{o}})\right)\right.$$
$$\left. -(1-\kappa_w)(\beta_{pu}(u-\bar{u}) + \beta_{pv}\ln(v/v_{\mathrm{o}}))\right], \tag{8.14}$$

$$\dot{\pi}^c = \beta_{\pi^c}(\hat{p} - \pi^c), \tag{8.15}$$

with the supplementary equations (we recall that $\kappa = 1/(1-\kappa_w\kappa_{\mathrm{p}})$)

$$i - \hat{p} = (i-\hat{p})_{\mathrm{o}} + \alpha_{iw}(\hat{w} - \pi^c) + \alpha_{iu}(u-\bar{u}) + \alpha_{iv}(v - v_{\mathrm{o}}), \tag{8.16}$$

$$\hat{w} - \pi^c = \kappa\left[\beta_{we}(e-\bar{e}) + \beta_{wu}\left(\frac{y^P}{zl_{\mathrm{o}}}\frac{u}{e} - \bar{u}^w\right) - \beta_{wv}\ln(v/v_{\mathrm{o}})\right.$$
$$\left. + \kappa_w(\beta_{pu}(u-\bar{u}) + \beta_{pv}\ln(v/v_{\mathrm{o}}))\right], \tag{8.17}$$

$$\hat{p} - \pi^c = \kappa\,[\beta_{pu}(u-\bar{u}) + \beta_{pv}\ln(v/v_{\mathrm{o}})$$
$$+ \kappa_p(\beta_{we}(e-\bar{e}) + \beta_{wu}(u^w - \bar{u}^w) - \beta_{wv}\ln(v/v_{\mathrm{o}}))] \tag{8.18}$$

to be inserted into these laws of motion. Note here that the reduced form of the PPC must be used in the law of motion for the inflationary climate of the economy, but that this law does not feed back into the first three laws of motion for the state variables u, e, v, which therefore can be studied in their interaction independently of this climate expression and the PPC (due to the type of inflation gap that is considered in the interest rate policy rule).

Note finally that we have tailored the Taylor rule in view of the central feedback channels that characterize this economic structure, in particular for the case where the economy is wage- as well as labor-market-led and thus unstable from the perspective of this partial real wage feedback chain. This exemplifies that an

---

22 As the model is formulated we have no real anchor for the steady state rate of interest (via investment behavior and the rate of profit it implies in the steady state) and thus have to assume here that it is the monetary authority that enforces a certain steady state value for the nominal rate of interest.

understanding of the important feedback channels of the private sector is essential for a proper formulation of interest rate policy rules. It is hard to see how a New Keynesian framework could fulfill such a requirement, since it tends to imply trivial deterministic core dynamics in general and therefore nothing systematic in the working of the economy.

The stability features of this dynamical model are totally different from the NK model with staggered wage and price setting, as will be shown in the following section, though its structural equations from a formal perspective are in close correspondence to the ones of its New Keynesian counterpart. This implies that it is not possible that both types of approaches can be considered as explanations of the economic world in which we are living.

8.5 The 3D Core Dynamics: Some Stability Results

In this section, we formulate some simple assumptions regarding the model of the preceding section and shall derive on this basis the local asymptotic stability of the steady state of the implied reduced form dynamics. In addition we shall include some observations on feedback channels and their theoretical implications. We stress again that the core dynamics are three-dimensional, since the state variable π^c does not feed back into them due to our choice of the Taylor rule.

Assumption.[23]

1. *Assume that $\hat{v}_e > 0$ holds, that is, the parameter β_{we} is chosen sufficiently large such that it dominates the effect of changes in e on the utilization rate of the workforce of firms (a labor market led economy of type 1).*
2. *Assume that $\hat{v}_u > 0$ holds, that is, the parameter β_{pu} is chosen sufficiently small (relative to β_{wu} in this case, a labor market led economy of type 2).*
3. *Assume that $\hat{u}_v < 0$ holds, that is, the parameter α_{iv} is chosen sufficiently large (which is only needed in the case of a wage-led economy where monetary policy thus must be sufficiently determined in this respect)*

On the basis of these three assumptions the following stability propositions holds true (see the mathematical appendix for their proofs).[24]

Proposition 8.1.

1. *The assumptions made imply that of the Jacobian of the considered 3D system at the steady state has the sign structure:*

$$J = \begin{pmatrix} - & - & - \\ + & - & 0 \\ + & + & - \end{pmatrix}$$

[23] The κ parameters are always assumed to lie between zero and one.

[24] Note that propositions on parameter changes always assume that all other parameters are kept fixed in the considered situation.

2. *This sign structure implies for the Routh–Hurwitz stability conditions (see the appendix):* $a_1, a_2, a_3 > 0$. *The remaining Routh–Hurwitz stability condition* $b = a_1a_2 - a_3 > 0$ *is fulfilled if the term* $J_{13}J_{21}J_{32}$ *in the determinant of the matrix* J *is dominated by the remaining items in* a_1a_2.[25] *Under this additional assumption the steady state is locally asymptotically stable.*[26]
3. *An increase in the parameter* α_{iu} *supports the assumed partial dynamic multiplier stability, that is, the negative term* J_{11} *in the trace of the matrix* J, *and an increase in the parameter* α_{iv} *does the same for the entry* J_{33} *in the trace of the Jacobian matrix* J.
4. *Setting the parameter* $\alpha_{iw} = 0$ *implies* $J_{12} = 0$. *This parameter, representing the inflation gap control of the interest rate, is thus not essential for the control of the private sector of the economy.*[27]

We have indeed designed the Taylor rule such that the Mundell or real rate of interest channel in the dynamics of the goods market is turned from instability towards stability (even without inflation targeting). This holds, since – when our Taylor rule is inserted into the law of motion for capacity utilization – the real rate of interest is totally replaced by the gaps included into the working of the Taylor rule and since all these gaps have a negative impact on the growth rate of u. The only remaining feedback channel in this model type is therefore the real wage channel discussed in Sect. 8.3, which presents no problem in the case where the economy is profit-led, since we have assumed above that the real wage dynamics are labor market led. In the case of wage-led goods market dynamics there is a positive influence of v on the growth rate of capacity utilization and thus we need as a sufficient (not necessarily a necessary) condition that the parameter α_{uv} must be chosen sufficiently large in order to turn the effect of v on $\hat{u}$ into a negative one. Here the gap term $\hat{w} - \pi^c$ can be of additional help, due in particular to that fact that it includes the Blanchard and Katz (1999) error correction terms.

The outcome of this stability analysis is that monetary policy should take into account the feedback channels that characterize the economy to which it is applied, that is, in the present case the real rate of interest channel and the real wage or wage share channel. These feedback chains should guide the choice of the primary gaps (and the degree of interest rate smoothing) that are to act on the setting of the interest rate, which in fact are here not so much the output gap and the inflation gap (the central gaps in the conventional formulations of the Taylor rule and the Taylor principle that is implied by them). The understanding of the central feedback channels of Keynesian macrodynamics, as they are discussed in Chiarella and Flaschel

[25] When the identical expressions in a_1a_2 and $\det J$ – with opposite signs – have been canceled against each other.

[26] This situation is in particular fulfilled if the parameter β_{we} is close to zero, that is, in the case where the outside labor market conditions are not relevant for the dynamics of nominal wages or, see the appendix, if the parameter β_{eu} is sufficiently small.

[27] This also holds if $\hat{p} - \pi^c$ is used in the place of $\hat{w} - \pi^c$ in the Taylor rule, that is, the main component of conventional types of Taylor rules is not really essential for its proper working in the present context (where the real wage channel represents an important feedback chain).

(2000) and the later work they have developed with various coauthors on this behavioral disequilibrium approach to Keynesian monetary growth, may therefore be crucial for the proper conduct of monetary policy (and also fiscal policy).

We note finally that the hiring and firing parameter β_{eu} is not really of importance for the qualitative features of the considered dynamics (the same holds for the parameter β_{π^c}, which however may become of importance if the inflation climate does not enter the formulation of the Taylor rule as we have done it in the preceding section). Under the conditions of Proposition 8.1 we have what we would call a consent economy, see Flaschel, Franke, and Semmler (2008), where there is no real conflict between a flexible hiring and firing economy and the existence of a satisfactory stable balanced growth path, since also wage flexibility (with respect to its demand pressure items) is stabilizing. The most important threat to stability in this case is demand pressure driven price flexibility (relative to the adjustment speed of wages) and here in particular the danger of a deflationary spiral and the economic breakdown that may result from it.

Proposition 8.2.

Assume that $\alpha_{iw} = 0$ holds. Then a sufficient increase in the parameter β_{pu} gives rise to a Hopf-bifurcation leading to local asymptotic instability by way of the birth of a stable limit cycle or the death of a stability corridor (and will also imply global instability sooner or later).[28]

The proof of this proposition is straightforward, since we get in this case $J_{31} < 0$ and since this entry of the Jacobian of the dynamics at the steady state is the only one that depends on the parameter β_{pu}. If one wishes to use monetary policy to avoid the resulting deflationary spirals (in the case of a global loss of stability), it is necessary to increase its reaction to the utilization gap, α_{iu}, to a sufficient degree.

Proposition 8.3.

Consider now the case of a wage-led economy where monetary policy is sufficiently inconclusive with respect to the wage gap, that is, where the entry J_{13} is positive. Then a sufficient increase in the parameter β_{uv}, representing the degree to which the economy is wage-led), will destabilize the steady state of the dynamics.

Remark (see Proposition A2 in the appendix): The same result can be achieved through an increase in the parameter β_{wu} characterizing the behavior of labor market insiders in the case of a weak reaction of the central bank to the wage inflation gap by way of the Routh–Hurwitz parameter a_2, that is, by way of an unstable feedback chain reaction between capacity utilization u and the wage share v. Similarly, instability can also be generated through an increase in the parameter β_{we} characterizing the role of the external labor market (in the case of a weak reaction of the central bank to the wage inflation gap), here by way of the Routh–Hurwitz parameter $a_3 = \det J$, that is, by way of an unstable three stage feedback chain reaction between capacity utilization u, the employment rate e, and the wage share v. The case

[28] Proposition 8.A3 in the appendix shows the same result for a value of the parameter β_{uv} that is chosen sufficiently large.

of a wage led goods demand can thus become a problem if this effect is too strong or if wages are too flexible with respect to their demand pressure terms. It thus appears that the profit led situation is the more robust one in the case where the markups of firms on their cost pressure items are not very responsive to demand pressure on the market for goods. This result casts some doubt on the wage-led scenarios often found or favored in Post-Keynesian economics.

Wage-led scenarios with an indeterminate monetary policy may have characterized the evolution in the late 1960s and early 1970s where accelerating wage and price inflation were observed in many countries. However, on average we would expect a profit led situation to have prevailed for the major industrialized countries after World War II, and we will investigate this situation briefly in the following section.

Before closing this section we briefly consider the 4D extension of the model when the interest rate policy rule is of a more conventional type, so that (8.11) is replaced by

$$i - \hat{p} = (i - \hat{p})_o + \alpha_{ip}(\hat{p} - \bar{\pi}) + \alpha_{iu}(u - \bar{u}) + \alpha_{iv}(v - v_o). \tag{8.19}$$

The Central Bank here pursues a given inflation target $\bar{\pi}$ and uses the conventional inflation gap. We need not assume that it chooses the parameter α_{iu} such that $\hat{u}_v < 0$ holds again as in the case of an economy that is wage-led. However, we simplify Okun's law to the form $\hat{e} = \beta_{eu}(u - \bar{u})$, where the recruitment policy of the firms only depends on the degree of capacity utilization of their capital stock. On this basis we can establish the following proposition:

Proposition 8.4.

1. *The dynamics (8.12)–(8.15) (with (8.16) replaced by (8.19)) are now 4D, since π^c appears in the law of motion of the goods market.*
2. *The determinant of the Jacobian matrix of the system at the interior steady state (which in this case is easily shown to be uniquely determined) is positive.*
3. *The stable 3D core dynamics (where the influence of π^c is neglected) remain stable in their 4D form if the parameter β_{π^c} is sufficiently small.*
4. *The dynamics may not lose stability (by way of a Hopf bifurcation) if the parameter β_{π^c} becomes larger and larger, that is, the Mundell effect is here neutralized by way of the chosen interest rate policy rule.*

To prove this proposition one has simply to note that the result

$$\det J = \begin{pmatrix} 0 & 0 & 0 & - \\ + & 0 & 0 & 0 \\ 0 & + & 0 & 0 \\ 0 & 0 & 0 & + \end{pmatrix} > 0$$

can be achieved by adding or subtracting rows in the original form of the Jacobian appropriately. This result implies that the three eigenvalues with negative real parts of the 3D core system are augmented by a fourth one, which must be negative for small β_{π^c} due to the continuity of eigenvalues with respect to the entries of the Jacobian. Assertion 4 finally follows from the fact that the goods market dynamics $\hat{u}$ are negatively dependent on the inflation climate π^c (after insertion of the Taylor rule given by (8.19)) and not positively as would be the case of a given nominal rate of interest. However, instability may occur in such a case when the economy is wage-led (and $\beta_{uv} = 0$ holds), when the Blanchard and Katz error correction is missing and the economy is goods-market-led in addition.[29] In the next section we shall, however, show that these conditions are not likely to be met in actual economies. This shows again the importance of the real wage feedback channel for the overall stability of the economy under consideration.

8.6 Estimation and Simulation of the Model

For the econometric estimation of the model for the UK, we use the aggregate time series available from the International Financial Statistics database and the National Statistics database (www.statistics.gov.uk) (Fig. 8.2). The data, described in Table 8.2, is quarterly, seasonally adjusted and concerns the period from 1980:1 to 2003:4.

The logarithms of wages and prices are denoted $\ln(w_t)$ and $\ln(p_t)$, respectively. Their first differences (backwardly dated), that is the current rate of wage and price inflation, are denoted $\hat{w}_t$ and $\hat{p}_t$. The inflationary climate π^c of the theoretical part of this chapter is approximated here in a very simple way by a linearly declining moving average of CPI price inflation rates (measured by p_c in Table 8.2) with linearly decreasing weights over the past twelve quarters, denoted π_t^{12}.

To be able to identify in a structural manner the dynamics of the system and especially of the wage and price inflation (since as discussed in Sect. 8.3, the law of motion for the real wage rate, given by (8.7) represents a reduced form expression of

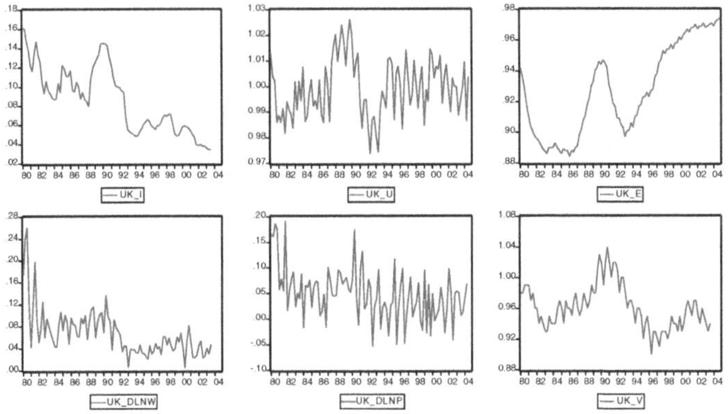

Fig. 8.2 UK aggregate time series

[29] This result follows easily by considering the principal minors of the Jacobian J of order 3.

Table 8.2 UK Data Set

Variable	Description of the original series
e	Employment rate
u	Industrial production Hodrick–Prescott cyclical term (calculated with a smoothing factor of $\lambda = 1{,}600$)
w	Average earnings in industrial production, seasonally adjusted (Index: year 2000 = 100)
p	Gross domestic product: implicit price deflator, year 2000 = 100
p_c	CPI index, all items, year 2000 = 100
z	Labor productivity, year 1996 = 100
v	Real unit wage costs (deflated by the GDP deflator), year 2003 = 100
i	Treasury bill rate

the two structural equations for $\hat{w}_t$ and $\hat{p}_t$), we estimate the following discrete time reformulation of our continuous time theoretical model (described in Sect. 8.3):[30]

$$\begin{aligned}
\hat{w}_t &= \beta_{we}(e_{t-1}-e_o)+\beta_{wu}\chi\left(\frac{u_{t-1}}{e_{t-1}}-\frac{u_o}{e_o}\right)-\beta_{wv}\ln(v_{t-1}/v_o)+\kappa_{wp}\hat{p}_t \\
&\quad +(1-\kappa_{wp})\pi_t^{12}+\kappa_{wz}\hat{z}_t+\varepsilon_{wt}, && (8.20)\\
\hat{p}_t &= \beta_{pu}(u_{t-1}-u_o)+\beta_{pv}\ln(v_{t-1}/v_o)+\kappa_{pw}(\hat{w}_t-\hat{z}_t)+(1-\kappa_{pw})\pi_t^{12}+\varepsilon_{pt}, && (8.21)\\
\ln u_t &= \ln u_{t-1}-\beta_{uu}(u_t-u_o)-\beta_{ui}(i_{t-1}-\hat{p}_t)\pm\beta_{uv}(v_{t-1}-v_o)+\varepsilon_{ut}, && (8.22)\\
e_t &= e_{t-1}+\beta_{eu}\chi\left(u_{t-1}-\frac{u_o}{e_o}\cdot e_{t-1}\right)+\varepsilon_{et}, && (8.23)\\
i_t &= i_{t-1}-\alpha_{ii}i_{t-1}+\alpha_{iw}\hat{w}_t+\alpha_{iu}(u_{t-1}-u_o)+c_i+\varepsilon_{it}, && (8.24)
\end{aligned}$$

with $\chi = \frac{y^p}{zl_o}$ for notational simplicity and all variables with a subscript o denoting sample averages (interpretable as the analogue to the steady state values in the theoretical model). The statistical error terms in each equation are represented by the respective ε.

It should be noted that rather than using the intensive form dynamics for the wage share v (8.14) we use the structural forms for $\hat{w}$ and $\hat{p}$ given by (8.5) and (8.6), of which (8.20) and (8.21) are discretized versions. Equations (8.22) and (8.23) are discretized versions of (8.12) and (8.13). Finally we use the Taylor rule (8.11), for simplicity without the term $\alpha_{iv}(v-v_O)$, and also using a lagged adjustment policy rule with α_{ii} being the speed of adjustment. Whilst this increases the dynamic dimensions of the system to be estimated it has the advantage of setting up interest rate lags that improve the empirical estimations.

To account for regressor endogeneity, we estimate the discrete time version of the structural model formulated above by means of instrumental variables system GMM (Generalized Method of Moments), which has the advantage of not relying on a specific assumption with respect to the distribution of the error terms. The weighting

[30] We here assume that the growth rate of labor productivity $\hat{z}$ enters the wage equation with a coefficient that need not be unity and that wage cost pressure in the price Phillips curve of firms is reduced by the growth rate of labor productivity.

matrix in the GMM objective function was chosen to allow the resulting GMM estimates to be robust against possible heteroskedasticity and serial correlation of an unknown form in the error terms. Concerning the instrumental variables used in our estimations, since at time t only past values are contained in the information sets of the economic agents, for all five equations we use, besides the strictly exogenous variables, the last four lagged values of the employment rate, the labor share (detrended by the Hodrick-Prescott Filter) and the growth rate of labor productivity. To test for the validity of the overidentifying restrictions, the J-statistics for both system estimations were calculated.

Since the formulation of the monetary policy rule in the theoretical part of this chapter was primarily ad hoc – with wage instead of price inflation as the target variable of the monetary authorities – to keep the dimension of the model low, we also estimate our model with the current price inflation as the target variable (note that the corresponding coefficient becomes α_{ip} in plane of α_{iw}) as is usually done in the literature. We present the structural parameter estimates under these two specifications for the UK economy (t-statistics in brackets), as well as the J-statistics in Tables 8.3 and 8.4.

At a general level the GMM parameter estimates shown in Tables 8.3 and 8.4 deliver empirical support for the specification of our theoretical Keynesian disequilibrium model and confirm for the UK to a large extent the empirical findings of Flaschel and Krolzig (2006) and Flaschel, Kauermann, and Semmler (2006) for the U.S. economy, as well as Proaño et al. (2006), there also for the Euro area.

Table 8.3 GMM parameter estimates (with $\hat{w}$ in the monetary policy rule)

Estimation Sample: 1980:1–2003:4 Kernel: Bartlett, Bandwidth: variable Newey-West (6)							
	β_{we}	β_{wv}	κ_{wp}	$\beta_{wu}\chi$	u_o/e_o	$\bar{R}^2$	DW
$\hat{w}_t$	1.283 [17.706]	−0.227 [8.623]	0.297 [7.575]	1.005 [15.657]	1.082 [1078.1]	0.494	1.592
	β_{pu}	β_{pv}	κ_{pw}			$\bar{R}^2$	DW
$\hat{p}_t$	0.358 [3.336]	0.227 [4.408]	0.386 [9.884]			0.353	2.334
$\hat{u}_t$	β_{uu}	β_{ui}	β_{uv}			$\bar{R}^2$	DW
	−0.367 [15.854]	−0.014 [2.166]	−0.097 [7.036]			0.426	1.986
	$\beta_{eu}\chi$	u_o/e_o				$\bar{R}^2$	DW
$\dot{e}_t$	0.030 [7.744]	1.068 [182.71]				0.979	1.197
	α_{ii}	α_{iw}	α_{iu}	c_i		$\bar{R}^2$	DW
i_t	0.113 [84.002]	0.084 [7.119]	0.049 [3.868]	0.002 [6.138]		0.939	1.849
Determinant Residual Covariance					1.80E-19		
J-Statistic					0.156		

Table 8.4 GMM parameter estimates (with $\hat{p}$ in the monetary policy rule)

Estimation Sample: 1980:1–2003:4
Kernel: Bartlett, Bandwidth: variable Newey-West (6)

	β_{we}	β_{wv}	κ_{wp}	$\beta_{wu}\chi$	u_o/e_o	$\bar{R}^2$	DW
$\hat{w}_t$	1.287	−0.227	0.296	1.010	1.082	0.494	1.592
	[17.835]	[9.181]	[7.781]	[15.374]	[1117.4]		
	β_{pu}	β_{pv}	κ_{pw}			$\bar{R}^2$	DW
$\hat{p}_t$	0.350	0.224	0.388			0.353	2.338
	[2.992]	[4.318]	[9.323]				
$\hat{u}_t$	β_{uu}	β_{ui}	β_{uv}			$\bar{R}^2$	DW
	−0.365	−0.013	−0.096			0.426	1.989
	[15.099]	[2.176]	[6.857]				
	$\beta_{eu}\chi$	u_o/e_o				$\bar{R}^2$	DW
$\dot{e}_t$	0.030	1.068				0.979	1.197
	[7.488]	[178.53]					
	α_{ii}	α_{ip}	α_{iu}	c_i		$\bar{R}^2$	DW
i_t	0.058	0.024	0.051	0.002		0.933	1.816
	[109.90]	[2.745]	[4.251]	[4.904]			
Determinant Residual Covariance					1.87E-19		
J-Statistic					0.156		

In particular, we find empirical support for the specification of cross-over expectational terms, with the wage inflation entering in the price Phillips curve and the price inflation entering in the wage Phillips Curve, as well as for the inclusion of the inflationary climate term in both equations. These results stand in stark contrast to the parameter estimates based on New Keynesian wage and price Phillips curves, where no cross-over expectations are assumed and not the present, but the future expected wage and price inflation rate determine the present wage and price inflation, in that order.

Also in line with the previously mentioned studies, we find a statistically significant influence of the Blanchard–Katz error correction terms (the log deviation of the wage share from its steady state value) in both the wage and price inflation equations. Concerning the IS equation, the coefficient of the wage share is negative and statistically significant in both countries, leading to the presumption that the UK like the US- and the Eurozone economies (see Proaño, Flaschel, Ernst, and Semmler (2006)) are profit led economies. Our differentiation between "outside" and "inside" employment also finds support in our estimation not only in the wage inflation equation but also in the employment equation. A remarkable result concerning this term is the nearly identical estimated values for u_o/e_o as predicted by our formulation of Okun's law. It is also remarkable that the parameter estimates in all equations are quite robust to the alternative specification of the monetary policy rule, and that both specifications deliver quite plausible results, with the wage inflation coefficient (α_{iw} in Table 8.3) being actually higher than the price inflation coefficient (denoted by α_{ip} in Table 8.4).

By inserting the estimated parameters of Table 8.3 into the continuous time intensive form dynamic equations given by (8.12)–(8.14), we find support for the characterizations of the sign structure of the Jacobian matrix of our Keynesian disequilibrium AD-AS model, namely

$$J = \begin{pmatrix} - & - & - \\ + & - & 0 \\ + & + & - \end{pmatrix}$$

and more importantly, for the validity of the Routh–Hurwitz conditions for local asymptotic stability $a_1 > 0$, $a_2 > 0$, $a_3 > 0$ (see the appendix for a thorough analytical calculation of these conditions), as well as

$$b = a_1 \cdot a_2 - a_3 = 0.3162 > 0.$$

To confirm this result and also to show the qualitative responses of the model with the estimated parameter values we show in Fig. 8.3 its dynamic adjustments to a one percent monetary policy shock under a wage and a price inflation targeting scheme (the latter is using the estimated coefficients of the monetary policy rule of Table 8.4).

As Fig. 8.3 shows, our calibrated model delivers dynamic adjustment paths that are quite plausible from the qualitative perspective under both specifications, showing that a theoretical framework based on disequilibrium considerations, which concern both goods and labor markets can be indeed used to analyze the effects of monetary policy in modern economies. Figure 8.4 in addition shows a phase plot for the variables wage share and employment rate, which can be usefully compared with the numerical simulations of the real wage channel as shown in Fig. 8.5, and to be discussed in the next section.

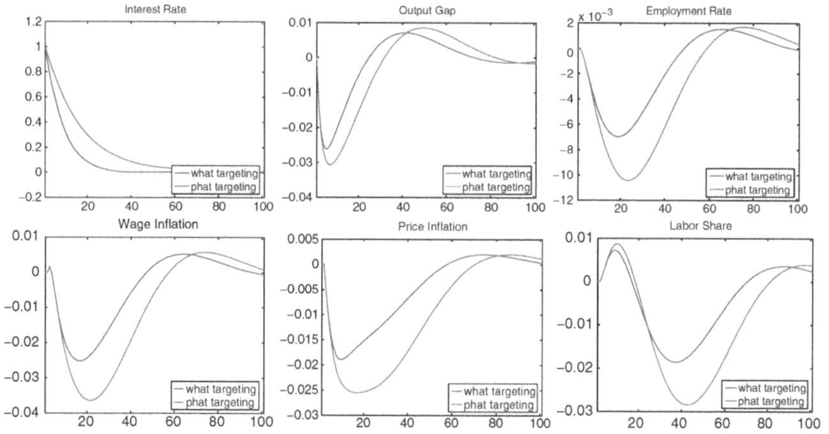

Fig. 8.3 Simulated quarter responses to a one percent monetary policy shock (annualized values)

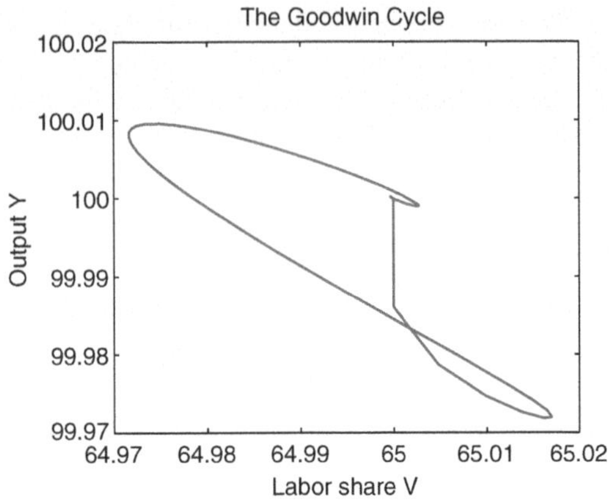

Fig. 8.4 A stable Goodwin growth cycle (simulated from a response to a one percent monetary policy shock)

8.7 Numerical Investigation of the Model

In this section we investigate the estimated general model of the preceding section from the numerical point of view. We also consider various partial models or core models that can be obtained by setting certain parameters equal to zero. We concentrate here on the Taylor rule that is based on the wage inflation gap and thus more labor market oriented than the conventional type of Taylor rule. We will recall that $\kappa = \frac{1}{1-\kappa_w \kappa_p}$ and $\chi = \bar{u}^w \bar{e}/\bar{u}$ and will use the abbreviations

$$z^w = \beta_{we}(e-\bar{e}) + \beta_{wu}\chi\left(\frac{u}{e} - \bar{u}^w/\chi\right) - \beta_{wv}(\ln v - \ln \bar{v}), \tag{8.25}$$

$$z^p = \beta_{pu}(u-\bar{u}) + \beta_{pv}(\ln v - \ln \bar{v}). \tag{8.26}$$

We stress that the term multiplying β_{wu} introduces a significant nonlinearity into the dynamics, which may give rise to further isolated interior steady state solutions (since $\det J \neq 0$) that still remain to be investigated. We here just concentrate on the interior steady state, which is given exogenously in this chapter.

Using (8.25) and (8.26) the dynamics for w and p may be written as

$$\hat{w} = \kappa[z^w + \kappa_w z^p] + \pi^c, \qquad \hat{p} = \kappa[z^p + \kappa_p z^w] + \pi^c.$$

The dynamical system is then given by[31]

$$\hat{u} = -\beta_{uu}(u-\bar{u}) - \beta_{ui}((i-\hat{p}) - \bar{r}) \pm \beta_{uv}(v-\bar{v}), \tag{8.27}$$

$$\dot{e} = \beta_{eu}\chi(u - \bar{u}^w/\chi e), \tag{8.28}$$

$$\hat{v} = \hat{w} - \hat{p}, \tag{8.29}$$

[31] Note that in contrast to the dynamical systems (8.12)–(8.15), we in addition have the interest rate smoothing Taylor rule (8.31), the continuous time version of (8.24).

$$\dot{\pi}^c = \beta_{\pi^c}(\hat{p} - \pi^c), \tag{8.30}$$
$$\mathrm{d}i/\mathrm{d}t = -\alpha_{ii}(i - i_o) + \alpha_{iw}(\hat{w} - \bar{\pi}) + \alpha_{iu}(u - \bar{u}) + \alpha_{iv}(v - \bar{v}), \tag{8.31}$$

which we simulate around the exogenously given interior steady state $u_o = \bar{u}$, $e_o = \bar{e}$, $v_o = \bar{v}$.

The empirical estimates of the preceding section suggest that the interest rate channel in the goods market dynamics is fairly weak compared to the real wage channel and that Okun's law provides only a weak connection between goods and labor markets when insiders dominate. We therefore set the parameters β_{ui}, β_{eu} equal to zero, which implies that we get a 2D subsystem in the state variables v, u if we start this system from its steady state values and shock it at time $t = 1$ by a contractive 1% capacity utilization shock. We see in Fig. 8.5 top left and right the impulse response in the v, u phase space and in time when all other parameters are chosen as estimated in the preceding section. This figure mirrors the empirical impulse-response representations shown in Figs. 8.3 and 8.4, where all five state variables are interacting.

In Fig. 8.5 bottom left we show how the dynamics change when the Blanchard and Katz error correction terms are suppressed (by setting $\beta_{wv} = \beta_{pv} = 0$) and the dynamic multiplier parameter β_{uu} is set equal to 0.05. These changes move the trace of the Jacobian matrix close to zero (from below) and the dynamics close to Goodwin's (1967) cross-dual overshooting growth cycle dynamics with their clockwise orientation in the v, u phase space. The strong stability properties of the real wage channel as estimated for the UK are then much less pronounced and become in fact the weaker the closer the diagonal terms in the Jacobian J are to zero. Figure 8.5 bottom right finally shows the maximum of the real parts of the eigenvalues of J when the parameter β_{pu}, measuring the adjustment speed of prices on the market for goods, is increased (in the situation considered in Fig. 8.5 bottom left), we see that local stability is lost at around $\beta_{pu} = 0.95$. Since the trace of J is always negative the loss of stability does not occur by way of a Hopf bifurcation, but by way of the establishment of saddlepoint dynamics, which happens when the real wage dynamics become goods market led to a sufficient degree.

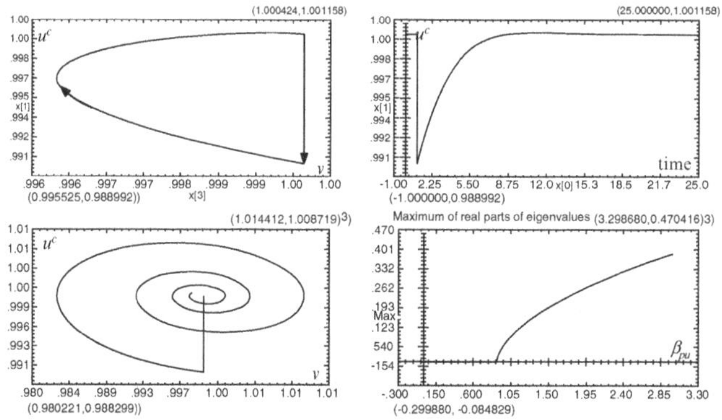

Fig. 8.5 The real wage channel of DAD-DAS macromodeling

The considered sub-dynamics in the two state variables v and u represents a fundamental integration of Keynesian demand dynamics with the Classical growth cycle, the estimates of which in the preceding section show that it is at their core. These dynamics can be made 3D in various ways:

1. By assuming $\beta_{eu} > 0$, which adds the dynamics of the employment rate e and outside effects to the insider distribution cycle,
2. By assuming $\beta_{ui} > 0$ and $\alpha_{ii} = \infty \beta_{\pi^c} > 0$, which adds the dynamics of the inflation climate π^c, but treats the interest rate i as a static variable as in the 3D dynamics we investigated in Sect. 8.5,
3. By assuming $\beta_{ui} > 0$ and $\beta_{\pi^c} = 0$, which adds the dynamics of the nominal rate of interest i, but not those of the inflation climate to the 2D dynamics.

In the first case the insider dynamics are augmented by an outsider effect of a similar type as the insider, which should not change the local behavior of the 2D system very much. However, because of the term u/e in the insider wage dynamics there is now the possibility of multiple interior steady state solutions, that is, the global behavior of the dynamics may be changed considerably. This model can be considered a special case of the model of Sect. 8.5 when an interest rate peg is assumed in this section.

In the second case, we have in addition the law of motion $\dot{\pi}^c = \beta_{\pi^c}(\hat{p} - \pi^c)$, which in its relationship with the law of motion for the real wage ω allows us to show that the determinant of the Jacobian matrix at the steady state is always negative (if the economy is labor market led, due to the linear dependencies that would then exist in the Jacobian matrix J). We then have the result that loss of stability can only occur via Hopf-bifurcations, which changes the 2D situation significantly.

The third situation exhibits again an unambiguously negative determinant of its Jacobian if the degree of interest rate smoothing is assumed to be sufficiently low (and, of course, if the economy is again labor market led), since the case of no interest rate smoothing gives a third column in J that has only one nonzero entry ($J_{13} < 0$). There are various destabilizing mechanisms in this case, in particular one that makes the entry J_{11} positive through the inflation term in the dynamics of the goods market (this situation was not possible in the case of Sect. 8.5).

Of course we can go on to dimension 4 in this way, but will instead now immediately go to the general 5D case and compare it with what we have obtained in Fig. 8.5. We start with a simulation of the 5D case that uses the estimated parameter values and a free parameter β_{π^c} as far as the speed of adjustment of the inflationary climate is concerned.

In Fig. 8.6 we show top left and right – again by way of eigenvalue diagrams – how the system loses its stability if either prices or the inflationary climate become too flexible. We do this by assuming $\beta_{\pi^c} = 0$ in both situations and see a significant degree of flexibility is needed to destabilize the dynamics by such a partial change. Assuming for the bottom figures $\beta_{\pi^c} = 0.3$ we know from the above that the steady state of the dynamics must be stable at this value. Indeed the phase plot bottom left shows this in a particular way, namely by rapid cyclical convergence to an intermediate point A in the phase space and from there by very slow convergence back to the

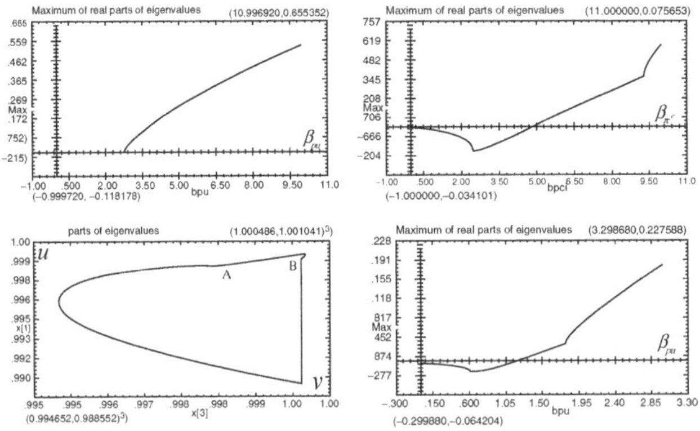

Fig. 8.6 The estimated 5D DAD-DAS macromodel

steady state position B. There is thus an intermediate "steady state" that is strongly attracting but then still a small negative root that brings the dynamics back to the true steady state. Bottom-right we show the role of price flexibility for $\beta_{\pi^c} = 0.3$ and see that a smaller value for the adjustment speed of prices with respect to demand pressure is now sufficient to make the dynamics locally unstable.

In the case of a wage-led economy ($\beta_{uv} > 0$) that exhibits explosive behavior, we can add a downward floor to the money wage Phillips curve, that is, a kink in the WPC, which means that the structural form of the WPC is modified as follows:

$$\hat{w} = \max\{z^w + \kappa_w \hat{p} + (1-\kappa_w)\pi^c, f\}.$$

Such a kink should stabilize the economy from below, since falling prices and rigid wages imply rising real wages and thus a recovery of the economy from a depression (the economy generally becomes goods market led in such a case).

When the rule of downwardly rigid nominal wages applies, that is, in the case where we get – in the model that was simulated so far – the condition

$$\kappa[z^w + \kappa_w z^p] + \pi^c \leq f,$$

we have for wage and price inflation the new expressions

$$\hat{w} = f,$$
$$\hat{p} = z^p + \kappa_p f + (1-\kappa_p)\pi^c$$

in the determination of the dynamics of the wage share, in the interest rate policy rule and in the law of motion for the inflationary climate π^c. The latter now feeds back into the real part of the economy through the monetary policy rule of the central bank. We stress again that we could also have used $\hat{p} - \pi^c$ as the inflation gap in the interest rate rule and would then have faced a similar situation to the present one. If, however, the central bank uses a fixed benchmark $\bar{\pi}$ for measuring the inflation gap, $\hat{p} - \bar{\pi}$, the fourth law would always feed back into the three others and the system would have been 4D right from the start (and thus more difficult to analyze in its stability properties, see Sect. 8.5). Note finally that the system changes between regimes in a continuous fashion, since the growth rate of money wages simply stays at f in all expressions if the system reaches this floor.

In a profit-led regime ($\beta_{uv} > 0$) we avoid explosiveness in the kinked situation by assuming that this situation only applies to a limited range (which stops existing strong volatility in capacity utilization, but would lead the economy slowly into a major depression, since real wages are rising at this floor). This floor is however assumed to be operating only as long as the employment rate is above some lower limit $\underline{e}$, while the original WPC with flexible wages comes into action again if the employment rate falls below this lower bound. We thus now have

$$\hat{w} = f,$$
$$\hat{p} = z^{\mathrm{p}} + \kappa_{\mathrm{p}} f + (1 - \kappa_{\mathrm{p}})\pi^{c}$$

only if the conditions

$$\kappa[z^{w} + \kappa_{w} z^{\mathrm{p}}] + \pi^{c} \leq f \quad \text{and} \quad e \geq \underline{e}$$

apply. All other situations are identical to the unkinked dynamics.

If employment falls below the threshold $\underline{e}$ wages become downwardly flexible again as described by the original WPC. In this situation we may get a downward jump in the growth rate of money wages, which improves the situation since the economy reacts positively to falling real wages. The kinked situation of the profit led regime is regained again if $\underline{e}$ is chosen sufficiently small, that is, the last "if" case can also be used to handle the case of a wage led economy.

In the profit led situation we get loss of stability in 2D by way of the establishment of a saddlepoint in which case the kinks in the WPC are of no help. Figure 8.7 shows, however, in this regard that the higher dimensional case may lead us back to the case of a cyclical loss of stability by way of a Hopf bifurcation.

In Fig. 8.7 we see a Goodwin (1967) type cycle that is slightly explosive in the case of the 4D dynamics of Sect. 8.5 with an inflation gap that is measured by

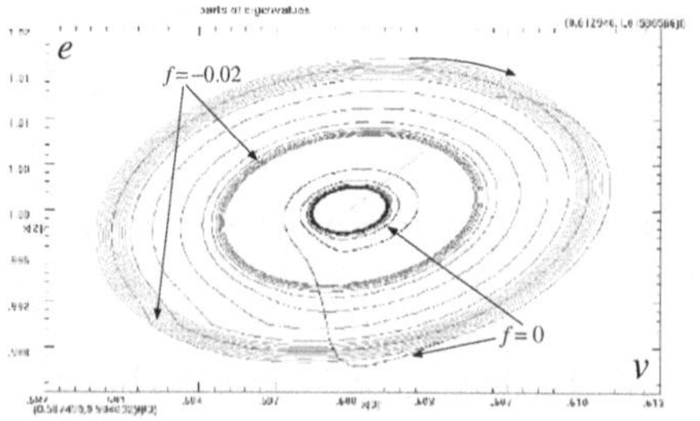

Fig. 8.7 An example of a profit led situation that can be stabilized by downward money wage rigidity

$\hat{w} - 0.02$.[32] Adding a floor of $f = -0.02$ to the dynamics moves the explosiveness inside and creates the larger limit cycle shown in Fig. 8.7, while a zero floor gives rise to the smaller limit cycle shown in this figure.

8.8 Conclusions and Outlook: E pur si muove

In this chapter we have considered two competing approaches to Keynesian macrodynamics, which are similar in their formal structure, but diametrically opposed in their views on and in their implications for the working of the economy on the macrolevel.

The well-established New Keynesian approach is rigorously microfounded and stochastic in nature, but is generally built on log-linear approximations and uses rational expectation algorithms to determine the reaction of the economy to macroeconomic shocks of various types. Its deterministic core is in the baseline cases of a purely forward looking economy with both staggered wages and prices (if determinacy would apply) completely trivial and thus completely void of interesting economic statements. Moreover, its determinacy is not guaranteed if Taylor rules of a conventional type are used. The baseline case for a Keynesian analysis of adjusting wages and prices in a staggered manner is thus not yet properly formulated in the New Keynesian research program and needs further discussion both from the analytical as well as from the empirical point of view. Adding elements of inertia-like habit formation, indexing, and the like may make this approach more applicable, but is often coupled with a loss of rigor as far as microfoundations are concerned. The New Keynesian approach, the new Neoclassical synthesis, in our view represents a complete renunciation from anything that characterizes Keynes (1936, Chap. 22) analysis of the trade cycle, but rather represents a new type of by and large a stochastic approach to macrodynamics based on imperfect competition and staggered adjustment processes.

Its theoretical fundament, the jump variable technique of the rational expectations school, stands on very shaky ground, since economic agents are assumed to move in an unstable environment in an ideal fashion that lets them find the stable submanifold in a unique way after the occurrence of (un-)anticipated shocks, exactly at the time were these shocks actually occur (as far as the deterministic core of the models is concerned). This methodology is designed to always produce convergence to the steady state of the dynamics, but does so in a way that in general is of a black-box type, with no representation or understanding of Keynesian feedback channels anymore. It demands the ad hoc addition of backward-looking behavior, processes of habit formation, indexing, and more to reconcile its theoretical starting point with the facts.

[32] The parameter values that generate this figure are $\beta_{uu} = 0.3$, $\beta_{ui} = 0.2$, $\beta_{uv} = 1$, $\beta_{eu} = 0.3$, $\beta_{we} = 1$, $\beta_{wu} = 0.36$, $\beta_{wv} = 0$, $\beta_{\pi^c} = 0.5$, $\beta_{pu} = 0.3$, $\beta_{pv} = 0$, $\alpha_{iu} = 0.2$, $\alpha_{iw} = 0.2$, $\alpha_{iv} = 0$, $\kappa_w = 0.5$, $\kappa_p = 0.5$.

Our alternative traditional, but matured approach to Keynesian AD-AS dynamics builds on the old Neoclassical synthesis, the microfoundations of which were of a quite different type as compared to the New Neoclassical synthesis. We add theory-based wage-price dynamics[33] in the spirit of Blanchard and Katz (1999), see also Flaschel and Krolzig (2006) in this regard. We obtain thereby a wage-price module that is formally seen similar to the one employed in the New Keynesian approach. It is only based on model-consistent short-run expectations (of crossover type, using neoclassical dating procedures in discrete time) and medium-run inflation inertia instead of the non-crossover purely forward-looking expectations of the New Keynesian framework.

We moreover employ a dynamic IS-curve and a Taylor rule as in the New Keynesian approach and thus have a macrostructure that is easily compared with its New Keynesian counterpart. Yet, rational expectation solution procedures are completely absent in this alternative approach, since all variables (inflation rates, output and interest rates) are predetermined variables now and allow us to analyze the model in the way ordinary differential equations are usually analyzed in the mathematical literature. We get interesting deterministic implications of this matured approach to Keynesian macrodynamics (also when it is estimated and thus quantified, see also the next chapter). However, its extension by exogenous stochastic disturbances is still missing here and is therefore left for future research. In the next chapter we shall, however, investigate an extended version of our Disequilibrium AD-AS model and apply it to a study of the US economy as well as the Eurozone.

Summing up, our conclusion is that the framework proposed here not only overcomes anomalies of the old Neoclassical Synthesis by a proper synthesis of Keynesian effective demand with Goodwinian wage-price dynamics and the distributive cycle it implies, see also Asada, Chen, Chiarella, and Flaschel (2006), but also provides a coherent alternative to its new formulation, the New Keynesian theory of the business cycle, as, for example, sketched in Galí (2000). Our alternative to this approach to macrodynamics is based on disequilibrium in the market for goods and labor, as it is reasonable in a continuous time framework,[34] and thus on sluggish adjustment of prices as well as wages (in the context of model-consistent short-run inflationary expectations, which are interacting with a sluggishly changing expression for the inflationary climate). The dynamic outcomes of our model exhibit significant potential for further generalizations, such as an advanced Metzlerian inventory approach to goods market dynamics and a Tobinian portfolio approach to financial markets (with the short-term interest rate being determined by the central bank), also in the framework of an open economy. Some of these generalizations have already been considered in Chiarella, Flaschel, Groh, and Semmler (2000), Asada, Chiarella, Flaschel, and Franke (2003), and Chiarella, Flaschel, and Franke (2005) and related work. Because of their descriptive nature, these routes to more an advanced modeling of the interaction of real and financial markets, with gradual adjustment at least on the real markets of the economy, are in principle much easier to

[33] In place of a monetarist type of wage Phillips curve and a marginal cost determination of the price level.

[34] See again Asada, Flaschel, and Proaño (2008).

establish than their equivalents in the New Keynesian representative agent approach to macrodynamics with its stability generating rational expectations (if determinacy can be shown to hold true).

Appendix: Stability Proofs and the Occurrence of Hopf Bifurcations

Substituting (8.16) in (8.12), we obtain the following three-dimensional system of equations.

$$\begin{aligned}
\dot{u} &= u\Big[-(\beta_{uu}+\beta_{ui}\alpha_{iu}+\kappa\kappa_w\beta_{ui}\beta_{pu}\alpha_{iw})(u-\bar{u})-\beta_{ui}\alpha_{iv}(v-v_0)\\
&\qquad -\kappa\beta_{ui}\beta_{we}\alpha_{iw}(e-\bar{e})-\kappa\beta_{ui}\beta_{wu}\alpha_{iw}\left(\frac{y^p}{zl_0}\frac{u}{e}-\bar{u}^w\right)\\
&\qquad +\kappa\beta_{ui}\alpha_{iw}(\beta_{wv}-\kappa_w\beta_{pv})\ln(v/v_0)\pm\beta_{uv}(v-v_0)\Big]\\
&\equiv F_1(u,e,v), \qquad (8.32)\\
\dot{e} &= \beta_{eu}\left(\frac{y^p}{zl_0}u-\bar{u}^w e\right)\equiv F_2(u,e), \qquad (8.33)\\
\dot{v} &= v\kappa\Big[(1-\kappa_{pw})\left\{\beta_{we}(e-\bar{e})+\beta_{wu}\left(\frac{y^p}{zl_0}\frac{u}{e}-\bar{u}^w\right)-\beta_{wv}\ln(v/v_0)\right\}\\
&\qquad -(1-\kappa_{wp})\{\beta_{pu}(u-\bar{u})+\beta_{pv}\ln(v/v_0)\}\Big]\equiv F_3(u,e,v). \qquad (8.34)
\end{aligned}$$

The Jacobian matrix of this system *at the equilibrium point* may be written

$$J=\begin{pmatrix} F_{11} & F_{12} & F_{13}\\ F_{21} & F_{22} & 0\\ F_{31} & F_{32} & F_{33}\end{pmatrix}, \qquad (8.35)$$

where

$$F_{11}\equiv\frac{\partial F_1}{\partial u}=-u\left(\beta_{uu}+\beta_{ui}\alpha_{iu}+\kappa\kappa_w\beta_{ui}\beta_{pu}\alpha_{iw}+\kappa\beta_{ui}\beta_{wu}\alpha_{iw}\frac{y^p}{zl_0}\frac{1}{e}\right)<0, \qquad (8.36)$$

$$F_{12}\equiv\frac{\partial F_1}{\partial e}=-u\kappa\beta_{ui}\beta_{we}\alpha_{iw}+\frac{\kappa u\alpha_{iw}\beta_{ui}\beta_{wu}y^p}{zl_0e^2}<0, \qquad (8.37)$$

$$F_{13}\equiv\frac{\partial F_1}{\partial v}=u\left[-\beta_{ui}\alpha_{iv}+\kappa\beta_{ui}\alpha_{iw}(\beta_{vw}-\kappa_w\beta_{pv})\frac{1}{v}\pm\beta_{uv}\right], \qquad (8.38)$$

$$F_{21}\equiv\frac{\partial F_2}{\partial u}=\beta_{eu}\frac{y^p}{zl_o}>0, \qquad (8.39)$$

$$F_{22}\equiv\frac{\partial F_2}{\partial e}=-\beta_{eu}\bar{u}^w<0, \qquad (8.40)$$

$$F_{31}\equiv\frac{\partial F_3}{\partial u}=v\kappa\left[\beta_{wu}\frac{y^p}{zl_0}\frac{1}{e}-(1-\kappa_{wp})\beta_{pu}\right], \qquad (8.41)$$

$$F_{32} \equiv \frac{\partial F_3}{\partial e} = v\kappa(1-\kappa_{pw})\left[\beta_{we} - \beta_{wu}\frac{y^p}{zl_0}\frac{u}{e^2}\right], \tag{8.42}$$

$$F_{33} \equiv \frac{\partial F_3}{\partial v} = -\kappa[(1-\kappa_{pw})\beta_{wv} + (1-\kappa_{wp})\beta_{pv}] < 0.(A12) \tag{8.43}$$

Under the Assumptions in the text, we have $F_{13} < 0$, $F_{31} > 0$, and $F_{32} > 0$. In this case, the sign structure of the Jacobian matrix becomes like that in 1 of Proposition 1, and the characteristic equation of this system becomes

$$\Delta(\lambda) \equiv \lambda^3 + a_1\lambda^2 + a_2\lambda + a_3 = 0, \tag{8.44}$$

where

$$a_1 = -\text{trace } J = -\underset{(-)}{F_{11}} - \underset{(-)}{F_{22}} - \underset{(-)}{F_{33}} > 0, \tag{8.45}$$

$$a_2 = \text{sum of all principal second-order minors of } J = \begin{vmatrix} F_{22} & 0 \\ F_{32} & F_{33} \end{vmatrix} + \begin{vmatrix} F_{11} & F_{13} \\ F_{31} & F_{33} \end{vmatrix} + \begin{vmatrix} F_{11} & F_{12} \\ F_{21} & F_{22} \end{vmatrix}$$

$$= \underset{(-)(-)}{F_{22}F_{33}} + \underset{(-)(-)}{F_{11}F_{33}} - \underset{(-)(+)}{F_{13}F_{31}} + \underset{(-)(-)}{F_{11}F_{22}} - \underset{(-)(+)}{F_{12}F_{21}} > 0, \tag{8.46}$$

$$a_3 = -\det J = -\underset{(-)(-)(-)}{F_{11}F_{22}F_{33}} - \underset{(-)(+)(+)}{F_{13}F_{21}F_{32}} + \underset{(-)(-)(+)}{F_{13}F_{22}F_{31}} + \underset{(-)(+)(-)}{F_{12}F_{21}F_{33}} > 0, \tag{8.47}$$

$$b = a_1a_2 - a_3$$

$$= \Big(-2\underset{(-)(-)(-)}{F_{11}F_{22}F_{33}} - F_{11}^2\underset{(-)}{F_{33}} + \underset{(-)(-)(+)}{F_{11}F_{13}F_{31}} - F_{11}^2\underset{(-)}{F_{22}} + \underset{(-)(-)(+)}{F_{11}F_{12}F_{21}} - F_{22}^2\underset{(-)}{F_{33}}$$

$$-\underset{(-)}{F_{11}}F_{22}^2 + \underset{(-)(+)(-)}{F_{12}F_{21}F_{22}} - \underset{(-)}{F_{22}}F_{33}^2 - \underset{(-)}{F_{11}}F_{33}^2 + \underset{(-)(+)(-)}{F_{13}F_{31}F_{33}}\Big) + \underset{(-)(+)(+)}{F_{13}F_{21}F_{32}}. \tag{8.48}$$

Therefore, we have $b > 0$ if the negative term $F_{13}F_{21}F_{32}$ ($J_{13}J_{21}J_{32}$ in 2 of Proposition 1 in the text) is dominated by the remaining positive terms in (B17). In this case, all of the Routh–Hurwitz conditions for local stability ($a_1 > 0$, $a_2 > 0$, $a_3 > 0$, $a_1a_2 - a_3 > 0$) are satisfied. This proves 2 of Proposition 1. Assertion 3 of Proposition 8.1 follows from (B5). We can easily see that this condition is in fact satisfied if the positive parameter value β_{eu} is sufficiently small.

Proposition A1. *The equilibrium point of the three-dimensional dynamical system (B1)–(B3) is locally asymptotically stable for all sufficient small values of* $\beta_{eu} > 0$ *under the Assumptions in the text.*

Proof. Suppose that $\beta_{eu} = 0$. In this case, we have $F_{21} = F_{22} = 0$ so that

$$b = -\underset{(-)}{F_{11}^2} F_{33} + \underset{(-)}{F_{11}} \underset{(-)}{F_{13}} \underset{(+)}{F_{31}} - \underset{(-)}{F_{11}} F_{33}^2 + \underset{(-)}{F_{13}} \underset{(+)}{F_{31}} \underset{(-)}{F_{33}} > 0. \tag{8.49}$$

This inequality implies that we have $b > 0$ for all sufficiently small values of $\beta_{eu} > 0$ by continuity. On the other hand, all of the inequalities $a_j > 0$ $(j = 1,2,3)$ are satisfied under the Assumptions in the text. This proves the assertion.

Let us consider the comparative dynamic analysis of the changes of the parameter β_{uv}. First, we consider the case of wage-led goods demand, which means that the effective demand is an increasing function of the wage share v. In this case, we must replace the term $\pm\beta_{uv}$ in (B7) with $+\beta_{uv}(\beta_{uv} > 0)$, and we have $F_{13} > 0$ for sufficiently large values of the parameter β_{uv}. This means that 3 of the Assumptions in the text is no longer satisfied.

Proposition A2. *Let us consider the case of wage-led goods demand and suppose that 1 and 2 of the* ***Assumptions*** *in the text are satisfied. In this case, the equilibrium point of the system (B1)–(B3) is unstable for all sufficiently large values of $\beta_{uv} > 0$. More accurately, the characteristic equation (A13) has at least one positive real root if $\beta_{uv} > 0$ is sufficiently large.*

Proof. In this case, we have $\lim_{\beta_{uv} \to +\infty} F_{13} = +\infty$, so that $\lim_{\beta_{uv} \to +\infty} a_3 = -\infty$, if 1 and 2 of the Assumptions in the text are satisfied. Therefore, by continuity, we have $a_3 < 0$ for all sufficiently large values of $\beta_{uv} > 0$. In such a case, one of the Routh–Hurwitz conditions for local stability is violated. We also have $a_3 = -\lambda_1\lambda_2\lambda_3$, where $\lambda_j (j = 1,2,3)$ are three roots of the characteristic equation (A13). Therefore, $a_3 < 0$ means that $\lambda_1\lambda_2\lambda_3 > 0$, which implies that the characteristic equation (B13) has at least one positive real root.

1 of the Assumptions in the text corresponds to the case of labor market-led real wage adjustment. Therefore, Proposition A2 implies that the combination of wage-led goods demand and labor market-led real wage adjustment tends to destabilize the macroeconomic system through direct noncyclical divergent. This conclusion is consistence with Table 8.1 in the text.

Next, let us consider the case of profit-led goods demand, which means that the effective demand is a decreasing function of the wage share v. In this case, we must replace the term $\pm\beta_{uv}$ in (B7) with $-\beta_{uv}(\beta_{uv} > 0)$. Such a case is consistent with all of the Assumptions in the text, and in this case the inequalities $a_j > 0 (j = 1,2,3)$ are satisfied, which means that the direct destabilizing effect through negative value of a_3 is shut out. This observation is consistent with Table 8.1 in the text, which asserts that the combination of profit-led demand and labor market-led wage adjustment tends to stabilize the macroeconomic system. However, the following proposition reveals that the indirect destabilizing mechanism through cyclical movement can work even in this case.

Proposition A3. *Let us consider the case of profit-led goods demand and suppose that all of the Assumptions in the text are satisfied. Furthermore, suppose that the* *parameter value $\beta_{eu} > 0$ is sufficiently large and $b = a_1 a_2 - a_3 = b(\beta_{uv}) > 0$ when $\beta_{uv} = 0$. Then, we have the following properties (i) and (ii).*

(i) There exists a parameter value $\beta_{uv}^0 > 0$ such that the equilibrium point of the system (B1)–(B3) is locally asymptotically stable for all $\beta_{uv} \in (0, \beta_{uv}^0)$, and it is unstable for all $\beta_{uv} \in (\beta_{uv}^0, +\infty)$.

(ii) The point $\beta_{uv} = \beta_{uv}^0$ in (i) is a Hopf bifurcation point. In other words, there exists a family of nonconstant closed orbits at some parameter values β_{uv}, which are sufficiently close to β_{uv}^0.

Proof. (i) In this case, $b(\beta_{uv})$ becomes a strictly decreasing function of β_{uv} with the properties $b(0) > 0$ and $\lim_{\beta_{uv} \to +\infty} b(\beta_{uv}) = -\infty$. Therefore, there exists a parameter value $\beta_{uv}^0 > 0$ such that $b(\beta_{uv}) > 0$ for all $\beta_{uv} \in (0, \beta_{uv}^0)$, $b(\beta_{uv}^0) = 0$, and $b(\beta_{uv}) < 0$ for all $\beta_{uv} \in (\beta_{uv}^0, +\infty)$. On the other hand, all of the inequalities $a_j > 0 (j = 1, 2, 3)$ are satisfied under the Assumptions in the text. This means that all the Routh–Hurwitz conditions for local stability are satisfied for all $\beta_{uv} \in (0, \beta_{uv}^0)$, and one of the Routh–Hurwitz conditions is violated for all $\beta_{uv} \in (\beta_{uv}^0, +\infty)$.

(ii) At the point $\beta_{uv} = \beta_{uv}^0$ we have $a_1 > 0$, $a_2 > 0$, and $b = a_1 a_2 - a_3 = 0$. These properties imply that at $\beta_{uv} = \beta_{uv}^0$ the characteristic equation (A13) has a pair of pure imaginary roots and one negative real root (cf. Asada, Chiarella, Flaschel, and Franke (2003, p. 522)). Furthermore, we have $\partial b / \partial \beta_{uv} < 0$, which means that the real part of the complex roots is not stationary with respect to the change of β_{uv} at $\beta_{uv} = \beta_{uv}^0$. These properties imply that the point $\beta_{uv} = \beta_{uv}^0$ is in fact the Hopf bifurcation point (cf. Asada, Chiarella, Flaschel, and Franke (2003, p. 521)).

Chapter 9
Keynesian DAD-DAS Modeling: Baseline Structure and Estimation

9.1 Introduction

With the introduction of the Euro as the single official currency of the Member States of the European Monetary Union (EMU) in 1999, a great currency area of similar dimensions as the US economy was created. The economic size, nevertheless, is not the only feature that these two large currency areas have in common: the increased synchronization of the national business cycles of the EMU Member States caused by the economic integration and the process of monetary and fiscal convergence determined by the Maastricht Treaty, the structure of the goods, and labor markets, as well as the relative degree of closeness of these two economic systems are also important macroeconomic characteristics that both common currency areas share to a significant degree. In this chapter[1] we formulate for both of these economies a Keynesian Disequilibrium AD-AS model (DAD-DAS model)[2] based on gradually adjusting quantities, wages, and prices and hybrid, cross over inflation expectation formation. The model consists of a dynamic IS as well as employment adjustment equation, a wage and a price Phillips curve, and a Taylor interest rate rule. Through GMM system estimation with aggregate data of the US and the Euro area, we obtain structural parameter estimates that support the general specification of the model. They show, in addition to the conventional real rate of interest channel, the importance of the real wage feedback chain and of related Blanchard–Katz (1999) error correction terms, and thus of income distribution, for the dynamics of wage and price inflation, and of the macroeconomy, in the US and the Euro area.

[1] This chapter is an abbreviated and to a certain degree reformulated version of Proaño, Flaschel, Ernst, and Semmler (2006). Disequilibrium macroeconomic dynamics, income distribution, and wage-price Phillips curves. Evidence from the US and the Euro area. Düsseldorf: IMK Working Paper No. 4. In this chapter we use as notation w for nominal wages, ω for real wages, u for the rate of capacity utilization, e for the rate of employment, v for the wage share, z for labor productivity, y for the output-capital ratio, and finally i for the rate of interest.

[2] See Day and Yang (2008) for a related approach, based on a similar perception of the forces that are driving the macroeconomy.

P. Flaschel, *The Macrodynamics of Capitalism: Elements for a Synthesis of Marx, Keynes and Schumpeter, Second Edition,*

9.2 Contemporaneous Keynesian AD-AS Modeling

During the last decade, Dynamic Stochastic General Equilibrium (DSGE) models in the line of Erceg, Henderson, and Levin (2000), Smets and Wouters (2003), and Christiano, Eichenbaum, and Evans (2005) have become the workhorse framework for the study of monetary policy and inflation in the academic literature. Based on solid microfoundations, the representation of the dynamics of the economy by theoretical frameworks of this type is derived from first principles (which result from a rational, forward-looking maximizing behavior by firms and households) and the condition of general equilibrium holding at every moment in time. This approach, though intellectually appealing at first sight, has nevertheless been questioned from both the theoretical and empirical point of view by a numerous amount of researchers like Mankiw (2001), Estrella and Fuhrer (2002), and Solow (2004), among others, primarily due to its highly unrealistic assumptions concerning the alleged "rationality" in the forward-looking behavior of the economic agents. Indeed, as discussed in Fuhrer and Moore (1995), Mankiw (2001), and more recently in Eller and Gordon (2003), empirical estimations of wage and price Phillips curves based on the New Keynesian approach have had, despite their sound microfoundations, only a poor performance in fitting the predictions of the underlying theoretical models of this approach with actual aggregate time series of both the United States and the Euro area. As Mankiw (2001) states, "although the new Keynesian Phillips curves has many virtues, it also has one striking vice: It is completely at odd with the facts."

As an alternative framework we propose a behavioral, semi-structural Keynesian macroeconomic model, where wages and prices react sluggishly to disequilibrium situations in both the goods and labor markets. As we discuss in this chapter, despite the apparent similarity that our gradual wage and price inflation adjustment equations share with their recent New Keynesian and DSGE analogues (which, among other things, also include elements of forward and backward looking behavior concerning the inflation dynamics of the economy), our approach is based on the notion of nonclearing goods and labor markets, and therefore of underutilized labor and capital stock. We think that our formulation of the wage-price dynamics permits an interesting comparison to New Keynesian work which, as stated before, usually models the dynamics of wage and price inflation as the result of the reoptimization by the economic agents under a staggered wage and price Calvo (1983) setting.

Some of the questions to be addressed in this chapter on this basis are To what extent is our semi-structural Keynesian macromodel able to fit the behavior of wages, prices, and other macroeconomic variables in the US and the Euro area? Are there significant differences in wage and price inflation (the wage-price spiral) in both economies observable over the past 30 years? Which ones and how strong are the main Keynesian transmission channels in the US and the Euro area? And what are the implications of the wage-price spiral for the dynamics of income distribution in both economies?

The remainder of the chapter is organized as follows. In Sect. 2 we briefly discuss the Keynesian semi-structural macromodel as introduced in Chen, Chiarella,

Flaschel, and Semmler (2006) and highlight its main conceptual differences from the New Keynesian approach. In Sect. 3 we estimate the model with aggregate time series of the US and the Euro area to find out sign and size restrictions for its behavioral equations and to study which type of feedback mechanisms may apply to the US and the Euro area after World War II. Section 4 concludes the chapter.

9.3 A Baseline Keynesian D(isequilibrium)AD-D(isequilibrium) AS Model

In this section we formulate a simplified Keynesian macromodel within the framework of Chiarella, Flaschel, and Franke (2005) and Chen, Chiarella, Flaschel, an Semmler (2006). As we will discuss later in more detail, this theoretical framework builds on gradual wage and price level adjustments as recent New Keynesian macroeconometric models, but assumes in contrast to those models that such adjustments are not the result of the agents' reoptimization to new economic conditions, but instead occur as reaction to disequilibrium situations in both the goods and the labor markets.

9.3.1 The Goods and Labor Markets

Since the focus of our theoretical framework is set on the wage-price dynamics, we model the goods and labor markets in a rather parsimonious manner. Concerning the goods markets dynamics, we assume a dynamic IS-equation, see also Rudebusch and Svensson (1999) in this regard, where the growth rate of output gap is determined by

$$\hat{u} = -\alpha_u(u-u_o) + \alpha_v(v-v_o) - \alpha_r((i-\hat{p}) - (i_o - \pi_o)). \tag{9.1}$$

Equation (9.1) has three important characteristics: (i) it reflects the dependence of output changes on aggregate income by assuming a negative, that is, stable dynamic multiplier relationship in this respect, (ii) it shows the joint dependence of consumption and investment on the real wage, where joint parameter may in the aggregate be positive ($\alpha_v > 0$) or negative ($\alpha_v < 0$), depending on whether consumption or investment is more responsive to real wage changes),[3] and (iii) it shows finally the negative influence of the real rate of interest on the evolution of economic activity.

Concerning the labor market dynamics, we assume a simple empirical relationship that links output and employment (in hours) according to

$$e_h/\bar{e}_h = (u/\bar{u})^b.$$

[3] This simplifying formulation helps to avoid the estimation of separate equations for consumption and investment.

Obviously, the growth rate of employment (in hours) is then given by

$$\hat{e}_h = b\,\hat{u}. \tag{9.2}$$

Employment in hours is in fact the relevant measure for the labor input of firms and therefore for the aggregate production function in the economy. Nevertheless, because of the lack of available time series of this variable for the Euro area (this series is available only for the US) and for the sake of comparability of the parameter estimates in the next section, we assume that the dynamics of employment in hours and actual employment are quite similar, so that (9.2) in fact describes the dynamics of actual employment e, so that $\hat{e} = b\,\hat{u}$ holds.

9.3.2 The Wage-Price Dynamics

As stated before, the core of our theoretical framework, which allows for nonclearing labor and goods markets and therefore for under- or over-utilized labor and capital stock, is the modeling of the wage-price dynamics, which are specified through two separate Phillips Curves, each one led by its own measure of demand pressure (or capacity bottlenecks), instead of a single one as is usually done in many New Keynesian models as, for example, by Galí and Gertler (1999) and Galí, Gertler, and López-Salido (2001).

The approach of estimating two separate wage and price Phillips curves is not altogether new: While Barro (1994) observes that Keynesian macroeconomics are (or should be) based on imperfectly flexible wages and prices and thus on the consideration of wage as well as price Phillips Curves, Fair (2000) criticizes the low accuracy of reduced form price equations. In the same study, Fair estimates two separate wage and price equations for the United States, nevertheless using a single demand pressure term, the NAIRU gap. In contrast, by the modeling of wage and price dynamics separately from each other, each one determined by its own measures of demand pressure in the market for labor and for goods, namely $e - e_o$ and $u - u_o$, respectively, where e denotes the rate of employment in the labor market (e_o being the NAIRU-level of this rate) and u the output gap (knowingly closely related with the rate of capacity utilization of the capital stock) (u_o being its potential level), we are able to circumvent the identification problem pointed out by Sims (1987) for the estimation of separate wage and price equations with the same explanatory variables.[4] By these means, we can analyze the dynamics of the real wages in the economy and identify oppositely acting effects as they might result from different developments on labor and goods markets. Indeed, we would suggest that a Keynesian model of aggregate demand fluctuations should (independently of whether justification can be found for this in Keynes' General Theory) allow for under- (or over-)utilized labor *as well as* capital, in order to be general enough from the descriptive point of view.

[4] See Erceg, Henderson, and Levin (2000) and Sbordone (2004) for other alternative approaches.

The structural form of the wage-price dynamics in our framework is given by

$$\hat{w} = \beta_{we}(e-e_o) - \beta_{wv}\ln(v/v_o) + \kappa_{wp}\hat{p} + (1-\kappa_{wp})\pi_c + \kappa_{wz}\hat{z}, \tag{9.3}$$

$$\hat{p} = \beta_{pu}(u-u_o) + \beta_{pv}\ln(v/v_o) + \kappa_{pw}(\hat{w}-\hat{z}) + (1-\kappa_{pw})\pi_c, \tag{9.4}$$

where $\hat{w} = \dot{w}/w$ and $\hat{p} = \dot{p}/p$ denote the growth rates of nominal wages and prices, respectively, that is, the wage and price inflation rates.

The demand pressure terms $e-e_o$ and $u-u_o$ in the wage and price Phillips Curves are augmented by three additional terms: the log of the wage share v or real unit labor costs (the error correction term discussed in Blanchard and Katz (1999, p. 71), a weighted average of corresponding expected cost-pressure terms, assumed to be model-consistent, with forward looking, cross-over wage and price inflation rates $\hat{w}$ and $\hat{p}$, respectively, and a backward looking measure of the prevailing inertial inflation in the economy (the "inflationary climate," so to say) symbolized by π_c, and labor productivity growth $\hat{z}$ (which is expected to influence wages in a positive and prices in a negative manner, due to the associated easing in production cost pressure). Concerning the latter variable we assume for simplicity that it is always equal to the growth rate of trend productivity, namely $\hat{z} = g_z =$const.[5]

Concerning the inertial inflation term, this may be formed adaptively following the actual rate of inflation (by use of some linear or exponential weighting scheme), may be based on a rolling sample (with hump-shaped weighting schemes), or on other possibilities for updating expectations. For simplicity of exposition we shall make use of the conventional adaptive expectations mechanism in the theoretical part of this chapter, namely

$$\dot{\pi}_c = \beta_{\pi_c}(\hat{p} - \pi_c). \tag{9.5}$$

Note that here our approach differs again from the standard New Keynesian approach based on the work by Taylor (1980) and Calvo (1983). Instead of assuming that the aggregate price (and wage) inflation is determined in a profit maximizing manner solely by the expected future path of nominal marginal costs, or in the hybrid variant discussed in Galí, Gertler, and López-Salido (2001), also by lagged inflation, we assume that not only the last period inflation, but instead the medium run inflationary development in the economy is taken into account by the economic agents. Indeed, while the agents in our model have myopic perfect foresight with respect to future values, there is no reason to assume that they also act myopically with respect to the past, "forgetting" whole sequences of fully observable and highly informational values.

The microfoundations of our wage Phillips curve are thus of the same type as in Blanchard and Katz (1999), see appendix B and also Flaschel and Krolzig (2006), which can be reformulated as expressed in (9.3) and (9.4) with the unemployment gap in the place of the logarithm of the output gap if hybrid expectations formation is in addition embedded into their approach. Concerning the price Phillips curve, a similar procedure can be applied, based on desired markups of firms. Along these

[5] Even though explicitly formulated, we assume in the theoretical part of this chapter $g_z = 0$ for simplicity and leave the modeling of the labor productivity growth for future research.

lines one in particular gets an economic motivation for the inclusion of – indeed the logarithm of – the real wage (or wage share) with negative sign in the wage PC and with positive sign in the price PC, without any need for log-linear approximations. We furthermore use the employment gap and the output gap in these two Phillips Curve equations, respectively, in the place of a single measure (the log of the output gap). Our wage-price module is thus consistent with standard models of unemployment based on efficiency wages, matching and competitive wage determination, and can be considered as an interesting alternative to the – theoretically rarely discussed and empirically questionable – New Keynesian form of wage-price dynamics.

Note that we have assumed model-consistent expectations with respect to short-run wage and price inflation, incorporated into our Phillips curves in a cross-over manner, with perfectly foreseen price – in the wage – and wage inflation in the price-Phillips curve. We stress that we can include forward-looking behavior here, without the need for an application of the jump variable technique of the rational expectations school and the New Keynesian approach as will be shown in the next section.[6]

Slightly different versions of the two Phillips curves given by (9.3) and (9.4) have been estimated for the US economy in various ways in Flaschel and Krolzig (2006), Flaschel, Kauermann, and Semmler (2007), Chen and Flaschel (2006), and Chen, Chiarella, Flaschel, and Semmler (2006), and have been found to represent a significant improvement over the conventional single reduced-form Phillips curve. A particular finding of those studies was that wage flexibility was greater than price flexibility with respect to their demand pressure measure in the market for goods and for labor,[7] respectively, and also found workers were more short-sighted than firms with respect to their cost pressure terms.[8]

The corresponding across-markets or *reduced-form Phillips Curve* equations resulting from (9.1) and (9.2) are given by (with $\kappa = 1/(1-\kappa_{wp}\kappa_{pw})$):

$$\begin{aligned} \hat{w} &= \kappa[\beta_{we}(e-e_o) - \beta_{wv}\ln(v/v_o) + \kappa_{wp}(\beta_{pu}(u-u_o) + \beta_{pv}\ln(v/v_o)) \\ &\quad +(\kappa_{wz} - \kappa_{wp}\kappa_{pw})g_z] + \pi_c, \qquad (9.6) \\ \hat{p} &= \kappa[\beta_{pu}(u-u_o) + \beta_{pv}\ln(v/v_o) + \kappa_{pw}(\beta_{we}(e-e_o) - \beta_{wv}\ln(v/v_o)) \\ &\quad +\kappa_{pw}(\kappa_{wz} - 1)g_z] + \pi_c, \qquad (9.7) \end{aligned}$$

with pass-through terms behind the κ_{wp} and κ_{pw}-parameters, which represent a considerable generalization of the conventional view of a single-market price PC with only one measure of demand pressure, namely the one in the labor market.

Note that for our current version of the wage-price spiral, the inflationary climate variable does not matter for the evolution of the labor share $v = w/(pz)$, whose law of motion is given by

[6] For a detailed comparison with the New Keynesian alternative to our model type see Chiarella, Flaschel, and Franke (2005).

[7] For lack of better terms we associate the degree of wage and price flexibility with the size of the parameters β_{we} and β_{pu}, though of course the extent of these flexibilities will also depend on the size of the fluctuations of the excess demand expression in the market for labor and for goods.

[8] Note that such a finding is not possible in the conventional framework of a single reduced-form Phillips curve.

$$\begin{aligned}\hat{v} &= \hat{w} - \hat{p} - \hat{z} \\ &= \kappa\big[(1-\kappa_{pw})(\beta_{we}(e-e_o) - \beta_{wv}\ln(v/v_o)) - (1-\kappa_{wp})(\beta_{pu}(u-u_o) \\ &\quad + \beta_{pv}\ln(v/v_o)) + (\kappa_{wz}-1)(1-\kappa_{pw})g_z\big]. \end{aligned} \tag{9.8}$$

Equation (9.8) shows the ambiguity of the stabilizing property of the real wage channel discussed by Rose (1967), which arises – despite the incorporation of specific measures of demand and cost pressure on both the labor and the goods markets – if the dynamics of the employment rate are linked to the behavior of the output and if inflationary cross-over expectations are incorporated in both Phillips curves. Indeed, as sketched in Fig. 9.1, a real wage increase can act, taken by itself, in a stabilizing or destabilizing manner, depending on whether the output dynamics depend positively or negatively on the real wage (i.e., if consumption reacts more strongly than investment or viceversa) *and* whether price flexibility is greater than nominal wage flexibility with respect to its own demand pressure measure.

These four different scenarios can be jointly summarized as in Table 9.1. As it can be observed, there exist two cases where the Rose (1967) real wage channel operates in a stabilizing manner: in the first case, aggregate goods demand (proxied in our analysis by the output gap) depends negatively on the real wage, which can be denoted in a closed economy as the profit-led case[9], and the dynamics of the real wage are led primarily by the nominal wage dynamics and therefore by the developments in the labor market. In the second case, aggregate demand depends positively on the real wage, and the price level dynamics, and therefore the goods markets, primarily determined the behavior of the real wages.[10]

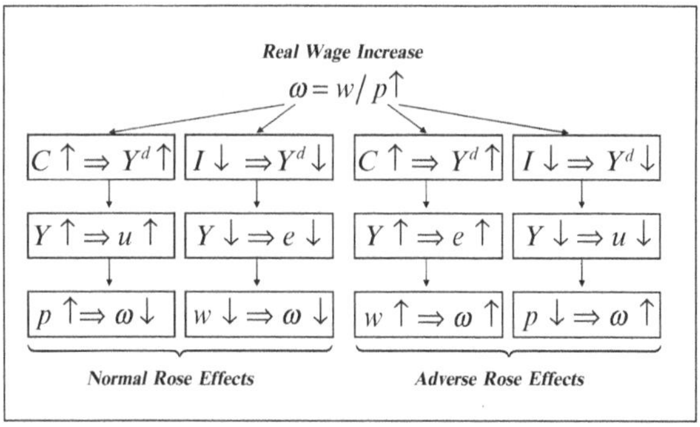

Fig. 9.1 Normal (convergent) and adverse (divergent) Rose effects: the real wage channel of Keynesian macrodynamics

[9] In an open economy other macroeconomic channels, such as the real exchange rate channel, would also be influenced by the real wage and in turn influence the aggregate demand dynamics, so that the designation "profit led" would not be appropriate anymore. Nevertheless, since we restrict our theoretical analysis to closed economies (or relatively closed as in our econometric analysis of the United States and the Euro area), we will adhere to the designation used in Table 9.1.

[10] Note here that the cost–pressure parameters also play a role and may influence the critical stability condition of the real wage channel, see Flaschel and Krolzig (2006) for details.

Table 9.1 Four baseline real wage adjustment scenarios

	Wage-led goods demand	Profit-led goods demand
Labor market-led real wage adjustment	Adverse (divergent)	Normal (convergent)
Goods market-led real wage adjustment	Normal (convergent)	Adverse (divergent)

These two cases are in turn to be combined with two additional constellations concerning the dynamics of the real wage resulting from the joint dynamics of wages and prices: while in the first one the real wage dynamics are primarily driven by nominal wage adjustments and therefore by the labor markets, in the second case they follow mainly the developments of the price dynamics, and therefore of the goods markets. As Table 9.1 clearly shows, the combination of these four possibilities sets up four different scenarios where the dynamics of the real wage (in their interaction with the goods and labor markets) might turn out to be per se convergent or divergent. One of the goals of this chapter will thus be the categorization within this setup of the real wage dynamics in the US and the Euro area.

9.3.3 Monetary Policy

Finally, we no longer employ a law of motion for real balances (an LM Curve) as was still the case in Asada, Chen, Chiarella, and Flaschel (2006). Instead we endogenize the nominal interest rate by using a type of Taylor rule as is customary in the literature, see, for example, Svensson (1999). Indeed, as Romer (2000, p. 154–155) states, "Even in Germany, where there were money targets beginning in 1975 and where those targets paid a major role in the official policy discussions, policy from the 1970s through the 1990s was better described by an interest rate rule aimed at macroeconomic policy objectives than by money targeting."[11] The target rate of the monetary authorities and the law of motion resulting from an interest rate smoothing behavior by the central bank are defined as

$$i^* = (i_o - \pi_o) + \hat{p} + \alpha_{ip}(\hat{p} - \pi_o) + \alpha_{iu}(u - u_o)$$
$$\dot{i} = \alpha_i(i^* - i).$$

The target rate of the central bank i^* is here made dependent on the steady state real rate of interest $i_o - \pi_o$ augmented by actual inflation back to a nominal rate, and is as usual dependent on the inflation and the output gap.[12] With respect to this target there are interest rate smoothing dynamics with strength α_i. Inserting i^* and rearranging terms we obtain from this expression the following dynamic law for the nominal interest rate:

[11] See also Clarida and Gertler (1997).

[12] All of the employed gaps are measured relative to the steady state of the model to allow for an interest rate policy that is consistent with it.

$$\dot{i} = -\alpha_i(i - i_o) + \gamma_{ip}(\hat{p} - \pi_o) + \gamma_{iu}(u - u_o), \tag{9.9}$$

where we have $\gamma_{ip} = \alpha_i(1 + \alpha_{ip})$, thatis, $\alpha_{ip} = \gamma_{ip}/\alpha_i - 1$ and $\gamma_{iu} = \alpha_i \alpha_{iu}$.

Furthermore, the actual (perfectly foreseen) rate of inflation $\hat{p}$ is used to measure the inflation gap with respect to the inflation target $\bar{\pi}$ of the central bank. Note finally that we could have included (but have not done this here yet) a new kind of gap into the above Taylor rule, the labor share gap, since we have in our model a dependence of aggregate demand on income distribution and the labor share, that is, the state of income distribution matters for the dynamics of our model and thus should also play a role in the decisions of the central bank.

Taken together, the model of this section consists of the following five laws of motion (with the derived reduced form expressions as far as the wage-price spiral is concerned and with reduced form expressions by assumption concerning the goods and the labor market dynamics):[13]

$$\begin{aligned}
\hat{v} &\overset{\text{LaborShare}}{=} \kappa[(1-\kappa_p)(\beta_{we}(e-e_o) - \beta_{wv}\ln(v/v_o)) \\
&\qquad -(1-\kappa_w)(\beta_{pu}(u-u_o) + \beta_{pv}\ln(v/v_o)) + \delta g_z], \\
&\qquad \text{with } \delta = (\kappa_{wz} - 1)(1 - \kappa_{pw})
\end{aligned} \tag{9.10}$$

$$\hat{u} \overset{\text{Dyn.IS}}{=} -\alpha_u(u-u_o) + \alpha_v(v-v_o) - \alpha_r((i-\hat{p}) - (i_o - \pi_o)), \tag{9.11}$$

$$\dot{i} \overset{\text{T.Rule}}{=} -\alpha_i(i-i_o) + \gamma_{ip}(\hat{p} - \pi_o) + \gamma_{iu}(u-u_o), \tag{9.12}$$

$$\dot{\pi}_c \overset{\text{I.Climate}}{=} \beta_{\pi_c}(\hat{p} - \pi_c) \tag{9.13}$$

$$\hat{e} \overset{\text{O.Law}}{=} b\,\hat{u}, \tag{9.14}$$

The above equations[14] represent, in comparison to the baseline model of New Keynesian macroeconomics, the law of motion (9.10) for the labor share $\hat{v} = \hat{w} - \hat{p} - \hat{z}$ that makes use of the same explanatory variables as the New Keynesian approach (but with inflation rates in the place of their time rates of change and with no accompanying sign reversal concerning the influence of output and wage gaps), the IS goods market dynamics (9.11), the Taylor Rule (9.12), the law of motion (9.13) that describes the updating of the inflationary climate expression, and finally Okun's Law (9.14) as link between the goods and the labor markets. Note that the model can be reduced to a 4D system if we recover from (9.14) the actual level of employment by making use of the original formulation of Okun's Law, see the equation preceding (9.2), and insert the resulting functional relationship in the remaining equations of the system. We can thus abstract from (9.14) (and the influence of e as an endogenous variable) in the stability analysis to be discussed below.

[13] As the model is formulated we have no real anchor for the steady state rate of interest (via investment behavior and the rate of profit it implies in the steady state) and thus have to assume that it is the monetary authority that enforces a certain steady state value for the nominal rate of interest.

[14] Which are very close to a linear system.

To get an autonomous nonlinear system of differential equations in the state variables, labor share v, output gap u, the nominal rate of interest i, and the inflationary climate expression π_c, we have to make use of (9.7) (the reduced-form price Phillips Curve equation), which has to be inserted into the remaining laws of motion in various places.

With respect to the empirically motivated restructuring of the original theoretical framework, the model is as pragmatic as the approach employed by Rudebusch and Svensson (1999). By and large we believe that it represents a working alternative to the New Keynesian approach, in particular when the current critique of the latter approach is taken into account. It overcomes the weaknesses and the logical inconsistencies of the old Neoclassical synthesis, see Asada, Chen, Chiarella, and Flaschel (2006), and it does so in a minimal way from a mature, but still traditionally oriented Keynesian perspective (and is thus not really "New"). It preserves the problematic stability features of the real rate of interest channel, where the stabilizing Keynes effect or the interest rate policy of the central bank is interacting with the destabilizing, expectations driven Mundell effect. It preserves the real wage effect of the old Neoclassical synthesis, where – due to an unambiguously negative dependence of aggregate demand on the real wage – it was the case that price flexibility was destabilizing, while wage flexibility was not. This real wage channel, summarized in the Fig. 9.1, is not really discussed in the New Keynesian approach, due to the specific form of wage-price and IS dynamics there considered.

9.4 Econometric Analysis and Evaluation of the Model

In this section we report the estimation results of the theoretical model of the previous section obtained with aggregate time series data of the US and the Euro area.[15] While, on the one hand, we intend to demonstrate the consistency of our theoretical model with the empirical data, on the other hand, we expect to identify the main similarities and differences of the determinants of wage and price dynamics in the two economies. At this stage we would like to point out nevertheless that the parameter estimates for the Euro area must be handled with care since, despite the many similarities in the macroeconomic development of the participant economies and the possibility of cross-country aggregation, they represent the theoretical values of an artificial economy. Indeed, since country-specific labor market conditions such as the respective bargaining power of national labor unions have played an important role in the wage and price differentials among the member countries of the Euro area before and after the introduction of the Euro, a different development of the competitiveness and of the economic performance of the respective economies has taken place that cannot be identified through the estimation of aggregate data.

[15] From the theoretical point of view, the Euro area could be considered as a single economy also before the introduction of the Euro 1999 due to the economic convergence process which led to it, as well as due to the high degree of economic integration of the participating countries.

The estimated parameters serve the purpose of confirming the parameter signs we have specified in the initial theory-guided formulation of the model and to determine the sizes of these parameters in addition. However, as discussed in the previous section, we have three different situations where we cannot specify the parameter signs on purely theoretical grounds and where we therefore aim to obtain these signs from the empirical estimates of the equations whenever this happens: the ambiguous influence of labor share on (the dynamics of) the output gap, see (9.11), on the nominal interest rate (through its effect on the price inflation) as well as on the inflationary climate. Mundell-type, Rose-type, and Blanchard–Katz error-correction feedback channels therefore make the dynamics indeterminate on the general level.

In all of these three cases empirical analysis will now indeed provide us with definite answers as to which ones of these opposing forces will be the dominant ones. Furthermore, we shall also see that the Blanchard and Katz (1999) error correction terms do play a role in the US economy, in contrast to what has been found out by these authors for the money wage PC in the US However, we will not attempt to estimate the parameter β_{π_c} that characterizes the evolution of the inflationary climate in our economy. Instead, we will approximate inflationary climate π_c of the theoretical model by a linearly declining moving average of price inflation rates with linearly decreasing weights over the past 12 quarters (denoted as π_t^{12}),[16] what allows us to bypass the estimation of the law of motion (9.5). We consider this as the simplest approach to the treatment of our climate expression (comparable with recent New Keynesian treatments of hybrid expectation formation), which should later on be replaced by more sophisticated ones, for example, one that makes use of the Livingston index for inflationary expectations as in Laxton, Rose, and Tambakis (2000), which in our view mirrors some adaptive mechanism in the adjustment of inflationary expectations.

9.4.1 Data Description: The US Economy and the Eurozone

The empirical data of the corresponding time series stem from the Federal Reserve Bank of St. Louis data set (see `http:/www.stls.frb.org/fred`) and the OECD database for the US and the Euro area, respectively. The data are quarterly, seasonally adjusted and concern the period from 1961:1 to 2004:4 for the US and from 1975:1 to 2004:4 for the Euro area (Table 9.2).

The logarithms of wages and prices are denoted $\ln(w_t)$ and $\ln(p_t)$, respectively. Their first differences (backwardly dated), that is, the current rate of wage and price inflation, are denoted $\hat{w}_t$ and $\hat{p}_t$.

In Fig. 9.2 we can observe the remarkably similar pattern of the macroeconomic dynamics of the US and the Euro area over the last two decades. Nevertheless, an important difference in the macroeconomic performance of the United States and

[16] We also estimated the structural model shown in Table 9.4 with other proxies for the inflationary climate, which also covered the four, six, and eighteen last quarters. The resulting estimates could be rejected even at the 10% significance level.

Table 9.2 Data description

Variable	Description of the original series
e	US : Employment Rate
	EZ : Employment Rate
u	US : Capacity Utilization: Manufacturing, Percent of Capacity
	EZ : Output Gap
w	US : Nonfarm Business Sector: Compensation Per Hour, 1992 = 100
	EZ : Business Sector: Wage Rate Per Hour,
p	US : Gross Domestic Product: Implicit Price Deflator, 1996 = 100
	EZ : Gross Domestic Product: Implicit Price Deflator, 2000 = 100
z	US : Nonfarm Business Sector; Output Per Hour of All Persons, 1992 = 100
	EZ : Labor Productivity of the business economy,
v	US : Nonfarm Business Sector: Real Compensation Per Output Unit, 1992 = 100
	EZ : Business Sector: Real Compensation Per Output Unit,
i	US : Federal Funds Rate
	EZ : Short Term Interest Rate

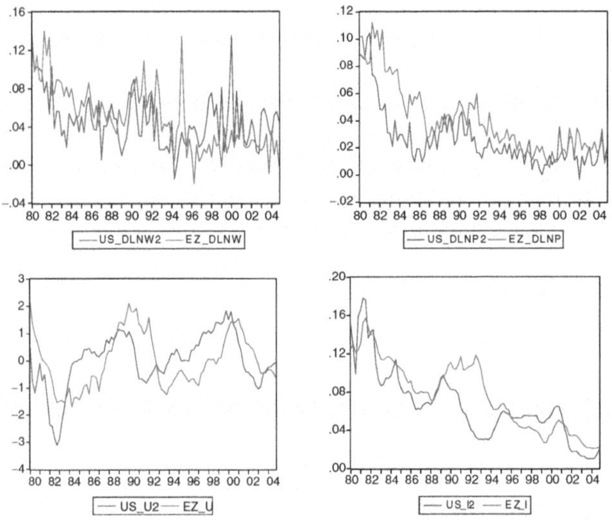

Fig. 9.2 US and Euro area wage and GDP deflator inflation, capacity utilization, and nominal interest rates

the Euro area in the last 20 years can be observed in Fig. 9.3: while the US unemployment rate has fluctuated, roughly speaking, around a constant level (which would suggest a somewhat constant or at least for a not all too varying NAIRU) over the last two decades, the European employment (unemployment) rate has described a persistent downwards (upwards) trend over the same time period.

This particular European development has been explained by Layard, Nickell, and Jackman (1991) and Ljunqvist and Sargent (1998) by an over-proportional increase in the number of long-term unemployed (i.e., workers with an unemployment duration over 12 months) with respect to short-term unemployed (workers with an unemployment duration of less than 12 months) and the phenomenon of

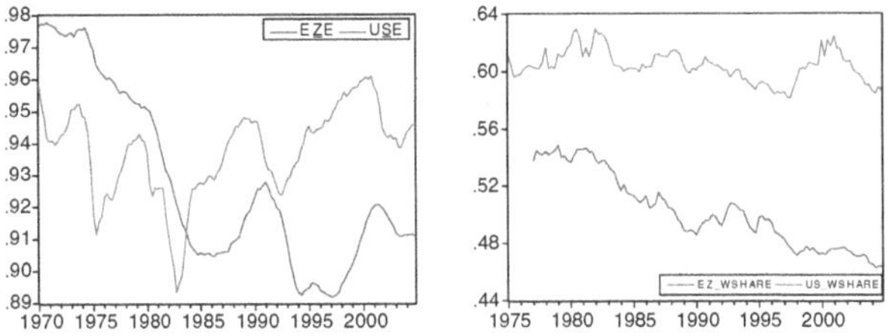

Fig. 9.3 US and Euro area aggregate employment rate and wage share

hysteresis especially in the first group. One main explanation for the persistence in long-term unemployment is that human capital, and therefore the productivity of the unemployed, tend to diminish over time, which makes the long-term unemployed less "hirable" for firms, see Pissarides (1992) and Blanchard and Summers (1991). Because long-term unemployed become less relevant, and primarily the short-term unemployed are taken into account in the determination of nominal wages, the potential downward pressure on wages resulting from the unemployment of the former diminishes, with the result of a higher level of the NAIRU.[17] When long-term unemployment is high, the aggregate unemployment rate of an economy thus, "becomes a poor indicator of effective labor supply, and the macroeconomic adjustment mechanisms – such as downward pressure on wages and inflation when unemployment is high – will then not operate effectively."[18] Indeed, Llaudes (2005), for example, by using a modified wage Phillips curve, which incorporates the different influences of long- and short-term unemployed in the wage determination, finds empirical evidence for some OECD countries of the fact that the long-term unemployed have only a negligible influence on the wage determination.

Since time series data for long-term unemployment in the Euro area are not available, we try to approximate it in a rather simple way: We first run the HP-filter on the Euro area unemployment rate with a high smoothing factor ($\lambda = 640,000$). We normalize the resulting smoothed series so that the 1970:1 value equals zero, implicitly assuming that in 1970:1 the number of long-term unemployed was not too different from zero, since before the oil shocks in the 1970s unemployment (and also long-term unemployment) were extremely low on the European continent. We interpret this smoothed series as a proxy for the actual development of long-term unemployment. The difference between this series and the aggregate unemployment rate, denoted u^{st}, can then be interpreted as a proxy for the short term unemployment rate, which is the relevant variable in the wage bargaining process. With this series we calculate for the Euro area the alternative employment rate measure $e = 1 - u^{st}$.[19] In our econometric estimation, thus, we implicitly assume the existence of a variable NAIRU in the Euro area, despite the fact that we did not explicitly model it in the theoretical framework of the previous section.

[17] See Blanchard and Wolfers (2000).

[18] OECD (2002, p. 189).

[19] Note nevertheless that, by the construction of the Hodrick–Prescott filter, the calculated course of the proxy for the long-term unemployed (the smoothed series) depends on the whole sample period.

Concerning the wage share in the Euro area (normalized to 0.60 in 1970), we see in Fig. 9.5 that it possesses a pronounced downward trend over the whole sample period. To focus on the cyclical implications of changes in income distribution, and along the way to ensure the stationarity of the time series, we use again the cyclical component calculated by the Hodrick–Prescott filter with the same smoothing factor $\lambda = 640,000$. We depict the considered short- and long-term time series in Fig. 9.4.

We carry out Phillips–Perron unit root tests for each series in order to account, not only for residual autocorrelation as is done by the standard ADF Tests, but also for possible residual heteroskedasticity when testing for stationary. The Phillips–Perron test specifications and results are shown in Table 9.3.

The applied unit root tests confirm our presumptions with the exception of the nominal interest rate i. Nevertheless, although the Phillips–Perron test on this series cannot reject the null of a unit root, there is no reason to expect both time series to be unit root processes. Indeed, we reasonably expect these rates to be constrained to certain limited ranges in the Euro area and the US economy. Because of the generally low power of the unit root tests, we interpret these results as providing only a hint of the possibility that the nominal interest rates exhibit a strong autocorrelation.

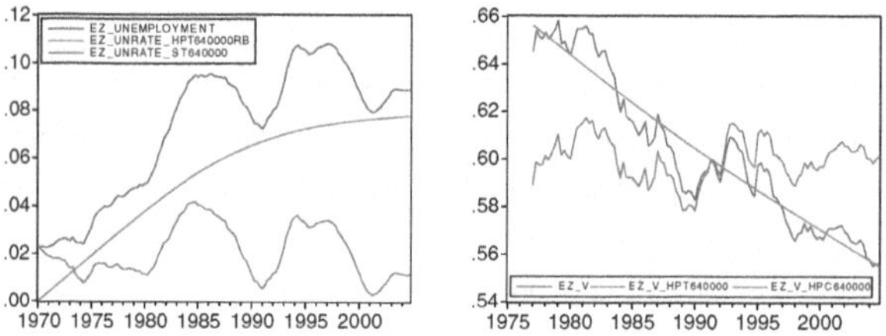

Fig. 9.4 Modified Euro area long- and short-term unemployment rate and wage share

Table 9.3 Phillips–Perron unit root test results

Sample: 1980:1–2004:4					
Country	Variable	Lag Length	Determ.	Adj. Test Stat.	Prob.*
	$\mathrm{dln}(p)$	1	–	−2.106	0.034
US	$\mathrm{dln}(w)$	1	–	−2.589	0.010
	$\mathrm{d}(e)$	–	–	−4.821	0.000
	$\mathrm{d}(u)$	1	–	−7.122	0.000
	i	1	–	−1.8557	0.061
	$\mathrm{dln}(p)$	1	–	−2.3362	0.0183
Euro area	$\mathrm{dln}(w)$	1	–	−2.197	0.027
	$\mathrm{dln}(e)$	1	–	−3.152	0.001
	$\mathrm{d}(u)$	1	–	−8.089	0.000
	i	1	–	−1.481	0.129

*McKinnon (1996) one-sided p-values.

9.4.2 Estimation of the Feedback Channels of the Model

As discussed in Sect. 2, the law of motion for the real wage rate, given by (9.10), represents a reduced form expression of the two structural equations for $\hat{w}_t$ and $\hat{p}_t$. Noting again that the inflation climate variable is defined in the estimated model as a linearly declining function of the past twelve price inflation rates, the dynamics of the system (9.3)–(9.9) can be reformulated as

$$\begin{aligned}
\hat{w}_t &= \beta_{we}(e_{t-1} - e_o) - \beta_{wv}\ln(v_{t-1}/v_o) + \kappa_{wp}\hat{p}_t + (1-\kappa_{wp})\pi_t^{12} + \kappa_{wz}\hat{z}_t,\\
\hat{p}_t &= \beta_{pu}(u_{t-1} - u_o) + \beta_{pv}\ln(v_{t-1}/v_o) + \kappa_{pw}(\hat{w}_t - \hat{z}_t) + (1-\kappa_{pw})\pi_t^{12},\\
\ln u_t &= \ln u_{t-1} + \alpha_u(u_{t-1} - u_o) - \alpha_{ui}(i_{t-1} - \hat{p}_t) + \alpha_{uv}(v_t - v_o),\\
\hat{e}_t &= \alpha_{eu-1}\hat{u}_{t-1} + \alpha_{eu-2}\hat{u}_{t-2} + \alpha_{eu-3}\hat{u}_{t-3},\\
i_t &= \phi_i i_{t-1} + \varphi_{ip}\hat{p}_t + \varphi_{iu}(u_{t-1} - u_o) + \varepsilon_{it},
\end{aligned}$$

with sample means denoted by a subscript o.

To account for regressor endogeneity, we estimate the discrete time version of the structural model formulated above (accounting for the parameter restrictions resulting from the theoretical model) by means of instrumental variables system GMM (Generalized Method of Moments).[20] The weighting matrix in the GMM objective function was chosen to allow the resulting GMM estimates to be robust against possible heteroskedasticity and serial correlation of an unknown form in the error terms. Concerning the instrumental variables used in our estimations, since at time t only past values are contained in the information sets of the economic agents, for all five equations we use, besides the strictly exogenous variables, the last four lagged values of the employment rate, the labor share (detrended by the Hodrick–Prescott Filter), and the growth rate of labor productivity. To test for the validity of the overidentifying restrictions, the J-statistics for both system estimations were calculated. We present the structural parameter estimates for the US and the Euro area economies (t-statistics in brackets), as well as the J-statistics (p-values in brackets) in Table 9.4.[21] In-sample, one-period ahead forecast for the US and the Euro area, which show the fit of the structural model in the estimation sample, are depicted in Fig. 9.5.[22]

---

[20] As stated in Wooldridge (2001, p. 92), a GMM estimation possesses several advantages with respect to more traditional estimation methods such as OLS and 2SLS, especially in time series models, where heteroskedasticity in the residuals is a common feature: "The optimal GMM estimator is asymptotically no less efficient than two-stage least squares under homoskedasticity, and GMM is generally better under heteroskedasticity." This and the additional robustness property of GMM estimates, of not relying on a specific assumption with respect to the distribution of the residuals, make the GMM methodology appropriate and advantageous for our estimation.

[21] Estimation results with different sample sizes for the US and the Euro economies deliver similar parameter values and are available upon request.

[22] Del Negro, Schorfheide, Smets, and Wouters (2004) also use in-sample, one-period ahead forecasts when discussing the fit and forecasting performance of New Keynesian models. Note here that we find only partial productivity pass-through in the wage Phillips curve.

Table 9.4 GMM parameter estimates of the structural model

Estimation Sample: 1980:1–2004:4
Kernel: Bartlett, Bandwidth: Andrews(U.S.: 2.62, Euro area: 3.20)

$\hat{w}$	β_{we}	β_{wv}	κ_{wp}	κ_{wz}	const.	$\bar{R}^2$	DW
U.S.	0.679	−0.208	0.421	0.233	0.012	0.355	1.824
	[10.735]	[4.614]	[3.839]	[7.629]	[8.763]		
Euro area	0.326	−0.383	0.886	0.223	0.005	0.692	1.606
	[4.724]	[8.613]	[7.579]	[9.587]	[8.027]		
$\hat{p}$	β_{pu}	β_{pv}	κ_{pw}	const.		$\bar{R}^2$	DW
U.S.	0.294	0.113	0.044	–		0.763	1.264
	[13.581]	[5.260]	[2.921]				
Euro area	0.291	0.089	0.075	–		0.887	1.389
	[9.320]	[3.551]	[4.229]				
$\hat{u}$	α_u	α_{ui}	α_{uv}	const.		$\bar{R}^2$	DW
U.S.	−0.078	−0.042	−0.173	0.001		0.901	1.517
	[9.137]	[4.423]	[8.225]	[3.689]			
Euro area	−0.104	−0.061	−0.238	−0.068		0.926	2.012
	[10.997]	[−6.968]	[−14.889]	[14.622]			
$\hat{e}$	α_{eu-1}	α_{eu-2}	α_{eu-3}	α_{eu-4}		$\bar{R}^2$	DW
U.S.	0.201	0.113	0.039	–		0.387	1.634
	[23.492]	[8.012]	[3.730]				
Euro area	0.128	0.115	0.057	0.159		0.645	1.501
	[28.448]	[19.691]	[7.972]	[14.994]			
i	ϕ_i	φ_{ip}	φ_{iu}			$\bar{R}^2$	DW
U.S.	0.830	0.369	0.072			0.929	1.915
	[71.523]	[12.064]	[5.362]				
Euro area	0.936	0.0981	0.113			0.981	1.385
	[105.06]	[5.414]	[10.591]				

Determinant Residual Covariance	U.S.: 7.99E-21, Euro area: 2.18E-22
J-Statistic [p-val]	U.S.: 0.372 [0.975], Euro area: 0.316[0.996]

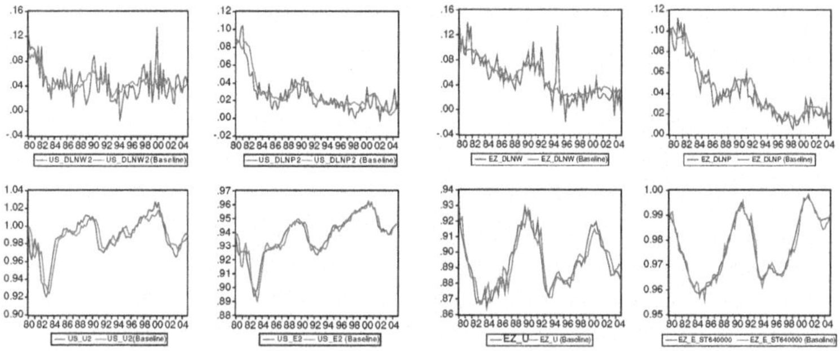

Fig. 9.5 US and Euro area in-sample one-period-ahead forecasts

At a general level the GMM parameter estimates shown in Table 9.4 deliver empirical support for the specification of our theoretical Keynesian disequilibrium model and confirm, for the Euro area, some of the empirical findings of Flaschel and Krolzig (2006) and Flaschel, Kauermann, and Semmler (2007) for the US economy. Especially, we find empirical support for the specification of cross-over expectational terms, with the wage inflation entering in the price Phillips curve and the price inflation entering in the wage Phillips Curve, as well as for the inclusion of the inflationary climate term in both equations. This findings stand in stark contrast to those based on standard New Keynesian Phillips curves as in Galí, Gertler, and López-Salido (2001, p. 1256), where nominal wages are assumed to be perfectly flexible and prices depend only on future expected marginal costs.

We also confirm the results of Flaschel and Krolzig (2006) and Flaschel, Kauermann, and Semmler (2007) and find that wage flexibility is greater than price flexibility (with respect to their demand pressure terms in the labor and goods markets, respectively) in both economies (though we have a greater fluctuation amplitude in the capacity utilization than in the employment rate). In addition, we find that the estimated parameter β_{we}, which measures the wage flexibility with respect to labor market developments, is not significantly higher in the United States than in the Euro area, as pointed out by Nickell (1997), if we make use of our proxy variable for the Euro area short-term unemployed (which as stated before is the relevant group in the wage bargaining process) instead of using the aggregate unemployment rate.

Concerning the (log of the) wage share, the Blanchard–Katz error correction term, we find a similar influence on the price inflation dynamics in both economies, and a higher effect of this variable on the wage dynamics in Europe is observable, confirming (at least from a qualitative point of view) the empirical findings of Blanchard and Katz (1999). Income distribution, thus, indeed seems to play indeed a more important role in the determination of wage inflation in Euro area than in the United States. Concerning the role of monetary policy in both economies, our empirical estimates confirm other studies such as Gerlach and Schnabel (2000) and Carstensen (2006), for example, where the validity of the Taylor principle, that is, of an active interest rate policy with respect to the inflation gap is confirmed, since $\alpha_{ip} = \varphi_{ip}/(1-\phi_i) > 1$.

By inserting the estimated values of the structural parameters in the reduced-form price Phillips curve (which must be included at several places in the dynamical system given by (9.10), (9.11), (9.12), and (9.13)), a positive and unambiguous dependency of price inflation $\hat{p}$ with respect to capacity utilization u and the (log of the) labor share v for the United States and the Euro area is found (the net effect of the (log of the) labor share is 0.099 and 0.026 respectively), so that

$$\hat{p} = f(\underset{+}{u}, \underset{+}{v}).$$

Focusing on the three main equations of the dynamical system given by (9.10), (9.11), and (9.12), these parameter estimates provide us, after their inclusion in the resulting reduced form price Phillips curve of the dynamical system, with the following signs for the core 3D Jacobian for the United States and the Euro area (for the variables v, u, i):

$$\text{U.S.: } J = \begin{pmatrix} - & + & 0 \\ - & - & - \\ + & + & - \end{pmatrix} \qquad \text{Euro area: } J = \begin{pmatrix} - & + & 0 \\ - & - & - \\ + & + & - \end{pmatrix}.$$

These Jacobians deliver some additional interesting insights into the macroeconomic interaction of the analyzed variables: In the first place we find that, because the trace of both Jacobians is unambiguously negative, the endogenous system variables v, u, i, and π^c in both economies do not act per se in a destabilizing manner, implying that both systems are intrinsically stable and that possible unstable scenarios are thus generated by cross-effects. Additionally, the fact that all elements of the estimated Jacobians for the US and the Euro area economies possess the same sign, supports the notion that no significant differences in the basic macroeconomic interaction of the analyzed variables between the US and the Euro area economies can be detected. The calculated influence of the capacity utilization (our proxy for the output gap) on the labor share, which implies a pro-cyclical income distribution in favor of workers in both economies, is nevertheless very weak in both countries and probably cannot be considered as determining its actual outcome.

Concerning the output gap equation, we find evidence for principally profit led goods markets dynamics in both countries (determined by the negative sign of J_{21}), a result that supports the Classical point of view, see Goodwin (1967), whereby lower real wages lead to a higher employment and production levels. Taken together, these two empirical findings allow us to identify in Table 9.1 the upper right case as the relevant one for the US and the Euro area economies, where the Rose real wage channel operates in a convergent and therefore not destabilizing manner. Additionally, we find empirical evidence for the positive influence of the Mundell effect (J_{14}) – which influences aggregate production through the real interest rate channel – in both economies.

Taken together, these results deliver an insight into the role of interacting price – wage determination. While the New Keynesian approach is based on the assumption that only next period expected values are relevant for the respective wage and price determination, our estimation results deliver a twofold innovation: indeed, the crossover expectation formation (where future price (wage) inflation influences the future wage (price) inflation rate) as well as the inflationary climate cannot be rejected as significant explanatory variables in the wage and price Phillips Curves. In sum, the system estimates for the US and the Euro area discussed in this section provide us with a result that confirms the theoretical sign restrictions for both economies. They moreover provide definite answers with respect to the role of income distribution in the considered disequilibrium AS-AD or DAS-DAD dynamics, confirming in particular the orthodox point of view that economic activity is likely to depend negatively on real unit wage costs. We have also a stabilizing effect of real wages on the dynamics of income distribution in the US and the Euro area, in the sense that the growth rate of the real wages (see our reduced form real wage dynamics in Sect. 2) depends – through Blanchard–Katz error correction terms – negatively on its own level. Its dependence on economic activity levels, however, is somewhat ambiguous, but in any case small. Real wages therefore only weakly increase in the US and the Euro area, with increases in the rate of capacity utilization, which in turn, however, depends in an unambiguous way negatively on the real wage, implying in sum that the Rose (1967) real wage effect is present, but may not dominate the dynamic outcomes in both economies.

9.5 Conclusions and Outlook

We have considered in this chapter a significant extension and modification of the traditional approach to AS-AD growth dynamics, primarily by means of an appropriate reformulation of the wage-price block of the model, which principally allows us to avoid the empirical weaknesses and theoretical indeterminacy problems of the so-called New Keynesian approach that arise from the existence of only purely forward-looking behavior in baseline models of staggered price and wage setting. The DAD-DAS baseline model we have obtained in this way out of the old Neoclassical Synthesis represents what we would call a Keynes–Marx synthesis, which astonishingly enough came about as an extension of the Neoclassical Synthesis, stage I towards a coherent disequilibrium approach to macrodynamics (as far as real markets are concerned). There is therefore nothing of unconventional type involved in our Keynes–Marx synthesis. Quite the contrary, it is the outcome of a meaningful extension of traditional macrodynamic theory, in striking difference to the radical break with any Keynesian tradition that is characteristic for the New Keynesian approach to macrodynamics.

The empirical estimation of the structural model equations with aggregate time series data for the US and the Euro area economies, besides confirming the theoretical signs of the dynamical system, delivered some interesting insights into the similarities and differences of both economies with respect to the analyzed macroeconomic variables. In the first place we found a remarkable similarity in nearly all of the estimated coefficients in the structural equations. This is a somewhat surprising result if we keep in mind that the Euro area became a factual currency union with a unique and centrally determined monetary policy only 7 years ago, on 1st January 1999, so that for a long interval of the estimated sample the estimated coefficients reflect only the theoretical values of an artificial economy. Nonetheless, the US and the Euro area economies seem to share more common characteristics than is commonly believed, especially concerning the wage inflation reaction to labor market developments, once a proxy for the rate of short-term unemployed rather than the aggregate unemployment rate is taken into account.

Despite the fact that more empirical work is needed to check for the model's parameter stability, we think, given the empirical results discussed in this chapter, that our framework (which may be called a disequilibrium approach to business cycle modeling of mature Keynesian type) provides an interesting alternative to the

DSGE framework for the study of monetary policy and inflation dynamics. As other researchers such as Zarnowitz (1999), we also stress the message that the dynamic interaction of many traditional macroeconomic building blocks, which might take place even without an explicit theoretical "microfoundation," should be considered by economists to really understand the high complexity of modern economies.

In Appendix D to this chapter we briefly indicate some further characteristics of the economic evolution that has taken place in the US economy after World War II. They suggest that this evolution has been characterized by the interaction of (at least) two cycle generators, the Keynesian trade cycle mechanism, bringing about business fluctuations of approximately 8 years length, and the Goodwin distributive cycle mechanism, which seems to have generated just one cycle of about 50 years length in this period. We stress that this confirms the analysis we have conducted in Part II of the book (and extended in its Part III) in a striking way. However, the outcome on the long-phased cycle described in Appendix D needs, of course, more detailed investigation in future research. For the time being we just take it as a further characteristic of the working of dissent-driven capitalism, a form of capitalism that the next chapter will question from the perspective of socio-economic reproduction processes that are sustainable in the long-run in a democratic society. On this basis, Chap. 10 will therefore provide an alternative to this form of capitalism by modeling in detail what is now called a flexicurity economy in the literature.

Summing up, our general conclusion is that the here proposed DAD-DAS framework does not only overcome the anomalies of the old Neoclassical Synthesis, but also provides a coherent alternative to its new stage, the New Keynesian theory of the business cycle, as, for example, sketched in Galí (2000). Our alternative to this approach to macrodynamics is based on disequilibrium in the market for goods and labor, on sluggish adjustment of prices as well as wages in view of these disequilibria and on myopic perfect foresight interacting with a medium-run inflationary climate expression. The rich array of possible dynamic outcomes based on the central feedback channels of our model (somewhat restricted when parameter estimates are taken into account) provides a sound basis for further generalizations. Some of these generalizations have already been considered in Chiarella, Flaschel, Groh, and Semmler (2000), Chiarella, Flaschel, and Franke (2005), and Flaschel, Groh, Proaño, and Semmler (2008).

Appendix A: 4D Feedback-Guided Stability Analysis

In this section we illustrate a method to prove local asymptotic stability of the interior steady state of the dynamical system given by (9.10)–(9.13) (with (9.7) inserted wherever needed) through partial considerations from the feedback chains that characterize this empirically oriented baseline model of Keynesian dynamics. The Jacobian of the 4D dynamic system, calculated at its interior steady state, is

$$J = \begin{pmatrix} - & \pm & 0 & 0 \\ \pm & + & - & + \\ \pm & + & - & + \\ \pm & + & 0 & 0 \end{pmatrix}.$$

Since the model is an extension of the standard AS-AD growth model, we know from the literature that the real rate of interest, first analyzed by formal methods in Tobin (1975) (see also Groth (1992)) typically affects, in a negative manner, the dynamics of the economic activity (J_{23}). Additionally, there is the activity stimulating (partial) effect of increases in the rate of inflation (as part of the real rate of interest channel) that may lead to accelerating inflation under appropriate conditions (J_{24}). This transmission mechanism, known as the Mundell effect, is the stronger the faster the inflationary climate adjusts to the present level of price inflation, since we have a positive influence of this climate variable both on price as well as on wage inflation and from there on rates of employment of both capital and labor. Concerning the Keynes effect, because of our use of a Taylor rule in the place of the conventional LM curve, it is here implemented in a more direct way towards a stabilization of the economy (coupling nominal interest rates directly with the rate of price inflation) and it works the stronger, the larger the choice of the parameters γ_{ip}, γ_{iu}.

As it is formulated, the theoretical model also features further potentially (at least partially) destabilizing feedback mechanisms due to the Mundell-effect and the Rose-effect in the dynamics of the goods-market and the opposing Blanchard–Katz error correction terms in the reduced form price Phillips curve. There is first of all J_{12}, see (9.10), the still undetermined influence of the output gap (the rate of capacity utilization) on the labor share, which depends on the signs and values of the parameter estimates of the two structural Phillips curves, and therefore on the cross-over expectations formation of the economic agents. In the second place, see (9.11), we have J_{21}, the ambiguous influence of the labor share on (the dynamics of) the rate of capacity utilization, which should be a negative one if investment is more responsive than consumption to real wage changes and a positive one in the opposite case. Concerning also the effects of the labor share on capacity utilization, we have aggregate price inflation determined by the reduced form price Phillips curve given by (9.7). Thus there is an additional, though ambiguous channel through which the labor share affects the dynamics of the output gap, on the one hand, and the inflationary climate of the economy (J_{41}) through (9.13) on the other hand. Mundell-type, Rose-type, and Blanchard–Katz error-correction feedback channels therefore make the dynamics indeterminate on the theoretical level.

The feedback channels just discussed will be the focus of interest in the following stability analysis of our D(isequilibrium)AS-D(isequilibrium)AD dynamics. We have employed reduced-form expressions in the above system of differential equations whenever possible. We have thereby obtained a dynamical system in four state variables that is in a natural or intrinsic way nonlinear (due to its reliance on growth rate formulations). We note furthermore that there are many items that reappear in various equations, or are similar to each other, implying that stability analysis can exploit a variety of linear dependencies in the calculation of the conditions for local asymptotic stability. A rigorous proof of the local asymptotic stability for the original model version and its loss by way of Hopf bifurcations can be found in Asada, Chen, Chiarella, and Flaschel (2006).

To focus on the interrelation between the wage-price and the output gap dynamics, we make use of the following proposition.

Proposition A1.

Assume that the parameters β_{π^c}, β_{wv}, β_{pv}, as well as g_z are not only close to zero but in fact equal to zero. This decouples the dynamics of π^c from the rest of the system and the system becomes 3D. Assume furthermore that the partial derivative of the second law of motion J_{22} depends negatively on v, and that $(1-\kappa_p)\beta_{we} > (1-\kappa_w)\beta_u$ holds. Then, the interior steady state of the implied 3D dynamical system

$$\hat{v} = \kappa[(1-\kappa_{pw})(\beta_{we}(e(u)-e_o)) - (1-\kappa_{wp})(\beta_{pu}(u-u_o))], \tag{9.15}$$

$$\hat{u} = -\alpha_u(u-u_o) - \alpha_v(v-v_o) - \alpha_r((i-\hat{p}) - (i_o-\pi_o)), \tag{9.16}$$

$$\dot{i} = -\alpha_i(i-i_o) + \gamma_{ip}(\hat{p}-\pi_o) + \gamma_{iu}(u-u_o), \tag{9.17}$$

is locally asymptotically stable.

Sketch of proof. In the considered situation we have for the Jacobian of the reduced dynamics at the steady state:

$$J = \begin{pmatrix} - & + & 0 \\ - & - & - \\ 0 & + & - \end{pmatrix}.$$

According to the Routh–Hurwitz stability conditions for the characteristic polynomial of the considered 3D dynamical system, asymptotic local stability of a steady state is fulfilled when

$$a_i > 0, \quad i = 1,2,3 \quad \text{and} \quad a_1 a_2 - a_3 > 0,$$

where $a_1 = -\text{trace}(J)$, $a_2 = \sum_{k=1}^{3} J_k$ with

$$J_1 = \begin{vmatrix} J_{22} & J_{23} \\ J_{32} & J_{33} \end{vmatrix}, J_2 = \begin{vmatrix} J_{11} & J_{13} \\ J_{31} & J_{33} \end{vmatrix}, J_3 = \begin{vmatrix} J_{11} & J_{12} \\ J_{21} & J_{22} \end{vmatrix},$$

and $a_3 = -\det(J)$. The determinant of this Jacobian is obviously negative if the parameter γ_i is chosen sufficiently small. The sum of the minors of order 2: a_2 is unambiguously positive. The validity of the full set of Routh–Hurwitz conditions then easily follows, since trace $J = -a_1$ is obviously negative. ■

Proposition A2.

Assume now that the parameter β_{π_c} is positive, but chosen sufficiently small, while the error correction parameters β_{wv} and β_{pw} are still kept at zero. Assume furthermore that α_r is sufficiently small, and that $\gamma_{ip} > 1$. Then, the interior steady state of the resulting 4D dynamical system (where the state variable π^c is now included)

$$\hat{v} = \kappa[(1-\kappa_{pw})(\beta_{we}(e(u)-e_o)) - (1-\kappa_{wp})(\beta_{pu}(u-u_o))], \tag{9.18}$$
$$\hat{u} = -\alpha_u(u-u_o) - \alpha_v(v-v_o) - \alpha_i((i-\hat{p})-(i_o-\pi_o)), \tag{9.19}$$
$$\dot{i} = -\alpha_i(i-i_o) + \gamma_{ip}(\hat{p}-\pi_o) + \gamma_{iu}(u-u_o), \tag{9.20}$$
$$\dot{\pi}^c = \beta_{\pi^c}(\hat{p}-\pi^c) \tag{9.21}$$

is locally asymptotically stable.

Sketch of proof. Under the mentioned stated assumptions, the Jacobian of the 4D system is equal to

$$J = \begin{pmatrix} - & + & 0 & 0 \\ - & - & - & + \\ 0 & + & - & + \\ 0 & + & 0 & 0 \end{pmatrix}.$$

We can clearly see that J_{34} describes the reaction of the nominal interest rate with respect to inflation. According to the Taylor (1993) principle, as long as $\gamma_{ip} > 1$, monetary policy stabilizes the economy. Together with sufficiently small β_{π^c} and α_r, the incorporation of the inflationary climate as a state variable in the dynamical system does not disturb the local stability properties of the system. ■

Summing up, we can state that a weak Mundell effect, the neglect of Blanchard–Katz error correction terms, a negative dependence of aggregate demand on real wages, coupled with higher nominal wage than price level flexibility, and a Taylor rule that stresses inflation targeting therefore are here (for example) the basic ingredients that allow for the proof of local asymptotic stability of the interior steady state of the dynamics (9.10)–(9.13). We expect, however, that indeed a variety of other and also more general situations of convergent dynamics can be found, but have to leave this issue here for future research and also numerical simulations of the model.

Appendix B: Wage Dynamics: Theoretical Foundation

This subsection builds on the paper by Blanchard and Katz (1999) and briefly summarizes their theoretical motivation of a money-wage Phillips curve, which is closely related to our dynamic wage equation.[23] Blanchard and Katz assume – following the suggestions of standard models of wage setting – that real wage expectations of workers, $\omega^e = w_t - p_t^e$, are basically determined by the reservation wage, $\bar{\omega}_t$, current labor productivity, $y_t - l_t^d$, and the rate of unemployment, e_t:[24]

$$\omega_t^e = \theta\bar{\omega}_t + (1-\theta)(y_t - l_t^d) - \beta_w e_t.$$

[23] In this section, lower case letters (including w and p) indicate logarithms.

[24] Level magnitudes are expressed in logarithms here and represented by lowercase letters.

Expected real wages are thus a Cobb–Douglas average of the reservation wage and output per worker, but are departing from this normal level of expectations by the state of the demand pressure on the labor market. The reservation wage in turn is determined as a Cobb–Douglas average of past real wages, $\omega_{t-1} = w_{t-1} - p_{t-1}$, and current labor productivity, augmented by a factor $a < 0$:

$$\bar{\omega}_t = a + \lambda\omega_{t-1} + (1-\lambda)(y_t - l_t^d).$$

Inserting the second into the first equation results in

$$\omega_t^e = \theta a + \theta\lambda\omega_{t-1} + (1-\theta\lambda)(y_t - l_t^d) - \beta_w e_t,$$

which gives after some rearrangements

$$\begin{aligned}\Delta w_t &= p_t^e - p_{t-1} + \theta a - (1-\theta\lambda)[(w_{t-1} - p_{t-1}) - (y_t - l_t^d)] - \beta_w e_t \\ &= \Delta p_t^e + \theta a - (1-\theta\lambda)v_{t-1} + (1-\theta\lambda)(\Delta y_t - \Delta l_t^d) - \beta_w e_t\end{aligned}$$

where Δp_t^e denotes the expected rate of inflation, v_{t-1} the past (log) wage share, and $\Delta y_t - \Delta l_t^d$ the current growth rate of labor productivity. This is the growth law for nominal wages that flows from the theoretical models referred to in Blanchard and Katz (1999, p. 70).

In this chapter, we proposed to operationalize this theoretical approach to money-wage inflation by replacing the short-run cost push term Δp_t^e by the weighted average $\kappa_w \Delta p_t^e + (1-\kappa_w)\pi_t$, where Δp_t^e is determined by myopic perfect foresight. Thus, temporary changes in the correctly anticipated rate of inflation do not have full impact on temporary wage inflation, which is also driven by lagged inflation rates via the inflationary climate variable π_{ct}. Adding inertia to the theory of wage inflation introduced a distinction between the temporary and persistent cost effects to this equation. Furthermore, we have that $\Delta y_t - \Delta l_t^d = \hat{z}_t$ due to the assumed fixed proportions technology. Altogether, we end up with an equation for wage inflation of the type presented in Sect. 9.3.2, though now with a specific interpretation of the model's parameters from the perspective of efficiency wage or bargaining models.[25]

Appendix C: Price Dynamics: Theoretical Foundation

We here follow again Blanchard and Katz (1999, Sect. IV) and start from the assumption of normal cost pricing, here under the additional assumption of our

[25] Note that the parameter in front of v_{t-1} can now not be interpreted as a speed of adjustment coefficient. Note furthermore that Blanchard and Katz (1999) assume that, in the steady state, the wage share is determined by the firms' markup $\bar{\mu}$ to be discussed in the next appendix. Therefore, the NAIRU can be determined endogenously on the labor market by $\bar{e} = \beta_w^{-1}\left[\theta a - (1-\theta\lambda)\bar{\mu} - \theta\lambda(\Delta y_t - \Delta l_t^d)\right]$. The NAIRU of their model therefore depends on both labor and goods market characteristics in contrast to the NAIRU levels for labor and capital employed in our approach.

chapter of fixed proportions in production and of Harrod neutral technological change. We therefore consider as rule for normal prices:

$$p_t = \mu_t + w_t + l_t^d - y_t, \quad \text{i.e.,} \quad \Delta p_t = \Delta \mu_t + \Delta w_t - \hat{z}_t,$$

where μ_t represents a markup on the unit wage costs of firms and where again myopic perfect foresight, here with respect to wage setting, is assumed. We assume, furthermore, that the markup is variable and responding to the demand pressure in the market for goods $\bar{u} - u_t$, depending in addition negatively on the current level of the markup μ_t in its deviation from the normal level $\bar{\mu}$. Firms therefore depart from their normal cost pricing rule according to the state of demand on the market for goods, and this the stronger, the lower the level of the currently prevailing markup has been (markup smoothing). For sake of concreteness let us here assume that the following behavioral relationship holds:

$$\Delta \mu_t = \beta_p(\bar{u} - u_{t-1}) + \gamma(\bar{\mu} - \mu_{t-1}),$$

where $\gamma > 0$. Inserted into the formula for price inflation this in sum gives

$$\Delta p_t = \beta_p(\bar{u} - u_{t-1}) + \gamma(\bar{\mu} - \mu_{t-1}) + (\Delta w_t - \hat{z}_t).$$

In terms of the logged wage share $v_t = -\mu_t$, we then get

$$\Delta p_t = \beta_p(\bar{u} - u_{t-1}) + \gamma(v_{t-1} - \bar{v}) + (\Delta w_t - \hat{z}_t).$$

As in the preceding subsection of the chapter, we again add persistence to the cost pressure term $\Delta w_t - \hat{z}_t$ now in the price Phillips curve in the form of the inflationary climate expression π_c and thereby obtain in sum the price inflation equation of this chapter.

Appendix D: Business and Long Phase Cycles in Inflation and Income Distribution

Econometric studies often investigate on the methodological level as well as in empirical research the problem of how to separate the business cycle from the trend in important macroeconomic time series. Yet, economic growth theory in its advanced form provides us with insights on which economic ratios may exhibit a secular trend (like capital intensity when not measured in efficiency units) and which ones will not (like the output-capital ratio or the rate of employment as two measures of macroeconomic factor utilization). In contrast to a variety of econometric studies, macrodynamic growth theory therefore generally uses appropriate ratios or growth rates in its analytical investigations and there in particular the ones that allow for the determination of steady state positions and which therefore should not exhibit a trend in the very long run when the macrodynamic theory is formulated in a sufficiently general way.

In using the methodology developed in Kauermann, Teuber, and Flaschel (2008) – and their illustrations in their empirical appendix – we will in fact concentrate on secularly trendless magnitudes, namely the employment rate on the external labor market, the wage share in national income, and the inflation rate (here of producers' prices). There are a variety of smaller as well as larger macrodynamic models in the tradition of Goodwin (1967), which show the existence of persistent cycles in the interaction between the employment rate and the wage share, on the one hand, and the employment rate and the inflation rate, on the other hand, which tend to long phased when simple constant parameter estimates are used for their numerical investigation. In these models the ordinary business cycle fluctuations must therefore be explained by something else, namely by systematic variations in the parameters of the model, which then add cycles of period lengths of about 8 years to the 50 years cycles these models are generating when used with average or constant parameter values.

We have considered in Flaschel, Kauermann, and Teuber (2005) models of the Friedman unemployment/inflation cycle and the Goodwin employment/income distribution cycle in isolation as well as in their direct interaction or more indirect interactions in a five-dimensional model of goods market, labor market, and interest rate dynamics, and have calculated numerically the long phase cycles these models generate under plausible parameter values. We take from these models the working hypothesis that there should be long phase cycles interacting with business cycles in the data as far as employment, income distribution, and inflation is concerned. The method developed in Kauermann, Teuber, and Flaschel (2008) now in fact allows us to test this hypothesis in a way much more refined then just by using Hodrick–Prescott filters with an arbitrarily given λ parameter. Moreover, it can do this by using an econometric approach that is close in spirit to the two-dimensional phase plots of the employment – inflation cycle and the employment – income distribution cycle of the literature on the Friedman inflation cycle and the Goodwin growth cycle, see Flaschel, Kauermann, and Teuber (2005) for details.

Applying the technique developed in Kauermann, Teuber, and Flaschel (2008) then gives rise to the collection of time series and phase plots shown in Figs. D1 and D2 (where the long cycle is not yet shown as a phase plot). With respect to inflation dynamics in Fig. D1, we see that the unemployment rate is leading compared to the inflation rate in the long phase cycle (the solid lines in the two time series plots top-left), since it, for example, starts rising much before inflation starts falling again. In the middle of the bottom figures (showing the radius) we see, moreover, that there are approximately six business cycles surrounding these long phase cycles, in line with what is shown to hold for the US economy in Chiarella, Flaschel, and Franke (2005) and other work. The figure bottom-right shows in addition the anti-clockwise rotation of the long phase cycle is by and large also characterizing the business cycles surrounding it (shown as phase plots top-right), though there are exceptions to this rule (periods at the beginning and the end of the considered time span), see also the figure top-right in this regard.[26] We note that we follow the

[26] For the details of this econometric estimation approach (using polar coordinates) we refer the reader to Kauermann, Teuber, and Flaschel (2008).

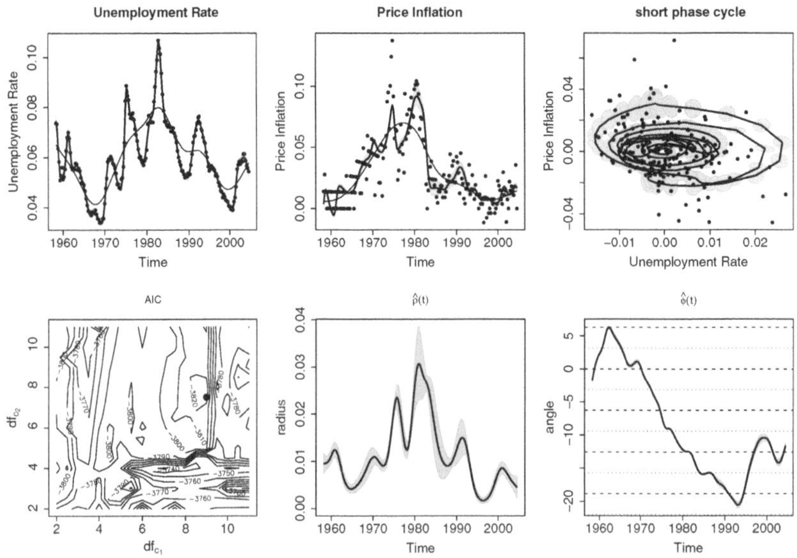

Fig. D1 Short phase and long phase inflation cycles

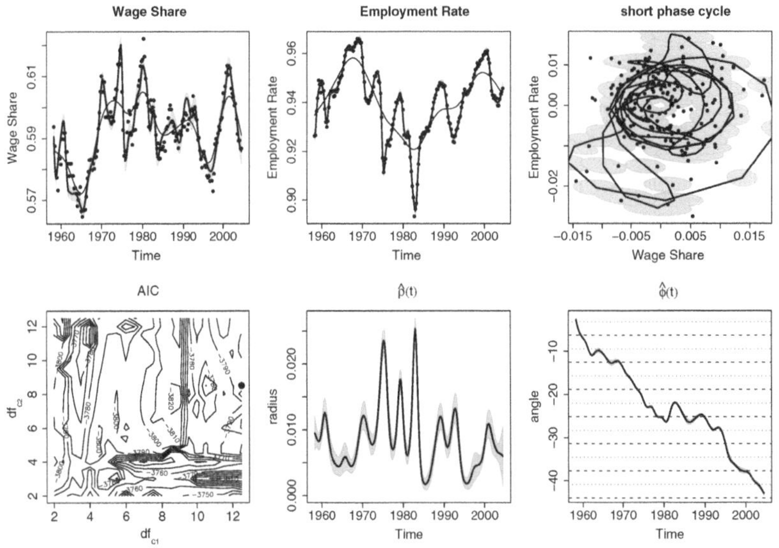

Fig. D2 Short phase and long phase income distribution cycles

tradition here that uses the unemployment rate in place of the employment rate on the horizontal axis (the latter would give rise to an anti-clockwise orientation of the business and the long phase cycles shown in these figures and Fig. D3). Figure D3 in the present section shows in addition for better visibility the long-phase cycle in isolation and it indicates that indeed 50 years of data are needed to get the indication

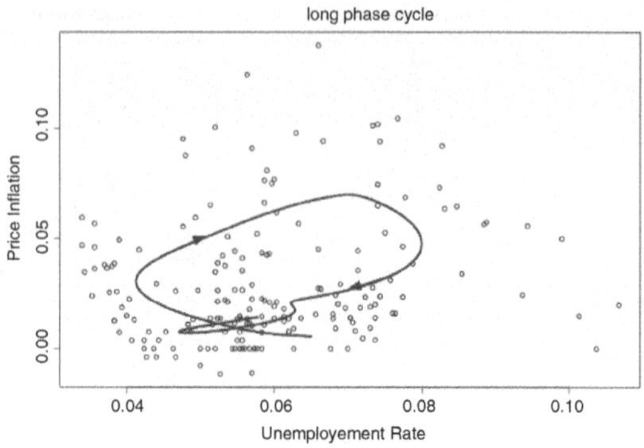

Fig. D3 The long phase inflation cycle

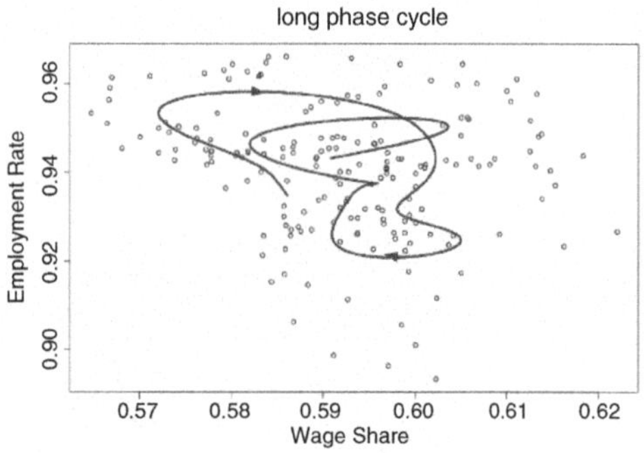

Fig. D4 The long phase income distribution cycle[27]

of the existence of such a cycle. We observe in Fig. D3 periods where unemployment and inflation are both rising (i.e., where stagflation occurs) and also periods where the opposite takes place and therefore falling unemployment rates do not lead to rising inflation rates immediately.

We stress again that our extraction of the business cycle component as shown in Fig. 5 in Kauermann, Teuber, and Flaschel (2008) through a phase as well as a radius plot is an integral part of our treatment of the long phase evolution of the economy.

With respect to the other long phase cycle model, the Goodwin (1967) growth cycle model, we have in Fig. D2 the following situation. As far as the evolution of the wage share, shown top-left, is concerned we have now more volatility as was the case with the inflation rate. This may be due to the involvement of labor productivity as constituent part of the definition of the wage share. Nevertheless, one can see a single long phase cycle in the solid line shown in the time series presentation of the wage share. Again, the employment rate is leading with respect to this long phase cycle in the wage share. We know from Goodwin (1967) and the numerous articles that followed his approach that the interaction of the employment rate with

[27] See Flaschel, Tavani, Teuber, and Taylor (2008) for a detailed motivation of the specific shape of this cycle.

the wage share is generating a clockwise motion in the v, e phase space, see Flaschel, Kauermann, and Teuber (2005) for details. In Fig. D2 we can in this regard only see that the cycles of business cycle frequency are also moving in a clockwise fashion as it is suggested by the again basically downward sloping angle line bottom-right. To the right of this figure we again see (if minor cycles are neglected) now by and large seven business cycles overlaid over the long phase cycles as they are also shown in the figure top-right.

Figures D3 and D4 finally show the long phase cycle in isolation (for the inflation as well as for the wage share dynamics). We see with respect to the latter indeed a Goodwin cycle that is nearly closed (and thus approximately of 50 years length), moving clockwise as suggested by the simple Goodwin (1967) growth cycle model. This cycle can of course be related to the one shown for the interaction of the inflation rate with the unemployment rate, if inflation dynamics is added to the Goodwin growth cycle framework (as described in the Appendices B and C).

We conclude that the method developed in Kauermann, Teuber, and Flaschel (2008) provides an important approach to the separation of long-phased cycles – which describe the evolution from high-to-low inflation regimes and from high-to-low wage share regimes – from cycles of business cycle frequency. This method therefore allows in a distinct way the discussion of long waves in inflation and income distribution in modern market economies after World War II.

Chapter 10
Modeling Our Future: Flexicurity Capitalism

10.1 From Marx's Law of Capitalist Accumulation to Schumpeter's Competitive Socialism and Beyond

This chapter[1] starts from the hypothesis that Goodwin's (1967) Classical Growth Cycle, modeling the Marxian Reserve Army Mechanism, does not represent a process of social reproduction that can be considered as adequate and sustainable in a social and democratic society in the long-run. The chapter derives on this background a basic macrodynamic framework where this form of cyclical growth and economic reproduction of capitalism is overcome by an employer of "first" resort, added to an economic reproduction process that is highly competitive and flexible and thus not of the type of the past Eastern socialism. Instead, there is high capital and labor mobility (concerning "hiring" and "firing," in particular), and thus flexibility, where fluctuations of employment in this first labor market of the economy (the private sector) are made socially acceptable through the security aspect of the flexicurity concept, that is, by a second labor market where all remaining workers (and even pensioners) find meaningful occupation. The resulting model of flexicurity capitalism with its detailed transfer payment schemes is in its essence comparable to the flexicurity models developed for the Nordic welfare states and Denmark in particular.

We show that this economy exhibits a balanced growth path that is globally attracting. We also show that credit financed investment, and thus more flexible investment behavior, can be easily added without disturbing the prevailing situation of stable full capacity growth. We do not yet get, however, demand- but only supply-driven business fluctuations in such an environment with both factors of production always fully employed. This combines flexible factor adjustments in the

[1] This chapter is based on Flaschel, Greiner, and Luchtenberg (2008). Flexicurity capitalism, skill formation, and the equal opportunity principle. Bielefeld: CEM working paper. In this chapter we use as notation w for nominal wages, ω for real wages, u for the rate of capacity utilization, e for the rate of employment, v for the wage share, z for labor productivity, y for the output-capital ratio, and finally i for the rate of interest.

P. Flaschel, *The Macrodynamics of Capitalism: Elements for a Synthesis of Marx, Keynes and Schumpeter, Second Edition*, private sector with high employment security for the labor force and shows that the flexicurity variety of a capitalist economy, protected by the government, can work in a fairly balanced manner.

A similar framework for the modeling of flexicurity capitalism is also investigated in Flaschel, Greiner, Luchtenberg, and Nell (2008). We here go beyond this modeling by the consideration of two types of workers in the first (and the public) labor market: skilled and high-skilled ones (as baseline representation of a full set of skill differentials). This makes the model comparable to the discussion of unskilled vs. skilled labor under contemporaneous capitalism and is intended to show that there is no systematic need for unskilled labor in a model of flexicurity growth. We do not deny, however, that there may also exist an employer of last resort (in addition to the employer of first resort) in such a framework, since there may always exist some people that are unwilling or incapable for providing work within the schemes set up in this model. Yet, the primary task of the schooling system is to provide equal opportunities for all school students in primary and secondary education and to minimize thereby the number of people who by one reason or another do not contribute to labor markets of the flexicurity model though illness or refusal may occur after school. The chapter here only considers the situation of where everybody passes successfully through the schooling system (as investigated in its components and environment in a later section of the chapter) and thus leaves the consideration of an employer of last resort to future research. It, however, adds a tertiary education sector to the model where access is limited and that is responsible for the education of high-skilled workers of the model.

Solow's (1956) famous growth model is to a certain degree also of the flexicurity type, since competitive firms are always operating there on their profit-maximizing activity level and since the labor market is assumed to always guarantee full employment. We thus have employment flexibility again coupled with wage income "security," through the assumed behavior of firms and through the assumption of perfectly flexible money wages (which may give rise to wage income fluctuations). The monetarist critique of Keynesianism and recent work by Blanchard and Katz (1999) and others suggest, however, a wage Phillips curve which, when, for example, coupled with the assumption of myopic perfect foresight regarding the price inflation rate, implies a real wage Phillips curve where the growth rate of real wages depends positively on the employment rate and negatively on the level of the real wage rate. Adding such empirically supported real wage rigidity to the Solow model then gives rise to two laws of motion, now for labor intensity and the real wage, a dynamical system that approaches the situation of the overshooting Goodwin growth cycle mechanism if factor substitution in production is sufficiently inelastic and if the Blanchard and Katz (1999) real wage error correction term in the Phillips curve is sufficiently weak. Solow's growth model thus becomes thereby a variant of the Classical distributive growth cycle and its overshooting reserve army mechanism, the adequacy of which for a democratic society is questioned in this chapter. An empirical example of what is meant by this latter statement is provided by Fig. 10.1.

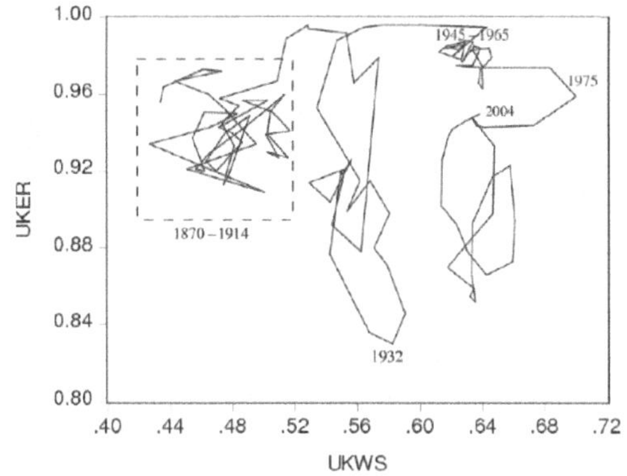

Fig. 10.1 UK distributive cycles 1870–2004: *WS* wage share, *ER* employ.t rate

The important insight that can be obtained from Fig. 10.1 for the UK 1855–1965 is that the Goodwin cycle must have been significantly shorter before 1914 (with larger fluctuations in employment during each business cycle), and that there has been a major change in it after 1945. This may be explained by significant changes in the adjustment processes of market economies for these two periods: primarily price adjustment before 1914 and primarily quantity adjustments after 1945. Based on data until 1965 one could have expected that the growth cycle had become obsolete (and maybe also the business cycle as it was claimed in the late 1960s). Yet, extended by the data shown in Fig. 1, taken from Groth and Madsen (2007), it is now obvious that nothing of this sort took place in the UK economy. In fact, we see in Fig. 10.1 two periods of excessive over-employment (in the language of the theory of the NAIRU), which were followed by periods of dramatic underemployment, both started by periods of the more or less pronounced occurrence of stagflation.

Generating order and economic viability in market economies by large swings in the unemployment rate (mass unemployment with human degradation of part of the families that form the society), as shown above and as described and analyzed in detail in Marx (1954, Chap. 23), is one way to make capitalism work, but it must surely be critically reflected with respect to its social consequences (social segmentation or even social class clashes). Such a reproduction mechanism is not compatible with an educated and democratic society in the long-run, as we shall describe it in this chapter, which is supposed to provide equal opportunities to all of its citizens.

This situation must therefore be contrasted with an alternative social structure of accumulation that allows to combine the situation of a highly competitive market economy with a human rights bill that includes the right (and the obligation) to work and to get income from this work that at the least supports basic needs and basic happiness.

Criticizing the at his time existing Eastern state socialism from the viewpoint of immaturity, Schumpeter (1942) developed a concept of socialism for countries in the state of maturity that can be characterized as competitive socialism built on foundations erected unconsciously through the big enterprises created by the Rockefeller, the Vanderbilts, and other famous dynasties in the Western industrialized countries. In Part II of his book, Schumpeter discusses the question of whether this type of socialism can work, how the corresponding socialist blueprints should look like, and to what extent they are superior to the capitalist mark II blueprints that Schumpeter conceived as having made obsolescent the entrepreneurial functioning of the capitalism mark I, the dynamic entrepreneur, and the process of creative destruction conducted by this leading form of an economic agent. Monopolistic practices, vanishing investment opportunities, and growing hostility in the social structure of capitalism where part of the reasons that characterized the decomposition of capitalism in his analysis of capitalism, socialism, and democracy. Against this scenery he described the superiority of the socialist blueprint of Western competitive type, the transition to this form of social structure of accumulation, and the comparative efficiency of such economies. In a separate chapter he discusses the human element in this type of economy, the problem of work organization, and the integration of bourgeois forms of management under capitalism into this type of socialism and the incentive problems this creates for the behavior of these economic agents.

The central message of Schumpeter's (1942) work on "Capitalism, Socialism and Democracy" is that Socialism is created out of Western capitalist economies, and not on the basis of (the now past) Eastern type of socialism (which he characterized as "the case of premature adoption of the principle of socialism," p. 223). Instead, socialism had to be competitively organized through large production units and their efficient – though bureaucratic – management, a form of management that is developed out of the principles used under capitalism in the efficient conduct of large (internationally oriented) enterprises. Schumpeter viewed his type of socialism as culturally indeterminate, but then discusses extensively the possibility of democracy under socialism, organized as dynamic competition for political leadership under majority voting, leading to specific rules for a strong government. It is one of the great contributions of Schumpeter's (1942) book to not only have initiated a new concept of socialism, but also of having established a new type of democracy theory and its principles under a socialist type of accumulation structure.

After World War II the discussion of how to incorporate welfare principles in the conduct of existing capitalist economies has, however, become more or less the focus of interest, formulated as "social market economy" by Ludwig Erhard in Germany, in particular. The rise of the welfare state was thus the central topic, at least in European market economies, by which they responded to the strengthened influence of the Eastern socialist economies on world politics and on the evolution of socialism in various parts of the world. Types of welfare states were, for example, discussed in detail in Esping-Anderson's (1990) "The Three Worlds of Welfare Capitalism" among others. But Kalecki (1943) already pointed to limitations in the evolution of the welfare state and its full employment concept in his essay on the "Political aspects of full employment." Deregulation principles and the fall of the welfare indeed took place in Western market economies after the stagflationary period of the 1970s in a more or less intensive way, with the gradual fall of the welfare state often being associated with an insufficient recovery from the inflationary episodes and their implication for unemployment after World War II.

Yet, labor market deregulation theories and policy proposals have meanwhile also created a situation where questions are raised concerning the social consequences of such policies when they are conducted a "cold turkey" strategies as they are often suggested by neoclassical mainstream economists. Social degradation, social segmentation processes, and the progressive evolution of social conflicts based on them may indeed be incompatible with the proper conduct of democracy in the Western type of economies where labor market deregulation processes and the cutback of the welfare state occurred to a significant degree – at least in the longer-run. "Workfare" has therefore become one of the keywords that attempts to combine efficient labor market performance with welfare principles, see, for example, Vis (2007) on "States of welfare or states of workfare? Welfare state restructuring in 16 capitalist democracies, 1985–2002."

In this chapter we, however, favor another concept that attempts to overcome the deficiencies of the purely economically oriented process of labor market deregulations, the concept of flexicurity capitalism (in place of the Schumpeterian concept of competitive socialism, to which it is in fact not related in the literature and in the current numerous political discussions of flexicurity principles), see, for example, the discussion "Towards Common Principles of Flexicurity – Council Conclusions" conducted by the Council (Employment, Social Policy, Health, and Consumer Affaires) of the European Union.

The Danish flexicurity discussion may provide a typical example on the way to such an alternative, see, for example, the newsletter "Future Watch, October 2006: Flexicurity Denmark-Style" of the Center for Strategic and International Studies (CSIS). However, the discussion led so far lacks rigorous and formal model building of the principles, the economic structure, and the dynamics of flexicurity capitalism. To build a model of the reproduction schemes of this future type of an economy needs a presentation of its system of national accounts and the behavior of economic agents within such a system. Moreover, the adjustment processes on the market for labor and for goods as well as the functioning of financial markets in such an economy needs detailed investigations. Analysis of this type is surely at best in its state of infancy. The present chapter intends to contribute to such an analysis and does so on the background of the models of capitalism we have developed in this book, in particular, concerning Marx's general law of capitalist accumulation. In modeling our future in this way we hope to show that there is a variety of capitalism that not only pays respect to the Human Rights, in particular, their article 23,[2] but that is compatible with the evolution of democracy in the long-run.

By contrast, a laissez-faire capitalistic society that ruins family structures to a considerable degree (through alienated work, degrading unemployment, and education- and value-decomposing visual media) cannot be made compatible with a democratic society in the long-run, since it produces conflicts that may range from social segmentation to class conflicts, racial clashes, and more. We argue in this chapter that stable balanced reproduction is possible under a socially regime of flexicurity capitalism that is in addition backed by reflected educational principles concerning skill formation, equal opportunities, and citizenship education in a democratic society.

The abstract vision of a new reproduction scheme of capitalism as it is formulated in this chapter can be compared – as already indicated in part – with work of Quesnay, Marx, Schumpeter, and Keynes. It may be considered as radical and fundamental (but also as infeasible) as Quesnay's design of the Tableau Économique for the French economy, an ideal system where the productive sector was at the center of interest and all taxes were paid out of rent (by the landlords). It may be compared with Marx's reproduction schemes, in Capital Volume II, for a capitalist economy of his times (not considered feasible under capitalism by him). It may also be compared with Schumpeter's vision in his work on Capitalism, Socialism, and Democracy, where he claimed that socialism would be the consequence of Western type capitalism (as created by the Rockefeller and other industrial dynasties) and not the result of the Eastern socialism that existed at his times. It may finally also be compared with the Social Philosophy of Keynes' General Theory and his discussion of the means by which the trade cycle of conventional Western capitalism might be tamed. All these aspects may play a role in the understanding and the appraisal of the model of flexicurity capitalism that is designed in this chapter.

In Sect. 2 we consider the accounts of such an economy with particular emphasis on the distinction between skilled and high-skilled workers both in the private and the public sector. Section 3 considers the stability of such an economy, where wages dynamic is determined by high-skilled workers according to a Blanchard and Katz type Phillips curve and where labor intensity growth is determined by realized profits. Section 4 considers stylized presentations of the schooling system for Finland as an existing example as well as our hypothetical flexicurity model. In Sect. 5 such systems are considered in more detail and from the perspective of the equal opportunity principle and the life-long learning hypothesis. In Sect. 6 we discuss the role of real credits in such an economy. This discussion is extended to a treatment of nominal financial assets and resulting Keynesian business cycle fluctuations in Sect. 7. Section 8 reconsiders the Schumpeterian dynamic entrepreneur in the framework of flexicurity capitalism and also other forms of firm behavior. Section 9 concludes the chapter.

[2] See United Nations (1998, article 23): Universal Declaration of Human Rights, 1948 (http://www.un.org/Overview/rights.html).

10.2 Flexicurity: A Spectre is Haunting Europe

> The concept of flexicurity attempts to find a balance between flexibility for employers (and employees) and security for employees. The Commissions 1997 Green Paper on Partnership for a new organisation of work stressed the importance of both flexibility and security to competitiveness and the modernisation of work organisation. The idea also features prominently in the "adaptability pillar" of the EU employment guidelines, where "the social partners are invited to negotiate at all appropriate levels agreements to modernise the organisation of work, including flexible working arrangements, with the aim of making undertakings productive and competitive and achieving the required balance between flexibility and security." This "balance" is also consistently referred to in the Commissions Social Policy Agenda 2000–2005 (COM (2000) 379 final, Brussels, 28 June 2000).[3]

We now design, as a rigorous modeling proposal for the flexicurity debate in Europe and as an alternative to the Goodwin growth cycle representation of capitalism, a model of economic growth that rests in place of overaccumulation (in the prosperity phase) and mass unemployment (in the stagnant phase) on a second labor market, which through its institutional setup guarantees full employment in its interaction with the first labor market, the employment in the industrial sector of the economy, which is modeled as highly flexible and competitive. This model of flexicurity capitalism extends the approach of Flaschel et al. (2008) towards a treatment of heterogeneous skills and the skill formation processes this requires in an advanced macroeconomy.

In the basic framework we are considering an economy where the workforce (and all of its components) are growing with a given natural rate n. We first consider the sector of firms of the economy (which is indexed by 1):

Firms

Production and Income Account:

Uses	Resources
δK	δK
$\omega_{1a}L^{\mathrm{d}}_{1a}$, $L^{\mathrm{d}}_{1a} = Y^{\mathrm{p}}/z$, $\hat{z} = \bar{m}$	$C_1 + C_2 + C_r$
$\omega_{1b}L^{\mathrm{d}}_{1b}$, $L^{\mathrm{d}}_{1b} = Y^{\mathrm{p}}/z$, $\omega_{1b} = \alpha_{1b}\omega_{1a}$	G
$\Pi \quad (=Y^f)$	$I \quad (=Y^f)$
$\delta_1 R + \dot{R}$	S_1
Y^{p}	Y^{p}

this account is still a simple one. Firms use their capital stock (at full capacity utilization Y^{p} as we shall show later on) to employ the amount of high-skilled labor (in hours, indexed by a): $L^{\mathrm{d}}_{1a} = Y^{\mathrm{p}}/z_a$, at the real wage ω_{1a}, the law of motion of which is to be determined later on from a model of the wage-price interaction in the manufacturing sector. They in addition employ normal (skilled) labor force (in hours, indexed by b): $L^{\mathrm{d}}_{1b} = Y^{\mathrm{p}}/z_b$ at the wage ω_{1b}, which is a constant fraction α_{1b} of

[3] http://www.eurofound.europa.eu/areas/industrialrelations/dictionary/definitions/FLEXICURITY.htm.

the market wage in the high-skill labor market. Both skilled and high-skilled workers are working overtime or undertime depending on the size of the capital stock in comparison to the size of skilled and high-skilled workers currently employed by firms. The rate $u_x^{rmw} = L_{1x}^{\mathrm{d}}/L_{1x}^{\mathrm{w}}, x = a, b$ is the utilization rate of the workforce L_{1x}^{w} in the primary labor markets, the industrial workers of the economy (all other employment originates from the work of households occupied in the second labor market by the government). We assume that there is exogenous technical progress of Harrod-neutral type at the rate $\bar{m} = \hat{z} = \dot{z}/z$ with respect to the output employment ratios of both types of workers and a given output capital ratio $y^{\mathrm{p}} = Y^{\mathrm{p}}/K$.

Besides primary labor markets (in the privately organized industrial sector), we have a second labor market for both skilled and high-skilled workers (that is organized by government agencies and indexed by 2) and indirectly also a third labor market (where the government acts as employer of first resort, indexed by 3). These third labor markets are, however, operated under the same remuneration and workload conditions as the second labor markets (which gives the reason why we do not consider here the government as being an employer of last resort).

Firms produce full capacity output[4] $Y^{\mathrm{p}} + \delta_1 R = C_1 + C_2 + C_r + I + \delta K + G$, that is sold to three types of worker households: the industrial workers who have to pay all taxes and government transfer out of their salaries, the workers in the public sector, and the retired households, to the investing firms and to the government. The demand side of the model is formulated in a way such that this full capacity output can indeed be sold. Deducting from this output Y^{p} of firms their real wage payments to skilled and high-skilled workers (and depreciation),[5] we get the profits of firms that are here assumed to be fully invested into capital stock growth $\dot{K} = I = \Pi$. We thus have Classical (direct) investment habits in this model with an employer of first resort.

We have assumed a fixed proportions technology with $y^{\mathrm{p}} = Y^{\mathrm{p}}/K$ the potential output-capital ratio and with $z = Y^{\mathrm{p}}/L_{1x}^{\mathrm{d}}$, $x = a, b$, the output-labor time ratios (which determine the employment L_{1x}^{d} of the workforce L_x^{w} of firms and which grows at a uniform given rate $\bar{m}$).

We next consider the skilled and high-skilled household sectors, which are composed of two types of workers one working in the private sector and the remaining part in the public sector of the economy. The total number of high-skilled workers is $L_a^{\mathrm{w}} = \alpha_s t_a L_{\mathrm{o}}$ and that of skilled workers is given by $L_b^{\mathrm{w}} = (1 - \alpha_s) t_b L_{\mathrm{o}}$. We are assuming here a given population L with constant deterministic age structure $L = tL_{\mathrm{o}}$, where T is the given lifetime of an individual household and where L_{o} denotes the number of people of a certain year of age. This number is assumed as constant for all vintages between 0 and T. We moreover assume here that the work life of skilled workers is t_b years and that of high-skilled ones $t_a (< t_b)$ years. We finally have assumed here that there is a given ratio α_s of students[6] having just finished their (comprehensive and all day) schooling years who are (by exit or entry exams)

[4] Augmented by company pension payments $\delta_1 R$.

[5] The term S_1 is equal to $\delta_1 R + \dot{R}$.

[6] The determination of which will be discussed later on.

qualified to enter the phase of higher education (leading to high-skilled degrees at "universities" and other tertiary education institutions). Given the constant vintage structure within the population, we thus have a workforce $L_b^w = (1-\alpha_s)t_b L_o$ of skilled workers in the economy (who start their working life directly after (primary and secondary) schooling, while $L_a^w = \alpha_s t_a L_o$ is the number of high-skilled workers of the considered model economy. Year-in year-out the economy has therefore a given amount of school students L_s, university students L_u, high-skilled workers L_a^w, skilled workers L_b^w, and retired workers L_r (contributing work according to their willingness and capability) for whom it must organize education and work in the primary and the secondary labor markets (including the government activities as an employer of first resort).

Households I: high-skilled (a) and skilled (b) workers in primary labor markets
Income Account (Households A, B)

Uses	Resources
$C_1 = c_1(1-\tau_1)(\omega_{1a}L_{1a}^d + \omega_{1b}L_{1b}^d)$	
$T = \tau_1(\omega_{1a}L_{1a}^d + \omega_{1b}L_{1b}^d)$	
$\omega_{2a}L_{3a}^w,\ L_{3a}^w = L_a^w - (L_{1a}^w + L_{2a}^w)$	
$\omega_{2b}L_{3b}^w,\ L_{3b}^w = L_b^w - (L_{1b}^w + L_{2b}^w)$	
$\omega_{2b}L_r, L_r = t_r L_o$	
S_1	$\omega_{1a}L_{1a}^d + \omega_{1b}L_{1b}^d$
$Y_1^w = \omega_{1a}L_{1a}^d + \omega_{1b}L_{1b}^d$	Y_1^w

Households II: Secondary high-skilled (a) and skilled (b) workers
Income Account (Households A, B):

Uses	Resources
C_{2a}	$\omega_{2a}(L_{2a}^w + L_{3a}^w) = Y_{2a}^w,\ \omega_{2a} = \alpha_{2a}\omega_{1a}$
C_{2b}	$\omega_{2b}(L_{2b}^w + L_{3b}^w) = Y_{2b}^w,\ \omega_{2b} = \alpha_{2b}\omega_{1b}$
$Y_2^w = Y_{2a}^w + Y_{2b}^w$	$Y_2^w = Y_{2a}^w + Y_{2b}^w$

Both households of type I are taxed at the same tax rate τ_1 and consume with the same marginal propensity to consume c_1 goods of amount C_1. They pay (all) income taxes T and they pay in addition – via further transfers – all workers' income in the labor markets that is not coming from firms and from government tax revenues (which is equivalent to an unemployment insurance and therefore indexed with an index 3.) Moreover, they pay the pensions of the retired households ($\omega_{2b}L_r$) and accumulate their remaining income S_1 in the form of company pensions into a fund R that is administrated by firms (with inflow S_1, see the sector of households and with outflow $\delta_1 R$). Wage rates are determined by wage-negotiations of high-skilled workers in the industrial sector, while all other real wages are constant fractions of these negotiated wages and are uniform for all skilled workers in the government sector and for retired persons (who, however, receive extra company pension payments according to their accumulated contributions to the work, their occupation time in the primary sector).

The transfers $\omega_{2a}(L_a^w - (L_{1a}^w + L_{2a}^w))$ and $\omega_{2b}(L_b^w - (L_{1b}^w + L_{2b}^w))$ can be considered as solidarity payments, since workers from the primary labor markets who lose their job will automatically be employed in the second labor market where full employment is guaranteed by the government (as employer of first resort). We consider this employment as skill preserving, since it can be viewed as ordinary office or handicraft work (subject only to learning by doing when such workers return to the first labor market).

The secondary sector of households is here modeled in the simplest way that is available: households employed in the secondary labor markets, that is, $L_{2a}^w + L_{3a}^w, L_{2b}^w + L_{3b}^w$ pay no taxes and totally consume their income. We have thus Classical saving habits in this household sector, while households of type I may have positive or negative savings S_1 as residual from their income and expenditures. We assume as law of motion for pension funds R

$$\dot{R} = S_1 - \delta_1 R,$$

where δ_1 is the rate by which these funds are depreciated through company pension payments to the "officially retired" workers L_r assumed to be a constant fraction of the "active" workforce L^w. These worker households are added here as not really inactive, but offer work according to their still existing capabilities and willingness that can be considered as an addition to the supply of work already organized by the government $L_{2a}^w + L_{3a}^w + L_{2b}^w + L_{3b}^w$, that is, the working potential of the officially retired persons remains an active and valuable contribution to the working hours that are supplied by the members of the society. It is obvious that the proper allocation of the work hours under the control of the government needs thorough reflection from the microeconomic and the social point of view, which, however, cannot be a topic in a chapter on the macroeconomics of such an economy.

The income account of the retired households, shown below, shows that they receive pension payments as if they would work in the secondary skilled segment of the economy and they get in addition individual transfer income (company pensions) from the accumulated funds R in proportion to the time (and type as which) they have been active in the first labor market as portion of $\delta_1 R$ by which the pension funds R are reduced in each period.

Income Account (Retired Households)

Uses	Resources
C_r	$\omega_{2b}L_r + \delta_1 R, L_r = t_r L_o$
Y^r	Y^r

There is finally the government sector that is also formulated in a very simple way:

The Government

Income Account: Fiscal Authority/Employer of First Resort

Uses	Resources
$G = \alpha_g T$	$T = \tau_1(\omega_{1a} L^{d}_{1a} + \omega_{1b} L^{d}_{1b})$
$\omega_{2a} L^{w}_{2a} = \alpha_a T$	
$\omega_{2b} L^{w}_{2b} = ((1 - \alpha_g) - \alpha_a)T$	
$\omega_{2a} L^{w}_{3a}, L^{w}_{3a} = L^{w}_{a} - (L^{w}_{1a} + L^{w}_{2a})$	$\omega_{2a} L^{w}_{3a}$
$\omega_{2b} L^{w}_{3b}, L^{w}_{3b} = L^{w}_{b} - (L^{w}_{1b} + L^{w}_{2b})$	$\omega_{2a} L^{w}_{3a}$
$\omega_{2b} L^{w}_{r}$	$\omega_{2b} L^{w}_{r}$
Y^{g}	Y^{g}

The government receives income taxes, the solidarity payments (employment benefits) for the secondary labor markets paid by workers in the primary labor markets, and old-age pension payments. It uses the taxes to finance government goods demand G and the surplus of taxes over these government expenditure to actively employ both skilled and high-skilled workers in the government sector. In addition it employs the workers receiving "unemployment benefits" and it in fact also employs the "retired" persons to the extent they can still contribute to the various employment activities. We therefore have that the total labor force in the secondary labor markets is employed through the government that is organized by government in the way it does this in the administration of the state in all modern market economies.

We assume that real wages in the public sector are limited by the following conditions:

$$\omega_{2a} \geq \bar{\omega}_{2a}, \quad \omega_{2b} \geq \bar{\omega}_{2b},$$

where $\bar{\omega}_{2a}$ and $\bar{\omega}_{2b}$ are the levels of real wages where the expressions L^{w}_{3a} and L^{w}_{3b} are zero, that is, where the planned employment in the private and the public sector are just sufficient to clear the labor market. This condition therefore provides lower bound for public real wages, which prevent that there are supply constraints from the side of the labor market in this model of flexicurity capitalism.

In sum we get that workers are employed either in the primary labor market and if not there then by the government sector concerning public administration, infrastructure services, educational services, or other public services (in addition there is potential labor supply L_r from the retired households, which due to the long-life expectancy in modern societies can remain effective suppliers of specific work over a considerable span of time). In this way the whole workforce is always fully employed in this model of social growth (and the retired persons according to their capabilities and willingness) and thus does not suffer from human degradation in particular. Of course, there are a variety of issues concerning state organized work that point to problems in the organization of such work, but all such problems also exist in all actual industrialized market economies in one way or another. We thus have a Classical growth model where full employment is not assumed, but actively constructed and where – due to the assumed expenditure structure – Say's law holds true, that is, the capital stock of firms is also always fully utilized, since all savings are additions to the pension fund in terms of commodities and since all profits are invested. For the inclusion of debt financed investment (which is excluded here) see Flaschel et al. (2008).

10.3 Dynamics: Stable Balanced Reproduction

Based on Flaschel et al. (2008) we have in this model type a real wage Phillips curve as it was described here in the introductory section, which can be represented in stylized form as follows ($G^1(1)=0, G^2(0)=0$):[7]

$$\hat{v}_{1a} = G^1\left(\frac{v_{1a}}{v^o_{1a}}\right) + G^2\left(\frac{y^{\mathrm{p}}}{l^{\mathrm{w}}_{1a}} - \bar{u}_w\right) = \tilde{G}^1(v_{1a}) + \tilde{G}^2(l^{\mathrm{w}}_{1a}), \tag{10.1}$$
$$\tilde{G}^{1'}, \tilde{G}^{2'} < 0,\ v_{1a} = \frac{\omega_{1a}}{z}.$$

The first term on the right hand side represents the Blanchard and Katz (1999) real wage error correction term, while the second one derives from the utilization rate $u_w = L^{\mathrm{d}}_{1a}/L^{\mathrm{w}}_{1a} = l^{\mathrm{d}}_{1a}/l^{\mathrm{w}}_{1a}$ of the workforce employed by firms expressed in per unit of capital form, see the next law of motion), where l^{d}_{1a} is here assumed a given magnitude due to fixed proportions in production and due to full capacity growth. The assumption $\tilde{G}^{2'} < 0$ thus simply states that real wage dynamics depends positively on the utilization rate of the high-skilled workers employed by firms. We stress again that all other types of work exhibit fixed wage differentials with respect to the high-skilled workers of the primary labor market. This allows to consider only their real wage in the dynamical investigations that follow below – in place of the full array of real wages represented by $0 < \omega_{2b} < \omega_{2a} < \omega_{1b} < \omega_{1a} < z$. The growth rate of the high-skilled workforce of firms (the recruitment of new high-skilled workers), $\hat{L}^{\mathrm{w}}_{1a}$ also depends positively on the rate of capacity utilization $u_w = l^d/l^{\mathrm{w}}_1$, more precisely: the above shown utilization gap, as suggested by Okun's law, and thus also negatively on its own level. Moreover, since the second state variable of the model l^{w}_1 is to be defined by zL^{w}_{1a}/K, we get a negative effect from the rate of profit on the growth rate of this state variable (through the investment behavior of firms) and thus a positive effect of real wages in the second law of notion of the economy, which in general terms therefore reads

$$\hat{l}^{\mathrm{w}}_1 = -\hat{K} + \hat{z} + \hat{L}^{\mathrm{w}}_{1a} = H^1(v_{1a}) + H^2(l^{\mathrm{w}}_1), H^{1'} > 0, H^{2'} < 0\, l^{\mathrm{w}}_{1a} = zL^{\mathrm{w}}_{1a}/K. \tag{10.2}$$

[7] See Flaschel et al. (2008) for the details of the derivation of this real wage (or better wage share) Phillips curve and note that this equation implicitly assumes that v^{o}_{1a} describes the situation where capital stock growth is equal to natural growth n.

We assume that the steady state value of $v^{\rm o}_{1a}$ is given (by social compromise) in such a way that we get for the rate of profit of firms in the steady state the equation

$$\hat{K} = \rho^{\rm o} = y^{\rm p} - \delta - v^{\rm o}_{1a} l^{\rm wo}_{1a} - v^{\rm o}_{1b} l^{\rm wo}_{1b} = y^{\rm p} - \delta - v^{\rm o}_{1a} l^{\rm wo}_{1a} - \alpha_{1b} v^{\rm o}_{1a} l^{\rm wo}_{1b} = \hat{z} = \bar{m},$$

with $l^{\rm wo}_{1a} = l^{\rm wo}_{1b} = y^{\rm p}/\bar{u}^{\rm w}$. Under this assumption we indeed have that the laws of motion (10.1) and (10.2) indeed exhibit the values v^{o}_{1a} and l^{wo}_{1a} as their in general unique interior steady state position. Moreover, all ratios of the type zL/K are then constant in the steady state, since all possible l-values that can be considered here are constant in time.[8]

The 2D dynamics (10.1) and (10.2) allow for the application of the following Liapunov function to be used in the stability proof that follows:

$$V(v_{1a}, l^{\rm w}_{1a}) = \int_{v^{\rm o}_{1a}}^{v_{1a}} H^1(\tilde{v}_{1a})/\tilde{v}_{1a}\, {\rm d}\tilde{v}_{1a} + \int_{l^{\rm wo}_{1a}}^{l^{\rm w}_{1a}} -\tilde{G}^2(\tilde{l}^{\rm w}_{1a})/\tilde{l}^{\rm w}_{1a}\, {\rm d}\tilde{l}^{\rm w}_{1a}$$

This function describes by its graph a 3D sink with the steady state of the economy as its lowest point, since the above integrates two functions that are negative to the left of the steady state values and positive to their right. For the first derivative of the Liapunov function along the trajectories of the considered dynamical system we, moreover, get

$$\begin{aligned}
\dot{V} &= {\rm d}V(v_{1a}(t), l^{\rm w}_{1a})/{\rm d}t = \left(H^1(v_{1a})/v_{1a}\right)\dot{v}_{1a} - \left(\tilde{G}^2(l^{\rm w}_{1a})/l^{\rm w}_{1a}\right)\dot{l}^{\rm w}_{1a}\\
&= H^1(v_{1a})\hat{v}_{1a} - \tilde{G}^2(l^{\rm w}_{1a})\hat{l}^{\rm w}_{1a}\\
&= H^1(v_{1a})(\tilde{G}^1(v_{1a}) + \tilde{G}^2(l^{\rm w}_{1a})) - \tilde{G}^2(l^{\rm w}_{1a})(H^1(v_{1a}) + H^2(l^{\rm w}_{1a}))\\
&= H^1(v_{1a})\tilde{G}^1(v_{1a}) - \tilde{G}^2(l^{\rm w}_{1a})H^2(l^{\rm w}_{1a})\\
&= -H^1(v_{1a})(-\tilde{G}^1(v_{1a})) - (-\tilde{G}^2(l^{\rm w}_{1a}))(-H^2(l^{\rm w}_{1a}))\\
&\le 0 \qquad [=0 \quad \text{if and only if} \quad v_{1a} = v^{\rm o}_{1a}, l^{\rm w}_{1a} = l^{\rm wo}_{1}],
\end{aligned}$$

since the multiplied functions have the same sign to the right and to the left of their steady state values and thus lead to positive products with a minus sign in front of them (up to the situation where the economy is already sitting in the steady state). We thus have proved that there holds:

Proposition 1

The interior steady state of the dynamics (10.1) and (10.2) is a global sink of the function V, defined on the positive orthant of the phase space, and is attracting in this domain, since the function V is strictly decreasing along the trajectories of the dynamics in the positive orthant of the phase space, that is, its economic part.

---

[8] The reader is referred to Flaschel et al. (2008) for details.

There is a further law of motion in the background of the model that needs to be considered to provide a complete statement on the *viability* of the considered model of flexicurity capitalism. This law of motion describes the evolution of the pension fund per unit of the capital stock $\eta = \frac{R}{K}$ and is obtained from the defining equation $\dot{R} = S_1 - \delta_1 R$ as follows:

$$\begin{aligned}\hat{\eta} &= \hat{R} - \hat{K} = \frac{\dot{R}}{K}\frac{K}{R} - \rho = \frac{S_1 - \delta_1 R}{K}/\eta - \rho, \quad \text{i.e.,} \\ \dot{\eta} &= \frac{S_1}{K} - (\delta_1 + \rho)\eta = s_1 - (\delta_1 + \rho)\eta,\end{aligned}$$

with savings of households of type I and profits of firms per unit of capital being given by[9]

$$\begin{aligned}s_1 &= (1-c_1)(1-\tau_1)(v_{1a}+v_{1b})y^{\mathrm{p}} - v_{2b}l_{\mathrm{r}} \\ &\quad -[v_{2a}l_a^{\mathrm{w}} - (v_{1a} + v_{2a}\alpha_a\tau_1(v_{1a}+v_{1b}))y^{\mathrm{p}}] \\ &\quad -[v_{2b}l_b^{\mathrm{w}} - (v_{1b} + v_{2b}((1-\alpha_{\mathrm{g}}) - \alpha_a)\tau_1(v_{1a}+v_{1b}))y^{\mathrm{p}}] \\ \rho &= y^{\mathrm{p}}[1-(v_{1a}+v_{2a})] - \delta.\end{aligned}$$

For the ratio of savings to GDP $\theta_1 = S_1/Y^{\mathrm{p}} = s_1/y^{\mathrm{p}}$, we therefore get in the steady state of the economy the expression

$$\begin{aligned}\theta_1^{\mathrm{o}} &= (1-c_1)(1-\tau_1)(v_{1a}^{\mathrm{o}}+v_{1b}^{\mathrm{o}}) - v_{2b}^{\mathrm{o}}y_r^{\mathrm{o}} \\ &\quad -[v_{2a}^{\mathrm{o}}y_a^{\mathrm{wo}} - (v_{1a}^{\mathrm{o}} + v_{2a}^{\mathrm{o}}\alpha_a\tau_1(v_{1a}^{\mathrm{o}}+v_{1b}^{\mathrm{o}}))] \\ &\quad -[v_{2b}^{\mathrm{o}}y_b^{\mathrm{wo}} - (v_{1b}^{\mathrm{o}} + v_{2b}^{\mathrm{o}}((1-\alpha_{\mathrm{g}}) - \alpha_a)\tau_1(v_{1a}^{\mathrm{o}}+v_{1b}^{\mathrm{o}}))],\end{aligned}$$

with $y_{\mathrm{r}} = l_{\mathrm{r}}/y^{\mathrm{p}} = zL^{\mathrm{r}}/Y^{\mathrm{p}}, y_a^{\mathrm{w}} = zL^{\mathrm{w}}/Y^{\mathrm{p}}, y_b^{\mathrm{w}} = zL_b^{\mathrm{w}}/Y^{\mathrm{p}}$. For $v_{2a}^{\mathrm{o}} = \bar{v}_{2a}, v_{2b}^{\mathrm{o}} = \bar{v}_{2b}$, that is, the case where wages in the government sector are clearing the labor market without any need for employment of first resort, this gives

$$\boxed{\theta_1^{\mathrm{o}} = (1-c_1)(1-\tau_1)(v_{1a}^{\mathrm{o}}+v_{1b}^{\mathrm{o}}) - \bar{v}_{2b}l_r^{\mathrm{o}}, \quad \text{i.e.,}}$$

this ratio is positive if $L_{\mathrm{r}}/(Y^{\mathrm{p}}/z) = L_{\mathrm{r}}/L_{1a}^{\mathrm{d}}$ is sufficiently small. We therefore need a condition that limits the ratio $L_{\mathrm{r}}/L = t_{\mathrm{r}}L_{\mathrm{o}}/L = t_{\mathrm{r}}/t$ from above in combination with conditions that limit (from above) the real wages $\omega_{2a}^{\mathrm{o}} \geq \bar{\omega}_{2a}, \omega_{2b}^{\mathrm{o}} \geq \bar{\omega}_{2b}$ paid in the government sector to get a positive ratio θ_1^{o}. This shows that such upper limits on wages in the public labor markets as well as in base pension payments are needed and provide sufficient conditions for positive savings ratio with respect to GDP Y^{p}. If this is given, we will have a positive steady state value for company pension funds per unit of capital $\eta^{\mathrm{o}} = s_1^{\mathrm{o}}/(\delta_1 + \bar{m})$ and also a positive value for the percentage of

[9] $l_a^{\mathrm{w}} = zL_a^{\mathrm{w}}/K, l_r = zL_r/K, s_1 = S_1/K$.

company pension payments as a fraction of base pension payments $\gamma_1^{\rm o}$, which is given by

$$\gamma_1^{\rm o} = \theta_1^{\rm o}/\sigma_r \leq (1-c_1)(1-\tau_1)\frac{v_{1a}^{\rm o}+v_{1b}^{\rm o}}{v_{2b}^{\rm o}}\frac{y^{\rm p}}{y_{\rm r}} - 1,$$

where $\sigma_{\rm r} = \omega_{2b}^{\rm o} L_{\rm r}/Y^{\rm p}$ is the share of base pension payments in GDP. The establishment of a desired ratio between company pension payments and base pension payments therefore demands (besides a viable ratio $t_{\rm r}$ concerning the age structure of the economy) for the choice of appropriate real wages in the public sector and it is in any case limited from above by the expression on the right hand side in the above equation.

10.4 Educational Systems: Basic Structures and Implications

In this section we extend the flexicurity model towards the integration of an educational sector. We assume as in the preceding sections that there are only two types of workers, skilled (b) and high-skilled (a) ones. We stress that we assume a stationary population $L = tL_{\rm o}$ in this and the next section, where $L_{\rm o}$ is the stationary number of people of age τ, $\tau = 1, \cdots, t$, with t denoting the given lifespan of each individual agent of the economy. There are $L_{\rm r} = t_{\rm r} L_{\rm o}$ retired people in each given year, $L_{\rm s} = t_{\rm s} L_{\rm o}$ students on the primary and secondary education level, $L_{\rm u} = \alpha_{\rm g} t_{\rm u} L_{\rm o}$ students on the tertiary education level, $L_{\rm b} = t_{\rm b} L_{\rm o}$ skilled workers, and $L_a = t_a L_{\rm o}$ high-skilled workers (and $L_{\rm c} = t_{\rm c} L_{\rm o}$ children in the background of the model). The natural rate of the preceding sections is thus set equal to 0 here for reasons of simplicity. The t_x-coefficients express the number of years an agent will be part of this population group.[10] Finally, it is assumed that the current system allows a fraction $\alpha_{\rm s}$ of $t_{\rm s} L_{\rm o}$ to go to University to become high-skilled workers, while the remainder enters the workforce as a member of $L_b^{\rm w}$ after having finished school with a final certificate. To keep the model simple, we abstain from vocational schools, apprenticeships or dual systems.

Before we come to a graphical representation and analysis of such a stylized educational system, we provide in Fig. 10.2 a brief representation of an existing example: the Finnish educational structure as it is provided by the National Board of Education in Finland.[11] Distinguishing marks of this school systems are (1) A comprehensive compulsory school for all students with no differentiation between good

[10] With respect to concrete numbers one therefore could, for example, assume $t_{\rm c} = 6, t_{\rm s} = 12, t_{\rm u} = 5, t_b = 47, t_a = 42, t_{\rm r} = 15$. We stress here that the considered age structure is still a very stylized one in view of what is shown in Fig. 10.2.

[11] Source: http://www.edu.fi/english/SubPage.asp?path=500,4699.

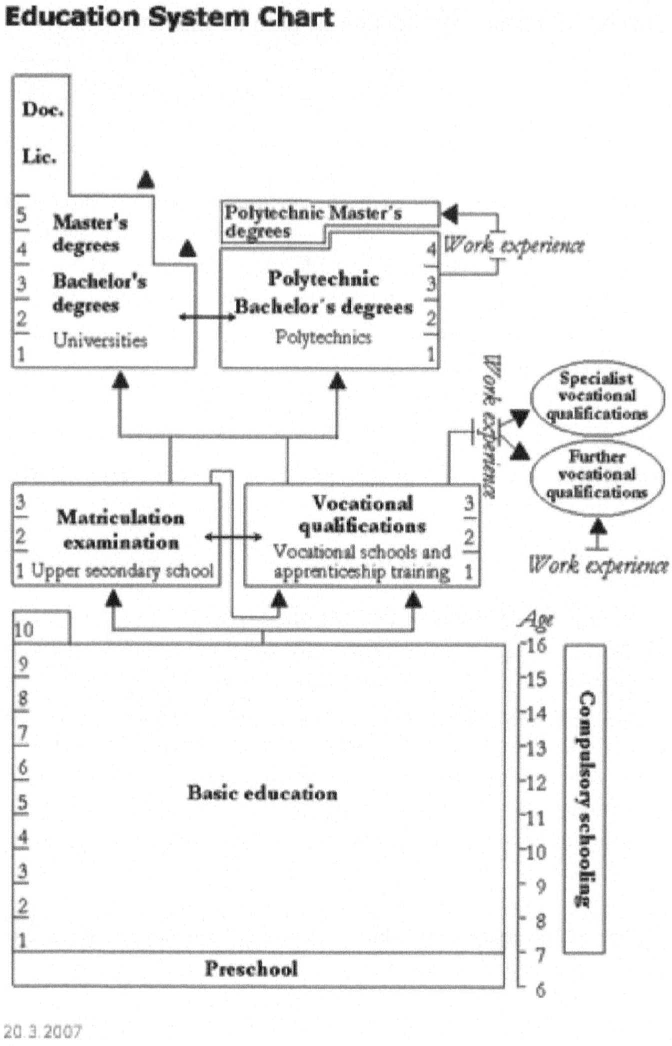

Fig. 10.2 The education system of Finland: stylized representation. (Source: http://www.edu.fi/english/SubPage.asp?path=500,4699)

learners and those with learning difficulties, (2) two ways to finish secondary school, which both can lead to a higher qualification (to enter universities or polytechnics), (3) further details that are not to be seen in this figure such as the renouncement of grading until the last 2 years of basic education.

For our purposes we, however, use the somewhat simplified structure for an educational system underlying our model of flexicurity capitalism, as shown below.

Education in the Flexicurity Model: Baseline Case of a Stationary Population

Retired People $t_r L_o$ (base pensions and company pensions) (labor market contribution acc. to willingness and capability)				
Occup 1b: active	Occup 2b (part EFR)	Occup 2b (EFR)	Occup 2a	Occup 1a
		Tertiary Education (at 'Universities')		
Secondary School Education: $t_s L_o$ (aggregated)				
Primary School Education: $t_s L_o$ (aggregated)				
Pre-School (not modeled)				

Note with respect to this table that workers of type b can only be in one of the two situations as far as their salary group is concerned, since employment of first resort is remunerated at the same level as workers of type b actively employed in the government sector. For workers of type a this, however, implies that they can be in one of the three states concerning their salaries, since they are paid higher wages when actively employed in the public sector. Note that we will consider only a steady state situation in the following and thus investigate the implications of balanced reproduction in this type of capitalism (shown to be an attractor of situations of unbalanced growth in an earlier section).

With respect to the above stationary subdivision of the population of the economy, let us consider now the situation where this workforce reproduction scheme allows for the case where there is no employment of first resort needed for the workforce of type a. If $\alpha_s L_o$ is the number of students that go from primary and secondary education to tertiary education after finishing school we get for the parameter α_s in the considered situation on the one hand the definitional relationship

$$L^w_a = \alpha_s t_a L_o, \quad L^w_b = (1-\alpha_s) t_b L_o$$

On the other hand, we have as active employment rules for workers of type a

$$L^w_{1a} = Y^p/z, \quad L^w_{2a} = \alpha_h T/\omega_{2a} = \alpha_h \tau_h \left(\frac{\omega_{1a}}{\omega_{2a}} L^w_{1a} + \frac{\omega_{1b}}{\omega_{2a}} L^w_{1b} \right)$$

The equilibrium condition $L^w_a = L^w_{1a} + L^w_{2a}$ then implies

$$\alpha_s t_a L_o = Y^p/z(1+\alpha_h \tau_h) \left(\frac{\omega_{1a}}{\omega_{2a}} + \frac{\omega_{1b}}{\omega_{2a}} \right),$$

which in turn gives[12]

$$\boxed{\alpha_s = (1+\alpha_h \tau_h) \left(\frac{\omega_{1a}}{\omega_{2a}} + \frac{\omega_{1b}}{\omega_{2a}} \right) \frac{L^d_{1a}}{t_a L_o}}$$

[12] The ratio $\frac{L^d_{1a}}{t_a L_o}$ compares employment in the first sector (of high skilled workers) with the common core employment of all workers.

This ratio must be applied for the access to Universities if the reproduction of high skilled workers is such that no first resort employment is necessary for them. A numerical example may help to understand this condition in more detail. Since workers employed in the industrial sector pay all taxes, we may assume the following crude estimates for the expressions that determine the equilibrium α_s

$$\alpha_h = 1/3, \tau_h = 0.5, \frac{\omega_{1a}}{\omega_{2a}} = 4, \frac{\omega_{1b}}{\omega_{2a}} = 2, \quad \frac{L_{1a}^{d}}{t_a L_o} = 0.5.$$

This gives for α_s the value $\alpha_s = 0.5$, a value that coincides with what is suggested by studies of the OECD. The above formula for the university access ratio α_s clearly shows the possibilities by which this ratio may be increased (if desirable).

Even though we divide the working population into two groups – skilled and high skilled workers – it should be taken into consideration that skilled workers have finished their schooltime on the same level as high skilled ones, only with lesser results in their final examinations that are equal to "Abitur" in Germany, "Baccalaureate" in France, or "A-Levels" in Great Britain. Thus, it is guaranteed that the workforce as a whole is well educated and trained far above basic skills. To gain such high qualifications might be regarded as an exaggerated aim, but examples, especially from the Scandinavian countries, show that a strict concept of "demand and support" will be able to get such results in the school population.

10.5 Education, Equal Opportunities, and Life-Long Learning

In this section, we first discuss the conditions of a suitable educational system (preschool and school, yet with an emphasis on school education). To gain the described results demands a strict support of the rules of "equal opportunities" to eliminate all hindrances for children to participate in an education that fits their abilities and allows them to meet the requirements of the schools. Furthermore, we discuss the competitive way in which students in their final exams gain University access or not. This concludes the relationship of equal opportunities and competition in a more general aspect.

Second, we deal with the demand of life-long learning assuming that part of all the peoples' leisure time is used for keeping their skill up to date as well as accepting skills enhancements offered by their employers. A generally accepted necessity of lifelong learning will allow for a continuous high skill level in all sectors where skilled or high-skilled workers are doing their job, but it holds true in a similar way for all pensioners who still feel fit to take an active part in the workforce.

We will finally deepen our reflections on education by discussing the role of equal opportunities in its close relationship to Human Rights, which are strongly related to democracy. This leads to the discussion of democracy and citizenship education as well as Human Rights education. It should be clarified that we can here only outline these questions, which will be discussed in more detail in future work.

10.5.1 The School System

To become, and be, a member of the workforce demands great engagement even if employment is guaranteed, although the industrial sector is free to hire and fire, since the employer of first resort will take over the fired workers, both skilled and high-skilled persons. All workers owe their education and welfare expenses to the tax payers, the industrial workers in this model type. Thus, the system is extremely supportive by giving work to all, but it is also highly demanding by expecting full commitment by everyone due to the fact that it depends on the mutual giving and taking in this society. This demands a high consensus within the society with regard to the necessity of work and the working conditions. It is the task of education to provide students in (pre)schools not only with the necessary skills to become adequate workers in their later professions and jobs, but also to help them to understand this system and to integrate themselves into it. This kind of integration is not to be misunderstood as a simple adaption but it concludes – as does socialization – the development of an independent, mature, and responsible personality, which is part of the aim of education as described in this chapter. A positive view on work is a necessity in a society where all persons are assumed to find work, but are also obliged to engage in their work, even after their retirement. A contradicting attitude towards work in the public and media discourse where consumption and leisure time are often more favored than work is not compatible with the demands of our model. Based on these underlying assumptions, skills are here understood in a broad sense, which transcends intellectual or technical competencies, but include work attitudes, teamwork etc.

As we have made clear earlier, all students will be led to leave school on the level of "Abitur." This demands a good education from the very beginning. Therefore, in our society "school" starts in an early stage, also due to the fact that the mother will normally return to work 2 years after the birth of the child. Our educational system – named school system for reasons of simplicity – begins for children at the age of 2, though nursery schools may be available for younger kids if parents prefer so. All forms of schooling are thought to be all-day institutions though families may have a choice of lesser schooling until the child is 3 years old. In nursery schools children are cared for by trained personnel. Even if there is no formal training, they already learn first – mainly social – skills, which include first behavior rules in a community such as how to share toys, how to behave during meals in an age-adequate way, etc.

Further skills that are learnt in this age are linguistic and communicative ones. This happens in families, too, but in an educational setting as in a nursery school more support will be given by guiding the children. As in kindergarten, children also learn at the age of 2 to use materials and thus train their fine motor skills. They are also trained to use their bodies and exercise their movements. This demands caretakers with a good training on a University level. This holds as well true for the following kindergarten period, which should last for 3years. Skills that are already trained in a first approach in the nursery schools will now be deepened in a more and more systematic way though, of course, the stages of development of a child have to be kept in mind as well as the necessity of formal and especially informal play. When the last kindergarten year is either transferred to primary schools or organized together with them, it is possible to allow for a gradual transition into school.

Following the Scandinavian role Model of schooling, all children will be together in a general school at least until grade 8 or 9 when they are about 15 or 16 years old (cf., e.g., Ministry of Education and Science of Sweden, 2004). Any earlier division into different school types would lead to a selection before all main abilities will be developed so that young people would be bereaved of the chance to evolve into the skilled person that they are. A longer time of learning together will furthermore help them to develop social skills. Finally, a selection before or just when they have reached puberty would probably intensify the general problems to that time. When students have to opt for different types of secondary or high school thereafter, they can be aware that all types will lead them to a matriculation certificate though with different focuses (either more academic or more technical) and a different length of schooling (between 2 and 4 years depending on the preferences of a student), so that they are able to plan their secondary school time with the help of their teachers, following their individual abilities and interests.

This school system needs to bring to light all abilities and interests a child may have, since otherwise the ambitious aim of a final certificate for all cannot be reached. This means that the school education works in a way such that educational support for the differently talented students obeys the principle of equal opportunities. We have a double task resulting from the principles of equal opportunities, where each child will be given the optimal support. The one task is to eliminate social or structural hindrances such as family income, level of education of the parents, social stratum, migration background, etc. In our system, these forms of disadvantages should become less important when all – or at least most – parents will be skilled or high-skilled persons with an adequate income. Yet, disadvantages – which are often connected with discrimination – may remain due, for example, to the social, regional, or political background of a family. Here, it is an important task of all forms of schooling to overcome these disadvantages by giving the necessary support.

While this is also a task to be fulfilled by the state and the society, it is the domain of schools and education to find the special abilities of a child and support them as the second task. Education has to improve its didactic and methods, so that each child can be supported in its special competencies, and furthermore that each child can be supported individually so that he/she will be able to pass a successful school career. This strong focus on individual support in relationship with the common aim of reaching the final certificate demands not only a well-equipped school with regard to teaching personnel, further personnel such as social workers, psychologists, librarians, medical helpers, and close relationships with professionals from outside such as sport trainers, artists, etc., but it also demands a well equipped school with attractive rooms and interior. Special support will be given for students with disabilities within integrative classes (cf. Report 2006). Equal opportunities are thus an aim in the school system and also the way in which the ambitious aim of a final certificate for all can be reached.

It has to be asked how the competitive end of school, when only those with the best results will be allowed to go to University, fits into this approach, even if this could be about 50%. This is surely a more general question of whether equal opportunities are compatible and if so, in which way, with competition. Competition is part of school life and in most cases it is a planned part of education, for example, in those sports where naturally a winner will be declared at the end, such as sprinting or high jumping, where students are not equally quick. In schools where individual abilities are detected and supported, competition in this sense will do no harm since students learn that they have different abilities, which makes them winners in different disciplines, yet education has to make sure that there are no obvious losers.

This attitude is supported when students are not ranked within their class but measured by their individual progress. Then there will be a winner after the 100 m sprinting, but each child will learn about his or her individual successes or be supported to further improve itself, since all children will take part in sports even if their main abilities are, for example, in music. The competition at the end of the school time is of a different character, since it is a competition due to the fact that there are not enough University places and subsequent job opportunities for all – following the idea that the society needs only a certain amount of high-skilled persons with University degrees.

10.5.2 Tertiary Education, Lifelong Learning, and Equal Opportunities

This is not the place to discuss the question whether a society and workforce can be imagined where all persons may go to University mainly to complete their personal education, though the division into skilled and high-skilled positions will not be abandoned. The graded high school where students attend different types of either mainly academic or mainly technical education will already lead to a kind of preliminary decision between those who want to go to University and those who will enter only the skilled workforce after receiving their certificate. It will certainly be a task of school education to prepare students to such situations of competition and the possibility of not gaining the wanted position. This has to be compensated by developing individual abilities and skills some of which may be more valid for leisure time, for example, playing an instrument without reaching the top level for orchestra music.

The selection for University will be based on school results in the final certificate, though entry exams are also an option. According to recent results by OECD, there exist realistic expectations of about 50% of students going to University (cf. OECD 2007). About half of the students with the final certificate can thus be supposed to become high skilled workers in our model. This is not the place to go into the details of University education and the distribution of students to different studies, but concluding this discussion of the school system we want to stress the necessity of an education that allows for individual development and support under the principles of equal opportunities.

Students who finish school with the final certificate and enter the workforce as well as those who do so after having finished University are already well trained in organizing their learning processes, since one of the principles of teaching will be to teach students how to adopt learning competencies, that is, how to learn to organize a learning program, how to work together with others, and to learn how to find out about special skills as well as about weak points. The aim is to lead students to an independent learning style that fits best for the individual learner. Learning portfolios may be a recommendable way to keep records of this learning process. It can be assumed that young adults will be able to continue with this procedure as well as to continue documenting it.

The European Union had already declared the year 1996 as the European year of lifelong learning and passed a resolution on "Lifelong Learning" in 2002 (Council 2002). It is here stressed that learning starts in the pre-school age and lasts until post-retirement. Furthermore, it is relevant here that the resolution refers not only to all kinds of learning, including the entire spectrum of formal, nonformal, and informal learning, and that the aim of learning is not restricted to skills and competencies with regard to later employment. Instead it is regarded as important within a personal, civic, or social perspective as well. While school education and thus learning in schools follows a common curriculum where the highest possible grade of individualization and interest-dependence is guaranteed though a general curriculum remains to be followed, lifelong learning after school and University is far more guided by individual interests and the needs of a person, though there will also be on-the-job training in most professions, since skills and knowledge have to be updated on a regular basis.

The idea of lifelong learning adds to the concept of equal opportunities, since the personal access to knowledge and competencies is increased by the possibilities of learning independently of age or position. Therefore, it is necessary that the educational system offers a variety of learning procedures after school and University, such as adult education centers and also the possibility of access to arts, museums, nature, and its learning opportunities. Mobility will add to lifelong learning of languages and cultures, but also of professional skills. Lifelong learning includes all forms of social learning and is also highly important for political learning.

Political learning plays an important role in education, especially in a model where the state has a major role as employer and provider of social services. Political learning, which is often referred to as citizenship education, is of high relevance in a system that depends on the individual skills and knowledge of its workforce, but at the same time demands a high amount of social commitment and acceptance of different work places though no unemployment. Furthermore, the principles of equal opportunities, on which we have commented earlier, are integrated in political concepts such as Human Rights so that the necessity of political learning is again underlined. Political learning will be part of school education as well as of lifelong learning. Human Rights education provides all necessary contents and skills to cope with in a democratic society, especially since Human Rights and democracy are inseparably interconnected. Thus, democracy as the underlying state model as well as equal opportunities as the adequate principle for social justice can be deduced from Human Rights. Democracy education, citizenship education, and human rights education are well-established and partly overlapping forms of education, which provide not only an introduction into the necessary knowledge of political structures, but prepare furthermore for different kinds of participation in democratic procedures. Additionally, they intend to increase media competence to allow students as well as adult learners to understand actual political decision making processes.

10.6 Pension Funds and Credit

In this section we investigate the implications of the situation where existing pension funds are used for real capital formation (instead of remaining idle except of being used for company pension payments of amount δR at each point in time). The productive use of part of the existing pension fund R is here assumed to be rewarded at the constant interest rate r applied to the debt level D accumulated by the firms in the private sector of the economy. To simplify the presentation we assume that tertiary education is provided to all members of the workforce (during their education). The generalization to the case of two types of workers in the industrial as well as in the government sector is straightforward, but makes the presentation of the model more complex (since we have to distinguish then again between workers of type a and b and their income and consumption patterns).

10.6.1 Accounting Relationships

Pension funds here act as quasi-commercial banks who give credit to firms out of their funds and thus allow firms to invest in good times much beyond their retained earnings, that is, profits net of interest payments on loans.

Firms

Production and Income Account

Uses	Resources
δK	δK
$\omega_1 L_1^d = \omega_1 Y^p / z$	$C_1 + C_2 + C_r$
rD	$\tilde{G}$
Π	$I = (i_\rho(\rho - \rho_o) - i_d(d - d_o) + \bar{a})K$
Y^p	Y^p

The behavior and financing of gross investment is shown in the next account.

Investment and Credit:

Uses	Resources
δK	δK
$I = (i_\rho(\rho - \rho_o) - i_d(d - d_o) + \bar{a})K$	Π
	$\dot{D} = I - \Pi$
I^g	I^g

We assume as investment behavior of firms the functional relationship

$$I/K = i_\rho(\rho - \rho_o) - i_d(d - d_o) + \bar{a}.$$

This investment schedule states that investment plans depend positively on the deviation of the profit rate from its steady state level and negatively on the deviation of the debt to capital ratio from its steady state value. The exogenous trend term in investment is $\bar{a}$ and it is again assumed that it represents the influence of investing firms "animal spirits" on their investment activities.

Firms Net Worth

Assets	Liabilities
K	D
	Real Net Worth
K	K

In the management of pension funds we assume that a portion sR of them is held as minimum reserves and that a larger portion of them has been given as credit D to firms. The remaining amount are idle reserves D^s, not yet allocated to any interest bearing activity.

Pension Funds

Pension Funds and Credit (stocks)

Assets	Liabilities
R	sR
	D
	X excess reserves
R	R

Pension funds receive the Savings of households of type 1 (the other households do not save) and they receive the interest payments of firms. They allocate this into required reserve increases, payments to pensioners, new credit demands of firms, and the rest as an addition or substraction to their idle reserves.

Pension Funds and Credit (flows)

Resources	Uses
S_1	$s\dot{R}$
rD	$\delta R + rD$
	$\dot{D} = I - \Pi$
	$\dot{X}$
$S_1 + rD$	$S_1 + rD$

The above representation of the flows of funds in the pension funds system implies for the time derivative of accumulated funds R the relationship

$$\dot{R} = S_1 - \delta R - (I - \Pi) = S_1 + \Pi - \delta R - I, \quad \text{i.e.,}$$

it is given by the excess of savings of households of type I over current company pension funds payments to retired households and the new credit that is given to firms to finance the excess of investment over retained profits.

Households I and II (primary and secondary labor market)
Income Account (Households I)

Uses	Resources
$C_1 = c_{h1}(1 - \tau_h)Y_1^w$	
$\omega_2 L_{2h}^w = c_{h2}(1 - \tau_h)Y_1^w$	
$T = \tau_h Y_1^w$	
$\omega_2(L - (L_1^w + L_{2h}^w + L_{2g}^w))$	
$\omega_2 L^r$	
S_1	$\omega_1 L_1^d$
Y_1^w	Y_1^w

Households in the first labor market consume with a constant marginal propensity out of the income after primary taxes and they employ households services in constant proportions to the consumption habits. They pay the wages of the workers in the second labor market that are not employed by firms, by them, and the government as a quasi-unemployment benefit insurance (a generational solidarity contribution) and they pay the common base rent of all pensioners (as intergenerational contribution). The remainder represents their contribution to the pension scheme of the economy, from which they will receive $\delta R + rD$ when retired. We consider this as a possible scheme of funding the excess employment and the pensioners, not necessarily the only one, however.

Income Account Households II

Uses	Resources
C_2	$\omega_2 L_2^w$
Y_2^w	Y_2^w

Income Account (Retired Households):

Uses	Resources
C_r	$\omega_2 L^r + \delta R + rD$
Y^r	Y^r

The Government

Income Account – Fiscal Authority/Employer of First Resort:

Uses	Resources
$G = \alpha_g \tau_h Y_1^w$	$T = \tau_h Y_1^w$
$\omega_2 L_{2g}^w = (1-\alpha_g)\tau_h Y_1^w$	
$\omega_2 L_x^w$	$\omega_2(L - (L_1^w + L_{2h}^w + L_{2g}^w))$
$\omega_2 L^r$	$\omega_2 L^r$
Y^g	Y^g

Government gets primary taxes and spends them on goods as well as services in the government sector (which are here determined residually). It administrates the common base rent payments as well as the payments of those not yet employed in the sectors of the economy. Its workforce consists of all workers who are not employed by firms of households of type 1 and also of all pensioners who are still capable to work. The model therefore assumes not only that there is a work guarantee for all, but also a work obligation for all members in the workforce, with the addition of those that are retired but still able and willing to work.

10.6.2 Investment and Credit Dynamics in Flexicurity Growth

For simplicity we assume again that the steady state value of the real wage is fixed at a level that implies $n = \hat{K}$ in the steady state, as was already assumed in the investigation of the stability of the basic reproduction schemes.[13] We thus do determine the steady state value of the real wage ω_1 from the law of motion for $l = L/K$, and supply it here from the outside through a given $\omega_1^o = \bar{\omega}_1$. We can ignore the fluctuations of the state variable l outside the steady state, since they do not feed back into the rest of the dynamics.[14] This, however, no longer also provides us with the steady state value of the rate of profit, since profits are now to be determined net of interest payments: $\rho = y^p[1 - (1 + \alpha_\omega \alpha_f)\bar{\omega}_1/z] - \delta - rd$, where $d = D/K$ denotes the indebtedness of firms per unit of capital. We assume again as trend term in

[13] Moreover, any fluctuations away from the steady state ratio $l_o = \bar{l}$ are here also ignored in the remainder of this chapter, which allows to save one law of motion in the subsequent stability analyses, see Flaschel et al. (2008) for a motivation of this situation. We stress, however, the need to treat this issue explicitly in the case where skill formation and heterogeneous skills are considered.

[14] Moreover, we ignore now the originally considered $-\hat{K}$ in the following first law of motion without loss of generality.

Okun's law the growth rate of the capital stock (i.e., this part of the new hiring is just determined by the installation of new machines or whole plants under the assumption of fixed proportions in production). The normal level of the rate of employment of the workforce employed by firms is again set equal to "1" for simplicity.

On the basis of these assumptions we get from what was formulated in the preceding subsection (where investment was already assumed to be given by $I/K = i_\rho(\rho - \rho_o) - i_d(d - d_o) + \bar{a}$):

$$\begin{aligned}
\hat{l}_1^{\mathrm{w}} &= H(l_1^{\mathrm{w}}), \quad H' < 0, \\
\hat{\omega}_1 &= G^1\left(\frac{\omega_1}{\bar{\omega}_1}\right) + G^2\left(\frac{y^{\mathrm{p}}}{l_1^{\mathrm{w}}} - \bar{u}_w\right), \quad G^{1'}, G^{2'} < 0, \\
\dot{d} &= [i_\rho(\rho - \rho_{\mathrm{o}}) - i_d(d - d_{\mathrm{o}}) + \bar{a}](1 - d) - \rho, \\
\hat{\eta} &= s_1 + \rho - (\delta\eta + (1+\eta)[i_\rho(\rho - \rho_{\mathrm{o}}) - i_d(d - d_{\mathrm{o}}) + \bar{a}]) \\
&= (1 - c_{\mathrm{h}1}(1 - \tau_{\mathrm{h}}) - \alpha_{\mathrm{g}}\tau_{\mathrm{h}})\omega_1 y^{\mathrm{p}}/z - ((1+\alpha_{\mathrm{r}})\bar{l} - (l_1^{\mathrm{w}} + \alpha_{\mathrm{f}} y^{\mathrm{p}}/z))\alpha_\omega\omega_1 \\
&\quad + [y^{\mathrm{p}}[1 - (1 + \alpha_\omega\alpha_{\mathrm{f}})\bar{\omega}_1/z] - \delta - rd] \\
&\quad - (\delta\eta + (1+\eta)[i_\rho(\rho - \rho_{\mathrm{o}}) - i_d(d - d_{\mathrm{o}}) + \bar{a}]).
\end{aligned}$$

The introduction of debt financing of firms thus makes the model considerably more advanced in its economic structure, but not so much from the mathematical point of view, due to the recursive structure that characterizes the dynamical system at this level of generality. We note that there is not yet an interest rate policy rule involved in these dynamics, but the assumption of an interest rate peg: $r = \text{const}$.

We make use of the following abbreviations:

$$s_1^{\mathrm{o}} = (1 - c_{\mathrm{h}1}(1 - \tau_{\mathrm{h}}) - \alpha_{\mathrm{g}}\tau_{\mathrm{h}})\bar{\omega}_1 y^{\mathrm{p}}/z - ((1+\alpha_{\mathrm{r}})\bar{l} - y^{\mathrm{p}}/z(1+\alpha_{\mathrm{f}}))\alpha_\omega\bar{\omega}_1$$

and

$$\rho_{\max} = y^{\mathrm{p}}[1 - (1 + \alpha_\omega\alpha_f)\bar{\omega}_1/z] - \delta.$$

On the basis of such expressions we then have:

Proposition 2

The interior steady state of the considered dynamics is given by

$$l_1^{\mathrm{wo}} = \frac{y^{\mathrm{p}}}{z}/\bar{u}_w, \; \omega_1^{\mathrm{o}} = \bar{\omega}_1, \; \eta_{\mathrm{o}} = \frac{s_1^{\mathrm{o}} + \rho_{\mathrm{o}} - \bar{a}}{\delta + \bar{a}},$$

where d_{o} and ρ_{o} have to be determined by solving the two equations

$$\rho_{\mathrm{o}} = \rho_{max} - rd_{\mathrm{o}}, \quad \rho_{\mathrm{o}} = \bar{a}(1 - d_{\mathrm{o}}),$$

which gives for the steady state values of d, ρ, η the expressions:

$$\begin{aligned}
d_{\mathrm{o}} &= \frac{\bar{a} - \rho_{\max}}{\bar{a} - r}, \quad \rho_{\mathrm{o}} = \bar{a}\frac{\rho_{\max} - r}{\bar{a} - r}, \\
\eta_{\mathrm{o}} &= \frac{s_1^{\mathrm{o}} + \bar{a}\frac{\rho_{\max} - r}{\bar{a} - r}}{\delta + \bar{a}} = \frac{s_1^{\mathrm{o}}(\bar{a} - r) - \bar{a}(\bar{a} - \rho_{\max})}{(\delta + \bar{a})(\bar{a} - r)}.
\end{aligned}$$

We assume that both the numerator and the denominator of the fraction that defines d_o are positive, that is, the trend term in investment is sufficiently strong (larger than the rate of profit before interest rate payments $\rho_{\max}$ and larger than the rate of interest r). Moreover, it is also assumed that $\rho_{\max} > r$ holds so that all fractions shown above are in fact positive. In the case where $\bar{a} = \rho_{\max} = y^p[1-(1+\alpha_\omega\alpha_f)\bar{\omega}_1/z] - \delta$ holds, we have $d_o = 0$ and $\rho_o = \bar{a}$ in which case the value of η_o is the same as in the sections on investment without debt financing. Nevertheless, the dynamics around the steady state remain debt-financed and are therefore different from the one of the preceding section. We thus can have a "balanced budget" of firms in the steady state while investment remains driven by $I/K = i_\rho(\rho - \rho_o) - i_d(d - d_o) + \bar{a}$ outside the steady-state position.

For the fraction of company pension funds divided by base pension payments, we now get as relationship in the steady state

$$\alpha_c = \frac{\delta\eta_o + rd_o}{\alpha_\omega\alpha_r\bar{\omega}_1\bar{l}},$$

an expression that in general does not give rise to unambiguous results concerning comparative dynamics. In the special case $d_o = 0$ we, however, can state that this fraction depends positively on s_o^1 (also in general) and negatively on $\bar{a}, \delta, \bar{l}$.

The Jacobian at the interior steady state of the here considered 4D dynamics reads

$$J^o = \begin{pmatrix} - & 0 & 0 & 0 \\ ? & - & 0 & 0 \\ ? & ? & -(i_\rho + i_d)(1-d_o)) - (\bar{a} - r) & 0 \\ ? & ? & ? & -\bar{a}(1+\delta) \end{pmatrix}.$$

This lower triangular form of the Jacobian immediately implies that the elements on the diagonal of the matrix J^o are just equal to the four eigenvalues of this matrix, which are therefore all real and negative. This gives:

Proposition 3

The interior steady state of the considered dynamics is locally asymptotically stable and is characterized by a strict hierarchy in the state variables of the dynamics.

Because of the specific form of the considered laws of motion, we conjecture that the steady state is also a global attractor in the economically relevant part of the 4D phase space. We then would get again monotonically convergent trajectories from any starting point of this part of the phase space and thus fairly simple adjustment processes also in the case where investment is jointly financed by profits (retained earnings) and credit.

The stability of the steady state is increased (i.e., the eigenvalues of its Jacobian matrix become more negative) if the speed parameter characterizing hiring and firing is increased, if Blanchard and Katz-type error correction becomes more pronounced, and if the parameters $i_\rho, i_d, \bar{a}$ in the investment function are increased.

Summing up, we thus can state that the adjustment processes and their stability properties remain very supportive for the working of our model of flexicurity type, which is generally monotonically convergent with full capacity utilization of both capital and labor to a steady state position with a sustainable distribution of income between firms, our three types of households, and the government. We conclude that flexicurity capitalism may be a workable alternative to current forms of capitalism and can avoid in particular severe social deformations and human degradations caused by the reserve army mechanism and the mass unemployment it implies for certain stages in a long-phase distributive and welfare state cycle, in the US and the UK, more of as a neoclassical cold turkey type, and in Germany and in France more, gradualistic in nature.[15]

10.7 Flexicurity and the Keynesian Trade Cycle

So far the economy was a purely supply driven, with growth of the capital stock driven by net profits and credit from pension funds such that Say's law remained true, that is, aggregate demand has always been equal to potential output due to the expenditure behavior of households, the government, and the firms. In this section we now briefly sketch a situation where capacity utilization problems as well as stability problems may arise within the flexicurity variant of a capitalistic economy. We modify the baseline credit model of the preceding section in a minimal way to obtain such results. In place of its pension funds as well as the credits they give to firms, we now consider the situation where firms finance their investment plans through their profits and through the issuing of corporate paper bonds. We assume these bonds to be of the fixprice variety and we also keep the rate of interest that is paid on these bonds fixed for simplicity.

Despite this simple change we will now get the situation that actual goods market equilibrium will now depart from potential output (here reinterpreted by a normal rate of capacity utilization of potential output) and may now fluctuate around the assumed normal capacity output. We therefore have the first real problem – here on the macrolevel – the flexicurity society has to cope with, namely the possibility of severe recessions or even depressions when aggregate demand is behaving accordingly, but also the possible situation of an overheated economy. Clearly, there is now need for economic policy, that is, fiscal, monetary, or even income distribution policy to avoid large swings in economic activity and thus large imbalances between the industrial and the public labor markets. This section, however, only provides the basics for such an analysis and leaves policy consideration for future research.

The amount of corporate bonds that firms are now assumed to have issued in the past is denoted by B and their price is 1 in nominal units. Firms thus have to pay rB as interest at the current point in time and they intend to use their real profits net of interest rate payments and in addition the issue $\dot{B}^s/p$ to finance their rate of investment $I/K = i_\rho(\rho - \rho_o) - i_b(\frac{B}{pK} - (\frac{B}{pK})_o) + \bar{a}$. This rate of investment is

[15] We refer the reader back to what is shown in Fig. 10.1 where the postwar period up into the 1960s seemed to suggest that the working of the reserve army mechanism had been overcome, a suggestion that was disproved in the subsequent years in a striking way.

assumed to depend positively on excess profitability compared to the steady state rate of profit and negatively the deviation of their debt from its steady-state level.

Firms

Production and Income Account:

Uses	Resources
δK	δK
$\omega_1 L_1^d, L_1^d = Y/z$	$C_1 + C_2 + C_r$
	G
rB/p	$I = i_\rho(\rho - \rho_o)K - i_b(\frac{B}{p} - (\frac{B}{p})_o) + \bar{a}K$
$\Pi(= Y^f)$	$[I = \Pi + \dot{B}^s/p]$
Y	Y

Households of type I behave as was assumed so far, but now attempt to channel their real savings into corporate bond holdings as shown later. They will be able to exactly satisfy their demand for new bonds when there is goods market equilibrium prevailing ($I = S$), since only firms and these households act on this market, while all other economic units just spend what they get (with balanced transfer payments organized by the government). The real return from savings in corporate bonds rB/p, at each moment in time, will be added below to the base rent payments of retired households, who receive these benefits in proportion to the bonds they have allocated during their worklife in the private sector of the economy. The bonds allocated in this way thus only generate a return when their holders are retired and then – as in the pension fund scheme of Sect. 2 – at the then prevailing market rate of interest (which is here a given rate still). The pension fund model is therefore here only reformulated in terms of nominal paper holdings (coupons) and thus no longer based on the storage of physical magnitudes. Hence, corporate bonds are here not only of a fix-price variety, but also provide their return only after retirement. This is shown in the income account of retired persons below. The income account of the workers in the second labor market is unchanged and therefore not shown here again.

Households I (primary labor market) and Retired Households

Income Account (Households I)

Uses	Resources
$C_1 = c_{h1}(1 - \tau_h)\omega_1 L_1^d$	
$\omega_2 L_{2h}^w = c_{h2}(1 - \tau_h)\omega_1 L_1^d$	
$T = \tau_h \omega_1 L_1^d$	
$\omega_2(L - (L_1^w + L_{2h}^w + L_{2g}^w))$	
$\omega_2 L^r, L^r = \alpha_r L$	
$S_1[= \dot{B}^d/p]$	$\omega_1 L_1^d$
$Y_1^w = \omega_1 L_1^d$	$Y_1^w = \omega_1 L_1^d$

Income Account (Retired Households)

Uses	Resources
C_r	$\omega_2 L^\mathrm{r} + rB/p, L^\mathrm{r} = \alpha_\mathrm{r} L$
Y^r	Y^r

The government income account (not shown) is also kept unchanged and in particular balanced in the way used in the preceding model types. The modifications of the model of Sect. 2 are therefore of a minimal kind, largely concerning a different type of investment behavior of firms and a new type of organizing the formerly assumed company pension funds. However, the assumed flexicurity system becomes now of real importance, since we here will get demand determined (Keynesian) business cycle fluctuations in the dynamics implied by the model, whereas firms did not face capacity under- or over-utilization problems in the earlier model types. Keynesian IS-equilibrium determination has to be considered now and gives rise to the following equation for the effective output per unit of capital (characterizing goods market equilibrium):[16]

$$
\begin{aligned}
Y/K = y &= C_1/K + C_2/K + C_r/K + \delta + I/K + G/K \\
&= c_h(1-\tau_h)\omega_1\frac{y}{z} + \alpha_\omega\omega_1(\bar{l} - l_1^\mathrm{w}) + \alpha_\omega\alpha_r\omega_1\bar{l} + rb \\
&\quad + \delta + i_\rho(\rho - \rho_\mathrm{o}) - i_b(b - b_\mathrm{o}) + \bar{a} + \alpha_\mathrm{g}\tau_\mathrm{h}\omega_1 y/z, \\
\rho &= y - (1 + \alpha_\mathrm{f}\alpha_\omega)\omega_1 y/z - \delta - rb, \qquad b = B/(pK), \\
&\text{which taken together gives} \\
y &= \frac{\alpha_\omega\omega_1(\bar{l} - l_1^\mathrm{w}) + \alpha_\omega\alpha_\mathrm{r}\omega_1\bar{l} + (rb + \delta)(1 - i_\rho) - i_\rho\rho_\mathrm{o} - i_b(b - b_\mathrm{o}) + \bar{a}}{1 - [c_\mathrm{h}(1-\tau_\mathrm{h}) + \alpha_\mathrm{g}\tau_\mathrm{h} - i_\rho(1 + \alpha_\mathrm{f}\alpha_\omega)]\omega_1/z - i_\rho} \\
&= y(l_1^\mathrm{w}, \omega_1, b, \ldots).
\end{aligned}
$$

Note that we have modified the investment function in this section to $i(\cdot) = i_\rho(\rho - \rho_\mathrm{o}) - i_b(b - b_\mathrm{o}) + \bar{a}$. Note also that we have again assumed that natural growth n is always adjusted to the growth rate of the capital stock $\hat{K}$. We also assume that the denominator in the above fraction is positive and now get the important result that output per unit of capital is no longer equal to its potential value, but now depending on the marginal propensity to spend as well as on other parameters of the model. This is due to the new situation that firms use corporate bonds to finance their excess investment (exceeding their profits) or buy back such bonds in the opposite case and that households of type I buy such bonds from their savings (and thus do not buy goods in this amount anymore to increase the pension fund). We thus have independent real investment and real savings decisions which – when coordinated by the achievement of goods market equilibrium as shown above – lead to a supply of new corporate bonds that is exactly equal to the demand for such bonds at this

[16] Standard Keynesian assumptions will again ensure that $y^\mathrm{o} > 0$ holds true.

level of output and income. This simply follows from the fact that only firms and households of type I are saving, while all other budgets are balanced. Households of type I thus just have to accept the amount of the fixed price bonds offered by firms and are thereby accumulating these bonds (whose interest rate payments are paid out to retired people according to the percentage they have achieved when retiring).

Assuming the accumulation of corporate bonds in the place of real commodities and an investment function that is independent from these savings conditions thus implies that the economy is subject to Keynesian demand rationing processes (at least close to its steady state). These demand problems are here derived on the assumption of IS-equilibrium and thus represented in static terms in place of a dynamic multiplier approach that can also be augmented further by means of Metzlerian inventory adjustment processes. We stress once again that the possibility for full capacity output is here prevented through the Keynesian type of under-consumption assumed as characterizing the household type I sector and the fact that there is then only one income level that allows savings in bonds to become equal to bond financed investment in this simple credit market that is characterizing this modification of the flexicurity model, due to the now existing effective demand schedule $y(l_1^w, \omega_1, b, \ldots)$. We assume that the parameters are chosen such that we get for the partial derivatives of the effective demand function y

$$y_{l_1^w}(l_1^w, \omega_1, b, \ldots) < 0, \quad y_{\omega_1}(l_1^w, \omega_1, b, \ldots) > 0, \quad y_b(l_1^w, \omega_1, b, \ldots) < 0$$

holds true. This is fulfilled, for example, if the expression in the denominator of the effective demand function is negative and if the parameter i_b is chosen sufficiently large. Effective demand is then wage led and flexible wages therefore dangerous for the considered economy.

As now significantly interacting laws of motion we have in the considered case:

$$\hat{l}_1^w = H\left(\frac{y}{zl_1^w} - \bar{u}_w\right), \quad H' > 0,$$
$$\hat{\omega}_1 = G^1\left(\frac{\omega_1}{\bar{\omega}_1}\right) + G^2\left(\frac{y}{l_1^w} - \bar{u}_w\right), \quad G^{1'}, G^{2'} < 0,$$

$$\dot{b} = (1-b)(i_\rho(\rho - \rho_o) - i_b(b - b_o) + \bar{a}) - \rho - \hat{p}b,$$
$$\hat{p} = \kappa\left[\beta_{py}\left(\frac{y}{y^p} - \bar{u}_c\right) + \beta_{p\omega}\ln\left(\frac{\omega_1}{\omega_1^o} + \kappa_p\right)\beta_{wu}\left(\frac{y}{zl_1^w} - 1\right) - \beta_{w\omega}\ln\left(\frac{\omega_1}{\omega_1^o}\right)\right] + \pi^c,$$

where $\hat{p}$ has to be inserted into the other equation (where necessary) to arrive at an autonomous system of fourordinary differential equations. This particular formulation of the debt financing of firms thus makes the model considerably more advanced from the mathematical as well as from an economic point of view. We note that there is not yet an interest rate policy rule involved in these dynamics, but that the assumption of an interest rate peg is maintained still: $r = \text{const.}$

Since the model is formulated partly in nominal terms, we have to consider now the price inflation rate explicitly. We do this on the basis of a wage-price spiral mechanism as it has been formulated in Flaschel et al. (2008) with respect to the industrial sector of the economy

$$\hat{w} = \beta_{wu}\left(\frac{y}{zl_1^{\mathrm{w}}} - \bar{u}_w\right) - \beta_{w\omega}\ln\left(\frac{\omega}{\omega^{\mathrm{o}}}\right) + \kappa_w\hat{p} + (1-\kappa_w)\pi^{\mathrm{c}},$$

$$\hat{p} = \beta_{py}\left(\frac{y}{y^{\mathrm{p}}} - \bar{u}_{\mathrm{c}}\right) + \beta_{p\omega}\ln\left(\frac{\omega}{\omega^{\mathrm{o}}}\right) + \kappa_{\mathrm{p}}\hat{w} + (1-\kappa_p)\pi^{\mathrm{c}}.$$

In these equations, $\hat{w}$ and $\hat{p}$ denote the growth rates of nominal wages w and the price level p (their inflation rates) and π^c a medium-term inflation-climate expression, which, however, is of no relevance in the following due to our neglect of real interest rate effects on the demand side of the model (and thus set equal to zero). We denote again by $\bar{u}_w$ the normal ratio of utilization of the workforce within firms and now by $\bar{u}_c$ the corresponding concerning the utilization of the capital stock. Deviations from these normal ratios measure the demand pressure on the labor and the goods market, respectively. In the wage Phillips curve C as well as the price Phillips curve we in addition employ a real wage error correction term $\ln(\omega/\omega_0)$ as in Blanchard and Katz (1999), see Flaschel and Krolzig (2006) for details, and as cost pressure term a weighted average of short-term (perfectly anticipated) wage of price inflation $\hat{w}, \hat{p}$, respectively, and the medium-term inflation climate π^c in which the economy is operating.

The above structural equations of a wage-price spiral read in reduced form as follows:

$$\hat{w} = \kappa\left[\beta_{wu}\left(\frac{y}{zl_1^{\mathrm{w}}} - \bar{u}_{\mathrm{w}}\right) - \beta_{w\omega}\ln\left(\frac{\omega_1}{\omega_1^{\mathrm{o}}}\right) + \kappa_w\left(\beta_{py}\left(\frac{y}{y^{\mathrm{p}}} - \bar{u}_{\mathrm{c}}\right) + \beta_{p\omega}\ln\left(\frac{\omega_1}{\omega_1^{\mathrm{o}}}\right)\right)\right] + \pi^{\mathrm{c}}$$

$$\hat{p} = \kappa\left[\beta_{py}\left(\frac{y}{y^{\mathrm{p}}} - \bar{u}_{\mathrm{c}}\right) + \beta_{p\omega}\ln\left(\frac{\omega_1}{\omega_1^{\mathrm{o}}}\right) + \kappa_{\mathrm{p}}\left(\beta_{wu}\left(\frac{y}{zl_1^{\mathrm{w}}} - \bar{u}_{\mathrm{w}}\right) - \beta_{w\omega}\ln\left(\frac{\omega_1}{\omega_1^{\mathrm{o}}}\right)\right)\right] + \pi^{\mathrm{c}}$$

which give the above equation for the price inflation rate and also the above real dynamics when the price equation is deducted from the wage equation.

Note that our model only considers the utilization rate of insiders (within firms) in the wage dynamics, since the markets for labor are always cleared in flexicurity capitalism. We thus now use the output-capital ratio $y = Y/K$ to measure the output gap in the price inflation PC and the deviation of the real wage $\omega = w/p$ from the steady state real wage ω^{o} as error correction expression also in the price PC. Cost pressure in this price PC is formulated as a weighted average of short-term (perfectly anticipated) wage inflation and our concept of an inflationary climate π^{c}, see Flaschel and Krolzig (2006) for details. In this price Phillips curve, we have three elements of cost pressure interacting with each other, a medium term one (the inflationary climate) and two short term ones, basically the level of real unit-wage labor costs (a Blanchard and Katz (1999) error correction term) and the current rate of wage inflation, which taken by itself would represent a constant markup pricing rule. This basic rule is, however, modified by these other cost-pressure terms and in particular also made dependent on the state of the business cycle by way of the demand pressure term $y/y^{\mathrm{p}} - \bar{u}_{\mathrm{c}}$ in the market for goods.

The laws of motion describe again (in this order) our formulation of Okun's law, the real wage dynamics as it applies in a Keynesian environment (see Sect. 3), the debt dynamics of firms and a simple regressive expectations scheme concerning the inflationary climate surrounding the wage-price spiral where it is assumed (and in fact also taking place) that inflation converges back to a constant price level. There is therefore not yet an inflation accelerator present in the formulation of the dynamics of the four state variables of the model. Nevertheless, price level inflation is now explicitly taken account of, indeed for the first time in this chapter.

Steady state and stability analysis is no longer straightforward in this Keynesian variant of flexicurity capitalism. With respect to steady state positions we have to solve now a simultaneous equation system in the variables ω_1, ρ, b. Because of the structure of the effective demand function we have moreover no longer zero entries in the Jacobian of the dynamics at the steady state of the first three state variables (the last law of motion is a completely trivial one). As economic mechanism we can identify a real wage channel as in the Kaleckian dynamics of Flaschel et al. (2008) (working here in a wage led environment by assumption). There is furthermore the dynamic of the debt to capital ratio of firms. These feedback channels can be tamed through appropriate assumptions, but are even then working in an environment that gives no straightforward economically plausible stability assertions, due to the strong interactions present in the dynamics. We therefore have to leave the stability analysis here for future research.

The conclusion of this section therefore is that effective demand problems can make flexicurity capitalism significantly more difficult to analyze (and to handle) and therefore demand a treatment of much more depth – including inflation and interest rate policy rules, government deficits, and fiscal policy rules, etc. – than was possible in this short section. Moreover, credit relationships may be looked for that can avoid the increase in complexity of the dynamics of this section.

10.8 Schumpeterian Creative Destruction in Flexicurity Capitalism

After having considered the macroeconomic problems a flexicurity economy might face, we now come to a brief discussion of the microeconomic problems it has been constructed for as a solution, namely the socially acceptable handling of exit and entry problems with respect to the real capital stock as well as labor supply. The most remarkable feature of existing capitalism is definitely its property to revolutionize the technological foundations and the product frame of such market economies. The first in depth treatment of this fundamental tendency was given in Marx's (1954) Capital, Vol. I based on what he called the law of value. Schumpeter knew Marx's work very well, but developed his own vision of the microdynamics of capitalism, which in place of some questionable monotonic tendencies asserted by Marx, with the exception of the secular law of increasing labor productivity, led him to the consideration of long waves in his work on business cycles (see Schumpeter, 1939).

Marx, of course, had not lived long enough to become aware of long phased cyclical changes in the economic and social structure of capitalist economies, but was nevertheless able, on the basis of his value theory, to discuss the secular tendencies of the concentration and centralization of capital and this even on a globalized scale.

Schumpeter's (1912) "Theory of Economic Development" started from a quite different theoretical apparatus as compared to the classical theory of labor values and production prices, namely from the Walrasian concept of a perfectly competitive market economy, which for him described the circular flow of economic life in given circumstances. To this he then added economic development and credit and most fundamentally the dynamic character of the entrepreneur who is initiating spontaneous and discontinuous changes, which forever alter and displace the previously existing equilibrium state.

> These spontaneous and discontinuous changes in the channel of the circular flow and these disturbances in the center of equilibrium appear in the sphere of industrial and commercial life, not in the sphere of the wants of the consumer of final products.
>
> (Schumpeter, 1912, p. 65).

Concerning today's Walrasian theory of general equilibrium where production is but an appendix to consumption theory, this is a totally different perspective and this may also give one reason why Schumpeter (1942) later on used the theory of monopolistic competition as the starting point of his analysis of the dynamics of capitalism. Defining development as driven by the spontaneous action of the dynamic entrepreneur Schumpeter (1912, p. 66) then classifies the possibilities for such actions as follows:

> Development in our sense is then defined by the carrying out of new combinations. This concept covers the following five cases: (1) The introduction of a new good that is one with which consumers are not yet familiar or of a new quality of a good. (2) The introduction of a new method of production, that is one not yet tested by experience in the branch of manufacture concerned, which need by no means be founded upon a discovery scientifically new, and can also exist in a new way of handling a commodity commercially. (3) The opening of a new market, that is a market into which the particular branch of manufacture of the country in question has not previously entered, whether or not this market has existed before. (4) The conquest of a new source of supply of raw materials or half-manufactured goods, again irrespective of whether this source already exists or whether it has first to be created. (5) The carrying out of the new organization of any industry, like the creation of a monopoly position (for example through trustification) or the breaking up of a monopoly position.

To realize these various activities the role of credit is essential, since it allows to start such projects with a degree of innovation, often created by new ideas of new entrants in certain markets. Credit helps to redirect labor and capital from old combinations to definitely new ones through process or product innovation and more, see the above list given by Schumpeter. It is therefore not just the use of idle resources of the economy, but the redirection of the employed resources towards new projects and the extra profits they can generate in comparison to their competitors. A typical example here is the railroadization discussed at length in Schumpeter (1939).

The innovative character of the Schumpeterian entrepreneurs thus alters the way the economy has been functioning so far and this the more rapidly the larger the scale on which such entrepreneurs enter the scene. Of course there are subsequent processes of the diffusion of the newly created technology or products, which in the course of time reduce extra profits and these new projects have become a routinized economic activity. Yet processes of innovation and diffusion may cluster in historical time and may thus lead to the long phased evolution of social structures of accumulation as they are described historically in Schumpeter (1939) as three Kondratieff waves (superimposed by shorter cycles in addition).

It is not our intention here to go into the details of Schumpeter's analysis of the forces that drive the evolution of capitalist economies. We refer the reader instead to the paper by Swedberg (1991) on Schumpeter's work and biography and to a voluminous edition on Schumpeter and Neo-Schumpeterian Economics edited by Hanusch and Pyka (2007). Our interest instead is to go on from Schumpeter's analysis of capitalism to his analysis of competitive socialism and the implications it may have for the model of flexicurity capitalism that is the subject of this chapter.

Questioning the viability of (at his time) existing Eastern state socialism from the viewpoint of immaturity, Schumpeter (1942) developed a concept of socialism for Western countries in the state of maturity characterized as a type of competitive socialism built on foundations erected unconsciously through the big enterprizes created by the Rockefellers, the Vanderbilts, and other famous dynasties in the Western industrialized countries. Schumpeter discusses the question of whether this type of socialism can work, how the corresponding socialist blueprints should look like, and to what extent they are superior to the capitalist mark II blueprints (of the mega-corporations) that Schumpeter conceived as having made obsolescent the entrepreneurial functioning of his view of capitalism mark I, the dynamic entrepreneur, and the process of creative destruction, which is conducted by this leading form of an economic agent.

Monopolistic practices, vanishing investment opportunities, and growing hostility in the social structure of capitalism where part of the reasons that in Schumpeter's view characterized the decomposition of capitalism as he investigated it in 1942. Against this scenery he described the superiority of the socialist blueprint of Western competitive type, the transition to this form of social structure of accumulation and the comparative efficiency of such economies. In a separate chapter he discusses the human element in this type of economy, the problem of work organization, and the integration of bourgeois forms of management under capitalism into this type of socialism, including the incentive problems concerning the behavior of these economic agents.

A typical statement with respect to the latter situation is:

> It is not difficult however to insert the stock of bourgeois extraction into its proper place within that machine and to reshape its habits of work. ⋯ Rational treatments of the ex-bourgeois elements with a view to securing a maximum performance from them will then not require anything that is not just as necessary in the case of managerial personnel of any other extraction
>
> Schumpeter (1942, p. 65).

It may appear from today's perspective that his focused and provocative discussion of these points in Sect. III of the chapter "The Human Element" can be questioned to a certain degree. However, the managerial element in existing Western capitalism has become more and more the focus of public debate ranging from the salaries to the ethics the (top) managerial personal should receive and adopt, respectively. Actual discussions on the behavior of industrial management therefore are already preparing the ground for a situation where these persons may be attributed an appropriate level of exclusiveness, that may completely suffice to motivate their efforts to a sufficient degree with a problem-adequate perspective. We do not, however, claim here that such short characterizations suffice as considerations of the issue. On the contrary, detailed microeconomic and other investigations are absolutely necessary here to deal with such issues, yet, these issues have to be dealt with in actual capitalist management problems anyway. The important point in Schumpeter's arguments is that Western capitalism may transform itself automatically into some kind of competitive socialism on the basis of Western management principles. Such a statement can also be applied to the evolution of the Nordic European countries, which may be en-route on a progress path towards a kind of social structure of accumulation we have modeled as flexicurity capitalism in this chapter.

With respect to the workforce of firms – in capitalism as well as in his type of socialism Schumpeter (1942, p. 213) states:

> Second, closely allied to the necessity of incessant training of the normal is the necessity of dealing with the subnormal performer. This term does not refer to isolated pathological cases, but to a broad fringe of perhaps 25% of the population. So far as subnormal performance is due to moral or volitional defects, it is perfectly unrealistic to expect that it will vanish with capitalism. The great problem and the great enemy of humanity, the subnormal, will be as much with us as he is now. He can hardly be dealt with by *unaided* group discipline alone - although of course the machinery of authoritarian discipline can be so constructed as to work, partly at least, through the group of which the subnormal is an element.

In view of our discussion of the working of Marx's general law of accumulation under today's conditions in Western type economies, we would, however, point here to the fact that capitalism itself is in part responsible for the existence of the subnormal element as characterized in the above quote from Schumpeter's work. Mass unemployment, and its consequences for family life much beyond the current status on the labor market, alienation from human types of work organization, degradation of part of the workforce as the unskilled element in an otherwise flourishing economy, the rise and the fall of the welfare state and the latter's consequences for basic income needs, sufficient health care, sufficient care for the children and the elderly, and adequate schooling systems are just some of the reasons why the "subnormal" element in the population is a persistent fact of life. In this respect, we would claim that the social acceptance of a system of flexicurity and its educational substructure – as we have sketched it in this chapter – would be one way to eliminate the subnormal segment from the population gradually, but maybe not totally.

We therefore assert here that a system of flexicurity capitalism – based on the principles we have modeled in this chapter – would progressively tend towards social acceptance and social learning processes that put it on a progress path towards viable economic reproduction, sufficient income and care for everybody, and – if security is well developed to cope with flexibility of a Schumpeterian kind (creative destruction) – that leads it into a situation where it can easily compete with societies that are subject to the Marxian reserve army mechanism and the ruthless capitalism that derives from it.

The central message of Schumpeter's (1942) work on "Capitalism, Socialism and Democracy" – that socialism is created out of Western capitalist economies, and not on the basis of (the now past) Eastern type of socialism – thus can be carried over to the current debate on the possibility of flexicurity capitalism. Also this form of socio-economic reproduction may be organized through large production units and their efficient – though bureaucratic – management, a form of management that is developed out of the principles used under capitalism in the efficient conduct of large (internationally oriented) enterprizes. Equally well, as we currently experience this in the service sector (both for industrial production as well as for private consumption), there may be sufficient room for the dynamic entrepreneur of Schumpeterian type, in particular through the flexible entry and exit conditions the flexicurity variant of capitalism may allow for.

It is certainly true that contemporaneous capitalism (often of the ruthless type, but in certain countries also of a socially acceptable kind) is not likely to be forced into a defensive position, at least from its performance on the goods and on the labor markets (though the current operation of financial markets may produce extremely undesirable results). Yet, the consciousness that ruthless, unrestricted capitalism is producing significant negative external social and environmental effects is increasing throughout the world economy and this gives the hope that an alternative form of capitalism – based on flexicurity principles – may be superior in its socio-economic performance, at least when approached in the state of maturity as it was already considered a necessity in Schumpeter's vision of a democratic society based on competitive socialism.

To a certain degree this alternative variety of capitalism also is of a ruthless type, if Schumpeterian creative destruction processes are allowed for, but as in any democratic society there are of course more or less close limits to the choice of techniques (e.g., in bio-genetics) and the choice of products (e.g., in war-games), limits that are to be set by the elected political leadership of each country.

Marx viewed the general law of accumulation and its perpetual reserve army mechanism as the element that not only allowed, but was also needed for the reproduction of capitalism. Schumpeter considered changes towards a competitive socialism as a possible alternative to the form of capitalism of his times. We think that there is a chance for an alternative to current forms of ruthless capitalism that not only adopts some welfare principles, but that is founded on a coherently based socio-economic structure that is socially accepted, but that is flexible enough to quickly adjust to the changing world market conditions. The foundations are social acceptance in an educated democratic society. The problems are given by the mastering of Keynesian types of business fluctuations and Schumpeterian types of creative process and product revolutions and – of course – of the control of financial markets such that the real activities of an economy do not just become the side-product of a casino as it was already observed in Keynes's (1936) General Theory.

10.9 Conclusions and Outlook

Starting from the problematic features and the social consequences of the reserve army dynamics characterizing the evolution of the labor markets of many contemporaneous developed capitalist economies, this chapter tried to demonstrate that a combination of ideas of Marx, Keynes, and Schumpeter on the future of capitalism can provide an alternative to the ruthless form of competition that is currently ruling the world (in developed as well as developing countries). In place of the multilayered degradation of a significant proportion of the population also of democratically governed societies, we designed economic reproduction schemes (including education and skill formation) of a competitive form of capitalism that combines flexicurity of a very high degree with security of income as well as employment for the workforce. Schumpeter's investigation of the workability of a competitive type of socialism is thereby carried one step further towards a social vision, which preserves to a greater extent the advantages of the existing capitalist forms of production and circulation, but which nevertheless creates a social structure of accumulation, which in its essence is liberated from the human degradation we can even observe in leading industrialized countries in the world economy.

The essential ingredients along the progress path towards such a social structure are not only a basic income guarantee of the workfare type (which includes the obligation to work), but also a reorganization of the labor market towards an employer of first (not last) resort who organizes in a decentralized way the work for all people not employed within privately run industries, but also the work of officially retired person who are still willing to offer their human capital on the labor markets of the economy. The workability of the designed reproduction scheme of flexicurity type of course depends – in the same way as many other actual organizational problems – on detailed microeconomic analyses of the labor relations within large, medium-sized, and small business firms as well as in the public sector. Yet, economic incentives need to be coupled with an educational system that not only creates the basis for skill formation, but also provides the proper foundations for citizenship education in a democratic society, where citizens essentially approve the high degree of flexibility in the industrial part of the economy (and not only there) on the basis of the security aspects of the flexicurity concept and the equal opportunity principles during primary and secondary education.

There are of course many microproblems to be solved on the way towards a proper design of working of the Schumpeterian process of creative destruction in the flexicurity economy, problems that were only touched upon in our presentations of the barebones of flexicurity capitalism. There are also many macroproblems to be solved on this way, since Keynesian effective demand constraints may lead to unwanted fluctuations in the industrial sector of the economy, caused by malfunctions in the financial sector of the economy in particular. It is far from clear at the present stage of our investigation whether these micro- and macroproblems can indeed all be coped with on the way to a well-educated democratic society, which provides income and employment guarantees (and therewith interrelated obligations), but no job guarantees, but maybe significant job discontinuities coupled with a process of life-long learning.

The main support for the need of an evolution towards such a flexicurity society in our view comes from the fact that the currently existing alternative reproduction schemes of capitalism do not provide a social structure of accumulation that is compatible with an educated and democratic society in the longer run, since their reoccurring situations of mass unemployment undermine social cohesion in many ways in such societies (if this cohesion did exist in them at all), leading to social segmentation, social class clashes, and more. The evolution in the Nordic states of the European Union provide examples how such a development towards socially accepted flexicurity based on a modern schooling system may be approached. We close the chapter, however, with the observation that it does not yet say much on how the modeled situation can in fact be reached in actual economies, at current primarily in the Nordic countries. We here simply assume that the individual experience with progress in educational systems (towards equal opportunities in particular), with the need for flexibility as well as security during the working life, and with democratic institutions on all levels of the society will implement ratchet effects in individual and social choice mechanisms, which prevent return to the Marxian reserve army mechanism as it has been and continues to be investigated in the many contributions to the original Goodwin Growth Cycle model in view of what happens in actual capitalist economies.

We have started, in Chap. 1 of this book, from a very basic model of a capitalist economy which, on the one hand, used microfoundations (in a very simple manner) as relevant modeling tool, but which stressed, on the other hand, the need to have at least two agents (capitalist and workers) if the model is really meant to represent a capitalistic society. The model therefore rejected the representative agent approach of mainstream macroeconomics, where the conflict between labor and capital is integrated into a single "soul." In the chosen continuous time framework we moreover argued, as in Asada, Flaschel, and Proaño (2008), that the assumption of permanent market clearing (at any "microsecond") is not an appropriate hypothesis to characterize the working of (at least) the real markets of the economy. We therefore used an expectations-augmented wage Phillips curve (with model-consistent expectations) as adjustment process on the market for labor (but left out Keynesian demand problems on the market for goods to keep the model simple). The implied differentiated saving habits of workers and capitalists led in this model to a law of motion for the distribution of the capital stock between workers and pure capitalists, so that in particular the savings of workers out of wage income and profit income did not rule out the existence of pure capitalists in the steady state.

The limiting extremely Classical situation where workers do not save and where capitalists do not consume and where therefore the latter own the whole capital stock of the economy may be considered an approximation of the situation before World War I, and be characterized as constituting Capitalism, Mark I, while the above case with differentiated saving habits may be called Capitalism, Mark II.[17] Both types of capitalism can be characterized by and large as being dissent-driven. For the latter type this dissent may be emblematized by the rise and the subsequent

[17] This is not identical to the way these terms are used to characterize the evolution of Schumpeter's theory of capitalism, which was focused on the figure of the dynamic entrepreneur.

fall of the welfare state in most Western capitalist economies (corresponding to a certain degree to the rise and the fall of Eastern socialism).

In the present chapter, by contrast, we have attempted to formulate a model of Capitalism, Mark III, where essentially consent (on macroeconomic issues) between the management of firms and the workers is one of the pillars of the economy and the considered society, while the Chaps. 8 and 9 considered the working of Capitalism, Mark II.[18] It may well be that Capitalism, Mark III may be difficult to reach in the globalized world we are now living in. But there are – for example, in the Nordic Countries of Europe – elements of a progress path towards flexicurity capitalism already visible, and the debate on such transformational processes is a lively one in the European Union at present. It is the hope of the author of this book that it can contribute to such a debate by showing that aspects of Marx's, Keynes,' and Schumpeter's work can be successfully combined to model and understand the current situation of World capitalism and its future evolution. Such a MKS system – as called by Richard Goodwin, see the appendix for details – in our view provides a proper synthesis for the analysis of the macrodynamics of capitalism, a synthesis of very differing research profiles, that at first sight seems to be impossible, but which indeed unifies complementary approaches to the understanding of capitalism, widespread enough not to allow to characterize such a system as just one (and even overcome) school of economic thought.

[18] Without studying the consequences of the savings of workers, however, as in Chap. 1.

The M-K-S System. The Functioning and Evolution of Capitalism (by Richard M. Goodwin)

What I wish to sketch[19] is an analytic system consisting of selected elements, suitably combined, of the concepts of the three great economists, Marx, Keynes, and Schumpeter. What a strange conjunction of the stars, which could combine the dates of three such totally disparate individuals: Jewish intellectual revolutionary, English liberal reformer, and Central European reactionary. Incompatible though they are, I have found in each of them the most illuminating insights; furthermore, whilst their integral systems are quite incompatible, certain central elements from each seem to me to be essential to the understanding of the behavior of industrial capitalism. Marx had the particular advantage of being totally hostile to capitalism whilst accepting the necessity of understanding it the better to foretell its passing. Schumpeter approved of capitalism but agreed, though for different reasons, that its dynamism would bring it to an end. Keynes wanted nothing better than to save capitalism from its own irrational behavior, though he did foresee the euthanasia of the rentier. Marx, and like him, Schumpeter, were deeply concerned with the wider social aspects of capitalist evolution: I shall, however, limit myself to the narrowly economic side.

In my view it is illuminating to regard capitalism as an example of perpetual morphogenesis: *Capital* (vol. I) appeared in the same year as Darwin's *Origin of Species* and Marx felt they were fellow adventurers in uncharted territory (a feeling not reciprocated). Were he alive today, would he not hail Rene Thom as a fellow spirit? Seeing capitalism not as timeless wonder but rather an evolving system, which has to be seen as an intermittent but persistent generator of changing morphology. The analysis cannot be of the familiar dynamics of a given system, but rather of a system characterized by continuing alteration of its essential technological structure.

Darwin missed joining our astrological group by only one year, but he must be considered an honorary member, since he did for natural history what Marx did for social history. Beyond the essential point of view of evolutionary morphology, all similarity ends: Marx was a critical admirer of Darwin but did not fall victim to simple-minded translation of concepts; he was, of course, violently hostile to the social Darwinism of bourgeois apologists. As Schumpeter carefully puts it: "Marx may have experienced satisfaction at the emergence of Darwinist evolution. But his own had nothing whatever to do with it, and neither lends any support to the other", p. 441, the *History*.

The problem, then, is how to conceptualize the evolutionary aspect of capitalism. The economic structure of previous societies changed, if at all, very slowly. In industrial capitalism there are elements of structural stability along with instability: they must be kept distinct and both are needed analytically. Human economic behavior has shown many examples of continuity over long periods. By contrast the striking characteristic of the bourgeois revolution was laissez-faire: the potent harnessing of

[19] Essay 6 in R.M. Goodwin (1989). Essays in Nonlinear Economic Dynamics. Bern: Peter Lang. I thank the publisher Peter Lang for the permission to reprint this essay here.

man's greed to the generation of new forms of production. Never before has there been such rapid and profound alteration of inherited ways of working and living, carried out with ruthless disregard for the effect on the lives of those involved. Biological concepts can be no more than suggestive for the study of social organisms: thus one might consider the familial structure, father to son and mother to daughter, as the genetic programming that gave continuity for so long to earlier social structures. Bourgeois society has seriously emasculated the family and substituted innovative, extra-familial education for the traditional ways.

To model this problem, I assume that there are costs that vary linearly with prices and demands that vary linearly with outputs: these constitute dual transmission mechanisms. Then there are given costs and demands that vary autonomously over time. For any set of given costs and demands, there will exist a set of equilibrium prices equal to total costs and outputs equal to total demands. I assume that the transmission mechanisms are asymptotically stable.

Schumpeter elaborated Marxian theory by investigating the impact on such a system, of innovations, broadly defined as any new, cost-reducing process, consisting of either a new method of producing an existing good or service, or a new good, better than existing ones. A single innovation becoming operational constitutes a shock to the system, shifting the equilibrium position, thus creating a disequilibrium state. In a competitive system there will ensue a distributed lagging reaction, a long train of adjustments, as prices fall (or fail to rise), leading to falling costs, and so on. If the innovation is quantitatively important, for example, in energy (steam, electricity, oil, nuclear) or in transport (railways, canals, steamships, motor cars, airplanes), it will affect seriously a large number of industries. Some of them, in view of the changing constellation of input costs, will then be led to making induced changes in production processes, Reality is not, of course, so simple. Most important innovations occur at first in crude form and only subsequently, in the course of a long series of small improvements, reach their full potential.

Marx was the first economist seriously to study the cyclical aspect to capitalism, and to point out that fluctuations were an essential, not peripheral, feature of the functioning of the system. Although he phrased it differently, Schumpeter took the same view. Unfortunately, Marx never got around to formulating a unified, explicit theory of the cycle. Schumpeter did, and it posed for him, as it would have for Marx, a difficult problem. If, as is surely the case, technical innovation consists of a large number of small changes, why does it not result in the steady state growth, so beloved of orthodox economists? Schumpeter tried to deal with this by his conception of "swarms," but, in my opinion, it is all too frail a construction to bear the weight of explaining fluctuations in the general level of activity.

The issue is a central one in dynamical analysis. No linear theory, like the transmission mechanism, can explain the generation and maintenance of oscillations. Both Marx and Schumpeter firmly maintained that cycles were endogenous to the system, and that they did not come from the weather, bad government, misbehavior of the banking system, etc., but that they were an inherent consequence of the very nature of capitalism. It follows therefore that in the structure of capitalism itself must be found the source of fluctuations.

One of the most illuminating ways to view oscillators is as frequency convertors. A steady source of energy of action is converted into a pulsating response. Therefore, what Schumpeter needed was an analysis of how a roughly steady stream of innovations, along with their many improvements, got altered into the ups and downs of capitalism. For me, Keynes's theory of effective demand supplied the missing link in Schumpeter's model. To make an innovation operational requires prior investment outlays. The transmission mechanism magnifies and distributes this demand amongst the other sectors. Thus occurs a general, as distinct from a sectoral, rise in outputs, which will in turn help the expansion of the new process. If the innovation and its secondary effects are large enough, the economy may be lifted to the region of full capacity. Then the accelerator becomes effective, which constitutes a *bifurcation* of behavior, changing the transmission mechanism from stability to instability. To put it as simply as possible, in aggregative real terms

$$\varepsilon\dot{y} = I - S = I - (1-\alpha)y,$$

where I is real innovational investment plus all other real outlays independent of the level of output, y, with α and ε as constants. The accelerator introduces a new dynamic term, $\beta\dot{y}$, with $\beta > \varepsilon > 0$, yielding

$$\varepsilon\dot{y} = I + \beta\dot{y} - (1-\alpha)y$$

so that

$$(\beta - \varepsilon)\dot{y} = (1-\alpha)y - I$$

and the system becomes unstable. Beyond this point we are treading on the Harrod–Keynes razor's edge. The economy grows at a rate that gradually reduces the Industrial Reserve Army to low levels, which will make it impossible to continue at the same rate of expansion. After a time the growth rate necessarily decelerates, which cuts out the accelerator and inhibits any remaining innovational investment. The economy relapses either to a lower growth rate or declines, but in the new equilibrium state it will have a different structure and a higher productivity with lower employment for any given output level, thus renewing the Industrial Reserve Army.

As a young economist I felt this Keynesian-type cycle theory was the natural, essential completion of Schumpeter's "vision." I spent much effort to convince him of it. About cycle theory he was reasonably open-minded, and even went so far as to agree that, if I would give a course of lectures on mathematical cycle theory, he would attend ... which he did (along with Gottfried Haberler). But on the subject of Keynes's *General Theory* his mind was closed: nothing would convince him that it was anything but clever nonsense. I was baffled then and still am, to some extent: how could so acute, and so unprejudiced, a mind be so blind? I offer some possible explanations. Keynes's grasp of economic orthodoxy, never very great, (especially of the continental variety), had become ossified: it had, happily, been replaced by some sense of the real functioning of capitalism. By contrast, Schumpeter, having begun as an outrageous, semi-Marxist rebel (ejected from Böhm–Bawerk's seminar and denied a job in the university), had, by the 1930s, so immersed himself in teaching what academics wrote that he was quite unable to conceive of anything radically different. For example, he firmly believed that Walras was the greatest of all economists because of his methodology and in spite of his essentially trivial dynamics. Whilst Schumpeter, unlike Wicksell, did not explicitly assume full employment, nonetheless the cast of his thought was that technological progress, not effective demand, determined the variations of output, as controlled by resources.

In an unpublished lecture on Ricardo, given in Japan, he developed one of those brilliant half-truths, maintaining that Ricardo had four unknowns, for which he needed to solve four equations: but, being like Schumpeter himself, no mathematician, he reduced the problem to one unknown. The wage level he took as fixed by the Malthusian iron law, profits disappeared into rents and were determined by them. This left output, the level of which he simply did not discuss, instead, concerning himself solely with distributive shares in output. Distributive shares, since they add to unity, yield inverse relations necessarily: if one goes up another goes down. One can find this strain of thought in Marx, deeply influenced as he was by Ricardo, and it is still visible, in all its purity, in the work of Sraffa. Accumulation drives wages up and profits down, leading to crisis, depression and the search for labor saving innovations. This is true for shares but not for levels of wages and profits. After Keynes we all know that, on the contrary, with unemployed resources, higher wages can, and usually do, lead to higher profits: or, higher profits can, and usually do, lead to higher wages. Profits depend not only on the difference between prices and wage costs, but even more potently on the scale of output relative to capacity. The neoclassical assumption of market-clearing and the determination of output by resources, not by effective demand, disastrously confused a whole generation of economists. However, once the region of full employment is reached, the Ricardo–Marx assumption becomes operative.

The impact of Keynes was to produce a new form of denial of the Marxian breakdown theory. The existence of a steady-state, exponential growth path was established, for which it seemed that all that was needed was a sophisticated demand management which could realize it. The quite exceptional post-war boom gave strong support to the view of its feasibility. Marx is, however, not so easily dismissed: long before Keynes he attacked Say's Law and the facile optimism, which maintained that it guaranteed full employment. The post-war maintenance of near full employment brought a growing intensity of the conflict between worker and employer over the shares of product – a conflict which has only been resolved either by inflation or by massive unemployment. It is by now clear that the Industrial Reserve Army has all along played the essential role in capitalism that Marx ascribed to it: the economy needs unemployment to restore labor "discipline" and the conditions for further growth.

Once the economy has collapsed into depression, the question arises as to what will bring about a recovery. Keynes has no answer: Marx has one or two, not altogether convincing, answers. The growth of the Industrial Reserve Army weakens the bargaining power of labor: the difficulty is that this does not restore profits, since they depend on output as well as cost. Then he refers to the irrational drive to accumulate – but accumulate for what? Here we need Schumpeter. It is rational to accumulate and profitable to invest in an innovation, even if excess capacity exists and even if demand is low; there ensues "creative destruction" of existing, capacity.

By calling in economic history to be an essential part of economic analysis, Schumpeter, like Marx, made a profound change, though one not too much to the liking of either economic historians or of economic theorists. As an aspiring young theorist, I was much upset to discover, after his unexpected death, that Schumpeter's last paper urged economists to study the records of the great business enterprizes! Superficially very un-Marxian, it is in fact very much in the line of the master's thinking: the industrial tycoon, unappealing though he is, is the dynamo of capitalism and the generator of new social structures In this way, and in this way only, we can explain the total lack of any form of strict periodicity, hidden or overt, in economic time series. If an innovation is small, or if it has already been substantially completed, when the economy collapses, it may "bump along the bottom" for some considerable time before rising again. On the other hand, if, following the collapse of a boom, a large innovation still has much development left in it, then, though the slump will temporarily inhibit investment, it will quickly be resumed when the economy ceases to decline. In this manner it is possible not only to explain the variable periodicity, but also the so-called "long waves." There can be no question of establishing the existence of Kondratieff cycles, since the run of data is too short. Indeed it may be pointless to try to develop a theory of long cycles. On the other hand, technological history, being mainly exogenous to the economy, can explain everything. Thus a big thing like the railways can explain why a relatively long span of time will have vigorous booms and short, sharp slumps; the lack of such an event will explain why other periods have weak booms and prolonged stagnations.

I agree with Schumpeter that in Marx it is not the detail of his analytic apparatus but in his over-all "vision" that his greatness and his unique contribution lies. He saw society as an organism evolving historically along a path determined dynamically by, and determining, its productive structure. Starting from this evolutionary viewpoint, he avoided the errors of the "vulgar" economists who gave a rosy, timeless view of capitalism.

Particularly important, and unique to him, was the conception of the Industrial Reserve Army. Connecting this with distributive shares – or more polemically, exploitation – he saw that if wages were too high, accumulation slackened; the urge to save labor increased and the demand for labor weakened. Consequently, there follows a period of wages lagging behind productivity; potential profitability increases and accumulation accelerates again, leading back to the initial situation of rising demand for labor, rising wages, and declining reserves of unemployed. Thus capitalism chases but never finds a "natural," or dynamically equilibrated, level of unemployment. Again, Marx, unlike most economists, took the simple view, fully borne out by later statistics, that profits, not some intertemporally maximized utility, were the source and explanation of most saving and investment.

A great deal depends on whether the system is constrained exogenously by factor supply, or endogenously by demand. Generally, capacity, natural resources, and labor supply, if fully employed, constitute parametric constraints. However, unfortunately for orthodox theory, most of the time the system is not so constrained:

the problem is to sort out how and when the constraints do, and do not, operate. Capacity, of course, is not at all a constraint in the long-run, nor, much of the time, in the short-run: this has to be resolved by the Marxian accumulation analysis. Natural resources, contrary to the Classical view, have not proved to be a serious constraint (though this may change in the future). Labor is the crucial element, much more complex: it is sometimes a constraint and sometimes not. In the course of a vigorous expansion, the supply of trained and disciplined labor tends to be exhausted. But in the longer time span it has not been so: capitalism has been able to grow exponentially for two centuries, uninhibited by labor shortages. To begin with it inherited the endemic, rural surplus population; then came the natural increase through falling death rate, then large scale migration, and, finally, the extraordinary technological efflorescence, which "liberated" workers for the expansion of production. On the other hand, there clearly have been periods when demand pressed heavily on the labor supply, and others where it was not so. Thus whilst in the short-run, there is always an upper limit to growth, given by the effective labor supply, in the long-run, there is little or no limit: labor becomes more or less an endogenous variable, growth being set by the rate of accumulation. As Marx indicated, labor shortage and high wages are a potent stimulant to the search for labor-saving innovations, and these stretch the labor supply to accommodate more growth. This complex behavior of labor supply clearly transforms the problem and the solution: we get *no* limit to growth except the rate of accumulation, which thus helps to explain the great variations in the growth rate of capitalist economies.

Taking a simple view, one might characterize the history of industrial capitalism as follows: in the previous century capitalists enjoyed a highly elastic, cheap labor supply from agriculture, handicrafts, and domestic labor. In our own century the rate of accumulation has been sufficient, largely to exhaust this source, leading to a tendency for rising real wages to press on profits, with sharpened conflict over distribution. With the gradual introduction of automation, it is conceivable that there may be a reversion to the earlier condition. The original industrial revolution consisted essentially in the substitution of natural energy for human and animal energy. Animals were eliminated but not man, needed as machine minded: now machines can mind machines. Though it is too soon to say, it is possible that a substantial portion of the labor force may be set "free," thus creating a truly formidable Industrial Reserve Army.

Precisely this danger was foreseen, over 30 years ago, by Norbert Wiener, one of the principal creators of control theory. "Perhaps I may clarify the background of the present situation if I say that the first industrial revolution ... was the devaluation of the human arm by the competition of machinery ... the modern industrial revolution is similarly bound to devalue the human brain at least in its simpler and more routine decisions ... I have said that this new development has unbounded possibilities for good and for evil ... It gives the human race a new and most effective collection of mechanical slaves to perform its labor. Such mechanical labor has most of the economic properties of slave labor, although unlike slave labor, it does not involve the direct demoralizing effects of human cruelty. However, any labor that accepts the conditions of competition with slave labor, accepts the conditions of slave labor, and is essentially slave labor." *Cybernetics*, Preface, 1947. This scenario raises the spectre of really massive unemployment and with it a new and more violent form of class conflict. The climate of the labor market under these conditions would probably be very different from that in the nineteenth century. Having finally tasted power and high wages, the working class is not likely to be as weak as formerly. On the other hand, the great wealth of the modern world may, and probably will, be deployed to blunt protest by lavish social subventions.

Without attempting an explicit model, I may try to summarize what I have been trying to say. By combining elements from all three of our thinkers, one attains one good schemata for the analysis of capitalism as a system in variable states of turmoil.

(1) Marx – the law of Moses and the prophets is profits and accumulation. But accumulation by itself would lead to falling profits, so another aspect of his theory was elaborated by

(2) Schumpeter – The driving force of capitalism is innovation in production (not in consumption, which is passive).

(3) The economic transmission mechanism is substantially constant over shortish periods, so that we can analyze its reactions to

(a) new processes and goods and the resulting changes in relative prices, and

(b) how other sectors shift to lower cost processes in response to the changes in relative prices. Thus innovations, particularly in energy and transport, gradually infect the whole economy.

Also necessary is

(4) Keynes, who taught us that effective demand, as well as, and more often than, the existing resources, determines the level and rate of change of output. This supplies the essential ingredient to Schumpeter's elaboration of Marx, showing how particular technological progress becomes generalized into a broad upsurge in the whole economy, thought at very different rates for each sector.

The upper turning point creates little difficulty: we meet the accelerator in the middle of the upswing, so that the system becomes unstable. This means growth rates that cannot be sustained. The system becomes constrained by resources, by high relative prices for labor, and for raw materials. Simultaneously, the growth rate decelerates and the real cost of production rises, which leads directly to inflation as the reaction of producers. This masks but cannot remove the real trouble, which is deceleration. So investment is cut, expectations collapse dramatically, and the economy becomes stable downward to the level set by unsystematic expenditures, for example, government outlays, foreign trade. There the economy sits until the arrival of a new innovation large enough to get it off the bottom. In this way we explain the historical specificity of each fluctuation. These movements are not strictly speaking cycles; they appear to be similar because the capitalist drive for profit means an eternal search for cost-reducing innovations, so that sooner or later growth is always renewed; but then it proceeds too rapidly and breaks down.

Mathematical Appendix: Some Useful Theorems

1 The Concepts of Local Stability and Global Stability in a System of Differential Equations

Let $\dot{x} \equiv \frac{dx}{dt} = f(x), x \in R^n$ be a system of n-dimensional differential equations that has an equilibrium point x^* such that $f(x^*) = 0$, where t is interpreted as "time." The equilibrium point of this system is said to be *locally asymptotically stable*, if every trajectory starting sufficiently near the equilibrium point converges to it as $t \to +\infty$. If stability is independent of the distance of the initial state from the equilibrium point, the equilibrium point is said to be *globally asymptotically stable*, or *asymptotically stable in the large*, see Gandolfo (1996, p. 333)

2 Theorems that are Useful for the Stability Analysis of a System of Linear Differential Equations or the Local Stability Analysis of a System of Nonlinear Differential Equations

Theorem A.1 (Local stability theorem, Gandolfo (1996, pp. 360–362)). *Let $\dot{x}_i = f_i(x)$, $x = [x_1, x_2, \ldots, x_n] \in R^n \mid (i = 1, 2, \cdots, n)$ be an n-dimensional system of differential equations that has an equilibrium point $x^* = [x_1^*, x_2^*, \ldots, x_n^*]$ such that $f(x^*) = 0$. Suppose that the functions f_i have continuous first-order partial derivatives, and consider the Jacobian matrix evaluated at the equilibrium point x^**

$$J = \begin{bmatrix} f_{11} & f_{12} & \cdots & f_{1n} \\ f_{21} & f_{22} & \cdots & f_{2n} \\ \vdots & \vdots & \ddots & \vdots \\ f_{n1} & f_{n2} & \cdots & f_{nn} \end{bmatrix},$$

where $f_{ij} = \partial f_i / \partial x_j$ $(i, j = 1, 2, \ldots, n)$ are evaluated at the equilibrium point.

(i) The equilibrium point of this system is locally asymptotically stable if all the roots of the characteristic equation $|\lambda I - J| = 0$ *have negative real parts.*

(ii) The equilibrium point of this system is unstable if at least one root of the characteristic equation $|\lambda I - J| = 0$ *has positive real part.*

(iii) The stability of the equilibrium point cannot be determined from the properties of the Jacobian matrix if all the roots of the characteristic equation $|\lambda I - J| = 0$ *have nonpositive real parts but at least one root has zero real part.*

Theorem A.2 (See Murata (1977, pp. 14–16)). *Let* A *be an* $(n \times n)$ *matrix such that*

$$A = \begin{bmatrix} a_{11} & a_{12} & \cdots & a_{1n} \\ a_{21} & a_{22} & \cdots & a_{2n} \\ \vdots & \vdots & \ddots & \vdots \\ a_{n1} & a_{n2} & \cdots & a_{nn} \end{bmatrix}.$$

(i) We can express the characteristic equation $|\lambda I - A| = 0$ *as*

$$|\lambda I - A| = \lambda^n + a_1\lambda^{n-1} + a_2\lambda^{n-2} + \cdots + a_r\lambda^{n-r} + \cdots + a_{n-1}\lambda + a_n = 0, \quad (10.3)$$

where

$$a_1 = -(\text{trace } A) = -\sum_{i=1}^{n} a_{ii}, \quad a_2 = (-1)^2 \sum_{i<j} \begin{vmatrix} a_{ii} & a_{ij} \\ a_{ji} & a_{jj} \end{vmatrix}, \ldots,$$

$$a_r = (-1)^r \sum_{i<j<\cdots<k} \underbrace{\begin{vmatrix} a_{ii} & a_{ij} & \cdots & a_{ik} \\ a_{ji} & a_{jj} & \cdots & a_{jk} \\ \vdots & \vdots & \ddots & \vdots \\ a_{ki} & a_{kj} & \cdots & a_{kk} \end{vmatrix}}_{(r)}, \ldots, \quad a_n = (-1)^n \det A.$$

(ii) Let λ_i $(i = 1, 2, \ldots, n)$ *be the roots of the characteristic equation (10.3). Then, we have*

$$\text{trace } J = \sum_{i=1}^{n} a_{ii} = \sum_{i=1}^{n} \lambda_i, \quad \det A = \prod_{i=1}^{n} \lambda_i.$$

Theorem A.3 (Routh–Hurwitz conditions for stable roots in an n-dimensional system, cf. Murata (1977, p. 92), Gandolfo (1996, pp. 221–222)).[1] *All of the roots of the characteristic equation (10.3) have negative real parts if and only if the following set of inequalities is satisfied:*

$$\Delta_1 = a_1 > 0, \quad \Delta_2 = \begin{vmatrix} a_1 & a_3 \\ 1 & a_2 \end{vmatrix} > 0, \quad \Delta_3 = \begin{vmatrix} a_1 & a_3 & a_5 \\ 1 & a_2 & a_4 \\ 0 & a_1 & a_3 \end{vmatrix} > 0, \ldots,$$

[1] See also Gantmacher (1954) for many details that can be associated with and Brock and Malliaris (1989) for a compact representation of these conditions.

$$\Delta_n = \begin{vmatrix} a_1 & a_3 & a_5 & a_7 & \cdots & 0 \\ 1 & a_2 & a_4 & a_6 & \cdots & 0 \\ 0 & a_1 & a_3 & a_5 & \cdots & 0 \\ 0 & 1 & a_2 & a_4 & \cdots & 0 \\ 0 & 0 & a_1 & a_3 & \cdots & 0 \\ \vdots & \vdots & \vdots & \vdots & \ddots & \vdots \\ 0 & 0 & 0 & 0 & \cdots & a_n \end{vmatrix} > 0.$$

The following Theorems A.4–A.6 are corollaries of Theorem A.3.

Theorem A.4 (Routh–Hurwitz conditions for a two-dimensional system). *All of the roots of the characteristic equation*

$$\lambda^2 + a_1\lambda + a_2 = 0$$

have negative real parts if and only if the set of inequalities

$$a_1 > 0, \quad a_2 > 0 \qquad \textit{is satisfied.}$$

Theorem A.5 (Routh–Hurwitz conditions for a three-dimensional system). *All of the roots of the characteristic equation*

$$\lambda^3 + a_1\lambda^2 + a_2\lambda + a_3 = 0$$

have negative real parts if and only if the set of inequalities

$$a_1 > 0, \quad a_3 > 0, \quad a_1 a_2 - a_3 > 0 \tag{10.4}$$

is satisfied.

Remark on Theorem A.5.
The inequality $a_2 > 0$ is satisfied if the set of inequalities (10.4) is satisfied.

Theorem A.6 (Routh–Hurwitz conditions for a four-dimensional system). *All roots of the characteristic equation*

$$\lambda^4 + a_1\lambda^3 + a_2\lambda^2 + a_3\lambda + a_4 = 0,$$

have negative real parts if and only if the set of inequalities

$$a_1 > 0, \quad a_3 > 0, \quad a_4 > 0, \quad \Phi \equiv a_1 a_2 a_3 - a_1^2 a_4 - a_3^2 > 0, \tag{10.5}$$

is satisfied.

Remark on Theorem A.6. The inequality $a_2 > 0$ is always satisfied if the set of inequalities (10.5) is satisfied.

3 Theorems that are Useful for the Global Stability Analysis of a System of Nonlinear Differential Equations

Theorem A.7 (Liapunov's theorem, cf. Gandolfo (1996, p. 410)). *Let* $\dot{x} = f(x), x = [x_1, x_2, \ldots, x_n] \in R^n$ *be an n-dimensional system of differential equations that has the unique equilibrium point* $x^* = [x_1^*, x_2^*, \ldots, x_n^*]$ *such that* $f(x^*) = 0$. *Suppose that there exists a scalar function* $V = V(x - x^*)$ *with continuous first derivatives and with the following properties (1)–(5):*

(1) $V \geqq 0$,
(2) $V = 0$ *if and only if* $x_i - x_i^* = 0$ *for all* $i \in \{1, 2, \ldots n\}$,
(3) $V \rightarrow +\infty$ *as* $\|x - x^*\| \rightarrow +\infty$,
(4) $\dot{V} = \sum_{i=1}^{n} \frac{\partial V}{\partial (x_i - x_i^*)} \dot{x}_i \leqq 0$,
(5) $\dot{V} = 0$ *if and only if* $x_i - x_i{*} = 0$ *for all* $i \in \{1, 2, \ldots, n\}$.

Then, the equilibrium point x^* *of the above system is globally asymptotically stable.*

Remark on Theorem A.7. The function $V = V(x - x^*)$ is called the "Liapunov function."

Theorem A.8 (Olech's theorem, cf. Olech (1963), Gandolfo (1996, pp. 354–355)). *Let* $\dot{x}_i = f_i(x_1, x_2)(i = 1, 2)$ *be a two-dimensional system of differential equations that has the unique equilibrium point* (x_1^*, x_2^*) *such that* $f_i(x_1^*, x_2^*) = 0\ (i = 1, 2)$. *Suppose that the functions* f_i *have continuous first-order partial derivatives. Furthermore, suppose that the following properties (1)–(3) are satisfied:*

(1) $\frac{\partial f_1}{\partial x_1} + \frac{\partial f_2}{\partial x_2} < 0$ *everywhere,*
(2) $(\frac{\partial f_1}{\partial x_1})(\frac{\partial f_2}{\partial x_2}) - (\frac{\partial f_1}{\partial x_2})(\frac{\partial f_2}{\partial x_1}) > 0$ *everywhere,*
(3) $(\frac{\partial f_1}{\partial x_1})(\frac{\partial f_2}{\partial x_2}) \neq 0$ *everywhere, or alternatively,* $(\frac{\partial f_1}{\partial x_2})(\frac{\partial f_2}{\partial x_1}) \neq 0$ *everywhere.*

Then, the equilibrium point of the above system is globally asymptotically stable.

4 Theorems that are Useful to Establish the Existence of Closed Orbits in a System of Nonlinear Differential Equations

Theorem A.9 (Poincaré–Bendixson theorem, Hirsch and Smale (1974, 11)). *Let* $\dot{x}_i = f_i(x_1, x_2)(i = 1, 2)$ *be a two-dimensional system of differential equations with the functions* f_i *continuous. A nonempty compact limit set of the trajectory of this system, which contains no equilibrium point, is a closed orbit.*

Theorem A.10 (Hopf bifurcation theorem for an n-dimensional system, cf. Guckenheimer and Holmes (1983, pp. 151–152), Lorenz (1993, p. 96) and Gandolfo (1996, p. 477)).[2] *Let $\dot{x} = f(x;\varepsilon), x \in R^n, \varepsilon \in R$ be an n-dimensional system of differential equations depending upon a parameter ε. Suppose that the following conditions (1)–(3) are satisfied:*

(1) The system has a smooth curve of equilibria given by $f(x^*(\varepsilon);\varepsilon) = 0$,
(2) The characteristic equation $|\lambda I - Df(x^*(\varepsilon_0);\varepsilon_0)| = 0$ has a pair of pure imaginary roots $\lambda(\varepsilon_0), \bar{\lambda}(\varepsilon_0)$ and no other roots with zero real parts, where $Df(x^*(\varepsilon_0);\varepsilon_0)$ is the Jacobian matrix of the above system at $(x^*(\varepsilon_0), \varepsilon_0)$ with the parameter value ε_0,
(3) $\left.\frac{\mathrm{d}\{Re\lambda(\varepsilon)\}}{\mathrm{d}\varepsilon}\right|_{\varepsilon=\varepsilon_0} \neq 0$, where $Re\lambda(\varepsilon)$ is the real part of $\lambda(\varepsilon)$.

Then, there exists a continuous function $\varepsilon(\gamma)$ with $\varepsilon(0) = \varepsilon_0$, and for all sufficiently small values of $\gamma \neq 0$ there exists a continuous family of nonconstant periodic solution $x(t,\gamma)$ for the above dynamical system, which collapses to the equilibrium point $x^*(\varepsilon_0)$ as $\gamma \to 0$. The period of the cycle is close to $2\pi/Im\lambda(\varepsilon_0)$, where $Im\lambda(\varepsilon_0)$ is the imaginary part of $\lambda(\varepsilon_0)$.

Remark on Theorem A.10. We can replace the condition (3) in Theorem A.10 by the following weaker condition (3a) (cf. Alexander and York (1978)).

(3a) For all ε that are near but not equal to ε_0, no characteristic root has zero real part.

The following theorem by Liu (1994) provides a convenient criterion for the occurrence of the so called "simple" Hopf bifurcation in an n-dimensional system. The "simple" Hopf bifurcation is defined as the Hopf bifurcation in which all the characteristic roots *except* a pair of purely imaginary ones have negative real parts.

Theorem A.11 (Liu's theorem, see Liu (1994)). *Consider the following characteristic equation with $n \geqq 3$:*

$$\lambda^n + a_1\lambda^{n-1} + a_2\lambda_{n-2} + \cdots + a_{n-1}\lambda + a_n = 0.$$

This characteristic equation has a pair of pure imaginary roots and $(n-2)$ roots with negative real parts if and only if the following set of conditions is satisfied:

$$\Delta_i > 0 \; for \; all \; i \in \{1,2,\ldots,n-2\}, \quad \Delta_{n-1} = 0, \quad a_n > 0,$$

where $\Delta_i (i = 1,2,\ldots,n-1)$ are Routh–Hurwitz terms defined as

$$\Delta_1 = a_1, \quad \Delta_2 = \begin{vmatrix} a_1 & a_3 \\ 1 & a_2 \end{vmatrix}, \quad \Delta_3 = \begin{vmatrix} a_1 & a_3 & a_5 \\ 1 & a_2 & a_4 \\ 0 & a_1 & a_3 \end{vmatrix}, \ldots,$$

[2] See also Strogatz (1994), Wiggins (1990) in this regard.

$$\Delta_{n-1} = \begin{vmatrix} a_1 & a_3 & a_5 & a_7 & \cdots & 0 & 0 \\ 1 & a_2 & a_4 & a_6 & \cdots & 0 & 0 \\ 0 & a_1 & a_3 & a_5 & \cdots & 0 & 0 \\ 0 & 1 & a_2 & a_4 & \cdots & 0 & 0 \\ 0 & 0 & a_1 & a_3 & \cdots & 0 & 0 \\ \vdots & \vdots & \vdots & \vdots & \ddots & \vdots & \vdots \\ 0 & 0 & 0 & 0 & \cdots & a_n & 0 \\ 0 & 0 & 0 & 0 & \cdots & a_{n-1} & 0 \\ 0 & 0 & 0 & 0 & \cdots & a_{n-2} & a_n \\ 0 & 0 & 0 & 0 & \cdots & a_{n-3} & a_{n-1} \end{vmatrix}.$$

The following theorems A.12–A.14 provide us with some convenient criteria for two-dimensional, three-dimensional, and four-dimensional Hopf bifurcations, respectively. It is worth noting that these criteria provide us with useful information on the "non-simple" as well as the "simple" Hopf bifurcations.

Theorem A.12. *The characteristic equation*

$$\lambda^2 + a_1\lambda + a_2 = 0$$

has a pair of pure imaginary roots if and only if the set of conditions

$$a_1 = 0, \quad a_2 > 0 \qquad \textit{is satisfied.}$$

In this case, we have the explicit solution $\lambda = \pm \mathrm{i}\sqrt{a_2}$, *where* $\mathrm{i} = \sqrt{-1}$.

Proof. Obvious because we have the solution $\lambda = (-a_1 \pm \sqrt{a_1^2 - 4a_2})/2$.

Theorem A.13 (cf. Asada (1995), Asada and Semmler (1995)). *The characteristic equation*

$$\lambda^3 + a_1\lambda^2 + a_2\lambda + a_3 = 0$$

has a pair of pure imaginary roots if and only if the set of conditions

$$a_2 > 0, \quad a_1a_2 - a_3 = 0$$

is satisfied. In this case, we have the explicit solution $\lambda = -a_1,\ \pm\mathrm{i}\sqrt{a_2}$, *where* $\mathrm{i} = \sqrt{-1}$.

Theorem A.14 (cf. Yoshida and Asada (2001), Asada and Yoshida (2003)). *Consider the characteristic equation*

$$\lambda^4 + a_1\lambda^3 + a_2\lambda^2 + a_3\lambda + a_4 = 0. \tag{10.6}$$

(i) The characteristic equation (10.6) has a pair of pure imaginary roots and two roots with nonzero real parts if and only if either of the following set of conditions (A) or (B) is satisfied:

(A) $a_1 a_3 > 0, \quad a_4 \neq 0, \quad \Phi \equiv a_1 a_2 a_3 - a_1^2 a_4 - a_3^2 = 0.$
(B) $a_1 = a_3 = 0, \quad a_4 < 0.$

(ii) The characteristic equation (10.6) has a pair of pure imaginary roots and two roots with negative real parts if and only if the following set of conditions (C) is satisfied:
(C) $a_1 > 0, \quad a_3 > 0, \quad a_4 > 0, \quad \Phi \equiv a_1 a_2 a_3 - a_1^2 a_4 - a_3^2 = 0.$

Remarks on Theorem A.14.

(1) The condition $\Phi = 0$ is always satisfied if the set of conditions (B) is satisfied.

(2) The inequality $a_2 > 0$ is always satisfied if the set of conditions (C) is satisfied.

(3) We can derive Theorem A.14 (ii) from Theorem A.11 as a special case with $n = 4$, although we cannot derive Theorem A.14 (i) from Theorem A.11.

References

Ackley, G. (1969). *Macroeconomic Theory*. New York: Macmillan.

Alexander, J. C., & York, J. A. (1978). Global bifurcation of periodic orbits. *American Journal of Mathematics*, 100, 263–292.

Allen, R. G. D. (1967). *Macro-Economic Theory*. London: Macmillan.

Amann, H. (1983). *Gewöhnliche Differentialgleichungen*. Berlin: Walter de Gruyter.

Andronov, A. A., & Chaikin, C. E. (1949). *Theory of Oscillations*. Princeton: Princeton University Press.

Armstrong, H., & Taylor, J. (1981). The measurement of different types of unemployment. In J. Creedy (Ed.), *The Economics of Unemployment in Britain* (pp. 99–121). London: Butterworth.

Arrowsmith, D. K., & Place, C. M. (1982). *Ordinary Differential Equations*. London: Chapman and Hall.

Asada, T. (1995). Kaldorian dynamics in an open economy. *Journal of Economics*, 2, 1–16.

Asada, T., & Franke, R. (1990). Expectations dynamics in a Keynes–Goodwin model of the business cycle. Bielefeld University: Discussion paper.

Asada, T., & Semmler, W. (1995). Growth and finance: An intertemporal model. *Journal of Macroeconomics*, 17, 623–649.

Asada, T., & Yoshida, H. (2003). Coefficient criterion for four-dimensional Hopf-bifurcations: A complete mathematical characterization and applications to economic dynamics. *Chaos, Solitons & Fractals*, 18(3), 421–423.

Asada, T., Chiarella, C., Flaschel, P., & Franke, R. (2009). *Lectures on Monetary Macrodynamics*. London: Routledge, forthcoming.

Asada, T., Chiarella, C., Flaschel, P., & Franke, R. (2003). *Open Economy Macrodynamics. An Integrated Disequilibrium Approach*. Berlin: Springer.

Asada, T., Chen, P., Chiarella, C., & Flaschel, P. (2006). Keynesian dynamics and the wage-price spiral. a baseline disequilibrium model. *Journal of Macroeconomics*, 28, 90–130.

Asada, T., Flaschel, P., & Proaño, C. (2008). Expectations, monetary policy and the real wage feedback channel. Two competing baseline approaches. Working paper, CEM, Bielefeld University.

Asada, T., Flaschel, P., & Proaño, C. (2008). *On the Indeterminacy of New Keynesian Models with Wage and Price Staggering in Continuous Time*. Bielefeld: Bielefeld University, mimeo.

Ball, L. (1991). The genesis of inflation and the costs of disinflation. *Journal of Money, Credit, and Banking*, 23, 439–461.

Barro, R. J. (1990). *Macroeconomics*. New York: John Wiley.

Barro, R. (1994). The aggregate supply/aggregate demand model. *Eastern Economic Journal*, 20, 1–6.

Barro, R. J., & Grossman, H. (1971). A general disequilibrium model of income and employment. *American Economic Review*, 61, 82–93.

Batchelor, R. (1981). A natural interpretation of the present unemployment. *Paper presented to the City University Conference on 'Monetarism in the United Kingdom'*. London: The City University.

Beltrami, E. (1987). *Mathematics for Dynamic Modeling*. London: Academic Press.

Benassy, J. -P. (1984). A non-walrasian model of the business cycle. *Journal of Economic Behaviour and Organization*, 5, 77–89.

Bergstrom, A. R. (1962). A model of technical progress, the production function and cyclical growth. *Economica*, 29, 1–16.

Black, F. (1974). Uniqueness of the price level in monetary growth models with rational expectations. *Journal of Economic Theory*, 7, 53–65.

Blanchard, O. (2006). *Macroeconomics*. New York: Prentice Hall.

Blanchard, O., & St. Fischer (1989). *Lectures on Macroeconomics*. Cambridge, MA: The MIT Press.

Blanchard, O. J. (1981). Output, the stock market and interest rate. *American Economic Review*, 71, 132–43.

Blanchard, O. J. & Kahn, C. M. (1980). The solution of linear difference models under rational expectations. *Econometrica*, 48(5), 1305–1312.

Blanchard, O. J., & Katz, L. (1999). Wage dynamics: Reconciling theory and evidence. *American Economic Review. Papers and Proceedings*, 89, 69–74.

Blanchard, O. J., & Summers, L. H. (1991). Hysteresis and unemployment. In G. N. Mankiw, & D. Romer (Eds.), *New Keynesian Economics. Coordination Failures and Real Rigidities* (pp. 235–243). Vol. 2, Cambridge, MA: MIT Press.

Blanchard, O. J., & Wolfers, J. (2000). The role of shocks and institutions in the rise of European unemployment: the aggregate evidence. *The Economic Journal*, 110, 1–33.

Boggess, T. E. (1983). A generalized Keynes–Wicksell model with variable labor force growth. *Journal of Macroeconomics*, 5, 197–209.

Brock, W. A., & Malliaris, A. G. (1989). *Differential Equations, Stability and Chaos in Dynamic Economics*. Amsterdam: North Holland.

Bronfenbrenner, M., (Ed.) (1969). *Is the Business Cycle Obsolete?* New York: Harper & Row.

Calvo, G. A. (1977). The stability of models of money and perfect foresight: A comment. *Econometrica*, 45, 1737–1739.

Calvo, G. A. (1983). Staggered prices in a utility maximizing framework. *Journal of Monetary Economics*, 12, 383–398.

Carlin, W., & Soskice, D. (2005). *Macroeconomics. Imperfections, Institutions and Policy*. Oxford: Oxford University Press.

Carstensen, K. (2006). Estimating the ECB policy reaction function. *German Economic Review*, 4.

Chang, W. W., & Smyth, D. J. (1971). The existence and persistence of cycles in a non-linear model: Kaldor's 1940 model re-examined. *Review of Economic Studies*, 38, 37–44.

Chen, P., & Flaschel, P. (2006). Measuring the interaction of wage and price Phillips Curves for the U.S. economy. *Studies in Nonlinear Dynamics and Econometrics*, 10, 1–35.

Chen, P., Chiarella, C., Flaschel, P., & Semmler, W. (2006). Keynesian macrodynamics and the Phillips Curve. An estimated baseline macromodel for the U.S. economy. In C. Chiarella, P. Flaschel, R. Franke, & W. Semmler (Eds.), *Quantitative and Empirical Analysis of Nonlinear Dynamic Macromodels*. Contributions to Economic Analysis. Amsterdam: Elsevier.

Chiarella, C. (1986). Perfect foresight models and the dynamic instability problem from a higher viewpoint. *Economic Modelling*, 3, 283–292.

Chiarella, C. (1990). *The Elements of a Nonlinear Theory of Economic Dynamics*. Heidelberg: Springer.

Chiarella, C., & Flaschel, P. (1996). Real and monetary cycles in models of Keynes-Wicksell type. *Journal of Economic Behavior and Organization*, 30, 327–351.

Chiarella, C., & Flaschel, P. (1998). Dynamics of 'natural' rates of growth and employment. *Macroeconomic Dynamics*, 2, 345–368.

Chiarella, C., & Flaschel P. (2000). *The Dynamics of Keynesian Monetary Growth: Macro Foundations*. Cambridge, UK: Cambridge University Press.

Chiarella, C., Flaschel P., & Franke, R. (2005). *Foundations for a Disequilibrium Theory of the Business Cycle. Quantitative Analysis and Qualitative Assessment*. Cambridge, UK: Cambridge University Press.

Chiarella, C., Flaschel, P., Franke, R., & Semmler, W. *Financial Markets and the Macroeconomy. A Keynesian Perspective*. London: Routledge, forthcoming.

Chiarella, C., Flaschel, P., Groh, G., & Semmler, W. (2000). *Disequilibrium, Growth and Labor Market Dynamics*, Heidelberg: Springer Verlag.

Chick, V. (1983). *Macroeconomics after Keynes*. Oxford: Philip Allan.

Christiano, L., Eichenbaum, M., & Evans, C. (2005). Nominal rigidities and the dynamic effects of a shock to monetary policy. *Journal of Political Economy*, 113, 1–45.

Clarida, R., & Gertler, M. (1997). How the Bundesbank conducts monetary policy. In C. D. Romer, & D. H. Romer (Eds.), *Reducing Inflation: Motivation and Strategy* (pp. 363–406). Chicago: Chicago University Press.

Coddington, E. A., & Levinson, N. (1955). *Theory of Ordinary Differential Equations*. New York: McGraw-Hill.

Colander, D., (Ed.) (2006). *Post Walrasian Macroeconomics. Beyond the Dynamic Stochastic General Equilibrium Model*. Cambridge, UK: Cambridge University Press.

COUNCIL (2002). Council resolution of 27 June 2002 on lifelong learning. In Official Journal of the European Communities C 163/1 (`http://europa.eu/eur-lex/pri/en/oj/dat/2002/c_163/c_16320020709en00010003.pdf`) (read 11-18-2007).

Crouch, R. (1972). *Macroeconomics*. New York: Harcourt Brace Jovanovich.

Cukierman, A. (1984). *Inflation, Stagflation, Relative Prices, and Imperfect Information*. Cambridge, UK: Cambridge University Press.

Day, R., & Yang, C. (2008). An encompassing theory of macroeconomic growth and fluctuation. In P. Flaschel, & M. Landesmann (Eds.), *Mathematical Economics and the Dynamics of Capitalism*. London, Routledge, forthcoming.

Del Negro, M., Schorfheide, F., Smets, F., & Wouters, R. (2004). On the fit and forecasting performance of New Keynesian models. *Working Paper 2004-37*, Federal Reserve Bank of Atlanta.

Domar, E. D. (1946). Capital expansion, rate of growth, and employment. *Econometrica*, 14, 137–147.

Dornbusch, R. (1976). Expectations and exchange rate dynamics. *Journal of Political Economy*, 84, 1161–1176.

Dornbusch, R., & St. Fischer (1987). *Macroeconomics* (4th ed.). New York: McGraw-Hill.

Duguay, P., & Rabeau, Y. (1988). A simulation model of macroeconomic effects of deficit. *Journal of Macroeconomics*, 10, 539–564.

Dutt, A. K., & Skott, P. (2006). Keynesian theory and the AD-AS framework: A reconsideration. In C. Chiarella, R. Franke, & W. Semmler (Eds.), *Quantitative and Empirical Analysis of Nonlinear Dynamic Macromodels. Contributions to Economic Analysis*. Amsterdam: Elsevier.

Eller, J. W., & Gordon, R. J. (2003). Nesting the New Keynesian Phillips Curve within the mainstream model of U.S. inflation dynamics. Presented at the CEPR Conference. *The Phillips Curved Revisited*. Berlin, Germany, 5–6 June 2003.

Erceg, C., Henderson, D. W., & Levin A. T. (2000). Optimal monetary policy with staggered wage and price contracts. *Journal of Monetary Economics*, 46, 281–313.

Esping-Anderson, G. (1990). The Three Worlds of Welfare Capitalism. Cambridge, UK: Cambridge University Press.

Estrella, A., & Fuhrer, J. C. (2002). Dynamic inconsistencies: Counterfactual implications of a class of rational expectations models. *The American Economic Review*, 92, 1013–1028.

Evans, M. K. (1969). *Macroeconomic Activity. Theory, Forecasting, and Control*. New York: Harper & Row.

Fair, R. (2000). Testing the NAIRU model for the United States. *The Review of Economics and Statistics*, 82, 64–71.

Farkas, M., & Kotsis, M. (1992). Modelling predator-prey and wage-employment dynamics. In G. Feichtinger (Ed.), *Dynamic Economic Models and Optimal Control. Proceedings of the Fourth Viennese Workshop on Dynamic Economic Models and Optimal Control* (pp. 513–526). Amsterdam: North Holland.

Felderer, B., & Homburg, S. (1984). *Makroökonomik und neue Makroökonomik*. Heidelberg: Springer.

Fischer, S. (1972). Keynes–Wicksell and neoclassical models of money and growth, *American Economic Review*, 62, 880–890.

Flaschel, P. (1984). Some stability properties of Goodwin's growth cycle model. *Zeitschrift für Nationalökonomie*, 44, 63–69.

Flaschel, P. (1984). The inflation-based 'natural' rate of unemployment and the conflict over income distribution. In R. Goodwin, M. Krüger, & A. Vercelli (Eds.), *Nonlinear Models of Fluctuating Growth* (pp. 103–126) Heidelberg: Springer.

Flaschel, P. (1985). Macroeconomic dynamics and effective demand. Some corrections. *Metroeconomica*, 37, 135–156.

Flaschel, P. (1988). 'Fiscal policy in an accelerator-augmented classical growth cycle', In P. Flaschel, & M. Krüger (Eds.), *Recent Approaches to Economic Dynamics*. Berlin: Verlag Peter Lang, 80–99.

Flaschel, P. (1991). A Keynes-Wicksell model of the 'growth cycle'. The myopic perfect foresight case. University of Bielefeld: Discussion paper.

Flaschel, P. (1992). Adaptive expectations or myopic perfect foresight: The wrong alternative. Bielefeld University: Discussion paper.

Flaschel, P. (2001). Disequilibrium growth in monetary economies: basic components and the KMG working model. In L. Punzo (Ed.), *Cycles, Growth and Structural Change* (pp. 128–168). London: Routledge.

Flaschel, P., & Krolzig, H.-M. (2006). Wage-price Phillips curves and macroeconomic stability: Basic structural form, estimation and analysis. In0 C. Chiarella, P. Flaschel, R. Franke, & W. Semmler (Eds.), *Quantitative and Empirical Analysis of Nonlinear Dynamic Macromodels*. Contributions to Economic Analysis. Amsterdam: Elsevier.

Flaschel, P., & Landesmann, M. *Mathematical Economics and the Dynamics of Capitalism. Goodwin's Legacy Continued*. London: Routledge. Frontiers of Political Economy, forthcoming.

Flaschel, P., & Picard, R. (1986). Problems concerning the dynamic analysis of a Keynesian model with perfect foresight. In W. Semmler (Ed.), *Competition, Instability and Nonlinear Cycles* (pp. 269–288). Heidelberg: Springer.

Flaschel, P., Franke, R., & Proaño, C. (2008). On the (in-)determinacy of New Keynesian models with staggered wage and price setting. Working paper, IMK, Düsseldorf.

Flaschel, P., Franke, R., & Semmler, W. (2008). Kaleckian investment and employment cycles in postwar industrialized economies. In P. Flaschel & M. Landesmann (Eds.), *Mathematical Economics and the Dynamics of Capitalism*. London: Routledge, forthcoming.

Flaschel, P., Greiner, A., Luchtenberg, S., & Nell, E. (2008). Varieties of capitalism. The flexicurity model. In P. Flaschel, & M. Landesmann (Eds.), *Mathematical Economics and the Dynamics of Capitalism*. London, Routledge, forthcoming.

Flaschel, P., Groh., G., & Proaño, C. (2007). *Keynesianische Makroökonomik. Unterbeschäftigung, Inflation und Wachstum*. Heidelberg: Springer.

Flaschel, P., Groh, G., Proaño, C., & Semmler, W. (2008). *Topics in Applied Macrodynamic Theory*. Heidelberg: Springer Verlag.

Flaschel, P., Kauermann, G., & Semmler, W. (2006). Testing wage and price Phillips Curves for the United States. *Metroeconomica*, 58, 550–581.

Flaschel, P., Kauermann, G., & Teuber, T. (2005). Long cycles in employment, inflation and real unit wage costs. Qualitative analysis and quantitative assessment. *American Journal of Applied Sciences*, Special Issue on: Economic Sciences, Dynamics, Expectations and Learning, 69–77.

Flaschel, P., Tavani, D., Teuber, T., & Taylor, L. (2008). A Structuralist Model of the Wage-Price Spiral with Non-Linear Demand Pressure Terms. Bielefeld University: Working paper.

Flemming, J. S. (1987). Wage flexibility and employment stability. *Oxford Economic Papers*, 39, 161–174.
Franke, R. (1992). Stable, unstable, and persistent cyclical behaviour in a Keynes–Wicksell monetary growth model. *Oxford Economic Papers*, 44.
Friedman, M. (1968). The role of monetary policy. *American Economic Review*, 58, 1–17.
Friedman, B. M. (1979). Optimal expectations and the extreme information assumptions of "rational expectations" macromodels. *Journal of Monetary Economics*, 5, 23–41.
Frisch, H. (1983). *Theories of Inflation.* Cambridge: Cambridge University Press.
Frisch, H., & Hof, F. (1981). A "textbook" model of inflation and unemployment. *Kredit und Kapital*, 14, 159–179.
Fuhrer, J. C., & Moore, G. (1995). Inflation persistence. *Quarterly Journal of Economics*, 110, 127–59.
Galí, J. (2000). The return of the Phillips Curve and other recent developments in business cycle theory. *Spanisch Economic Review*, 2, 1–10.
Galí, J. (2008). *Monetary Policy, Inflation and the Business Cycle.* Princeton: Princeton University Press.
Galí, J., & Gertler, M. (1999). Inflation dynamics: A structural econometric analysis. *Journal of Monetary Economics*, 44, 195–222.
Galí, J., Gertler, M., & López-Salido, J. D. (2001). European inflation dynamics. *European Economic Review*, 45, 1237–1270.
Gandolfo, G. (1983). *Economic Dynamics: Methods and Models.* Amsterdam: North Holland.
Gandolfo, G. (1996). *Economic Dynamics* (Third Edition). Berlin: Springer.
Gantmacher, F. R. (1954). *Theory of Matrices.* New York: Interscience Publishers.
Gerlach, S., & Schnabel, G. (2000). The taylor rule and interest rates in the EMU area. *Economics Letters*, 67, 165–171.
Glahe, F. (1977). *Macroeconomics.* New York: Harcourt Brace Jovanovich.
Glombowski, J., & Krüger, M. (1984). Unemployment insurance and cyclical growth. In R. Goodwin, M. Krüger, & A. Vercelli (Eds.), *Nonlinear Models of Fluctuating Growth* (pp. 25–46). Heidelberg: Springer.
Goldman, S. M. (1972). Hyper inflation and the rate of growth in the money supply. *Journal of Economic Theory*, 5, 250–257.
Goodwin, R. (1951). The non-linear accelerator and the persistence of business cycles. *Econometrica*, 19, 1–17.
Goodwin, R. (1967). A growth cycle. In C. H. Feinstein (Ed.), *Socialism, Capitalism and Economic Growth* (pp. 54–58). Cambridge: Cambridge University Press.
Grasman, J. (1987). *Asymptotic Methods for Relaxation Oscillations and Applications.* Heidelberg: Springer.
Gray, J. A. (1984). Dynamic instability in rational expectation models: An attempt to clarify. *International Economic Review*, 25, 93–122.
Greiner, A. (2001). Distribution and endogenous growth: The two-class Pasinetti model. *Jahrbücher für Nationalökonomie und Statistik*, 22, 309–321.
Groh, G. (1991). Kaufkraft- vs. Kosteneffekte in der Neokeynesianischen Konjunkturtheorie Malinvauds. Bielefeld, Faculty of Economics, Diploma thesis.
Grossman, H. (1980). Rational expectations, business cycles, and government behavior. In St. Fischer (Ed.), *Rational expectations and Economic Policy* (pp. 5–22). Chicago: University of Chicago Press.
Groth, C. (1992). Some unfamiliar dynamics in a familiar macromodel. *Journal of Economics*, 58, 293–305.
Groth, C., & Madsen, J. B. (2007). Medium-term fluctuations and the "Great Ratios" of economic growth. Working Paper, University of Copenhagen.
Guckenheimer, J., & Holmes, P. (1983). *Nonlinear Oscillations, Dynamical Systems, and Bifurcation of Vector Fields.* Heidelberg: Springer.

Hadjimichalakis, M. G. (1981). Expectations of the "myopic perfect foresight" variety in monetary dynamics. *Journal of Economic Dynamics and Control*, 3, 157–176.

Hahn, F. (1972). *The Share of Wages in the National Income*. London: Weidenfeld and Nicolson.

Hall, R. E. (1988). The relation between price and marginal cost in U.S. industry. *Journal of Political Economy*, 96, 920–947.

Hanusch, H., & Pyka, A. (2007). *The Elgar Companion to Neo-Schumpeterian Economics*. Aldershot: Edward Elgar.

Harrod, R. (1939). An essay in dynamic economic theory. *The Economic Journal*, XLIX, 14–33.

Hartman, P. (1964). *Ordinary Differential Equations*. New York: John Wiley.

Hicks, J. (1950). *A Contribution to the Theory of the Trade Cycle*. London: Claredon Press.

Hillier, B. (1991). *The Macroeconomic Debate*. Oxford: Basil Blackwell.

Hirsch, M. W., & Smale, S. (1974). *Differential Equations, Dynamical Systems, and Linear algebra*. New York: Academic Press.

Hommes, C. (1991). *Chaotic Dynamics in Economic Models*. Groningen: Wolters-Noordhoff.

Ito, T. (1978). A note on the positivity constraint in Olech's theorem. *Journal of Economic Theory*, 17, 312–318.

Ito, T. (1980). Disequilibrium Growth Theory. *Journal of Economic Theory*, 23, 380–409.

Jones, H. G. (1975). *An Introduction to Modern Theories of Economic Growth*. London: Thomas Nelson & Sons.

Jordan, D. W., & Smith, P. (1977). *Nonlinear Ordinary Differential Equations*. Oxford: Claredon Press.

Kaldor, N. (1940). A model of the trade cycle. *Economic Journal*, 50, 78–92.

Kalecki, M. (1943). Political aspects of full employment. Reprinted in M. Kalecki, *Selected Essays on the Dynamics of the Capitalist Economy*, Cambridge: Cambridge University Press, 1971.

Kauermann, G., Teuber, T., & Flaschel, P. (2008). Exploring US Business Cycles with Bivariate Loops using Penalized Spline Regression, Bielefeld University: Working paper.

Kemp, M., & Kimura, Y. (1978). *Introduction to Mathematical Economics*. Heidelberg: Springer.

Keynes, J. M. (1936). *The General Theory of Employment, Interest and Money*. New York: Macmillan.

Kiguel, M. A. (1989). Budget deficits, stability, and the monetary dynamics of hyperinflation. *Journal of Money, Credit, and Banking* 21, 148–157.

Laidler, D. (1981). Monetarism: An interpretation and an assessment. *Economic Journal*, 91, 1–28.

LaSalle, J. (1949). Relaxation oscillations. *Quarterly of Applied Mathematics*, 7, 1–19.

Laxton, D., Rose, D., & Tambakis, D. (2000). The U.S. Phillips-curve: The case for asymmetry. *Journal of Economic Dynamics and Control*, 23, 1459–1485.

Layard, R., & Bean, C. (1989). Why dose unemployment persist. *Scandinavian Journal of Economics*, 91, 371–396.

Layard, R., Nickell, S., & Jackman, R. (1991). *Unemployment: Macroeconomic Performance and the Labor Market*. Oxford: Oxford University Press.

Liu, W. M. (1994). Citerion of Hopf bifurcations without using eigenvalues. *Journal of Mathematical Analysis and Applications*, 1982, 250–256.

Ljungqvist, L., & Sargent, T. J. (1998). The European unemployment dilemma, *Journal of Political Economy*, 106, 514–550.

Llaudes, R. (2005). The Phillips Curve and long-term unemployment, Working Paper 441, European Central Bank.

Lorenz, H. -W. (1993). *Nonlinear dynamical economics and chaotic motion* 2nd ed. Heidelberg: Springer.

Lorenz, H. -W. (1989). *Nonlinear Dynamical Economics and Chaotic Motion*. Heidelberg: Springer.

Lorenz, H. -W., & Gabisch, G. (1989). *Business Cycle Theory*. Heidelberg: Springer.

Malinvaud, E. (1977). *The Theory of Unemployment Reconsidered*. Oxford: Basil Blackwell.

Malinvaud, E. (1980). *Profitability and Unemployment*. Cambridge: Cambridge University Press.

Malinvaud, E. (1984). *Mass Unemployment*. Oxford: Basil Blackwell.

Mankiw, N. G. (1994). *Macroeconomics*. New York: Worth Publishers.
Mankiw, G. (2001). The inexorable and mysterious tradeoff between inflation and unemployment. *Economic Journal*, 111, 45–61.
Marx, K. (1954). *Capital* (Vol I). London: Lawrence and Wishart.
Matthews, R. C. O. (1970). *The Trade Cycle*. Cambridge: Cambridge University Press.
McCallum, B. (1989). *Monetary Economics*. New York: Macmillan.
McCallum, B. T. (1978). Price level adjustments and the rational expectations approach to macroeconomic stabilization policy. *Journal of Money, Credit, and Banking*, 10, 418–436.
Meade, J. (1982). *Stagflation, Vol. I: Wage Fixing*. London: George Allen & Unwin.
Minford, P., & Peel, D. (1983). *Rational Expectations and the New Macroeconomics*. Oxford: Martin Robertson.
Ministry of Education and Science of Sweden. (2004). Equity in education. Thematic review. Country analytical report. Sweden. `http://www.oecd.org/dataoecd/30/22/38697408.pdf` (read 11-18-2007).
Mill, J. S. T. (1965). Principles of Political Economy. In J. M. Robson (Ed.), *Collected Works of John Stuart Mill*. London: Routledge and Kegan Paul.
Modigliani, F. (1944). Liquidity preference and the theory of interest and money, *Econometrica*, 12, 45–88.
Moggridge, D. (1973). The Collected Writings of John Maynard Keynes. Volume XIV: *The General Theory and After. Part II: Defense and Development*. London and Basingstoke: Macmillan.
Murata, Y. (1977). *Mathematics for Stability and Optimization of Economic Systems*. New York: Academic Press.
Nickell, S. (1997). Unemployment and labor market rigidities. *The Journal of Economic Perspectives*, 11, 55–74.
Nikaido, H. (1980). Harrodian pathology of neoclassical growth: The irrelevance of smooth factor substitution. *Zeitschrift für Nationalökonomie*, 40, 111–134.
OECD (2002). The ins and outs of long-term unemployment. *OECD Employment Outlook*, OECD, 189–239.
OECD (2007). Education at a Glance 2007. `http://www.oecd.org/document/30/0,3343,en_2649_39263294_39251550_1_1_1_1,00.html` (read 11-18-2007).
Okun, A. M. (1970). *The Political Economy of Prosperity*. Washington, D.C.: The Brookings Institution.
Olech, A.M. (1963). On the global stability of an autonomous system in the plane. In: P. Lasalle and P. Díaz (eds.): *Contributions to Differential Equations*, 1, 389–400.
Patinkin, D. (1965). *Money, Interest and Prices*. New York: Harper and Row.
Phillips, A. W. (1954). Stabilization theory in a closed economy. *The Economic Journal*, 64, 290–323.
Phillips, A. W. (1961). A simple model of employment, money and prices in a growing economy. *Economica*, 73, 360–370.
Pissarides, C. A. (1990). *Equilibrium Unemployment Theory*. Oxford: Basil Blackwell.
Pissarides, C. (1992). Loss of skill during unemployment and the persistence of unemployment shocks. *Quarterly Journal of Economics*, 107, 1371–1391.
Poston, T., & Stewart, I. (1978). *Catastrophe Theory and its Applications*. Boston: Pitman.
Proaño, C., Flaschel, P., Diallo, M.B., & Teuber, T. (2008). Short Run Distributive Cycles, Business Cycles and the Wage-led/Profit-led Debate. Working paper. Bielefeld: CEM.
Proaño, C. R., Flaschel, P., Ernst, E., & Semmler, W. (2006). Disequilibrium Macroeconomic Dynamics, Income Distribution and Wage-Price Phillips Curves: Evidence from the U.S. and the Euro Area. Macroeconomic Policy Institute (IMK) Working Paper 04/2006.
Puu, T. (1991). *Nonlinear Economic Dynamics*. Heidelberg: Springer.
Quirk, J., & Saposnik, R. (1968). *Introduction to General Equilibrium Theory and Welfare Economics*. New York: McGraw-Hill.
Report of the special rapporteur on education, Vernor Muñoz, on his mission to Germany (13–21 February 2006) `http://www.netzwerk- bildungsfreiheit.de/pdf/Munoz_Mission_on_Germany.pdf` (read 11-18-2007).

Romer, D. (2000). Keynesian macroeconomics without the LM curve. *The Journal of Economic Perspectives*, 14, 149–169.

Rose, H. (1967). On the non-linear theory of the employment cycle. *Review of Economic Studies,* 34, 153–173.

Rose, H. (1990). *Macrodynamics. A Marshallian Synthesis*. Oxford: Basil Blackwell.

Rose, H. (1990). *Macroeconomic Dynamics*. Oxford: Basil Blackwell.

Rowthorn, B. (1980). Conflict, inflation and money, In B. Rowthorn, *Capitalism, Conflict and Inflation. Essays in Political Economy*. London: Lawrence and Wishart.

Rudebusch, G. D., & Svensson, L. E. (1999).: Policy rules for inflation targeting. In J. B. Taylor (Ed.), *Monetary Policy Rules*. Chicago: The University of Chicago Press, Ch. 15.

Samuelson, P. (1939). Interactions between the multiplier analysis and the principle of acceleration, *Review of Economic Statistics,* 21, 75–78.

Samuelson, P. (1978). The canonical classical model of political economy. *Journal of Economic Literature*, XVI, 1415–1434.

Santomero, A. M., & Seater, J. F. (1978). The inflation–unemployment trade-off: a critique of the literature. *Journal of Economic Literature*, 16, 499–544.

Sargent, T. (1987). *Macroeconomic Theory*, New York: Academic Press.

Sargent, T. (1988). *Dynamic Macroeconomic Theory*. Harvard: Harvard University Press.

Sargent, T., & Wallace, N. (1973). The stability of models of money and growth with perfect foresight. *Econometrica*, 41, 1043–1048.

Sargent, Th. J. (1973a). Interest rates and prices in the long run: A study of the Gibson paradox. *Journal of Money, Credit, and Banking*, 83, 385–449.

Sargent, Th. J. (1973b). Rational expectations, the real rate of interest, and the natural rate of unemployment. *Brookings Papers on Economic Activity*, 2, 429–472.

Sargent, Th. J., & Wallace, N. (1975). Rational expectations, the optimal monetary instrument, and the optimal money supply rule. *Journal of Political Economy*, 83, 385–449.

Sbordone, A. M. (2004). A limited information approach to simultaneous estimation of wage and price dynamics. Rutgers University, mimeo.

Schumpeter, J. (1912). *The Theory of Economic Development.* London: Oxford University Press.

Schumpeter, J. (1939). *Business Cycles* (Vol. I and II). Philadelphia: Porcupine Press.

Schumpeter, J. (1942). *Capitalism, Socialism and Democracy.* New York: Harper & Row.

Sen, A., (Ed.) (1970). *Growth Economics*. London: Penguin Economics Readings.

Sims, C. (1987). Discussion of Olivier J. Blanchard, aggregate and individual price adjustment. *BPEA*, 1, 117–20.

Sims, C. (1998). "Stickiness." Carnegie-Rochester Conference Series on Public Policy, 49, 317–356.

Sims, C. A. (2002). Solving linear rational expectations models. *Computational Economics*, 20, 1–20.

Smets, F., & Wouters, R. (2003). An estimated dynamic stochastic general equilibrium model for the euro area. *Journal of the European Economic Association*, 1, 1123–1175.

Snower, D. J. (1984). Rational expectations, nonlinearities, and the effectiveness of monetary policy. *Oxford Economic Papers*, 36, 177–199.

Solow, R. (1956). A contribution to the theory of economic growth. *The Quarterly Journal of Economics*, 70, 65–94.

Solow, R. (1990). Goodwin's growth cycle: Reminiscence and rumination. In K. Velupillai (Ed.), *Nonlinear and Multisectoral Macrodynamics* (pp. 31–41). London: Macmillan.

Solow, R. (2004). Introduction: the Tobin approach to monetary economics. *Journal of Money, Credit and Banking*, 36, 657–663.

Soyka, D. (1991). Der Realkasseneffekt bei Malinvaud. Bielefeld, Faculty of Economics, Diploma thesis.

Sraffa, P. (1970). *The Works and Correspondence of David Ricardo. Vol. I: On the Principles of Political Economy and Taxation*. Cambridge: Cambridge University Press.

Stein, J. (1982). *Monetarist, Keynesian and New Classical Economics.* London: Basil Blackwell.

Strogatz, S. H. (1994). *Nonlinear Dynamics and Chaos*. New York: Addison-Wesley.

Svensson, L. E. (1998). Inflation targeting as a monetary policy rule. Working Paper 6790, National Bureau of Economic Research.

Swedberg, R. (1991). *Schumpeter. A Biography.* Princeton: Princeton University Press.

Taylor, J. B. (1980). Aggregate dynamics and staggered contracts. *Journal of Political Economy*, 88, 1–23.

Taylor, J. B. (1993). Discretion versus policy rules in practice. *Carnegie-Rochester Conference Series on Public policy*, 39, 195–214.

Tobin, J. (1965). Money and economic growth, *Econometrica*, 33, 671–684.

Tobin, J. (1975). Keynesian models of recession and depression. *American Economic Review*, 45, 195–202.

Tobin, J. (1980). *Asset Accumulation and Economic Activity*. Oxford: Basil Blackwell.

St. Turnovsky (1977). *Macroeconomic Analysis and Stabilization Policies*. Cambridge: Cambridge University Press.

van Rijckeghem, W. (1966). The stability of the Domar model. *Econometrica*, 34, 724–726.

Varian, H. R. (1979). Catastrophe theory and the business cycle. *Economic Inquiry*, 17, 14–28.

Vis, B. (2007). States of welfare or states of workfare? Welfare state restructuring in 16 capitalist democracies, 1985–2002. *Policy & Politics*, 35, 105–122.

Wiggins, S. (1990). *Introduction to applied nonlinear dynamical systems and chaos*. Heidelberg: Springer.

Wolfstetter, E. (1977). *Wert, Profitrate und Beschäftigung*. Frankfurt a.M.: Campus Verlag.

Wolfstetter, E. (1982). Fiscal policy and the classical growth cycle. *Zeitschrift für Nationalökonomie*, 42, 375–393.

Woodford, M. (2003). *Interest and Prices. Foundations of a Theory of Monetary Policy.* Princeton: Princeton University Press.

Wooldridge, J. M. (2001). Applications of generalized method of moments estimation. *Journal of Economic Perspectives*, 15, 87–100.

Yan-Qian, Y. et al. (1984). *Theory of Limit Cycles*. Providence - Rhode Island: American Mathematical Society.

Yoshida, H., & Asada, T. (2007). Dynamic analysis of policy lag in a Keynes-Goodwin model: Stability, instability, cycles and chaos. *Journal of Economic Behavior & Organization*, 62(3), 441–469.

Zarnowitz, V. (1999). Theory and history behind business cycles: are the 1990s the onset of a golden age. Working Paper 7010, NBER.

Zhang, W. -B. (1991). *Synergetic Economics*. Heidelberg: Springer.

The manufacturer's authorised representative in the EU is Springer Nature Customer Service Centre GmbH, Europaplatz 3, 69115 Heidelberg, Germany. If you have any concerns regarding our products, please contact ProductSafety@springernature.com

Printed and bound by CPI Group (UK) Ltd, Croydon, CR0 4YY
01/10/2026
02225968-0013